# Ecumenical Documents V

# GROWING CONSENSUS

## Church Dialogues in the United States, 1962-1991

Edited by
Joseph A. Burgess and
Jeffrey Gros, FSC

Preface by
Leonid Kishkovsky

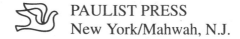

PAULIST PRESS
New York/Mahwah, N.J.

25 7

The publisher is grateful to the following for permission to include their documents in this publication: the United States Catholic Conference, the United Methodist Church, the Executive Council of the Episcopal Church, the Consultation on Church Union, the Office of Theology and Worship/Congregational Ministries Division/Presbyterian Church (USA), the National Council of the Churches of Christ in the U.S.A./Commission on Faith and Order, *American Baptist Quarterly,* March 1988, with permission of The American Baptist Historical Society, Valley Forge, PA, *The Covenant Quarterly, The Theological Educator,* Forward Movement Publications, Thomas Nelson Inc., Augsburg Fortress for selections from Paul C. Empie and James L. McCord, eds., *Marburg Revisited,* copyright © 1966; James E. Andrews and Joseph A. Burgess, eds., *An Invitation to Action,* copyright © 1984; William A. Norgren and William G. Rusch, eds., *Implications of the Gospel,* copyright © 1988; William A. Norgren and William G. Rusch, eds., "Toward Full Communion" and "Concordat of Agreement," copyright © 1991; H. George Anderson, J. Francis Stafford, and Joseph A. Burgess, eds., *The One Mediator, the Saints, and Mary,* copyright © 1992; John Meyendorff and Robert Tobias, eds., *Salvation in Christ,* copyright © 1992.

Library of Congress Cataloging-in-Publication Data

Growing consensus: documents from church conversations in the United States / [edited] by Joseph A. Burgess and Jeffrey Gros; [preface by Leonid Kishkovsky}.
    p.   cm.—(Ecumenical documents; 5)
   Includes index.
   ISBN 0-8091-3382-2 (pbk.)
   1. Christian union—United States—History—20th century—Sources. 2. Interdenominational cooperation—United States—History—20th century—Sources. 3. United States—Religion—1960- —Sources. 4. Church—Unity. I. Series.
BR516.5.G76   1990
280'.042—dc20                              93-27753
                                                  CIP

Published by Paulist Press
997 Macarthur Boulevard
Mahwah, New Jersey 07430

Printed and bound in the
United States of America

# Contents

# Abbreviations

| | |
|---|---|
| *AAS* | *Acta Apostolicae Sedis* |
| AB | Anchor Bible |
| AELC | Association of Evangelical Lutheran Churches |
| ALC | The American Lutheran Church |
| ALERC | Anglican-Lutheran European Regional Commission |
| ALICC | Anglican-Lutheran International Continuation Committee |
| Ap | Apology of the Augsburg Confession |
| ARCIC | Anglican-Roman Catholic International Commission |
| ARC/USA | Anglican-Roman Catholic Dialogue in the USA |
| *A.V.S.* | *Acta Synodalia Sacrosancti Concilii Vaticani Secundi* |
| BAGD | *A Greek-English Lexicon of the New Testament and Other Early Christian Literature* (Walter Bauer's 5th ed.) |
| *BC* | *The Book of Concord. The Confessions of the Evangelical Lutheran Church* (tr. and ed. T. Tappert); within *An Invitation to Action*, BC = Book of Confessions |
| *BCO* | *Book of Church Order* |
| *BCP* | *Book of Common Prayer* |
| BelC | Belgic Confession |
| *BEM* | *Baptism, Eucharist and Ministry* |
| *BkC* | *The Book of Concord* (within *An Invitation to Action*); cp. *BC* |
| *BO* | *Book of Order* |
| *BS* | *Die Bekenntnisschriften der lutherischen Kirche* |
| *BU* | *Building Unity* |
| C'67 | Confession of 1967 |
| *CA* | *Confessio Augustana* (Augsburg Confession) |
| Cambridge Platform | Cambridge Platform of 1648; see Williston Walker, ed., *The Creeds and Platforms of Congregationalism* |
| *CCL* | *Corpus Christianorum, Series latina* |
| COCU | Consultation on Church Union |

| | |
|---|---|
| *C.O.D.* | *Conciliorum Oecumenicorum Decreta* (ed. G. Alberigo et al.) |
| CR | *Corpus Reformatorum* (ed. C. G. Bretschneider and H. E. Bindsell) |
| CS | Common Statement |
| CSEL | *Corpus scriptorum ecclesiasticorum latinorum* |
| d. | died |
| DS | *Enchiridion Symbolorum* (33rd ed.; H. Denzinger and A. Schönmetzer) |
| DV | *Dei Verbum* (Vatican II) |
| ELCA | Evangelical Lutheran Church in America |
| ER | *Encyclopedia of Religion* |
| EWNT | *Exegetisches Wörterbuch zum Neuen Testament* (ed. H. Balz and G. Schneider) |
| FC Ep | Formula of Concord, Epitome |
| FC SD | Formula of Concord, Solid Declaration |
| GCS | *Die Griechischen Christlichen Schriftsteller der ersten drei Jahrhunderte* |
| GiA | *Growth in Agreement,* Ecumenical Documents II |
| HCat | Heidelberg Catechism |
| IA | *An Invitation to Action* |
| IS | *Information Service of Pontifical Council for Christian Unity* |
| JB | Jerusalem Bible |
| JBC | *Jerome Biblical Commentary* |
| LA | Leuenberg Agreement |
| LBW | *Lutheran Book of Worship* |
| LC | Large Catechism |
| LCA | Lutheran Church in America |
| LCL | *Loeb Classical Library* |
| LCMS | The Lutheran Church—Missouri Synod |
| LCUSA | Lutheran Council in the U.S.A. |
| LED | Lutheran-Episcopal Dialogue |
| LG | *Lumen Gentium* (Vatican II) |
| LR | Lutheran-Reformed |
| L/RC 6 | *Teaching Authority and Infallibility in the Church* (Lutherans and Catholics in Dialogue 6) |
| L/RC 7 | *Justification by Faith* (Lutherans and Catholics in Dialogue 7) |
| L/RC 8 | *The One Mediator, the Saints, and Mary* (Lutherans and Catholics in Dialogue 8) |
| LThK | *Lexikon für Theologie und Kirche* (2nd ed.) |

| | |
|---|---|
| *LW* | *Luther's Works* (general ed. J. Pelikan and H. Lehmann) |
| LWF | Lutheran World Federation |
| *Mary in the New Testament* | *Mary in the New Testament. A Collaborative Assessment by Protestant and Roman Catholic Scholars* (ed. R. E. Brown, K. P. Donfried, J. A. Fitzmyer, and J. Reumann) |
| NAB | New American Bible |
| NABRNT | New American Bible Revised New Testament |
| NCCB | National Conference of Catholic Bishops |
| NCCCUSA | National Council of Churches of Christ in the USA |
| *NIDNTT* | *New International Dictionary of New Testament Theology* |
| *NJBC* | *New Jerome Biblical Commentary* |
| PC(U.S.A.) | Presbyterian Church (U.S.A.) |
| PCUS | Presbyterian Church in the United States |
| PECUSA | Protestant Episcopal Church in the U.S.A. |
| *PG* | *Patrologiae cursus completus, Series graeca* (ed. J. P. Migne) |
| *PL* | *Patrologiae cursus completus, Series latina* (ed. J. P. Migne) |
| PNCC | Polish National Catholic Church |
| RCA | Reformed Church in America |
| RCC | Roman Catholic Church |
| RSV | Revised Standard Version |
| SA | Smalcald Articles |
| SC | Small Catechism |
| SCOBA | Standing Conference of Canonical Orthodox Bishops |
| ScotsC | Scots Confession |
| II HC | Second Helvetic Confession |
| S.P.C.K. | Society for Promoting Christian Knowledge |
| *S.T.* | *Summa theologiae* |
| Tappert | See *BC* |
| *TDNT* | *Theological Dictionary of the New Testament* (ed. G. Kittel) |
| TR | Treatise on the Power and Primacy of the Pope |
| *TRE* | *Theologische Realenzyklopädie* |
| *TWNT* | *Theologisches Wörterbuch zum Neuen Testament* (ed. G. Kittel) |
| UCC | United Church of Christ |
| UFMCC | Universal Fellowship of Metropolitan Community Churches |
| UMC | United Methodist Church |
| UPUSA | United Presbyterian Church in the U.S.A. |

| | |
|---|---|
| USCC | United States Catholic Conference |
| *WA* | Martin Luther, *Werke* (Kritische Gesamtausgabe: "Weimarer Ausgabe") |
| WA TR | WA Tischreden |
| WC | Westminster Confession |
| WCC | World Council of Churches |

# Preface

American ecumenism is characterized by two tendencies—perhaps these tendencies may even be called temptations. One is the temptation to extreme individualism. In the individualistic pattern, Christians articulate their own, individual views, not seeking to embody and interpret the theological traditions of their churches. American Christians often appear not to know and even not to respect these traditions.

The second temptation is that of reducing ecumenism to pragmatic, practical cooperation. In this model of ecumenism Christians bring together their resources and concerns in order to work together on social and humanitarian issues.

It must be noted that neither temptation can be limited to American ecumenism. Both are powerfully present in all of American religious life and indeed represent strong and enduring currents of American history and society.

This volume, presenting Documents from Church Conversations in the United States, reveals churches and traditions in encounter, in dialogic conversation one with another. It thus represents the stream of U.S. ecumenical life which is the least visible but most promising factor of American ecumenism. It is in this record of conversation that we hear the Christian traditions and churches of America in dialogue regarding Christian faith, mission, and responsibility. It is here that we are encouraged in the hope that the tendencies of extreme individualism and the reduction of Christian faith and Christian ecumenism to pragmatic activism may not be irresistible.

In the fall of 1991, the newly-elected Ecumenical Patriarch, Batholomew I, observed in an interview that ecumenism today is clearly facing a crisis, but that the achievements of ecumenism during the past decades are real, are important, and must not be lost. This collection of documents will be of real service both in the facing of the crisis and in the affirmation and strengthening of the ecumenical achievements.

Why is it accurate today to speak of an ecumenical crisis? What is the evidence for this crisis, and what is its nature?

During the World Council of Churches' Seventh Assembly (Canberra,

1

February 1991), it was clear that the question of the "limits of diversity" is at the heart of ecumenical life and theological debate today. We all know that the unity to which Christ calls us is not uniformity. We know that within unity there is room for legitimate diversity—diversity which does not divide but rather bears witness to unity. Christians are ready enough to affirm this notion of "legitimate diversity." Yet to affirm legitimate diversity is also to suggest that some forms of diversity do divide, must divide, and are in fact illegitimate forms of diversity undermining the integrity of the Christian faith. Christians have appeared to shrink from facing the challenge of "illegitimate diversity."

The tensions in the World Council of Churches, reflected in Orthodox and Evangelical concerns at Canberra and afterward, are evidence that the world ecumenical movement has entered a decisive stage in its life, a period in which fundamental issues of ecumenical vision and Christian theology are at stake.

In the United States 1991 was also a milestone year in the ecumenical journey. Four Eastern Orthodox member churches of the National Council of the Churches of Christ in the USA suspended their participation in the council. They raised questions about the fundamental theological and ecclesial convictions of the council and its member communions.

What is at issue is the very core of the Christian witness: Trinitarian faith, the divinity of Christ, biblical language as expressing biblical faith. The Orthodox concerns are based on the anxiety that on every one of the core questions there has been an erosion in the ecumenical reality and experience. The evidence for this erosion has centered on such factors as the inclusive language debate (particularly as it affects language about God) and questions of sexual morality (particularly church teaching on sexual morality).

Parallel to the theological debate about the direction of ecumenism and the very spirit of ecumenism, other evidence of ecumenical crisis has appeared in inter-Christian conflicts. Explosive examples of such conflicts are to be found now in the realities of an Eastern Europe ridding itself of communism. Currently the most painful conflict situations are ones in which Eastern Orthodox and Catholics (especially the Eastern rite) are in friction one with another. The greater tensions in this regard appear to exist in the Ukraine, Romania, and Slovakia. In the Serbo-Croat violence the religious dimension of the struggle is represented by the Eastern Orthodox Serbs and the Latin rite Roman Catholic Croats. The root question that Christian persons and churches face in the midst of these conflicts is the power or powerlessness of the Christian faith, of the gospel itself, in moving toward repentance, forgiveness, and reconciliation.

The quest for Christian unity is a quest for discernment and insight. It is a quest for the faithful and truthful way toward the oneness of his disciples which is willed by Christ. Such a quest, while deeply personal for everyone engaged in it, is not individualistic. It is a quest both in community and for the fullness of community in Christ. Thus the quest for Christian unity, when it is most authentic, is a quest for spiritual discernment and theological insight. The ecumenical task is not solitary, a matter of private insight. It is, rather, a vocation of Christian communities, communions, churches, a vocation carried out on their behalf by faithful Christian persons.

The documents here presented bear witness to the steady and serious spiritual and theological labor which undergirds the ecumenical vocation— not at its most visible level, but at its deepest and most authentic level. Jaroslav Pelikan, a great contemporary Lutheran scholar, called Tradition the living faith of the dead, and traditionalism the dead faith of the living. May this book help the American churches and American Christians to grow in our understanding of the Tradition of the Christian faith so that we may be united with the faith of the "cloud of witnesses" who went before us and may hand on the Christian Tradition undiluted and even enriched to those who will follow us.

*Father Leonid Kishkovsky*
Ecumenical Officer,
Orthodox Church in America
President (1990-1991),
The National Council of the
Churches of Christ in the USA

# Introduction

## The American Context

The alert reader will have noted that not all of the churches involved in the dialogues reported in this volume are restricted to the borders of the United States. Thus it is appropriate to use "American" rather than "United States" in the subtitle for this paragraph. In order to understand these dialogues, it is useful to keep in mind the sweep of history on the North American continent—from the waves of exploration, settlement, and expansion, with all of the ambiguities of the frontier, democracy, and the separation of church and state, to the successive attempts to establish something "new" in a new world, including complex histories of Puritanism, revivalistic movements, battles against racism, the tensions between fundamentalism and modernism, and the like.[1]

## The International Context

Each dialogue is aware of being part of a larger context, the ecumenical movement, and particularly that phase of the ecumenical movement called Faith and Order, both within the World Council of Churches and within the National Council of Churches of Christ in the United States of America. At this point in history delegates of the World Council of Churches at the meeting of Assembly in Canberra, 1991, have focused efforts for unity on the concept "conciliar communion."[2] Although not all of the churches represented in this volume are members of the WCC and the NCCC, each contributes to the larger unity Christ wills for his church.

Most of the World Christian Communions not only have ties with each other, but the Conference of Secretaries of Christian World Communions has also met yearly since 1957 under the auspices of the WCC. The Faith and Order Commission of the WCC keeps track of such union negotiations, assists when asked, publishes a list of such negotiations every two years, and, beginning in 1967, periodically has brought together a Consultation of

United and Uniting Churches. Regional, national, and local councils of churches are often in contact with each other and coordinate their work, as, e.g., with the WCC at the regional and national levels. The NCCUSA, of course, is an independent entity with a history reaching back through its predecessor, the Federal Council of Churches, to 1908.

Beginning in 1978, the Faith and Order Commission of the WCC has periodically conducted Forums on Bilateral Conversations in order to assist in coordinating dialogues throughout the world.[3] Further, the WCC Faith and Order consensus document, *Baptism, Eucharist and Ministry* (1982), has effectively challenged both the churches and ecumenical dialogues.[4] At the same time a complex set of relationships exists between BEM and the Consultation on Church Union in the United States because of overlapping membership; at times even phrasing is similar. And a study process within the Faith and Order Commission of NCCUSA has also evaluated ecumenical dialogues.[5] Recently, to be sure, ecumenical dialogue has seemed to have become less effective; perhaps dialogues have treated symptoms rather than the disease. Efforts have been made to solve this problem by uncovering a fundamental consensus as well as possibly fundamental differences.[6]

## This Volume in Context

Dialogues carried out in the United States are perhaps more pragmatic and concrete, yet, like all dialogues, they ultimately have to do with questions of theological method and authority. More importantly, these dialogues must be understood in their diversity. One is a full church-to-church conversation, calling for organic unity: the Consultation on Church Union. Another is a confederation dialoguing with a similar confederation: The Lutheran Council in the U.S.A. and the Caribbean and North American Area Council of the World Alliance of Reformed Churches. Still another is a dialogue between a national church and part of a worldwide communion: the U.S. Roman Catholic and Polish National Catholic dialogue. Then there is a dialogue between parts of a worldwide communion and an ecumenical confederation: The Orthodox-Reformed dialogue. Finally, there are both the multilateral Faith and Order dialogues and the rather informal evangelical coalitions, whose purposes vary and whose relationships to the churches are much more remote. Some have produced convergence texts that do not claim to be sufficient for church union, some are consensus texts calling for full unity, others are agreements on faith and order proposed as the basis for action.

What is important is to keep in mind who is talking to whom and what sort of result is offered to the churches. Neither bilateral and multilateral dialogue nor national and international dialogue should be played off against one another. No type of dialogue ranks above another, and all types are necessary. What is decisive is not the external status of a dialogue but whether the results of the dialogue do in fact lead to greater insight. The gift of theological insight and dialogue is one of God's many gifts to the church and to the ecumenical movement; it is a resource for that insight and renewal to which the Spirit of God calls his church.

Words of thanks are due to David Taylor for his introduction to the COCU materials and Donald Dayton for his introduction to the Evangelical materials, to Joanne Barbiere, Stacey Andres, and Elizabeth Mellen for their work in collating the documents, and to Paulist Press for its concern that these materials, often out of print and hard to find, be made available. In most cases, in order to avoid unnecessary duplication, introductory material and bibliographies found in *Building Unity* have not been reprinted.[7]

## Notes

1. Don Herbert Yoder, "Christian Unity in Nineteenth-Century America," in Ruth Rouse and Stephen c. Neill (eds.), *A History of the Ecumenical Movement 1517-1948* (2nd ed.; Philadelphia: Westminster, 1967) 1:221-59; Thaddeus Horgan (ed.), *Apostolic Faith in America* (Grand Rapids: Eerdmans, 1988).

2. W. A. Visser 't Hooft, *The Genesis and Formation of the World Council of Churches* (Geneva: WCC, 1982); Lukas Vischer (ed.), *A Documentary History of the Faith and Order Movement 1927-1963* (St. Louis: Bethany Press, 1963); Thomas F. Stransky, "A Basis Beyond the Basis: Roman Catholic/World Council of Churches Collaboration," *Ecumenical Review* 37 (1985) 213-22; Vitaly Borovoy, "The Ecclesiastical Significance of the WCC: the Legacy and Promise of Toronto," *Ecumenical Review* 40 (1988) 504-18; *Signs of the Spirit:* Official Report, Seventh Assembly, Canberra, Australia, 7-20 February 1991/World Council of Churches (ed. M. Kinnamon; Geneva: WCC; Grand Rapids: Eerdmans, 1991).

3. *The Three Reports of the Forum on Bilateral Conversations* (Faith and Order Paper 107; Geneva: WCC, 1981); *Fourth Forum on Bilateral Conversations: Report* (Geneva: WCC, 1985); *Fifth Forum on Bilateral Conversations: Report* (Geneva: WCC, 1991).

4. Cf. *Churches Respond to BEM: official responses to the "Baptism, Eucharist and Ministry," text:* vol. 1 (1986), Faith and Order Paper 129; vol. 2 (1986), Faith and Order Paper 132; vol. 3 (1987), Faith and Order Paper 135; vol. 4 (1987), Faith and Order paper 137; vol. 5 (1988), Faith and Order Paper 143; vol. 6 (1988), Faith and Order Paper 144; ed. M. Thurian (Geneva: WCC, 1986-88); Paul Schrotenboer (ed.), "An Evangelical Response to *Baptism, Eucharist and Ministry*" (prepared by the World Evangelical Fellowship), *Evangelical Review of Theology* 13 (1989) 291-313; *Baptism, Eucharist & Ministry 1982-1990. Report on the Process and Responses* (Faith and Order Paper 149; Geneva: WCC, 1990).

5. See below, pp. 629-48.

6. Joseph A. Burgess, (ed.), *In Search of Christian Unity. Fundamental Consensus—Fundamental Differences* (Minneapolis: Augsburg Fortress, 1991).

7. Lukas Vischer and Harding Meyer (eds.), *Growth in Agreement. Reports and Agreed Statements of Ecumenical Conversations on a World Level* (Ecumenical Documents 2; New York/ Mahwah: Paulist, 1984); Joseph A. Burgess and Jeffrey Gros (eds.), *Building Unity. Ecumenical Dialogues with Roman Catholic Participation in the United States* (Ecumenical Documents 4; New York/Mahwah: Paulist 1989); Giovanni Cereti and Sever J. Voicu (eds.), *Enchiridion Oecumenicum. Documenti del Dialogo Theologico Interconfessionale. 2. Dialoghi Locali 1965-1987* (Bologna: Edizioni Dehoniane, 1988); James F. Puglisi and Sever J. Voicu

(eds.), *A Bibliography of Interchurch and Interconfessional Theological Dialogues* (Rome: Centro Pro Unione [Via dell'Anina, 30, 00186 ROME, ITALY], 1984); *Ecumenical Relations of the Lutheran World Federation. Report of the Working Group on the Interrelations between the Various Bilateral Dialogues* (Geneva: LWF, 1977); "The Bilateral Consultations Between the Roman Catholic Church in the United States and Other Christian Communions. A Theological Review and Critique by the Study Committee Commissioned by the Board of Directors of the Catholic Theological Society of America. Report of July 1972," *Proceedings of the Catholic Theological Society of America* 27 (1973) 180-232; "The Bilateral Consultations Between the Roman Catholic Church in the United States and Other Christian Communions (1972-1979). A Theological Review and Critique by the Study Committee Commissioned by the Board of Directors of the Catholic Theological Society of America. Report of June 1979," *Proceedings of the Catholic Theological Society of America* 34 (1979) 253-85; "Lutheran-Roman Catholic Dialogues: Critique by the Committee on Doctrine of the National Council (*sic*) of Catholic Bishops," *Lutheran Quarterly* ns 1(1987) 125-136; "Observations on the Critique Submitted by the Committee on Doctrine of the National Conference of Catholic Bishops," ibid., 137-58; "Evaluation of the U.S. Lutheran-Roman Catholic Dialogue by the Roman Catholic Bishops' Committee for Ecumenical and Interreligious Affairs," ibid., 159-69; "An Evaluation of the Lutheran-Catholic Statement *Justification by Faith* by the Roman Catholic Bishops of the United States," *Lutheran Quarterly* ns 5(1991) 63-72; Joseph A. Burgess (ed.), *Lutherans in Ecumenical Dialogue. A Reappraisal* (Minneapolis: Augsburg Fortress, 1990); N. Lossky et al. (eds.), *Dictionary of the Ecumenical Movement* (Geneva: WCC; Grand Rapids, MI: Eerdmans, 1991).

# CHURCH UNION DOCUMENTS, CONSULTATION ON CHURCH UNION

# Introduction

The broadest church union effort of a multilateral and intraconfesssional character that has emerged on this continent within the past fifty years is the Consultation on Church Union. It involves nine churches: African Methodist Episcopal Church, African Methodist Episcopal Zion Church, Christian Church (Disciples of Christ), Christian Methodist Episcopal Church, the Episcopal Church, International Council of Community Churches, Presbyterian Church (U.S.A.), United Church of Christ, and United Methodist Church. These churches are seeking a form of visible and organic church unity that is at once "truly catholic, truly evangelical, and truly reformed."[1]

The two documents which follow are major excerpts from the final report of the Consultation of Church Union, submitted for adoption and implementation to its nine member churches. They are the culmination of more than two decades of theological reflection, accompanied by several rounds of churchwide discussion and response.[2]

The first selection is from the *COCU Consensus*.[3] Issued in 1985, it functions as the theological basis for a plan of covenant communion. The second selection, from *Churches in Covenant Communion*,[4] was issued four years later (1989) and is the plan itself. Together they comprise the proposal of the Consultation to the churches. Both documents contain other materials than those excerpted here—particularly the material in the Introduction and Preface and (in the latter document) the full text of the liturgies by which covenant communion is to be established.

The work of the Consultation has been informed not only by the traditions there represented, but also by wider ecumenical impulses. These have included the bilateral dialogues in which several of the member churches have been involved.[5] It has included also the work of the Faith and Order Commissions of the World Council of Churches and the National Council of Churches, many COCU participants serving simultaneously in both.[6] Moreover, the Consultation has been consistently represented in the several International Consultations of United and Uniting Churches convened by the World Council of Churches,[7] and the World Council has periodically published progress reports on the work of the Consultation on Church Union.[8] Further, the work of the Consultation has been significantly informed by the active participation of non-member churches, including Roman Catholic, Lutheran, and international partner churches.

Of particular importance in the development of the Consultation's proposal has been the presence and participation of three historically African American churches in the Consultation. Many issues heretofore regarded as "non-theological factors" affecting church union are now seen more clearly as having to do with the very essence of the unity we seek.[9] Much the same may be said of the participation in the Consultation of other ethnic minorities as well as of women and of persons who are physically impaired.[10]

The work of the Consultation on Church Union is well documented in its own publications.[11] It has given rise as well to a wealth of public commentary from other sources both within and beyond the circle of its member churches.[12]

## Notes

1. Cf. Eugene Carson Blake, "A Proposal Toward The Reunion of Christ's Church" (Philadelphia; General Assembly Office of the United Presbyterian Church in the USA, 1961). Copies of this sermon are currently available from the Consultation on Church Union. It appears also in Robert McAfee Brown and David H. Scott, *The Challenge to Reunion* (New York: McGraw-Hill, 1963), pp. 271-83.

2. Draft texts issued by the Consultation on Church Union for churchwide study and response have included *A Plan of Union* (1970), *In Quest of a Church of Christ Uniting* (1976, revised 1980), and *From Consensus to Communion* (1985).

3. *The COCU Consensus: In Quest of a Church of Christ Uniting* (Princeton: COCU, 1985).

4. *Churches in Covenant Communion: The Church of Christ Uniting* (Princeton: COCU, 1989).

5. Among the bilateral dialogues between the Roman Catholic Church and particular churches participating in COCU may be mentioned the Reformed/Roman Catholic dialogue (both regional and international), the Anglican/Roman Catholic dialogue (both regional and international), the Methodist/Roman Catholic dialogue, and the Disciples/Roman Catholic dialogue. In addition, there have been less well publicized dialogues between the Orthodox churches and some of the member churches of the Consultation. Moreover, the Consultation has benefited from NCC dialogues with Pentacostals and with conservative evangelicals.

6. E.g., see *The COCU Consensus,* ch. I, par. 6: ch. VII, pars. 32, 39-43. See also *Churches in Covenant Communion,* ch IV, par. 24 (incl. n. 24) and par. 26. Further reference to wider ecumenical indebtedness is referenced in the Introduction and Preface to *The COCU Consensus* in addition to the excerpts found in this section.

7. E.g., see Thomas F. Best, *Living Today Towards Visible Unity* (Faith and Order Paper 142; Geneva: WCC, 1988).

8. "Survey of Church Union Negotiations," published biennially by the Faith and Order Commission of WCC. This material appears also in the WCC journal, *The Ecumenical Review.*

9. Cf. *The COCU Consensus,* ch.I, pars. 13-17. Cf. also *Churches in Covenant Communion,* ch. IV, par. 43.

10. Cf. *Churches in Covenant Communion,* ch. IV, pars. 5-12.

11. The publications of the Consultation are too extensive for listing here; a bibliography is available from its office in Princeton, NJ. The most comprehensive summary of its work is contained in the published reports of the seventeen plenary assemblies of the Consultation, comprising a set of seventeen volumes, each similarly titled, *Digest of the Proceedings of the [numbered] Meeting of the Consultation on Church Union, Volume [number]* (Princeton: COCU, 1962-1988).

12. Commentary appearing in periodical journals is too numerous to cite. The following books are of significance:

Robert McAfee Brown and David H. Scott, *The Challenge to Reunion* (New York: McGraw-Hill, 1963).

*COCU; A Catholic Perspective* (Washington, DC: United States Catholic Conference, 1970).

Paul A. Crow, Jr. and William Jerry Boney (eds.) *Church Union at Midpoint* (New York: Association Press, 1972).

Thomas P. Rausch, S.J., *Authority and Leadership in the Church* (Wilmington: Glazier, 1989).

# The COCU Consensus

**Foreword**

This document is the first of three parts of a proposal of the Consultation on Church Union for enabling the participating churches to continue on their way toward visible unity. The other two parts of the proposal are found in the emerging work of the Consultation's Commission on Church Order and its Commission on Worship. It is the intent of the Consultation that these parts be understood together. Each constitutes an essential aspect of the process of "covenanting for unity" among the COCU churches: a step in the direction of the ultimate achievement of life together in a Church of Christ Uniting.

This document, THE COCU CONSENSUS: *In Quest of a Church of Christ Uniting,* is being referred by the Consultation to the participating churches for wide study and appropriate action by their highest policy-making bodies. This document will serve as one basis for an emerging convenantal relationship. It is the counsel of the Consultation that ample time be taken for full discussion in each church before the moment of decision is reached, and that the process leading to decision in each church be thoroughly understood by all and coordinated in the fullest possible degree.

*The Context of the Covenanting Proposal*

In 1970, the Consultation approved and submitted to the participating churches a full Plan of Union. It was clear from the responses of the churches that they were not yet ready to enter immediately into full and organic church union. But neither were they willing to disband the Consultation. Hence, beginning in 1973, the Consultation entered upon a process of "living our way toward unity," through encouraging the development of Generating Communities, Interim Eucharistic Fellowships, and joint study and action. What the Consultation now refers to as "covenanting" is a fuller development of that process.

Covenanting entails a number of deliberate actions by the participating churches. The claiming of this document, THE COCU CONSENSUS, is one of those actions. Other actions of covenanting include a mutual and formal recognition by the participating churches of their respective members, churches, and ministries. There will also be acts designed to reconcile the presently differing forms of ministry, to enable regular eucharistic fellowship, and to create various interim bodies for common life and action at each level of the churches' life. Covenanting, its steps and actions, are more fully described in the report of the Commission on Church Order.

Covenanting, therefore, is an act of solemn commitment to one another by the participating churches. It is embodied in a process of identifying and taking certain mutually agreed actions which will move them toward becoming a visibly united church. The covenanting process is thus a new interim stage in the life of the participating churches together. The act of covenanting does not itself effect visible church union. Formation of one church at this time could prevent our being open to the creative work God may do among us and through us in the process of covenanting. The goal of this process is to let our participating churches become one in the essentials of faith, worship, order, and witness. At the same time, it allows the churches to recognize and embrace the gifts of continued diversity our churches bring in their particular traditions, ethos, and racial and ethnic heritage, while we are spiritually renewed through these relationships and commitments.

By means of this document and the other reports, the Consultation on Church Union now calls its participating churches to a new relationship of commitment which is not yet full and organic union, but which is far more than a consultative relationship such as that which has constituted the life of COCU thus far. The ultimate goal of the Consultation remains: a faithful response to Jesus' call to unity in one visibly united church.

### The Meaning of Claiming this Document

This document, THE COCU CONSENSUS: *In Quest of a Church of Christ Uniting,* is a key element in the covenanting process. Therefore, it is important to understand what the act of "claiming" it means.

The 16th Plenary adopted the following resolution:

RESOLVED: that the 16th (1984) Plenary of the Consultation on Church Union approves this text and asks the participating churches, by formal action, to recognize in it

1) an expression, in the matters with which it deals, of the Apostolic faith, order, worship, and witness of the Church,

2) an anticipation of the Church Uniting which the participating bodies, by the power of the Holy Spirit, wish to become, and

3) a sufficient theological basis for the covenanting acts and the uniting process proposed at this time by the Consultation.

The three purposes stated in this resolution should be held firmly in mind. The churches are asked to find in this document "an expression" of the great Apostolic tradition they hold in common, an anticipation of what they intend together to become, and an expression of those things "sufficient" to make next steps in covenanting possible. Each body should be able to find the Apostolic faith reflected here.

As the churches consider their actions with regard to the process of claiming, the following points are to be considered:

1) The document, THE COCU CONSENSUS, is intended to build confidence in the process of covenanting. It is also intended to encourage the development of a common language for the expression of a common faith.

2) The question before each church is, "Do you recognize in this text an expression of the faith of the Church?" The question is not, "How does this consensus agree or disagree with our particular communion's theology?"

3) Consensus as used here does not imply complete unanimity or uniformity of doctrinal understanding. "Consensus" does, however, point toward that fuller confession of our common faith that can be made only on the basis of life together within one ecclesial fellowship.

4) It is important to remember that this consensus is "emerging"; it is an ecumenical witness of a group of churches that are on a pilgrimage of faith and reconciliation.

### A Note on Matters of Terminology

An attempt has been made to use terminology consistently throughout the consensus statement. The term "participating churches" is used, as the By-Laws direct, to refer to churches officially related to COCU, and therefore as accepting its aim to "explore" the establishment of a "uniting church" (By-Laws II and III).

In the 1980 edition of this consensus, the term "uniting churches" (plural) was used "with great discretion," for it was desired not to suggest, in a loose manner, commitment to aspects of a plan of union by the participating churches prior to their own decisions. This discretion in the use of terms is still important. But there is need now for a term with which to refer to the state of affairs which will exist when the participating churches, by "claiming" this consensus within the context of a Covenant, agree to live together in ways which will envision the sort of unity the document describes. At the

moment they adopt the Covenant, and thereby commit themselves to a series
of steps leading to the establishment of Councils of Oversight, the participating churches will become "uniting churches."

This document has adopted the term "Church Uniting" to refer to the
union COCU hopes to achieve, with emphasis on its continued openness to
new participating churches. This term replaces, throughout, the former term
"uniting church." The new term has the advantage of referring to the body
which is the eventual goal of this effort by an abbreviated form of its intended proper name, *The Church of Christ Uniting*.

## I. Why Unity?

1) Division in the life of the Church is a contradiction of its very
nature. Christ's reconciling work is one, and members of the Church fail as
Christ's ambassadors in reconciling the world to God if they have not been
visibly reconciled to one another.

2) The means by which the good news is preached must be congruous
with the content of the good news: a "making whole," a healing of all things
in Christ Jesus. The Church, as described in the Bible, is to be a family created by God in Christ out of all tribes and nations and peoples, a family set by
God as a sign to the world of the direction in which all creation and history
are moving: the summing up of all things in Christ and the coming of the
reign of God.

### The Imperative for Unity

3) The reasons for seeking unity among the churches are found in the
Bible, in Tradition, and in the imperatives of witness and world-wide mission. Unity is a characteristic of the Church into which we are called by
Christ's gospel; unity is a characteristic of the vision of the Church held by
the great saints and theologians over the centuries. For the Church to be a
concrete embodiment of Christ's message and an authentic witness of
Christ's mission to the contemporary world, some visible expression of unity
is indispensable. Let us consider each of these areas of concern in turn.

4) The New Testament repeatedly affirms the essential, the intrinsic,
unity of Christ's Church. In John 17, Jesus prays for his people "that they
may all be one...so that the world may believe that thou hast sent me" (Jn.
17:21); thus the unity desired is both a harmony of mind and spirit, and a
form which is visible to the world, capable of sustaining the life and mission
of the body of Christ (I Cor. 12:12-31).

5) Similarly, in John 11 we have already been told that Jesus should
die, not for the nation of Israel only "but to gather into one the children of

God who are scattered abroad" (Jn. 11:52). Paul enjoins the Philippians to "stand firm in one spirit, with one mind striving side by side for the faith of the gospel" (Phil. 1:27). Such unity is an omen or sign of their salvation from God (Phil. 1:28). To the Galatians Paul writes that they, despite being of different theological persuasions, must eat together as a sign of their unity in the gospel (Gal. 2:11-16). The Corinthians, as Paul sees them, are denying the gospel by gathering around party names, saying "'I belong to Paul,' or 'I belong to Apollos,' or 'I belong to Cephas,' or 'I belong to Christ.'" The apostle's rejoinder is swift: "Is Christ divided? Was Paul crucified for you?" (I Cor 1:12-13). And Paul takes up the argument again two chapters later: "For while there is jealousy and strife among you, are you not of the flesh and behaving like ordinary men? For when one says 'I belong to Paul,' and another 'I belong to Apollos,' are you not merely men? What then is Apollos? What then is Paul? Servants through whom you believed, as the Lord assigned to each. I planted, Apollos watered, but God gave the growth" (I Cor.3:3-6).

6) Finally, all Christians acknowledge their membership in a community of *one* Lord, *one* faith, *one* baptism, and *one* God (Eph. 4:5a). This is why, with many others, "we believe that the unity which is both God's will and his gift to his Church is being made visible as all in each place who are baptized into Jesus Christ and confess him as Lord and Saviour are brought by the Holy Spirit into one fully committed fellowship, holding the one apostolic faith, preaching the one Gospel, breaking the one bread, joining in common prayer, and having a corporate life reaching out in witness and service to all and who at the same time are united with the whole Christian fellowship in all places and all ages in such wise that ministry and members are accepted by all, and that all can act and speak together as occasion requires for the tasks to which God calls his people" (*The New Delhi Report*, p. 116).

7) The post-biblical Tradition also witnesses powerfully to the essential unity of the Church given in Jesus Christ. The oneness of the Church was early recognized as one of its four "marks," the others being apostolicity, catholicity, and holiness. We find this, for example, in the Nicene (i.e., Constantinopolitan) Creed: "We believe...in one holy catholic and apostolic Church. We confess one baptism for the remission of sins..." Scholars and church leaders also speak forcefully for unity; for example, Ignatius of Antioch exhorted the Ephesians that they should "form a choir, so that joining the symphony by your concord and by your unity, taking your keynote from God, you may with one voice through Jesus Christ sing a song to the Father." Irenaeus of Lyons described the Church as "having received this (apostolic) preaching and this faith, although scattered throughout the world, yet as if occupying but one house, carefully preserves it." Similarly, Cyprian of Carthage emphasized that "God is one, and Christ is one, and his Church

is one; one is the faith, and one the people cemented together by harmony into the strong unity of a body."

*Historic Sources of Division*

8) Despite such affirmations, divisions appeared early in the history of the church and have multiplied in subsequent centuries. Even in apostolic times, divisions occurred between Jewish and Gentile Christians, In medieval times, schism occurred between Eastern and Western Christians. Differing doctrinal formulations were not the only causes of these divisions. Discord and disunity also resulted from political preferences, cultural differences, social and economic polarizations, and various forms of discrimination on the basis of race, sex, physical or mental condition, and age.

9) Even as these divisions appeared, many in the Church struggled to maintain and restore Christian unity. Today a world-wide effort has begun to discern the meaning of the unity that Christ intended, and to recover, or to achieve for the first time, such unity on a global basis.

10) There are many reasons why efforts toward unity have become a vital concern in the twentieth century. Perhaps the most important single reason is a growing consciousness of the sinfulness of division. The disunity of the Church is a stumbling block to the world. It is a scandal that calls into question the being of God and the resurrection of Christ, and so imperils the credibility of the gospel. A united church will be able to develop a more nearly responsible ecumenical strategy which will give a more a credible witness in the world. A united church will be able to exert a genuinely transforming force in society. For example, the injustices which hinder peace among nations and which threaten the very survival of humankind are in part the inevitable effect of disunity upon the Church's social mission.

11) Secondly, the revolution in communications and increased mobility of large numbers of people have raised the churches' awareness of Christian communions other than their own. But still more important has been the impact of religious pluralism. No longer can it be assumed that all the people in a given area are Christian; no longer is there the luxury of "one church for every theological viewpoint." "Christendom" is gone; everywhere Christians are in a missionary situation. Christians must find a way of being together in such a way that the very form of the church in the world will communicate its message to the world, and still make room, within consensus, for a great range of theological points of view, practices, worship, and forms of organization.

12) Thirdly, after the church union in Canada (1925), the real impact of our now universal missionary situation was largely felt outside Europe and North America. It is here that the most extensive and successful church unions have been achieved, especially in India, certain parts of Africa, Asia,

and Australia. In these regions it became evident by the early twentieth century that transplanted church divisions made little sense. Not only were the issues involved hard to express, or even irrelevant, in such new countries and cultures, but it became clear that Christians could not invite people of other religions to recognize and follow Jesus as the Lord and Savior when they themselves, by their divisions, were proclaiming that they did not believe in his sufficiency to reconcile all people in one body to God. Today Christians are learning from these "mission fields" that the "household" they exhibit to the world is an indispensable vehicle of witness.

### Contemporary Church-Dividing Issues

13) Unity today is a task that requires resolutions not only of old but also of new divisions. Divisions must be overcome between the different forms of catholicism and protestantism. But there is also need for a reconciliation of long-standing estrangements in the Church which now have surfaced in forms echoing tensions in the modern world: estrangements between the sexes, and among races, cultures, classes, political opinions, and visions of the meaning of justice.

14) Divisions of this sort are of central concern to the Consultation on Church Union. By its very nature the Consultation stands against every sort of division in the Church of Jesus Christ. Often that division has been viewed only in terms of disagreement in such matters as the sacraments, ministry, or church order. But these things do not exist in a vacuum. The Church participates in, and reflects, the sources of division between human beings in society and culture. COCU was born at a time, the early sixties, when the United States was being compelled to reach a new consciousness concerning the feelings of alienation experienced by a number of its citizens: at a time when this country could no longer pretend that certain of its historic inequities were non-existent.

15) Early in the Consultation's life, moreover, it was joined by three major historic branches of Black Methodism. The racism which brought about the existence of these churches is one of the grave sins of persons and religious institutions in the United States. There are other churches within the COCU communions which arose historically as racially/ethnically separated churches. These churches arose despite being ignored by the larger community of faith and flourished as language-speaking churches. They often attached themselves to existing denominations and communions but to this day remain alienated. These churches—along with minority members of the other COCU churches—bring to the Consultation a distinctive perspective on theology and ethics, on ecclesiology and the Kingdom. Thus they keep the Consultation aware of the relevance of these distinctive perspectives to the work that needs to be done to rid ourselves of the sin of racism.

Furthermore, in several successive drafts of this Consensus, a series of warnings concerning the church-dividing potential of such realities as racism, sexism, institutionalism, and congregational exclusivism have appeared as appendices called "Alerts."

Much more work needs to be done in defining institutionalism and congregational exclusivism.[1] However, the matters of racism, sexism, and prejudice against persons with disabilities are now addressed throughout this text. Statements regarding these problems will be found particularly in the treatments of creation in the image of God, and of the new creation into which Christians enter by Baptism. Nevertheless, these issues need to be discussed at this point in the document because of their relevance to every element in it.

16) "One way of describing these issues," the original authors of the Alerts wrote, "would be to say that our deepest differences reach beyond sacraments and ministry into the divisions that tragically separate the human family." But such differences "are themselves theological in that they distort God's plan to bring all creation together, everything in heaven on earth, with Christ as head" (Eph. 1:10).

> [a] Where racism is concerned, the Alerts asked, "Why ought we expect to be brothers and sisters of equal status in the Church of Christ Uniting when members of the majority refuse to live next door as neighbors? How can we have 'brotherhood' and 'sisterhood' without neighborhood?" While COCU documents insist on equal representation and voice for racial and ethnic communities, Black Christians and churches have observed or experienced the divisive and demoralizing consequences of merger for the black experience, institutions, and community. Many Blacks feel that integration or merger causes fundamental and serious disruptions resulting in the elimination of leadership and loss of black self-control, absorption and the loss of identity, accommodation and the loss of self-reliance. And while some of these are offered up in the body of Christ, it all too often is assumed that they must not be given up in the body of white Christianity. Blacks ask, "If a church is not willing to risk too much of itself prior to union on the scale envisioned by COCU, will it practice equality and representation after union matters of race, sex, and age?"
>
> [b] As for the issue of sexism, the language of the Alerts is equally striking. "The most subtle and significant threat sexism poses for the future of COCU is the possibility of a loss of new life— the new life, the gift of God, that is being generated by the movement of women and men into full partnership in the task of

creating a new human community." And again, "COCU's task in relation to sexism is urgent because the loss of new life has already begun. Growing numbers of women and men who are committed to liberating styles of human partnerships are becoming unable to participate in the life of the churches as they now exist. These creative Christians can no longer give any legitimacy to the polarizing sexism that permeates the language and practice of worship, theology, styles of ministry, and the governing structures of all denominations. The Consultation may live its way toward union, therefore, only to discover within five or ten years that many of its members have been so alienated along the way that 'unity' has become a gentlemen's agreement within the dominant group, rather than an agreement of partners who have struggled together toward true mutuality in every expression of their personal and institutional lives."

[c] Even though none of the Alerts deals specifically with the role of persons with disabilities, this concern has nevertheless been present in the thinking of the Consultation. Since the Louvain meeting of the World Council of Churches' Faith and Order Commission (1971), full inclusion of persons with disabilities in the life of the church has been understood as a central, not a peripheral, ecumenical issue. It continues to be so understood in this document. Physical access to facilities is an indispensable starting point, but it is not enough. Subtle patronizing of persons with disabilities, the refusal to receive such sisters and brothers as full human beings and contributing members of Christ's body, is a form of apostasy. It has no place in the Church of Christ Uniting. Such forms of rejection appear not only in attitudes and structures, but also in patterns of language and other forms of communication which convey excluding assumptions. We must be constantly vigilant so that we do not give ground in these matters, as well as loving and creative in our attempt to overcome new obstacles to inclusiveness, as we become aware of them.

17) There is no easy solution to these dilemmas. The Church, however, is called to be a community of reconciliation in the modern world. Hence it must continually find ways of bringing its differing interpretations of the gospel into one community of faith. As a community of hope and love, it must also find means for healing the division among people who are alienated as a result of such unchristian attitudes as racism, sexism, ageism, and handicapism. The challenges of the modern world offer new possibilities for seeing and overcoming the old divisions. This includes a mutually enriching

appropriation of the theological and spiritual impulses which gave birth to the uniting denominations. Insofar as Christians have been divided from one another, they have suffered by being deprived of each other's gifts, help, and correction. Even when communication must consist of protest or rebuke (e.g., "speaking the truth in love," Eph. 4:15), it cannot be fully accomplished in isolation, but requires visible unity. Further, it is the traditions and practices over which we have become divided that contain the rich diversity of gifts that we must offer to the modern world, gifts whose power for the reconciliation of humankind can be released if we live them out as one People.

## II. Unity: A Gift To Be Made Visible

1) The unity of the Church is a gift of God in Jesus Christ to be made visible before the world. Diverse as the People of God are by reasons of race, sex, physical or mental condition, nationality, tongue, politics, vocation, and religious heritage, they belong to one another by their creation in the image of God and by Baptism into the one body of Christ (I Cor. 12:12-13). Just as Christ is one and undivided, so it is essential for his body to be one.

2) Each of the participating churches justifiably seeks to preserve the heart of its heritage and tradition in which is has received gracious gifts from the Lord.

3) The particular traditions, however, have on occasion been distorted by false claims of exclusiveness and even of ultimacy. Thus, while church union involves preservation and sharing, it also requires repentance, conversion, and a new commitment by all to the enrichment coming from the gifts and experience of the other uniting churches. Indeed, for the sake of unity, it may be necessary for a church to modify some of its historic customs in order to incorporate into its life the contributions of other traditions joining in the Church Uniting.

4) That which would be modified in the process of union, if anything, would be upon the decision of the church involved in the change; it would not be imposed from the outside.

5) The Church Uniting may find that it will need the contributions of traditions other than those of the presently participating churches, in order to become visibly a fuller and more diversified community of reconciled persons and gifts. The call is to a new and growingly inclusive form of the Church. In this spirit what is envisioned is a Church Uniting bearing enough family resemblance to the separate traditions to manifest its continuity with them, yet unlike any of the churches in their past separateness.

6) There can be no precise blueprint for the form which a Church

Uniting will eventually attain. But inasmuch as the participating churches are already bound by years of Bible study, theological reflection, shared mission, and common prayer, it can be said that the Holy Spirit has led the churches to identify a number of distinctive characteristics that should mark the reconciling and liberating community which is being sought, in anticipation of which they are already beginning to act. Each of these seven following characteristics is seen as fundamental to the quest for the visible unity of a Church Uniting which is truly catholic, truly evangelical, and truly reformed.

[a] *Celebration of God's grace shall be central to our life together.* Celebration means rendering glory to God and giving joyful expression to the love by which we are bound together. As we celebrate God's grace in Christ, we who were formally strangers offer ourselves back to God as a reconciled family (Eph. 2:12-21). God has provided the very means of grace by which we are forgiven, reconciled to God and one another, renewed in life, and given our common identity and mission. These are the saving gospel of Jesus Christ, the one apostolic faith, the sacraments of Baptism and Eucharist. Through these gifts the Holy Spirit leads us into all truth and empowers us to grow more and more into the likeness of Christ.

[b] *Christ's ongoing mission of salvation for the whole world will mark every endeavor of a Church Uniting.* Salvation is deliverance from sin and entrance into *shalom:* peace with God, health, and liberation. The risen Christ, to whom all power has been given in heaven and on earth, is at once Savior and Lord of persons and of history. The closing words of Jesus as recorded in the Gospel according to Matthew, "Go, therefore!", leave no human sphere outside of God's claim (Matt. 28:18-19a). As servant, the Church's mission is to the whole of human life, societies, and social structures, including individuals and their religious needs. But sin is at work, denying men and women the fruition of their calling as children of God, both within and without the Church, in such practices and attitudes as racism, sexism, ageism, prejudice toward persons with disabilities, institutionalism, and congregational exclusiveness. The Christian faith clearly assumes that converted and baptized individuals become transformed persons. This should mean freedom from discrimination in all relationships, social and institutional, as well as personal. The Church Uniting will take this assumption very seriously in theology and practice. Since "in Christ God was reconciling the world to himself" (II Cor. 5:19), there are no such things as "off-limits zones" for Christians in

mission. At the same time, it ought not to surprise Christians when they find allies for social mission among those who do not confess Christ's name (Mk. 9:38-40).

[c] *Each member of a Church Uniting will be called to an apostolic and priestly ministry.* A mission of such dimensions and promise will require of each member of a Church Uniting an apostolic identity, i.e., the identity of one sent to share with others the experience of wholeness which he or she, and the believing community, have found in Christ (Eph. 4:15-16). This is one of the chief implications of what is called the priesthood of all believers. In a Church Uniting, the distinction between ordained and non-ordained ministries will not mean the establishment of a ladder of dignities. Rather it will mean the ordering under Christ of the gifts and special callings of all for the sake of the ministry with which all are charged—that of loving and healing the world as Jesus did. In this way a Church Uniting will offer persuasive witness that it is indeed the People of God.

[d] *The structures of a Church Uniting will mirror the diversity of its membership in every aspect of its fellowship and ministry* (III:7b). Its racial and ethnic multiplicity will be held forth both as one of its richest gifts and the most persuasive witness that the reconciliation it offers to the world in the name of Christ is already at work in its midst (I Cor. 12:12-27). The same may be said for the contribution of male and female, of young and old, and of persons with disabilities. A Church Uniting will seek, both within and outside its own fellowship, to redress that imbalance of power and powerlessness which results from the fact that people have been, and are being, oppressed by reason of class, race, sex, age, physical disability, or any other such factor.

[e] *Because of the mutual enrichment of its several traditions, a Church Uniting will more faithfully reflect the universality of the body of Christ.* It is recognized that each of the participating churches, with its particular traditions and history, genuinely manifests the reality of Christ's one body (I Cor. 1:12-13; 3:4-13, 21-22). For this reason, a Church Uniting will value and maintain everything in these separate heritages which serves the gospel. Each particular church will find, by union with the others, not loss but expansion of identity, through giving and receiving in a renewed life of faith, worship, fellowship, and ministry. Yet many forms of church life which are valued as precious or even essential may have to be modified so that a

Church Uniting can be born. The new humanity of our Lord's risen body required suffering and death. Participation in that body requires no less. The most painful instance of such dying may be the overcoming of present narrow denominational identities.

[f] *Previous ecumenical relationships shall be maintained and strengthened.* A Church Uniting should be a uniting church. The bonds now existing between the participating churches and other Christian bodies (confessional, conciliar, and the like) will be preserved. A Church Uniting should seek to maintain communion with those churches with which the participating churches now enjoy communion. The unity of Christ's body is indivisible. To manifest it in the local community without expressing it in a broader area would defeat ecumenical aims just as surely as would preoccupation with world denominational or confessional unity alone (Acts 15:1-34). Relationships to other bodies cannot remain separate and private matters, but belong to the whole Church Uniting. The goal of a Church Uniting will be to add to existing associations new relationships which have hitherto been inaccessible to the separated churches, and thus to extend through visible forms and vital experience its solidarity with the People of God in all places and ages.

(i) Because a Church Uniting is only a step toward the reunion of Christ's Church, its commitment is toward a wider unity both within this nation and outside its borders. There is danger in a church organized solely within one nation, since nationalistic attitudes may pervert or silence the judgment of God's Word on the cultural, social, and political shape of national life. Nevertheless a church is sent to the society within which it is called, and apart from this society, it cannot bear true and responsible witness in this world (Gal. 2:7-10).

(ii) The participating churches desire to become more than a new and more inclusive denomination. They seek full reconciliation with all Christian bodies—with those whose separate identities stem from the very ancient divisions, as well as with those of more recent origin. This pilgrimage has as its ultimate goal the unity of the universal Church.

[g] *Maximum openness shall be provided for our continuing renewal and reformation* (III:13). No visible, earthly body, however idealistically planned, can ever be safe from the corruption of human folly, prejudice, ignorance, and sin. From such corruption, God has repeatedly saved the Church through those who

under the freedom of the gospel opposed its aberrations, checked its excesses, or summoned it to repentance (Jn. 2:13-22; Gal. 2:11-16). Provision for dissent is essential so that order may not stifle conscience nor prohibit the expression of viewpoints, particularly by minorities, who can easily be ignored or coerced by the majority. Provision for diversity and openness in decision-making sufficient to recognize and include both minority and majority opinions and interest will thus be made. As Christians continue to listen to one another, improvising new structures in the transitional period, building flexibility in the emerging organization, experiencing new ways of worship, and expressing obedience to Christ in joint action in society with all persons of good will, they will awaken to new understandings of the great work God is doing and calling us to share. What is essential is that every possible channel be open by which the purifying action of God's Holy Spirit may be experienced (II Cor. 3:17; Gal. 5:13-25). Power must, then, be checked by vigilant conscience, and authority balanced by accountability. Decisions must be made in the open and shared by the entire body. In so doing, a Church Uniting will come closer to realizing the wholeness, unity, and mission of the pilgrim community of Christ.

### III. Toward A Church Catholic, Evangelical, and Reformed

1) Christ the risen and reigning Lord has one body and many members in this world. These members are all baptized by the one Spirit into his body, the Church (I Cor. 12:13). By dying to their old selves and rising to new life with Christ and in Christ, they belong to the community of suffering and service, of faith, hope, and love which carries Christ's saving mission to all people (Rom. 6:5;Phil. 1:20;I Cor. 13:13). If they will put old divisions behind them, the churches can bear witness to the unity of the Church and its mission by becoming uniting churches. As they press forward to what lies ahead they can become a Church Uniting. Moving in the unity of the Spirit to the unity of faith, they must seek the structural forms and institutions which will make manifest their fundamental oneness in Christ.

2) In what spirit, though, and with what guiding principles, shall this search for an institutional expression of unity in Christ be undertaken? Such a united and uniting body will be truly catholic—that is, to manifest in the forms of its life and action the wholeness of the Christ who is its life. At the same time, such a body will be truly evangelical—that is, to know the Christ

in whom it lives as one who is to be received and proclaimed to the world as God's transforming good news. Finally, such a body will be truly reformed—that is, to recognize in Christ, whose identity it shares, one who calls it ever and again to change and to purify its ways.

3) In the history of the Church, to be sure, these three adjectives— "catholic," "evangelical," and "reformed"—have frequently been used to describe separate and sometimes warring traditions. Each of them, however, indicates an essential dimension of the Church's common life in Christ; and for just that reason the Church Uniting will strive to embody in its life and structures the qualities to which these terms refer.

*Truly Catholic*

4) "Catholicity" means universality, inclusiveness, unity. The Church is catholic, then, to the extent that it has these characteristics (Eph. 4:4-5).

5) The catholicity of the Church is rooted in the fact that it is a People whose shared life is a participation, through the Spirit, in the person and work of Jesus Christ.

6) The Church treasures its essential institutions—the Scriptures and the exposition of them; common and individual prayer and praise; confession of God in Christ through the Spirit. By these means Christians know and receive the "grace and truth" of the Word made flesh (Jn. 1:14) and so enter on a new kind of existence. As catholic, therefore, the Church is not ashamed to value and even to venerate these visible and human institutions, because they are also the means by which it lives in Christ.

7) For the Church to be catholic, then, means for it to embody and express in the forms of its life and action the fullness of the Christ who is "our wisdom, our righteousness and sanctification and redemption" (I Cor. 1:30). Thus the idea of catholicity includes the following components:

[a] The Church catholic manifests Christ's *universality*. Each local church—itself the Church catholic in its own place—is a part of the greater communion of saints which extends over the whole world and throughout all ages. Each assembly of Christians shares the calling, the problems, and the faith of other such assemblies in other times and places, and from their witness it learns and is built up (I Cor. 14:12), even as it makes its own witness and its own contribution to the life of the whole body. In this sense, to be catholic means to be in spiritual, intellectual, and institutional communion with all others who share or have shared the calling of God in Christ, and thus to live in a fellowship of mutual affection, responsibility, and correction.

[b] The Church catholic, because it lives in the new humanity which is the risen Christ, is *inclusive*. As Jesus' ministry embraced all

and was directed in a special way to those whom the world rejected, so the Church embraces those who are adjudged of little value by the world, regardless of distinctions of sex, race, physical or mental condition, nationality, or social rank (I Cor. 1:26-31). All members are given the same gift of faith and the same promise of the gospel, attested and sealed in Baptism. All share in the life and work of the Church, having a common identity and forming a single people in Christ (II:6,d). Hence the Church catholic is comprehensive in its capacity to embrace and sustain diversity in the expression of its faith and of its life of witness and service. Refusing deadening conformity and sterile uniformity, it welcomes the full range of the gifts which the Holy Spirit distributes among its members (I Cor. 12:4-11) just as it values the varieties of natural endowment in sex, race, age, physical or mental condition, culture, and linguistic or ethnic identity (IV:6).

[c] The Church catholic lives in the *one faith* which was delivered by the witnessing apostles to the first Christians, and which has been kept in continuity ever since (Jude 3; Gal.1:9, 12). The meaning of this faith can be, and has been, expressed in a variety of legitimate ways (V:8-9). The Church, however, because it lives and understands itself only through the nurture and disciplines of the authentic apostolic witness, guards continually against distortion and denial of this foundation. The apostolic faith and witness is binding and normative just because it points always to Jesus Christ, who is ever faithful and ever present. The Church's rich and many-sided continuity of confession is maintained within the community by faithful preaching of the Word and celebration of the sacraments. It is maintained beyond the community by the mission and ministries of its members.

[d] *Corporate discipline* in Christian life and teaching is necessary to maintain and nurture the catholic integrity of the Church (IV:14). Christian freedom comes as a gift in and with the gospel, delivering people from servitude to self and bondage to the alienating and destructive powers of sin. Such freedom, however, is experienced in the shape of a new kind of servitude—servitude to the power of love (Gal. 5:1,13), and in fidelity to the truth (II Cor. 13:8).

(i) Constrained by the love of Christ (II Cor. 5:14), members who are entrusted with responsibility and authority for preserving the integrity of the Church need at the same time to seek the restitution and welfare of the failing member (Gal. 6:1-2;Heb. 12:7-11;James 5:19-20). Nevertheless attitudes, words, and actions that are clearly contrary to the truth which is in Christ, or injurious to the life and mission of the community, must be judged and corrected.

(ii) The Church catholic has established means by which appropriate discipline may be exercised: the normative canon of Scriptures, presenting the will of God revealed in Christ; an acknowledged rule of faith and life aimed at growth in grace; a theological tradition which freely and continually reinterprets the faith for effective mission; transmission of ministerial responsibility; faith for effective mission; and constitutions and canons for maintaining order and wholeness.

8) The Church catholic stands within a form of the world which is passing away. Nevertheless it affirms the significance in God's sight of that world's common life in all of its dimensions. It values in that world everything which is of God's creation and seeks to inform the whole realm of culture and society with the spirit of the redeeming Christ. In those who hear its message it inspires new vision—for political and social order, for philosophical understanding, as well for literature, music, and the visual arts. Because the world is made in Christ and for him, the Church catholic accepts the fact that it is of the world and responsible in and for it.

## Truly Evangelical

9) The evangelical character of the Church means that it is constantly informed and empowered by the Gospel of Jesus Christ, and that it is commissioned to share its message of new life and hope with all people (Jn. 17:17-21). By initiation into faith, Christians are, in a true sense, ordained to a caring priesthood and to a company of witnesses to Christ (VII:28). Spreading the good news in ways which speak to the varieties of the human condition, the Church offers new possibilities and resources for both individuals and institutions (I Tim. 2:1-4). It conveys the sure promise that God forgives, reconciles, heals, and calls us to a new order of life in the risen Lord. Despite its own shortcomings, of which it constantly repents, the Church holds forth this news and this promise, and endeavors to realize and embody them in its communal life.

10) Being truly evangelical, the church will manifest certain characteristic emphases:

[a] *The Gospel means Jesus Christ.* Christ is both its bearer and its content. Recognizing this, the Church repeats Jesus' own message of the present and coming reign of God, with all of its radical requirements and hopeful promises (Mk. 1:14-15). This con-

tinuing recital of Jesus' message to the world is at the same time complemented by witness to his ministry, suffering, death, resurrection, and saving power (I Cor. 2:2). The evangelical faith and message touch upon every dimension of human experience, but in every point they confess Jesus Christ as Lord.

[b] *The Scriptures have authority.* The Scriptures are the normative authority for knowledge of Jesus Christ and of God's dealing with the people of Israel and the Church (Jn. 5:39). That authority, understood in the light of the living Tradition (V:6) and reasoned exegesis, and illumined by the Holy Spirit, always remains primal and effectual (I Cor. 11:2; 15:1-11). The Church lives by the promises of God in the Bible and stands under God's judgment and discipline.

[c] *Through the working of the Holy Spirit the Church evangelical experiences the power of the gospel in its own life.* The Spirit seals God's promise in the hearts of believers (Eph. 1:13-14). The Spirit conforms the life of individual and community to that of Christ (Rom. 8:1-17). By this work of the Spirit the Church is separated from the idolatries of this world, and built up in love through the gifts and charisms given its members (Jn. 4:1-3;I Cor. 12:1-11). The mark of its life is thus mutual participation in the gifts of God: in the presence and fruit of the Holy Spirit, in the prayers of common worship and the communion of Christ's Body and Blood, in the suffering which comes with service and witness, and in the joys and hopes of the new life in Christ (Gal. 5:22-23;Acts 2:42-44;I Cor. 10:16-17).

[d] God's mission to the world through Jesus Christ and the Holy Spirit has become *the evangelical mission of the Church.* The mandate for mission is for the whole Church, in every place, by every member. Mission and evangelism are inseparable, just as there is no antithesis between action and word (Jn. 3:21;I Jn. 1:6). Even during his earthly ministry Jesus began sending his disciples with the power to preach and to heal (Mk. 6:7). As the risen Lord, he commissioned them to share the gospel and the power of the Spirit (Jn. 20:21-23;Acts 1:8). In the centuries which have followed, the purpose of this mission has remained the same: that all people and nations may hear the gospel and respond by faith in Jesus Christ as the incarnate, serving, crucified, risen, and exalted Lord, and may know the transforming power of Christ in their individual and common lives.

11) The gospel is not only heard, It is seen and experienced in actions which are sacrificial, redemptive, and empowering (Matt. 5:16). Through the

Spirit's enabling presence, such actions are addressed to the whole range of human need. Personal and individual needs are met by sharing goods, showing care, offering community in love, and exemplifying forgiveness and hope (Matt. 25:35-40). Social needs are met by struggling to overcome oppression and exploitation, by working for human liberation and for justice, and by taking economic and political action to correct inequities in the distribution of life's necessities (Micah 6:8;Lk. 4:17-21;Matt. 23:23).

12) In all these ways the Church evangelical is employed by God, who acts through it for the welfare and salvation of the whole human family, and for the redemption of all creation (Rom. 8:19-23). In all these ways, the Church keeps inviting people to believe, receive, and celebrate God's work.

*Truly Reformed*
13) To say that the Church is truly reformed is to recognize that Christ continually calls it to repentance and reform As the Church is sustained by the Holy Spirit, it preserves continuity, through its form of doctrine, polity, and ministry, with the Church of all times and places. These traditional forms, however, are always subject to critical judgment which asks about their conformity and usefulness to the apostolic Gospel of Jesus Christ. In this way the Church, both in its reality and in its appearance, is constantly being reformed, and is always to be reformed, by the Word of God (Rev. 3:14-22;Gal. 3:1-5). Whether in the manner of the papal and monastic reforms of the Middle Ages, the evangelical Reformation of the sixteenth century, the evangelical revivals of the eighteenth and nineteenth centuries, the global reformation represented by the ecumenical movement of the twentieth century, or the numerous local and regional movements for purification and renewal, the Word of God is never without effect on the Church (Isaiah 55:10-11;Heb. 4:12). What then are the marks of a Church truly reformed?

[a] Drawing an analogy from the nomadic tribes of desert lands, the Bible portrays the Church as a *people on pilgrimage* (I Cor. 10:1-4;Heb. 11:29, 37-12:2). This analogy is not meant to point simply to geographical movement; rather, it suggests the Church's restless quest for the realization of God's reign (Matt. 6:10). As the people of Israel were called and led by the Lord through the wilderness and into a promised land, so the Church is on the move in history, anticipating that "city which has foundations, whose builder and maker is God" (Heb. 11:10). When the Church is called a pilgrim People, however, equal emphasis falls on both words in this phrase. The pilgrims are truly *a People,* the People of God reconstituted in Christ (Rom. 9:6-8;Gal. 6:16;Eph. 2:11-13;I Pet. 2:9-10). The Church is capable of "pitching its tent" in every place and culture. Yet as a pilgrim

People it can never be fully at home in any place (Phil. 3:20; Heb. 13:13-14). This means, in modern terms, that the Church must not become encrusted in traditionalism or carry unnecessary ecclesiastical baggage. It means also that Christianity cannot become a culture-religion, or a civil religion, or a nationalistic and imperialistic cult.

[b] The Church reformed expects to stand under the constant *judgment of God,* even in its identity as the body of Christ. By reason of its special vocation, it is the place where divine judgment begins (I Pet. 4:17). Everything treasured by the Church—attitudes and institutions, customs and practices—are constantly re-examined and reconstituted for the sake of greater faithfulness in thought, life, and work. The Church must accept this judgment responsibly. It must practice self-examination without self-justification, and self-criticism without self-repudiation. The judgment of God's Word finds its fruit in creative discontent, rooted in the conviction that a pilgrim People is one which continually grows in grace and fidelity. Because the Holy Spirit precedes the Church in its mission, the Church is ready to accept new forms and expressions of life and faith.

[c] The reformed Church is always a *servant Church.* Only a community which resists and rejects temptations to self-exaltation and grandeur can assume "the form of a servant" as Jesus Christ did (Phil. 2:1-11). No admonition about the true nature of discipleship, whether for the community or for individuals, is more clearly conveyed in Scripture than this. Christians have always regarded Jesus's humiliation and death on the cross as a supreme act of servanthood, enacting quite literally the prophecy about the servant of God in Isaiah 53 (I Pet. 2:22-24). The Church, then, can carry out its prophetic function in human society only insofar as it is ready to experience the sacrifices and share the abuses accorded the oppressed.

[d] To be reformed by the Word of God means *to be renewed* for God's future and not only to be reprimanded for past sins. The Church has a vigorous memory (II:6,g). It remembers with encouragement its past fidelities, but it recalls as well its dreadful apostasies in both faith and action. For the latter it must accept God's judgment and forgiveness, and then, "forgetting what lies behind and straining forward to what lies ahead" (Phil. 3:13), place full confidence in the God who makes all things new (Rev. 21:5). To be reformed, then, means that the Church

corporately, and, its members individually, need continually to be reconverted to God in faithfulness to the gospel.

14) The passing of outmoded forms and ways heralds the expectation and coming of *the new creation* for any persons who are in Christ (II Cor. 5:17). The pilgrim Church, subject to judgment and open to transformation, partakes of that new creation; it lives in tension between the already and the not yet (Lk. 11:20;Matt. 6:10). In many ways the Church is thus already catholic (affirming its apostolic rootage and seeking to be inclusive), evangelical (under the rule of Scripture and engaged in God's mission), and reformed (open to judgment and renewal of life and faith). But in none of these dimensions can it be said yet to express fully what God intends. God's promise to the Church is that it will become Christ's body on earth more authentically, God's pilgrim People in mission more zealously, God's partner in covenant more faithfully. The Church thus lives in joyous anticipation of God's reign over all people.

15) The Church can be a sign or foretaste of this Kingdom to the extent that it willingly subjects itself to reform (I Cor. 11:26-27). The time of the Church in history is between the times of life, death, and resurrection of Jesus Christ and his final coming in glory. In proclamation, celebration, fellowship, common life, and mission the Church invites all men and women to participate in provisional experience of the destiny which Christ its head offers to all. God calls the Church between these times to be faithful and loving in building up the body of Christ, in witnessing to the gospel and engaging in the total mission to all persons and institutions, and indeed to the whole of creation. As long as the Church is responsive to this call, it will lead persons to faith and salvation, and "the powers of death will not prevail against it" (Matt. 16:18).


## IV. Membership: The Unity of the Body and the Diversity of Its Members

1) The word "member," in Christian understanding, derives from the Apostle Paul's image of "the body of Christ," into which we are incorporated by faith through Baptism. "Now you are the body of Christ and individually members of it" (I Cor. 12:27). Through incorporation as members into this body, we receive our identity as Christians (I Cor. 12:12-13;Rom. 6:3-4;Gal. 2:20). As the human being has many parts, so this body has many individual members, each of whom is valuable to the work of Christ, who is the head of the one body and the source of its unity (Col. 1:18).

2) Concretely, membership involves entrance into a visible community of believers in a given locality, with a corresponding recognition of that

community as a particular realization of the universal body of Christ. Membership in the body of Christ and in any given community of believers is voluntary in the sense that faith, as response to God's initiative, is a free act, and in the sense that membership is developed by willing participation in the Church's ministry and witness.

3) Among these members, there are varieties of gifts, but the same Spirit, varieties of service, but the same Lord, varieties of working, but the same God who inspires them all in every one (I Cor. 14:4-6). This God-given diversity of talent and calling in its members is essential both to the Church's mission and to its unity as a living body (Eph. 4:11-16),(III:7,b). Moreover, such differences as those of race, sex, age, physical or mental condition, tongue, and nationality manifest the richness of Christ's purpose in creation and redemption (Rom. 10:11-13;Eph. 2:11-15;Rev. 21:24).

4) This diversity, too, therefore, must not merely be acknowledged and admitted, but appreciated as treasures with which God has endowed the Church. Rather than ignoring or suppressing such differences, Christians have the privilege of cherishing them. They must resist the temptation to discriminate and divide (James 2:1-5). They must permit the controversy which such diversity occasions to find its just and proper issue in fellowship (Eph. 4:15). They must insure that no one is deprived of place or participation. In this way, because of the grace by which they are already at one in Christ, believers must bear witness in a divided world to the richly diversified unity which God intends for human society under his Word.

5) While the Church celebrates diversity, it does not forget that in Christ Jesus there are no longer distinctions to be made on the basis of race, gender, physical, mental, or social condition (Gal. 3:28). The Church cannot permit practices in its corporate life which betray this oneness in Christ.

6) Membership in the Church, therefore, is for all persons who receive and believe the gospel (III:7,b). The Church has all too often practiced discrimination against racial minorities, women, the young and old, socially marginal and persons with disabilities, and others who are oppressed. Consequently, a vigorous struggle must be waged against all such abuses of human diversity, within the Church itself as well as in the larger society. The Church Uniting will receive into membership persons with developmental or accidental disabilities whose only response in faith may be spiritual or mystical, but in the sight of God real and dynamic.

*Membership in the Body*
7) To be a Christian is to be a member of the community of Christian faith. The word "membership" is commonly used in several senses—incorporation into the body of Christ as the one Church universal, enrollment in one of the particular churches in the divided state of the one Church univer-

sal, and participation in a local parish or congregation of a specific church. Both within and among the churches there exists a variety of conceptions about how these meanings are interconnected. The full meaning of life together with Jesus Christ and with one another exceeds the limited conceptions which the churches, in their divisions, have devised. The Church Uniting will not grant exclusive validity, or impose on anyone an obligation, to any of those specific historical conceptions. It does affirm that membership in a particular church is membership in the whole People of God. The Church Uniting will dedicate itself to the removal of any and all impediments in its life which prevent it from receiving into full membership all members of the particular churches.

8) Scripture gives a rich and varied picture of the meaning and implications of this membership. Because they are united to Jesus Christ in his living body, the Church's members are united to one another and grow together by the power of the Holy Spirit in the bond of peace (Eph. 4:15-16). Because the members care for one another, all suffer together if even one member suffers; and if one member is honored, all rejoice together (I Cor. 12:26). Because all are children in the household of God, they are constrained by love to live as brothers and sisters, and also, as they accept divine discipline and instruction, to express their love for God in worship and work (Eph. 2:19-22). Because all are members of a priestly people, whose High Priest is Christ alone, they are endowed with varieties of gifts for the exercise of service to one another and to all people (I Pet. 2:9;Heb.10:19-25;I Cor. 12:7). Because they are the universal People of God, they are commissioned to proclaim and share the gospel, and to be a leavening influence for reconciliation among peoples and nations (Matt. 28:18-20). Since God sent the Son so that we might realize in him that human oneness which was intended in creation, this community strives, by the fellowship of its members, to symbolize God's intention for all humanity (Jn. 3:16-17;Phil. 1:27).

9) The Church Uniting which we envision would accept as outward and visible bonds or marks of Church membership those confessions, attitudes, and acts which derive from the living traditions of the Church in all ages and places, and which are consistent with Scripture. Among such bonds or marks, normally present in unison, are the following:

[a] *Baptism with Water in the Name of Father, Son, and Holy Spirit* (Matt. 28:19). Baptism effects or signifies the union of the one baptized with Christ, and in Christ, with all members of his body, the universal Church. Thus our baptism is a basic bond of unity. Baptism in the case of adults is the enactment of a personal decision of faith, repentance, and loving obedience, which is a response in the power of the Spirit to the gracious call of God in Christ. In the case of infants it is the act by which the

child of a Christian family is sacramentally placed within the sphere of God's grace and the Church's pastoral nurture, with a view to being taught and led to a subsequent act of personal faith in Christ (VI:10-13).

[b] *Public Confession of Faith* (I Tim. 6:12;Rom. 10:9-10). Public confession of faith means the confession of Jesus Christ as Lord and Savior, of the One who raised him from the dead, and of the Spirit by which Christ dwells in our hearts. Normally it takes place in the presence of the congregation, either at the time of Baptism in the case of professing believers, or at the time of confirmation by those who were baptized as infants. Such confession, rooted in the experience of grace and repentance, involves deep and persistent commitment to learn the way of Christ while striving to walk within it (VI:4).

[c] *Faithful Participation in the Life of the Church* (Acts 2:42-47; I Cor. 16:1-3). Members participate in the life of the Church in the first instance through active sharing in worship both public and private, and in particular through faithful worship in the context of the Lord's Supper. They further participate in its life through study of Scripture and earnest thought concerning God's will for the world and the Church, and through the generous support of its life and mission by gifts, by work, and by active devotion.

[d] *Faithful Participation in the Life of the World.* Members of Christ's body bear witness, in action and speech, to God's presence in the world (Matt. 24:14;Jn. 8:12,17:11,14:21). This mission they carry out by the way in which they participate not only in affairs connected with their family and their job, but also in those of the community at large: politics, education, leisure, and art. By personal acts of service and sometimes resistance, which aim to actualize justice, mercy, and peace, and by active work to alter structures which deny God's will for humanity, they participate in the life of Christ.

### The Development of Membership

10) Membership develops as people "grow up in every way into him who is the head, into Christ, from whom the whole body, joined and knit together by every joint with which it is supplied, when each part is working properly, makes bodily growth and upbuilds itself in love" (Eph. 4:15-16).

11) A person enters upon this membership through a many-sided sharing in the life of the Christian community, within which, as the gospel is heard and received in faith, he or she freely and personally appropriates the

grace of Christ conveyed in Baptism. A person continues in this membership by continual sharing in the grace which creates and animates the Christian community. This involves participation in the preaching of the Word and the celebration of the sacraments. It involves learning and sharing a spirituality and a manner of life worthy of the gospel. It involves having an active part in the life of mutual concern and care which characterize brothers and sister in Christ. It involves accepting the common Christian life of service, reconciliation, and witness. A person manifests this membership by allowing the Spirit of Christ to nurture and develop the talents and vocation which are the seeds of a unique individual life of ministry and witness to God (Rom. 6:3-13).

12) Christian nurture is fundamentally a sharing in the life of Jesus who says: "I am the vine, you are the branches. He who abides in me, and I in him, he it is that bears much fruit" (Jn. 15:5). It is thus the Church's provision for the growth of all its members in all aspects of Christian life, understanding, and witness, throughout their entire lives. It manifests an impulse which is inherent in Christian faith: to seek growth in knowledge, love, and discernment for the sake of maturity in Christ, a manner of life worthy of the gospel, and "a spirit of wisdom and revelation in the knowledge of him" (Eph. 1:17).

13) Christian nurture is also an indispensable instrument of the Church's mission. Children and other persons who look forward to confession of faith and church membership need instruction in the meaning of Christian faith and discipleship and in the challenge to commit their lives to Christ. Persons who are already members need continuing Christian education and training to develop the maturity, understandings and skills needed in the life of discipleship and witness. It is especially important in the present time that members learn how to develop and express their own contemporary interpretations of the Christian message and life, so that when called to do so, they "account for the hope that is in them" (I Pet. 3:15).

14) The recovery and clarification of Christian discipline—considered by our forebears in the faith to be a mark not only of the individual believer but of the Church—is an essential task as churches work towards union. A Church which knows that there is no discipleship apart from a disciplined life will be equipped to face the divisions and discriminations that too frequently infect Christian fellowship. Within the freedom of those who have been set free in Christ, the Church relies not so much on rules and church laws as on the power of the gospel to shape communal and personal life and spirituality. Yet the Church must be prepared to root out barriers within its life due to race, sex, age, disability, and other such factors. Fundamentally, Christian discipline is also a sharing in the life of the Jesus who says: "As a branch cannot bear fruit by itself, unless it abides in the vine, neither can you, unless you abide in me." "Every branch of mine that bears no fruit, he

takes away, and every branch that does bear fruit, he prunes, that it may bear more fruit" (Jn. 15:2). Such fruit—love, joy, peace, patience, kindness, goodness, faithfulness, gentleness, self-control (Gal. 5:22-23)—contributes to the credibility of the Church's witness. The discipline of Christ by which this fruit is cultivated is indispensable in the Church's ministry of shepherding, safeguarding as it does the apostolic message and worship, and guiding the life and witness of its members. Today, moreover, it is important to stress the corporateness of this ministry of discipline by encouraging the mutual care and concern of Church members (III:7,d).

15) As a cherished aspect of its internal diversity and thus as a contribution to the richness of its unity, the Church Uniting will recognize a call to certain of its members to associate together in special covenantal communities, sharing a common life under a rule of prayer, service, and growth. Undertaken in unity with the Church, the establishment and maintenance of such communities will be of great value to the whole Church's life, witness, and work.

## Mutual Recognition of Members

16) Since all believers who are baptized into Jesus Christ are members of his body and share in his ministry, it is therefore appropriate that the covenanting churches have mutually recognized one another's members as sharing a common membership and ministry in the whole People of God (Acts 15:4;I Cor. 1:2;Rom. 15:25-27,16:1-23).

## V. Confessing the Faith

1) The Church lives and finds its identity in thankful confession of Jesus Christ as the one Lord and Savior (Col. 1:15-20). In Christ God's purpose for humanity is effectively made known (Eph. 1:9-10). Christ is God's self-giving in the Holy Spirit to be the life of the People of God (Jn. 1:4;Rom. 8:2). Christ therefore is "our wisdom, our righteousness and sanctification and redemption" (I Cor. 1:30). Being justified by faith in Christ, we are reconciled to God and to one another through the faith and love which is bestowed in the Spirit (II Cor. 5:18-19;I Cor. 13). The Church thus confesses and worships in glad celebration the one triune God (Matt. 28:19;II Cor. 13:14).

2) The content of the Church's confession is the apostolic preaching and faith which it continuously hears, believes, and expresses anew (I Cor. 15:1-15). This essential Tradition is handed on by being confessed not only in Scripture and creeds, but also in preaching and teaching, in forms of praise and prayer, and in witness and action obedient to the Lord.

3) The Church Uniting will acknowledge that the Head of the Body has made it a steward and trustee of this gospel (I Cor. 4:1). As it seeks to protect the integrity of the gospel, it will not merely preserve the common faith, but also will allow it to bear fruit in the personal commitment and action of individuals. It will seek the gospel's meaning not only in the witness of Scripture and Tradition but also in interpretations of faith made in the light of personal and communal experience and of careful reasoning. It will seek to grasp the fullness of the one Christ in and through the historical and cultural diversity of human expressions of the "grace and truth" which are his (Eph. 1:22-23).

*Scripture*

4) The source and basis of this faith and the confession of it is the creative and redemptive action of God in Christ, known through the prophetic and apostolic witness definitively borne in the Bible. The Church Uniting will therefore acknowledge the unique and normative authority of Holy Scripture. Scripture is the supreme rule of the Church's life, worship, teaching, and witness. It conveys all that is necessary for salvation to those who seek it in faith. The inspired testimony of Scripture belongs to the saving event by which God has, in Christ, constituted the Church and promised his final reign (Lk. 4:17-21;II Tim. 3:16;I Cor. 4:6). The Holy Scripture is the norm of the Church's confession, and therefore of its identity. It is the source of new life and light as the Holy Spirit makes fruitful in the Christian community the Word of God (III:10,b).

5) The Word incarnate is Jesus Christ, the living Lord, the Head of the Church (Jn. 1:14). Christ is the truth which the community seeks and finds in the Holy Scriptures (Jn. 5:39;Lk. 24:27,32). In Christ the promises of God are fulfilled; to Christ the Apostolic writings bear witness. Christ is the Word to whom the Scriptures and the Spirit testify (Acts 18:28;Jn. 16:13-15).

*Tradition*

6). There is an historic Christian Tradition to which every Christian body inevitably appeals in matters of faith and practice. In this Tradition three aspects can be distinguished, although they are inseparable. [a] By "*Tradition*" (with a capital "T") is meant the whole life of the Church insofar as, grounded in the life of Christ and nourished by the Holy Spirit, it manifests, confesses, and testifies to the truth of the gospel (I Jn. 1:1-4). This uniting Tradition comes to expression in teaching, worship, witness, sacraments, way of life, and order. [b] Tradition is also the *process of transmitting* by which this living reality of Christ is handed on from one generation to another. [c] And, since Tradition is this continually flexible and growing reality as it is reflected, known, and handed on in the teaching and practice of the

Church, Tradition is also embodied and expressed more or less adequately in a variety of concrete historical *traditions* (lower case "t").

7) In the Church, Scripture and Tradition belong together, since each is a manifestation, by and for faith, of the reality of Christ. They are related in at least three ways. [a] Scripture is itself included in the Tradition. Christian Tradition, drawing on and in many ways continuous with the traditions of Israel, antedated the formation of the Church's biblical canon. [b] Scripture is the focal and definitive expression of the Tradition of the apostles. As such, it is the supreme norm and corrector of all traditions. The Church has acknowledged this by binding itself to the Scriptures as its canon. The use of Scripture in worship and the authority of Scripture over the teaching of the Church are essentials in the life of the Christian community.

## Creeds and Confessions of the Church

8) The Church Uniting will acknowledge the Apostles' Creed and the Nicene (Constantinopolitan) Creed as unique, ecumenical witnesses of Tradition to the revelation of God recorded in Scripture. These are ancient and widely accepted statements in which community and individual alike enact their identity by confessing their faith. Both of these creeds grew out of baptismal confessions of faith as the early Church struggled to test and clarify its understanding of the gospel, and have been used as short affirmations and summaries of the Church's witness and belief. Although conditioned by the language and thought of their time, these symbols (creeds) have transcended such limitations by their continuing power to set forth the reality and mystery of God's reconciling work in Jesus Christ.

9) The Church Uniting will use these creeds in worship as acts of praise and allegiance to the Triune God, thus binding itself to the apostolic faith of the one Church in all centuries and continents (Acts 2:42). In its duties as a guardian of the truth of the gospel, the Church will teach the faith of these creeds, recognizing the historically conditioned character of their language, their corporate nature, and the principle that they are witnesses to and instruments of God's New Covenant with humanity in Christ (II Cor. 3:5-6).

10) The Church Uniting will acknowledge that every member has a direct relationship with God within the community of faith. It will, therefore, seek to respect the conscientious conviction of individual members and to enhance the deeply personal character of Christian faith. Only by the costly, individual choice and obedience which grace enables can a person trust in Jesus Christ and be fully committed to him. Corporate confessions are intended to guard, guide, and embody this personal commitment within the community. Although individual belief must be responsive to the public con-

fession of the Church, formal assent to a creed cannot substitute for personal commitment (Matt. 15:1-3;Col. 2:8-10).

11) The Church Uniting will honor the distinctive understandings of the faith which God has historically committed to the uniting churches and which they have sought to express in formal confessions (Rom. 1:18;Col. 1:3-5;I Pet. 2:21-24;Eph. 4:4). Each of them has ordered its life under the authority of Scripture. Each has made its own the apostolic testimony to God's redemption. Each has responded in special ways to the truth of the gospel, and embodied the theological insight thus achieved in corporate covenants and confessions. The tradition represented by each of these will enrich corporate understanding of the gospel. In the diversity of its life, the Church Uniting has room for those confessions which are cherished by any of the covenanting bodies. It will value such confessions as they serve the renewal and revitalization of the Church in a common scriptural faith. It will not permit any such confession to become an exclusive requirement for all its members, or to become a basis for divisions within its community. As it grows in unity, it will outgrow or resolve such diverse disputes as are no longer compelling to faith or theology.

12) The responsibility of the Church Uniting as a guardian of the apostolic Tradition will include, as a part of its preaching and teaching office, an obligation to confess and communicate from time to time the substance of the faith in new language to meet new occasions and issues (II Cor. 3:4-6; I Pet. 3:15). In formulating such fresh confessions, it will work under the authority of the Scriptures, seeking the guidance of the Holy Spirit (I Jn. 4:1-2).

13) Faithful guardianship also entails an obligation to help the members of each covenanting church to rediscover a more comprehensive tradition of covenants and confessions (Eph. 3:14-19). There are other churches, not represented in the Consultation, to whom we are bound in one Lord, one faith, one Baptism (Eph. 4:5). These churches have expressed their stewardship of the gospel in their own symbols and creeds. A Church Uniting will study these confessions, and where possible, join in them, thus enhancing the strength and richness of the common faith and expressing the fuller uniting of the Body of Christ.

*Worship as Confession*

14) Confession of faith takes place not only, or even primarily, in the setting forth of doctrinal confessions, but also in the forms and acts of common public worship (Jn. 4:22-24;Acts 2:46-47). The Church Uniting will therefore order its services of worship to express faith in Christ. By its celebration of the Word of God—through the reading of Scripture and the response of prayer and praise, through preaching and responsive hearing,

through the ministry of the sacraments, and also through expression in music, architecture and other arts—it will confess Christ as the source and foundation of life.

## Mission as Confession

15) Because it inherits the apostolic and evangelical calling, the Church Uniting will be summoned to exercise toward individual persons as well as society a mission which is both prophetic and reconciling (Acts 1:8;Rom 1:5;Eph. 3:7-10;Lk. 4:18-21; 12:49-56; II Cor. 5:18-20). The carrying out of this calling is a further essential form of its confession of Christ. The Church will therefore seek continually to clarify its understanding of the eternal gospel, and to convey that understanding in its public appeal to the world. It will aim to set forth the essentials of Christian faith in terms intelligible to the people among who it is called, without at the same time weakening the demands which follow from Christ's work as Judge and Redeemer of all (I Cor. 2:1-5). It will aim to address the contemporary issues of public life, knowing the conflict between "the wisdom of God" and "the wisdom of the world," and knowing also that Christ has reconciled the world to God (I Cor. 1:20-21).

16) Serving in Christ's name and following his example, the Church will seek to confess its faith by giving itself in suffering love for the world. By translation of faith into deeds in this way the Church can participate in the suffering and glory of the crucified and risen Lord (Col. 1:24). In each situation, while keeping open to new knowledge and sincere criticism by others, it will seek to bear witness to the presence of God, who rules and overrules in all human affairs and enterprises.

## Inclusiveness as Confession

17) The Church knows and acknowledges that humanity is both diverse and one, because it confesses that in Jesus Christ all men and women are offered redemption. Therefore, every person who confesses Christ as Lord is by that very confession bound to other persons as neighbors (I Jn. 4:11, 19-21). For this reason, the Church Uniting must not only call to mind the judgments of God upon the injustices and sins of the past, but also address itself to contemporary wrongs which alienate people from themselves, from their neighbors, from the created order of which they are a part, and from God.

18) To be faithful to its confession of faith, therefore, the Church must stand against all forms of prejudice, hatred, false nationalism, or discrimination based upon supposed social, racial, mental, physical, or sexual superiority. The Church Uniting will confess that such discrimination denies the unity of the God whose love is the same for all human beings, obscures the

truth of one Lord and one humanity, and degrades the oppressor even while it inflicts injustice upon the oppressed (Matt. 22:37-40;Eph. 1:9-10;James 2:1-7;Acts 17:24-28;Gal. 3:28). Congregations, individuals, or groups of Christians who exclude, exploit, or patronize any of their sisters or brothers, however subtly, offend God and place the profession of their faith in doubt (III:7,b).

19) The Church Uniting will affirm the diversity, equality, and dignity of all persons. It will identify itself with those for whom justice has been thwarted, and will support them in their struggle (Matt. 25:31-46;James 2:15-17). Rectification of past inequities is urgently needed. Thus the Church Uniting will insist upon freedom from discrimination due to race, sex, age, class, physical or mental condition within its own life, and will work for the abolition of injustice in society at large. In this effort to express the love of God for all people and to eliminate the idolatry which is implicit in every kind of human discrimination, the educational program of the Church Uniting will stress continually the inclusiveness of the People of God, as that is given in the Christ whom it confesses as Lord.

## VI. Worship: The Meaning of Worship

1) The essence of worship is a response of thanksgiving for God's holy love revealed supremely in Jesus Christ (Phil. 4:6-7;I Cor. 11:24). Through worship we are enabled to join those who in all times and places have offered the sacrifice of praise and obedience to God through "Christ Jesus, who died, yes, who was raised from the dead, who is at the right hand of God, who indeed intercedes for us" (Rom. 8:34).

2) It is Christ who has made this sacrifice on our behalf (Heb. 9:24-26). We are joined to Christ in our worship by the renewing power of the Holy Spirit, through whom we are enabled to offer the response of praise for which the universe and humanity were created (Rom. 8:26-27, 19-23). Since the God who creates and saves also governs according to his own purpose, the worship of the Church is an act of confident hope that the kingdom shall come and God's will be done on earth as it is in heaven (Matt. 6:10).

*Forms of Worship*

3) Corporate worship centers in the proclamation of the Word and the celebration of the sacraments. The individual believer's prayer, obedience, and service are essential components of the entire community's worship.

4) The public worship of the Church is an act by which the Church offers itself to God (1 Pet. 2:5). It includes corporate acts of praise, confession of sin, thanksgiving and prayer, the reading and hearing the Scriptures,

the preaching and hearing the Word of God, affirmation of faith, and the celebrating of the sacraments. Because public worship is an act of the entire
People of God, it involves the lively participation of all members, not only in
hymns and prayers but also in the acts of preaching and hearing, and in
sacramental worship as corporate celebrants and communicants (Acts 2:42-
47;I Tim. 2:1).

5 ) Forms of worship are important in the life of the Church for several
reasons. They guard and transmit the Church's faith and witness; they foster
the unity of God's people in its diversity; and they enable the familiar participation of all in public worship. As churches unite, new forms will be
encouraged and old forms both used and cherished, or revised as seems wise.
A variety of forms—especially as regards matters of ceremony, church fur-
nishings, vesture, music, and the like—is both natural and valuable. Forms of
worship must be in accord with scriptural standards, which govern every
expression of the Church's life and witness.

*Corporate Worship*

6) The Word of God, made flesh in Jesus Christ our Savior, is attested
in the Scriptures of the Old and New Testaments (Jn. 1:14; 5:39,46). It is the
right and duty of believers to hear the full testimony of this prophetic and
apostolic witness publicly and clearly read, and to bear witness in their own
right to the truth and power of the apostles' message (I Tim. 4:13).

7) The apostolic message realizes its inherent aim only when it is interpreted, proclaimed, and applied in the present. In this way it awakens the
faith and witness which constitute the living Church. Through preaching, the
Word evokes hearing, repentance, faith, love, and witness. Such hearing,
active as well as receptive, is an essential congregational contribution to corporate worship under the Word of God (Rom. 10:14-15;I Jn. 1:1-3; Matt.
13:23).

8) Congregational worship in which the preaching of the Word is con-
joined with the celebration of the Lord's Supper is the constitutive and representative service of the community of apostolic faith (I Cor. 11:23-26;Acts
2:42). A sacrament is an effective sign and seal of the grace of God which is
in Christ (Rom. 4:11;I Cor. 11:26). That is, it not only signifies God's
redemption of humanity in Christ, but also, by God's faithful gift through the
Spirit, it conveys that which it signifies as this is appropriated in the response
of faith (Gal. 5:22-26;Acts 2:38). Christ may be called the fundamental
sacrament of God's gracious encounter with humankind (Rom. 6:3-11;I Cor.
11:23-26).

9) The Church, then, as the body of Christ, may be seen as a sacrament
of the Kingdom of God, appropriating its identity in Christ through faithful
celebration of its most characteristic sacramental actions: Baptism and the

Eucharist. The Church recognizes the central importance of the sacraments of Baptism and Holy Communion, which derive their authority from Christ as witnessed by the Scriptures (Matt. 28:19-20;I Cor. 11:23-26), and are integrally related to the founding events of the Christian community.

*The Sacrament of Baptism*

10) As an act of Christ and a proclamation of the gospel, Baptism is not a private affair but a corporate act of worship (Gal. 3:27-29). The act of Baptism effects, or signifies, the incorporation of the baptized into Christ's death and resurrection (Rom. 6:3-11;Col. 2:11-15), makes them living members of the Church universal (I Cor. 12:13), and by the power of the Holy Spirit enables them to confess their faith, to renounce sin and overcome death (Acts 2:38;Rom. 6:8), and in their new identity to commit themselves in a new life and ministry of love and righteousness, which are a foretaste here and now of the life of the Kingdom (Eph. 1:13-14). Baptism as symbol, ordinance, and sacrament is a divine mystery and forms the visible basis of our unity in Jesus Christ. In Baptism all persons are made one in Christ Jesus. Human distinctions of race, class, gender, and physical and mental conditions are overcome (IV:9,a).

11) Scripture and Tradition are united in their witness that there is one Baptism (Eph. 4:5). Diversity of baptismal practice in the churches reflects different dimensions of the meaning of Baptism into the body of the one Lord. It is therefore appropriate that alternative practices be maintained within a Church Uniting. Infant Baptism calls attention to human need and helplessness, and to the reality of God's gracious initiative and action on our behalf. Baptism of confessing believers emphasizes the personal response to grace and the forgiveness of sin. It bears witness to the Church as a community reborn in the Spirit. Both infants and adults need responsible sponsorship by church members and adequate provision for Christian nurture.

12) Following instruction, Baptism is administered with water (by immersion, pouring, or sprinkling) in the name of the Father, the Son, and the Holy Spirit (Matt. 28:19.20;Jn. 3:5;Eph. 5:26). The rite includes an act of repentance on the part of the persons, or their sponsors; a confession of faith in God the Creator, in Jesus Christ and in the Holy Spirit; and a commitment by the person baptized or their sponsors, to a continuing life of obedience to Christ in the fellowship of the Church. Baptism is administered only once, normally by a presbyter with the participation of the sponsoring congregation.

13) The new life of membership in Christ and his Church must be continually and responsibly reaffirmed by the baptized persons so that they may fulfill the responsibilities of being called in Christ as ministers and witnesses in the world (Rom. 6:4,12-14).

14) This lifelong reaffirmation of baptismal vows may include an act of worship, which at times has been called confirmation, consisting of prayer and the laying on of hands of those having been baptized as infants. Confirmation may also be understood as an effective sign of the continuing and growing incorporation into the life of Christ (Eph. 4:13-16), of which Baptism is the foundation and the Eucharist is the regular renewal. Baptism and confirmation signify both membership in the body of Christ and entrance into the ministry of the whole People of God (VII: 29).

## The Lord's Supper

15) The sacrament of the Lord's Supper proclaims and recalls the life, death and resurrection of Christ while looking forward to Christ's return (I Cor. 11:23-26). In so doing it actualizes the unity and mission of the redeemed community, and thus, understood as including the preaching of the Word, it stands at the heart of the Church's worship (I Cor. 10:16-17;Acts 2:42,20:7).

16) The liturgy of the Holy Communion is an act of congregational thanksgiving for the perfect sacrifice of Jesus Christ (Matt. 26:27;Heb. 9:24-26). By reason of his real presence in the action, believers truly share the gifts and fellowship of his table (Mk. 14:22-24; I Cor. 11:24-25). Christ's high priestly act of sacrifice gathers up our self-offerings of praise, thanksgiving, and service, and unites them with his own (Heb. 10:19-25). In this way the Church's work of prayer and service in the world anticipates the fulfillment of God's ultimate purpose "to unite all things in him, things in heaven and things on earth" (Eph. 1:10).

17) Thus Christ in the Lord's Supper effectually shares with his People all that has been accomplished in his incarnation, atoning death, resurrection, and exaltation. "The cup of blessing which we bless, is it not a participation in the blood of Christ? The bread which we break, is it not a participation in the body of Christ?" (1 Cor. 10:16) God renews us corporately and individually in the life of the Spirit, and creates with us before the whole creation a visible and effectual sign of the reconciliation and liberation provided for humankind (Lk. 4:18-19;Eph. 1:13-14;II Cor. 5:16-21). Because Jesus Christ is its host and embodies the whole gospel, the Lord's Supper, wherever it is celebrated, is the communion of the universal Church of God (I Cor. 10:16-I7).

18) In the celebration of the Eucharist the bread and cup are taken, they are blessed as thanks is given over them for God's creation and redemption of the world in Christ, the bread is broken, and the elements are shared among the congregation. The act of giving thanks includes recitation of Christ's Words of Institution as well as prayer invoking the Holy Spirit. The

action is presided over by a bishop or presbyter, and deacons and lay persons assist in appropriate ways.

19) All of life, indeed, may be understood as invested with a certain sacramental quality through the activity of the creative and redemptive Word incarnate in Jesus Christ by the power of the Holy Spirit (Col. 1:15-20). A Church Uniting will recognize and respect different views as to whether there are other ordinances which merit to be called sacraments in the strict sense, such as confirmation, marriage, ordination, declaration of the forgiveness of sins, and anointing of the sick. The Church Uniting will recognize a sacramental quality in the Word of God preached, heard, or expressed through the visual arts, footwashing, feeding the hungry, giving of drink to the thirsty, welcoming the stranger, clothing the naked, and visiting the sick and the imprisoned.

### VII. Ministry: A Note on the Function of Chapter VII in the Covenanting Process

The covenanting process proposed by the Church Order Commission of COCU and outlined in the Foreword to this Consensus document offers the participating churches a way to grow together toward a renewed and reconciled ministry. The shape of that new ministry, as envisioned by the Theology Commission, is sketched in the pages that follow. This sketch points toward an ordering of ministry which may well be different from that now found in any of the participating church bodies. But the indications offered here do not amount to a constitution. Many details are deliberately left unsettled. There is room for the participating churches to grow together in unforeseen ways as they work out the implications of the covenant.

The Theology Commission assumes that the ordering of ministry outlined in this chapter will first begin to appear concretely in the Councils of Oversight. (For more details see the Report of the Church Order Commission.) These bodies will be the initial bridges thrown across the chasms that now separate the churches from each other. As the covenanting churches give the Councils additional responsibilities, the provisions of this chapter will begin to be embodied in more detail. The details will also be modified in the light of experience, new insights, and the decisions made by the churches in their relations to each other.

In preparation for covenanting, and through the period of growing together in covenant, each church will be responsible for the enabling actions needed to permit it to designate representatives to the Councils of Oversight. Whatever offices these representatives may hold in their own churches, within the Councils they will be laypersons, deacons, presbyters, and bishops.

The different nomenclatures and understandings concerning these ministries in the various churches will at the same time continue to exist. The old and the new orderings of ministry will thus exist side by side, informing and deepening each other. Certain polity changes in the participating churches may be needed to make this possible, but churches will make such changes only when they are ready to do so according to their own procedures. The anomalies in this situation will be frankly acknowledged. They will be minor in comparison to the anomaly of division itself.

The Consultation accordingly has not attempted to say where any particular ministerial office of any particular church finds its place. The Consultation assumes that each covenanting body will decide where in its own polity to find persons whose ministries correspond to those represented in the Councils of Oversight.

### The Ministry of Jesus Christ and the Ministry of God's People

1) The life, death, and resurrection of Jesus Christ was a ministry of God to all humankind. Through the Holy Spirit, God's People are called to share that ministry and are empowered to fulfill what it requires. By the power of same Spirit, the ministry of God's People appropriates and continues what God sent Jesus to be and do.

2) The ministry of Jesus Christ summed up and brought to focus all that God has done in the history of Israel and of all peoples to set men and women free and to reconcile them to one another and to God. His was therefore a liberating and reconciling ministry.

3) Sent by God to be and proclaim the fulfillment of all things in God's kingdom, Jesus Christ spoke with the authority of the Servant of God and humanity. Accordingly, Christ's mission was to preach good news to the poor, to proclaim release to the captives and recovering of sight to the blind, to set at liberty those who are oppressed, to proclaim the acceptable year of the Lord (Lk. 4:18;Isaiah 61:1). In Christ God began to put down the mighty from their thrones, and exalt those of low degree, to scatter the proud in the imagination of their hearts, to fill the hungry with good things and to send the rich empty away (Lk. 1:51-53).

4) Christ's authority was displayed in his healing the sick, forgiving sins, comforting the afflicted, challenging the arrogant, transforming traditions, and bringing into being a new covenant People in the midst of the old. Christ's authority was also made manifest in his announcement of the end of oppression and of the overturning of unjust power structures through the assertion of God's rule.

5) In solidarity with the outcast, and also with compassion for those who oppressed and executed him, Jesus Christ called all humankind to conversion and to repentance and summoned all to glorify God and love one

another. The ministry of the risen Christ continues both through the life of the Church and through the intercessory role he now exercises in the presence of God.

6) Christ's ministry was also a reconciling ministry. In Christ, God was reconciling the world to God, not counting (our) trespasses against (us). For the sake of the human race God made Christ, who knew no sin, to be sin, so that in Christ we might become the righteousness of God (II Cor. 5:21). Therefore if anyone is in Christ, that person is a new creation (II Cor. 5:17).

7) God showed self-giving love for us, sending Christ to die for human sin (Rom. 5:8). We are justified by faith. As justified sinners we have peace with God through Christ and his sacrifice on the cross (Rom. 5:1).

8) All this is from God, who through Christ reconciled us to God and gave us the ministry of reconciliation. Through Christ we have obtained access to God's grace in which we stand, and we rejoice in our hope of sharing the glory of God (Rom. 5:2).

9) Answering Christ's gracious summons, Christians by the Spirit are gathered into a ministering community, held together and empowered for service in love, hope, and faith.

10) In Christ, this People's life is vulnerable to suffering, yet strong in the midst of wickedness. This life offers and requires relationships of mutuality in need and service, and overcomes despair in the power of hope. This ministry is not confined to those of any one social or ethnic group. It is for and with the whole of humanity. Whenever obedience to Jesus Christ calls God's People to be in the world as he was in the world, they are led further by the Spirit into the truth of the gospel.

11) Enabled by grace, the People of God enters upon ministry by taking its stand where Christ is at work in the midst of humanity, in a continuing struggle against the powers of this age.

12) This struggle leads to both suffering and joy. Christ's People complete what is lacking of Christ's afflictions for the sake of his body, that is, the Church (Col. 1:24). They also know a foretaste of the joy that was set before him who endured the cross and is set down at the right hand of the throne of God (Heb. 12:2).

13) Therefore, where women and men struggle against poverty and oppression, ministry means entering into that struggle with oppressor and oppressed alike to overcome the causes of suffering. When men and women engage wittingly or unwittingly in oppressive actions and decisions, ministry means acting compassionately toward them for the eradication of these evils. Where people undergo affliction, pain, disease, and death, ministry means sharing witness with them in the calling to bear one anothers' burdens (Gal. 6:2). Where persons suffer because of their choice to work for liberation, jus-

tice, and peace, ministry means supporting them in their witness (Phil. 1:29,30;Matt. 25:31-45).

14) Yet, ministry is not simply to those who suffer and struggle. All who struggle and suffer with hope minister to the world and offer compelling testimony to the power of the cross and resurrection. Such ministries may express to the Church the privilege of "dying daily" with Christ, and at the same time of rising with Christ to new life. For the ministry of God's people is at the same time joyful. Those who minister in the midst of suffering are called "blessed" (Matt. 5:1-11). They begin to inherit now a kingdom prepared for them before the foundations of the earth (Matt. 25:34). They are offered a foretaste of that messianic banquet at which the poor, the maimed, the blind, and the lame, have the privileged place (Lk. 14:13-14).

15) In all its forms and functions, ministry is a rich interweaving of word and worship, work and witness. In different ways, members of the same body share responsibility for the Church's government, administration, discipline, instruction, worship, and pastoral care.

16) These activities are to be held together in a visible ordering through which the Church is equipped for its ministry. "Having gifts that differ according to the grace given to us" (Rom. 12:6), the several members bring to the one body a wide diversity of gifts, functions, and services. "To each is given the manifestation of the Spirit for the common good" (I Cor. 12:7). Each is a distinctive form of the single ministry of Christ as it is realized in diverse yet mutually complementary ways in the whole life of the Church and in the world (II:6,d;III:7,b;IV:3).

17) As the People gather to worship under the direction of the Word, all members both receive God's grace and make their contribution to the continuation of Christ's ministry before God.

18) There is a ministry of faithful hearing and proclaiming God's Word, of rightly administering and receiving the sacraments, of responsibly celebrating and living out the Church's worship. These are actions of the entire People of God. All members, including those with physical or mental impairments, are endowed with special gifts and vocations, and exercise particular functions, thus adding to the richness of Christ's ministry as it takes form in the worship of the gathered community.

19) Members of the Church are also called to labor as a People whose action manifests the ministry of Christ in the world. God's People bear witness to the world in and through the organized life of the Church (II:7-8;III:11). They are also summoned to be faithful witnesses in daily life: in trades, industry, agriculture, and commerce; in political life, education, and the family; in professional activity of every kind. They are summoned to forward God's redemptive ministry to humanity, to share in the ministry as a "living sacrifice" (Rom. 12:1), and to "prove what is the will of God"

through the "renewal of (our) minds" on the way toward "what is good and acceptable and perfect" (Rom. 12:2).

20) The ministry of Jesus Christ, and the ministry of the Church in him, are intelligible only in relationship to God. In ministry the People enter into a cycle of life in the Spirit that leads from God and to God. Through the ministry of Christ and of his People, God's purpose of uniting all things in heaven and earth is being accomplished (Eph. 1:10).

*The Sharing and Ordering of Ministry*

21) The ordained and lay ministries of the Church are differing forms of the one ministry of Christ that is shared by the whole People of God. Because they are forms of one ministry, they complement one another. Thus, they must be ordered in relation to one another in the life of the Church.

22) All ministries, lay as well as those of bishop, presbyter, and deacon, are to be understood as at once personal, collegial, and communal. In attempting to actualize the personal, collegial, and communal character of ministry, the Church Uniting will seek to incorporate "catholic" and "protestant" concerns, as well as the experience of the different uniting polities, drawing sustenance and admonition from the several converging streams of tradition.

> [a] All ministry in the Church Uniting will be *personal*. In every minister, lay and ordained, Christ and the gospel are made present as personal reality and are the source of that life of holiness and devotion which is a mark of ministry. Ministry is exercised by men and women who have been individually called and baptized, and in certain cases, also ordained. They continue, in their activities, the ministry of Christ to the Church and to the world and, in turn, manifest the ministry of the Church to humanity. In their varying personal capacities, they serve individuals and groups within and outside the Church.

> [b] All ministry in the Church Uniting will be *collegial*. Baptism and ordination alike associate the individual with others who share the same call. Ministry is inherently a shared responsibility. Thus no minister is independent or autonomous. Just as collegial relationships obtain among persons in the same ministry, so too they obtain among those in different ministries. Such relationships include lay persons as well as bishops, presbyters, and deacons. The interpersonal character of collegiality is a basis for partnership in governance and gives life and substance to the institutional structures of the Church.

> [c] All ministry in the Church Uniting will be *communal*. The intimate relation between the different ministries and the Christian

community as such should find expression in relationships through which the exercise of ministry is rooted in the life of the worshipping and witnessing congregation and requires the local church's effective participation in the discovery of God's will and the guidance of the Spirit.

23) All ministry in the Church Uniting will be constitutionally or canonically ordered and exercised in such a way that each of these three dimensions can find adequate expression. A person enters ministry through formal procedures of membership or ordination, accompanied by election or appointment. No individual's ministry can be regarded as representative of the Church unless it is constitutional or canonical, and remains in communion with and accountable to, other ministers in ordered assemblies in which all ministries are represented.

## The Ministry of Lay Persons

24) Lay persons are called by their Baptism and membership in the Church to manifest and bear witness to Christ's presence in the world in all their activities. Through their Baptism, lay persons are called into the ministry of Jesus Christ, into a personal relationship to God in Christ, and at the same time into a relationship to other Christians. Lay persons who are subsequently ordained continue to bear responsibility for the ministry common to all Christians to which they were called at Baptism.

25) The terms "laity" and "laypersons" continually give rise to confusion, in part because of their apparent connection with *laos* or people, a term applicable to the entire body of the Church, whether "lay" or "ordained." The derivation of the term "lay" is from the Greek *laos* or *laikos*, meaning "the people" or "of the people." But in common English usage the term "lay" means either "not ordained," or "not professional," and hence carries with it not only an inherent equivocation about the status to which it is the antonym, but also the suggestion of a deprived or residual character in the status to which it refers. In the list of Christian ministries, the "layperson" may thus be perceived as "none of the above," as one who does not have the duties or prerogatives of ordained persons. We wish to overcome this implication. Lay status in the Church is not a residual status, but rather the primary form of ministry apart from which no other Christian ministry can be described.

26) The ministry received in Baptism is at once personal, collegial, communal, and therefore also constitutional. Lay persons may be formally appointed to various functions, thereby being acknowledged by the Church, and, in turn, acknowledging their responsibility for particular tasks. They carry out their ministries in a variety of ways.

[a] *Witnessing to the Gospel in Worship and in the World.* Lay persons hear the gospel and proclaim it. They participate in the

worship of the community by offering words and actions of praise, by taking part in the preaching whether by speaking or by responding, by reading the Scriptures, offering prayers, and bringing the eucharistic gifts. They fill lay offices in the congregation. They participate in educational programs, pursue private study, teach and bear witness to others. They inform and test current theological understandings. They discern and practice the implications of the gospel by word and action in their families, in the congregation, and in all places of daily living. In evangelism, they share their faith in Christ with others.

[b] *Seeking Justice and Reconciliation in the World.* Through active involvement in the world, lay persons represent Christ's ministry of justice and reconciliation. As agents of God's purpose, they speak from within the world to the world for a society both just and humane, where the needs of "the least" are met with sensitivity and dignity. They seek to discern the signs of the Kingdom wherever they may be manifest in human affairs as they bear witness to the gospel with boldness, courage, hospitality, and love.

[c] *Bringing the World before God.* The laity makes the connections between Christ, the Church, and the world real and visible. In their devotional practices and through their liturgical life, these persons offer to God their public and personal concerns and celebrate the mighty acts of God. By adoration, confession, thanksgiving, intercession, and supplication, they bring themselves and others under the transforming justice and mercy of God.

[d] *Providing Pastoral Care for Persons.* Lay persons are called to care for each other, for the ordained, and for persons outside the Church. Such caring means sensitive listening and discerning counseling. It means visiting the sick, the prisoners, those confined by age or poverty. It means participation in congregational and other programs that enhance pastoral sensitivity to the hurts and dilemmas faced by social groups, families, and individuals. It also means the effort to address systemic social causes of human suffering.

[e] *Serving the Cause of Unity.* In virtue of their Baptism and membership in the body, lay persons constitute an inherently ecumenical ministry. In all they do, they embody this reality and raise the question of unity for the Church Universal. Lay persons meet across denominational lines in prayer and common mission. Thus they can bring new expressions of the Church into being, acting out forms of unity which the institutional

churches cannot yet express. They transcend divisions and express in anticipation the fulfilled reality of the one body in Jesus Christ.

[f] *Participation in Governance.* Lay persons, bishops, presbyters, and deacons share in the governance of the Church locally, regionally, and nationally.

### The Ministry of Ordained Persons

27) The ministry of the one People of God, with all its diversity, is the continuation of the saving ministry of Jesus Christ, and this ministry is the context within which what is usually called ordained ministry must be discussed.

28) According to growing ecumenical understanding, all members of the Church are in a certain sense ordained to the whole, corporate ministry (III:9): "As persons are initiated into the faith, they are, in a true sense, ordained to a caring priesthood and to a company of witnesses to Christ" (VI:14). The ministry is "a royal priesthood, a holy nation, a people for God's own possession" (I Peter 2:9). Thus all Christians are called to ministry, to a life of faithful discipleship in and beyond the Church. The Church itself, indeed, was first known in New Testament Greek as *ekklesia,* having been called together from all peoples to be the People faithful to God.

29) This calling of each Christian is sealed effectually by Baptism/confirmation, when vows are taken and the responsibilities of discipleship conferred. There are distinctions of function, but a shared dignity or worth here, inasmuch as all are called to minister to one another and to all persons.

30) Within the one ministry of the whole People, God calls forth in the Church particular ministries of persons to serve the People through proclamation of the Word and administration of the sacraments (Lk. 22:25-27; I Cor. 3:5;Acts 1:21-26,6:1-6;II Tim. 1:11,1:6). These ministries share in the ministry of Christ by representing in and for the Church its dependence on, and its identity in, the Word of God (Jn. 20:21-23). For this reason they symbolize and focus the ministry of Christ and the apostles as well as the ministry of the whole Church. Those called to such public ministries are ordained, in the usual sense of the term, by the Church through the authority and power of the Holy Spirit (Acts 20:28). Minister, pastor, and preacher are general names for these persons; presbyter, priest, elder, deacon, and bishop are particular names.

31) These women and men share the whole ministry of witness and service with all the People of God. Their ordination marks them as persons who represent to the Church its own identity and mission in Jesus Christ. In this capacity they are authorized to undertake services in, with, and for the Church, preaching and teaching the gospel, presiding over the liturgical and

sacramental life of the congregations, assembling, equipping, and watching over the community.

32) The authority of the ordained minister is rooted in Jesus Christ, who received it from God (Matt. 28:18) and who confers it by the Holy Spirit in the act of ordination. This act takes place within a community which accords public recognition to a particular person. Because Jesus came as one who serves (Mk. 10:45,Lk. 22:27), to be set apart means to be consecrated to service. Since ordination is essentially a setting apart with prayer for the gift of the Holy Spirit, the authority of the ordained ministry is not to be understood as the possession of the ordained person, but as a gift for the continuing edification of the body in and for which the minister has been ordained. (This paragraph is adapted from the WCC *Baptism, Eucharist and Ministry* document, Faith and Order Paper 111, 1982.)

33) Ordination is not to be confused with "professional" status within the Church. Some who are ordained will derive their salaries from the Church, while others will perform their ministries without leaving their occupation or employment. Requirements of education or specialized training will vary among participating churches and between the three offices. Regardless of these variations, ordination to the offices of deacon, presbyter, and bishop represents the call of God through the voice of the one Church rather than the "professional" achievement of a given individual.

34) People are called in differing ways. Sometimes persons are mistaken about the reality of their calling. From its beginnings however, the Church has recognized that several elements are essential in the call to the ordained, representative ministry. First, there is an inner, personal awareness and call, as the Holy Spirit bears witness to one's spirit (Rom. 8:16). Secondly, there is a recognition of the particular gifts and graces, both naturally and spiritually given, needed for ministry (Eph. 4:11). Thirdly, there is required the Church's public approbation that the call is an authentic call heard with good conscience. In the judgment of the Church, this call requires, for its fulfillment, possession and development of appropriate gifts for fruitful ministry.

35) The Church's act of ordination is performed in the name of Christ on the basis of God's call and gifts, which come without regard to disability, race, sex, mature age, social or economic status.

36) Those who are charged to make decisions about ordination, while seeking guidance of the Spirit, must rely on human wisdom and discretion. As fallible persons, they can err in accepting some and rejecting others, but faithfulness and serious purpose are presumed.

37) However the ordination ritual may be written or theologically interpreted, it consists essentially of prayer with the laying on of hands. (Prototypes of such practices in the New Testament are found, for example, in Acts 8:18, Hebrews 6:2, II Timothy 1:6.) The prayer is an invocation of

the Holy Spirit, asking for divine power to be bestowed on the candidate for the exercise of this ministry. Believing that the prayer will be answered, as representatives of the whole Church, bishops and other persons place their hands upon the head of the ordinand, making a visible and effective sign of the gift of the Spirit, attesting the Church's approbation, and commissioning this person to fulfill a particular ministry. In recognition of the God-given nature of ministry, ordination to any one of the representative ministries is never repeated, just as Baptism is never repeated.

38) By the act of ordination the community of faith thankfully acknowledges that God provides women and men equipped with gifts and graces to lead and care for the Church in its total mission. By this act the minister, whether bishop, presbyter, or deacon, who shares with all members in the dignity of the priesthood of all believers, acknowledges an obligation to be a servant of God's servants, to the church bodies which ordain, to the Church Universal, and to Jesus Christ, the head of the Church.

### The Threefold Pattern of Ordained Ministry

39) Several orderings of ordained ministry have arisen in the history of the Church. The exclusive warrant of the New Testament cannot be claimed for any one of them. They are adaptations of biblical forms to the needs of the Church in differing times and places. In the midst of this variety however, one ordering has emerged as predominant; the threefold ministry of bishop, presbyter, and deacon.

40) It is important to be aware of the changes the threefold ministry has undergone in the history of the Church. In the earliest instances, where threefold ministry is mentioned, the reference is to the local eucharistic community. The bishop was the leader of the community, was ordained and installed to proclaim the Word and preside over the celebration of the Eucharist. The bishop was surrounded by a college of presbyters and by deacons who assisted in his tasks. In this context, the bishop's ministry was a focus of unity within the whole community.

41) Soon, however, episcopal functions were modified. Bishops began increasingly to exercise oversight over several local communities at the same time in a manner analogous to the way the apostles has exercised oversight in the wider Church. Bishops thus began to provide a focus of unity in life and witness within areas comprising several eucharistic communities. As a consequence, presbyters and deacons were assigned new roles. Presbyters became the leaders of local eucharistic communities, and, as assistants of the bishops, deacons received larger responsibilities.

42) Although there is no single New Testament pattern, although the Spirit has many times led the church to adapt ministries to its contextual needs, and although other forms of the ordained ministry have been blessed

with the gifts of the Holy Spirit, the threefold ministry of bishop, presbyter, and deacon may nevertheless serve today as an expression of the unity we seek and as a means for achieving it. Historically, the threefold ministry became the generally accepted pattern, and is still retained, in a variety of forms, by many churches today. Whatever nomenclature they may use, the churches need persons who in different ways express and perform the tasks of ordained ministry in its diaconal, presbyteral, and episcopal aspects and functions.

43) Yet the threefold pattern stands evidently in need of reform. In some churches the collegial dimension of leadership in the eucharistic community has suffered diminution. In others, the function of deacons has been reduced to an assisting role in the celebration of the liturgy: they have ceased to fulfill any function with regard to the diaconal witness of the Church. The relation of the presbyterate to the episcopal ministry has been discussed throughout the centuries. The degree of the presbyter's participation in the episcopal ministry is still for many an unresolved question of far reaching ecumenical importance. In some cases, churches which have not formally kept the threefold form have, in fact, maintained certain of its original patterns.

(The five paragraphs above are adapted from the *Baptism, Eucharist and Ministry* document, Faith and Order Paper 111, World Council of Churches, Geneva, 1982.)

44) In full awareness of these facts and of a continuing need for thoughtful attention to them, the threefold ordering will be continued in the Church Uniting in ways appropriate to the differing traditions of the uniting churches and to the future needs of their common mission. The ministry of the Church Uniting will be intended to manifest visible historical continuity "with the whole Christian fellowship in all places and in all ages in such wise that ministry and members are accepted by all" (WCC *New Delhi Statement,* 1961).

## *The Ministry of Bishops*

45) Bishops are baptized members of the People of God, ordained to preach the Word, preside at the sacraments, and administer discipline in such a way as to be representative pastoral ministers of oversight, unity, and continuity in the Church.

46) Bishops, in communion with all the People of God, represent the continuity of the Church's life and ministry over the centuries, the unity of its communities and congregations with one another, and the oneness of its ministries in mission to the world. Bishops are a sign of, and are particularly responsible for, the continuity of the whole Church's Tradition (V:6), as well

as of its pastoral oversight (in Greek of the New Testament, *episkopé*), as they teach the apostolic faith.

47) Some churches have maintained episcopacy in the form of a succession of ordained ministers who combine in their ministries the functions of both bishop and presbyter. Some other churches do not claim a formal episcopal succession, but in fact exist with the express intention of maintaining a succession in the apostolic faith. It is the intent of the participating churches that the apostolic content of such ministries, as well as the existence in them of ministries of *episkopé* in various forms, be fully recognized.

48) The participating churches intend that in the Church Uniting, bishops shall stand in continuity with the historic ministry of bishops as that ministry has been maintained through the ages, and will ordain its bishops in such a way that recognition of this ministry is invited from all parts of the universal Church.

49) In doing so, the Church Uniting will not require any theory or doctrine of episcopacy or episcopal succession which goes beyond the consensus stated in this document. It will recognize that it inherits, from episcopal and non-episcopal churches alike, a variety of traditions about the ministry of oversight, unity, and continuity. It will seek to appropriate these traditions creatively, and so to move toward an episcopate reformed and always open to further reformation in the light of the gospel: an episcopate which will probably be different from that now known in any of the covenanting bodies.

50) The service for the ordination of bishops will be in the form of a renewal of the commitment implicit in the person's Baptism and will include prayer for the Holy Spirit with the laying on of hands and an appointment of the bishop to the tasks of ministry to which he or she has been called.

51) The ministry of bishops, like all other ministries in the Church Uniting, will be at once personal, collegial, and communal, and set within an appropriate constitutional or canonical framework. Bishops of the Church carry out their ministries in a variety of ways. They minster as:

[a] *Liturgical Leaders.* Bishops have responsibility for maintaining the apostolicity and unity of the worship and sacramental life of the Church.

[b] *Teachers of the Apostolic Faith.* Bishops have a responsibility, corporately and individually, to guard, transmit, teach, and proclaim the apostolic faith as it is expressed in Scriptures and Tradition, and, as they are led and endowed by the Spirit, to interpret that faith evangelically and prophetically in the contemporary world.

[c] *Pastoral Overseers.* Bishops have general pastoral oversight of all the people of the dioceses, districts, or jurisdictions to which they are called or appointed. They have particular responsibil-

ity, as shepherds, for other ordained ministers. Bishops are responsible for furthering the spiritual unity of their areas, for being available in as wide a range of personal relationships as possible, and for regular visitation of parishes, congregations, and communities in their districts. In such visitations, bishops will ordinarily preach, celebrate the Lord's Supper with the people, and preside at services of Baptism, confirmation, and the ordination of deacons within the congregation. Ordinarily, responsibility for administration of church discipline, especially as it applies to ordained ministers, will rest with the bishops— but always as they work in cooperation with presbyters, deacons, and lay persons in representative groups which have been given such responsibility.

[d] *Leaders in Mission.* It is an essential tasks of bishops, both collegially and individually, to further the mission of God's People in Christ to the whole world, in evangelizing, fostering, and nurturing communities of faith and in clarifying the demand for social justice which is directly involved in that mission. In company with other ministers, they take initiative in evolving new approaches for mission wherever they serve.

[e] *Representative Ministers in the Act of Ordination.* Bishops, with the participation of other ministers ordained and unordained, are responsible for the orderly transfer of ministerial authority in the Church. This means not only that bishops preside at ordinations, but also that they share pastoral and administrative responsibility for candidates for the ordained ministry (Acts 8:18;II Tim. 1:6;I Tim. 5:22).

[f] *Administrative Leaders.* Bishops also have responsibility for the supervision and administration of the Church's organized life and work (I Cor. 12:28;Eph. 4:11-12). In the context of the Church assemblies, bishops, as chief pastors, have either directly or by delegation, and always in cooperation with other officers of the Church, a central role in the development of administrative policy and are responsible for the effective carrying out of such policy.

[g] *Servants of Unity.* As personal representatives of the given unity of the Church in all places and all ages, bishops have, both individually and collegially, an obligation "to call the churches to the goal of visible unity in one faith and one eucharistic fellowship expressed in worship and in common life in Christ, and to advance toward that unity that the world may believe" (Constitution of the WCC, III, Functions & Purposes,i).

[h] *Participants in Governance.* As ministers serving within relationships of accountability, bishops have responsibility for taking their constitutionally or canonically defined role, alongside lay persons, presbyters, and deacons, in the governance of the Church.

## The Ministry of Presbyters[2]

52) Presbyters are baptized members of the People of God ordained to serve among the People as ministers of Word and sacraments. In this role they bear responsibility for the discipline of the Church and are teachers and preachers of the faith to the end both that the world may believe and that the entire membership of the Church may be renewed, equipped, and strengthened in its ministry.

53) All presbyters will be ordained by the Church through bishops, with the participation of other presbyters, deacons, and lay persons. The service of presbyteral ordination will be in the form of a renewal of the commitment to ministry implicit in the person's Baptism, and will include prayer for the gift of the Holy Spirit, with the laying on of hands, and an appointment of the presbyter to the task of ministry to which he or she has been called.

54) The presbyteral ministry is personal, collegial, and communal in character and is set within an appropriate constitutional or canonical framework. Presbyters personally represent to the Church its identity in mission in Christ. At the same time, presbyters are associated together in a corporate concern for life and government of the Church under the Word of God (Acts 15:2). Therefore they participate in decision-making assemblies of the Church in which all ministries, lay and ordained, are represented.

55) In order to provide the ministry of Word and sacrament to specific congregations or particular circumstances, the ministry of presbyter may include women and men who in view of their fitness for this service are chosen, approved, and ordained for such ministry without either leaving their occupations outside the organized structure of the Church or undergoing the normal educational preparation for ordained ministry. Normally the exercise of ministry in these cases will be limited to particular settings, and will require periodic review.

56) Presbyters, in virtue of their calling as ministers of Word and sacraments, serve the Church in a variety of ways. With allowance made for differing circumstances and specialized ministries, the functions of presbyters include the following:

[a] *Preachers of the Word.* Presbyters have a responsibility to proclaim the prophetic and apostolic word of the redemption and liberation wrought by God in Christ (Acts 6:2-4;Eph. 4:11; I Cor. 14:3;I Tim. 4:13-14).

[b] *Celebrants of the Sacraments.* Presbyters normally baptize and preside at the celebration of the Eucharist as recognized representatives of the Church's ministry in Christ, and thus offer, with all the people, spiritual sacrifices acceptable to God (I Peter 2:5). They also bear responsibility for other acts of the Church which for some have a sacramental nature, such as confirmation, marriage, ordination, declaration of the forgiveness of sin, anointing of the sick, and the announcement of God's blessing (VI:19). And they perform or make provision for funeral services and other rites of the Church.

[c] *Teachers of the Gospel.* Presbyters bear responsibility within and outside congregations for teaching the apostolic faith and for handing on the doctrine, discipline, and worship of the Church. They have particular responsibility for the preparation of members for Christian life and ministry. Presbyters may be called to teach in seminaries, divinity schools, theological colleges, and universities, to counsel students and to engage in scholarly research.

[d] *Pastoral Overseers.* Presbyters have responsibility under the Word of God for the pastoral care of persons. This includes spiritual direction of Church members, pastoral use of the Church's disciplines, counseling the troubled, and caring for the sick and needy. Since the members of the congregation have their own part to play in this pastoral ministry, it is the presbyter's responsibility to see that they are not only equipped for mutual pastoral care, but encouraged and enabled to carry it out. Such pastoral ministry has as its aim to nurture the unity and witness of the congregation. Presbyters may serve pastorally also in such settings as the hospital chaplaincy, the counseling center, the campus ministry, and so on.

[e] *Pastoral Administrators.* It is a responsibility of presbyters, when they are serving as leaders of congregations, to see that the many other ministries carried on in the congregation are adequately planned, prepared, and performed, and helped with every resource and support which the congregation can provide. Presbyters may also function as administrators in church boards, agencies, and organizations of all kinds, including ecumenical organizations.

[f] *Leaders in Mission.* Mission is a responsibility of all who share the ministry of Christ, Presbyters, accordingly, are called to leadership in mission. As evangelists they proclaim the gospel, teach God's purposes, and share their personal faith. They bear

witness to God's work in the world as well as in the Church. They lead the Church in calling persons to faith in Jesus Christ, and in establishing congregations. As ministers of Word and sacraments, they pioneer in new forms of mission. They enlist, renew, equip, and accompany God's People as they go out into the local community, the nation, and the world.

[g] *Servants of Unity.* As representative ministers of the Church, presbyters work ecumenically across the walls that continue to divide the one Church of Jesus Christ. Specifically it is important for them, by their personal relationships and leadership, to facilitate a vital communion with persons, congregations, and communities of other traditions. At the same time it is their responsibility to give active support and leadership to ecumenical worship, programs, coalitions, councils, and church unions in their local community and, as opportunity may come, at the levels of the region, the nation, and the world (Acts 15:2;II Cor. 8:1-4,20).

[h] *Participants in Governance.* As ministers serving within relationships of accountability, presbyters have responsibility for taking their constitutionally or canonically defined role, alongside lay persons, bishops, and deacons, in the governance of the Church.

## The Ministry of Deacons

57) Deacons are baptized members of the People of God, ordained to represent to the People its identity in Christ as a body of persons who are in service both to Church and world. It belongs to diaconal ministry to struggle with the myriad needs of societies and persons in Christ's name, and so to exemplify the interdependence of worship and mission in the life of the Church.

58) The nature of the diaconal ministry is classically symbolized by the special role of the deacon in worship. The deacon is the People's helper or servant as he or she is reader and proclaimer of the gospel, leader in intercession, presenter of the Church's offerings to God, minister of the eucharistic bread and wine, and organizer and guide for the People's worship.

59) This liturgical role of the deacon, in turn, finds its proper daily expression in a pastoral function of service and of helping directed to all who seek or need assistance. To the deacon is assigned a special role in the Church's ministry of teaching, in its assistance to those in need of any sort, and in its witness in the world on behalf of the forgotten, the oppressed, and the suffering. With these functions the deacon also assumes a special role in

the guidance, focusing, and administration of the Church's ministry of service.

60) The uniting churches recognize that the diaconal ministry has been exercised in a variety of ways at different times and places. This ministry, as a proper and independent ministry in its own right, with its own place in the governance, worship, and pastoral work of the Church, has for long been neglected or suppressed in almost all organized Christian bodies, including the denominations which are members of this Consultation. No doubt there are, in each of our bodies, vestiges of, or surrogates for, the diaconal ministry which in earlier times was central at once to the Church's self-understanding and to its work of shepherding and of witness. On these remains, slight as they may be, a Church Uniting will build with a view to achieving a full restoration of the diaconal office and order in a form suited to the needs and circumstances of the present time.

61) To undertake this work of restoration and reformation will require serious research, imaginative thought, and mutual consultation. This document cannot, therefore, specify ahead of time the exact form of a restored diaconate, or delineate the changes and reforms that a revitalization of the diaconate would entail for the churches.

62) There are, however, certain principles which can be used to guide any consultation to this end. Like all other ministries in and of the Church, the diaconate is at once personal, collegial, and constitutional. It is a ministry in its own right and not a stepping-stone to other offices. It is a ministry which has its basis in the worship, work, and witness of the local church, alongside and together with the ministries of presbyter, layperson, and bishop. It is neither "special," marginal, supplementary, nor compensatory. It has its place in the governance and administration of the Church's affairs as well as in its worship and service. There is a tradition in the Church which views the deacon as having a special relation to the bishop.

63) All deacons should represent and take leadership in the general diaconal responsibility of the congregation in which they worship. Some deacons will serve full-time or part-time in the employ of the Church, working out their particular diaconal callings through the duties they are called upon by the Church to do. Such deacons could come to be called "regular" deacons, after the traditional use of the word to mean "according to rule." Other deacons will work out their particular callings in the world, in and through their activities in commerce, industry, education, government, the professions, and the like. These deacons will model for other Christians ways and means of fulfilling their "secular" or "in-the-world" calling to serve Jesus Christ and could thus come to be called "secular deacons," again adapting the traditional usage. Some deacons may change, according to need,

from "regular" to "secular" status, or vice-versa. All deacons, whatever their place or status of ministry, will serve in the following ways:

[a] *Servants in Worship.* Deacons, whatever their particular arenas of activity, normally participate as leaders in the worship within local congregations. It is their responsibility to read the Scriptures, including the Gospel, preaching when called to do so, leading the assembled people in prayer, assisting in the administration of the sacraments.

[b] *Partners in Congregational Oversight.* Upon election by a congregation for that purpose, deacons share in the oversight of ministry of that congregation. Together with presbyters and lay persons, such deacons will be concerned with the discipline and deployment of their congregations as collective expressions of the gospel.

[c] *Participants in Governance.* As ministers serving within relationships of accountability, deacons have responsibility for taking their constitutionally or canonically defined role, alongside lay persons, bishops, and presbyters, in the governance of the Church.

[d] *Leaders in Administration.* Deacons carry administrative responsibility in the life of the Church. The "gift of administration," seen in the New Testament as a pastoral gift, is an indispensable ministry among the People of God for which deacons may be specially suited.

[e] *Leaders in Mission.* Deacons may carry a responsibility for the development of mission both within and beyond parishes and congregations. Some may find the focus of their ministry primarily in their regular employment. Some may be volunteers with regular responsibilities in mission.

[f] *Servants in Pastoral Care.* Deacons may have a responsible share in the Church's concern for the pastoral care of persons. This includes not only their traditional responsibility for the care of the sick and needy but also a responsibility for the spiritual life of the congregation and its discipline.

[g] *Servants of Unity.* With their special concern for mission in the world, deacons may be called to witness to the unity of humankind in Christ by bringing the Church into dialogue with the society in which it is set. In the midst of diversity, they further, through their witness, the practical acknowledgement of human community.

# Notes

1. Work on these issues lies outside the scope, but not the concern of the present document, and is referred by the 16th Plenary to The Commission on Church Order.

2. Presbyter is a biblical name for persons today designated pastors, elders, ministers, or priests.

# Churches in Covenant Communion

## I. What Kind of Unity?

1) Scripture makes clear that Jesus calls the church to become visibly one. On the night before his crucifixion, Jesus prayed for the disciples and for those who would follow:

> "I do not pray for these only, but also for those who are to believe in me through their word, that they may all be one; even as you, Father, are in me, and I in you, that they also may be in us, so that the world may believe that you have sent me."
>
> —John 17:20-21

2) Based on the conviction, grounded in Scripture and Tradition, that God wills the unity of the church, the following proposal describes a covenantal form of unity. Biblical examples of unity are expressed in metaphor, such as Isaiah's vision of the peaceable kingdom (Isaiah 11), and in parable, such as Jesus' story of the great feast. (Luke 14) Rooted in the nature and action of the triune God, who is revealed to us as unity in diversity, the covenanting churches of the Consultation on Church Union hold to the vision of a reconciled and reconciling household of faith. Scripture and Tradition provide guidance on matters of unity, even though no blueprint exists.

3) Attentive to the yearnings and insights discerned from ecumenical dialogues over many years, the partner churches have come to believe that such a form of unity bears at least the folowing characteristics.[3]

(a) Celebration of God's grace will be central to our life together. (Eph. 2:12-21)

(b) Working together in Christ's mission of salvation for the whole world will mark our endeavors. (Matt. 28:18-19a)

(c) Each member, by virtue of baptism, will be understood to be a member of the apostolic and priestly ministry. (I Peter 2:9-10)

(d) The form of unity will mirror the diversity of its membership in every aspect of its fellowship and ministry. (I Cor. 12:12-27)

(e) In seeking God's justice in church and world, the reconciled communions will embody the unity that is God's gift. (Lk.2:46-55)

(f) Because of the mutual enrichment of our several traditions, this covenantal form of unity will more faithfully reflect the universality of the body of Christ and include the strengthening of our previous ecumenical commitments. (I Cor. 1:12-17)

(g) Covenant communion assumes a new kind of ecclesial reality, an organic life that includes, in Pauline language, those "joints and ligaments" which enable the church to act as one body knit together under Christ the head. (Col. 2:19;Eph. 4:15-16)

4) Given such characteristics of the unity God wills for the church, the Consultation on Church Union calls upon its member churches to confess their complicity in the sin of the church's division, and to do all that can be done to exhibit that unity. Moreover, the Consultation proposes to the member churches, in the pages that follow, a form of unity which it believes to be at once faithful to God's will, appropriate to the present circumstances, and open to the future for renewal and reformation. It is a proposal which calls for unity of heart and mind, for unity in faith, in prayer, in the breaking of bread, in the Word of the gospel, in ministry, in sharing, and in witness and service to the world. (Acts 2:42-44) Such unity will be a visible witness to the world of God's saving power in Jesus Christ. The Consultation on Church Union calls the churches to communion in Christ—a covenantal communion in faith, sacraments, ministry, and mission. The name here given to the churches in covenant communion is *The Church of Christ Uniting,* and the means by which it comes into being is referred to as "covenanting."

## II. What is Covenanting?

1) "Covenanting," as the Consultation uses the term, is both an act and a process by which the churches come into a new relationship with one other.

2) It is an act of covenant by churches which, though one in Christ, are currently divided from one another. By this solemn act the churches will commit themselves, before God and each other, to live henceforth in one covenantal communion even though they continue to exist as distinct ecclesiastical systems.

3) Such a covenantal act will inaugurate also a *process* of deepening commitment by these churches to one another in which the Spirit's gift of unity in Christ will be enabled to grow and to flower. The process will be one of maturing in unity as the covenanting churches jointly identify and

take such mutually agreed actions as may serve to deepen their communion in faith, sacrament, ministry, and mission.

4) In covenanting, diversities remain even while the covenanting partners become truly one. Moreover covenant communion is itself a way of *being* one. The church is by its very nature a pilgrim people. Through covenant communion the relationship with one another will grow, deepen, and change as it matures over the years, as this covenant communion is drawn forward by the Holy Spirit into the fullness of God's perfect will for the church.

5) In covenant communion the churches may maintain, for so long as each may determine, their own church structures and traditions, including present forms of worship, systems of ministerial selection, training, and placement, their international, confessional, and communion relationships, and their mission programs.[4] What covenanting means is that these now separated churches will resolve to live as one in the most basic things—in faith, sacrament, ministry, and mission. Uniformity in structure is not essential to covenant communion.

6) Approaching Christian unity in this way will tend to focus the energy of the churches' shared life upon the local communities of now separated congregations. For it is in such towns, neighborhoods, and local areas that Christians most often gather about the Word and sacraments, served by their recognized ministers, in living communities of faith and mission. Covenanting will make it possible for these several congregations in each place to see themselves not only as members of a particular communion but also as members of a living and functioning communion of communions, sharing the one baptism, proclaiming the one faith, receiving together the one bread and cup, recognizing the ministry of each as a ministry to all, and reaching out as one in love and service to the world.

7) A covenant communion of churches is, by definition, committed to become truly inclusive. Each partner is enriched by sharing in the gifts that God has given to the other. Each partner works to take down walls of alienation that exist between the churches, and to overcome attitudes which tend to marginalize persons in regard to race, class, age, gender, disabilities, marital status, sexual orientation, and positions of power and powerlessness, and to live toward a church in which all participate in the wholeness of Christ.

8) In covenanting, the churches will make an act of common repentance for the sin of disunity among them, and for the sins which inhibit community within the human family.[5] In living out that repentance, the covenanting churches dare to believe that in sacramental communion these sins can be faced in a substantially new way. What is needed for reconciliation is a new and intentional community of the Spirit, rooted in one Lord, one faith, one baptism, and nurtured at one eucharistic table. Such unity anticipates God's

coming future, now unfolding in Jesus Christ. It is the promised gift of the Holy Spirit to those who penitently ask for it and diligently seek it.

9) Covenant communion is intended to be a sign and foretaste of the community God wills for the world. In its ultimate intent, it is for the salvation of each and all. It is for the redemption of the world.

### III. How To Initiate Covenanting

1) Faithfulness to God's mission in the world impels the member churches to enter into covenanting. To initiate covenanting, actions of several different kinds will be required. Just as doctrine, polity, and liturgy are basic to the church's life and mission, so also the initiation of covenanting has these same three interrelated dimensions:

–*Theological:* the churches receive and voice together the faith of the church through the ages.
–*Governmental:* the governing bodies of the church consider and act on commonly developed proposals for Christian unity.
–*Liturgical:* the churches' unity is declared and confirmed in corporate acts of worship.

To initiate covenanting, action in all three of these dimensions is required, in faith that it is God who moves the churches to act and who alone is able to sustain them in covenant communion. In Christ, the interrelationship between these three dimensions can be discerned: the church's theological *affirmation* is grounded in the joyful praise of God, with implications for the church's polity; its governmental *decision* has a theological grounding, with implications for the church's worship; and its liturgical action has a grounding in the church's polity, with implications for the church's theology.

2) *The theological dimension* of entering into covenanting is basic to the rest. The Consultation on Church Union has looked carefully at the differences which historically have divided the several traditions. Through the consultative process, confirmed by the claiming of *The COCU Consensus,* the churches have come to recognize in one another the apostolic faith of the church universal: the Tradition.[6] Through covenanting, the distinctive treasures of these several histories will he maintained, while their insights and emphases will be made increasingly accessible to others for the common good. The process of covenanting begins by joyfully affirming the Christian faith.

3) *The governmental dimension* of entering into covenanting is also essential. This has to do with the decision making process of each church. It

includes voting. For the church, however, voting is much more than an exercise of democratic rule. When Christians gather in church governing bodies and seek God's leading through prayer and careful listening to one another in faith, God is there in the midst of them. The formal decision by each church to enter into this new relationship is therefore much more than a preparation for covenanting, but is itself a dimension of covenanting. Such governing action by each church is, the Consultation believes, a manifestation of God's action through the Holy Spirit in drawing the churches together into covenant communion.

4) *The liturgical dimension* of entering into covenanting is crucial as well. It is God who effects reconciliation in the divided household of faith. Corporate expressions of mutual commitment, shared hope, and common will must therefore be lifted up together in words and actions appropriate to the worship of God. Agreements reached separately must be celebrated together. The liturgical action in covenanting is much more than a ceremonial capstone for a uniting covenant which has been successfully voted; the liturgical action itself will be a sign and means of church unity.

5) Each of these dimensions has both an internal and an external aspect, related respectively to the church's life and to its mission. Thus the church's *doctrinal* life, consisting in appropriation of apostolic faith through continual theological reflection and teaching, finds its missional aspect in the urgent proclamation of the gospel of Jesus Christ, by word and deed, in and to the world. Similarly, the church's *polity* as the pastoral pattern of its life in Christ at once stands under the constant judgment of the gospel of God's reign and is directed to active mission for a just and life-giving stewardship of creation. Also, the *worship* of God in the church's life issues in mission and service to the whole human community created in the divine image and redeemed by Christ from its multiple distortions. Mission illuminates each of these three dimensions.

6) Crucial to covenant communion, in all three of the dimensions by which it is initiated, is a deliberate process of reception of the covenanting agreements by the churches. Such reception includes the participation and nurture of the people of the church, enabling them to understand and to receive these agreements and to enter fully the covenant communion into which their churches are being drawn. No such communion is possible, whatever one's system of church government may be, without the willing and joyful assent of the people of God. To that end, it is essential that the membership of the churches be fully informed about what is being proposed, so that their AMEN may be from the heart. A strong educational effort, accompanied by relationships which anticipate covenant life, can be an important part of the reception process. These can serve as vehicles of the Holy Spirit for building and strengthening ecclesial communion, as the

churches find themselves increasingly beckoned of God to be and become one covenant people in Christ.

## IV. The Elements of Covenanting

1) Since the unity that we seek is not chiefly organizational, what then are the identifying characteristics of that covenant communion here described? Through the Consultation on Church Union, the participating churches have together identified eight elements of covenanting, none of which now consistently characterize the relationship between these churches. They are:

    1. claiming unity in faith;
    2. commitment to seek unity with wholeness;
    3. mutual recognition of members in one baptism;
    4. mutual recognition of each other as churches;
    5. mutual recognition and reconciliation of ordained ministry;
    6. celebrating the Eucharist together;
    7. engaging together in Christ's mission;
    8. formation of covenanting councils.

These are described more fully below. They are called "elements" because each is regarded as basic to a covenant communion of churches. Together, they comprise a single reality, and each in its own way is essential to the whole.

*Claiming Our Unity in Faith*

> There is one body and one Spirit, just as you were called to the one hope that belongs to your call, one Lord, one faith, one baptism, one God and Father of us all, who is above all and through all and in all.
>
> —Ephesians 4:4-6

2) The "one faith" which the church proclaims and by which it lives is the faith of the one holy catholic and apostolic church. This is the faith to which Scripture and Tradition bear witness. Notwithstanding differences of emphasis and interpretation, the covenanting churches dare to affirm their essential unity in the faith. Claiming that faith in common is basic to covenant communion.

3) The ancient ecumenical creeds are not only witnesses to the faith but also abiding symbols[7] of that faith. The divided voices of many churches, however, make it difficult today for the faith of the church to be heard by all as one. After more than two decades of theological work by officially desig-

nated persons responsible to the most authoritative bodies in the several churches, it is now evident that an essential core of theological agreement exists and continues to grow among these churches in matters of faith, worship, sacrament, membership, ministry, and mission. That agreement is expressed in *The COCU Consensus: In Quest of a Church of Christ Uniting* (1984). The existence of that document is a sign of these churches' basic unity in faith; their claiming of it is treated as an element of covenanting.

4) *The COCU Consensus* is not a complete exposition of every article of Christian doctrine. It is intended rather as a *sufficient* expression of the apostolic faith, order, worship, and witness to enable the participating churches to enter together into a covenanting relationship. It also is intended as the theological foundation for the vision of a covenant communion of communions which these churches seek by God's grace to become. It is therefore the theological basis of the document in hand, *Churches in Covenant Communion: The Church of Christ Uniting*. For a fuller expression of what it means to "claim" the consensus, see the Foreword of *The COCU Consensus*.

### Commitment to Seek Unity with Wholeness

5) Commitment to Christian unity is essential if churches are to become visibly one. The Consultation affirms that unity is a gift of God, to be made visible among the churches in response to the prayers and actions of those who diligently seek it.

6) Through patient and persistent work over many years, the covenanting churches have been led by God to overcome seemingly insurmountable obstacles to unity in matters of faith, sacraments, ministry, and mission. For this the church gives thanks to God. Yet the churches still are not one in other ways. Racism and sexism still live as idolatries in churches, continuing to divide and destroy. Handicapism marginalizes people with disabilities as the institutions of both church and society continue to value physical wholeness in divisive and destructive ways. Rich and poor seldom worship God together. These are theological issues, just as truly as those of sacrament and mission, for they demonstrate to the world the church's disobedience to the will of Christ "that they may all be one."[8]

7) Commitment to a living unity, therefore, requires a change of heart—"transformed by the renewal of your mind"[9]—not for the sake of the church alone, but ultimately for the sake of that larger oneness for which our Savior prays. To repent of sins that divide Christ's body is to turn from them to God, committed by God's grace to obey the clear will of Christ. It means being ready to change, especially in these idolatries which alienate and cause pain to sisters and brothers in Christ. It is to seek a unity that is inclusive of

all who are baptized into Christ, while rejoicing in the diversity of persons and gifts which the Spirit has given to the church.[10]

8) *In Christ "there is neither Jew nor Greek."* God abhors racism. It is essential to Christian unity that there be a redress of racism and a commitment to racial inclusiveness, both in our churches and our society. This is not alone a matter of justice or mission. This commitment is fundamental to Christian community itself, for the church is continually called to be and to become one living communion in Christ.

9) *In Christ "there is neither bond nor free."* God abhors all forms of oppression, whether it is economic oppression or that of society's exclusion of persons with disabilities. In a community where many enrich themselves at the expense of the poor, or exert power through the disadvantage of others, Christian unity cannot exist. The gospel which the church proclaims is "good news to the poor...release to the captives...recovery of sight to the blind...liberty to those who are oppressed."[11] Inclusiveness is not just a matter of goodwill, but of the justice which the gospel demands. It is therefore of the very nature of the church, which is called to be one living body in Christ.

10) *In Christ "there is neither male nor female."* God abhors sexism. Degradation or diminution of others on the basis of gender, whether intended or not, is an affront to them and an offense to their Creator. The church often has fostered attitudes which devalue women. Such attitudes are the root cause of many evils which the church deplores, such as domestic violence, pornography, and the disproportionate poverty of women. Opportunities for leadership and full participation in the church are in many instances still effectively closed to women. The church cannot be whole without the gifts both of women and men in covenant communion through Christ.

11) Inclusiveness is essential to Christian unity. The word "inclusive," however, must be used with some care. For example, ethnic minorities often hear the word as a patronizing invitation to become part of the dominant group—to enter another's reality, but one which the other continues to dominate. And gay and lesbian persons in most churches seldom are included at all, if they are open in acknowledging their sexual identity. The appeal to inclusiveness is heard by some as an invitation to give up one's distinctive identity and merge into a culture alien to one's own. So the word "inclusive" is not an altogether adequate word, though it is far better than any others that have yet been proposed to replace it. The Consultation uses it, therefore, sensitive to its possible misuses, being deeply persuaded that there can be no unity for the church unless it is truly inclusive. By "inclusiveness" is meant the catholicity of God's inclusiveness.

12) The goal of this covenant communion is not a homogenization of all differences into a new sameness, but a new community in Christ, in which differences are affirmed, accepted, and celebrated as the gifts of God

for the common good. This is a work of divine grace. The integrity, moral authority, and strength of witness that this covenant communion of churches will have within the nation and the world will be in significant measure related to its becoming, by God's grace, a truly inclusive communion in Christ.

### Mutual Recognition of Members in One Baptism

13) Scripture and Tradition are united in witness that there is one baptism with water in the name of the triune God. Baptismal practice among the churches, however, is quite diverse, including both a variety of baptismal modes and, for some, preliminary acts of dedication or blessing and, for others, additional acts of affirmation of baptismal vows such as confirmation.[12] This diversity reflects not different baptisms but different facets of the one baptism into the one body of the one Lord.[13] (Eph. 4:4-6)

14) At its 1974 plenary session the Consultation on Church Union proposed a "Mutual Recognition of Members," by which it invited the member churches to recognize that "all who are baptized into Christ are members of Christ's universal church and belong to and share in Christ's ministry through the people of the one God, Father, Son, and Holy Spirit." Over the next four years each of the participating churches took formal and official action approving this resolution. These acts were a dramatic witness to our unity in Christ.

15) In its 1979 plenary, the Consultation proposed to its member churches that each take actions to move "Beyond Affirmation to Action" in implementing such mutual recognition. Many suggestions were offered by the plenary, and a number of significant actions were taken in response by the several churches, but much remains to be done. Recovery of our unity in baptism is at the heart of the covenanting journey, for it is central to realization of genuine *koinonia* among the churches.[14] Mutual recognition of members in one baptism is of basic ecclesiological significance. It implies recognition of the ministry of all the others in the common priesthood in which and from which God calls those ministers who will be ordained. Membership in Christ and in Christ's church is for every believer a calling by God to ministry and witness in the world.[15]

### Mutual Recognition of Each Other as Churches

16) A church's membership in the Consultation on Church Union implies at least *some recognition* of the other member churches as participants in the one church of Jesus Christ. So, also, does membership in a council of churches. In local experience, congregations have sometimes achieved relationships which amount to mutual recognition in spite of certain canons and constitutions of their churches. The fact is, however, that the member churches of the Consultation on Church Union, acting in conformity with

their respective foundational documents and theological principles, have not yet recognized each other as churches truly catholic, truly evangelical, and truly reformed. The absence of mutual recognition comes as a surprise to many who have been unaware of the official positions of the churches, and compels us to press on until such mutual recognition is achieved.

17) Covenanting provides the occasion and the means whereby that which is implicit in the relationship among the churches may become explicit, that which is privately and unofficially acknowledged may be openly and joyfully declared before God and many witnesses. To that end, in the liturgical event in which covenanting is inaugurated, participating churches through their authorized representatives will together make affirmations of:

–faith in the one God who through the Word and in the Spirit creates, redeems, and sanctifies;
–commitment to Jesus Christ as Savior and as the incarnate and risen Lord;
–obedience to the Holy Scriptures which testify to Tradition and to which Tradition testifies, as containing all things necessary for our salvation as well as being the rule and ultimate standard of faith;
–commitment to faithful participation in the two sacraments ordained by Jesus Christ, baptism and the Lord's Supper;
–commitment to the evangelical and prophetic mission of God and to God's reign of justice and peace;
–grateful acceptance of the ministry which the Holy Spirit has manifestly given to the churches.

These affirmations are to be voiced together in the liturgical act by which covenanting will be inaugurated.[16] Through these words spoken together, each church will publicly and officially recognize the others as authentic expressions of the one, holy, catholic, and apostolic church of Jesus Christ. This liturgical action will fulfill the intention to confess the faith together affirmed in Chapter V of *The COCU Consensus,* where the fundamental sources of the doctrine of the faith are described in detail: Scripture, Tradition, and the creeds and confessions of the church, together with worship, mission, and inclusiveness as forms of confession.

### Mutual Recognition and Reconciliation of Ordained Ministry

18) Through their baptism all Christians are called and empowered by the Holy Spirit to share in the ministry of Jesus Christ in the church and in the world.[17] Those among them who are ordained to particular ministries share also in that common ministry of the people of God, and represent to every member the ministry of Christ to which all have been called.[18] Because the ministry of the baptized is affirmed already by each of the covenanting

churches, there appears to be no impediment to public recognition and reconciliation of this common ministry. Obstacles remain to be overcome, however, to effect the mutual recognition and reconciliation of our ordained ministries. In the paragraphs which follow, therefore, attention is focused largely upon the ordained because that is where obstacles to the mutual recognition and reconciliation of our ministries lie.

19) The theological understanding of ministry, both lay and ordained, which underlies covenanting is set forth in Chapter VII of *The COCU Consensus*. But it is important to remember how that chapter of the Consensus is intended to function in the covenanting process. It is not a constitution.

> Many details are deliberately left unsettled. There is room for the participating churches to grow together in unforeseen ways as they work out the implications of the covenant.[19]

In the realm of ministerial order, just as in the doctrines of faith, there is a historic tradition which these churches hold in common, despite their differing expressions of it; and it is this that the Consultation has sought to express in Chapter VII of *The COCU Consensus*. The concept of ministry expressed there is not embodied in quite this way in any of the participating churches. Yet there can be seen in the divergent polities of the member churches particular ministries which are in fact episcopal, presbyteral, diaconal, and lay in their essential nature. Chapter VII articulates this historic, underlying pattern, providing thereby a common frame of reference for recognizing in one another's ministries the ministry of the church through the ages, and thus for reconciling their ministries one to another. Uniformity among the several church polities is not essential to covenant communion; but mutual recognition and reconciliation of the ordained ministries is essential, for it is integrally related to the recognition of churches.

20) Mutual *recognition* of ordained ministries is intended to acknowledge in these ministries the manifest blessing of God and the fruit of the Spirit, and to affirm that they are rooted in the apostolic tradition.[20] Such recognition does not obscure real differences, but neither does it depend upon first setting those differences aright according to one's own tradition before recognition can be granted. To the contrary, the mutual recognition of ordained ministries is a way of acknowledging both the headship of Christ over every ecclesial tradition and the freedom of the Spirit to work in and through these traditions however the Spirit wills.

21) *Reconciliation* of ordained ministries is intended to refer to actions by the churches, both separately and together, whereby the ordained ministries of each covenanting church become one ministry of Jesus Christ in

relation to all. This is not intended to mean that the standard of ministerial training and certification must become the same for all the churches, nor that their call or appointment systems must change, but rather that the ministry of one may function, whenever invited, as a ministry to all. This is not now possible among all of the covenanting churches. Hence. covenanting will make possible an enrichment of the ordained ministry for each church, as well as provide a new and visible demonstration of our essential unity in faith, sacraments, ministry, and mission.

22) The method by which the covenanting churches intend to accomplish reconciliation of ordained ministries is, first, by setting this reconciliation in the context of mutual recognition of members in one baptism, mutual recognition of churches, and mutual recognition of ministries. Within the covenanting liturgy, these three acts will precede the reconciliation of ordained ministries and, taken together, are regarded as foundational to it. For the sake of reconciliation, the sequential order of these acts is important, and their close conjuncture with one another is equally important. This ordering is reflected in the accompanying liturgy for declaring covenant and reconciling ordained ministers.[21] Reconciliation of ministries enables full eucharistic sharing.

23) Having mutually recognized one another's ministries, these ministers will then offer themselves in mutual commitment to one another, so that their ministry in the wider covenant communion may be received and appropriately ordered in all of the covenanting churches. To this end, the accompanying liturgies provide that the reconciliation of bishops shall include words of mutual commitment to one another in covenant, and an act of mutually laying hands upon each other in acknowledgment of the authority of the other churches within which each will, from time to time, exercise elements of shared ministry through covenanting. So also, the accompanying liturgy for the reconciliation of presbyters and welcoming of deacons includes words which similarly acknowledge the authority of the other churches within which each is enabled to minister occasionally through covenant communion, and an act of laying on of hands by a reconciled minister *of episkopé*, together with other signs of reconciliation and peace.[22]

24) Lest there be any misunderstanding in regard to the sign of reconciliation which these liturgies employ—the laying on of hands by an authorized minister of oversight—the covenanting churches recognize and declare that these are not liturgies of ordination or reordination, but of reconciliation among those whose ordained ministry already has been mutually recognized. The act of laying on hands is used for many different purposes within the church. It is used in blessing, in confirmation, in dedication, in anointing the sick, in commissioning to tasks of education or of mission, as well as in ordination. In each case, it is the context which defines its purpose. In the

covenanting liturgies, the laying on of hands is administered in silence. The context, especially the prayer which precedes or follows, leaves no doubt as to its meaning: it is an act of reconciliation.[23]

25) The Consultation is persuaded that no other sign serves that purpose as well as the ancient sign of the laying on of hands by the churches' authorized ministers of oversight. From the beginning of their journey together, the covenanting churches have sought a distinctively new communion: one that is simultaneously catholic, evangelical, and reformed. However evangelical and reformed this covenant communion may be, it will not effectively invite recognition of its ordained ministries by all parts of the universal church if the reconciliation of ordained ministries does not include the historic sign of episcopal succession—the laying on of hands. Its use under the circumstances here defined has to do, not with ordination, but with the recovery of a visible and widely valued sign of unity and continuity within the church of God, a sign that in this case signifies the mutual sharing of our ordered ministries. This understanding is in harmony with increasingly universal ecumenical understanding.[24]

26) Just as the use of this sign is judged to be essential, so also the way it is used is equally essential: by the mutual laying on of hands. It is in the mutuality of this act that each tradition gives to the other a sign of acceptance and of deepened or enriched understandings of ordination and *episkopé* as they have been preserved and practiced in the separate churches.

27) When reconciliation of ordained ministries has been achieved at the regional level,[25] everyone who is ordained thereafter in that region will be ordained into an already reconciled ministry. No further act will be required to accomplish reconciliation. Nonetheless, the ordination of women and men to the ministry is such a highly visible act in life of the churches that it provides for our covenant communion an unparalleled opportunity to demonstrate before the church and the world the unity which God has given. From the date of inauguration of covenant communion, there will be no more ordinations carried our in denominational isolation from the other covenanting churches. The Covenanting Councils[26] will enable the conduct of all ordination of persons, credentialed by the churches, through the laying on of hands and prayer by reconciled bishops together with the presence and participation of ministers, both lay and ordained, from as many of the covenanting churches as possible. Moreover, it is the desire of the covenanting churches that these ordinations be conducted according to mutually acceptable rites, in order to facilitate participation from all parts of the covenant communion.[27]

28) All of the participating churches in COCU already have a ministry of Word and sacrament, but not all now have a personalized ministry of *episkopé* at the middle judicatory level where ordination and pastoral care of pastors is lodged. Nor do all now have a regularly constituted office of dea-

con. It will be the responsibility of each participating church, prior to the COCU liturgy in which covenant is declared and ministries are reconciled, to determine how its present categories of ordained ministry relate to the historic categories set forth in *The COCU Consensus,* Chapter VII.[28]

29) Among the several functions of deacons listed in paragraph VII.63 of *The COCU Consensus,* the one function which may be regarded as *sine qua non* in identifying persons who are to be put forward initially for reconciliation as deacons is: "(f) Servants in Pastoral Care." Among the several functions of presbyters listed in *The COCU Consensus* VII.56, those which may be regarded as *sine qua non* in identifying persons who are to be put forward initially for reconciliation as presbyters are: "(a) Preachers of the Word," and "(b) Celebrants of the Sacraments." Among the several functions of bishops listed in paragraph VII.51 of *The COCU Consensus,* those which may be regarded as *sine qua non* in identifying those who are to be put forward initially for reconciliation as bishops are: "(c) Pastoral Overseers" of districts or regions,[29] "(e) Representative Ministers in the Act of Ordination,"[30] and "(g) Servants of the Christian Unity of the Church."

30) Each covenanting church may find these ministerial offices already existing within its polity, or may make amendment of existing offices to the extent necessary to fulfill the intention of ministry reconciliation through covenanting, or may create a new office within the integrity of its continuing polity but in a manner conformable to the intention of ministry reconciliation through covenanting. Each church may assign or continue to use such names for these offices as it may desire; however, in the shared life of the churches they commonly will be identified as deacons, presbyters, and bishops of the covenant communion of the churches.[31]

31) By reconciliation through covenanting, a presbyter or bishop does not acquire new rights, powers, or authority within his or her own denomination or communion. Such decisions about authority are properly left to the member churches. Rather, through ministry reconciliation it becomes possible to act in ecclesial unity with other lay and ordained ministries of the covenanting churches to make manifest in new and wider ways the visible and organic unity of the church.

*Celebrating the Eucharist Together*

32) The Lord's Supper is the sacred feast of the people of God. In communion with Christ, members of the church are renewed in their communion with one another in Christ, and are commissioned afresh to be Christ's agents of reconciliation in the world. The sacrament is at the heart of the church's life. Regular celebration of the Eucharist together is at the heart of covenanting as well.[32]

33) Observance of the Lord's Supper is a sign of the church's unity in

Christ. In the present divided state of the churches, it is an ironic witness against their disunity as well. As Christians gather in all their diversity at one Table of the Lord, they give evidence that their communion is with Christ, and hence that they are in communion with one another in Christ. But when Christians are unable or unwilling to partake together of the one Eucharist, they witness against themselves and give visible demonstration of the brokenness of Christ's body. Common celebration of Holy Communion is essential to the unity we seek.

34) The sacrament of the Lord's Supper exhibits a richness of meaning that is larger than the tradition of any single church. Its essential meaning is briefly stated in *The COCU Consensus,* Chapter VI, paragraphs 15-19. Without obscuring differences which remain, the covenanting churches find in *The COCU Consensus* sufficient agreement regarding the meaning of the Lord's Supper to enable partaking of it as one, while allowing for diversity of administration and practice. At the same time, they share in an increasingly universal convergence of Christian understanding that includes the following elements which should characterize all eucharistic liturgies:

–it is a great *thanksgiving* to God for everything accomplished in creation and redemption;
–it is a *memorial* of the crucified and risen Christ and a sign of Christ's redeeming love for all humankind;
–it is an *invocation* of the Holy Spirit who makes the crucified and risen Christ really present to us in the sacramental meal;
–it is a *communion* of the faithful who, in communion with Christ, are in communion with one another in Christ;
–it is a *meal* of the kingdom, a foretaste of the final redemption of all things in Christ.[33]

The eucharistic liturgies already authorized by the churches of the Consultation reflect such a mutually accepted pattern.

35) Shared celebration of the Eucharist is both a sign and a means of unity in Christ.[34] Even before the inauguration of covenanting, the churches' experience of interim eucharistic fellowship over more than a decade has demonstrated the dynamism of regular eucharistic sharing for the sake of Christian unity.[35] The power of reconciling grace made present in the sacrament has been compelling in furthering a new degree of unity between churches which have been deeply separated for many years along racial lines. It is that same power which has long been evident at the Lord's Table within each church, effecting the reconciliation of those who have become personally, politically, or theologically estranged from one another.

36) The Lord's Supper also is a powerful centering reality for the

church's mission. The church always is tempted to pursue either institutional or ideological ends in mission, substituting its own will for the will of Christ. Some even regard Christian unity as an enemy of the church's mission, in the belief that unity draws energy away from cherished causes. But at the eucharistic table, we "show forth the Lord's death until he comes." That is in itself a powerful act of gospel proclamation, providing the spring for Christian witness and action. Indeed, it is the paradigm of all that the church is called to say and do in mission in the world. Unity and mission are one at the Lord's Table.

37) In covenanting, it is important that common celebrations of the Eucharist be planned with intentional regularity. The frequency of such occasions is left to the discretion of the covenanting partners in each place.

*Engaging Together in Christ's Mission*

38) Mission is essential to the church's apostolicity. The church is apostolic not only because it continues in the faith and teaching of the apostles, but also because it is sent, like the apostles, to carry out Christ's mission to all people. Mission is essential to life in the church. It is essential as well to life in covenant communion among the churches.

39) The mission of the church takes many forms. In simplest terms, it is a mission of reconciliation and redemption. It is participation as a commissioned servant in God's mission, which is "to unite all things in Christ, things in heaven and things on earth." (Eph. 1:10) The church engages in mission through *worship*, through *proclamation* of the gospel, and through *action* which embodies God's justice, peace and love.

40) *In worship,* the church recalls and celebrates the might acts of God in creation, redemption and providence; is graciously forgiven and renewed in faith, hope and love; and is sent out in the power of the Holy Spirit, individually and collectively, to be ambassadors, witnesses and servants of Christ to the world. But in worship the church does more than just prepare for mission. Worship itself is one of the ways the church engages in its mission until the end of time. Even in places where some forms of mission are forbidden by the state, the faithful assembling of the people for Christian worship is a mighty witness to the gospel. What happens in worship is of vital significance for the world; the church intercedes for the world, and Christ is present for the life of all people. There is no such thing as Christian mission not rooted and renewed continuously in the church's worship. Worship is mission.

41) *Proclamation of the gospel* also is mission. Beyond the gathered worshipping community, faithful telling of the story by which the church lives is an essential part of its apostolate to the world. The church has been entrusted with the story that is life for the world. It is preserved and sent into

the world to proclaim that story. The church can never be content simply to signify its faith by deeds done in silence, however essential such deeds are. The church is called as well to confess unambiguously the Christ in whom it lives, and to invite all who will to enter the fellowship of life in Christ through the church, and thus be faithful to its evangelistic task. Proclamation is mission.

42) *Action which embodies Christ's mission* of justice, peace and love is the church's mission, too. Without such action, the church's worship and proclamation are betrayed, "for the tree is known by its fruit."[36] This action is described in many ways in Scripture; it is relief for the poor, release for prisoners, sight for the blind, liberty for the oppressed;[37] it is food for the hungry, drink for those who thirst, welcome for strangers, clothes for those who have none, companionship for those who are sick, imprisoned, or alone.[38] God in Christ has a special concern for those whom the world mistreats or overlooks: the poor, the weak, the oppressed, those excluded from full participation in society, and those who by reason of physical or mental disability, race, language or culture (such as African American, Asian, Pacific Islander, Hispanic, Native American) are dehumanized. Faithful participation in Christ's mission of justice, peace and love for all people, and the integrity of creation, requires repentance of the church: a deliberate turning away from all the various expressions of unconscious racism—individual, corporate, systemic—naming them and renouncing them. But such repentance is not enough unless it results in actions for justice, focused on eliminating those conditions which permit racism to fester and violate human life.

43) It is appropriate to add something more specific regarding the church's action in mission, in view of the racial and ethnic diversity of the covenant communion.[39] Christian unity, for churches of predominantly African American membership, is a subject never far removed from struggles to overcome poverty and to achieve social, economic, and racial justice. The struggle for civil rights in this country was rooted in the African American churches, and it became the greatest contribution of these churches to Christian unity in this century. With its holistic concern for the civic, spiritual and material well-being of every person, this evangelical movement for human rights gave new meaning to the word from which "ecumenical" is derived, *oikoumene:* "the whole inhabited earth." It embodied "ecumenical altruism": love that leaps all boundaries out of a profound respect for all people. This movement has taught us that where there is no condemnation of idolatry and no call to social justice, there can be no positive or prophetic ecumenical vision of unity or of peace. The covenant communion upon which we enter deliberately claims and shall seek by God's grace to embody this understanding of what it means to be the body of Christ in mission to the world.

44) The Consultation desires that its unity in mission find expression in all three of these dimensions of mission. For the sake of the world, these churches wish to find occasions for worshipping together in covenant communion, and celebrating the eucharist together. For the sake of the world, they seek ways in which their proclamation of the gospel may be made with one voice in covenant communion. For the sake of the world, they seek opportunities for acting together in the service of God's justice, peace and love in the world, that the unity and diversity of this covenant communion may be a sign to all people of God's redemptive will "to unite all things in Christ, things in heaven and things on earth."[40]

*Formation of Covenanting Councils*

45) Wherever covenanting occurs—nationally, regionally, or locally, one of the inaugural covenanting acts will be the formation of a covenanting council in each such "place." The reason for doing this is that church unity will be neither visible nor organic if it is not embodied in tangible form. The church exists not alone in the mind. It takes up space on the earth. It can be seen. It can act, and be accountable for its actions. In a covenant communion of churches, therefore, it is essential that there be a company of persons who representatively give expression and leadership to its common life. Such groups we refer to as covenanting councils.

46) The primary purpose of these covenanting councils will be to enable the communion of churches in covenant. Several of their functions are of a distinctly ecclesial nature. By giving visible expression to the unity of the churches in covenant communion, the covenanting councils create the corporate ecclesial setting for the ordering of the covenanting ministries of bishops, presbyters, deacons, and lay persons. Among the functions of covenanting councils are:

—ordering the sacrament of Holy Communion in ways that are faithful to the Tradition as claimed in the covenanting agreements, and assembling the people from time to time to celebrate it as one;
—enabling joint ordinations among all the covenanting churches in which reconciled bishops lay on hands with prayer together with the presence and participation of representative ordained and lay persons from as many of the covenanting churches as possible.[41]
—giving joint spiritual oversight (*episkopé*) of the things which enable covenant communion among the churches, including
  –pursuit of inclusiveness,
  –pursuit of a fuller embodiment within each church of the full vision of ministry described in Chapter VII of *The COCU Consensus*,
  –provision of public occasions which visibly bear witness to unity in Christ,

such as common baptisms, confirmations, ordinations, and other sacred occasions;

–acting as one in the service of justice on behalf of all for whom justice is delayed or denied, doing so within existing ecumenical bodies where appropriate; and,

–providing opportunity for shared decision-making in our common engagement in Christ's mission in the world.

The covenanting councils may also be given other tasks which the participating churches find appropriate to give them. Covenanting councils will not have authority over the churches. They will derive their authority to act from the judicatories which brought them into being. They will exercise a shared oversight of the covenanting process upon which the churches will enter.

47) This list of functions makes clear that the primary focus of the covenanting process is the local worshiping community, gathered around the Word and sacraments, and giving expression to the church's missionary vocation in the world. It is the local covenanting council, more than the regional or the national, on which primary attention falls in the covenanting process.

48) *Local covenanting councils* will exist to enable congregations of the covenanting churches, located in close proximity to one another (in the same town or in an urban or rural neighborhood), to live and act as one covenant communion in that place, even while maintaining their distinct existences and traditions. Through a shared life of Word and sacrament, publicly confessing the one faith together, and served by ordained ministers who are fully reconciled and hence fully accessible to all, these congregations will be able to reach out in mission as one people in Christ in ways not possible before they entered into covenant communion.

49) *Regional covenanting councils* bring together representatively those judicatories of the covenanting churches where ordination and oversight is located.[42] They are a collegial expression of shared oversight of the covenanting commitment of the churches, particularly in relation to the ordained ministries, congregations of the faithful, and common mission. Additionally, they facilitate formation of local covenanting councils, and encourage and assist those which have been formed.

50) *The national covenanting council* will encourage regional judicatories to enter into covenanting, and will assist those that have been formed. It will invite other communions of Christ's church to enter the covenant. The national covenanting council will provide a forum where churchwide concerns may be considered, including concerns that arise from local and regional covenanting experience. It will enable the churches to think together about matters of worship, including mutually acceptable liturgical norms for

shared worship. It will enable churches to think together about matters of ecclesiastical polity as each church seeks increasingly to embody the vision of ministry contained in partnership with the other covenanting churches. Any necessary amendments to the two documents embodying the basic agreements of the covenant communion shall be recommended to the participating churches by the national covenanting council. In sum, it will give collegial guidance to the covenanting process in matters of a general nature.

51) The covenanting churches will continue to participate fully in the life of other ecumenical bodies. The relationships nurtured through the conciliar movement have done much to bring the covenanting churches into closer relations with each other, and it is anticipated that the ecclesial depth of relationship among the covenanting churches will mean much to the conciliar movement as well. Councils of churches represent a broader constituency than do covenanting councils; hence, councils of churches will continue to be of great importance to the covenanting churches. It is intended that the relationship between covenanting councils and the councils of churches will be a cooperative, complementary, and mutually enriching one. It is intended that the funding and human resources now committed by the churches in their present separateness will not be eroded when they enter into covenant communion. Covenanting councils are not a substitute for councils of churches; rather, they give expression to a covenantal form of church union.

52) Each covenanting council may be organized in such manner as seems appropriate to the consenting covenanting churches in that "place," provided only that the following basic agreements be observed:

–covenanting councils shall be composed of elected representatives of churches which have formally entered into covenanting through affirmative action on *The COCU Consensus* and *Churches in Covenant Communion*, and through participation in the inaugurating liturgies of covenanting;
–covenanting councils shall be composed in such a way as to be representative of the total ministry of the people of God, lay ministries as well as ordained ministries, within these churches; the churches, with appropriate consultation, will determine in what way their existing ministries will be represented in the councils, and the particular persons who will be sent to them;
–covenanting councils shall be composed in such a way as to be inclusive of the diversity which God has given to the churches which form them.[43]

The size, organization, and frequency of meeting of the several covenanting councils, as well as their geographical territories or boundaries, shall be determined in the joint discretion of the ecclesiastical bodies which form them in each "place."[44]


## V. The Process of Covenanting

1) The process of covenanting is intended to be implemented by the churches through a series of deliberate steps and stages.

*Claiming the Theological Consensus*
2) The first formal act of covenanting is for each church to claim *The COCU Consensus: In Quest of a Church Uniting* (1984). What that means specifically is stated in the Foreword to that document, namely that each participating church is asked, by formal action, to recognize in it:

> [1] an expression, in the matters with which it deals, of the Apostolic faith, order, worship, and witness of the Church,
> [2] an anticipation of the Church Uniting which the participating bodies, by the power of the Holy Spirit, wish to become, and
> [3] a sufficient theological basis for the covenanting acts and the uniting process proposed at this time by the Consultation.[45]

The churches' action on these resolutions began in 1986. It is expected that by 1989 all of the member churches of the Consultation will have had an opportunity to consider and act upon them.


*Approving the Covenanting Proposal*
3) The second formal act of covenanting is for the participating churches to receive, study, and take formal action upon the document, *Churches in Covenant Communion: The Church of Christ Uniting* (1988). What that means specifically is stated in the resolution of transmittal of this document to the churches, issued by the 1988 Plenary of the Consultation on Church Union (see Preface). This document contains the essentials of the covenanting agreements, together with the liturgies by which the covenant is to be inaugurated.


*The Consultation Considers Next Steps*
4) After the participating churches have considered and acted upon the proposals of the Consultation contained in the two documents, *The COCU Consensus* and *Churches in Covenant Communion,* the Consultation on Church Union will carefully examine the actions of the churches on these recommendations, and determine next steps accordingly. No judgment has been made in advance regarding the number of churches that must approve the proposals in order for them to be implemented, nor on other questions

concerning the nature of the churches' actions upon them. Such matters will be addressed together by the churches, through the Consultation on Church Union, after the participating churches have acted upon the proposals now before them. If the decision of the Consultation is that the actions of the churches justify implementation of the covenanting proposals as presented, the following two sections of this chapter on "The Process of Covenanting" then apply. If the decision is other than that, the Consultation on Church Union in plenary session will itself determining what action to recommend to the churches.

*Preparations to Implement Covenanting*

5) The fourth step in the covenanting process may be somewhat different for each church. It has to do with the particular preparations that each church will need to make in order to participate fully in the inaugurating liturgies of covenanting. Each church which takes affirmative action on the first two steps described above will then need to take other steps as promptly as possible, internal to its own polity, to prepare itself in whatever ways it may deem to be necessary for the acts of recognition and of reconciliation which are described in the covenanting document and its accompanying liturgies. Specifically this could mean as many as four things:

    (a) discovering what categories of ordained ministry within one's polity correspond most closely to that of "bishop," "presbyter," and "deacon" as described in the two documents named above;

    (b) making such amendment of one's polity or ecclesiastical system as may be necessary—in good faith, in dialogue with other participating churches, and in the spirit of the covenantal commitment—in order:

        [1] to make possible the participation of one's church in a covenantal form of church union as here proposed,

        [2] to delegate to covenanting councils (upon their formation) sufficient authority to act in the ways described in this document, and

        [3] to make possible, through whatever changes may need to be made, full participation within the covenant communion of those who are to be put forward for reconciliation as covenanting bishops and presbyters—utilizing the collegial processes of the Consultation on Church Union to assure mutual acceptability of these forms of ministry within the covenant communion of churches;

    (c) naming its representatives to the national service of covenanting, and its representatives to the national covenanting council which will be inaugurated soon thereafter; and

(d) encouraging its regional bodies to name their representatives for participation in regional services of covenanting.

*Participation in the Covenanting Liturgies*

6) The fifth step in the covenanting process is the act of consummating a new relationship of covenant communion among the churches. Each church will participate representatively in the liturgies of covenanting, by which covenant will be declared, ministries reconciled, covenanting councils inaugurated, and the Eucharist shared by all. The full text of these three liturgies is attached.[46] These covenanting acts are parts of a single reality. Though they occur in three liturgical settings, each is integrally related to the others. These three liturgical actions are described as follows.

7) *The first will be the national service of declaring covenant.* This liturgy will include an act of mutual recognition of each other as churches, together with an act for the reconciliation of a small but representative number of ordained ministries (a bishop, a presbyter, and a deacon) from each church. The primary services for the reconciliation of ordained ministries will be held later, in many regional and local settings: bishops will ordinarily be reconciled in regional liturgies, presbyters and deacons in local liturgies. The national liturgy, however, is chiefly focused upon the formal declaring of the covenant on behalf of the participating churches as a whole. Nonetheless, in so doing, it will anticipate as well the reconciliation of ministries which is to follow both there and elsewhere. The national service will not include an act for the inauguration of a national covenanting council, but will instead express the commitment of these to do so later after recognition and reconciliation of ministry has occurred in several regions. The liturgy for declaring covenant among the churches will conclude with the celebration of the Lord's Supper, done in a manner that expresses the new relationship among the participating churches, under the leadership of a reconciled covenanting bishop.

8) *The second liturgical action will be the regional service for the reconciliation of bishops.* This action is intimately related to the first. Therefore, the first of these regional services will occur in close conjunction with the national service. The choice of location for the national service will be in part made in light of the readiness of the middle judicatories of the covenanting churches in that place to enter promptly into the implementation of the covenant through the reconciliation of their ordained ministers of regional *episkopé*. It is hoped that several of these regional services will be held immediately following the national service, perhaps simultaneously with one another at different places across the country. The reconciliation of bishops will be accomplished through the mutual recognition of one another's ministry of *episkopé* and through a mutual laying on of hands among the bish-

ops, together with other appropriate signs, and prayer. The regional service will include an act for the inaugurating of a regional covenanting council. The regional service will conclude with the celebration of the Holy Communion, done in a way that expresses the new relationship among the participating churches.

9) *The third liturgical action will be the local service for celebrating the covenant, for reconciling presbyters, and for welcoming deacons and other ordained ministers of governance.* These local services will occur within regions where there has already been a regional service for the reconciliation of bishops. They will of course occur in many localities throughout the region. The first such local celebration may well occur on the same day as the regional service of reconciliation of bishops, and possibly in the same place. The local service will include an acknowledgment of the reconciliation of bishops that has occurred in that region. It will then move to the reconciliation of presbyters, this being essential to eucharistic fellowship. To that end, the liturgy will include the laying on of the hands of a reconciled bishop upon each of the presbyters there gathered, together with the giving of the hand of fellowship and other appropriate signs of welcome.

10) The diaconal ministries of the churches are now so dissimilar to one another that a meaningful act of reconciliation into a single ministry of deacon is difficult to contemplate at this time. Nonetheless, every church does engage in diaconal ministry; some of these diaconal ministers are ordained and others are unordained. So also, each church provides in some manner for the participation of other persons in ecclesial governance—persons variously defined as Elders, members of the Vestry or of the Official Board. For some, these ministries of governance are an ordained office, and for others they are not. Hence, no meaningful act of reconciliation into a single ministry of governance can be effected at this time. Nonetheless, the local liturgy will include a public act for the mutual welcoming of all ordained deacons and all ordained ministers of governance within the shared life of the covenant communion of churches, but it will not include a liturgical act of the reconciliation of these varied ministries,

11) The service will include an act for the inauguration of a local covenanting council, and will be concluded with the celebration of the Eucharist, done in a way that expresses the new relationship among the participating churches.

*The Expanding Process of Covenanting*

12) It is not anticipated that covenanting will commence in all places at the same time. While the national church bodies will declare covenant and will proceed sometime thereafter to form a national covenanting council, regional church judicatories will in turn celebrate covenant, reconcile min-

istries, and form a regional covenanting council when they are ready to do so. Even after the regional judicatories of the churches have entered into covenanting, groups of congregations within the region will celebrate the covenant and form a local covenanting council when they are prepared so to do. Relationships can be encouraged but not compelled.

13) For an indefinite period, therefore, there may be some unevenness and indeed some anomaly in this covenant communion of churches. One may judge, however, that the anomaly will not be greater than the divisions which now fracture the one body and the one Table of Christ. Covenanting provides a means whereby the Holy Spirit may draw the churches into an ever widening and deepening unity, where and when the Spirit wills.

## Appendix

### *The Reason for an Appendix*

1) The matters dealt with in this appendix are not a part of the covenanting agreements. They are suggestions offered to those who will bear responsibility for the organization of covenanting councils in each place. Locating these suggestions in an appendix rather than among the covenanting agreements themselves reflects the understanding that, while such councils are indeed an element of covenanting, their precise structural form is not. The organizational arrangement of these bodies is seen as a matter of local judgment which may well vary from time to time and from place to place.

### *Composition of Covenanting Councils*

2) It is suggested that the covenanting councils be composed of representatives of each of the reconciled and welcomed ordained ministries (in such numbers, in such proportions among the ministries, and for such terms of service as the covenanting bodies shall themselves jointly decide in each place) together with representative lay members of the covenanting churches, in number at least equal to the sum of the representative ordained ministers.[47] In local covenanting councils, it may be considered permissible for bishops to be represented by deputies either from their own or from another covenanting communion. Since the covenanting council is to be a model of inclusiveness for all the covenanting churches, the composition of each communion's representation in the council should be negotiated in advance, so that the council will reflect the diversity of the church's membership.[48]

### *Accountability of Covenanting Councils*

3) It is suggested that the accountability of the covenanting councils be regarded as a collective accountability to the bodies which brought them into

being: the national covenanting council to the national governing bodies of the covenanting churches, the regional covenanting councils to the ecclesiastical middle judicatories which formed them, and the local covenanting council to the worshipping congregations of the covenanting churches which entered into covenant communion located in that place. The relationship between different levels of covenanting councils—local, regional, or national—is suggested to be one of mutual caring and encouragement, but not of power, as they together seek to further the integrity of the covenant communion of churches, of which they are the most tangible embodiment.

*Administration of Covenanting Councils*

4) Administrative structures are not an inherent aspect of these proposals at any level: local, regional, or national. The covenanting churches in any place or at any level may choose to organize themselves as they deem appropriate and to provide for themselves such administrative help as they may need, if any. The churches themselves—locally, regionally, or nationally—will know when or whether they need any administrative assistance in pursuing their covenant communion, and such matters are left entirely in their discretion.

*Worship in Covenanting Councils*

5) In light of the essentially ecclesial nature of the covenanting councils, it is suggested that their meetings be regularly marked by corporate acts of worship, including from time to time the celebration of the Eucharist. Through the Consultation on Church Union, the churches have developed many resources for such common worship, among which may be mentioned the COCU Liturgy for the Lord's Supper (approved by all the participating churches). *Guidelines for Interim Eucharistic Fellowship,* the COCU lectionary of agreed texts (now serving a much larger consistency in a modified form), and the COCU Lenten Booklet of devotional readings.

## Notes

[The text in which notes 1 and 2 appear is not included in material presented herein. Page 2 has the following important clarification:]

Of the many changes made during the process of revising the document, the most significant has to do with the way that the goal of the covenanting process is now stated. Covenanting was described in 1984 as an interim step on the way toward becoming one church. Though appreciative of such unions in the past, the responses to the 1984 text revealed profound resistance to that expression of the goal for the Consultation. Yet paradoxically that resistance was coupled with a genuine yearning for the unity of the church. On closer examination it became apparent that what was being resisted was any commitment to an eventual merger of Church structures. In the present document, therefore, all reference to the goal as an "interim step" toward something else has been removed from the text; and "church union" has been defined in a new way. In this document it implies, not consolidation of forms and structures, but what the early church referred to as "communion in sacred things." That means becoming one in faith, sacraments, ministry, and mission. This kind of unity is visible and organic, whether or not organizational structures are consolidated. In a word, it is covenant communion—a form of church unity broad enough and deep enough to permit an ever-widening circle of churches to manifest their unity in Christ. In the present understanding of the churches, the Church of Christ Uniting referred to in the *The COCU Consensus* means this covenant communion.

3. Adapted from *The COCU Consensus*, pp. 25-28.

4. *The COCU Consensus*: p. 24, par. 4; also pp. 26-27 par. 6(e) and 6(f).

5. See pp. 47-48 ("A National Service for Declaring Covenant..."), the Prayer of Confession on the first and second pages of this liturgy in *Churches in Covenant Communion*.

6. *The COCU Consensus*, pp. 41-42, par. 6-7.

7. The original meaning of "symbol" is: "an authoritative summary of faith or doctrine." For centuries it has been used in this way to refer to the creeds of the church. Other meanings of the word, such as a token or arbitrary sign, are of more recent development. The word derives from Greek (*syn* + *ballein*) meaning literally to "cast together"—that is, to hold two things side by side for comparison, as proof of authenticity.

8. *The COCU Consensus*, pp. 22-23, par. 16.

9. Romans 12:2.

10. "For as many of you as were baptized into Christ have put on Christ. There is neither Jew nor Greek, there is neither bond nor free, there is neither male nor female; for you are all one in Christ Jesus." (Galatians 3:27-28)

11. Luke 4:18.

12. The rite of confirmation is addressed under the heading of the renewal of baptismal vows in *The COCU Consensus*, pp. 47-48, par. 13-14. See also the document, *An Order for an Affirmation of the Baptismal Covenant (Also Called Confirmation)*, produced by the Consultation on Church Union and available from its office.

13. *The COCU Consensus*, p. 47, par. 11.

14. *The COCU Consensus*, p. 47, par. 10.

15. *The COCU Consensus*, p. 53, par. 21; also p. 54, par. 24.

16. See *Churches in Covenant Communion*, p. 53.

17. *The COCU Consensus*, p. 54, par. 24-25. See also *Baptism, Eucharist, and Ministry* (Faith and Order paper no. 111), Geneva: World Council of Churches, 1982: "Ministry," sections I and II.

18. *The COCU Consensus*, pp. 56-57, par. 27-31.

19. From "A Note on the Function of Chapter VII in the Covenanting Process," *The COCU Consensus*, p. 49.

20. *The COCU Consensus*, p. 60, par. 47 and see also *Baptism, Eucharist, and Ministry*, "Ministry," par. 34 and 37-38.

21. See *Churches in Covenant Communion*, pp. 51-54, 56-60.

22. See the accompanying liturgies, ibid., pp. 56-63. For the meaning of *episkopé*, see *The COCU Consensus*, pp. 59-60, paragraphs 46 and 47.

23. See *Churches in Covenant Communion*, pp. 58, 60, 62-63.

24. *Baptism, Eucharist and Ministry*, "Ministry" paragraph 53: "In order to achieve mutual recognition, different steps are required of different churches. For example:

 a) Churches which have preserved the episcopal succession are asked to recognize both the apostolic content of the ordained ministry which exists in churches which have not maintained such succession and also the existence in these churches of a ministry of *episkopé* in various forms.

 b) Churches without the episcopal succession, and living in faithful continuity with the apostolic faith and mission, have a ministry of Word and sacrament, as is evident from the belief, practice, and life of those churches. These churches are asked to realize that the continuity with the Church of the apostles finds profound expression in the successive laying on of hands by bishops and that, though they may not lack the continuity of the apostolic tradition, this sign will strengthen and deepen that continuity. They may need to recover the sign of the episcopal succession."

25. This refers to that level of ecclesiastical jurisdiction where ordination to ministry occurs, variously described as the diocese, presbytery, region, conference, or association. (See also footnote 42 below.)

26. Covenanting Councils are described later, on pp. 85-88.

27. The phrase, "mutually acceptable rites," refers to the existing ordination rites of the covenanting churches, adapted if necessary to facilitate the full and willing participation of representative ministers from other covenanting churches in the ordination rite of one's own church. The phrase is not meant to imply the necessity of a common ordinal for the churches, nor is it meant to foreclose the possibility that the churches may wish at some time to develop together such a common rite.

28. *The COCU Consensus*, pp. 58-59, par. 39-44.

29. The ministry of bishops as preachers of the Word and celebrants of the sacraments is included under the heading of "Pastoral Overseers" in the indicated paragraph of *The COCU Consensus*.

30. In *The COCU Consensus*, p. 61, par. 51(e) (which refers to bishops as "Representative Ministers in the Act of Ordination"), the statement that "bishops preside at ordinations" is understood by the covenanting churches to imply (1) the personal leadership of the bishop, (2) the direct participation of the bishop in the laying on of hands, and (3) the participation of others in the act of ordination (pp. 57-58, par. 37).

31. *The COCU Consensus*, pp. 58-59, par. 42.

32. It is understood that every reference to the sacrament in this document implies its inseparable connection with the reading and preaching of the Word. See *The COCU Consensus*, p. 46, par. 8; also p. 48, par. 15.

33. *Baptism, Eucharist and Ministry*, "Eucharist" II.2-26.

34. *The COCU Consensus*, p. 48, par. 15.

35. *Guidelines for Interim Eucharistic Fellowship*, Princeton, NJ: Consultation on Church Union, 1973. 11p. (A useful resource offering suggestions and liturgical guidelines for shared celebrations of the Eucharist.) Available from the COCU office.

36. Matthew 12:33.

37. Luke 4:18.

38. Matthew 25:35-40.

39. Three of the nine churches in the Consultation on Church Union are composed predominantly of African American membership. A fourth is approximately half black and half white in its composition. The remaining five churches, while having a predominantly Caucasian membership, are racially and ethnically diverse in significant measure.

40. Ephesians 1:10.

41. See p. 80, par. 27 below; see also middle of p. 52 in *Churches in Covenant Communion*.

42. This refers to the ordination of ministers of Word and sacrament (presbyters) and ministers of *episkopé* (bishops). In all of the COCU churches, these are ordained at the middle judicatory level (see footnote 25 above). It is recognized, however, that in some of the member churches there are other ministries in which ordination occurs at the level of the local congregation

43) *The COCU Consensus*, p. 21, par. 13; pp. 22-24, par. 16-17; and pp. 27-28, par. 6(g).

44. An illustration of how the covenanting churches in any "place" might wish to organize their Covenanting Council is described in an Appendix, attached hereto for information on pp. 92-93 below.

45. *The COCU Consensus*, pp. 16-17

46. See *Churches in Covenant Communion*, pp. 41 ff.

47. *The COCU Consensus*, p. 54, par. 25; also p. 56, par. 26(f).

48. *The COCU Consensus*, p. 21, par. 13; also pp. 22-24, par. 16-17; and pp. 27-28, par. 6(g).

# BILATERAL DIALOGUES IN THE UNITED STATES

# Introduction

The ecumenical documents in this section are the result of theological conversations between theologians representing two churches or families of churches. The Introduction to this volume outlines some of this diversity.[1] The *Building Unity* volume outlines in some detail the methodology followed in developing these dialogues and the diversity of goals facing the dialogue partners.[2] That volume also includes brief descriptions of all of the dialogue partners except the Polish National Catholic Church, for which a more extended note is included here. As noted in the preface and the introduction to *Building Unity*, the background documentation, the intention of the documents, and their place within the worldwide context of discussions between the two partners is to be taken into account if the texts are to be read in the spirit with which they were prepared for the churches.

These dialogues are related to the international conversations between churches and Christian World Communions. In some cases, the national bilaterals provide leadership and a context for enabling the worldwide discussions to move forward. In other cases, the worldwide conversations generate national discussions and provide leadership to local churches in improving their relationship. When a worldwide agreement is proposed, the national and local discussions and evaluation of these texts is an integral element of the reception process.[3] The Lutheran statements with Baptists and Methodists included here, for example, parallel the international conversations of the Lutheran World Federation with the Baptist World Alliance and the World Methodist Council.[4] The Lutheran-Reformed international agreements have engendered extensive dialogue, some of which are included here, but their reception is still the subject of extensive debate.[5] The Lutheran-Episcopal dialogues, reports, and proposed Concordat are also part of the worldwide discussions between these two communions.[6] Similar recommendations have been reported to the Church of England and the German Lutheran Churches.[7]

The Episcopal-Orthodox statements in the United States are national expressions of the relationships of these two Communions worldwide. The Anglican-Orthodox Conversations have produced a rich harvest of agree-

99

ment.[8] The Reformed-Orthodox dialogues have also produced international results which complement those included here.[9] Major Lutheran-Catholic documents from the United States are carried in *Building Unity I*, and these relate to the Lutheran World Federation/Roman Catholic conversations as well.[10]

Roman Catholic/Eastern Orthodox relationships have been document-ed in the volume *Towards the Healing of Schism* in this series.[11] However, there have been several important documents between these two churches produced since that volume was published.[12] The Lutheran/Easter Orthodox international dialogue has also produced some important results.[13]

The Anglican/Roman Catholic report contained here is to be seen in the context of a rich national and international heritage of dialogue and research over the last three decades.[14] The United Methodist/Roman Catholic report contained here is to be seen as the fruit of the dialogue chronicled in *Building Unity I* and the World Methodist Council/Roman Catholic Conversations.[15] Finally, the first international Roman Catholic/Baptist World Alliance dialogue was released in 1988.[16] These documents, and the wide array of research and supporting literature, provide the context for God's call to reconciliation in truth and common life in Christ.

In order to understand the chronology, personnel involved, and specific context of the documents below, notes have been provided to enable the reader to consult the original sources and place them in the context out of which they emerged.

## Notes

1. "Introduction," pp. 5-7 above.

2. "Introduction," in BU, 2-4; see also John Hotchkin, "Preface," BU ix-xii; *Directory for the Application of Principles and Norms on Ecumenism* (Washington DC: National Conference of Catholic Bishops, 1993), also printed in *Origins* 23 (1993) 129, 131-160.

3. BU, 5-7; *GiA*, 7-9.

4. Report of the Joint Commission of the Baptist World Alliance and the Lutheran World Federation, *Baptist and Lutheran Conversation: Message to the Churches* (Geneva: BWA/LWF, 1990). Cf. also Joseph Burgess, ed., *Lutherans in Ecumenical Dialogue* (Minneapolis: Fortress Press, 1990).

5. W.G. Rusch, and D.F. Martensen, eds., *The Leuenberg Agreement and Lutheran-Reformed Relationships* (Minneapolis: Augsburg, 1989); Lutheran World Federation/World Alliance of Reformed Churches, *Toward Church Fellowship* (Geneva: LWF/WARC, 1989).

6. GiA, 13.

7. Anglican-Lutheran Dialogue, "The Report of the Anglican-Lutheran European Regional Commission, Helsinki, September 1982" (London: SPCK, 1983): "The Meissen Common Statement: On the Way to Visible Unity," *Ecumenical Bulletin* 103 (January 1991) 4-9.

8. GiA, 39-60; "The International Commission of the Anglican/Orthodox Theological Dialogue, Communique of the Meeting Held in New Valamo, Finland, 20-26 June, 1989," *Ecumenical Bulletin* 97 (December 1989) 11.

9. T. Torrance, *Theological Dialogue Between Orthodox and Reformed Churches* (Edinburgh: Scottish Academic Press, 1985).

10. GiA 167-276; Lutheran-Roman Catholic Dialogue, *Facing Unity* (Lutheran World Federation, 1980); Karl Lehmann and Wolfhart Pannenberg, eds., *The Condemnations of the Reformation Era: Do They Still Divide?* (Minneapolis: Fortress Press, 1990).

11. E.J. Stormon, SJ, ed., *Toward the Healing of Schism: The Sees of Rome and Constantinople,* Ecumenical Documents III (New York: Paulist Press, 1987).

12. "The Mystery of the Church and the Eucharist in the Light of the Mystery of the Holy Trinity," IS, 49:II/III (1982) 107-111; "Faith, Sacraments and the Unity of the Church," IS, 64:II (1987) 82-87; "The Sacrament of Order in the Sacramental Structure of the Church, with Particular Reference to the Importance of the Apostolic Succession for the Sanctification and the Unity of the People of God," IS, 68:III-IV (1988) 173-78, Cf. IS 66:I (1988).

13. Lutheran-Orthodox Joint Commission, *Agreed Statements 1985-1989.* Divine Revelation. Scripture and Tradition. Canon and Inspiration (Geneva: LWF, 1992); 63 pp., in English, German, and Greek.

14. GiA, 61-130; J. Witmer and J.R. Wright, eds., *Called to Full Unity*, Documents on Anglican-Roman Catholic Relations, 1966-1983 (Washington, DC: U.S. Catholic Conference, 1986); "Salvation and the Church," IS, 63:I (1987) 33-40; "Church as Communion," *Origins* 20:44 (April 11, 1991) 719-27.

15. GiA, 307-388; "Toward a Statement on the Church. Report of the Joint Commission between the Roman Catholic Church and the World Methodist Council, Fourth Series, 1982-1986," IS 62:IV (1986) "The Apostolic Tradition: Report of the Joint Commission of the Roman Catholic Church and the World Methodist Council, 1986-1991, Fifth Series," in Joe Hale, ed., *Sixteenth World Methodist Council, 1991, Singapore* (Waynesville: World Methodist Council Press, 1992).

16. "Summons To Witness to Christ in Today's World: A Report on the Baptist-Roman Catholic International Conversation 1984-1988," IS I:72 (1990) 13-14

# Lutheran-Baptist Dialogue*

## Three Common Statements
## November 17, 1981

### DIVINE INITIATIVE AND HUMAN RESPONSE

Baptists and Lutherans are evangelical Christians. Together they believe in Jesus Christ as the gracious Savior of the world. Both churches are shaped by the acceptance of Scripture as the basis for Christian doctrine and life. Both also enjoy rootage in the Reformation heritage and seek to be grounded in, live by, and proclaim the Gospel of the saving act of God in Jesus Christ.

1. *Common Understandings of Faith.*—Lutherans and Baptists alike describe faith as being both divine gift and human response. Faith is made possible only by divine initiative, yet it is realized only through human response. In this human response it is recognized that the act of the human will in believing is itself regarded as a work of God. It is the Father's drawing the sinner to himself; it is the work of the Holy Spirit in the life of the believer.

The work of God does not, however, set aside the person's voluntary faculty and reduce the believer's participation to a passive, undynamic, and impersonal role. God's work enables a person to respond actively to the invitation of Christ, setting free, begetting anew (the new birth) and transforming the sinner. Faith is the work of the Spirit of Christ wrought in the heart by the gospel. No one is able to believe without the prior work of God who frees a person from the bondage of sin and enables an unwilling person to do the will of Christ.

The concern involved throughout this discussion of the nature of faith is to avoid the implication that the act of believing is made possible by an

*Introduction on Baptists and Lutherans included in *BU*, pp. 37-38, 85-87. "Lutheran-Baptist Dialogue," *American Baptist Quarterly,* 1:2 (December 1982) 103-112.

innate human power. Because our salvation is by the gracious justification of God through faith in Christ, all human boasting is excluded. True righteousness in us is accomplished by God's righteousness in Jesus Christ and is bestowed freely through faith in Christ. While it is true that as sinners we cannot believe without the work of God's Spirit which imparts new life, it is equally true that God does not believe for us nor cause us to believe without the exercise of our wills. The divine act of bestowal and human act of believing are in the closest union. Both Lutherans and Baptists wish to avoid a position which sets aside or minimizes either the divine or the human aspects of faith.

2. *Backgrounds to Differences.*—The historical situation which is most influential for *Baptist* formation is seventeenth century English Congregationalism in the context of an Anglican state church. It is in this context of early Puritan formation that the original impetus to the development of a truly regenerate and committed church membership took on its distinctive character. It was to be based on the hearing of the gospel, the experience of regeneration, purity in doctrine and life, and freedom from ecclesiastical and secular encroachment.

On American soil these original concerns of Baptists also found expression. Credible evidence of the new life in Christ served as a qualification for church membership. The church is thus experience centered in its expectations and standards of fellowship. This commitment to the experience of regeneration has an influence on other related beliefs and practices in the church.

*Lutheranism*, on the other hand, is shaped by its reaction to legalism in the sixteenth century. Lutheran origins can be traced to the quest for a gracious God expressed in terms of justification of the sinner, a doctrine which has continued to stamp this confessional family. The necessity of God's free act of justifying the sinner is clearly seen against the background of sin. Each person is born having no fear of nor trust in God and is unable to make the first move toward salvation. This condition, understood as original sin, is not overcome by human efforts but through rebirth by the Holy Spirit in baptism. There is a consistent rejection of any notion that a person can achieve righteousness by one's own powers.

For Lutherans justification is the work of God and is therefore "by grace." To say that it is "through faith" is to insist that the human response is a response of reception. We do not attract or merit it. Reception is a matter of trust and an acknowledgment of God's favor, which comes to us by means of word and sacrament. Faith can then never be misunderstood as a meritorious act by which one has a claim on God and is saved.

*These two developmental patterns have conditioned each church.* The

Lutheran concern for giving glory to God and comfort to repentant sinners led to an emphasis on the action of God in justification.

The Baptist concern for repentance and conversion led to an emphasis on faith as the human response to God's initiative.

Baptists and Lutherans agree that it is the gracious activity of a loving God which awakens faith in human beings. It is in defining the nature of that faith that our traditional difference in emphasis has emerged. Lutherans, in their concern to affirm the primacy of redeeming grace, have emphasized the powerlessness to initiate life in God. Baptists, on the other hand, in their concern to affirm the place of human responsibility in relation to God, have emphasized the element of decision with regard to faith.

3. *Baptism as an Illustration.*—These differences of emphasis with regard to divine initiative and human response become especially apparent with respect to the understanding and practice of baptism. *Baptists* see believer's baptism as most consonant with the concept of a regenerate church. Baptism is understood primarily as a sign of the gospel and the believer's response to it. It publicly attests the redemptive deed of God in Christ and the baptized person's trust in Christ as Savior, identification with him in his death and resurrection, and confession of him as Lord. Since faith involves a conscious, informed and voluntary decision, and baptism is an act of obedience in following Christ as Lord and Savior, an infant is considered to be incapable of such an act and is, therefore, not a proper candidate for baptism. Baptists understand the scriptural order to be: repent, believe, and be baptized. For Baptists, personal faith on the part of the candidate is therefore a prerequisite for the administration of baptism.

In the practice of infant and adult baptism *Lutheran* theology continues to carry through the theme that the action is primarily divine. God is the giver of the promise and the human being is the receiver. The baptized person receives what the promise offers and is incorporated and accepted into the body of Christ. In adults the Spirit works faith through the hearing of the word and through baptism. For infants the activity of the Spirit begins with baptism and leads to their confession of Jesus as Lord. For both adults and infants the priority of divine action is emphasized.

4. *Faith and Works.*—Lutherans and Baptists are agreed that the proper human response to God's gracious initiative is one of thanksgiving and service. Lutherans and Baptist agree that faith leads to good works, the indispensable demonstration of faith's reality: "faith apart from works is dead," or it is no faith at all. The faith in Christ by which alone we are saved is the faith which is sure to produce good works. Faith that works by love calls each believer to a life of investment in others out of a sense of indebtedness and thanksgiving for what it has received. In this perspective faith is characterized by dedicated discipleship.

## Baptism and the Theology of the Child

1. *Baptism.*—While Lutherans and Baptists differ with respect to the role and place of baptism, we both see baptism as embodying the whole gospel of God's grace and the response it calls forth. The importance of baptism is that which it signifies in relation to the gospel and the response it calls for. Baptism attests the redemptive work of God in Christ and the promise of salvation to believers, which is life in the kingdom of God. This promise must be appropriated by faith, but it is experienced in the community of the Spirit and of faith, where the gospel is proclaimed and people respond in faith. There baptism is seen as truly functioning in prospect of the day of final redemption. Baptism unites the effective gospel and the responding individuals in the community of faith. The church which baptizes is prior to the individuals in their believing and sustains them in their believing.

The essential relationship between faith and baptism is clearly recognized among both Lutherans and Baptists, but this relationship is viewed differently.

The fact that baptism embodies the word of God with its promise is interpreted by Lutherans to mean baptism effects what it signifies because it embodies the word of God with its promise. When they say baptism effects salvation, they understand that to say that God effects salvation through his promise in the baptismal context. Therefore, faith can never be made a prior condition of baptism, for faith itself is of grace. It is the work of God and the fruit of God's promise to human beings, irrespective of the age of the recipients. Hence infants can receive baptism.

Baptists also acknowledge baptism as embodying the word of God with its promise, but they emphasize that it also embodies the faith which confesses God in his saving grace. Hence the rite of baptism should not be seen as effecting what it signifies, unless it is seen as symbolizing the divine grace and help which leads to repentance and faith. Baptists, however, gratefully recognize the operation of grace in faith that turns to the Lord, but they see that as exhibited precisely in the baptism of a believer who has responded to grace.

2. *Theology of the Child.*—The fundamental issue of the theology of the child is the relation of the child in the human race to God. The child is a member of the race which is created by God in his image and fallen into corruption yet not abandoned by God, for the Son of God has wrought salvation for all humanity. The solidarity of humanity with the first Adam is matched by its solidarity with the last Adam—but more than matched, since God's grace in Christ is greater than the corrupting power of Adam's sin (Rom. 5:14-17;I Cor. 15:20-22, 45-49). The child is included in both solidarities, including all the dimensions of Christ's saving work, in which he offered a

sacrifice for the sins of the whole world, wrought a redemption from sin for the whole world, and achieved a reconciliation between God and the whole world.

Lutherans and Baptists affirm first of all that corporate sin is a reality that engulfs humanity, but it expresses itself in individual transgression. Second, Christ's work for humanity stood in its perfection apart from and prior to a person's knowledge of it. But the gospel proclamation is God's way of making the all-encompassing work of Christ *for* people effective *in* people; the gospel is "the power of God to save everyone who believes." Third, the whole race suffers death in the first Adam and is raised through the last Adam. But resurrection in the last Adam is a resurrection to judgment, in which the response to the revelation of God in Christ is the supreme criterion.

While Baptists recognize a child's solidarity with Adam manifested in death, most deny that children are culpable before God until of their own will they depart from God, and affirm that until that time the redemptive work of Christ embraces the young. Children of believing parents are born within the bosom of the church, and they are to be nourished and taught the faith in the Christian community until they are prepared to make their own confession to Christ in baptism.

Lutherans believe that sin's reality is expressed in individual transgression from the beginning of a person's life. Those born in solidarity with Adam need to be reborn in solidarity with Christ. While God's saving work in Christ is for all, God binds us, though not himself, to the place where he has promised to be present for salvation. Children need to have God's promise in Jesus' death and resurrection effectively applied to them. This application takes place in baptism, where they are incorporated into Jesus Christ and receive new life in him.

To put it sharply, while Baptists regard the believing response of infants to be an unwarranted hypothesis, Lutherans regard the idea that there is a time when infants are not culpable before God to be an unwarranted hypothesis.

3. *The Practice of Baptism in the Light of the Theology of the Child.*— Both Lutherans and Baptists agree that the issue of children and baptism is more a theological problem than a historical one.

Both Lutherans and Baptists recognize the involvement of the child in a solidarity with a race that is both fallen and redeemed. The reality of the solidarity of corruption is more than matched by the reality of the redemption that has been accomplished for every child in Christ.

To Lutherans this duality of solidarity emphasizes the rightness of including children within the command to baptize and the promises that go with the command. The child needs what is signified in baptism and receives it in baptism. Baptism signifies and effects incorporation into Christ, and so it "effects forgiveness of sins, deliverance from death and the devil, and grants eternal salvation to all who believe" (Luther's *Small Catechism*). It is recognized that baptism is the beginning of a life long process, initiated and maintained by grace until it is completed in death and resurrection. But the beginning is of decisive importance. It is an eloquent expression of the priority of grace over response but also of the reality that faith grows as it is nourished within the body of believers. Baptism and faith certainly belong together, but faith is the effect of grace given in baptism, and it is nurtured within the church, the community of faith.

Baptists believe that the involvement of children in the solidarity of a corrupt race is a reality attested by the subjection of children to death. But their solidarity with Christ in his redeeming acts is prior to baptism and independent of it, since it is real in virtue of their belonging to the race for which Christ died and rose. Similarly the relation of the children of believers to the church, the community of the Spirit as well as of faith, is a reality prior to baptism and independent of it. For a child to be nurtured in the fellowship of the Spirit and of faith is a blessed privilege, since the grace of God speaks within the child long before it can know its source. But it can learn to recognize and be grateful for grace in its early years and so, in the goodness of God, come to own that grace in confession of Christ and baptism. Prevenient grace is a concept beloved also in Baptist circles, but it is seen not as stemming from baptism but from the cross of Christ and the Spirit of God, leading to a baptism wherein that grace is gratefully acknowledged and its source in Christ the Redeemer confessed.

Many Baptists express the need of their children for redeeming grace and the importance of the church as the community wherein that grace is experienced by bringing their children to a service of infant blessing and dedication, wherein prayer is made for the child's welfare and salvation and the solemn responsibility of parent and the church in nurturing the child is declared and accepted. Lutherans express the need for a public confession of faith through nurture and the rite of confirmation, which they interpret as a reaffirmation of baptism.

Both Lutherans and Baptists seek to accomplish the same things with children in different ways, and they recognize that while they cannot accept one another's baptismal practice as normative, each can gain valuable insights from the practice of the other. Is it possible to recognize ourselves to be members of one church with one baptism in which some of us incorporate children into a catechumenate culminating in baptism and some of us baptize children into a catechumenate culminating in a responsible, articulated confession of faith in Christ? Both of us would want to understand the catechumenate as a life-long process with many points of confession and commitment.

**Church and Ministry**

Baptists and Lutherans represent significant differences in terms of the Protestant spectrum and they emerge from quite different historical contexts. In their forms of worship, theological emphases, ecclesiastical structures, types of piety, and cultural ethos these differences are evident. Despite the divergences, however, we find profound bases for commonality and strong reasons for recognizing each other's churches and ministry as authentic manifestations of the whole body of Christ.

1. *Commonality.*—Both of our churches are evangelical, that is, centered in the Gospel of God's saving act in Jesus Christ. Christ alone is Lord of the church and the ultimate ground of faith and life.

For both of us, the church is primarily the fellowship of the people of God, the body of the living Christ, and not merely an association of like-minded people. We understand ourselves to be a divinely called community whose reason for being is to glorify God and serve Christ in the world.

For both of us, the church is the company of those who have been justified by God's grace, regenerated by the Holy Spirit, and incorporated by baptism into a visible community of faith. Given our foundation and unity in the Gospel, we deem of secondary importance that there be agreement among us regarding such matters as forms of worship, patterns of Christian piety, or styles of church polity.

For both of us, the priesthood of all believers emphasizes the quality of all Christians before God and their obligation to serve one another and the world with the Gospel. The apostolic vocation is laid upon all believers by the Lord in the Gospel through the Holy Spirit and cannot be usurped or diminished by a qualitative or elitist distinction between clergy and laity. However the relationship between the universal ministry of all Christians and the particular ministry of the ordained may be defined, the responsibility and care of the Gospel rests with the whole community of faith.

For both of us, we believe there is a special office of the ordained ministry which has a divine calling and a particular function within the common ministry of the whole body of believers.

For both of us, the credal affirmation of the church as "one, holy, catholic and apostolic" is both an article of faith and a goal to be achieved through the power of the Holy Spirit.

For both of us, true marks of the church include the right preaching of the Word and the administration of baptism and the Lord's Supper.

For both of us, the church is the fellowship of believers in Christ, his living body in the world. It exists not for its own sake but to do the will of God. Therefore, it must continually understand itself in terms of God's will and expectation for the whole created order. Its interests cannot be merely parochial, ecclesiastical, or institutional. Its mission and witness for Christ must be seen in terms of the total needs of humanity.

2. *Divergence.*—The affirmation of bases for commonality does not minimize the points of divergence between Baptists and Lutherans. Many of these divergences reflect differences in our histories and the contexts out of which our traditions arose. Any serious and continuing dialogue between us must not neglect, therefore, the importance of historical backgrounds. For example, the Lutheran theological tradition was shaped by a fresh discovery of the priority of the Word of God and a perceived conflict between the Lutheran interpretation of the Word and the Roman Catholic, Reformed, and Anabaptist theological positions. The Baptist theological tradition was formed by a biblical interpretation of the nature of the church in a context of and in conflict with 16th and 17th century Anglican, Reformed, Roman Catholic, and other continental traditions. Not all divergences, however, between the two denominational traditions can be explained merely on the grounds of logical perceptions, regardless of contexts, and these must be openly acknowledged and critically examined, e.g., baptism, regeneration, and the Lord's Supper. Often, the divergences between the churches are not outright contradictory positions but differences of emphasis. Even in those areas of commonality dealt with above, there are often nuances of emphasis which mark off one tradition from the other.

Our dialogue has disclosed commonality in our understanding of the church as the fellowship of believers in Christ. Yet here there is divergence in emphasis. Baptists historically have emphasized the "new life" of regenerate baptized believers and the restriction of membership into the church to those who have professed the experience of divine grace. Lutherans have stressed the priority of the proclamation of the Gospel in Word and sacrament for identifying the community of believers.

Baptists and Lutherans seek to be faithful to the apostolic witness of the church. Lutherans in their theological formulations, their credal statements and liturgical practices stress their continuity with the Christian community in history. While some Baptists have emphasized an historical continuity with groups outside the Roman Catholic tradition, their understanding of apostolicity focuses primarily on their perception of the New Testament pattern of the church and their attempt to embody this pattern in their church life and work.

Baptists and Lutherans affirm the importance of the divine calling to the ordained ministry. There are differences, however, between and within both traditions regarding adequate preparation and examination for ordination. Lutherans require certification of a special call to a congregation, agency, or institution of the church. Some Baptists do not require such certification for ordination.

While the Gospel takes precedence over all matters of organizational structure and authority, Baptists and Lutherans evidence considerable diversity in matters of church polity. Baptists give great weight to the importance and rights of the local congregation, but they see these modified by the local association of churches and by the larger denominational body to which it belongs, both of which gain their authority from the churches convened in assembly. Lutherans are not committed to one form of ecclesiastical polity. The variety within Lutheranism ranges from the episcopal forms more common in some European countries to those in North America in which more authority is maintained by the local congregations.

A very significant point of divergence between Baptists and Lutherans appears in the area of sacraments or ordinances. Lutherans speak of sacrament as enacted Word and visible means of grace, stressing thereby God's command and redemptive action on their behalf. Most Baptists in North America prefer the term ordinance, which emphasizes Christ's command, and they recognize the power of Christ's transforming presence in their midst. With respect to baptism we have major differences. This subject has been treated at length in other parts of our dialogue. With respect to the Lord's Supper a major difference seems to lie in the interpretation given to the meaning of Christ's presence and to the objective and subjective character of the meal. Baptists stress the aspects of the Supper as a remembrance of our Lord's dying and rising, as a present fellowship with the crucified and risen Lord and with one another, and as an anticipation of the fulfillment of the meal in the future Kingdom of God. Lutheran priority fastens on the promise of the Word, "This is my body," which cannot be invalidated by the recipient, though unbelieving reception brings judgment. Both of us agree that there is great need for further dialogue on the doctrine of the Lord's Supper.

Commonality and divergence are both realities among Baptists and Lutherans on the subject of the church and the ministry. Commonality must be joyfully celebrated and accentuated. Divergence must be continually and sympathetically examined and discussed, in the hope that divergences may lead in the direction of convergence and commonality, and in any event not become destructive of fellowship and common witness.

## Recommendations: Baptist-Lutheran Dialogue

*Recommendation to the North American Baptist Fellowship and the Lutheran Council in the United States of America.*—The dialogue participants, both Lutheran and Baptist, voted to recommend to our sponsoring bodies that a second series of dialogues be instituted to carry on the good beginning that has been started on the North American continent between representatives of the largest Protestant group in the world and the largest Protestant group in the United States.

*Recommendations to the Baptist World Alliance and the Lutheran World Federation.*—1. We recommend that the Baptist World Alliance and the Lutheran World Federation investigate the possibility of holding a series of international dialogues with each other, using and building upon the insights discovered in this North American dialogue. This dialogue was initiated as an alternative to an international conversation, and has proved the worth of such an international dialogue between our two communions.

2. We also recommend that, should an international dialogue not be feasible at this time, a Baptist-Lutheran dialogue be held in Europe, with the European Baptist Federation serving as the Baptist sponsor.

*Reasons for Continuing and Expanding the Dialogue.*—1. To share more fully the important heritage each tradition brings to dialogue. For example, the importance to Lutherans of grace, gospel, the priority of God, nurture, a corporate focus, and the ability to explicate theologically their actions; Baptists contribute a theology of the laity, a passion for mission and evangelism, and the importance of a considered response to Christ.

2. To maintain the momentum achieved in this dialogue. Rapport has been deepened and should not be lost.

3. To offset incomplete pictures of both our traditions contained in media reports. Continuity is needed to correct false impressions of each other. Our traditions are more than the few controversial figures covered by the media.

4. Population mobility brings us more in contact with each other. In the United States, the sunbelt movement and missionary expansion make our conversation and understanding of each other more urgent.

5. To aid in theological self-understanding through cooperative theology.

6. To explore means of cooperative action.

7. To further clarify each other's vocabulary.

8. The promise of possible future breakthroughs in the recognition of each other as manifestations of the body of Christ without compromise of convictions.

*Possible Future Topics for Dialogues.*—1. The authority of the New Testament for practice (Scripture and tradition, biblical hermeneutics); 2. The place of creeds and confessions; 3. The Lord's Supper; 4. Immersion; 5. Church and state; 6. The nature of the church and polity; 7. Faith.

# A Lutheran-United Methodist Statement on Baptism*

## The Lutheran-United Methodist Bilateral Dialogue December 11, 1979

### I. Introduction

1. As participants in the Lutheran-United Methodist bilateral consultation, which has met six times since 1977 and has now concluded its work, we report with gratitude to our churches the pastoral, liturgical, and evangelical concord and concern which we have discovered in our discussions.

2. It is fundamental to this report to note that our Lutheran and United Methodist churches acknowledge Scripture as the source and the norm of Christian faith and life and share with the whole catholic Church in that Christology and that Trinitarian faith which are set forth in the ecumenical Apostles' and Nicene Creeds. We also share the biblical Reformation doctrine of justification by grace through faith. We are agreed that we are justified by the grace of God for Christ's sake, through faith alone and not by the works demanded of us by God's law. We also recognized the common emphasis on sanctification as a divinely promised consequence of justification. We affirm that God acts to use the sacraments as means of grace. As heirs of the Reformation, we share a heritage of scriptural preaching and biblical scholarship. We also share a hymnic tradition, care for theological education, and concern for evangelical outreach.

3. We have continually recognized the validity of the acts of Baptism administered in accord with Scripture in our churches. While this recognition testifies to our considerable agreement in doctrine and practice, it rests final-

---

*Introduction on United Methodist, *BU*, 293-94. Text in Jack Tuell and Roger Fjeld, eds., *Episcopacy: Lutheran-United Methodist Dialogue II* (Minneapolis: Augsburg, 1991) 24-29; also in *Perkins Journal* 34 (1981) 2-5.

ly upon the shared acknowledgement of Baptism as an effective sign of God's grace. First and foremost, Baptism is God's gift, act, and promise of faithfulness. The entire life of faith and even our attempts to articulate a common understanding of God's prior act of grace are but a response of praise and thanksgiving.

4. The acknowledgement of God's gift as validly bestowed in the acts of Baptism administered in United Methodist and Lutheran churches entails the recognition of the shared benefit of the work of the Holy Spirit among us. Thus we are called to confess the scandal of whatever disunity or party spirit may still exist among us and between us lest we are found to despise God's gift. Our unity in Christ and in one Spirit is the unity of those who have been washed and forgiven, incorporated into Christ's death and resurrection, and called together for witness and service in his world until he comes again. This unity made manifest in Baptism is an inauguration and foretaste of the rule of God in all of life.

Thus we are offering to our churches the following Affirmations, Implications, and Recommendations as tangible expressions of our hope that our churches and congregations will seek further means for achieving a fuller manifestation of our God-given unity in Christ, of our sharing in one Spirit and one Baptism.

## II. Affirmations

5. We accept as valid all acts of Baptism in the Name of the Trinity using water according to Christ's command and promise (Matt. 28:18-20).

6. We affirm that Baptism is the sacrament of entrance into the holy catholic Church, not simply a rite of entrance into a particular denomination. Baptism is therefore a sacrament which proclaims the profound unity of the Church (I Cor. 12:13;Gal. 3:27-28). Baptism is a gift of God for the upbuilding of the Christian community.

7. We affirm that grateful obedience to the divine invitation obligates all believers to be baptized and to share the responsibility for baptizing.

8. We affirm that Baptism is intended for all persons, including infants. No person should be excluded from Baptism for reasons of age or mental capacity.

9. We affirm with Scripture that God gives the Holy Spirit in Baptism:
–to unite us with Jesus Christ in his death, burial and resurrection (Rom. 6:1-11;Col. 2:12);
–to effect new birth, new creation, newness of life (John 3:5;Titus 3:5);

–to offer, give, and assure us of the forgiveness of sins in both cleansing
and life-giving aspects (Acts 2:38);

–to enable our continual repentance and daily reception of forgiveness, and
our growing in grace;

–to create unity and equality in Christ (I Cor. 12:13;Gal. 3:27-28);

–to make us participants in the new age initiated by the saving act of God in
Jesus Christ (John 3:5);

–to place us into the Body of Christ where the benefits of the Holy Spirit are
shared within a visible community of faith (Acts 2:38;I Cor. 12:13).

10. We affirm that in claiming us in Baptism, God enables the
Christian to rely upon this gift, promise, and assurance throughout all of life.
Such faithful reliance is necessary and sufficient for the reception of the ben-
efits of Baptism.

11. We affirm that Baptism is both the prior gift of God's grace and the
believer's commitment of faith. Baptism looks toward a growth into the measure of the stature of the fullness of Christ (Eph. 4:13). By this growth, baptized believers should manifest to the world the new race of a redeemed
humanity which puts an end to all human estrangement based, for example,
on race, sex, age, class, nationality, and disabling conditions. In faith and
obedience, the baptized live for the sake of Christ, of his Church, and of the
world which he loves. Baptism is a way in which the Church witnesses to the
faith and proclaims to the world the Lordship of Jesus Christ. (See World
Council of Churches Statement, "One Baptism, One Eucharist, and a
Mutually Recognized Ministry.")

## III. Implications and Recommendations

12. *Baptism is related to a Christian community and (except in unusual
circumstances) should be administered by an ordained minister in the service of public worship of the congregation.*

We agree that Baptism should not be a private act. In communities
where United Methodist and Lutheran congregations exist, they can support
one another as they resist pressure for private, family baptisms. Normally,
for reasons of good order, the ordained officiate at Baptisms, but any person
may administer the sacrament in unusual circumstances.

13. *Lutherans and United Methodists agree that pre-baptismal instruction of candidates or their parents (or surrogate parents) is of crucial importance.*

Therefore we encourage ministers and congregations to take this instruction seriously and to support one another as they resist pressure to minimize such instruction.

14. *The Christian community has the responsibility to receive and nurture the baptized. When infants or children are baptized we regard it as essential that at least one parent, surrogate parent, or other responsible adult make an act of Christian commitment to nurture them in the Christian faith and life.*

There may be circumstances in which the refusal of Baptism is appropriate because this condition has not been met. Both United Methodist and Lutheran pastors can support one another by respecting and interpreting the action of one of them who has refused to administer Baptism.

Sponsors (or Godparents) may support the parent, surrogate parent, or other responsible adult in this act of commitment, but are not substitutes for such a committed individual.

15. *When a Christian family is partly Lutheran and partly United Methodist, the nurture of the baptized child is of primary importance. Here an opportunity also exists to display Christian unity in the midst of diversity.*

It is important for one congregation to assume primary responsibility to nurture the child in the Christian life.

Where one parent is more active than the other, it is recommended that the sponsoring congregation be the congregation of the more active parent.

It is recommended that the prebaptismal instruction be given by the pastor of the sponsoring congregation; or joint instruction under both pastors can take place, as this will enrich both traditions.

16. *We believe Baptism is not repeatable.*

Because we understand Baptism as entrance into the Church, we do not condone rebaptism of persons on any grounds, including new Christian experience or change of denominational membership.

Since United Methodists and Lutherans recognize one another's Baptism, we violate the integrity of our faith, pervert the meaning of Baptism, and impair our relation with other baptized Christians if we rebaptize.

17. *When instructed persons have made their profession of faith for themselves in the act of Baptism, their Christian initiation requires no separate rite of confirmation.*

Baptism is sacramentally complete even though the baptized Christian looks forward to a lifetime of Christian instruction and growth through regular reaffirmations or renewals of the baptismal covenant.

18. *We respect each other's practice of confirmation.*

We rejoice that both communions have an appreciation for the lifelong need for a pastoral and educational ministry. The baptized should be given frequent opportunity to reflect upon the meaning of their covenant through confirmation, sermons, curricula, and other such means.

While orientation to the history, liturgy, and practice of the denomination and a particular congregation is appropriate for persons who transfer from one of our denominations to the other, a further confirmation rite should not be required.

19. *Baptism witnesses to Christian unity, and therefore it enables transfer between our denominations.*

Because we believe that Baptism is the fundamental initiation into the Church, we affirm our oneness in Jesus Christ as taking precedence over our denominational divisions.

When persons transfer their membership between our denominations, they should not feel that they have thereby broken their earlier baptismal and confirmation promises. Pastors should provide opportunity for those transferring to make public reaffirmation of their baptism with the new congregation and denomination in an appropriate manner.

Each denomination affirms the pastoral and nurturing ministry of the other denomination and gladly commits members to the care of the other denomination when its own denomination does not provide an adequate congregational family for those members.

Because we are baptized not into a denomination nor into a particular congregation only, but into the one Church of Jesus Christ, therefore in communities where both Lutheran and United Methodist congregations exist, efforts may be made to share mutually in baptismal celebrations, thereby showing forth our essential unity.

20. *United Methodist and Lutheran theology and practice allow Baptism to be administered in various modes, including immersion, pouring and sprinkling.*

We agree that whatever mode is used, Baptism is an act in which the use of water is an outward and visible sign of the grace of God. The water of baptism, therefore, should be administered generously so that its sign value will be most effectively perceived by the congregation.

21. *The celebration of Baptism should reflect the unity of the Church which Baptism proclaims.*

Because in Baptism the contemporary Church is united to the historic Church, baptismal rites should draw upon the ancient traditions of the Church and also should serve to illustrate the catholicity of the Church in our time. In addition to the normative Trinitarian Baptismal formula in accordance with Matthew 28:19, the renunciation, the Apostles' Creed, and the prayer of thanksgiving over the water are also recommended.

We urge the common development of liturgical formulations for the rite of Baptism by the liturgical agencies of our respective churches.

## IV. Conclusion

22. This document represents the consensus of the undersigned members of the dialogue team after three years of intense discussion and prayerful deliberation. We commend it to our churches for their study and action. We hope it will serve as an impetus and resource for dialogue among Lutherans and United Methodists in local communities and throughout our churches.

# Episcopacy: A Lutheran-United Methodist Common Statement to the Church*

## Preface

The Lutheran Council in the United States of America (LCUSA), an agency composed of five Lutheran bodies in the U.S. (the Association of Evangelical Lutheran Churches, the American Lutheran Church, the Lutheran Church—Missouri Synod, the Latvian Evangelical Lutheran Church in America, and the Lutheran Church in America), and The United Methodist Church (UMC), a worldwide church body, jointly agreed in 1983 to hold a second series of dialogues, this time on the theme of episcopacy.

The first series between Lutherans and United Methodists was held between 1977 and 1979 on the theme of baptism. The common statement and supporting papers were published in a special issue of the *Perkins Journal* (34) (1981) and a separate printing of the common statement in pamphlet form was widely distributed.

The second series on episcopacy brought participants together for six times between 1985 and 1987. During this time, the new Evangelical Lutheran Church in America was forming and therefore the Common Statement was distributed by that body and The United Methodist Church.

This Common Statement was first published and distributed in pamphlet form, parallel with the earlier pamphlet on baptism. Selected papers prepared for the dialogue are now included in this volume and should contribute considerably to the ongoing discussion on episcopacy within the larger ecumenical movement.

*Jack M. Tuell and Roger W. Fjeld, eds., *Episcopacy. Lutheran-United Methodist Dialogue II* (Minneapolis: Augsburg, 1991) 11-22.

**Introductory Notes**

Theological documents sometimes reveal more in what is omitted than in what is stated. Sometimes critical agreements are reached which the reader merely takes for granted. These notes are intended to help the reader review the agreed statement with an eye to a more careful reading.

The Introduction sets the context of the dialogue, reminding the reader of the continuity with the previous United Methodist-Lutheran round on baptism and the relationship of the topic to the World Council of Churches' convergence text on "Baptism, Eucharist and Ministry." It declares two primary themes of the discussion: that episcopacy is an *office* of the Church (not of its essence) and that it is the *mission* of the Church that determines the shape of that office.

Responsibility and accountability are explored as part of the meaning of oversight (*episcopé*) in Part I A, but there is acknowledgement of other forms of oversight within the Church as well. Paragraph 20 lifts up some of the differences between the two traditions and affirms together in Par. 21 that episcopacy is not of the *essence* of the Church nor does it hold an inherent hierarchical understanding.

Part I C suggests that both traditions take a position of openness to the ordering of the Church in other forms. While each may believe that their form of oversight is both biblical and functional, neither believes that *episcopé* can only be structured as each has known it.

With regard to the practice of the *episcopé* (Part II), there are some clear differences between the traditions, particularly in the conciliar way in which United Methodists understand the collegiality of oversight. The bishops, in their prophetic witness and as symbols of unity, remind the Church of its own nature, but the Dialogue Team concluded that the unity of the Church is not dependent on the unity of the episcopate.

**Introduction**

1. The Lutheran and Methodist churches alike arose as reform movements within a large church body. Both sought a renewal in the life of the Church. Neither movement set out to create an independent body. Nevertheless, each finds expression today in distinct churches bearing the names "Methodist" and "Lutheran."

2. For historical and geographical reasons, Lutheran and Methodist churches have had little contact with each other. Our history has been characterized neither by mutual condemnation nor by mutual recognition and fellowship. Over the last twenty years, however, ecumenical dialogues between

Methodists and Lutherans have occurred in a variety of settings. Dialogues sponsored by the Lutheran World Federation and the World Methodist Council culminated in 1984 in the common statement "The Church: Community of Grace." This statement discussed an extensive range of topics and recommended "that our churches take steps to declare and establish full fellowship of Word and Sacrament" (¶ 91). Such fellowship was proposed between the (Lutheran) Church of Sweden and the Methodist Church of Sweden in 1985 and established between the United Evangelical-Lutheran Church of Germany and the Evangelical-Methodist Church in the Federal Republic of Germany and West Berlin in 1987.

3. A series of dialogues between The United Methodist Church and the member churches of the Lutheran Council in the USA was held between 1977 and 1979 on the subject of baptism. "A Lutheran-United Methodist Statement on Baptism" was produced.[1] The experience and results of this dialogue have been an encouragement to the present series of conversations between representatives of The United Methodist Church and of the member churches of the Lutheran Council in the USA on the subject of episcopacy.

4. The nature of episcopacy has become a focus of ecumenical discussion and difficulty. What is the nature of the ministry of oversight exercised by bishops? In what way does this ministry relate to other ministries in the Church? How does this ministry relate to the unity and continuity of the Church? United Methodists and Lutherans approach these questions from similar situations. United Methodists and the majority of American Lutherans have clergy called bishops, who play prominent leadership roles.[2] As the following common statement makes clear, our traditions have understood the ministry of the bishop as a form of the office of ministry shared by all clergy and have not understood the episcopal office to be of the essence of the church. Methodists and Lutherans face similar difficulties in our relations with churches which place a different emphasis on the office of bishop. This series of dialogues began with the hope both of furthering Lutheran-Methodist understanding and of contributing to the wider ecumenical discussion of the ministry of oversight.

5. In the New Testament, the term "bishop" does not appear to have a single distinct meaning. At places, it appears to be interchangeable with presbyter (e.g., Acts 20:17, 28). By the end of the second century, however, "bishop" had come to refer to a head of the church in a particular place. The nature of the office has varied greatly over the history of the Church. Nevertheless, basic ecclesiastical structures (e.g., congregations and dioceses) were headed by bishops. This pattern remained that of almost all of Christianity before and after the Reformation.

6. In recent years, new attempts have been made to understand the nature of the office of bishop. Typical of these attempts is the understanding

of episcopal ministry in *Baptism, Eucharist and Ministry, The COCU Consensus,* and a variety of bilateral dialogues.[3]

7. Lutheran and Methodist understandings of episcopacy are colored by our respective histories. Both movements encountered resistance from bishops in their initial attempts to carry out their mission. Both Methodists and Lutherans finally faced a situation in which the only choice they could see was between remaining obedient to episcopal leadership and remaining true to their mission in the gospel. In each case, the latter option was chosen. Our relation to episcopal leadership has been an ecumenical difficulty for both of our churches ever since. Within our own churches, however, episcopal leadership, under a variety of titles, has been respected and valued. Out of our histories and theological reflection we offer this common statement in the continuing endeavor to clarify our own mind and practice, to deepen understanding between our traditions, and to further discussion in the wider Church that seeks to serve the God who makes all one.

## Part I. Ecclesiology, Ministry, and Episcopacy

A. *Episcopé, Mission, and the Nature of the Church*

8. Lutherans and United Methodists each understand themselves to belong to the one Church:

> a congregation of [the] faithful...in which the pure Word of God is preached and the Sacraments duly administered according to Christ's ordinance.[4]

> the assembly of all believers among whom the Gospel is preached in its purity and the holy sacraments are administered according to the Gospel.[5]

The life of the one Church is inseparable from the presence within it of the Spirit who moves it to mission. Stated succinctly, this mission is to be a witness to the gospel of the justifying, sanctifying, and liberating Reign of God which has come and still comes to us and to the world in Jesus Christ. In this mission, the unity, holiness, catholicity, and apostolicity of the Church are realized.

9. This mission is carried out in a variety of ministries, empowered by the diverse gifts of the Spirit. Through these ministries, the Spirit not only points to God's activity in Christ, but also effects the redeeming and reconciling presence of Jesus Christ and the Reign of God inseparable from Jesus Christ.

10. The most important standard by which all ministries within the Church are to be judged is the mission which they seek to further. This standard is to be applied both to the general nature and structure of a ministry and its concrete execution. All aspects of ministry are to be judged by the question: do they further the fundamental mission of the Spirit within the Church?

11. The constant application of this criterion is part of the necessary oversight (*episcopé*) of ministry that must occur within the Church. This oversight is carried out first of all and principally through the divinely ordained pastoral office but then also in many ways by various persons and groups of persons from the local congregation to the most inclusive international structures. We trust that through faithful oversight of ministry by the entire Church the Spirit is at work, preserving the Church in mission.

12. While responsibility for oversight must finally rest with the entire Church, some persons, conferences, assemblies, boards, etc., are given responsibility for specific tasks of oversight. Oversight is thus itself a form of ministry within the Church. That specific responsibilities of oversight are given to some, however, does not take from the wider community responsibility and authority to oversee those who carry out specific ministries of oversight. Those who carry out ministries of oversight remain accountable to the community of believers. Such "oversight of oversight" is one way the mutual accountability of all ministries within the Church is realized. Ultimate accountability, of course, is always to the Word of God.

13. Our churches and all churches throughout the world must ask whether present forms of oversight are adequate to mission in the present and the future. While being mindful of the importance of continuity and the wisdom of our forebears, we must be open to different forms of oversight, whether new or old, that will better aid present and future mission.

## B. Episcopacy and the Nature of Ministry

14. Every member of the Church is called to ministry through baptism. Ministry is an activity of the entire Church and of each individual within it.

15. While all Christians share the ministry of the Word, we acknowledge God's gift of an ordained ministry, the public pastoral office. United Methodists and Lutherans typically refer to this ministry with different terms (a ministry of Word, Sacrament, and Order or a ministry of Word and Sacrament). Although this difference in language points to differences in how we understand ordained ministry, we have come to see that our different terms refer to the same ministry. Lutherans and United Methodists alike affirm this ministry as necessary to the church. The ordained minister presides in the proclamation of the Word, the celebration of the sacraments, and the administration of churchly order.[6]

16. Every church must find ways in which oversight of ordained ministry can be exercised. This oversight is concerned with all aspects of ordained ministry; its administrative organization, its faithfulness to the mission of Christ, the pastoral care it gives and receives.

17. In our churches a primary means of oversight is the office of bishop. We find this means of providing for oversight theologically and practically desirable. We do not, however, understand this oversight to be the exclusive prerogative of the bishop. Oversight is to be carried out in cooperation with other persons within the church. In addition, we do not see the episcopal office as the only acceptable means by which oversight of ordained ministry can be realized. Ecumenical relations with churches which carry out oversight through, e.g., a presbytery, pose no special problems in themselves for Lutherans or United Methodists. The episcopal office is not of the essence of the Church.

18. Bishops are themselves ordained ministers. United Methodists and Lutherans understand the distinctive ministry of the bishop to be a form of the single ordained ministry. We have thus emphasized the unity of the ministry of bishops with the ministry of all the ordained. Our churches rightly grant authority to bishops with the ministry to carry out their necessary ministry. Some activities within our churches are typically performed only by bishops. Nevertheless, the authority of the bishop derives from the office and its responsibilities; it never inheres in the person of the bishop in distinction from the office. That certain activities are typically carried out only by bishops derives from the relation between the activity reserved to the bishop and the ministry of the bishop. We do not understand bishops in their persons and distinct from their offices to possess capacities and powers not possessed by all Christians.

19. As is true for all authority within the Church, any authority exercised by a bishop is subordinate to the authority of the Bible, which for Lutherans and United Methodists in the "primary source and guideline for doctrine."[7]

20. The bishop's ministry of oversight appropriately extends to the oversight of ordination itself. United Methodist bishops preside at ordinations by themselves ordaining the candidates. Lutheran bishops conventionally attest the call of the congregation and authorize the service of ordination. With different frequency in our different churches, they participate in the ordination. None of our churches requires that a person ordained in another church by someone other than a bishop undergo a Lutheran or United Methodist ordination before entering the ordained ministry within our churches. United Methodists and Lutherans thus do not understand episcopal ordination to be of the essence of ordained ministry.

21. Our churches and the Church throughout the world must under-

stand and organize episcopal and other ministries in ways that affirm their diversity and mutual accountability. An understanding in which other ministries become intrinsically subordinate to, under the control of, or derived from the ministry of the bishop is to be rejected.

### C. Episcopacy and the Universal Church

22. Lutherans and United Methodists today face similar ecumenical proposals concerning episcopacy (e.g., *Baptism, Eucharist and Ministry,* the *COCU* proposals, *Facing Unity*).[8] We face these proposals with similar understandings and practices of episcopacy. Our churches are also engaged in parallel studies of the nature of ministry and episcopacy.

23. Neither United Methodists nor Lutherans understand their ordering or structuring of ministry to be the only theologically acceptable one. Thus, we are open to the possibility of restructuring our ministries, including episcopacy, for the sake of more effective mission.

24. Any proposal for a reordering of episcopacy in our churches must a) indicate how such a reordering will serve the mission entrusted to our churches, b) in no way imply that the ordained ministry carried out by our churches has lacked anything essential, and c) not imply that the proposed reordering is of the essence of the Church. Additional criteria may be needed for judging proposals for a reordered episcopacy.

25. While Lutherans and United Methodists alike celebrate the achievements represented by the ecumenical proposals of recent years, whether these proposals meet the criteria specified in ¶24 is disputed within our churches.[9]

26. The detailed and critical discussion in our churches of these ecumenical proposals is a necessary step in the formation of an understanding and practice that will open us to the unity Jesus Christ desires for the Church. Further refinements of the proposals presently under discussion and the development of new proposals must continue.

## Part II. Practice of Episcopé in the Two Traditions

### A. Historic Practice

27. Lutherans and United Methodists developed our present structures of oversight through a combination of theological reflection and historical circumstance. Both traditions initially moved away from an episcopacy in historical succession with reluctance.[10]

28. United Methodists and Lutherans have learned from our differing histories that a ministry of oversight like that of bishops is a practical necessity. Such a ministry is needed for the empowering and equipping of the

entire body of the saints for mission. In recent years, the structure and practice of our ministries of oversight have become more similar. Many Lutherans have given greater recognition and authority to synodical and district ministries of oversight, while United Methodists have sought to strengthen the accountability of the episcopacy to other ministries.[11]

29. Both Lutherans and United Methodists have sought organizational structures that will both be efficient and embody ecclesiological principles to which we are committed. United Methodists and Lutherans in the United States have sought to preserve the accountability of bishops to the rest of the church, e.g., by protecting against individual abuses of power that obscure mission. We have found such structures of accountability important to our life. We offer the ways we elect and review bishops and interrelate episcopal and other ministries as a contribution to the ecumenical discussion.

30. Lutherans have not shared the United Methodist experience with bishops who are "itinerant, general superintendents," yet assigned to specific areas. United Methodists view each bishop as a bishop of the whole church and the Council of Bishops as an expression of the collegiality of oversight. The United Methodist practice of episcopacy raises issues about the universal responsibility of each bishop and of the college of bishops that need to be reflected on by all churches. Discussions about a reordering of the ministry of oversight should examine the particular experience of Lutherans and United Methodists.

31. Lutherans and United Methodists have in recent years appropriated new language and concepts in our thought about and practice of the ministry of oversight. We together recognize ourselves to be in a process of continual reform in our ministry of oversight and hope for structures that will more effectively aid the mission that unites us.

32. The United Methodist Church and the churches forming the Evangelical Lutheran Church in America call women and men to the ordained ministry. On the basis of Scripture, theological principle, and experience, these churches strongly affirm their commitment to the presence of women and men in all forms of ordained ministry, including the office of bishop. The Lutheran Church—Missouri Synod, on the basis of Scripture and theological principle, does not ordain women to the pastoral office.

*B. The Ministry of the Bishop*

33. Since the ministry of bishops is a form of the ministry shared by all ordained ministers, the common pastoral, liturgical, and proclamatory tasks of the ordained ministry should be central to the ministry of bishops. Our churches need to find ways in which the preaching of the Word and the celebration of the sacraments can be given greater priority within the total activity of our bishops.

34. We agree that the entire ministry of bishops has a pastoral character. However, our churches are organized in ways that hinder the development of pastoral relations between bishops and the clergy and laity.

35. As persons called to oversee and exercise the ordained ministry, bishops in their total ministry should serve the unity, holiness, catholicity, and apostolicity of the Church.

36. In their preaching and teaching, bishops serve the apostolicity and catholicity of the Church. In our churches, bishops have recently spoken out on issues of concern to the Church and the world. We have profited from their voice. Whether their ministry of oversight gives bishops a special voice in the decisions of the church is a question for both Lutherans and United Methodists.

37. As their ministry of oversight focuses on the pure preaching and teaching of the gospel, bishops serve the unity of the Church. United Methodists have in the past understood their bishops as an important symbol of the unity of the Church. Lutherans have understood that the unity of the Church is created by the Word of God, manifested in the preaching of the gospel and the administration of the sacraments. Lutherans are not of one mind on the ecumenical role of bishops, as recent studies indicate. Neither Lutherans nor United Methodists equate the visible unity of the Church with the unity of the episcopate. Nevertheless, we are open to discussion of the special ecumenical role that may be played by bishops and the episcopacy.

38. In the witness to the gospel of the grace of God which they share with all Christians and all pastors, bishops serve the holiness Christ shares with the Church. The visibility of bishops to the Church and the world gives their witness particular prominence within the Church's total witness. The words and lives of those who lead the church can have a profound effect. Our churches need to seek leaders who will reflect Christ in their total life and ministry.

## Conclusion

39. The Church looks to Jesus Christ as the Shepherd and Bishop of our souls (I Pt. 2:25). United Methodists and Lutherans reflect on episcopacy with this fundamental conviction in mind. We bring to this reflection practices of episcopacy that have much in common. Although we have each struggled with questions of authority and freedom, we have recognized the importance of a ministry of oversight as one ministry among others in the Body of Christ. Leadership from our bishops and presidents has often aided greater unity and effectiveness. Nevertheless, we have together insisted that no particular structure of oversight is of the essence of the Church. Church-

dividing difficulties have developed because of this insistence. We offer our common convictions in the hope that this obstacle can be overcome as all churches reconsider how they can serve the single and unifying mission of Christ.

## Notes

1. This statement was signed by all representatives, except those from the Lutheran Church—Missouri Synod (LC-MS).

2. A synodical or district president within the LC-MS carries out a ministry of oversight similar to that of bishops in the other participating churches. The term "bishop" is used throughout this statement to refer to LC-MS presidents. In Lutheran and Methodist churches in other parts of the world, other titles are also used for those who exercise episcopal leadership (e.g., praeses, superintendent, ephorus).

3. For example, *The Report of the Lutheran-Episcopal Dialogue Second Series 1976-1980* (Cincinnati: Forward Movement Press, 1981); James E. Andrews and Joseph A. Burgess, eds., *An Invitation to Action: A Study of Ministry, Sacraments, and Recognition,* The Lutheran-Reformed Dialogue Series III, 1981-1983 (Philadelphia: Fortress Press, 1984).

4. Article 13, The Articles of Religion of the Methodist Church. In *The Book of Discipline,* Part II, Section 2, 68. Cp. The Confession of Faith of the Evangelical United Brethren Church, Article 5.

5. Augsburg Confession, Article VII. In *The Book of Concord: The Confessions of the Evangelical Lutheran Church,* trans. and ed. by Theodore G. Tappert, et al. (Philadelphia: Fortress Press, 1959), p. 32.

6. Cp. Lutheran-Methodist Joint Commission, *The Church: Community of Grace* (Geneva: Lutheran World Federation; Lake Junaluska: World Methodist Council, 1984), 37. A typically greater Methodist stress on the administration of churchly order is reflected in Methodist language of a ministry of Word, Sacrament, and Order. Lutheran ministries of Word and Sacrament are also called upon, however, to administer churchly order.

7. "Our Theological Task," in *The Book of Discipline,* Part II, Section 3, 69, pg. 78. Cp. Formula of Concord, Epitome, Rule and Norm, 1.

8. See *Baptism, Eucharist and Ministry,* Faith and Order Paper 111 (Geneva: World Council of Churches, 1982); *Covenanting Toward Unity: From Consensus to Communion. A Proposal to the Churches from the Consultation on Church Union* (Baltimore: Consultation on Church Union, 1985); *The COCU Consensus: In Quest of a Church of Christ Uniting,* ed. Gerald F. Moede (Baltimore: Consultation on Church Union, 1985); Roman Catholic-Lutheran Joint Commission, *Facing Unity: Models, Forms and Phases of Catholic-Lutheran Church Fellowship* (Geneva: Lutheran World Federation, 1985). Typical of the understanding of episcopal ministry in these proposals is ¶29 of the third section of *Baptism, Eucharist and Ministry:* "Bishops preach the Word, preside at the sacraments, and administer discipline in such a way as to be representative pastoral ministers of oversight, continuity and unity in the Church. They have pastoral oversight of the area to which they are called. They serve the apostolicity and unity of the church's teaching, worship, and sacramental life. They have responsibility for leadership in the Church's mission. They relate the Christian community in their area to the wider Church, and the universal Church to their community. They, in communion with the presbyters and deacons and the whole community, are responsible for the orderly transfer of ministerial authority in the Church." (¶M 29)

9. Four of the participating churches have responded officially to BEM. The responses can be found in *Churches Respond to BEM: Official Responses to the "Baptism, Eucharist and Ministry" text,* 3 vols. Faith and Order Papers 129, 132, 135, ed. Max Thurian (Geneva: World Council of Churches, 1986-87), Vol. 1, pp. 28-38. Vol. 2, pp. 79-84, 177-199, Vol. 3, pp. 131-141.

10. Attitudes toward episcopacy were mixed among early Lutherans and early Methodists. While statements about the desire to retain episcopacy in historical succession can be found in the Lutheran Confessions (e.g., Ap. 14), their interpretation is a matter of dispute.

11. For this history, see James K. Mathews, *Set Apart to Serve: The Meaning and Role of Episcopacy in the Wesleyan Tradition* (Nashville: Abingdon Press, 1985), and Ivar Asheim and Victor R. Gold, *Episcopacy in the Lutheran Church? Studies in the Development and Definition of the Office of Church Leadership* (Philadelphia: Fortress Press, 1970). The Asheim and Gold volume does not cover important recent developments in American Lutheranism.

# Lutheran–Reformed Dialogue

# Marburg Revisited:
# Lutheran-Reformed
# Consultation Series, 1962-1966*

## Preface

Early in this decade the desirability of theological conversations between members of the Lutheran and the Reformed traditions was discussed informally. In the spring of 1961 sponsorship of such conversations was approved by the North American Area of the World Alliance of Reformed Churches Holding the Presbyterian Order and the U.S.A. National Committee of the Lutheran World Federation. A preliminary meeting was held in New York in February, 1962; annual consultations thereafter culminated in a meeting at Princeton, New Jersey in February, 1966, when the sessions were given over chiefly to summarizing and evaluating the previous discussions.

It was agreed that the objective would be "to explore the theological relations between the Lutheran and Reformed churches to discover to what extent the differences which have divided these communions in the past still constitute obstacles to mutual understanding." In order to encompass the concerns of groups within the two traditions not related to the two sponsoring organizations, invitations were extended to and accepted by the Orthodox Presbyterian Church, the Christian Reformed Church, and the Lutheran Church—Missouri Synod to take part. It was clear from the start that the individuals named to participate would speak for themselves, their conclusions neither necessarily representing nor binding the respective churches which appointed them.

The papers and summaries prepared in connection with each annual

*Introduction on Reformed Churches, BU, 373-74. Cf. also K.F. Nickle, T.F. Lull, eds., *A Common Calling*. The Report of the Lutheran–Reformed Committee for Theological Conversation, 1988-1992 (Minneapolis: Augsburg, 1993). Text in: Paul C. Empie, James I. McCord, eds., *Marburg Revisited: A Reexamination of Lutheran and Reformed Traditions* (Minneapolis: Augsburg Publishing House, 1966), i-iii, 37-38, 103-04, 151-52, 177.

consultation were printed in pamphlet form and given wide distribution among the clergy of the related church bodies in this country and Canada. The recommendation that this material be made available for use in theological seminaries led to the decision to have them printed together in a single volume.

The statement drawn up and unanimously approved at the final session is ample evidence that these theological conversations were fruitful. Although all discussions were "off the record" and it is not always easy to relate the summary statements to the papers discussed prior to their formulation, it can be said that as the participants become better acquainted and more effective in communication, caricatures disappeared and misunderstandings were rectified. Most important of all, distinctions were made between differences which were matters of relative emphases rather than contradictions in substance. Not all controversial points were touched upon nor were all differences resolved. However, the conclusion that each group recognized in the other a true understanding of the Gospel is significant and the implications of this fact are inescapable.

We suggest that the materials in this book be read in the light of the following statement adopted by participants in their final session:

> During these four meetings we have examined carefully the major issues which have aroused theological controversy between our traditions for generations past. At some points we have discovered that our respective views of each other have been inherited caricatures initially caused by misunderstanding or polemical zeal.
>
> In other instances it has become apparent that efforts to guard against possible distortions of truth have resulted in varying emphases in related doctrines which are not in themselves contradictory and in fact are complementary, and which are viewed in a more proper balance in our contemporary theological formulations.
>
> A number of differing views and emphases remain to be resolved, but we are encouraged to believe that further contacts will lead to further agreement between the churches here represented. We regard none of these remaining differences to be of sufficient consequence to prevent fellowship. We have recognized in each other's teachings a common understanding of the Gospel and have concluded that the issues which divided the two major branches of the Reformation can no longer be regarded as constituting obstacles to mutual understanding and fellowship.
>
> We are grateful to God that he brought us together for these discussions, acknowledging that such confrontation under the guidance of the Holy Spirit was long overdue. Although we can speak only for ourselves, we express our conviction that the work begun in this way must not be permitted to lapse, but should be carried on to fruition by the churches we represent.

We who have had the privilege during the course of these conversations of strengthening the bonds of Christian unity and brotherly affection thank God for the evident working of his spirit in our midst and pray that what was begun in this way will be carried on to a successful conclusion with all "deliberate speed."

James I. McCord, President          Paul C. Empie, Executive Director
Princeton Theological Seminary    National Lutheran Council

## Summary Statement on Gospel, Confession and Scripture

1. Both Lutheran and Reformed churches are evangelical in the sense that they are rooted in, live by, proclaim and confess the gospel of the saving act of God in Jesus Christ. They receive it as it is revealed in the prophetic and apostolic scriptures, attested through the witness of the Holy Spirit, and preserved in the tradition of the catholic faith as expressed in the commonly accepted creeds of the ancient church.

2. The churches of the Reformation confessed this gospel by means of the biblical concept of justification by grace through faith alone. The scriptures also present the same gospel in other concepts, such as reconciliation, regeneration, and redemption. An evangelical confession accordingly may be, and has been, framed in terms of one or more of these.

3. We are agreed that the new life of faith in Christ involves obedience, but there is some question concerning the place and meaning of law in the new life.

4. The Church is constrained by the gospel to confess its faith. Such confession takes the primary form of praise to God. It must also take the form of confession before man, testimony to and defense of the gospel in various historical situations.

5. Confession takes a variety of forms both in scripture and in the Church. The history of the Church exhibits such types as the doxological confession which celebrates the glory of the gospel, the kerygmatic which identifies and declares the gospel, the catechetical which serves for the instruction of believers, and the critical which distinguishes the gospel from errors and misunderstandings.

6. The confessions originated in different geographical and historical situations and they use different vocabularies. These differences do not of themselves preclude unity in the faith which is confessed in them.

7. Credal and confessional subscription is regarded seriously in both Lutheran and Reformed churches, but there is some diversity of opinion concerning its meaning.

8. We are agreed that in the canonical scriptures of the Old and New Testaments the acts of God which culminate in the revelation of Himself in Jesus Christ, His Son our Lord, are set forth by chosen witnesses under the leading of the Holy Spirit.

9. The confessions affirm the supreme authority of scripture as the norm for the proclamation of the gospel and provide authoritative guidance and direction in the interpretation of this normative scripture.

## Summary Statement on Christology, the Lord's Supper and Its Observance in the Church

1.In the present situation, in which windows are opening between Protestants and Roman Catholics as well as between Protestants and Eastern Orthodox, it is especially important that Lutheran and Reformed churches appreciate and bear witness to their common evangelical heritage in the Reformation.

2. We acknowledge the abiding significance of the recovery of the gospel granted to our churches in the Reformation. We confess that this gospel imposes on us the necessity of constant re-examination of our theological-formulations in the light of the word of God.

3. During the Reformation both Reformed and Lutheran churches tended to be one-sided in their teaching and practice, Unfortunately, they did not support or correct one another as they might have done if they had mutually recognized how much they had in common.

5. Ever since the sixteenth century Reformed and Lutheran churches have held the conviction that the same gift is offered in the preached word and in the administered sacrament. Each of these is both word and deed, for in preaching word is action and in the Lord's Supper action is word.

6. When by word is meant the proclamation of the gospel, the sacrament is a form of visible, enacted word through which Christ and his saving benefits are effectively offered to men. Accordingly, the sacrament is a means of peace.

The assurance of his presence is given in the self-witness of Christ in the instituting rite: This is my body, this is my blood. The realization of his presence in the sacrament is effected by the Holy Spirit through the word.

We are agreed that the sacrament does not simply serve to confirm a faith that is awakened by preaching; it also arouses faith through its presentation of the gospel.

7. An adequate doctrine of the Lord's Supper requires some reference to sacrifice. The perfect self-offering of the Son of God is the atoning sacri-

fice whereby our self-offering to God in worship and in loving gift to the neighbor is made possible and acceptable.

8. We are agreed that the presence of Christ in the sacrament is not effected by faith but acknowledged by faith. The worthy participant is one who receives in faith and repentance the Christ who offers himself in the sacrament. The unworthy participant is the one who fails to acknowledge the Lordship of Christ, his presence in the sacrament, and the fellowship of the brethren in the common Lord. Such unworthy participation brings judgment.

9. The significance of christology for the Lord's Supper is that it provides assurance that it is the total Christ, the divine-human person, who is present in the sacrament, but it does not explain how he is present.

10. Our churches are not in full agreement on the practice of intercommunion because they hold different views of the relation of doctrine to the unity of the Church.

## Summary Statement on Creation and Redemption, Law and Gospel, Justification and Sanctification

1. The Reformed and Lutheran traditions are agreed that creation is the work of God, the Father, Son, and Holy Spirit, and that, therefore, the creation is essentially good in spite of the presence and power of evil.

2. The God who creates also redeems and for this reason the creation must be understood in the light of redemption and redemption in the context of creation.

3. Some in our traditions tend to relate redemption too narrowly to man as sinner. We, however, are agreed that we should also bear adequate witness to the significance of redemption for the whole created order, inasmuch as creation and redemption have an eschatological dimension pointing to a new heaven and a new earth.

4. We observe that with respect to law and gospel there are different emphases in our traditions. In part these differences were and are semantic and arise out of different patterns of theological thought. For example, the Lutheran description of law as "always accusing" (*Apology IV*, 38) restricts the meaning of the term "law" more severely than is the case either in the totality of scripture or in the Calvinistic tradition.

5. We are agreed both that Jesus Christ is the fulfillment and end of the law, and that in the Christian life God continues to lay his claim upon the redeemed; but we are not agreed how to denominate that claim, whether law or gospel. Both Calvinists and Lutherans know themselves to be saved through the gospel and called to Christian obedience.

6. We are agreed that the doctrine of justification by faith is fundamen-

tal in both traditions. We recognize, however, that for Lutherans this doctrine has played a more formative role in the articulation of theology. This difference is due in part to the historical situations in which Luther and Calvin did their theological work.

7. We are agreed that each tradition has sought to preserve the wholeness of the gospel as including the forgiveness of sins and the renewal of life. Our discussions have revealed that justification and sanctification have been distinguished from each other and related to each other in rather different ways in our tradition.

8. Failure properly to interpret and relate justification and sanctification leads to the development of antinomian and legalistic distortions in both traditions.

In the light of these observations we acknowledge that differences exist between us, but we record our gratitude to God for the progress we have made toward mutual understanding and resolution of our differences. We also acknowledge the obligation laid upon us to submit ourselves to the guidance of the Word and Spirit in the further pursuit of these objectives.

## Summary Statement on Ethics and Ethos—Christian Service in the Modern World

1. We are agreed that there is a common evangelical basis for Christian ethics in the theology of the Reformers. Both the Lutheran and the Reformed traditions have emphasized the new obedience of Christians through faith active in love and the inseparability of justification and sanctification. Our dialogue leads us to conclude that differing formulations of the relation between law and gospel were prompted by a common concern to combat the errors of legalism on the one hand and antinomianism on the other. While there remains a difference among us as to the importance we attach to the need for the instruction of God's law in the Christian life, we do not regard this as a divisive issue. We affirm together that Christians are free from the bondage of the law in order to live in love under the direction of God's Word and Spirit to the end of good order and eternal life.

2. In attempting to translate Reformation theology into the twentieth century, however, we must take into account not only a clericalism that frustrates the ministry of the laity, but also a secularism which denies that the world is the creation of God and the object of his love. This world is the arena for Christian ethical service. The impersonal structures of power in modern society are morally ambiguous. While they tend to pervert the humanity of men and the proper use of things, they also offer untold possibilities for good. This situation compels us to search for new ways of loving our

neighbors. Recent technological and sociological developments intensify the urgency for translating personal love into social justice.

3. We believe that faithful obedience in modern life involves renewed stress on the vital interaction of Christian righteousness and civil righteousness. In response to the gospel of Christ, we welcome the opportunity for a united witness through Christian social action in service to the world. Such responsible public action will also involve us in cooperation with men of good will who are likewise committed to peace, freedom and justice in society.

# Lutheran-Reformed Consultation Series II, 1972-1974*

I

The first round of Lutheran-Reformed conversations was held from 1962 to 1966 and resulted in the publication of *Marburg Revisited: A Reexamination of Lutheran and Reformed Traditions.*[1] It covered gospel, confession and scripture; the Lord's Supper and christology; justification and sanctification; law and gospel; creation and redemption; and ethics. A summary statement followed each of the four sections, setting forth the consensus and remaining differences. In spite of important differences, on the basis of the consensus arrived at the group reported to the sponsoring confessional organizations (i.e., the North American Area of the World Alliance of Reformed Churches and the U.S.A. National Committee of the Lutheran World Federation) as follows: "As a result of our studies and discussions we see no insuperable obstacles to pulpit and altar fellowship and, therefore, we recommend to our parent bodies that they encourage their constituent churches to enter into discussions looking forward to intercommunion and the fuller recognition of one another's ministries."[2] Although *Marburg Revisited* was sent to the constituent churches, no official action was taken by any Reformed or Lutheran church "to enter into discussions looking forward to intercommunion and the fuller recognition of one another's ministries."[3]

1. In the remit for the second round of conversations, drawn up in July 1971 by the presidents of the church bodies participating in the Lutheran Council in the U.S.A., and by stated clerks of churches of the North American Area of the World Alliance of Reformed Churches (Presbyterian and Congregational), it was stated: "In resuming the Lutheran-Reformed conversations, it shall be the objective to assess the consensus and remaining differences in the theology and life of the participating churches as they bear upon the teaching of the Gospel in the current situation." It was our aim in these discussions to test and deepen this consensus in the current situation

*IA, 54-58.

136

without ignoring remaining differences. Although the report focused on "the teaching of the Gospel in the current situation, the results of the *Marburg Revisited* study regarding intercommunion, and recent developments affecting church relationships, brought us repeatedly back to problems of pulpit and altar fellowship. It became apparent to us that attention would have to be given to the sources of the diversity of theological understanding and to the differences of ecclesiastical life style that play into the separation between Lutheran and Reformed churches. It also became clear to us that some of the most intransigent theological differences run across denominational lines.

2. Representatives designated by the presidents of the church bodies participating in LCUSA and the North American Area of WARC held six meetings from 1972 to 1974. Papers were read and discussed on (1) Churches in Dialogue Today; (2) *Marburg Revisited*; (3) the Leuenberg Agreement of 1973; and (4) the official positions of the participating churches on matters of fellowship. At the first meeting in Princeton, New Jersey, 14-15 April 1972, papers were presented by Dr. William Weiblen on "The Church in Dialogue in 1972," with a response by Dr. Thomas Parker; by Dr. Daniel Migliore on "An American Looks at Leuenberg" with a response by Dr. George Forell; and Drs. Ralph Bohlmann and John Leith on "Marburg Revisited in the Light of 1972."

At the fall meeting in Chicago eight brief papers were read by Drs. Arnold Carlson and Thomas Parker on "Leuenberg's Hermeneutics and Theological Methodology"; by Drs. Henry Stob and James Burtness on "The Understanding of the Gospel in the Leuenberg Agreement"; by Drs. M. Eugene Osterhaven and James Burtness on "Problem Areas: Are Past Differences Still Issues?"; and by Drs. Eugene Klug and Roger Hazleton on "Achieving Church Fellowship."

At the spring meeting of 1973 in New York papers were presented by Dr. Walter Wietzke on "Identify and Identification" with a response by Dr. Daniel Migliore; by Dr. Ralph Bohlmann; and a discussion was led by Professor Peter Berger on sociological issues in the Protestant churches in America.

At the fall meeting in 1973 in Grand Rapids, Michigan, representatives of the participating churches presented papers on their churches' official positions with respect to: (1) requirements for admission to the Lord's Table and to pulpits; (2) the role of the Eucharist in the life of the church, with special attention to its juridical and disciplinary functions, and its relation to other doctrines; (3) ways to overcome obstacles to fellowship. The representative who presented papers were Drs. Howard Tepker (The Lutheran Church—Missouri Synod), George Forell (Lutheran Church in America), William Weiblen (The American Lutheran Church), Henry Stob (Christian Reformed Church), Eugene Osterhaven (Reformed Church in America),

John Leith ( Presbyterian Church in the United States), Thomas Parker (United Presbyterian Church in the U.S.A.), and Roger Hazleton (United Church of Christ). "Reactions and Forecasts" were given by Drs. Daniel Migliore and William Lazareth.

At the spring meeting in 1974 in New York a committee composed of Drs. Forell, Wietzke, and Bohlmann presented a paper on the "Lutheran Assessment of the Reformed," and Dr. Arthur C. Cochrane gave a paper on "Descriptive Assessment of the 'Consensus and Remaining Differences'" with responses by Drs. John Leith and Roger Hazleton.

3. The Leuenberg Agreement of 1973, which had been drawn up by representatives of Lutheran, Reformed, and United churches in Europe, has been sent to some ninety churches. "Full pulpit and altar fellowship" will be formally created among the churches signing. It is possible that a formal agreement among our churches in America might have been achieved if our group had recommended that Leuenberg be sent to them to be signed. But for a number of reasons this option was rejected: (a) Leuenberg was criticized by some because of its alleged ambiguities and compromises. (b) Others felt that it is inadequate for our pluralistic society. It does not take account of the sociological factors which have shaped our churches in America; culture, ethos, class, secularization, the protean character of modern existence, etc. An assessment of differences and common understanding of our Christian faith needs to take account of our peculiar and specific history in North America. It is for this reason that a document like the Leuenberg Agreement did not seem to be of particular help to the American situation. (c) Still others felt that the basis of church fellowship cannot be in the settlement of sixteenth-century disputes about the Lord's Supper but in a common confession of Jesus Christ in the face of contemporary issues facing our churches in America.

We attempted to express our unity in terms other than Leuenberg but were unsuccessful. In gratitude we recognize that we have learned much from one another; in penitence we acknowledge our common need to be open to the work of the Spirit in a fresh hearing of God's word, which alone can create genuine church fellowship in what is proclaimed in our pulpits, is celebrated around the Lord's Table, and is demonstrated in our witness and service.

## II

1. When the official positions of the participating churches with respect to pulpit and altar (table) fellowship were studied, it was found that there has existed and still exists a consensus among Lutheran and Reformed churches concerning the following *doctrinal* points: the Lord's Supper is (1) a sacrament; (2) a means of grace, in which (3) the true (proper) body and

blood of Jesus Christ are present and are eaten and drunk. Disagreement remains between Lutheran and Reformed churches, and even among Reformed churches, concerning the *mode* of Christ's presence.

Our discussions have revealed that one of the significant points of remaining differences is a different view in understanding what is meant by "pulpit and altar fellowship." We have discovered that Lutherans tend to give much more weight and significance to the concept "pulpit and altar fellowship" than do the Reformed. There is a variety of understandings that prevails among the churches in the Reformed tradition but overall amongst them there seems to be less packed into the meaning of this concept. It became apparent in this round of conversations that a great deal more attention was given to the question of "altar fellowship" than to any other dimension of relationship between the churches engaged in these conversations.

2. When the *practice* of the participating churches in regard to the Lord's Supper was reviewed, it was observed that most of the Reformed churches have for a long time taught and practiced Communion open to all Christians and recognized the ordination of ministers of other churches. A difference became apparent between The Lutheran Church—Missouri Synod on the one hand, and The American Lutheran Church and the Lutheran Church in America on the other. The Missouri Synod refrains for doctrinal reasons from pulpit and altar fellowship with other church bodies.[4] Although in The American Lutheran Church and the Lutheran Church in America the practice varies in individual congregations they have in fact been practicing pulpit and altar fellowship. They do not practice "close" Communion, nor do they adhere to a rule of Lutheran pulpits for Lutheran preachers alone, but function under the rubric of "selective fellowship" on these matters.

3. We observed that while The American Lutheran Church and the Lutheran Church in America and the Reformed churches adhere to the doctrine of the Lord's Supper expressed in their respective Confessions of faith, in *practice* they are saying that the confessional differences concerning the mode of Christ's presence ought not to be regarded as obstacles to pulpit and altar fellowship. The differences may involve error, but they do not amount to heresy and therefore to a denial of Jesus Christ as the one Lord and Savior of men. These churches practice a measure of pulpit and altar fellowship without formal agreement, and they have done so on the basis of their respective Confessions of faith.

4. In drawing this report to a close, we would again call attention to the fact that we were asked "to assess the consensus and remaining differences in the theology of the participating churches as they bear upon the teaching of the Gospel in the current situation." In fact, most of our time and energy was spent upon what pulpit and altar fellowship is actual and possible among us on the basis of our respective traditions.

Our inability to make theological headway may well be related to our concentration on our ecclesiastical traditions instead of a fresh and serious study of Scripture in the current situation.

### III. RECOMMENDATIONS

In view of our assessment of "the consensus and remaining differences in the theology and life of the participating churches," we recommend to the presidents of the church bodies participating in the Lutheran Council in the U.S.A., and to the North American Area of the World Alliance of Reformed Churches (Presbyterian and Congregational) the following:

1. That this present series of Lutheran-Reformed conversations be considered terminated;

2. That our churches be urged to approach each other, at every level of life, through a fresh hearing of the gospel declared in Holy Scripture, as well as in terms of their confessional and ecclesiastical traditions;

3. That if formal declarations of altar fellowship are desired, this question be dealt with on a church body to church body basis;

4. That in view of appalling needs in the world drawing us to speak and act concretely concerning hunger, oppression, poverty, and all other forms of human misery, our respective churches be urged to recognize and proclaim, in repentance and hope, the judgment and promise of the word of God in our contemporary situation;

5. That in view of the teaching of Scripture and the brokenness of society, we reaffirm our belief in the unity of the church, and express our fervent prayer and hope that the Holy Spirit will lead the whole body of Christ to repentance and renewal.

### Notes

1. Paul C. Empie and James I. McCord, eds. (Minneapolis: Augsburg Publishing House, 1966).

2. Ibid., p. 191.

3. Two church body actions should, however, be noted. The American Lutheran Church, at its 1966 convention, referred the report of this dialogue series to its Committee on Inter-church Relations. The Lutheran Church—Missouri Synod, at its 1967 convention, voiced appreciation that the conversations had proved fruitful, had manifested a measure of agreement upon the topics discussed, and had frankly recognized and discussed remaining differences. It requested its Commission on Theology and Church Relations, in cooperation with other Lutherans, to take whatever steps would be necessary for participation in further discussion on national and local levels.

4. Except, in North America, for The American Lutheran Church.

# An Invitation to Action*

## Introduction

This common statement and urgent invitation for action is addressed to the Lutheran and Reformed churches[1] of the United States which appointed us as official representatives for the third round of theological dialogue between our confessional families.

Our common statement is the product of two years of study and explicitly builds on the earlier work of the theologians of our churches. The first round of Lutheran-Reformed dialogue, which concluded in 1966, was also the first bilateral theological conversation authorized by our churches. Those Lutheran-Reformed conversations thus began a new era in ecumenism.

Both the first and second rounds of dialogue invited our respective churches to take specific positive actions[2] to encourage our two traditions of the continental Reformation to recognize significant theological convergence and to participate in specific common activities. We regret that our respective churches did not do so as early as 1966.

We affirm that it is now an appropriate time for our churches to take positive action.

### 1. "For God so loved the world..."

1.1 God enters history in the Son and the Spirit to save and liberate the world from the bondage of sin and death. Sin is evidenced in our alienation from God and from one another, in the misuse and scarring of the goodness of creation and in injustice all around us. "The whole creation groans and travails in pain together until now" (Rom. 8:22). In Christ, God robs death of its power over creation. Through the resurrection God reverses the decay of all things. God's own mission in the world among all peoples goes on constantly. The existence of the ongoing people of God offers hope in our culture gripped alternately by arrogant self-sufficiency and despair.

1.2 This mission of God in such a world addresses churches of common faith. Today there is a new urgency to unite in common proclamation of

*IA, 1-36.

141

the gospel, witnessing to the kingdom of God and its justice (Matt. 6:33). Humankind seems bent upon bringing the end of the world upon itself and all creatures of God by nuclear holocaust. Our churches are already enlisted in a common mission: participation in God's preservation of the world, God's struggle for justice and peace, and evangelization.

1.3 The people of our churches live in the same communities, work in the same buildings, perform the same tasks, suffer the same pains, celebrate the same joys, and are sustained by the same gospel.

1.4 Each of our churches independently has addressed issues common to our local communities, our nation, and the world, such as: nuclear armament, peace, justice for the poor of our country and the world, prison reform, sex, marriage, the family, economic justice, the yokes of race and class, ecology, and the advocacy of all persons denied their right to achieve their potential.

1.5 Our churches in varying degrees already cooperate with each other locally, nationally, and internationally in addressing the urgent needs of our world and in confessing God's work among us.

1.6 Because our churches are engaged in a consideration of the document on *Baptism, Eucharist and Ministry* developed within the World Council of Churches, we are obligated to explore again the heritage of ministry, sacraments, and missions we share as churches shaped by the Reformation of the sixteenth century.

1.7 Because we have commonality in our theological reflections and our social setting in spite of our separation, God's mission presses us on to a more visible unity rooted in God's word and sacraments.

1.8 Because God makes us all members of the holy catholic church by baptism, our churches are committed to work together officially toward full communion in each other's baptism, Holy Communion,[3] and ministry.

1.9 Our unity in word and sacraments will be one additional step for our churches as we pray for and accept the unity Christ has given us, so that the world might believe and be re-created.

2. Our unity in Christ compels us to claim our strong affinities in doctrine and practice. Both Lutheran and Reformed traditions:
>    a. Affirm themselves a living part of the church catholic.
>    b. Confess the Nicene and Apostles' Creeds.[4]
>    c. Affirm the doctrine of justification by faith as fundamental.[5]
>    d. Affirm the unique and final authority of Holy Scripture in the church.[6]
>    e. Affirm the real presence of Christ in the Lord's Supper. [7]
>    f. Affirm the priesthood of all believers and have interpreted this as our servanthood to God and our service to the world.[8]

g. Affirm the vocation of all the baptized, which is service (ministry) in every aspect of their lives in their care of God's world.[9]

h. Affirm that they are in faithful succession in the apostolic Tradition and that faithful succession in this Tradition is all that is necessary for mutual recognition as part of the church catholic.[10]

i. Share a common definition of a church in the apostolic Tradition: a community where the word is rightly preached and the sacraments rightly administered. [11]

j. Identify a ministry of word and sacrament as instituted by God.[12]

k. Ordain once to a ministry of word and sacrament, and the functions of such persons are identical.

l. Understand that ordination is to the ministry of the church catholic.[13] Such ordinations in both traditions have usually been by presbyters.[14]

m. Have granted the appropriateness under some circumstances of one ordained person exercising *episkopé*, oversight (under a variety of titles including that of bishop), but both traditions have ordinarily exercised the function of *episkopé* collegially through such structures as presbyteries and synods.

n. Affirm that the church always must be open to further growth and reformation. Both traditions have been willing to be self-critical. Both traditions have become increasingly open to a historical-critical understanding of the history of the church and of their respective traditions within the apostolic Tradition.[15]

3. Shared appreciation for the gifts and unique heritage of each of our traditions drives us to affirmation of our unity in Christ.

3.1 Our traditions, both rooted in the same reforming movement of the sixteenth century, have been strongly confessional. Our Confessions were often experienced and understood by our fathers and mothers in the faith as life-and-death testimonies on behalf of the gospel.

3.2 In that unique historic setting, such faith testimonies were often expressed in strong polemical language. Such polemic, we have all learned from our bilateral theological conversations among many traditions, often masked and distorted awareness of our common rootedness in the church catholic and its common faith.

3.3 Polemic often leads to caricature and polarization, rarely to careful appreciation of nuances. It is not strange that close cousins within the church catholic have been on occasion the objects of the sharpest polemic and the most unfair caricature. This has often been true for Reformed and Lutheran traditions.

3.4 Yet all of the churches represented in the present dialogue grew out of the same evangelical reform movement of the sixteenth century, and all addressed the same fundamental issues. Our theological reflections often have been expressed in different vocabularies and nuanced somewhat differently from place to place and from time to time in the past four and one-half centuries.

3.5 Our work together in this dialogue persuades us that such a basic consensus now exists among us to justify the conclusion that the condemnations pronounced by the Reformation Confessions are no longer appropriate.[16]

3.6 We affirm that both of our traditions have done their theological reflection from the same foundations and used the same classical vocabulary: Christ alone, faith alone, grace alone, Scripture alone.

3.7 Such affirmation of our unity in Christ is not new among Lutheran and Reformed churches. There have long been examples in America of joint Lutheran-Reformed congregations. We celebrate and call attention to the full fellowship in sacraments and ministries already experienced in Europe for more than ten years under the Leuenberg Agreement.[17]

4. From a common gospel, a common faith, a common theological conviction that Christ intends unity for the church as a faithful reflection of its essential nature, and in obedient response to our Lord's prayer "that they all may be one" (John 17:21);

From a common conviction of the urgency of God's mission confronting identical social, political, and cultural problems which require the united proclamation, witness, and service of Christians;

We therefore request all the members of the Caribbean and North American Area Council (CANAAC) of the World Alliance of Reformed Churches (WARC) and the Lutheran Council in the U.S.A. to receive our report and study it so that there will be the fullest possible use of the document in their own churches. More particularly we call upon the Presbyterian Church (U.S.A.), the Reformed Church in America, the Cumberland Presbyterian Church, the United Church of Christ, the American Lutheran Church, the Association of Evangelical Lutheran Churches, the Lutheran Church in America, and the Lutheran Church—Missouri Synod to take action at their highest levels of authority in order to:

    a. Recognize one another as churches in which the gospel is proclaimed and the sacraments administered according to the ordinance of Christ.

    b. Recognize as both valid and effective one another's ordained ministries which announce the gospel of Christ and administer the sacraments of faith as their chief responsibility.

    c. Recognize one another's celebrations of the Lord's Supper as a means of grace in which Christ grants communion with himself, assures us of the forgiveness of sins, and pledges life eternal.

d. Enter into a process of reception of this report so that it may become a part of the faith and life of each church at the deepest level, moving beyond purely administrative and intellectual action by taking such steps as:

(1) praying with and for one another, supporting one another's ministry, and where appropriate establishing relationships among presbyteries, classes, conferences, synods, and districts;

(2) common study at each judicatory level of the Holy Scriptures, the histories and traditions of each church, and current theological and liturgical renewal;

(3) joint celebrations of the Lord's Supper among congregations, presbyteries, classes, conferences, districts, and synods;

(4) invitations to the ordained pastors of each tradition to preach in the congregations of the other tradition, and, where local conditions make it necessary or possible, to preside at the Holy Communion of the other tradition;

(5) designation by each church, in cooperation with the others, of two or three geographical areas where Lutheran and Reformed judicatories serving the same territory might develop extended projects of cooperation, meeting together for joint study of common issues, mission planning, and common worship;

(6) designation by each regional judicatory of at least one congregation which may be linked in extended projects of cooperation with a congregation of the other tradition, meeting together for joint study of issues, mission planning, and common worship;

(7) requesting annual reports of such joint ministry, mission, and worship experiences to the national ecumenical offices of the judicatories;

(8) transmitting a copy of this report and its attached papers to all persons participating in the official response by church bodies to the Lima document on *Baptism, Eucharist and Ministry*;

(9) requesting appointment of a small planning team representing these several ecumenical offices to assemble and evaluate such reports, to report annually to the several churches, and to have responsibility for recommendation of further action appropriate to facilitate this ongoing process of reception;

(10) referring any unresolved theological issues, such as the rela-

tionship between faith and ethics, and church and world, to a
subsequent dialogue in the context of these new relationships;
(11) informing the World Alliance of Reformed Churches and the
Lutheran World Federation of activity and developments in
this process of reception.

## Notes

1. See *IA*, pp. 3-4 for background information.
2. Cf. Appendix I, Recommendations of LR I, *IA*, p. 52. Cf. Appendix 2, Recommendations of LR II, p. 140 above.
3. Various images and concepts have been used to describe the sacrament in which Christ gives himself anew to the believing community. Among Christians it has been referred to as the Lord's Supper, the Holy Communion, the Sacrament of the Altar, and the Eucharist. Motifs of remembrance, fellowship, thanksgiving, confession and forgiveness, and celebration have been incorporated. Whatever images and concepts are used,the intention and emphasis of the biblical witness and of our traditions have been to assert and affirm God's gift of grace through the body and blood of Christ, "given and shed for you." The several terms, common to our traditions, and to the church catholic, are used interchangeably in the following text: cf. ALC/LCA Statement on Communion Practices, 1978; PC (U.S.A.)BO S-3.0500.
4. See description of participating churches, *IA*, pp. 3-4, on the use of Confessions in the UCC.
5. Cf. pp. 148-51 below, Joint Statement on Justification.
6. FC, Epitome 1:1, BkC 464; WC, chap. 1, BC 6.001-6.010; BelC, Arts. 3-7;C'67,BC 9:27-30;Cumberland Confessions of Faith, chaps. 1-4;II HC, BC 5.001-2; ScotsC, chap. 19, BC 3:19; Constitution, American Lutheran Church, 401; Constitution, Association of Evangelical Lutheran Churches, Article II; Constitution, Lutheran Church in America, Article II, Section 3; PC (U.S.A.) BO G-14.0207, 14.0405; Cumberland Constitution chaps. 46,57. Cf. RCA *Liturgy and Psalms* (ordination service), p. 96.
7. Cf. above, *Marburg Revisited*, pp. 132-33, *IA*, p. 69; cf. Appendix 3, Leuenberg Agreement, *IA*, p. 69. Cf. Joint Statement on the Lord's Supper, pp. 151-59, below.
8. Cf. Joint Statement on Ministry, below.
9. Cf. Joint Statement on Ministry, below.
10. CA I and 2, *BkC* 27,29; II HC, chap. 17, *BC* 5.124-41;WC, chap. 25;*BC* 6.125-30; BelC, Arts. 27-28; ScotsC, chap. 16, 18, BC 3.16, 3.18; PC(U.S.A.) *BO* G-4.000. For this use of the word "Tradition," see n. 1 of the Joint Statement on Justification, below.
11. CA 7, *BkC* 32; BelC, Art, 29; II HC, chap. 17, BC 5.134-35; ScotsC, chap. 18, BC 3.18.
12. CA 5, *BkC* 31; BelC, chap. 30; ScotsC, chap. 22, BC 3:22; WC, chap. 25, BC 6.127; II HC, chap. 18, BC 5.142-63. According to the Reformed tradition, elders must authorize and be present at the Lord's Supper along with the minister(PC[U.S.A.]BO S-3.500).
13. Occasional Services (Companion to the LBW), Ordination (Minneapolis; Augsburg Publishing House; Philadelphia: Fortress Press, 1982), p. 193; PC(U.S.A.) BO G-11.0203, 14.0401, 15.0202; Cumberland Constitution, chap. 60B; RCA BCO I, II 18.
14. *The Ministry of the Church: A Lutheran Understanding* (Division of Theological Studies, Lutheran Council in the U.S.A., 1974), p. 4; II HC, chap. 18 BC 5.150-51; PC(U.S.A.) BO G-14.0401; Cumberland Constitution, chaps. 55-57; RCA BCO I, II 10.
15. C'67, BC 9.40; PC(U.S.A.) BO G-2.O200, 3.0401, 4.0303-4, 4.0401.
16. Cf. Appendix 3, Leuenberg Agreement, *IA*, pp. 66, 69-70, esp. paragraphs 5,20,23,and 26-28.
17. Cf. Appendix 3, Leuenberg Agreement, *IA*, pp. 61-73.

\* \* \*

## MINORITY REPORT

### From Lutheran Church-Missouri Synod Participants October 1, 1983

We, Lutheran Church—Missouri Synod participants, wish to express our gratitude and appreciation for having had the opportunity to participate in Lutheran-Reformed Dialogue III. We commend the participants for their willingness to discuss some of the basic doctrines of the Holy Scripture for the purpose of reaching a better understanding of the faith professed by fellow Christians in other church bodies—with a view toward recognizing their baptism, Lord's Supper, and ministry. We thank God for the amount of agreement which was discovered on the basis of an exchange of views.

A number of substantial issues, however, remain unresolved. Since Lutheran Church-Missouri Synod establishes altar and pulpit fellowship with other church bodies only after substantial agreement has been reached in all of the doctrines of Scripture, the LCMS participants cannot at this time concur in the opinion that "...Lutheran churches should, at the earliest appropriate time and at the highest level, officially recognize the Eucharists (Lord's Suppers) of those churches which affirm the Reformed Confessions and have them as a living part of their present witness and proclamation" [See A Statement of Lutherans to Lutherans Reflecting on This Dialogue, p. 110 of *An Invitation to Action*].

We do, however, recommend:
1. that the report of Lutheran-Reformed Dialogue III be forwarded to the president of The Lutheran Church—Missouri Synod with the suggestion that it be shared with the Synod for its information, edification, and mutually agreed-upon action;
2. that The Lutheran Church—Missouri Synod continue to participate in discussions of this kind with a view toward reaching a more complete agreement on the important doctrines of the Scripture; and
3. that we continue fervently to ask God for his guidance and blessing upon our efforts and thus hasten the day when believers everywhere will agree on the truth of God's Holy Word and live together in unity and Christian love.

## JOINT STATEMENT ON JUSTIFICATION

1. Both Lutheran and Reformed churches are evangelical. We are rooted in, live by, proclaim, and confess the gospel of the saving act of God in Jesus Christ. We accept the Tradition[1] of the catholic faith as expressed in the Nicene and Apostles' Creeds.

2. This gospel is the good news that for us and for our salvation God's Son became human in Jesus the Christ, was crucified and raised from the dead. By his life, death, and resurrection he took upon himself God's judgment on human sin and proved God's love for sinners, reconciling the entire world to God.

3. For Christ's sake we sinners have been reconciled to God, not because we earned God's acceptance but by an act of God's sheer mercy. The Holy Spirit calls and enables us to repent of our sin and accept God's gracious offer. Those trusting in this gospel, believing in Christ as Savior and Lord, are justified in God's sight.

4. Both the Lutheran and Reformed traditions confess this gospel in the language of justification by grace through faith alone. This doctrine of justification was the central theological rediscovery of the Reformation; it was proclaimed by Martin Luther and John Calvin and their respective followers.[2]

5. This doctrine of justification continues to be a message of hope and of new life to persons alienated from our gracious God and from one another. Even though Christians who live by faith continue to sin, still in Christ our bondage to sin and death has been broken. By faith we already begin to participate in Christ's victory over evil, the Holy Spirit actively working to redirect our lives.[3]

6. This gospel sets Christians free for good works and responsible service in the whole world. In daily repentance and renewal we praise God and serve others. As grateful servants of God we are enabled to do all those good works that God commands, yet without placing our trust in them. As a community of servants of God we are called and enabled to do works of mercy and to labor for justice and peace among individuals and nations.[4]

## CONCLUSION

7. We agree that there are no substantive matters concerning justification that divide us. We recommend that Lutheran and Reformed churches which subscribe to the classic Confessions of their traditions should at this time officially recognize and declare one another as churches in which the gospel is preached and taught.

# Notes

1. We distinguish between *Tradition* understood as the common deposit of the faith of the church catholic represented in the canon of Scripture, and *tradition* understood as the ecumenical creeds and traditions of the several faith communities as they have evolved in different periods of history and in different cultures.

2. WC, chap. 11, *BC* 6.060-61

> Those whom God effectually calleth, he also freely justifieth: not by infusing righteousness into them, but by pardoning their sins, and by accounting and accepting their persons as righteous; not for any thing wrought in them, or done by them, but for Christ's sake alone; not by imputing faith itself, the act of believing, or any other evangelical obedience to them, as their righteousness, but by imputing the obedience and satisfaction of Christ unto them, they receiving and resting on him and his righteousness by faith; which faith they have not of themselves: it is the gift of God. Faith, thus receiving and resting on Christ and his righteousness, is the lone instrument of justification; yet it is not alone in the person justified, but is ever accompanied with all other saving graces, and is no dead faith, but worketh by love.

II HC, chap. 15, BC 5.107, 5.109, 5.110:

> Now it is most certain that all of us are by nature sinners and godless, and before God's judgement-seat are convicted of godlessness and are guilty of death, but that, solely by the grace of Christ and not from any merit of ours or consideration for us, we are justified, that is, absolved from sin and death by God the Judge....
> But because we receive this justification, not though any works, but through faith in the mercy of God and in Christ, we therefore teach and believe with the apostle that sinful man is justified by faith alone in Christ, not by the law or any works....
> Therefore, we do not share in the benefit of justification partly because of the grace of God or Christ, and partly because of ourselves, our love, works or merit, but we attribute it wholly to the grace of God in Christ through faith.

CA 4, *BkC* 30 (German version):

> It is also taught among us that we cannot obtain forgiveness of sin and righteousness before God by our own merits, works, or satisfactions, but that we receive forgiveness of sin and become righteous before God by grace, for Christ's sake, through faith, when we believe that Christ suffered for us and that for his sake our sin is forgiven and righteousness and eternal life are given to us. For God will regard and reckon this faith as righteousness, as Paul says in Romans 3:21-26 and 4:5.

Further evidence of this confessional congruence may be observed: (a) during the Crypto-Calvinist controversy, 1560-74, justification was not an issue (cf. *Book of Concord* [St. Louis:Concordia Publishing House, 1922], pp. 172-92); (b) at Marburg, 1529, Zwingli, Oecolampadius, Bucer, Melanchthon, and Luther agreed on articles on justification (cf. *Book of Concord*, ed. H. E. Jacobs [Philadelphia: Frederick, 1883], II:70-71); (c) the first series of Lutheran-Reformed dialogue in the United States concluded: "We are agreed that the doctrine of justification by faith is fundamental in both traditions. We recognize, however, that for Lutherans this doctrine has played a more formative role in the articulation of theology. This difference is due in part to the historical situations in which Luther and Calvin did their theological work" (cf. Appendix 1, *Marburg Revisited*, pp. 133-34 above); (d) the Leuenberg

Agreement, in affirming consensus on justification, had no need to revoke condemnations, as it did on other matters of doctrine (cf. Appendix 3, Leuenberg Agreement, IA, pp. 67-68).

In regard to the United Church of Christ's position, it is understood that in 1957 it merged Congregational Christian Churches and the Evangelical and Reformed Church "without break in their respective continuities and traditions" (*Constitution and Bylaws*, p. 3). On the Lutheran side, for example, it thus claims as its own the CA and on the Reformed side the HCat, both confessional statements of the Evangelical and Reformed Church. Thus there is no need to quote again from the CA what already has been noted above. On the Congregational Christian side the Savoy Declaration puts the United Church of Christ in close touch with the WC. The Savoy Declaration was adopted by a Massachusetts Synod in Boston in 1680. Note the close agreement in language with the WC (above, n.2) on justification.

> Those whom God effectually calleth, he also freely justifieth not by infusing right-eousness into them, but by pardoning their sins and by accounting and accepting their person as righteous, not for anything wrought in them, or done by them, but for Christ's sake alone; not by imputing Faith itself, the act of believing, or any other Evangelical obedience to them, as their righteousness, but by imputing Christ's active obedience unto the whole Law, and passive obedience in his death for their whole and sole righteousness, they receiving and resting on him and his righteousness by Faith; which Faith they have not of themselves, it is the gift of God. (Savoy Declaration, chap. 11, in Williston Walker, ed., *The Creeds and Platforms of Congregationalism* [Boston: Pilgrim Press, 1960], pp. 378f.)

3. Both the Lutheran and the Reformed traditions continue to affirm in our confessional statements, our instruction, and our worship that sin is in essence the radical, inveterate, willful self-seeking by which we tend to use our fellow beings and even God for our selfish advantage. Humans are in bondage to sin and thus alienated from God and from one another. Only God through Christ's justifying work can liberate us from this bondage and alienation, reconcile us with God and our fellow humans, and restore the full integrity of all creation.

Both traditions affirm that, although Christians are truly justified in Christ—restored to God's family—our inveterate sinfulness is not eradicated. To describe this situation, Martin Luther occasionally used the paradoxical expression that a Christian is "at one and the same time a righteous person and a sinner" (*simul justus et peccator*). By this he meant that the Christian's life, though truly liberated and righteous in God's sight, is a constant struggle—with the Holy Spirit's help—to eradicate our persisting tendency to fall back into bondage to sin. Both Lutheran and Reformed theologies, however, have traditionally used the term "sanctifica-tion" to describe the continuing struggle of the justified Christian, with the Spirit's help, to elim-inate his or her sin and manifest a holy life (cf. FC SD 3:40-41, BkC 546). Cf. WC VI, BC 6.031-36;WC XI, 5, BC 6.064; WC XIII, BC 6.067-69; WC XV, 3-4, BC 6.075-76; II HC VIII-IX, BC 5.036-5.051; HCat, Part I, BC 4.003-4.011; HCat, Part III, BC 4.086-4.129; C'67, BC 9:21-26.

Illustrative of this theme in public worship would be the *LBW*, p. 56; *The Worshipbook* of the PC(U.S.A.) and Cumberland Presbyterian Church (jointly published), p. 26; *Book of Common Worship*, PC(U.S.A.), p. 136; *Ordinal and Service Book* of the Church of Scotland, pp. 1-2.

4. CA 6, BkC 31-32: "It is also taught among us that such faith should produce good fruits and good works and that we must do all such good works as God has commanded, but we should do them for God's sake and not place our trust in them as if thereby to merit favor before God..." Cf. also CA 20:27, *BkC* 45; "It is also taught among us that good works should and must be done, not that we are to rely on them to earn grace but that we may do God's will and glorify him. It is always faith alone that apprehends grace and forgiveness of sin" and CA 20:35, BkC 46: "Consequently this teaching concerning faith is not to be accused of forbidding good works but is rather to be praised for teaching that good works are to be done and for offering help as to how they may be done."

WC, chap. 16, *BC* 6.080-83:

These good works, done in obedience to God's commandments, are the fruits and evidences of a true and lively faith; and by them believers manifest their thankfulness, strengthen their assurance, edify their brethren, adorn the profession of the gospel, stop the mouths of the adversaries, and glorify God, whose workmanship they are, created in Jesus Christ thereunto:...Their ability to do good works is not at all of themselves, but wholly from the Spirit of Christ. And that they may be enabled thereunto, besides the graces they have already received, there is required an actual influence of the same Holy Spirit to work in them to will and to do of his good pleasure;...We cannot, by our best works, merit pardon of sin, or eternal life.

II HC chap. XVI, BC 5.118:

Therefore, although we teach with the apostle that a man is justified by grace through faith in Christ and not through any good works, yet we do not think that good works are of little value and condemn them. We know that man was not created or regenerated through faith in order to be idle, but rather that without ceasing he should do those things which are good and useful.

\* \* \*

## JOINT STATEMENT ON THE SACRAMENT OF THE LORD'S SUPPER

### Gospel

1. We are Christians because of the presence of Jesus Christ in our lives. This good news of Jesus Christ is the gospel. It is from the gospel that we understand the Lord's Supper. The Supper is a unique way in which Christ shares himself with us and in which we share in Christ with one another. Thus the Supper is itself a particular form of the gospel. The same gift is offered in the preached word and in the administered sacrament.[1]

1.1 The gospel is the good news of Jesus Christ, God's Son, who has been given to us because God loves the world and acts to reconcile the world to himself.

1.2 In Christ we are called, corporately and individually, to manifest the presence of our Lord Jesus Christ in our lives, witness, and service. It is this gospel which compels us to engage in God's mission in the world.

1.3 As churches we must see to it that the gospel we proclaim in word and action is indeed the true gospel of the Holy Scriptures and not a distortion or a substitute. This is why both of our communions regard fidelity to the gospel as the fundamental norm for church fellowship.

**Greatness of the Supper**

2. Appreciating what we Reformed and Lutheran Christians already hold in common concerning the Lord's Supper, we nevertheless affirm that both of our communions need to keep on growing into an ever-deeper realization of the fullness and richness of the eucharistic mystery.

2.1 Both Lutheran and Reformed churches affirm that Christ himself is the host at his table. Both churches affirm that Christ himself is truly present and received in the Supper. Neither communion professes to explain how this is so.

2.2 The Lord's Supper is inexhaustibly profound and awesome. We concur with the 1982 Lima Faith and Order statement *Baptism, Eucharist and Ministry,* which reminds all Christians that five features belong to the fullness of the Lord's Supper. The Eucharist is (1) thanksgiving to the Father; (2) anamnesis or memorial of Christ; (3) invocation of the Spirit; (4) communion of the faithful; and (5) meal of the kingdom.

2.3 While none of these features is alien to either of our traditions, both Reformed and Lutheran Christians need continually to grow in our understanding and experience of this joyful communion with Christ and with one another.

**The New Community**

3. By his real presence among us in word and sacrament and by the work of his Holy Spirit, Christ creates and nurtures a new community of faith, his holy church. Holy Communion richly nourishes us in our devotion to a life of faithful discipleship and calls us to grow in our understanding of what God intends the entire human family to become. Fed at Christ's table, we are drawn to care for one another in the fellowship of believers. Fed at Christ's table, we are called to become more sensitive to the needs of our sisters and brothers in the entire human family.

3.1 As we participate in Holy Communion we receive the benefit of the forgiveness of sins, life, and salvation through our trust in God's faithfulness.[2]

3.2 As we participate in Holy Communion with our Lord we experience our oneness in Christ. We become more sensitive to the sufferings of our brothers and sisters in Christ, and we are moved to minister to one another as Christ did.

3.3 As we participate in Holy Communion God commissions us to minister to the entire human family as Christ did. Christ summons us to share our bounty with all those whose physical and spiritual lives are burdened by poverty. He calls us to "...struggle with the oppressed towards that freedom and dignity promised with the coming of the Kingdom" (*BEM*, Ministry, I.4). He challenges us to commit ourselves to the cause of justice and peace for all people.[3]

3.4 As we participate in Holy Communion we are committed afresh to the ecumenical task, the effort to realize Christ's will that all his followers may be one, gathered around one table.

## Doctrine

4. We affirm that the Lutheran and Reformed families of churches have a fundamental consensus in the gospel and the sacraments which not only allows but also demands common participation in the Lord's Supper.

4.1 In the past Christians of the Reformed and Lutheran traditions have been deeply divided by controversy over the understanding of the Lord's Supper although both have strongly affirmed the real presence of Christ in the Sacrament. Today we cherish a high regard for our ancestors in the faith who stalwartly proclaimed the gospel according to their respective convictions. At the same time, through long and careful discussion, responsible commissions of Lutheran and Reformed representatives have concluded that our two communions do fundamentally agree on the gospel and on the sacraments of baptism and the Lord's Supper. We reaffirm these agreements, in particular the conclusions reached in *Marburg Revisited* in America (1966) and the Leuenberg Agreement in Europe (1973). We do not imagine that all differences in eucharistic doctrine between (and within) our two communions have thereby disappeared or become negligible, but we maintain that the remaining differences should be recognized as acceptable diversities within one Christian faith.[4]

4.2 The Christian doctrine of the Lord's Supper needs to present the clearest and fullest possible witness to the profound meaning of the Supper. We maintain that traditional Lutheran and Reformed doctrinal concerns are still valuable to help the wider Christian community appreciate the full significance of our Lord's Supper. We acknowledge meanwhile that our doctrinal formulations themselves cannot altogether grasp the fullness either of the mystery of Christ's gift of himself in the Supper or of our experience of communion with him.

## Practice

5. Mutual recognition of the Lord's Supper by our two communions also involves reconciliation in regard to our appreciation of each other's eucharistic practice.

5.1 As churches of the Reformation we share many important features in our respective practices of Holy Communion. Over the centuries of our separation, however, there have developed characteristic differences in practice, and these still tend to make us uncomfortable at each other's celebration of the Supper. These differences can be discerned in several areas, for example, in liturgical style and liturgical details, in our verbal interpretations of our practices, in the emotional patterns involved in our experience of the Lord's Supper, and in the implications we find in the Supper for the life and mission of the church and of its individual members.[5]

5.2 We affirm our conviction, however, that these differences should be recognized as acceptable diversities within one Christian faith. Both of our communions, we maintain, need to grow in appreciation of our diverse eucharistic traditions, finding mutual enrichment in them. At the same time both need to grow toward a further deepening of our common experience and expression of the mystery of our Lord's Supper.

## Ministry

6. Reconciliation at the Lord's Table also involves mutual recognition of our public ministries, since each church is responsible for authorizing and publicly regulating the celebration of the Lord's Supper.[6]

## Conclusion

7. We agree that there are no substantive matters concerning the Lord's Supper which should divide us. We urge Lutheran and Reformed churches to affirm and encourage the practice of eucharistic fellowship with one another.

## Notes

1. On the variety of names applied to this sacrament, see n.3 of *IA*, p. 146 above.

2. "...the forgiveness of sins, life, and salvation are given to us in the sacrament, for where there is forgiveness of sins, there are also life and salvation" (SC 6:6,*BkC* 352). Both Martin Luther and John Calvin stressed the benefits of the sacrament. Luther described the sacrament as "rich in grace...full of benefit and salvation, as well as innumerable and unspeakable blessings" (Admonition Concerning the Sacrament," *Luther's Works*, Vol. 38 [Philadelphia: Fortress Press, 1971], p. 105). Among such benefits and blessings he included being "present to the praise and glory of my God" (p. 109), having "faith and love stimulated, renewed and strengthened" (pp. 125f.), "the heart is refreshed anew in its love of the neighbor and is made strong and equipped to do all good works and to resist sin and all temptations" (p. 126). Calvin speaks of the Lord's Supper as a "spiritual banquet, wherein Christ attests himself to be the life-giving bread, upon which our souls feed unto true and blessed immortality" (*Institutes of the Christian Religion* IV,

xvii, 1, ed. J.T. McNeill [Philadelphia: Westminster Press, 1960], p. 1360). "Godly souls can gather great assurance and delight from this Sacrament; in it they have a witness of our growth into one body with Christ such that whatever is his may be called ours." We are assured of participation in eternal life, the Kingdom of Heaven, and forgiveness of sin (*Inst.* IV, xvii, 2, pp. 1361-62). Participation in the one body of Christ inspires "purity and holiness of life" and "love, peace, and concord"; so the Sacrament is a "bond of love" arousing mutual love in the community (*Inst.* IV, xvii, 38, pp. 1415-15). For Calvin's view of the real presence of Christ in the Eucharist, see *Inst.* IV, xvii, 1-33 esp. 7, 10, 14, 18, 19, 31, 32.

The Savoy Declaration (Williston Walker, ed., *The Creeds and Platforms of Congregationalism* [Boston: Pilgrim Press, 1960], p. 400) corresponds with the WC also on the Lord's Supper (see n.2, Joint Statement on Justification). The CA in the UCC of course offers the same tradition as noted here.

3. "God's reconciliation in Jesus Christ is the ground of the peace, justice, and freedom among nations which all powers of government are called to serve and defend. The church, in its own life, is called to practice the forgiveness of enemies and to commend to the nations as practical politics the search for cooperation and peace" (C'67, *BC* 9.45). "The reconciliation of man [sic] through Jesus Christ makes it plain that enslaving poverty in a world of abundance is an intolerable violation of God's good creation. Because Jesus identified himself with the needy and exploited, the cause of the world's poor is the cause of his disciples" (C'67, *BC* 9.46). "The Holy Communion is a service celebrating reconciliation. It is a Means of Grace by which the common life of God's new community is fostered and sustained and this new people is propelled into the world to engage in the mission which they have been given" (A Statement on Communion Practices, I.6, Appendix 4, p. 78).

One of the summary statements on ethics formulated and adopted by both Lutheran and Reformed theologians states: "This world is the arena for Christian ethical service. The impersonal structures of power in modern society are morally ambiguous. While they tend to pervert the humanity of men [sic] and the proper use of things, they also offer untold possibilities for good. This situation compels us to search for new ways of loving our neighbors. Recent technological and sociological developments intensify the urgency for translating personal love into social justice" ("Christian Service in the Modern World," *Marburg Revisited*, ed. Paul C. Empie and James I. McCord [Minneapolis: Augsburg Publishing House, 1966], p. 177).

4. Insistence on the importance of affirming real presence and sacramental union is prominent in both Lutheran and Reformed traditions. II HC asserts that "by the work of Christ through the Holy Spirit they (the faithful) inwardly receive the flesh and blood of the Lord, and are thereby nourished unto life eternal. For the flesh and blood of Christ is the true food and drink unto life eternal; and Christ himself, since he was given for us and is our Savior, is the principal thing in the Supper..." (*BC* 5.196). Similarly the ScotsC announces that "we utterly condemn the vanity of those who affirm the sacraments to be nothing else than naked and bare signs," and insists that "...in the Supper rightly used, Christ Jesus is so joined with us that he becomes the very nourishment and food of our souls" (*BC* 3.21). CA 10 affirms "that the true body and blood of Christ are really present in the Supper of our Lord under the form of bread and wine and are there distributed and received" (*BkC* 34), which the Ap 10 expands: "that in the Lord's Supper the body and blood of Christ are truly and substantially present and are truly offered with those things that are seen, the bread and the wine. We are talking about the presence of the living Christ, knowing that 'death no longer has dominion over him'" (*BkC* 179-80).

The controversy has focused on the mode of Christ's presence in the sacrament. The signers of FC SD 7 rejected "the denial of an oral eating of the body and blood of Christ in the Supper, and the contrary teaching that in the Supper the body of Christ is partaken only spiritually through faith and that in the Supper our mouth receives only bread and wine" (*BkC* 589). The WC holds that "worthy receivers, outwardly partaking of the visible elements in this sacrament, do then also inwardly by faith, really and indeed, yet not carnally and corporally, but spiritually, receive and feed upon Christ crucified, and all benefits of his death; the body and blood of Christ being then not corporally or carnally in, with, or under the bread and wine; yet, as really, but spiritually, present to the faith of believers in that ordinance as the elements themselves are to their outward senses" (*BC* 6.152).

Both traditions were trying to protect and preserve the dynamic of authentic sacramental union between Christ, the believer, and the other faithful over against the opposing extremes of mere symbolic recollection and the magic of transubstantiation. Each tradition suspected that the other veered too far toward one of the unacceptable extremes.

In recent times scholars have approached the problems from fresh and helpful directions. For example, the Lutheran scholar Regin Prenter gives the expected emphasis on divine promise: "In every sacrament there is a divine *promissio* expressed in the Word which accompanies the sacrament. This *promissio* is the decisive factor. It is what makes the sacrament a sacrament." Then Prenter continues: "By virtue of understanding the word of the sacrament as *promissio* faith enters into the concept of the sacrament in the sense that it thus forms the real connection between the Word and the external element. For the external element is the confirmation of the promise. But only faith in the promise can receive the confirmation" (*Spiritus Creator*, trans. J.M. Jensen [Philadelphia; Muhlenberg Press, 1953], pp. 138f).

Oscar Cullmann writes: "[Christ's] presence is understood to be as real as possible. He comes to participate in the meal...In the early Church, the Lord's Supper involved the presence of Christ in its threefold relation with Easter, with the cult and the Parousia. Alternatively expressed, this presence is at one and the same time that of Christ risen, of Christ living, and of Christ who is to come" ("The Meaning of the Lord's Supper," *Essays on the Lord's Supper*, trans. J.G. Davies [Atlanta: John Knox Press, 1958], p. 15). Reformed Christians feel at home with such formulations. A contemporary Reformed declaration of faith affirms:

> The Word has not only been read and preached,
> But also seen, tasted, and touched.
>
> We believe Christ is present through the Spirit of the Church,
> He makes himself known to us as the one who stood in our place and
> conquered our death for us.
> He offers us his broken body and shed blood.
> We offer ourselves to him in return.
>
> A Declaration of Faith, chap. 6, lines 93-94,
> 112-18, PCUS, Atlanta, 1974

David Willis focuses on Christ's real presence in "The Eucharist in the Reformed Tradition," prepared for the Russian Orthodox/Reformed Consultation (Leningrad, 1976).

Wilhelm Niesel describes a meeting of the Confessional Synod of the Evangelical Church of the Old Prussian Union which met in Halle in 1937 and affirmed "Our Lord and Savior Jesus Christ...is Himself the gracious gift in the Supper He instituted in His church...The differences still existing between us in the doctrine of the Holy Supper concern the mode and form in which the Lord gives Himself in the supper. They do not touch the fact that the gift of the Supper is the Lord Himself." Niesel further reports on the theses published in 1957 after eight years of study by a commission of theologians from the Lutheran, Reformed, and Union churches which states: "The words spoken by our Lord Jesus Christ, in offering to us the bread and the cup, tell us what He Himself gives in this supper to all who came to it. He, the crucified and risen Lord, permits Himself in His body delivered to death for all and in His blood shed for all, to be taken by us through His promised Word with the bread and the wine, and thereby associates us, by the power of the Holy Spirit, with the victory of His Kingdom so that, by faith in His promise, we have forgiveness of sins, life and salvation" (*The Gospel and the Churches*, trans. D. Lewis [Philadelphia: Westminster Press, 1962], pp. 282-83).

These affirmations led Niesel to conclude the "theologians of the different Reformation Churches can today bear common testimony on the basis of Scripture about the meaning of the Lord's Supper," and "Membership of one or the other of the Reformation Churches therefore constitutes no ground for exclusion from celebration of the Lord's Supper," (ibid.). Subsequent Lutheran-Reformed affirmations such as *Marburg Revisited*, (1966), the Leuenberg Agreement

(1973), and the Lima statement on *Baptism, Eucharist and Ministry* (1982) encourage us to embrace similar conclusions.

The difficulty of translating theological concepts and religious insights from one language to another has been expressed throughout the history of the church as it has grown and expanded among all peoples and cultures. Biblical translators such as Luther and Calvin and their successors struggled with the problems of finding appropriate words and phrases in Latin, German, and French, for example, that would accurately represent the Hebrew and Greek originals.

The framers of the *BkC*, as well as authors of other Reformation confessional statements, also faced this dilemma. As the preface to the *BkC* affirms: "we repeat once again that we are not minded to manufacture anything new by this work of agreement or to depart in any way at all, either in content or in formulation, from the divine truth that our pious forebears and we have acknowledged and confessed in the past" (p. 13). Nevertheless, the preface acknowledges honest differences of opinion and interpretation which required "a general convention…to discuss in a thorough and friendly way" such differences with the intent that such "offensive differences might be settled and brought to a conclusion (consensus) without violation of divine truth…" (pp.4-6).

There is a recognition that in technical theological questions such as the relation of the idea of omnipresence to the Lord's Supper, it is advisable "to stay with the plain words of Christ." "This," they say, "is the surest and most edifying way as far as the common layman is concerned, for he cannot comprehend this discussion." (*BkC*, p. 10).

Furthermore, changes in scientific and philosophical outlooks from one period of history to another also present problems of "translating" traditional doctrines. The truth of God's revelation in Jesus Christ is changeless, but the human language which gives it doctrinal expression undergoes constant modification. We realize that while the sixteenth-century formulations of doctrines such as the real presence represent faithful articulations of the biblical message, they also were conditioned by the worldview of the period. Our world is strikingly different from that of Luther and Calvin and their contemporaries, and the words and phrases now used to interpret the mysteries of our faith may take on unintended meaning or lose their original import. The task of "translating" traditional doctrines into a language which mirrors the worldview of our times presents both a challenge and new possibilities. The challenge of setting ancient formulations in the context of twentieth-century thought is formidable. But it is possible that this process will shed new light on ancient texts. We believe that as this "translating" continues, Lutheran and Reformed Christians will increasingly discover that what divided their forebears in regard to the Lord's Supper need not be divisive; to the contrary, classical Reformed and Lutheran concerns over the real presence may come to be seen as complementary and enriching for the lives of both traditions.

This does not settle the matter, of course, but it suggests that the deepest articles of faith, in whatever language, are ultimately, as the theologians of the *Book of Concord* admit, in the realms of "inscrutable mystery."

In A Statement on Communion Practices both The American Lutheran Church and the Lutheran Church in America exhorted Lutherans to "…uphold the reality of Christ's presence in the Sacrament, his body and blood being given 'in, with and under' the bread and the wine, in order to affirm by these means his saving work for us." To this point the paper comments, "It is the responsibility of our churches to teach clearly this Lutheran doctrine of the Lord's Supper and to witness to it in dealing with other churches. Fulfilling the obligation to the truth in this way makes it possible to express the unity of the Church at the Lord's table with those who affirm the Real Presence of Christ in the Sacrament *but who use formulations to describe it other than those used in the Lutheran Confessions*" (p. 4; or pp. 76-77 of IA; emphasis added).

5. Considerable diversity in the practices of celebrating the Lord's Supper exists among congregations of both the Lutheran and Reformed traditions. Partly this is a consequence of denominational divergence; partly it reflects the impact of regional custom. In recent years the influence of liturgical renewal (including recovery of the liturgical heritage of the tradition) and of liturgical experimentation has increased the rate of diversity.

For example, some Reformed and UCC congregations stand or even are seated around the communion table for the distribution of the elements. The more usual method in the United States, however, is for the communicants to serve each other from trays passed down the pews.

Even this more usual custom is ambiguous to worshippers. Some regard it as simply an arrangement of convenience. For others it is a moving visual enactment of the priesthood of all believers.

Lutheran practice at the Supper also varies: communicants may come to the altar and stand or kneel; administration may be by table or continuous; stations in several parts of the building may be used; communicants may stand in a circle and administer the bread and wine to each other; use of the chalice is preferred, but many congregations use individual glasses; wine is the norm, but some congregations use grape juice; either leavened or unleavened bread is used; intinction is occasionally used; it is normal to include lay persons in the distribution of the elements, but in many congregations only the pastor distributes. Lutherans have experienced a rich growth in practice over the past twenty-five years.

There are central features that are characteristic of Reformed observance as testified by the constitutional documents of the churches:

Regular or frequent celebrations of the sacrament: "at least once every three months" (RCA *BCO* 1.1.2.6.c); "frequently but at least quarterly" (PCUS *BCO* 211-12); "as frequently as each Lord's Day, and at least as often as quarterly" (PC[U.S.A.], *BO* S-3.05005); cf. also *Confession of Faith* of the Cumberland Presbyterian Church, p. 160, 18.

The sacrament is held in high regard—"an essential part of the public ministry of the church," PC(U.S.A.) *BO* S 3.0100; cf. also the WC chap. 27, 1, *BC* 6.134; UPCUSA, *BO* 21.

The unworthy are to be warned: PC (U.S.A.) *BO* S-3.0500d; cf. RCA "Orders for Public Worship," *Liturgy and Psalms*, p. 77; "The minister shall also warn the unprepared, the self-sufficient, the unrepentant, not to approach the holy table" (PCUS *BCO* 211-17).

The elements used are bread and wine, although many congregations substitute unfermented grape juice: PC(U.S.A.) *BO* s-3.0500e; *Confession of Faith* of the Cumberland Presbyterian Jesus Christ, pp. 161f., n.20; PCUS *BCO*, 211-18.

The distribution of the elements is preceded by an *epiklesis* and the repetition of the scriptural words of institution—"the minister...shall ask that the Holy Spirit sanctify the Sacrament to the people's benefit" PC(U.S.A.) *BO* S-3.0500F, G; PCUS *BCO* 211-12,18, "The invocation of the Holy Spirit signifies and seeks to ensure that what takes place in the sacrament is not accomplished by human endeavor, but is done by the grace of God" UPCUSA *BO*, 21.03. "Great God, give your Holy Spirit in the breaking of bread, so that we may be drawn together, joined in Christ the Lord, receive new life, and remain his glad and faithful people until we feast with him in glory" (The *Worshipbook* [Philadelphia: Westminster Press, 1970], p. 36).

The norm of Lutheran practice for the LCA and the ALC is contained in A Statement on Communion Practices, adopted in 1978 (Appendix 4 of IA). There is no comparable document for the AELC.

The Supper is described as a sacrament, "God's gift of Christ's presence and love to us"; "service celebrating reconciliation"; "a means of grace by which the common life of God's new community is fostered and sustained," and "this new people is propelled into the world to engage in the mission..."

Admission is open to the baptized who in the judgment of the church are ready to participate. Criteria for readiness include: "simple trust that the Crucified and Risen Lord is here truly present"; "basic understanding and appreciation of the gifts..."; "acceptance of one's place as a communicant in the fellowship of believers"; "self-examination...appropriate to the level of maturity and recognition of the need for forgiveness."

Corporate confession and absolution are of "great value" and a "normal preparation." Opportunity for private confession is recommended.

Participation as a visitor in non-Lutheran settings is "proper" and "a matter of personal judgment." Five criteria are offered. Lutheran clergy may be involved as presiding or assisting ministers in other churches if a "reciprocal relationship between the congregation and clergy involved should prevail."

Celebration of Holy Communion is recommended on every Sunday and on other festivals, and on weekdays for those "whose schedules make Sunday communion difficult."

Lutherans use the elements of bread and wine. The elements, according to the LBW, may be set aside by the words of institution alone, a prayer and words of institution, or a eucharistic prayer.

6. This brief section intends to direct attention to the companion statement by the Lutheran-Reformed dialogue entitled Joint Statement on Ministry, pp. 159-69 below.

\* \* \*

## JOINT STATEMENT ON MINISTRY

### Our Common Heritage

1. Traditions we represent are *rooted in a common understanding* of the gospel which developed at the time of the Reformation.

1.1 What we hold in common is fundamental to both Reformation traditions. For both Lutheran and Reformed believers the cornerstone of faith is expressed in the Reformation's Confession of *salvation through Christ alone*. Standing alongside of it are those other great affirmations of the sixteenth century, namely, faith alone (*sola fide*), grace alone (*sola gratia*), and Scripture alone (*sola scriptura*). That which is the ground for salvation is also the foundation for ministry. Ministry in our heritage derives from and points to the Christ who alone is sufficient to save. Centered in the proclamation of the word and administration of the sacraments, it is built on the affirmation that the benefits of Christ are known only through faith, grace, and Scripture. Ministry in the Reformation perspective always draws attention away from itself to the Lord it serves and at the same time to those the Lord loves and seeks to redeem.[1]

### The Servant Ministry of Jesus and Our Ministry

2. There is but *one ministry, that of Jesus Christ*. In all its aspects this was a *servant* ministry. All ministry in the church derives from the ministry of its Lord and is also characterized by service.

2.1 The relationship of the ministry of Jesus to ours has been well expressed by the dictum that speaks of the ministry of the church participating in the great ministry of its Lord. As he is the truth which frees men and women, so the church through its ministry by the power of the Holy Spirit proclaims this liberating truth in word and deed. As he is the sacrificial lamb offered for forgiveness and reconciliation, so the church announces this free gift of love and acts as an agent of healing and reconciliation. As he is the hidden ruler of the world, the church reveals to humankind its true Lord, calls all people to a life of worship, and participates in the divine acts of justice and mercy which witness to God's sovereign power and majesty.[2]

2.2 The biblical term "servant" best captures the understanding of ministry we hold in common. To speak of a servant ministry is redundant, for the word "ministry" *means* service in its own right. At the same time, it is necessary to tolerate this redundancy and join the words, for the unhappy truth is that today the word "ministry" does not always connote service.[3]

2.3 This is unfortunate, for the only way to participate in the ministry of the one who came not to be served but to serve is through engaging in a servant ministry. The writers of the New Testament saw Jesus as the servant par excellence. His life is presented as one of perfect obedience to God and consequently one of humble service to humanity. The Lord taught his disciple that greatness in his kingdom means becoming a servant of all (Mark 10:44). "Jesus made his own the nature, condition and cause of the whole human race, giving himself as a sacrifice for all. Jesus' life of service, his death and resurrection, are the foundation of a new community which is built up continually by the good news of the Gospel and the gifts of the sacraments" (*BEM*, Ministry, I.I).[4]

## Ministry and the Kingdom of God

3. Christian ministry is oriented to the kingdom of God. In the power of the Spirit it serves Christ both in the church and the world by seeking to manifest signs of the salvation to come.

3.1 The Holy Spirit calls, gathers, enlightens, and sanctifies a people to serve the lordship of Christ (the *regnum Christi*), which will come in its fullness only when Christ returns at the end of history. The kingdom of God is truly present here and now through signs created when the Spirit of Christ engages the people of God in the servant tasks of the Lord. By these signs the world is given testimony of the church's belief in the triumph of God's love and witness to its faith in the advent of a new age when all things shall be made new. These signs are established when the Church, in obedience to its Lord and in the power of the Spirit, becomes an agent of justice, mercy, peace, healing, and reconciliation in this world. But the signs of the new age are also present when within the church lives are reborn, healed, reconciled, and sanctified; when in Christian community persons are knit in love, united in service, and joined in proclaiming the gospel; when God's people gather to acknowledge their dependence on grace, openly confess Christ, and publicly glorify the triune God.[5]

## The Ministry of the Entire People of God

4. The entire baptized people of God, the body of Christ, is called to participate in Christ's servant ministry. The foundation for this vision of ministry is to be found in the Reformation doctrines of the universal priesthood of all believers and Christian vocation.

4.1 The servant ministry is the people of God engaged in God's mission (the *missio Dei*), the service of the kingdom. The call to this service is not limited to those who hold office in the church but is extended to all who are baptized. As stated above,the cornerstone for the Reformation doctrine of ministry is salvation through Christ alone. Union with Christ in baptism carries with it the call, power, authority, and promise of gifts requisite for the participation in his servant ministry. For example, immediately following the imposition of water, according to the baptismal liturgy of the Reformed Church in America, the officant declares: "In the name of the Lord Jesus Christ, the only King and Head of his Church, I declare that this child is now received into the visible membership of the Holy Catholic Church, and is engaged to confess the faith of Christ crucified, and to be his faithful servant unto his/her life's end." Here all distinctions are rejected. Male and female, young and old, impaired and unimpaired, educated and uneducated, rich and poor, people of every color, nation, and tongue—all who are baptized and confess Christ are also called to be part of the servant ministry. This ministry is the ministry of the entire people of God.[6]

4.2 The Reformation spoke of this doctrine as the universal priesthood of all believers. Formulated by Martin Luther, the notion of the universal priesthood was recognized as profoundly biblical by Reformation theologians, and it consequently became critical for the development of ministry in both traditions. All Christians are called and empowered by the Holy Spirit to be priests to their neighbors. This means that worship, intercession, service, and witness are not reserved for the clergy but are the responsibility of all believers. The pastoral office is instituted to strengthen and support the community of believers.[7]

4.3 The scope of the servant ministry of the entire people of God becomes apparent, however, only when the Reformation doctrine of vocation is also taken into consideration. Both the Lutheran and Reformed theologians of the Reformation rejected the medieval distinction between higher and lower occupations. God calls men and women to employment not only in the church but in the secular world as well. Any task that contributes to the preservation of the created order, the well-being of humankind, and the administration of justice is pleasing to God. Christians are called to engage their vocations honestly, justly, and as a service to God and neighbor. Then even the most humble and mundane tasks are rightly viewed as service to God.[8]

4.4 The implications for the mission of God of these two Reformation doctrines are far-reaching. The ministry of every baptized Christian is exercised through vocation in both church and world. Since the lordship of Christ is the priestly rule of the one who offers himself as the sacrificial lamb, the universal priesthood represents the self-offering of the people of God in the service of the kingdom. The Spirit bestows diverse gifts on God's people not only to build up the church but also to establish signs of the kingdom in the world. The church aids in the identification and development of these gifts both to strengthen the bond of love within its own fellowship and its witness in word and deed in the world. The church also learns from those who work in the secular order about pressing human needs and strategies to address them. Persons at work in the world are equipped by the church for their vocation in the larger society, but they in turn help to shape the church's understanding of its mission.

## The Pastoral Office

5. In the context of the ministry of the whole people of God, the pastoral office is accorded special servant responsibility.

5.1 To affirm the servant ministry of the entire people of God and the Reformation doctrines of the universal priesthood and Christian vocation does not mean that all are called to the same places and tasks in the church. Lutheran and Reformed Christians alike can agree with the Lima document, *Baptism, Eucharist and Ministry*, when it states: "In order to fulfil its mission, the Church needs persons who are publicly and continually responsible for pointing to its fundamental dependence on Jesus Christ, and thereby provide, within a multiplicity of gifts, a focus of its unity" (*Ministry*, IIA.8). For both the Lutheran and Reformed traditions the ordained office of pastor has borne much of the responsibility for this task.[9]

5.2 To set the pastoral office (minister of the word) in the context of the servant ministry of the baptized people of God does not deny its special character. Our Confessions speak of this as a divinely appointed office. While we do not contend that one particular form of this office has divine sanction to the exclusion of others, we do hold the office itself to be an expression of the will of God for the church. Indeed, the Reformation understanding of word and sacraments as means of grace is very closely tied to the Lutheran and Reformed doctrines of the pastoral office. God deigns to use ordained ministers as instruments to mediate grace through the preaching of the word and the administration of the sacraments.[10]

## The Servant Ministry of the Pastoral Office

6. The pastoral office is exalted by the service that characterizes it; in its every aspect this office is expressive of the servant ministry.

6.1 The pastoral ministry has been termed a high calling, and rightly so, but only because it serves a Lord exalted through humiliation and raised gloriously from the shame and ignominy of crucifixion. The paradoxical character of Jesus' ministry shapes the pastoral office. Its power is manifested not in strength but weakness; its authority does not reside in itself but is derived from its Lord. In a world that extols autonomy, the pastoral ministry is openly dependent; in an age that insists on pursuing its self-centered interests, this office finds its meaning in serving others. The exalted lowliness of the pastoral ministry is not only its glory but its freedom as well. Luther's dictum that the truly free person is one in servitude to Christ has special meaning in this connection.[11]

6.2 As effected in the universal priesthood, every aspect of the pastoral office should be marked by its participation in the servant ministry of Christ. Standing under the authority of the word, this ministry is exercised in concert with the congregation in witness to the world. The shape of the pastoral office as our churches have experienced it since the Reformation has many commonalities. The styles of exercise of pastoral ministry have always been adapted to changing historical and cultural circumstances. This process of adaptation of style and form will continue though the fundamental purpose remains. The pastoral office with special responsibility for upbuilding the congregation is a servant ministry enabling the baptized to become a servant community in the world. Pastors use their gifts and training to assist all the members of the community to grow in faith, to minister to one another in love, to discern their special gifts, and to develop their knowledge and skills for ministry. In this way the community can become one prepared to serve the world. But it is also for the sake of the world, so that the people of God may truly serve the Lord who claims sovereignty over all of creation, working for the transformation of the whole created order according to the will of God.

## Mission and Order

7. Structure serves the mission of the church.

7.1 One of the points at which the Lutheran and Reformed traditions have differed is church order. We are convinced that these differences are not church-dividing. Within each tradition, moreover, there is considerable diversity in order. Both our traditions have insisted that church order is not an end in itself and that no one order is biblically mandated to the exclusion of all others. Were one to speak of a biblical imperative on this matter, then it would be that structure must serve the mission of the church.[12]

## Ministry and Ordinations

8. Lutheran and Reformed Christians are in basic agreement concerning the nature and function of the ordained pastoral office. Churches of the Reformed tradition have also ordained elders and deacons.

8.1 The ordering of the serving community can be discussed under two headings: ordination and oversight. In regard to ordination to the pastoral office there are broad areas of agreement uniting Lutheran and Reformed Christians. Both traditions assert that men and women alike are eligible for this office but also must be called, examined for fitness, educated theologically, and approved by the appropriate judicatory. Both understand ordination to be the induction to an office in the church which carries with it certain necessary functions. For both Lutherans and Reformed ordination requires prayer and the laying on of hands and is viewed as a rite by which the candidate enters an office in the church universal. Reordination is rare in both traditions. The authority of the office is the word of God, and this is also its content. Both traditions have insisted that this apostolic office, which finds its center in the preaching of the word and the administration of the sacraments, be anchored in the Confessions and creeds of the church.

8.2 At the same time the Reformed tradition has set the pastoral office in a broader ministerium which includes ordained elders who share the government and oversight of the church and ordained deacons who are given responsibility for ministries of compassion and justice directed to those in need both in the church and in the world. While the Lutheran tradition has restricted ordination to the ministry of word and sacraments, it commissions or sets apart lay persons for particular ministries of leadership and governance in the church and compassion and justice in both church and world.[13]

## Ministry and Oversight

9. Both the Lutheran and Reformed traditions agree that oversight is necessary for the well-being of the church and the prosperity of its ministry.

9.1 Our two traditions also agree in the understanding that appropriate structures are requisite for proper oversight to be given to the church of Jesus Christ. The nomenclature, organization, and mode of operation may differ, but the objective of strengthening the church and giving guidance to its servant ministry is identical.[14]

9.2 Both Lutheran and Reformed traditions have believed it important for congregations to be related to one another. Structures have been developed in both traditions by which this has been accomplished and the oversight of congregations corporately exercised. In neither case is governance limited to pastors. In the Reformed tradition elders share with ministers the task of exercising oversight; in the Lutheran tradition lay leaders elected by the congregations share with those holding the pastoral office the responsibility of overseeing congregations on the synodical or district levels.

9.3 The title "bishop" is rarely used in Reformed churches to refer to one who exercises oversight, while it has become common in the Lutheran tradition. It should be noted that Lutheran polity, like Reformed, is constitutional, establishing procedures for electing and removing bishops, defining their responsibilities and authority, and expressing the manner in which those holding this office shall be held accountable. All the functions of the Lutheran bishop in North America are carried out in relationship to a synod, district, or church body.

Reformed Christians have on occasion spoken of their presbyteries (or associations or classes) as corporate bishops. Presbyteries or classes, comprised of ministers of the word and elders who share equally in the work, exercise oversight over a limited number of congregations clustered in a specified region. This oversight includes the supervising and ordaining of candidates for ministry, approving the call of a congregation to a minister, examining its provisions to see that the pastor is properly cared for, determining that a congregation is being properly served by its pastor, disciplining ministers, and granting the right of a congregation to acquire and dispose of property.

The bishop, together with the synod or district in the Lutheran tradition and the presbytery in the Reformed, bears responsibility for the general well-being of the congregations to which he or she gives oversight and assures that the activities of the churches are undertaken in an orderly fashion.[15]

9.4 Both our ecclesial families claim to stand in the historical and apostolic tradition by which the good news of the gospel is given witness generation after generation. Both traditions assert that proper oversight is requisite to ensure that the word is truly preached and sacraments rightly administered.

## Conclusion

10. We agree that there are no substantive matters concerning ministry which should divide us. We urge Lutheran and Reformed churches to affirm and recognize the validity of one another's ministries.[16]

# Notes

1. The Lutheran and Reformed Confessions of the sixteenth and seventeenth centuries abound in references to the *solus Christus*. For specific references see the frequently quoted first question of the HCat, *BC* 4.001, as well as Q.29 and Q.30 (4.029 and 4.030); the II HC which speaks of God being invoked ónly through Christ (*BC* 5.024) and Jesus as the only means of salvation (*BC* 5.077); and further the BelC, articles 20-22, and the WC, chap. 8, *BC* 6.043-6.050. For references in the Lutheran symbols see the CA 4 on justification, *BkC* 30, and also CA 21, *BkC* 47, 2-4; Ap 4, *BkC* 107-68, where in an extended discussion of the Reformation doctrine of justification the *solus Christus* is constantly asserted; and further the SA II, I, BkC 292.

For the Lutheran confessional affirmation of the *sola fide*, see CA 4, *BkC* 30; Ap 4, *BkC* 107-68; SA II, I, *BkC* 292. For the same doctrine in the Reformed standards see HCat Q.20 and Q.21, *BC* 4.020 and 4.021, and Q.53 and Q.61, *BC* 4.053 and 4.061; II HC, chaps. 15 and 16, *BC* 5.106-5.123; BelC, article 22; WC, chap. 11, *BC* 6.060 and 6.061. The doctrine of the *sola gratia* appears in many of the citations already given but see also Luther's LC on the third article of the Apostles' Creed for a forceful exposition of the relation of salvation to word and Spirit (*BkC* 415-16,##38-42). For references in the Reformed confessional statements in addition to the above, see HCat Q.60, *BC* 4.060, and II HC, chaps. 10 and 14, *BC* 5.052 and 5.094. Since it is well known that the *sola scriptura* is the foundational principle both for the theology of the Reformation and for both Lutheran and Reformed confessional statements, no specific citations will be offered.

In regard to the UCC position, see the introduction to An Invitation to Action and n.2 of the Joint Statement of Justification. The *sola scriptura* principle is quite clear also from the Congregational side: "The partes [*sic*] of Church-Government are all of them exactly described in the word of God...So that it is not left in the power of men, officers, Churches, or any state in the world to add, or diminish, or alter anything in the least measure therein" (Cambridge Platform, p. 203).

Cf. CA 7, *BkC* 32: "Also they teach that one holy church is to continue forever. The church is the congregation of saints, in which the Gospel is rightly taught and the Sacraments rightly administered. And to that true unity of the church, it is enough to agree concerning the doctrine of the Gospel and the administration of the Sacraments. Nor is it necessary that human traditions, that is, rites, or ceremonies, instituted by men, should be everywhere alike. As Paul says: 'One faith, one baptism, one God and Father of all.'" Cf. II HC, chap. 17, *BC* 5.141, a parallel Reformed statement.

2. Concerning the point that the ministry of the church participates in the ministry of the ascended Christ, see Ap 7 and 8, ##28 and 47, *BkC* 173 and 177, where the pastoral office is described as standing in Christ's stead. This is also implicit in CA 5 and 8, cf. 28, #22, *BkC* 31,33,84. See also the LCA Constitution, Article II (Confession of Faith), section 2: "In [Jesus Christ], the Word Incarnate, God imparts Himself to His people"; Article IV (Nature of the Church, section 1: "All power in the Church belongs to our Lord Jesus Christ, its head. All actions of this church [i.e., the LCA] are to be carried out under His rule and authority" (cf. ALC Constitution and Bylaws, 4.11). For the Reformed Confessions on this: II HC chaps. 14 and 18, *BC* 5.096-5.100 and 5.142-168, passim; BelC, articles 34 and 35 where the ministry of Christ is described as being effected by human agents; WC, chap. 25, *BC* 6.127, and the C'67, *BC* 9.33. See also the Preamble to the RCA BCO, p. 9, where it is stated: "The entire ministerial or pastoral office is summed up in Jesus Christ himself, in such a way that he is, in a sense, the only one holding that office." With the exception of the reference to C'67, these citations refer to the pastoral office; the principle expressed here, however, is applicable *mutatis mutandis* to every ministry in and through the church.

3. For the servant ministry see II HC, chaps. 18 and 16, *BC* 5.155, but also 5.114, C'67 speaks of the risen Christ as the savior of all persons and of those "...joined to him by faith...set right with God and commissioned to serve as his reconciling community" (*BC* 9.10); the Lutheran Confessions refer to ordained ministers as "church servants" (*Kirchendiener*). The 1970 LCA statement on the doctrine of the ministry, position statements, 1: "The Church exists to bring the grace of God in Jesus Christ to bear upon the whole of life. It is uniquely responsi-

ble for the redemptive relationship of faith to which all of its other concerns are subordinate, and it takes its place with other humanitarian servants to ameliorate the human situation." Cf. Preface, paragraphs 3 and 8, 1970 *LCA Minutes*, pp. 431ff., 428f., 430.

4. "The life, death, resurrection, and promised coming of Jesus Christ has set the pattern for the church's mission. His life as man involves the church in the common life of men. His service to men commits the church to work for every form of human well-being. His suffering makes the church sensitive to all the sufferings of mankind so that it sees the face of Christ in the faces of men in every kind of need. His crucifixion discloses to the church God's judgment on man's inhumanity to man and the awful consequences of its own complicity in injustice. In the power of the risen Christ and the hope of his coming the church sees the promise of God's renewal of man's life in society and God's victory over all wrong" C'67, *BC* 9.32. ALC "Definition of Terms" (for interpreting the constitution and bylaws, in *Handbook of the ALC*, 1983 ed., p. 12); "*Ministry*—The witness and service performed by this Church, its member congregations and their members in carrying out the mission given by Jesus Christ our Lord. *Mission*—The participation of the Church—its members, congregations, and other structures—in the redemptive work of the Triune God to bring wholeness to all persons, society, and his creation." LCA Constitution, Article V (Objects and Powers), section 1; "This church lives to be the instrument of the Holy Spirit in obedience to the commission of its Lord, and specifically a. To proclaim the Gospel through Word and Sacraments, to relate that Gospel to human need in every situation, and to extend the ministry of the Gospel to all the world...h. To lift its voice in concord and to work in concert with forces for good, cooperating with church and other groups participating in activities that promote justice, relieve misery, and reconcile the estranged."

5. While the understanding of the prominence of the kingdom of God in the New Testament and its relationship to the church and God's mission in the world largely developed after the period when the confessional statements of the Reformation were written, these documents are not without a sense of the importance of the concept of the kingdom of God and the call of the church to mission. See, for example, WC, chaps. 25 and 35, *BC* 6.126 and 6.175; BelC, article 36; HCat, Q.123, *BC* 4.123. For the kingdom in Lutheran documents of the sixteenth century: CA 17, *BkC* 38f; Ap 7 and 8, 12-19, *BkC* 170f; Ap 12, 176, *BkC* 210; and Ap 16, 2,*BkC* 222; SC, Creed, Second Article, *BkC* 345; LC, Lord's Prayer, Second Petition, sections 49-58, *BkC* 426-428.

6. "We believe that all members of the church are royal priests, enjoying full and free access to the throne of grace with no mediator save Jesus Christ. In calling a pastor to preach the Word of God and to administer the Sacraments in their midst and on their behalf, the members of a congregation exercise their royal priesthood and in no sense surrender it. The privilege and responsibility of ministering to the saints of God, of proclaiming his glory to all men, and of living victoriously in all the relationships of life, remain the privilege and responsibility of all members of the church." (From the ALC's *United Testimony on Faith and Life* [Part I, VI, *Handbook of the ALC*, 1983 ed., p. 153], an approved document between the uniting churches at their conventions in 1952, frequently referred to on matters of doctrine).

7. II HC seems to contradict the point made here when it insists that there is a distinction which must be drawn between the priesthood of all believers and ministry, the latter not being common to all Christians (*BC* 5.153). Ministry in this context refers to the pastoral office, and there is no intention here to suggest that some Christians participate in no ministry. The Reformed Confessions, while not often employing the phrase "priesthood of all believers," make much of the Christian's responsibility to serve the neighbor. The ScotsC ties this to admission to the Lord's Table (chap. 23, *BC* 3.23); cf, II HC, article 16, *BC* 5.114; see also the explications of the commandments in several of the Reformed Confessions. In the Lutheran Confessions the concept of the priesthood of all believers appears but only obliquely. To the church corporately, which is the royal priesthood instituted by God, has been given the gospel or the keys; therefore, "the church retains the right of electing and ordaining ministers" (Melanchthon's "Treatise on the Power and Primacy of the Pope," section 72, cf. 60-72 and 24, *BkC* 332, cf. 330-32 and 324). The ALC's *United Testimony on Faith and Life*, Part II, II, pp. 7-8 (*Handbook of the ALC*, 1983 ed., pp. 155-57) directly addresses the relation of the priesthood of believers and the public office of the ministry.

"The church will not restrain but will rather encourage all its members to private study of the Word of God, to bear Christian witness in word and in deed; to seek opportunities for mutual edification; to share in the teaching ministry, locally and in the church at large, when requested through regular channels; and to accept the responsibility of public proclamation of the Word when appointed to do so by the properly constituted authority of the congregation or of the church body" (from the ALC's *United Testimony on Faith and Life*, Part II, II [*Handbook of the ALC*, 1983 ed., p. 157], p. 9, an approved document between the uniting churches at their conventions in 1952, frequently referred to on matters of doctrine).

The Cambridge Platform (p. 208) speaks of a "mutual covenant" grounded "in the promises of Christ's special presence in the church; whence they have fellowship with him, and in him one with another" (p. 209).

8. It is interesting to note that while the Lutheran confessional statements of the sixteenth century abound in references to the doctrine of Christian vocation, the Confessions of the Reformed Reformation are silent on this matter, e.g., CA 26, *BkC* 65; CA 27, *BkC* 72-73; Ap 27, *BkC* 275; Ap 23, *BkC* 244; Ap 15, *BkC* 219. The silence of the Reformed Confessions on Christian vocation does not stem from an understanding that differs from the Lutheran. By the time the "second generation" of the Reformation had appeared on the scene, it was no longer necessary to assert this doctrine; it was assumed. There is mention of the doctrine in II HC, 19, *BC* 5.250; cf. C'67, *BC* 9.35-38.

Limited in scope though it was, the early congregationalist understanding of the ministry of the laity was strong. From the Cambridge Platform (p. 209) a fairly consistent line can be drawn to the present emphasis in the UCC on "the ministry of the laity" (*Minutes/Thirteenth General Synod/United Church of Christ*, 27 June-1 July 1981, p. 53).

9. There is no question that both the Reformed and Lutheran Confessions of the Reformation period called for a "set-apart" pastoral office. For Reformed references see: BelC, article 31; II HC, 18, *BC* 5.142-43; WC, chaps. 14 and 25, *BC* 6.070 and 6.127. The Lutheran Ap 13, 12f., speaks plainly on this: "The church has the command to appoint ministers; to this we must subscribe wholeheartedly, for we know that God approves this ministry and is present in it. It is good to extol the ministry of the Word with every possible kind of praise..." (*BkC* 212). More colorfully, from the preface to Luther's LC, section 6: "Indeed, even among the nobility there are some louts and skinflints who declare that we can do without pastors and preachers from now on because we have everything in books and can learn it all by ourselves. So they blithely let parishes fall into decay..." (*BkC* 359). These two quotations may be allowed to speak for the host of references to the necessity of the pastoral office in the Lutheran Confessions.

10. The necessity of a pastoral office is clearly taught in the Confessions of the Reformation; the form of that office, however, is not presented as a confessional matter.

11. Both Lutheran and Reformed Confessions teach that the authority of the pastoral office derives from the Lord, or the Word; cf. II HC, chap. 18, *BC* 5.165, for example, with Ap 28, 18, *BkC* 284.

Cambridge Platform (p. 209) sees the ministerial office derived from the Lord Jesus Christ as the *supreme* power in the church.

12. The churches of both traditions have since the time of the Reformation ordained their ministers in a rite which included the laying on of hands. "And those who are elected are to be ordained...with public prayer and laying on of hands" (II HC, chap. 18, *BC* 5.151; cf. C'67, *BC* 9.39). From the SA 3, 10, 3; "Accordingly, as we are taught by the examples of the ancient churches and Fathers, we shall and ought ourselves ordain suitable persons to this office"(*BkC* 314). See also Ap 13, 7-13, where ordination (with the laying on of hands) is presented in relation to the ministry of the Word (*BkC* 212).

For the teachings of the Lutheran Confessions concerning the apostolicity of the pastoral office, see Ap. 28, 18, *BkC*, p. 284; "Treatise on the Power and Primacy of the Pope," section 26 where, commenting on Matt. 16:18, Melanchthon states: "Besides,the ministry of the New Testament is not bound to place and persons, as the Levitical priesthood is, but is spread abroad through the whole world and exists wherever God gives his gifts, apostles, prophets, pastors, teachers. Nor is this ministry valid because of any individual's authority but because of the Word given by Christ" (*BkC* 324); Ap 7 and 8, 28, *BkC* 173. For the Reformed confessional statements: II HC, chap. 18, *BC* 5.147; HCat, Questions 83-85, *BC* 4.083-85; II HC, chap. 14, *BC* 5.096.

Consistently from the Cambridge Platform (ordination by "imposition of hands," p. 215) to the UCC *Constitution and Bylaws* (setting "apart by prayer and the laying on of hands," p. 5), there has been the same understanding of the rite of ordination.

13. For a description of office, ordination, and oversight in the Reformed tradition, see the essay, "Office and Ordination in the Reformed Tradition," by Paul R. Fries, which is found in Appendix 6, of IA.

14. It is remarkable that the question of oversight, which occasioned extensive discussion in the Lutheran confessional statements, receives so little comment in those of the Reformed tradition. References in the Lutheran BkC are so numerous that they need not be listed here. The II HC does state: "Nevertheless, for the sake of preserving order some one of the ministers called the assembly together, proposed matters to be laid before it, gathered the opinions of the others, in short, to the best of man's ability took precaution lest any confusion should arise." Thus, the II HC concluded, order is to be preserved (chap. 18, *BC* 5.161). In the Reformed tradition the form which oversight takes has rarely been a confessional issue.

Depending on what one means by "oversight," it is fair to say that in the Congregationalist strand of the United Church of Christ the form oversight takes has constantly been a "confessional" issue.

15. Today it is only in Hungary that the Reformed Church has bishops.

16. "Christian faith seeks fellowship, that is, the discovery and the practice of this spiritual fellowship with other Christians. It laments isolation; it yearns for communion. Christian faith seeks fellowship in prayer, in corporate worship, in the Communion, in doing the Lord's work, and even in suffering for the faith" (from the ALC's *United Testimony on Faith and Life*, Part II, VI[*Handbook of the ALC*, 1983 ed., p. 161], p. 2, an approved document between the uniting churches at their conventions in 1952, frequently referred to on matters of doctrine).

# Lutheran-Conservative/Evangelical Declaration*

## Introduction

In March 1978 the Division of Theological Studies of the Lutheran Council in the U.S.A.[1] passed a recommendation that a Lutheran-Conservative/Evangelical dialogue be arranged by staff. The recommendation was subsequently adopted by the council in May 1978. (The original request to give consideration to theological conversations with Conservative/Evangelicals was referred to the Council by the Lutheran Church in America in November 1974.)

Because no Conservative/Evangelical common agency corresponding to the Lutheran Council existed to co-sponsor this dialogue, the division invited several Lutheran and Conservative/Evangelical educational institutions, mostly seminaries, in the Midwest to select members from their faculties to participate. This "seminary-cluster" structure differed from the usual arrangement in other division-sponsored dialogues, such as the Lutheran-Baptist dialogue, where member churches of the council named participants officially to represent their respective church bodies and Baptist members were selected by the North American Baptist Fellowship. Participants in the Lutheran-Conservative/Evangelical dialogue spoke for themselves as theologians in their own right, not as official representatives of their respective church bodies. The "seminary-cluster" approach was new, experimental, and successful.

A series of four meeting was held over a two-year period. The goals of the dialogue were to correct stereotypes that may have existed and to increase mutual understanding of one another's traditions, not to plan for consensus.

At the initial meeting held October 19-20, 1979, the topic for discussion was new birth and baptism. One of the most difficult questions was: What is an evangelical? Topics for subsequent meetings were faith and expe-

*The Covenant Quarterly 41 (1983) 5-7.

rience (April 25-26, 1980); the Church in the world, or embodiment; how Christian faith is made incarnate in the world (December 5-6, 1980); and the authority (inspiration/inerrancy) and interpretation of Scripture (April 26-27, 1981). The method of conversing with one another usually took the form of presentations of formal, scholarly papers which members from both traditions had prepared. Responses to the major papers were sometimes presented by another person within that same tradition as well as from someone from the other tradition. A remarkable commonality and convergence of thought surfaced in the discussions.

At the conclusion of the dialogue the group drew up a common declaration plus recommendations, which were adopted by all those present. It should be noted that the statement and recommendations are the conclusions of the participants themselves and not of their respective church bodies. The same holds true for the essays published in this journal.

## Declaration

After a series of dialogues over a period of two years, we express our gratitude for the experience of encounter with one another and for the resulting awareness that we share a great measure of common vision concerning the mission and life of the Church of Christ in our world. We interpret the term evangelical in a variety of ways that cut across our denominational lines. Our dialogue has contributed to our understanding of one another and of ourselves, and we affirm the value of this process.

At the conclusion of this stage in our dialogues, we wish to go on record as in agreement in principle on the following issues:

We profess fidelity to the Gospel of the Lord Jesus Christ, whom we acknowledge to be true God and true man, according to the testimony of Scripture, the church universal, and the ecumenical creeds.

We acknowledge that salvation is by grace alone, through faith alone, and that those things which Christians believe are ultimately to be determined and tested by the standard of Scripture alone.

We acknowledge that true evangelical faith expresses itself in discipleship marked by devotion to God and loving service to our neighbors.

We acknowledge that as the Lutheran churches have defined themselves in part by distinction from the older Catholicism from which they emerged, and cannot be fully understood without reference to their Catholic antecedents, so the various conservative evangelical communities and fellowships have defined themselves in part in distinction from original churches of the Reformation, in part in distinction from Catholicism, and in part in distinction from one another, and also need to be seen in the context of those traditions.

We acknowledge the authority and fundamental importance of Holy Scripture in establishing Christian faith and life. We have not reached an understanding concerning the definition of that authority and the appropriate means of understanding and interpreting Scripture.

We acknowledge that our Lord has called us into his body, the Church. The Church lives by his gifts of grace. We acknowledge the importance of baptism, the Lord's Supper, and the exercise of spiritual discipline in the Church, without having attained a consensus concerning the definition of those ministries and offices.

## Note

1. Lutheran Council in the U.S.A. (LCUSA) is a common agency for several national Lutheran church bodies. At the time of the Lutheran-Conservative/Evangelical dialogue, Lutheran churches participating in the Council included the American Lutheran Church (ALC), Lutheran Church in America (LCA), The Lutheran Church-Missouri Synod (LCMS), and the Association of Evangelical Lutheran Churches (AELC).

# Lutheran-Episcopal Dialogue

# Lutheran-Episcopal Dialogue: Progress Report*

## Part One: Preamble

Over a period of two and one-half years we have held six meetings as designated participants from the Lutheran and Episcopal churches in the United States. The objective laid down in our mandate was to define the "possibilities and problems for a more extended dialogue having more specific fellowship or unity or union goals." We have gone somewhat beyond that objective because of the degree of unity of which we have become aware, as well as out of a sense of urgency arising form the Gospel itself. As we discussed the faith and the mission to which Christ calls us, we discovered both an existing unity and, in the face of massive cultural upheaval, an unavoidable imperative to manifest oneness. Moreover, we have been unable to ignore the many contemporary associations of Christians in worship, study, and service which we take to be manifestations of the Spirit's activity among God's people.

As our dialogues progressed our attention centered more and more upon the concept of *communio in sacris*—that is, intercommunion, or pulpit and altar fellowship. We found ourselves going beyond the usual question: Is intercommunion a means to unity or a goal of unity? On the basis of our explorations, the question that emerged in our dialogues was: Are we able mutually to affirm the presence of the Gospel and apostolicity in our respective communions sufficiently to agree that the renewal of the church is more likely to come in communion with one another than out of communion with one another? We believe that the question cannot be answered solely by comparison of inherited documents, or by intelligence operations conducted from afar, but only by such mutual explorations, under the judgment of the

*Introduction on Episcopal Church, *BU,* 13-14. Lutheran-Episcopal Dialogue. *A Progress Report* (Cincinnati: Forward Movement Publications, 1972), 13-25.

Gospel, as we have made in our meetings. We believe that we must take the risk of reporting that our answer to that question is "Yes." We base that answer on our assessment of how our respective traditions speak to us today and on our observation of what is in fact happening in places where the people of God find themselves together across denominational lines. It is toward the realization of *communio in sacris* that our conclusions and recommendations are directed, not to denominational mergers or merely institution ecumenism. We believe that the remaining problems between us could best continue to be explored within a relationship such as is hereinafter recommended.

Out of concern for responsible and orderly obedience to the Gospel and the Spirit, and with profound respect for authority, we present this report, and ask for its serious consideration.

## Part Two: Summary Statements Deriving from the First Four Dialogues

Dialogues I through IV, guided, we trust, by the promptings of the Holy Spirit, yielded the following four summaries. These summaries are in no way intended to be taken as complete expositions or definitions of the respective topics but as reflections of the various stages of discussion and the growing consensus which led us to make our later recommendations.

A. *Holy Scripture*—On October 14 and 15, 1969, the representatives of our respective communions met in Detroit, Michigan, and initiated our series of dialogues with a discussion of Holy Scripture.

1. For both Lutherans and Anglicans the Canonical Scriptures of the Old and New Testaments occupy a position of authority and primacy.

2. Lutherans and Anglicans, and both in varying degree, have been influenced by the development of the historical-critical approach to Scripture. This has made for some variety in both our communions as we have sought to employ the Scriptures in authoritative fashion but, in any case, would find us both using the Scriptures as normative in the proclamation of the Gospel. Inspiration per se has not yet been discussed.

3. The characteristic confessional basis of the Lutherans embraces
    (1) The Canonical Scriptures of the Old and New Testaments,
    (2) The symbols of the Lutheran Church:
        a. The Apostles', Nicene, and Athanasian Creeds
        b. The Augsburg Confession and the Apology of the same
        c. The Smalcald Articles
        d. The Large and Small Catechisms
        e. The Formula of Concord
There are varying degrees of official adherence to these symbolic documents.

4. The documents to which Anglicans, although less confessionally oriented than Lutherans, characteristically appeal include

    (1) The Canonical Scriptures of the Old and New Testaments,

    (2) The testimony of the Fathers and the definition of the Councils of the early Church,

    (3) The Apostles', Nicene, and Athanasian Creeds (note that while the Athanasian Creed has never been made formally authoritative for the Episcopal Church in the United States of America, there is no doubt that its Trinitarian affirmations are part of the faith of the Church),

    (4) The Book of Common Prayer,

    (5) The Thirty-Nine Articles of Religion (the ambiguous authority of the Articles was reviewed by Lambeth 1968; while not judged a complete confessional statement, the Articles have been retained by most provinces as an important historical document which most significantly bears clear witness to the primacy of Scripture and the centrality of the Gospel), and

    (6) For contemporary guidance in matters of faith, morals, and order, the Resolutions of successive Lambeth Conferences which, while not legally binding, have significant moral weight.

B. *Christian Worship*—Our second dialogue, meeting on April 7,8,9, 1970 in Milwaukee, Wisconsin, concentrated on a discussion of Christian Prayer and Worship.

    1. We agreed that the proclamation of the Gospel and the celebration of the Holy Eucharist constitute the distinctive and central act of Christian worship. We discovered, however, that more attention should be given to precisely what the Eucharist means and how it is to be celebrated.

    2. In viewing our several Eucharistic traditions in perspective, we agreed that unity in Eucharistic practice is to be found more in the "shape" of Eucharistic liturgies than in fixed texts.

    3. We agreed that further discussion as to just what is meant and not meant by the phrase "Eucharistic Sacrifice" would be generally helpful. Our attention was given to the significant discussion of the current issues in the *Lambeth Conference 1958* report, and the Lutheran-Roman Catholic report, *The Eucharist as Sacrifice.*

    4. We agreed that some measure of pulpit and altar fellowship between our communions is desirable. We asked ourselves whether inter-communion is one of the means of achieving the

unity of the church or is the expression of a unity already achieved. (Later discussion led us to go beyond this question and to pose the issue differently. See Preamble and Recommendations III and IV.)

5. Among the other matters discussed were: (a) the several formularies for absolution, blessing, and Eucharistic consecration to be found in our respective service books and the relationship between the spoken word and the gift bestowed; and (b) the varying emphases given to prayer and praise as purely a response to the divine initiative in Christ and as a general human religious activity.

C. *Baptism-Confirmation*—Our third dialogue, meeting on November 17, 18, 19, 1970, at Trinity Institute, New York City, considered our understanding and practice of Baptism and Confirmation.

1. We affirm the mystery of the New Birth in Christ by water and the Spirit. Holy Baptism, duly administered with water and in the Name of the Father, and of the Son, and of the Holy Spirit, and understood as God's action of adoption, initiates into the Body of Christ and (in principle at least) gives access to the Holy Eucharist and the reception of Holy Communion.

2. Adequate instruction is required whether before Baptism in the case of an adult, before Baptism for the parents and/or sponsors of a child to be Baptized in infancy, and following Baptism in the case of an infant.

3. Both communions baptize persons of any age. Strong representations were made by certain representatives of both communions urging experimentation which would advise delay in infant Baptism so that it might be received in conjunction with a personal and public confession of faith, *or*, at least until some guarantee of Christian nurture is given. (The matter of the Faith-Baptism relationship in both communions requires further exploration.)

4. Throughout most of our histories as separate communions there has been a practice of Confirmation. In both traditions, Confirmation has normally been preceded by a period of instruction of varying length, and has normally been received with prayer and the Laying on of Hands, followed by First Communion.

5. Prayer with the Laying on of Hands, whether as a separate Confirmation or as part of the Baptismal liturgy, is practiced in

both communions. The precise meaning of Confirmation and its appropriate ministration are under review in both communions.

6. In both traditions there has been much study of Baptism and the Laying on of Hands and now a willingness to experiment both in the interests of recovering a classical norm and meeting the needs of what are apparently the unique conditions of contemporary family life. Thus far, permission has been given for First Communion before Confirmation in the Episcopal Church, the Lutheran Church in America, and the American Lutheran Church. (Subsequently, the Lutheran Church-Missouri Synod left this issue to the local congregations for decision.)

7. Such theological differences as were noted were often within as well as across confessional lines and appear to be due in part to the challenge of cultural upheaval.

8. Looking to the future: The full ecumenical consequences of the fact that we share One Baptism remain to be spelled out.

D. *Apostolicity*—Our fourth dialogue, meeting April 15, 16, 17, 1971, at Luther Theological Seminary, Minneapolis, Minnesota, focussed on Apostolicity and arrived at the following five substantive agreements.

1. We agree that apostolicity belongs to the reality of the one holy catholic church; apostolicity is manifested in various ways in all areas of the church's life, and is guarded especially by common confession and through that function of the church designated as *episcope* (oversight).

2. We agree that both our communions can and should affirm that the Eucharistic celebrations held under the discipline of either communion are true occurrences of the Body of Christ in the world. We agree that the ordained ministries of both communions are true ministries of the one church of Christ, that is, that they are apostolic ministries. We agree that mutual recognition of ministries by each of the two traditions could enter that sort of relationship in which each would receive gifts from the other for greater service to the Lord and his Gospel.

3. We agree that the identity of our Gospel with the apostles' Gospel, and of our church with the apostles' church, is the personal identity of the risen Christ; He is always the one crucified under Pontius Pilate and just so the one whose word is new promise in every new historical occasion. The church is able to remain in conversation with this one Lord, and so to remain itself through the opportunities and temptations of its history, by the meditation of the whole continuous tradition of the Gospel in

word and sacrament. The church has, within the providence of God, enacted its responsibility that this succession shall be a succession of the Gospel, by the means of a canon of Scripture, the use and authority of creeds and confessions, sacramental-liturgical Reformation, and the institution of an ordered ministry and succession of ministers.

4. We agree that this substance of apostolic succession must take different forms in differing places and times, if the Gospel is intended to be heard and received. At the time of the Reformation, one of our communions in its place experienced the continuity of the episcopally ordered ministry as an important means of the succession of the Gospel; in various ways the other in its place was able to take its responsibility of the succession of the Gospel only by a new ordering of its ministry. We agree that by each decision the apostolicity of the ministry in question was preserved, and that each of our communions can and should affirm the decision of the other. Until the Lord of the church grants a new ordering of the church, each communion should respect the right of the other to honor the distinct history which mediates its apostolicity, and to continue that ordering of its ministry which its history has made possible. Within the one church, both the Anglican continuity of the episcopal order, and the Lutheran concentration on doctrine, have been means of preserving the apostolicity of the one church.

5. For the future, we agree that if either communion should be able to receive the gift of the other's particular apostolicity, without unfaithfulness to its own, the future of the church would surely be served. In any future ordering of the one church, there will be a ministry and within that ministry an *episcope*. The functional reality of *episcope* is in flux in both our communions. If we are faithful, we will *together* discover the forms demanded by the church's new opportunities, so that the church may have an *episcope* which will be an episcope of the apostolic Gospel. Similarly, any future unity of the church will be a unity of common confession. The functional reality of the common confessions of the past (their contemporary interpretation and use) is in flux in both our communions. Our faithfulness will be that we think and pray together seeking to be ready for a new common confession when the Lord shall give us the apostolic boldness to proclaim the Gospel with the freshness and vigor of our fathers in the faith.

**Part Three: Recommendations**

Two additional meetings were held at Trinity Institute, New York City, on November 10, 11, 12, 1971, and May 31 and June 1, 1972, respectively. At these sessions, members of the Dialogue gave their attention to the preparation and revision of this Report including the above Preamble, the following Recommendations, and the accompanying separate statements addressed to our respective Lutheran and Episcopal constituents.

In the light of the foregoing Preamble and Summary Statements, we recommend to our respective participating communions prayerful consideration of an action on the following proposals:

I. Recognition of agreement between Lutherans and Episcopalians on the following fundamentals of church life and doctrine:

    a. The primacy and authority of the Holy Scriptures

    b. The doctrine of the Apostles' and Nicene Creeds

    c. Justification by grace through faith as affirmed by both the Lutheran Confessions and the Anglican Book of Common Prayer and Thirty-Nine Articles of Religion

    d. The doctrine and practice of Baptism

    e. Fundamental agreement on the Holy Eucharist, though with some differences in emphasis

II. Agreement that our two communions have maintained the essential apostolicity of the church as set forth in Summary Statement IV.

III. Subject to the consent of the appropriate local authorities (the ordinary or those others responsible for recognizing and furthering agreement in the preaching of the Gospel and the ministration of the Sacraments):

> Commendation of communicants of each communion to the Eucharistic celebrations and gatherings around the Word of the other, including intercommunion between parishes or congregations which, by reason of proximity, joint community concerns, and/or activities, have developed such a degree of understanding and trust as would make intercommunion an appropriate response to the Gospel.

IV. As requisite accompaniments of the above, the creation of such structures as will enable Episcopalians and Lutherans, within their new fellowship, to assume joint responsibility for the proclamation of the Gospel with one accord and for an appropriate ministration of the Sacraments, these to include:

    A. Continuing joint theological study and conversation, at a level similar to that of the conversations just concluded, with such arrangements for broad discussion as will assure influence on the thought and practice of both communions. Topics for these discussions would include:

1. Continuing concentration on the nature of the Gospel and its effective proclamation,

2. Exploration of future common forms of ordered ministry and *episcope*, and

3. To further the continual reform and renewal of the church, close study of such features of the sacramental practices of our respective communions as may obscure or distort their character as Gospel, and

B. Participation of consultants from each communion in all deliberations of the other touching sacramental order or confessional status.

## Part Four: Enabling Legislation

In the interests of facilitating the above steps, we respectfully urge our respective communions to enact, as soon as may be feasible, such legislation, canonical or otherwise, as may be required.

# Lutheran-Episcopal Dialogue: Report and Recommendations*

## Joint Statement on Justification

A. We the participants in the Lutheran-Episcopal Dialogue understand that our respective churches confess the gospel of Jesus Christ as God's saving word of grace to a fallen world. Together, we affirm that the gospel is the good news that for us and for our salvation God's Son was made man, fulfilled all righteousness, died and rose again from the dead according to the scriptures. Through the proclamation of this gospel in word and sacraments, the Holy Spirit calls, works faith, gathers, enlightens and sanctifies the whole Christian Church on earth and preserves it in union with Jesus Christ in the one true faith. The Spirit thereby leads us into a life of service and praise of God, the Father, the Son, and the Holy Spirit.

B. At the time of the Reformation, Anglicans and Lutherans shared a common confession and understanding of God's justifying grace, i.e. that we are accounted righteous before God only for the merit of our Lord and Savior Jesus Christ, by faith, and not for our own works or deservings. This good news of salvation continues to comfort the people of God and to establish them in the hope and promise of eternal life. In preaching and teaching, in liturgy and sacraments, both communions confess the radical gift of God's grace and righteousness in the crucified and risen Jesus Christ to the human race, which has no righteousness of its own.

C. In the western cultural setting in which our communions, Episcopal and Lutheran, find themselves, the gospel of justification continues to address the needs of human being alienated from a holy and gracious God. Therefore, it is the task of the church to minister this gospel with vivid and fresh proclamation and to utilize all available resources for the theological enrichment of this ministry.

D. In both communions the understanding of the term "salvation" has

*Lutheran-Episcopal Dialogue. Report and Recomendations (Cincinnati: Forward Movement Publications, 1981) 22-43, 54-59.

181

had different emphases. Among Lutherans, salvation has commonly been synonymous with the forgiveness of sins; among Episcopalians, salvation has commonly included not only the forgiveness of sins but also the call to and promise of sanctification. As we continue to listen to each other, may God grant that justification by grace and the new life in the Spirit abound.

E. We rejoice in these common convictions, and recommend them to our churches for reflection and use.

## Joint Statement on the Gospel

God, who created and who continually sustains all that exists[1] out of that creation, brought forth humanity for eternal fellowship with himself.[2] Because such fellowship must be a relationship of freedom, humanity was originally given the free capacity to reject God's love. When human freedom was misused, as represented in Scripture by the story of the Fall,[3] this rebellion brought disorder to creation as a whole,[4] and in particular it brought disorder to human nature. God's love has sought constantly to reconcile humanity to himself[5] through the proclamation of the promise of salvation as he dealt with his people Israel. This divine activity has been effected by God's Holy Spirit,[6] and may be seen as the expression of grace. That grace has been fulfilled by God's entry into human life in the person of Jesus Christ.[7] He is the ultimate revelation of what God is like, whose actions and attitudes have shown what God intended human nature to be. As God made Man, Jesus Christ has been like us in all respects apart from sin,[8] but has identified himself with our sin and has claimed it for his own.[9] By taking that sin to the Cross, he has secured forgiveness for all sin. In raising Jesus Christ from death, God the Father has vindicated his sacrifice for our salvation. By grace, everyone who trusts entirely in God's mercy is set free from every burden of the past. In each life so redeemed God's Spirit operates through the gift of Christ who was uniquely anointed by the Holy Spirit for his saving work, for guidance, for perseverance and for the application of God's power in the world.[10] Thus fellowship with God and the divine image in humanity will be fully restored by a grace that can be received through faith that is not initiated by ourselves but is the gift of God.[11]

## Notes

1. Gen. 1:1
2. Gen. 2:15
3. Gen. 3:5
4. Gen. 3:17

5. John 3:16 & II Cor. 5:18
6. The Nicene Creed-"Who has spoken through the prophets"
7. Gal. 4:4
8. Heb. 4:15
9. II Cor. 5:21
10. John 16:13-14 & Eph. 1:13-14
11. Eph. 2:8-9

\*   \*   \*

## Joint Statement on Eucharistic Presence

1. In the period of the Reformation, the controversy over the Eucharist which affected Western Christendom as a whole was focused for Anglicans and Lutherans on the sacrifice of the Mass and Christ's presence in the sacrament. In the light of the recovery of the gospel of justification by faith, Lutherans rejected any notion of sacrifice which obscured the sufficiency and finality of Christ's sacrifice upon the cross and God's gracious gift of communion. Both traditions rejected a metaphysical explanation of the Real Presence (in particular the doctrine of transubstantiation), as well as interpretations of the Eucharist as a good work offered to God and meritorious for salvation. Both traditions affirmed a doctrine of the Lord's Supper conforming to the New Testament teaching in which Christ is both the gift and the giver. Lutherans defended the Real Presence of Christ's body and blood "in, with, and under" the forms of bread and wine in order to make the christological affirmation that God meets us in the humanity as well as the divinity of Christ in this means of grace. For them, this implied a two-fold eating of the sacrament, spiritually and orally (*Formula of Concord*, Solid Declaration VII:60-61). Anglicans, on the other hand, followed the Reformed emphasis on the spiritual eating by faith, thus denying that the wicked and unbelievers partake of Christ (*Articles of Religion* 28-29). It was Richard Hooker (1554?-1600) who gave Anglicanism its normative approach to eucharistic doctrine by teaching that the elements of bread and wine are the instruments of participation in the body and blood of Christ. In more recent times, biblical studies and liturgical renewal have led Lutherans and Anglicans to recognize a convergence on the essentials of eucharistic faith and practice.

2. The eucharistic celebration of Word and Sacrament is the heart and center of the life and mission of the Church as the body of Christ in and for the world. It nourishes the community of the New Covenant, the family of God, whose corporate life is characterized by thanksgiving (*eucharistia*). Such corporate life serves in the world as a sign of the new creation initiated

by God in Christ Jesus, so that through the Gospel the world may come to faith and that all people might be brought to unity with God and each other in Christ. The Eucharist enlivens the Church and strengthens our oneness in Christ. It is directly from the eucharistic table that we are sent forth into the world in the name of Christ, rejoicing in the power of his Spirit, strengthened and refreshed to do the work God has given us to do.

3. The presence of Christ in the Church is proclaimed in a variety of ways in the eucharistic liturgy. It is the risen Christ himself who presides at each assembly of his people: "where two or three are gathered together in my name, there am I in the midst of them." It is Christ who is promised and proclaimed in the readings of the Old and New Testaments. It is Christ who is represented by each of the baptized members and in a special way by the ordained ministers, as each fulfills a particular liturgical role, such diverse roles being complementary aspects of a single liturgical action. It is Christ who gives himself in his body and blood as both our sacrifice and our feast.

Throughout Western Christianity, the Words of Institution (*Verba Christi*) have been generally seen as the focus of the consecration, although all would acknowledge that the presence of the Holy Spirit is essential to the Eucharist whether or not it is explicitly expressed. Eucharistic prayer encompasses proclamation, remembrance, and supplication.[1] Within the framework of this thanksgiving, the Church proclaims its faith through the memorial of Christ in the events of salvation history and the supplication of the Holy Spirit to build up the unity of God's people through faithful reception of the body and blood of Christ.

4. The Church's celebration of the Eucharist rests upon the Word and authority of Christ, who commanded his disciples to remember him in this way until his return. According to his word of promise, Christ's very body broken on the cross and his very blood shed for the forgiveness of our sins are present, distributed and received, as a means of partaking here and now of the fruits of that atoning sacrifice. This is also the presence of the risen and glorified Christ who pleads for us before the throne of God. It is not our faith that effects this presence of our Lord, but by the faith we have received, the blessings of the Lord's suffering, death, and resurrection are sealed to us until he comes again in glory.

5. The Lord who comes to his people in the power of the Holy Spirit and by means of his Word "in, with, and under" the forms of bread and wine enables all Christians to avail themselves of the benefits of his saving death and life-giving resurrection. By partaking of the sacrament, the community of faith created by Baptism is manifested as the Body of Christ in and for the world, and empowered to live a godly life. We may speak of a sacramental transformation of the called and gathered people of God into the image of Christ, that we may be, in Luther's words, "Christ to our neighbor."

For this reason the Church has desired a steady access to the Word of God and the Sacrament of the Altar. In both of our Churches, more of our parishes are scheduling weekly celebrations of the Eucharist as the main Sunday and festival Service. As the frequency of celebration increases for the whole congregation, there is a desire to include the sick and the home-bound in the congregation's Eucharist. This is an ancient practice, and as an extension of the distribution of the sacrament it accords with the true use of the institution. (FC, Solid Declaration, VII, *passim*.) Both Lutherans and Episcopalians would want to disavow a veneration of the reserved elements that is dissociated from the eucharistic celebration of the congregation.[2]

The true use of the sacrament is to eat and drink the body and blood in the faith that our Lord's words give what they promise. Luther's *Small Catechism* asserts that "By these words the forgiveness of sins, life, and salvation are given to us in the sacrament, for where there is forgiveness of sins, there are also life and salvation" (Tappert, p. 352). The Catechism in the *Book of Common Prayer* amplifies the same benefits of the sacrament: "The benefits we receive are the forgiveness of our sins, the strengthening of our union with Christ and one another, and the foretaste of the heavenly banquet which is our nourishment in eternal life" (BCP, pp. 859-860).

6. In recent years, through biblical scholarship, there has been a growing appreciation of the eschatological dimension of the Lord's Supper. The Lord who comes to his people by the power of his Word and Spirit is the risen and glorified Lord. In Holy Baptism we are joined to the death and resurrection of Christ and made members of his body to be living signs of the new creation in Christ. In the eucharistic celebration we not only receive the strength to become what we are called to be, but also participate in the joys of the age to come when Christ will be all in all. The Eucharist manifests the unity of the Church in Christ here and now, and anticipates the oneness of all creation under the reign of Christ. For this reason, communion among separated Christians is to be sought wherever sufficient agreement on Word and Sacraments can be reached.[3]

## Notes

1. Eucharistic prayer encompasses the liturgical material between the *Sursum corda* and the distribution. The elements of proclamation, remembrance, and supplication are found in classical Lutheran communion rites, such as those in *The Common Service* (1888) and *The Lutheran Hymnal* (1941), in the eucharistic prefaces with their praise of God for redemption in Christ, the Lord's Prayer with its supplicatory petitions, and the Words of Institution, which are both proclamation and remembrance ("on the night in which He was betrayed, our Lord Jesus Christ took bread...").

2. "Differences arise between those who would practice reservation for (communion) only, and those who would also regard it as a means of eucharistic devotion. For the latter, adoration

of Christ in the reserved sacrament should be regarded as an extension of eucharistic worship, even though it does not include immediate sacramental reception, which remains the primary purpose of reservation. Any dissociation of such devotion from this primary purpose, which is communion in Christ of all his members, is a distortion in eucharistic practice." ('The Elucidations' of the Windsor Statement on Eucharistic Doctrine, par. 8; *Agreed Statements,* Cincinnati, Ohio: Forward Movement Publications, 1980, pp. 32-33. Cf. Lutheran/Roman Catholic Joint Commission: *The Eucharist:* Geneva: The Lutheran World Federation, 1980, par. 53, p. 19; and also *The Book of Common Prayer* (1979), pp. 408-409).

   3. The concluding sentence does not imply that all Lutherans and Episcopalians believe that such "sufficient agreement" has been achieved. Areas for further examination in future dialogues would laudably include:

   1) the theology of the consecration and its practical consequences in regard to the elements;
   2) the pastoral concern in administration (open and closed Communion);
   3) further clarification of the doctrine of the Real Presence;
   4) the concept of 'sacrifice' in the Eucharist;
   5) the relation of the Eucharist to the historic episcopate.


## Joint Statement on The Authority of Scripture

   We agree that the Holy Scripture of the Old and New Testament is the "rule and ultimate standard of faith" (Lambeth Conference of 1888, Resolution 11 a; cf. *Formula of Concord,* Epitome I: "the only rule and norm" (Tappert 464). Holy Scripture is the ultimate standard by which all of tradition, whether creeds, confessions, or Councils, is to be judged. Those who wrote Scripture were inspired by the Holy Spirit to put down the pure testimony of what God has said and done, and as the heart and center of Scripture, what he has said and done in our Savior Jesus Christ. Through the Holy Spirit the Church continues to hear the Holy Scripture as God speaking to his people. As a consequence, the Church has used Scripture as its normative guide for faith and life. Therefore the Church is able to proclaim the Word of God with authority and evaluate life with prophetic power.

   Holy Scripture needs to be expounded because language changes and because the Church faces problems which did not exist in Biblical times. But expositions vary, and sin corrupts; the pure testimony to Jesus Christ, our only Savior, is then endangered. The Holy Spirit, through means such as creeds, confessions, and Councils, has provided guides for correctly expounding Holy Scripture. These are secondary guides, subject to the ultimate standard of Holy Scripture, and they, like Holy Scripture, are also in need of exposition because language changes and new problems arise. Here, too, God through the power of his Word and Spirit continues to lead and guide his Church as he directs the Church's attention to Jesus Christ as found in Holy Scripture.

   All members of the Church share in expounding what Holy Scripture means for their faith and life, using all their gracious God has given them, including reason, to carry out this task. In addition, certain individuals have been given special gifts by the Spirit for discerning what Holy Scripture means for their place and time. Because of their authority or training, such individuals are able to be especially helpful in expounding Scripture for their time. On account of the vagaries of history and the corruption of sin, all members of the Church, even those with special gifts, remain subject for both faith and life to their Lord Jesus Christ as found in the ultimate standard of Holy Scripture.

In both communions there are varieties of understanding and application of Scripture. These differences and tensions are not without weight; however, they are not differences between Lutheran and Episcopalians. These are problems which we have in common and we might more helpfully face them together.

## Dissenting Statement Attached

Although there are excellent points in the paper on "Authority of Scripture," as a matter of conscience we herewith dissent from its adoption owning to perceived areas of ambiguity therein which we deem would cause confusion and be detrimental to the best interests of the Lutheran Church-Missouri Synod.

The Rev. Carl L. Bornman
The Rev. Jerald C. Joersz

## Joint Statement on Apostolicity

*Introduction*
During our discussion the Lutheran and Episcopalian participants have been happily surprised by the substantial agreement which we share with regard to the Church's apostolicity. The following statement indicates the lines of this convergence while pointing out areas of divergence where appropriate.

*Part One: Apostolicity: A New Appreciation*
(1) The Apostolicity of the Church refers to the Church's continuity with Christ and the apostles in its movement through history. The Church is apostolic as "devoted...to the apostles' teaching and fellowship, to the breaking of bread and the prayers." (Acts 2:42)

(2) Apostolicity or apostolic succession is a dynamic, diverse reality organically embracing a variety of elements and activities. It includes contin-

ued faithfulness to the apostles' teaching, which teaching found normative expression in Holy Scripture, and under Scripture, in the ecumenical creeds. It involves participation in baptism, in the apostles' prayers and the breaking of bread which continues in the liturgical and sacramental life of the Church. Abiding in apostolic fellowship is given expression through sharing in the Church's common life of mutual edification and caring, served by an ecclesiastically called and recognized pastoral ministry of Word and sacrament. Finally, apostolic succession involves a continuing involvement in the apostolic mission, in being sent into the world to share the Gospel of Christ by proclamation to all far and near and by neighborly service to those in need.

(3) It has been all too common for many to think of apostolic succession primarily in terms of historic episcopate. We must take care to avoid this narrowing of our view of the Church's apostolic succession to an exclusive concern with the historic episcopate. Such a reduction falsely isolates the historic episcopate and also obscures the fact that churches may exhibit most aspects of apostolicity while being weak or deficient in some. Recovery of appreciation for the wider dimensions of apostolicity has allowed us to see in each other a commonality which a narrow concentration on the historic episcopate would have obscured.

## Part Two: The Historical Development of Lutheran and Episcopalian Views and Expressions of Apostolic Succession

Different aspects of apostolicity have appeared throughout the Church's history and continue to shape the Church's faith, life and mission today. We note the following developments.

Three forms of apostolicity emerge in the early Church especially directed toward the threat of the Gnostics in the areas of (1) doctrine, (2) worship and (3) order. (1) The canon of prophetic and apostolic Scripture is set as the recognized authoritative norm or rule of doctrine. Apostolic "rules of faith" in creedal form develop, not only to guard against heresy and to instruct catechumens, but also (2) for use in baptismal liturgies as interrogatory creeds or as summaries of the faith for the newly baptized. Concomitant with this was the development of influential liturgies which helped protect apostolic authenticity in the celebration of Word and sacrament. (3) Apostolic succession was wedded to succession of bishops in sees so that bishops were looked to as guardians of apostolic faith and practice, representing the teaching authority of the apostles.

In the middle ages, mission became again clearly linked to apostolic succession, as in the missionary journeys of St. Paul. Missionary bishops were sent to spread Christianity throughout Europe; in other cases, missionaries like Boniface were subsequently made bishops.

The developments which led to a break between East and West in 1054 helped focus juridical authority in Rome, making the "Apostolic See" more and more the authoritative arbiter of theology and giving the Roman rite an increasingly normative character.

Both Lutheran and Anglican reformers rejected the Papacy as the primary focus of continuity in the Gospel. Lutherans saw faithfulness to the apostles' teaching in Scripture as the core of apostolicity. In England a similar recovery of biblical faith had been brewing. The Anglican reform began with polity when the problems of royal succession occasioned the break with Rome. Liturgical and doctrinal reform, which had been in ferment even before the break with Rome, followed. However, the metro-political government and diocesan structure remained intact in the Church of England. From this emerged the characteristic Anglican appeal to the bishops as signs and guardians of apostolicity in liturgy and doctrine. The German *Landeskirchen* and Scandinavian folk-churches were conditioned by princely prerogative (viz. *cuius regio, eius religio*). Sweden and Finland retained historic episcopal succession. For Lutheranism as a whole, the episcopate in apostolic succession did not function as the primary strand of apostolicity. The confessional writings, the Augsburg Confession and the Small Catechism in Scandinavia and the entire Book of Concord in Germany, served to focus the Lutheran understanding of apostolicity on *doctrinal continuity*. While the Anglicans had their 39 Articles (which showed significant Lutheran and some Reformed influence), the Book of Common Prayer tended to include liturgy as central to apostolic continuity.

In matters of reforming the doctrine, liturgy and polity of the Church, both communions showed high regard for tradition and resisted that version of *sola scriptura* which held that only what Scripture commands is to be retained. Rather, they kept whatever Scripture did not forbid if it had proved beneficial to the Church and consistent with the Gospel.

Cranmer, Hooker, and the Caroline divines of the 17th century were careful not to "un-Church" those continental Protestants who did not maintain the historic episcopate. Ironically it was the challenge of some of the Puritans who contended that episcopal government was not biblical which tended to harden certain Anglican defenses of Episcopacy in apostolic succession.[1] It was not until the Anglo-Catholicism of the 19th century Tractarian movement that serious argument was heard within the Church of England for the historic episcopate being of the essence (*esse*) of the Church in a way that tended to "un-Church" non-episcopal churches. In recent decades, most Episcopalians have argued either for the episcopacy as an order of ministry developed under the Spirit's guidance for the well-being (*bene esse*) of the Church or as an aspect of the fullness of the Church (*plene esse*)[2]—both groups holding it to be a sign, symbol and means of the Church's unity and continuity in mission and ministry, doctrine and worship.

The Lutheran reformers, while supportive of the office of bishop, were critical of abuses of episcopal power. Bishops have no power apart from the Word of God to make new laws, institute new rites or create traditions, as though one would sin by omitting them or could be justified by doing them (CA. XXVIII, p. 56; Apology, Art XV, p. 31; and XXVIII, pp. 8-14). Bishops ought not impose heavy burdens on people, taking no account of human weakness (CA XVIII, p. 16; Apology, Art IV, p. 233). On the contrary, "the power of bishops is a power or command of God to preach the Gospel, to remit or retain sins, and to administer sacraments" (CA, XXVIII, p. 5).

Lutheran Church life after the Reformation was focused around the ministry of Word and sacraments administered by those ecclesiastically called to the pastoral office. In the 19th century controversies arose in Europe and America over the doctrine of the ministry which have carried over into the 20th century. These controversies involved emphasizing *either* the functions of the pastor of proclaiming the Word and administering the Sacraments *or* the pastor's personal representation of Christ.[3] Another dimension of the controversy centers on ordination, understood *on the one hand* as delegation or even transference from the royal priesthood in a local congregation and *on the other hand* as a recognition by the larger Church (e.g., The Synod) of an office bestowed by the Lord through ordained clergy on persons ecclesiastically called.[4] All groups agreed that the call came ultimately from God.

During the modern era, all Scandinavian Lutherans retained the office and title of bishop. In the 20th century many German "general superintendents" were given the title bishop and three American churches have adopted the title since 1970 for their synod or district presidents. In Baltic and Slavic countries the title *bishop* is used. Some Lutheran churches in Africa have bishops and the Lutheran Church in Papua New Guinea has recently adopted the term.

*Part Three: An Analysis of the Agreement in Apostolic Succession to be Found in the Lutheran and Episcopal Churches*

It is important to state plainly the high degree of commonality which is to be found between the Lutheran and Episcopal Churches in the various aspects of the Church's apostolicity. We will look briefly at each of the main aspects, keeping in mind that these aspects interrelate and are treated separately only for purposes of analysis.

(1) Apostolic Mission

Preoccupation with things at home at the time of the Reformation delayed a vital engagement in overseas missions on the part of both

Anglicans and Lutherans. Subsequently both Lutherans and Anglicans have been extensively involved in missionary outreach. At the beginning of the modern missionary era there was a significant convergence of Anglican and Lutheran efforts. The first Protestant missionaries sent to India (German Lutherans named Plütschau and Ziegenbalg) were commissioned by the King of Denmark; later they came under the auspices of the S.P.C.K. The call of our Lord to "go into all the world" is clearly recognized by both churches. Actual participation has varied in both.

In an increasingly secular culture both communions must also recognize a new urgency in the call to evangelize those who live nearer to home. Social concern and acts of neighborliness are espoused by both Lutherans and Episcopalians in the name of Christ. The Lutheran doctrine of the "two kingdoms" (God's two-fold rule in all areas, secular and spiritual) has not always realized its social potential. The Episcopalian understanding of the church's social responsibility has in some places given way to the "suburban captivity of the churches." Both churches have experienced, in Europe and America, the negative Erastian effects of Caesaropapism—especially in times of war. Both Lutherans and Episcopalians have had glorious moments and sad declines in this aspect of apostolic succession.

## (2) Apostolic Scripture

The Lutheran churches and the Episcopal church acknowledge the writings of the Old and New Testaments to be the normative means of abiding in continuity with apostolic teaching. In this the two Communions are at one with each other and with the early Church which first recognized the canonical status of the inspired writings. By adhering to the same canonical writings, by assigning portions of them to be read in corporate worship, by sharing in large measure the same lectionary, by interpreting these writings in teaching and preaching, and by appealing to these writings as the Apostles' test of true doctrine and life, Lutherans and Episcopalians are at one.

## (3) Apostolic Creeds

Following a precedent already established in the days of the apostles, the church by the second century had formulated creeds. These creeds or "rules of faith," which were customarily trinitarian in structure, summarized the apostles' teaching and served as a guide and guard for the faith of the Church against errors such as Gnosticism. The use and the development of these rules of faith as doctrinal summaries and as interrogatory creeds in the baptismal rite was influenced by the catechumenate.

Due to the struggle with heresy and the attempt of the Church to interpret faith in the context of Hellenistic culture, the creeds of the ecumenical councils—unlike the earlier creedal formulations—used terminology not explicitly found in Scripture. Reflecting on Christological definitions of the Councils of Ephesus and Chalcedon, the Athanasian Creed (BCP, p. 864; LBW, pp. 54-55) of the 5th or 6th century described the mystery of Christ's person and expanded Nicene trinitarian theology.

Historically, both the Lutheran and Anglican communions have treasured and affirmed these creeds and confessed them in their worship, teaching, and preaching.

### (4) The Holy Sacraments

It is from the written apostolic testimony that we receive our Lord's commands to forgive sins, to commune, and to baptize. Lutherans and Episcopalians agree that Baptism and the Lord's Supper, ordained by Christ, are necessary to Christian life and worship.[5] Furthermore, the importance that absolution and ordination have had for both communions cannot be minimized historically, theologically, or liturgically. Remarkable similarities exist in the Lutheran and Episcopalian liturgies of Baptism, Holy Communion, Confession and Forgiveness, Ordination, and Morning and Evening Prayer. This is seen not only in the worship forms emerging from the liturgical movements of the 19th and 20th centuries (which demonstrate significant Anglican influence upon Lutheran rites) but also in the 16th century which saw Lutheran influences on the Book of Common Prayer.[6]

### (5) The Ordained Ministry or Pastoral Office

(a) This is a most controversial area in the discussions between Lutherans and Episcopalians regarding apostolicity. It is therefore important to note that even here we have a great measure of agreement not always found with other communions. The common aspects are:

(i) Both Lutherans and Episcopalians hold the ordained ministry of Word and Sacrament to be of divine institution. They distinguish this pastoral office from the priesthood of all believers, while holding at the same time that it is one of the primary tasks of the ordained ministry to equip the saints for their work of ministry (priesthood of all believers). (CA V; Articles of Religion XXIII).

(ii) The two communions both engage in the practice of ordination. Entrance into the pastoral office or holy orders is bestowed through a liturgical act which is not to be repeated.[7] Ordination is presided over by those set apart in the Church so to ordain in the Name of God. The language of sacrament is not always used of ordination in either Communion, but the ritual aspects of a sacramental act are always present in both (i.e., the Word of God, prayer and the laying-on-of-hands.).

(iii) Both Lutherans and Episcopalians intend by ordination to set apart ministers of both Word and Sacrament.

(iv) Both hold that the succession in office of ordained ministers shows the Church's continuity in time and space in the ministry of Word and Sacrament and the care of the Church.

(v) Both Lutherans and Episcopalians recognize the necessity of oversight (*episcopé*) which is embodied in an ordained office. Lutherans see *episcopé* exercised in the ministry of parish pastors as well as in bishops' supervision of local congregations and clergy, while Episcopalians see that *episcopé* as shared by bishops with their clergy.

(vi) Episcopalians recognize that Lutherans do affirm the full dignity of the pastoral office and are open to the historic episcopate as a valid and proper form of that office. Some Lutheran Churches are ordered in the historic episcopate. There is even a preference for the historic episcopate shown in the Lutheran confessional writings where and when that form could be maintained in accord with the Gospel, i.e., in the context of faithful preaching of the Word and the right administration of the Sacraments. Lutherans do not, however, hold the historic episcopate to be the only legitimate form of *episcopé*.

(b) Since both Lutherans and Episcopalians are in official bi-lateral discussions with Roman Catholics, we in this discussion take great encouragement from two findings of the Lutheran-Roman Catholic discussions which give strong support to the positions we have developed in our report.

First we note that the Roman Catholic-Lutheran discussions in the U.S.A. indicate large areas of agreement in the Faith. They further noted the diversity of church order found in the New Testament period. In the light of the practice of presbyteral succession found within the succession of the Roman Church, the Roman Catholic partners in the discussion recommend that Rome recognize the validity of Lutheran Orders as presently constituted.[8] (See Appendix 1 for excerpts.)

Next we note that in Roman Catholic theology, reflected in the international discussions between Lutheran and Roman Catholic Churches, a distinction is made between Apostolic Succession in substance (the apostolic succession of the whole Church in faith and life) and the apostolic succession of ministerial transmission (the succession of ministers) which is the sign and servant of the Apostolic Succession of the whole Church. This distinction is essentially the same as we have made. It allows the Roman Catholic partners to raise the question whether it is possible to affirm Lutheran orders to be within the true succession of the Church and therefore merely defective in form or lacking fullness and not invalid. (See Appendix 2, Malta N.57,58, and 63 and forthcoming statement on "The Ministry in the Church" of the international dialogue.)

Surely if Roman Catholics and Lutherans are coming to such an awareness of existing agreement in the area of the ordained ministry it behooves Episcopalians and Lutherans to see if such agreement does not also exist among us. We in this discussion have concluded that it does exist.

## Conclusion

There is, it is to be admitted, serious divergence in the actual ordering of the Pastoral Office in the two Communions as well as in the importance generally accorded to the historic episcopate. Futher, there are additional topics worthy of continued discussion.[9] However, despite that, we are profoundly impressed and encouraged by the basic and extensive elements of agreement which we have found in all of the aspects of apostolic succession, including that of the ordained ministry. We can declare together that both the Lutheran Church and the Episcopal Church stand in Apostolic Succession. "And they devoted themselves to the apostles' teaching and fellowship, to the breaking of bread and prayers." (Acts 2:42)

## Notes

1. At the Restoration of the English Monarchy and the Church of England as episcopally ordered (1660-62), a new phrase was added at the conclusion of the following statement from the Preface to the Ordinal in the 1662 Book of Common Prayer:

> And therefore, to the intent that these Orders may be continued and reverently used and esteemed in this Church, no man shall be accounted or taken to be a lawful Bishop, Priest, or Deacon, in this Church, or suffered to execute any of the said Functions, except he be called, tried, examined, and admitted thereunto, according to the Form hereafter following, *or hath had Episcopal Consecration or Ordination.*

Emphatically, this was not an attempt to un-Church continental Protestants, but rather to deal directly with a controverted point of polity within the English Church (in and after 1662 those clergy who could or would not accept this stipulation—Nonconformists—where legally ejected or barred from clerical office/livings within the Church of England as by law established). Certain difficulties within the Church of England that continued to touch upon this point of polity, e.g., the Bangorian Controversy (1717-19) and the Methodist Movement later in the century, resulted for some Highchurchmen in an increasingly rigorous interpretation of the necessity of episcopacy to authentic ecclesial life. But, again, this was understood not to un-Church continental Protestants.

2. It should be noted that the Consultation on Church Union (COCU), of which the Episcopal Church is a constituent member, has accepted the historical episcopate in its proposed order for a Church of Christ Uniting while not articulating any particular theory with regard to the terms mentioned in this paragraph. With respect to differing interpretations within contemporary Anglicanism, cf. Kenneth Kirk (ed.), *The Apostolic Ministry* (1946)—*esse* position; Stephen Neill (ed.), *The Ministry of the Church* (1947)—*bene esse* position; Kenneth Carey (ed.), *The Historic Episcopate in the Fullness of the Church* (1954)—*plene esse* position.

3. Holsten Fagerberg, *A New Look at the Lutheran Confessions* (St. Louis, Concordia, 1972), pp. 226-238.

4. Theodore G. Tappert (ed.), *Lutheran Confessional Theology in America*. 1840-1880 (New York: Oxford University Press, 1972), pp. 229-245, 279.

5. The XXXIX Articles, Articles XXV, and the Catechism of the Book of Common Prayer, p. 854, called these "the sacraments of the gospel." The usage of later Lutheranism limited the sacraments to two in number, but in the Apology of the Augsburg Confession (Book of Concord, Tappert edition, pp. 187.41, 211.4, 212.11-13; cf. pp. 310-313), Melanchthon includes Absolution among the sacraments and even allows that Ordination may be so designated. Melanchthon is operating here with a definition of sacraments in terms of Word-plus-*rite*. Luther tended to operate with a Word-plus-*element* definition, hence usually designated only two sacraments. (Cf. the Book of Common Prayer on other sacramental rites, p. 860.)

6. It is noted that the Lutheran law-gospel dialectic may have influenced the adoption of the reading of the Law in the 1552 BCP. Martin Bucer's influence here is clear, but the possible Lutheran theological roots of this practice (even though it did not take hold in Lutheran liturgical practice) hold out some fascinating comparisons between Anglicanism and Lutheranism.

7. This non-repeatability refers to orders recognized within the two communions and does not deal with the issue of a mutually recognized ministry as between Lutherans and Episcopalians.

8. *Eucharist and Ministry: Lutherans and Catholics in Dialogue IV* (Minneapolis: Augsburg Publishing House, 1979), especially pp. 7-22.

9. The following weighty matters we believe require further discussion: 1) the relationship between presbyteral succession and episcopal succession, including a discussion of the role and office of the bishop; 2) the relation of the pastoral office to the priesthood-of-all believers; 3) the possibility of a mutually recognized ministry of Word and Sacrament; and 4) the question of the ordination of women.

Several other matters are worthy of consideration and reflect issues which exist within both communions: 1) the exegetical basis of the institution of the ordained ministry; 2) the place of the charismatic ministry as found in the New Testament; and 3) the Papacy.

## Recommendations From LED II

The Report of the Lutheran-Episcopal Dialogue I (LED I) in the U.S.A. was subtitled "Exploration and Progress." Representatives of these two great ecclesiastical communities, which have a common heritage from the sixteenth century Reformation, similar styles of church life and liturgical worship, reverence for the catholic tradition, but only sporadic moments of historical interaction, came together to get better acquainted with one another to determine whether there was sufficient commonality to work toward closer relationships. The Report of LED I found substantial areas of agreement by comparing the respective requirements for intercommunion/pulpit and altar fellowship in the Chicago-Lambeth Quadrilateral and Article VII of the Augsburg Confession. While not recommending full pulpit and altar fellowship between the Protestant Episcopal Church in the U.S.A. (PECUSA) and the three participating Lutheran Church bodies (ALC-LCA-LCMS), the dialogue panel did recommend limited intercommunion between parishes or congregations "subject to the consent of the appropriate local authorities."

The LED I recommendations were not widely circulated among the membership of the respective churches and the hoped-for developments in the Lutheran-Episcopal relationship did not occur on any broad basis. We believe a number of factors account for this apparent lack of implementation. During the years 1972-76, the church bodies represented in the dialogue focused their attention on other issues; for example, within the Episcopal Church: the ordination of women to the priesthood, the revision of the Book of Common Prayer, and the study and response to the national and international dialogues with the Roman Catholic Church; within the Lutheran Church-Missouri Synod: the question of the ordination of women, the formation of Seminex and the separation of AELC; for Lutherans generally: the new Lutheran Book of Worship and Lutheran involvement in Roman Catholic-Lutheran dialogue on both national and international levels.

Because of the lack of wide distribution and study, the LED I recommendations were misunderstood or seen as too radical and/or inconsistent with the doctrine and practice of the participating churches; for example, some felt that the recommended interim eucharistic fellowship was at odds with the approaches followed in other dialogues and that all dialogues needed to be consistent with each other; many felt the need for more historical and theological documentation of the recommendations; others questioned the apparent interchangeability of Lutheran "confessionalism" with Anglican "historic episcopate" as a form of apostolicity.

Certain things have transpired in the meantime both among Lutherans and Episcopalians which affect our relationship; some of them are:

1. In 1976 the Joint Commission on Ecumenical Relations (now the Standing Commission on Ecumenical Relations) of the Episcopal Church adopted a restatement of Apostolicity, which moved in the direction of broader interpretation.[1]

2. The 1976 General Convention of the Episcopal Church adopted "Guidelines for Interim Eucharistic Fellowship" with the churches of the Consultation on Church Union. The Convention also, as had several previous General Conventions, reaffirmed the Chicago-Lambeth Quadrilateral as the basis for ecumenical dialogue with other Christian bodies.

3. In 1977 the Lutheran (ALC, AELC, LCA) and Episcopalian (Dioceses of Michigan and Western Michigan) judicatory heads in Michigan adopted a statement "Free to Share" on the basis of the 1972 LED I recommendations. More recently in Massachusetts, Lutheran and Episcopal parishes have received approval from regional church authorities for joint celebrations of the eucharist on "special ecumenical occasions."

4. The 1978 Ecumenical Consultation of the Episcopal Church (Detroit) urged an "intensified dialogue" with Lutherans because the 1977 Episcopal Diocesan Ecumenical Officers surveyed disclosed that the

Lutheran-Episcopal dialogue ranked second (after the Anglican-Roman Catholic Conversations) on the list of priorities among Episcopalians.

5. In 1978 the Lambeth Conference passed a resolution encouraging Anglican churches "to give special attention to our ecclesial recognition of the Lutheran Church" on the basis of the Anglican-Lutheran International Conversations (The Pullach Report, 1972), resolution 2 of the second meeting (Dublin, 1973) and resolution 5 of the third meeting (Trinidad, 1976) of the Anglican Consultative Council.

6. In 1978 the LCA and ALC adopted a new statement on "Communion practices," which provides guidelines for sharing the sacrament with baptized Christians of other churches.

7. The 1979 General Convention of the Episcopal Church adopted a new resolution and commentary on "Eucharistic Sharing," a statement of a "Goal of Visible Unity" and passed a resolution calling for "intensified dialogue with the Lutherans."

8. The 1978 Lutheran Book of Worship and the 1979 Book of Common Prayer share a similar structure for the Eucharistic Liturgy, similar material for the daily prayer offices, a common use of the historic church year, many of the same lesser festivals and commemorations, the three-year lectionary for Sundays and festivals, the two-year daily lectionary, the same translation of the Psalter, many of the same collects, and a use of texts translated by the International Consultation on English Texts for Creeds, Lord's Prayer, and canticles.

As a result of our studies and discussions in LED II:

A. We, the PECUSA, AELC, ALC, and LCA participants, are able to affirm the recommendations of LED I and move beyond them in recommending the following:

1. That our respective Church bodies "mutually recognize" one another as true churches where the Gospel is truly preached and the sacraments duly celebrated (cf. Article XIX of the Articles of Religion, Augsburg Confession, Article VII) by taking appropriate legislative action.

2. That, because of the consensus achieved in the discussions of LED I and II on the chief doctrines of the Christian faith, our respective churches work out a policy of interim eucharistic hospitality so that Episcopalians may be welcomed at Lutheran altars and Lutherans may be welcomed at Episcopalian altars.

3. That the kind of joint worship recommended in the Report of the International Lutheran-Anglican Conversations be authorized and encouraged: "In places where local conditions make this desirable, there should be mutual participation from time to time

by entire congregations in the worship and eucharistic celebrations of the other church. Anniversaries and other special occasions provide opportunity for members of the two traditions to share symbolic and eucharistic worship together."

4. That our church bodies take steps to cooperate in the publication and circulation of the reports and recommendations of LED I and LED II and other materials designed to popularize in the churches the findings of these dialogues.

5. That our respective church bodies encourage Episcopalian and Lutheran congregations to covenant together on the local level for the purpose of such things as: (a) mutual prayer and mutual support; (b) common study of the Holy Scriptures and the materials of LED I and LED II; (c) participation of Lutheran and Episcopal clergy at one another's services on special occasions; and (d) joint programs of religious education, theological discussion, mission, evangelism and social action.

6. That a third series of Lutheran Episcopal dialogues be held, with an emphasis on the means and models for implementing LED I and LED II, including such doctrinal discussions as may be pertinent. Discussion should focus on a mutually accepted order for ministry, with attention given to the role and office of bishop, diaconal ministry and the ministry of the laity.

B. We, the LCMS participants, recommend the following:

1. that we urge our constituent church bodies to publish and circulate the agreed statements for local discussion and dialogue among local pastors and parishes of the respective bodies for information, edification, reaction, and mutually-agreed-upon action;

2. that the unresolved issues listed in the documents calling for further amplification and clarification be commended to LED series III on the national level as well as to local dialogues urged above;

3. that we give thanks to God individually and corporately for His gift to us of one Lord, one faith, one Baptism, one God and Father of us all, even as we continue to pray that "all they who call upon your holy Name may come to agree in the truth of your holy Word and live in unity and godly love."

## Notes

1. See The Report of The Joint Commission on Ecumenical Relations to the 65th General Convention of the Episcopal Church, 1976.

# The Lutheran-Episcopal Agreement:
# September, 1982

The Episcopal Church/The American Lutheran Church, the Lutheran Church in America, and the Association of Evangelical Lutheran Churches voted to:

1. Welcome and rejoice in the substantial progress of the Lutheran-Episcopal Dialogues (LED) I and II and to the Anglican-Lutheran International Conversations, looking forward to the day when full communion is established between the Anglican and Lutheran churches.

2. Recognize now the (Episcopal Church/The American Lutheran Church, Lutheran Church in America, and Association of Evangelical Lutheran Churches) as churches in which the Gospel is preached and taught.

3. Encourage the development of common Christian life throughout the respective churches by such means as the following:

   a. Mutual prayer and mutual support, including parochial/congregational and diocesan/synodical covenants or agreements;
   b. Common study of the Holy Scriptures, the historical and theological traditions of each church, and the materials of LED I and II;
   c. Joint programs of religious education, theological discussion, mission, evangelism, and social action;
   d. Joint use of physical facilities.

4. Affirm now on the basis of studies of LED I and LED II and of the Anglican-Lutheran International Conversations that the basic teaching of each respective church is consonant with the Gospel and is sufficiently compatible with the teaching of this church that a relationship of Interim Sharing of the Eucharist is hereby established between these churches in the U.S.A. under the following guidelines:

   a. Extend a special welcome to members of the (Episcopal Church/The American Lutheran Church, Lutheran Church in America, and Association of Evangelical Lutheran Churches) to receive Holy Communion in it under [the Statement of

199

Communion Practices adopted in 1978(Lutheran)/Standard for Occasional Eucharistic Sharing of its 1979 General Convention (Episcopal)]. This welcome constitutes a mutual recognition of Eucharistic teaching sufficient for Interim Sharing of the Eucharist, although this does not intend to signify that final recognition of each other's Eucharists or ministries has yet been achieved.

b. Recognize that bishops of dioceses of the Episcopal Church and bishops/presidents of the Lutheran districts/synods may by mutual agreement extend the regulations of church discipline to permit common, joint celebration of the Eucharist in their jurisdictions. This is appropriate in particular situations where the said authorities deem that local conditions are appropriate for the sharing of worship jointly by congregations of the respective churches. The presence of an ordained minister of each participating church at the altar in this way reflects the presence of two or more churches expressing unity in faith and baptism as well as the remaining divisions which they seek to overcome; however, this does not imply rejection or final recognition of either church's Eucharist or ministry. In such circumstances the eucharistic prayer will be one from the *Lutheran Book of Worship* or the *Book of Common Prayer* as authorized jointly by the bishop of the Episcopal diocese and the bishops/presidents of the corresponding Lutheran districts/synods.

c. Request that the experience of this interim sharing of the Eucharist be communicated at regular intervals to the other churches of the Lutheran and Anglican communions throughout the world, as well as to the various ecumenical dialogues in which Anglicans and Lutherans are engaged, in order that consultation may be fostered, similar experience encouraged elsewhere and already existing relationships of full communion respected.

5. Authorize and establish now a third series of Lutheran-Episcopal Dialogues for the discussion of any other outstanding questions that must be resolved before full communion (*communio in sacris*/altar and pulpit fellowship) can be established between the respective churches, e.g., implications of the Gospel, historic episcopate, and ordering of ministry (bishops, priests, and deacons) in the total context of apostolicity.

# Implications of the Gospel*

## I. THE ESCHATOLOGICAL *GROUNDING* OF THE GOSPEL

### A. The Proclamation and Ministry of Jesus

6. When Jesus came preaching the gospel of God, he said, according to the Gospel of Mark, "The time is fulfilled, and the kingdom of God is at hand; repent, and believe in the gospel" (Mark 1:15). In the Lukan account Jesus begins his mission by reading in the synagogue a programmatic promise from the scroll of the prophet Isaiah and then announcing to the assembly, "Today this scripture has been fulfilled in your hearing" (Luke 4:17-21). The Gospels of the New Testament proclaim that the good news (gospel) is the advent in history of the redemptive reign of God. Jesus begins the consummation and realization of the great vision of Israel's prophet of the exile: "Your God reigns" (Isa. 52:7, cf. 61:1-2).

7. The documents of the New Testament use a variety of phrases, images, and concepts to give expression to the gospel. Paul, whose letters are among the earliest documents in the New Testament, proclaimed the gospel in terms of persons being "justified by faith in Christ, and not by works of the law" (Gal. 2:16). Paul condemned anything but "the grace of Christ" as a different gospel, no gospel at all, a perversion of the gospel (Gal. 1:6-7). Jesus is the justifier as the crucified one (Gal. 2:20-21). The Gospel of John, among the later documents in the New Testament, proclaimed the gospel as the eternal Word of God become flesh, dwelling among us, revealing grace, truth, and God (John 1:1-18). The "hour" for which he had come, and through which the "glory" of the Father and the Son would be revealed, and on the basis of which the Paraclete would be bestowed, was the cross, resurrection, and ascension of Jesus (John 14-17). The synoptic Gospels—Matthew, Mark, and Luke—although each is written from a unique perspective, proclaimed the mission and ministry of Jesus in terms of the breaking in

*William A. Norgren and William G. Rusch, eds., *Implications of the Gospel.* Lutheran-Episcopal Dialogue, Series III (Minneapolis: Augsburg; Cincinnati: Forward Movement, 1988) 16-95, 100.

of the reign of God. It is important to note that the central emphasis of the Gospel of Mark is to understand that the breaking in of the reign of God took place through the cross (Mark 8:27-35; 9:30-32; 10:32-45).

8. What identifies the proclamation of the cross as *good* news is the "eschatological" way of thinking in the New Testament. The writings of the New Testament are strongly focused in a future hope. That future hope is expressed by the theological term *eschaton* from which the word "eschatology" is derived. In traditional theological thought "eschatology" dealt with "last things," what would take place when history had come to an end. We are using the term "eschatology" in a closely related but nevertheless distinct sense, namely, as referring to the "outcome" of history, the ultimate goal or destiny or future toward which God is directing the history of the world. This "outcome" is present to us as the *promise* of the final victory of the reign of God. Most of the writings of the New Testament proclaim that in Christ the new age, the "eschatological age," has already begun, that the new age is now in tension with the ongoing "old age." The New Testament writings proclaim that the presence of the reign of God was already disclosed in the deeds, the teaching, and above all the death and resurrection of Jesus, the Christ.

## B. The Significance of the Resurrection of Jesus

9. The decisive event for opening Jesus's disciples to this conviction was the resurrection of Jesus. After his execution and burial the disciples were demoralized, defeated. The Gospel of Luke describes the two disciples on the way to Emmaus as assuming that Jesus had been discredited as Messiah by his crucifixion (Luke 24:21). What changed the disciples was their encounter with Jesus after his death. What they experienced was not a resuscitation, not their teacher resuming his life with them. Rather, Jesus encountered them now as the disclosure of the *eschaton* (outcome) proleptically, that is, in preview. Jesus encountered them as the beginning of the final hoped-for reign of God. The concepts available to them for describing what had happened to Jesus came from the eschatological expectations of Israel: that righteous sufferers would be vindicated, martyrs would be resuscitated (2 Maccabees 7:9-23). But the character of their encounters with Jesus after his death burst the framework of those expectations. They encountered someone and something radically *more*, not less, than those expectations. They experienced proleptically, that is, in preview, the outcome of history in the midst of history. They were let in on the disclosed promise of God's final salvation. The conviction of the earliest disciples eventually found expression in a variety of related convictions, implications

of the gospel in various documents of the New Testament. There would be "no condemnation" for those joined to the Christ (Rom. 8:1). The power of death was not to have the last word (I Cor. 15:54-56). The fallen (old) age and its powers had been subjected to the Christ (Eph. 1:15-23, especially vv. 21-23). The "world" as hostile to God's reign had been overcome (John 16:33). All tears would be wiped away (Rev. 7:13-17; cf. Isa. 25:6-8).

10. In their encounter with the resurrection of Jesus, the disciples at last understood something of the paradox that the crucified one was and is, despite all appearances, God's "Yes" to the world (2 Cor. 1:18-24). The good news which Jesus announced had indeed been an act as well as a teaching of grace, of unconditional promise (Luke 4:17-21; cf. Isa. 61:1-2). The resurrection disclosed that sin and death could not inhibit his freedom to be for the world or qualify his commitment to his creation (Rom. 8:18-39). The disclosure that the final consummation of history would be the reign of God meant the reaffirmation of the goodness of creation as well as effecting the reconciliation of an estranged humanity. The one who is Lord and Christ is also the one through whom "all things were created," in whom "all things hold together" (John 1:1-5; Col. 1:15-20).

11. The church confessed the death and resurrection of Jesus as good news for the world by rejecting the gnostic attempt to drive a wedge between creation and redemption. The following were among the ways the church affirmed the creation: the acknowledgment of the Scriptures of Israel as canonical Scriptures for the church; the continuity with Israel and its worship traditions (Psalter, Blessings, Thanksgivings); the creedal affirmation that the God of creation is identical with Jesus, his Father, and the Holy Spirit; the principle of sacramentality (that the creaturely is capable of being the vehicle for God's ultimate promise); and the expectation of the resurrection of all because the risen Jesus was the "first fruits." All of this testified to the conviction that the gospel as eschatological event was not a repudiation of the world but its fulfillment and hope.

## C. Baptism and the Eschatological Age

12. Baptism into the death and resurrection of Jesus was practiced by the earliest disciples on the basis of the resurrection of Jesus. It was both similar to and different from the baptizing of John the Baptist. John's was a baptism of *repentance* in anticipation of the coming reign of God. The baptism practiced by Jesus' disciples in his name recognizes that the reign of God is both "now" and "yet to be consummated." This comes to expression in two ways.

13. First, baptism in the name of Jesus or in the triune name is both *ini-*

*tiation* into the community of the *eschaton* already present in Jesus by means of being identified with Jesus' death and resurrection, and it is also *repentance* in anticipation of the final realization of the promise of Jesus. The baptized are grasped by the forgiving love of God, transferred to the kingdom of his beloved Son, in whom we have redemption, the forgiveness of sins (cf. Col. 1:13-14). Although repentance and faith often precede baptism, its character as initiation through identification with the death and resurrection of Jesus means that something happens *to* the candidate. This then becomes one reason for the baptism of infants. Because they share in the fallenness of humanity, their baptism is necessary. However, they also share in the present promise of the reign of God (Mark 10:14-16 and parallels; Matt. 18:3). Because the consummation of the reign of God is still awaited, candidates can also be summoned to "repent and be baptized" (e.g., Acts 2:38). Indeed, all who have been initiated into the eschatological community are called to repent in view of their still flawed and broken witness to the reign of God. Because they *have* died with Christ (Col. 2:20-23), they can be exhorted to "put to death" what is sinful (that is, whatever resists the reign of God), to "put away" whatever is characteristic of the "old nature" (Col. 3:5-11). Because they have been raised with Christ (Col. 3:1-4), they are exhorted to be clothed with all that is characteristic of the new nature (Col. 3:12-17).

14. Second, because the reign of God is both "now" and "yet to be consummated," the present existence of the eschatological community is characterized by temptation, that is, by assault on its identity, by struggle and conflict, by brokenness and lapses into unfaithfulness. Baptism is thus initiation into the *locus* of conflict between the old age and the new (Eph. 6:10-20). Because of baptism we can recognize that we are, in Martin Luther's phrase, simultaneously righteous and sinful. Baptism means that while we are grasped by the grace and power of the Holy Spirit, that is, by the gift and power of God's freedom for the future, we experience at the same time the continued power of the demonic. Hence baptism is the sacrament *par excellence* of justification *by faith*[2] for it initiates into a community which lives in the "land of promise" and which anticipates the city "whose builder and maker is God" (Heb. 11:10). Baptism plunges us into the situation in which the "old" (that is, the power of all that is hostile to the reign of God) has passed away (2 Cor. 5:17), but is still able to afflict, perplex, persecute, or strike down (2 Cor. 4:7-18).

15. Thus in the Lutheran rite of baptism those who are "set free from the bondage to sin and death" by being baptismally joined "to the death and resurrection of our Lord Jesus Christ" are asked to "renounce all the forces of evil, the devil, and all his empty promises" (*The Lutheran Book of Worship*, pp. 121-125). In the Episcopal rite of baptism those who are led by the Christ, "through his death and resurrection, from the bondage of sin into

everlasting life" are asked to renounce "Satan and all the spiritual forces of wickedness which rebel against God...the evil powers of this world which corrupt and destroy the creatures of God...the sinful desires that draw [us] from the love of God" (*The Book of Common Prayer*, pp. 301-308). Both liturgical traditions testify to the conviction that baptism links us with the death and resurrection of Jesus and therefore calls us to the struggle against evil and its power in ourselves and in the world.

## D. The Bondage of Sin

16. The "old aeon" from which we are delivered by God's eschatological salvation is characterized by our bondage to the power of sin and death, by our perversion of God's call to be creatures both finite and free, by our alienation from the image of God given with our creation. Our fallenness is disclosed when we deny either our finitude or our freedom or both; or when we refuse to be creatures or to be accountable or both; or when we use our best behaviors, insights, and achievements as occasions for idolatry or as a means of self-justification; or when we despair of God's mercy and engage in self-hatred. Our sin, in other words, is the bondage of misdirected trust, false faith. One sign of judgment upon such sin is that we are handed over to our idols. Captive to the powers of the fallen aeon, we reveal our bondage through attempts at exclusivistic self-preservation and self-protection, through our denial of the truth or our despair of God's mercy, or through our adherence to power and privilege at the expense of authentic peace and universal justice. This is the bondage from which the redemptive reign of God sets us free and at the same time the bondage which continues to assault and, at times, overwhelm the baptized.

## E. The Gospel as the Word and Way of the Cross

17. The resurrection is God's act of proclaiming that the "Christ" title is now qualified by, determined by, the cross (Acts 2:36; Rom. 1:4). Jesus the crucified one is the Christ (I Cor. 2:2). This proclamation calls into question every attempt of the church to pervert the gospel of God's reign into false "glory" or triumphalism. The word of the cross is the weapon given to the church in its struggle with various temptations, e.g., the temptation to substitute psychological manipulation, religious loyalty, or political and military power for the gospel.

18. The cross of Jesus defines the reign of God as an act of redeeming, sin-bearing suffering and death. Jesus incarnates the sovereign choice to be a

victim so that others need not be victimized. The reign of God is the reign of the one who consents to suffer in and with and for the world. The vision of such a God was given to Israel (e.g., Hos. 11:8-9;Jer. 31:18-20) and came to fulfillment when the Messiah of God was proclaimed as identical with the suffering servant of God. (Mark 1:11 and its parallels make a direct link between a messianic enthronement song, Psalm 2, and the Servant Song, Isa. 42:1-4). God's reign is therefore proclaimed as the reign of one who enters into solidarity with slaves and who dies the humiliating death of a slave (Phil. 2:5-11). It is the reign of the despised and crucified one (I Cor. 1:18-25;I Peter 2:21-25;Heb. 13:12-16;Mark 10:35-45 and parallels), whose crucifixion is also his exaltation (John 3:14;8:28; and 12:31-32). It is the reign of the abandoned one in whose death the Father and the Son experience the depths of condemnation and alienation and thus open the human future anew to the Spirit of creative love (Romans 8, esp. vv. 31-39;Gal. 3:13). It is the reign of "the Lamb of God, who takes away the sin of the world" (John 1:29). The cross of Jesus establishes God's redemptive reign. It is also the concrete way in which it engages in continued conflict with the powers of the "old aeon," that is, the powers of sin and death.

## II. THE *GOD* OF THE GOSPEL

### A. The History of Jesus and the Christological Dogma

19. The God of the church's confession. Father, Son, Holy Spirit, is the God of the gospel. The church is continuously led to that confession by the gospel and its implications. The church's path to its confession of God was historical in content; the history of Israel and the history of Jesus. The Scriptures of Israel grew out of Israel's history, where God is portrayed as one who calls, elects, and covenants with a people, who creates and redeems, who rules and judges the nations and the cosmos, who gives Torah and sends the prophets, whose very character is expressed in vulnerability and the determination to suffer with, for, at the hands of the world, whose involvement in history is directed toward such ends as peace (shalom), justice (righteousness), and wholeness (life).

20. Jesus of Nazareth appears in Israel's history as eschatological prophet with both implicit and explicit messianic claims. His enemies intended his crucifixion as judgment upon his claim to be the Christ of God, the one calling Israel to its mission on behalf of the reign of God. The crucifixion was intended as a rejection of the words and deeds by which Jesus proclaimed the reign of God and embodied its power. But the gospel declares that he is indeed the Christ, so designated by the resurrection (Rom. 1:3-

4;Acts 2:36). The resurrection points the church both forward toward the consummation of the redemptive reign of God and simultaneously directs attention back to the cross and its significance in the light of the entire ministry of Jesus.

21. In the wake of the resurrection encounters with Jesus, the community of his disciples moved through and beyond the recognition that he was inaugurating the reign of God to the confession that he and his history are to be regarded as one with God. In the words of an early Christian author (2 Clement 1:1), "we ought to think of Jesus Christ as we do of God." The history of Jesus, his ministry, cross, and resurrection, confirms, renews, and transforms Israel's experience and confession. That same history of Jesus is the basis for the church's trinitarian and christological dogmas. What the church *means evangelically* by confessing that Jesus has a divine nature is not that assumptions from philosophy about the qualities of deity (e.g., that the divine is "infinite" or "immortal" or "omnipotent") are applied to the historical Jesus. Rather, the evangelical meaning is that the historical person, Jesus, weak and crucified, is what we mean when we speak of God as redeemer (Col. 1:15-20). In his ministry the call to Israel to serve the reign of God comes to final and definitive expression. In his death God suffers with, for, or at the hands of his people and their enemies. In his resurrection the promise of the final triumph of God's reign is proleptically present.

22. There are three reasons why the way of thinking described above (pars. 19-21) is of decisive importance for our understanding of the gospel.

First, it serves the intelligibility of the church's witness. It must be noted that making the gospel understood does not make it easier to believe. Rather it makes evident the genuine alternatives with which humanity is confronted. It disclosed that our predicament is not ignorance of the gospel but sinful trust in false gospels. The church's recovery of the *historical* character of its gospel makes its proclamation more apparent to contemporary culture. The meaning of God in terms of ultimacy and of the gospel in terms of historical finality is both more faithful and more meaningful. Thus the historical meaning of the "two natures" dogma of Chalcedon witnesses to the ultimate and final redemptive quality of Jesus's death and resurrection.

23. Second, the history of Jesus is the grounding of the grace of God both in the world's history and in God's history. It is the grounding of grace within the world's history because in the cross of Jesus, God has made a final and unconditional commitment to the world. It is the grounding of grace within God's history because in the death and resurrection of Jesus something has happened to God that had not happened before. God's vulnerability and suffering was known in Israel (e.g., Hosea, Jeremiah). In Jesus that vulnerability and suffering receives its final expression, namely death itself. In Jesus God experiences the depth of sin (2 Cor. 5:21) and the power

of death (Rom. 5:8). Thus sin and death have been encountered and overcome in the being and history of God. With sin overcome and death behind
him, Jesus can and does make an unconditional promise to the world: the triumph of the reign of God will finally be manifested.

24. Third, the cross as central to the history of Jesus gives Christianity
an absolute or unconditional gospel which is not imperialistic, immoral, or
triumphalistic. Religion by definition is about absolutes. The tragic character
of inauthentic or false absolutes is that they establish themselves through
destructive power, the forced imposition of that which is alien. The reaction
to such imposition is the equally inappropriate and false assertion of autonomy. The absolute of the historical Jesus means the proclamation of a gospel
in which God reconciles the world by means of the absolute quality of suffering servanthood (2 Cor. 5:17-21;John 12:31-32;Phil. 2:5-11;Eph. 2:13-
22). The church commends its gospel with a servant ministry grounded in the
person and history of Jesus (2 Cor. 6:1-10).

## B. The Trinity and the Gospel

25. The church's name of God, "Father, Son, Holy Spirit," is grounded
in Jesus Christ. Among other things, *name* implies narrative, the story of the
one being named. Because the gospel is the historical narrative of God's
commitment to the world, God's determination to create and redeem the
world, and finally God's victorious promise of an unconquerable future for
the world, the church told the story of God in terms of the triune name. The
trinity is the way the church identifies and confesses God because of Jesus,
because of the gospel.

26. Jesus is identified as "Son," sent by one whom he called "Abba,"
an intimate term for "Father." He invited his disciples to use the name
"Father" when he taught them to pray the mission prayer of the present and
promised reign of God. Both names, "Father" and "Son," reflect and express
the gospel as the love of God for the world and the love within the triune
God. As we have learned in the self-giving love of Jesus, the Son, God's
love never turns in on itself. It is forever directed toward another. The act of
creating, of calling into existence a universe distinct from God, is expressive
of the love which is God. The act of reconciling a fallen humanity is consistent with a loving creator. Suffering will be the loss of both creator and rec-
onciler. Both the Son and the Father suffer, each in his own way, in the
cross.

27. The Son "gave himself for [us]" (Gal. 2:20) in a profound unity of
will with his Father, who "gave him up for us all" (Rom. 8:32). When the
Son's cry from the cross reveals his entry into forsakenness (Mark 15:34)

and condemnation (Gal. 3:13), it occurs under the darkness of his Father's hidden face (Mark 15:33). The death that is experienced goes to the very heart of God's being. The Son sacrificed his relationship to his Father, and his Father sacrificed his relationship to his Son. "God *so* loved the world that he gave his only Son" (John 3:16, italics added). That is, God loved the world *in this way*, the way of forsakenness in Jesus' death on the cross.

28. The farewell words of Jesus in the Gospel of John speak of the Holy Spirit as the one who "stands alongside of" (*paracletos*, John 14:16, 26; 15:26; 16:7) the persecuted community in its life in the world (John 15:18-25). In this role the Spirit of truth (John 14:17; 15:26; 16:13) continues to bear the witness of Jesus in the world concerning sin, righteousness, and judgment (John 16:8), and guides the community into the truth of Jesus' revelation of the Father (John 16:12-15). In the power of the Spirit the community is sent into the world by the risen Lord (John 20:17-18,21-23). Through the Holy Spirit the suffering Son and Father are thus united with the condemned and cursed, with helpless victims and helpless participants in the suffering of victims, finally even with oppressors in the overcoming of their sin. It is thus critical in the present missionary context of the church to understand that the proclamation of the suffering God aids mission. In terms of post-Holocaust Europe, this statement will be evident enough. In the case of middle-class America, much suffering is psychological and veiled, and it will therefore have to be exposed and named as "suffering." Then the liberating message of the suffering God will be at hand, and will be the tool for mission in our context of suffering. Because God is *Emmanuel*, God with us, there is now hope for the hopeless, forgiveness for sinners, comfort for the forsaken, vision for the victims, resurrection for the dead. In Christ God's holiness, that is, God's otherness and uniqueness, is not condemning and threatening. God's holiness is God's own and unique compassion. Paul expresses to the Galatian Christians that it is through the Spirit that faith has come in the hearing of the gospel (Gal. 3:2), in which the hearer receives God's promise of inheritance in Jesus: "God has sent the Spirit of his Son into our hearts, crying, 'Abba! Father!'" (Gal. 4:6). Being led by the Spirit is walking in the Spirit, putting to death the old enslavements, and living in the freedom of Christ to love and serve the neighbor (Gal. 5:1-6:6). The Ephesian letter takes up this theme by stating that the Holy Spirit represents the down payment (Eph. 1:13-14) which enables us to live in our inheritance "until we acquire possession of it." The dynamic of a new future is open to the world. The Holy Spirit is the power (*dynamis*) of that new and reconciled future. The trinity is the God of the gospel. The name of God, Father, Son, Holy Spirit, reflects the historical particularity of the gospel itself.

29. Our churches need to be concerned about the overuse of the term

"Father," especially in the address of God in prayer. When the term Father is not clearly used as part of the trinitarian name of God (cf. par. 31 below), it functions instead as a masculine image for God. While we recognize that the church has traditionally selected masculine images for God from the Scriptures, our churches need to advocate the use of feminine images as well as this traditional masculine imagery. We need all the imagery available to help us think about God. When the term Father is used as an image, as an analogy drawn from our experience, it must be supplemented by many other images and analogies in order to reflect the fullness of our experiences. Such supplementing will, of course, include feminine imagery. Especially in prayer, when it is appropriate to add modifying clauses in the address of God, the use of feminine imagery needs to be encouraged. (Examples: O God, whose love for us is like that of a mother, who suffers for us as woman in giving birth, who would gather us as mother hen gathers her chicks, etc.) There is ample precedent for such imagery in the Bible and the rest of the church's tradition (Deut. 32:18;Job 38:28-29;Ps. 123:2;Isa. 42:14;Hos. 13:8;Matt. 23:37; and Luke 13:34).[3] Strategies for introducing the feminine element into talk about God do not stop with the first Person of the Trinity. Scholars have recovered the biblical theme of Jesus as the "Sophia" of God. Others find feminine symbols to be appropriately descriptive of the Spirit's work. (The words for "spirit" vary in grammatical as distinct from sexual gender from language to language, being feminine in Hebrew and Aramaic, neuter in Greek, and masculine in Latin.)

30. We are aware that others advocate the substitution of gender-neutral terms, such as "creator," "redeemer," "sanctifier," for the trinitarian name. This reaction is understandable both because of the centuries of patriarchalism in the church and because, when the dogma of the trinity has been separated from the gospel and has instead been understood as a component of Christian ideology, it has been used in an oppressive manner. However the church *cannot* simply substitute the designations creator, redeemer, and sanctifier for the trinitarian name. We cannot do so because function is *not* identical with person and because each function is ascribed to all three persons encompassed by the one trinitarian name.

31. Furthermore, since the dogma of the trinity is a confession and naming of the God of the gospel, "Father" is not, on the one hand, just one image among other biblical images, nor, on the other hand, does it exhaust the church's name for God. It is the name by which Jesus addressed the one in whose mission and history he participates. Hence the church's full dogmatic name for God is "Father, Son, Holy Spirit." When we address the "Abba" of Jesus, we do so because we have been called to participate in the liberating mission of the gospel by the Father, Son, Holy Spirit.

For you did not receive the spirit of slavery to fall back into fear, but you have received the spirit of sonship. When we cry, "Abba! Father!" it is the Spirit himself bearing witness with our spirit that we are children of God, and if children, then heirs, heirs of God and fellow heirs with Christ, provided we suffer with him in order that we may also be glorified with him. (Rom. 8:15-17)

To abandon the "Abba" name given us by Jesus is to diminish the liberating mission of the gospel.

32. The uniqueness and finality of the God of the gospel must be confessed in such a way as to be grounded in the particular history of Jesus. God is *one* because the meaning of God's oneness is God's uniqueness, singularity, finality, ultimacy. The gospel defines and identifies that uniqueness, that singularity, that finality, that ultimacy. The gospel is the history of the Son, his Father, and the promised Spirit in, with, and for the world, a history which points back to the being of God as eternal Trinity.

## III. THE *CHURCH* OF THE GOSPEL

### A. The Church as Necessary Implication of the Gospel

33. It is to be expected that the issues of greatest sensitivity related to full communion between Episcopalians and Lutherans would occur in ecclesiology. On the basis of Article 7 (VII) of the Augsburg Confession Lutherans have traditionally emphasized that the preaching of the gospel "in its purity" and the administration of the sacraments "according to the gospel" are "sufficient for the true unity of the Christian church." Lutherans have asked whether doctrine, proclamation, and administration of the sacraments reflect an authentic understanding of the gospel before entertaining the prospect of full communion with non Lutheran churches. Anglicans have traditionally stressed the importance of order to assure the authentic administration of the sacraments. Episcopalians have asked, among other things, whether churches have the historic episcopate before entertaining the prospect of full communion with them.

34. In 1982, when the predecessor bodies of the Evangelical Lutheran Church in America and the Episcopal Church recognized each other as churches "in which the Gospel is preached and taught," this was done on the basis of official conversations both in Europe and the United States of America which revealed a significant shared understanding of the gospel of justification by grace for Christ's sake through faith (Anglican-Lutheran European Regional commission, 1983, pp. 8-10; Lutheran-Episcopal

Dialogue II, 1981, pp. 22-25; cf. pp. 181-82 above). The agreement on the sacraments (ALERC, pp. 10-14;LED II, pp. 25-29; cf. pp. 183-86 above) and on apostolicity (ALERC, pp. 14-20;LED II, pp. 31-43; cf. pp. 187-95 above) was sufficient to permit both churches to take the historic step of establishing "Interim Sharing of the Eucharist" as they continued to work toward full communion. These agreements encourage us to affirm together what we understand about the church. It is our conviction that the gospel of the reign of God means that the church is called to be an eschatological community. This does not mean that the church is identical with the reign of God. Understanding the church as eschatological community, however, confirms the fresh approach to apostolicity begun by LED II and opens new possibilities for understanding questions of order envisioned when LED III was mandated.

35. To begin, we confess and affirm the necessary relationship between the gospel and the church. While God calls each of us by name and gives each of us personal faith, this confession and affirmation requires special attention in the American context because of the pervasive presence of religious individualism in that context. Because many of the European immigrants who came to the North American continent were seeking to escape the oppressive qualities of established churches, and because post-Enlightenment culture often identified Christianity with morality, it became relatively easy for persons to identify themselves as Christians without becoming part of the church. The revival practice of asking hearers simply to "accept Jesus as personal savior" coupled with the scarcity of clergy on the frontier contributed to the separation of gospel from church. Currently, much religious television encourages and reinforces the individualism endemic to our religious history.

36. We must describe the necessary relationship between gospel and church with some care. The common history of our churches in the 16th century continues to remind us of the dangers of religious oppression, especially the insistence that *church* controls *gospel* or that the church believes something other than the gospel which calls it into being. We confess and affirm that church and gospel are necessarily related because both have to do with the reign of God. The gospel is grounded in the history of Jesus as the breaking in of the *end-time* reign of God. The goal and consequence of the mission of Jesus is nothing less than the renewed people of God now open to and called to include all peoples. Hence the church is the principal implication of the gospel in human history. The end-time reign of God implies and calls into being the end-time messianic community.

37. The mission of Jesus not only implies community. It requires community for its continuance. The church is called to be the explicit bearer of the gospel in history. There is no faith in Jesus, the Christ, as the grounding of the reign of God without the visible and audible proclamation of the

gospel in word and sacraments. And there is no proclamation of the gospel in word or sacraments without a community and its ministry (Rom. 10:14-20). Word and sacraments are embedded and embodied in the end-time community and its life. The call of the gospel is not to individualized and isolated faith. It is the call that persons be translated from communities dominated by the reign of death to the community created and liberated by the Christ's reign of life. The authentic alternative to oppressive religious institutionalism is not religious individualism but rather a community shaped by the gospel of the Christ as the crucified one.

## B. Israel as the Matrix of the Church

38. The church is rooted in the gospel of Jesus, the Christ, not because Jesus is the founder of a religious institution but because the church is the continuation of Jesus' mission to and through Israel. Jesus' announcement of the presence of the reign of God recalled for Israel themes long present in its history, particularly its vocation to be a light to the nations (cf. Isa. 49:1-6;60:1-7). Jesus' acts of healing are also to be seen in this context; they are effective signs (e.g., Luke 11:20;17:21) pointing to the presence of the reign of God so that Israel may fulfill its calling. They are intended to make for reconciliation of oppositions and opponents, to include the excluded, to embody the vision of the gathering of all humanity (e.g., Matt. 15:21-28;Luke 7:1-10; 13:29-30).

39. Yet the life and mission of Jesus also embodies the calling of Israel as "a kingdom of priests and a holy nation" (Exod. 19:6) to stand over against the idolatries of the nations. Hence the presence and acts of Jesus stand forth as a sign of contradiction, a sign of deprecation by others (Luke 2:34; Luke 12:51-53;Matt. 10:34-36). Thus, whether for those with no investment or expectation beyond the things of this world (cf. Phil. 3:17-20), or conversely, for those who regard the world as worthless, Jesus and the signs are themselves a cause for division and contradiction. Even though the vision of the messianic age is the gathering of all nations to and in the one people of God, this would occur, according to the mission of Jesus, only through the costly renewal of Israel as a prelude to the call and conversion of the Gentiles.

40. Hence Jesus and these active signs of the reign of God, implications of his teaching, serve as symbols of a renewed Israel consecrated by sacrifice. Thus Jesus' teaching, his proclamation of the reign of God, and especially collections of his sayings such as the Sermon on the Mount, were addressed to Israel, or the circle of disciples which represented Israel. His commitment was to a renewal of Israel, never more so than at his final meal

with the disciples before his passion. Jesus interpreted the meal in terms of his coming death as a pouring out of his blood for the "many." This is not a turning away from Israel to the world beyond but precisely a turning toward that very Israel determined upon his death.[4] Yet the same act of final commitment to Israel is simultaneously one of final, eschatological opening to the Gentiles, that is, to the entirety of humanity beyond Israel in every time and place.

41. Finally, the proximity of the reign of God to and within human society was represented by Jesus in his calling and constituting of the Twelve from among his disciples as an eschatological act and sign. The Twelve are not called to establish the church as distinct from Israel. They are rather called to serve in microcosm as symbols of a renewed Israel. After the resurrection of Jesus the community of the disciples took steps to perpetuate the Twelve (Acts 1:15-27) and chose one to become with them "a witness to his resurrection," that is, one who could witness with them to the breaking in of the *eschaton*. That the Twelve become part of the eventual apostles underscores Israel's mission of being the focus for the gathering of the Gentiles into the end-time people of God. They serve an ultimately wider apostolicity as a sign to the people of God of its continuity with Israel, its matrix in Israel (Mark 3:13-19 and parallels; Luke 22:28-30).

42. In the messianic vision the people of God is to be "Israel plus Gentiles." That this vision exists today in broken form, with a *church* which confesses Jesus as the Christ and a *synagogue* which does not, has significant implications for the church's proclamation of the good news that Jesus is indeed the Christ. It means, first, that the final consummation of the *eschaton* is still ahead of us. It means, second, that Christians cannot claim that God has abandoned the Jews (cf. Romans 9-11, especially 9:4-5 and 11:25-36). It means, third, that for us "new covenant" or "New Testament" does not mean replacing God's covenant with Israel but means rather the beginning of renewed or consummated covenant. It means, fourth, that we *churches* stand under a special call to offer love, care, commitment, and solidarity to *synagogue*. This is needed to overcome long centuries of oppression and persecution which have poisoned the relationship between church and synagogue and challenged the credibility of the church's confession that Jesus is the Christ, that the *eschaton* has begun. It means, finally, that together church and synagogue witness to humanity's flawed and broken capacity to be the bearer of the messianic vision and that we view our present ecclesial existence with appropriate modesty, humility, and repentance. Recognition of the brokenness with which church and synagogue bear witness to the dawning and vision of the messianic age places limitations upon the claims which the church can make about the continuity and *fullness* of its institutions.

## C. The Church's Liturgy Communicates
## the Identity and Mission of the Gospel

43. Shared narrative or story gives a community its identity. The identity of the Christian community is determined by the story (history) of the Scriptures with its climax in Jesus as the Christ. That story in turn shapes the three dimensions of the community's life; its *liturgy* or worship, its *polity* or disciplined life together, and its *doctrine* or normative teaching. All three terms—liturgy, polity, and doctrine—include aspects of the church's life in their definitions. Liturgy is worship. Etymologically, however, liturgy means one's duties as a citizen, that is, engaging in both the rites and responsibilities of citizenship. Participation in the church's liturgy entails ethics and mission as well as sharing in the rites of worship. Polity means more than governance. It means how the whole life together of the community is shaped by and witnesses to its story. Doctrine is, of course, normative teaching and includes the church's creeds, dogmas, and authorized proclamation. Doctrine, however, is to be understood not as a body of theory divorced from the common life of the church, but as what defines and makes sense of the church's story. The credibility of the church as witness to the gospel in its liturgy, polity, and doctrine is necessarily affected by the way it lives (cf. John 17:20-21). *Martyria*, it must be remembered, means "witness," but it soon and validly came to mean the witness of giving one's life as testimony that the power to inflict death was not the final power, that there was more to do with life than to prolong it. Attention is given to the church's life as mission in Section 5 of this document.

44. The Eucharist is the normative rite of the community of the baptized gathered for worship on the Lord's day. It is the rite by which the church is identified as the eschatological people of God and which shaped the church's mission of witness to the breaking in of the reign of God. In the last meal with the Twelve just before his execution, Jesus identifies the bread and the cup with his imminent death and promises his participation with the Twelve in the messianic meal of the inbreaking reign of God (Matt. 26:20-29;Mark 14:17-25;Luke 22:14-23). Both the eschatological hope of Israel as well as the meal dimension of Jesus' ministry are among the significant factors which provide the context for understanding the last meal. The prophet Isaiah sees the consummation of Israel's history in terms of a feast on Mount Zion to which all peoples will come when God has swallowed up death forever and wiped away tears from all faces (Isa. 25:6-8).

45. Because Jesus both made implicit messianic claims and was perceived to be making messianic claims by his contemporaries, the feedings of multitudes (Matt. 14:13-21 and parallels) are perceived and retold as messianic actions (cf. especially John 6:14-15). Jesus also uses the meal as a part

of his ministry in his teaching about his messianic mission (Matt. 8:11-12;Luke 13:28-30;Matt. 22:1-20;Luke 14:15-24) and his gathering of the lost sheep of Israel; for his eating with tax collectors and sinners was characteristic enough to become a primary accusation against him Luke 15:1-2;cf. Ezek. 34:1-24), In the community that gathers as the consequence of and witness to the resurrection of Jesus, the meal is central (Acts 2:42,46). "The breaking of bread" functions as a designation for the Eucharist in the Lukan literature. Paul's deals explicitly with the Lord's Supper in I Corinthians (e.g., 5:6-8; 10:14-22; 11:17-34), and the remaining letters of Paul together with other documents of the New Testament such as the Revelation to John presuppose the Eucharist. What all of this means is that from the beginning the community of Jesus' disciples understood itself to be the eschatological people of God and celebrated the Eucharist as the messianic banquet. The Eucharist is thus the rite through which the baptized continually receive the promise of the Christ that they are the community of the reign of God and are continually sent into the mission of the Christ on behalf of the reign of God.

46. In *Baptism, Eucharist and Ministry*, the document of the Faith and Order Commission of the World Council of Churches, all of the interpretive themes of the Eucharist are related to the eschatological identity of the people of God. The Eucharist is (A) *thanksgiving* "for everything that God will accomplish in bringing the Kingdom to fulfillment." It thus "signifies what the world is to become: an offering and hymn of praise to the Creator, a universal communion in the body of Christ, a kingdom of justice, love and peace in the Holy Spirit." The Eucharist is (B) an *anamnesis*, a remembering to which Christ attached the promise of his presence and thus "the foretaste of his *parousia* and the final kingdom." The Eucharist is (C) the *invocation of the Spirit*, that is, the divine presence and power of the new age through which "the Church receives the life of the new creation and the assurance of the Lord's return." The Eucharist is (D) the *communion* of the faithful, demonstrating and effecting "the oneness of the sharers with Christ and with their fellow sharers in all times and places." In the Eucharist "the community of God's people is fully manifested." Finally, the Eucharist is (E) the *meal of the kingdom*, the foretaste of the *eschaton*, "the church's participation in God's mission to the world." (*Baptism, Eucharist and Ministry*, Part II, Eucharist, pars. 2-26).

47. Two themes are of particular significance for our churches. Lutherans have historically emphasized the "real presence" of Christ's body and blood for the forgiveness of sins as the heart and center of the gospel character of the Eucharist. The intent behind such an emphasis was to trust the word and promise of Christ, assuring the faithful that it is not their believing which gives meaning to the bread and cup but rather the objective

body and blood promised by Christ which is offered to them. In short, faith does not effect the presence of Christ; rather, it receives the promise of Christ. We confess and affirm that the "once-for-all-time" offering of Christ, his body and blood, which has overcome the reign of sin and death and has inaugurated the final reign of God, is present, distributed to, and received by all who participated in the Eucharistic meal. Faith trusts the promise that sin is forgiven, that the reign of life has begun.

48. Episcopalians have historically emphasized that the Eucharist, as "the Church's sacrifice of praise and thanksgiving, is the way by which the sacrifice of Christ is made present, and in which he unites us to his one offering of himself" (*Book of Common Prayer*, p. 859). The intent behind such emphasis is to recognize that God initiates and offers expiation for sin in the sacrifice of Christ, the fruits of which are made available to us as an expression of God's gracious initiative and will to save. Christians receive this blessing of God through faith, not calling into question the historical uniqueness and completion, the "once-for-all-time" character of Christ's sacrifice on the cross. Lutherans can understand and appropriate this emphasis in terms of the words of Swedish Bishop Gustaf Aulen:

> When the living Lord meets his own in Holy Communion, he actualizes the sacrifice anew in the gifts of bread and wine. As the Lord on the last evening included and incorporated his disciples in his sacrifice of love about to be perfected in death, so now he includes his disciples everywhere and in all times in the eternally valid sacrifice in the new covenant established in his death. This participation involves dying to the old age and walking in the newness of life. In this sense it involves "dying with Christ" and living in the power of His resurrection" (Phil. 3:10). The sacrifice of Christ is victory. The Lord who is present in the Lord's Supper and there deals with his church is the heavenly Victor.[5]

In contemporary ecumenical dialogue, Lutherans have agreed that in the Lord's Supper Christ is present "as the once-for-all sacrifice for the sins of the world who gives himself to the faithful," and that "the celebration of the eucharist is the church's sacrifice of praise and self-offering or oblation." We therefore confess and affirm that in the Eucharist we share in Christ's "once-for-all-time" offering through faith's praise and thanksgiving, a praise and thanksgiving whose most faithful expression is that we are set free by Christ to offer ourselves as living sacrifices, taken up into his mission in and for the world (Rom. 12:1-2).[6]

49. In the Eucharist the church receives and renews not only its identity but also the shape of its mission. The church is called to be a witness to the breaking in of the *eschaton*. It is not only identified by the body of Christ

which it receives in the Eucharistic meal: it is called to be the body of Christ in and for the world. It not only receives the benefits of Christ's death and resurrection; when it eats and drinks in the Eucharistic meal, it proclaims the Lord's death until he comes (I Cor. 11:26). The themes of eschatological identity and mission come to special expression in the Gospel of John.

> He who eats my flesh and drinks my blood has eternal life, and I will raise him up at the last day. For my flesh is food indeed, and my blood is drink indeed. He who eats my flesh and drinks my blood abides in me, and I in him. As the living Father *sent* me, and I live because of the Father, so he who eats me will live because of me. (John 6:54-57, italics added)

The purpose of St. Paul's invoking of the liturgical tradition, the narrative of the Last Supper (I Cor. 11:23-25), was to recall the Corinthian church to is mission, its embodiment of the gospel, which it was denying when the more affluent did not share food with the less affluent. Because death and all that it symbolizes has been overcome in Jesus Christ, because death no longer has the last word for the community of faith in Jesus Christ, the church is nourished in its identity as witness to the reign of God and is thereby enabled to participate sacrificially in that transformation of the world which is the purpose of God's redemptive act in Jesus (John 3:16-17). On the basis of the gospel which it celebrates in the Eucharist, the church is called and enabled to serve the humanity and creation restored to the reign of God in Jesus Christ. The quality of that service should disclose in the world a more faithful stewardship of creation and a more authentic existence before God and in community with others than is possible on the terms of the powers dominated by death.

50. The Eucharist is the church's ritual narration of the story of Jesus, the eschatological meal in which the gathered people of God participate. The church is thus identified as Christ's end-time community and receives a Christ-like shape to its mission. Such an understanding not only serves to explain the centrality of the Eucharist in the life of the earliest church. It also provides the theological rationale for the recovery of the Eucharist as the normal Sunday liturgy for parishes today (cf. *Baptism, Eucharist and Ministry*, Part II, Eucharist, Par. 31). A significant implication of the gospel is the weekly and festival celebration of the Eucharist. We therefore urge the parishes of our respective churches to move deliberately and consciously toward renewal of the Eucharistic liturgy. That would mean celebration of the Eucharist at all Sunday and Festival gatherings of the people of the parish. The *Book of Common Prayer*, p. 13, identifies "The Holy Eucharist" as "the principal act of Christian worship on the Lord's Day and other major

Feasts." The *Statement on Communion Practices* of The American Lutheran Church and the Lutheran Church in America, Par. II.B.2, quotes the Apology of the Augsburg Confession, Article 24,1: "In our churches Mass is celebrated every Sunday and on other festivals when the Sacrament is offered to those who wish for it after they have been examined and absolved." Then the statement continues: "Congregations are encouraged to move toward this goal because the complete service of Holy Communion embodies the fullness of the Means of Grace, because it provides an excellent *focus for the whole Christian life and mission*, and because it witnesses to our confessional and ecumenical heritage" (italics added). Within a broader context, the recovery of the liturgy of the various members of the church can be freed of both clericalism and anti-clericalism, the whole people can be newly empowered for ministry, and the roles of all can be interdependently valued.

### D. The Church's Polity Is Life Together for Witness to the Gospel

51. This topic confronts our churches with the most obvious, although not the only, obstacle to full communion not only because there are actual differences in governance and ordination between our churches but also because there are differences in understanding the function of bishops and in the significance attached to the historic episcopate. When polity is understood in terms of specific forms, such understanding determines the way our respective churches raise questions about it. To Lutherans it seems that Episcopalian emphasis on the historic episcopate and its authority to ordain could be an unwarranted addition to the gospel. To Episcopalians the Lutheran view that, when there is agreement on the gospel, polity can become an *adiaphoron* seems an unwarranted indifference with regard to something that is at least an implication of the gospel. In this document we will not deal with all the issues related to polity. Another document of this dialogue will be devoted to the group of topics mandated by the 1982 resolutions authorizing Interim Sharing of the Eucharist, namely, "historic episcopate, and ordering of ministry (bishops, priest, and deacons) in the total context of apostolicity." If we understand polity as disciplined life together, then we can here give an account of how the gospel defines and shapes the polity of the church; how, in fact, the polity of the church is an implication of the gospel.

52. Polity is normally defined as a "politically organized community." But if the gospel is that the reign of God has begun and will triumph, then this cannot mean politics as usual. "You know that those who are supposed to rule over the Gentiles lord it over them, and their great men exercise authority over them. *But it shall not be so among you*" (Mark 10:42-43, ital-

ics added). Hence, polity in the church must mean the visible life together of the community which believes that Jesus is the Christ, that the messianic age has begun, that the reign of God will finally triumph. Polity includes governance, but it is more than governance. It included the ordering of ministries, but it is more than the ordering of ministries. It is the way the church as the body of Christ under historical conditions is freed by the gospel so to live together so that the patterns and powers of its life reflect and witness to the reign of God rather than to the patterns and powers of the "old age." Polity in the church thus testifies to the fact that the gospel gives life to a visible, historical community. Further, polity reflects to the church and the world at large the church's utter dependence on the one gospel. We therefore confess and affirm that the church witnesses to the gospel by the way its members live together, that the way its members live together should reflect both the resurrection victory of Jesus and his way of ministry up to and including the cross. Hence polity is fundamentally the gift of discipleship in its essential corporate dimension. The Messiah serves the people of God, calls that people to be the seed bed of the new reconciled and reconciling humanity, and shapes that people's life and mission by the power and character of his own ministry.

53. Two characteristics of Jesus' teaching about the ministry of the messianic community are represented by the terms "to send" (*apostellein*) and "to serve" (*diakonein*).[7] Because Jesus is sent as the Christ by the Father, he sends the community which confesses him as the Christ with his same mission (Mark 9:37 and parallels;Matt. 10:5-15 and parallels;John 3:17; 4:38; 17:3,8,18,21,23,25, 20-21). In a certain sense the church's "apostolicity" is its mission, the subject of Section 5 of this document. Equally important is the way the church engages in its mission. *Diakonia* "is the service performed for the unifying and preservation of the church, the service which establishes and maintains the faith."[8] In contrast to secular rule the church was not to be constituted by coercive power. Nor was it to be constituted by learned power (I Cor. 1:18-25), by magical power (Acts 8:18-24; Acts 16:16-24), or religious power (Heb. 13:10-16). Rather, Jesus brings in the reign of God as the one who serves (Luke 22:27 and parallels; John 13:1-20).

The reign of God did not come through visible power. It came through one who was a slave for slaves, one who was poor for the poor, one who was a servant for servants.[9] Even those who have been given the charism of leadership exercise their leadership "in the Lord" (I Thess. 5:12-13), as those whose worship is to present themselves as living sacrifices (Rom. 12:1-8, esp. 7 and 8).

54. Both mission and servanthood are characterized by diversity of concrete expression in the New Testament and other writings which take us well into the 2nd Century C.E.[10] The Twelve, resident in Jerusalem, represent

a corporate apostolate which witnessed to the messiahship of Jesus within Judaism and kept the emerging Gentile mission in contact with its Jewish matrix. Side by side was the ministry of the Seven (Acts 6-8), often regarded as the origin of the diaconate but more accurately described as a missionary ministry similar to an apostolate like that of Paul. Many of the Pauline churches were apparently led by a presbyter-bishop, while the corporate leadership of elders, derived from synagogue administration, seems to have functioned in the churches described by Luke and the Pastoral Epistles. The leadership of presbyters persisted even at Rome until well into the second century, long after the monarchial episcopate had established itself in Syria and Asia Minor. These offices did not exhaust the forms ministry took in earliest Christianity, for there is abundant evidence of the importance of "charismatic" leaders in both the Pauline (I Corinthians 12-14;Romans 12;Ephesians 4) and Johannine traditions (I John 2:20-27; 4:1; 3 John 9-10; Rev. 1:9-11).

55. The unity and reconciliation effected by the inbreaking reign of God embraces a fruitful, but sometimes turbulent, diversity among us. The church, from the beginning, knew a rich variety of activities in its life together, some of which served particularly to undergird its unity. We list a few of these.

a. *The sharing of goods* with those in need is held up in the New Testament writings as a characteristic of church life. Luke describe the earliest community in Jerusalem as exceptionally generous (Acts 4:32-5:11); Paul, later on, collected an offering from churches of his founding to help that church in a time of need (e.g., 2 Corinthians 8-9); and the letters of John (I John 3:16-18) and James (1:26-27) insist on such sharing as a fundamental Christian duty.

b. *Intercessory prayer* focused the Christians' concern for one another. Paul, for example, asked for such prayers for himself from the church at Rome (Rom. 15:30).

c. *Admonition and correction* were devoted to preserving community among those in disagreement. To accuse is to expose an enemy and break community. To admonish is to love a friend and preserve community in the midst of conflicts. Thus Paul could rebuke Peter (Gal. 2:11-15) without, it seems, breaking their partnership in the gospel.

d. *Suffering* for the sake of the gospel, for the sake of the community, also served to further the word of proclamation (Acts 5:41;2 Cor. 6:4-5; 11:23-29;Col. 1:24-29).

e. *Love and humility* were prominent themes of moral exhortation, for, by putting others first, we promote the unity of the church (I Corinthians 13;Phil. 2:1-11;I John 4:20;Mark 10:42-45).

In these and other ways, the church sought to practice the unity which is one of its cardinal characteristics (John 17-21) without obliterating the diversity which made its life vital.

56. In addition to mission, servanthood, diversity, and unity as dimensions of the church's life together, there is still another dimension that we believe can also be found in the life of the early church. A contemporary description of it is found in the agreed statement of Lutherans and Catholics in Dialogue V, *Papal Primacy and the Universal Church*, p. 20, which identifies collegiality and subsidiarity as norms of the renewal of the church's polity in general and the office of universal pastor in particular.

> *Collegial responsibility* for the unity of the church...is of utmost importance in protecting those values which excessive centralization of authority would tend to stifle.... The collegial principle calls all levels of the church to share in the concern and responsibilities of leadership for the total life of the church.
> The *principle of subsidiarity* is not less important. Every section of the church, each mindful of its special heritage, should nurture the gifts it has received from the Spirit by exercising its legitimate freedom. What can properly be decided and done in smaller units of ecclesial life ought not to be referred to church leaders who have wider responsibilities. Decisions should be made and activities carried out with a participation as broad as possible from the people of God. Initiatives should be encouraged in order to promote a wholesome diversity in theology, worship, witness, and service. All should be concerned that, as the community is built up and its unity strengthened, the rights of minorities and minority viewpoints are protected within the unity of faith.

57. It should be evident from the preceding paragraphs that the earliest centuries of the church's history hold before us a rich vision of the church's polity as life together in response to the gospel. Measuring its current life in terms of these examples, the church confesses by the power of the gospel that it exists in a broken and anticipatory form. It confesses its brokenness in its relation to Judaism; its own disunity; its too frequent identification with oppressing establishments; its failures of compassion, peacemaking, justice, inclusivity, stewardship, and pastoral discipline. The power of the gospel is seen not only in the church's freedom to confess its brokenness and sin but also in its freedom for reform. Indeed, the refusal to undertake evident and necessary reform is a possible indication that a community has hardened itself against the gospel. The ordination of women by our churches is a specific example of a recently undertaken reform. The importance of this action as an example of how our polity is a witness to the gospel of the reign of God calls for lengthier treatment.

58. The Lima statement, *Baptism, Eucharist and Ministry*, recognizes the role of both men and women in Christian ministry.

Where Christ is present, human barriers are being broken. The Church is called to convey to the world the image of a new humanity. There is in Christ no male or female (Gal. 3:28). Both women and men must discover together their contributions to the service of Christ in the Church. The church must discover the ministry which can be provided by women as well as that which can be provided by men. A deeper understanding of the comprehensiveness of ministry which reflects the interdependence of men and women needs to be more widely manifested in the life of the Church (p. 23, par. 18).

At the same time the Lima statement acknowledges that there is disagreement regarding the ordination of women. Lutheran and Episcopal churches in the United States have been ordaining women since the 1970s. Yet there is disagreement on this issue not only between our churches and those which do not ordain women but also within our churches and within our dialogue. We are encouraged by the fact that the Roman Catholic Church has expressed the willingness to continue the discussion of this topic and that the Orthodox churches have continued dialogue with us.

59. We on our part are mindful of the necessity of continuing to identify the profound doctrinal reasons which led us to ordain women. Such theological explication needs to be undertaken not only in order to inform our partners in ecumenical conversation but also to help us reappropriate what our churches have done. While social and cultural forces have obviously created a climate of readiness for the ordained ministry of women, our churches have not acted simply as a concession to such social and cultural forces. We have listened to the concerns of our ecumenical partners, but we have above all been persuaded by the freedom for radical newness given to women and men in Christ and by the Holy Spirit's gift of ministry so evidently bestowed on women and men.

60. There are statements in the New Testament, notably I Cor. 14:34-36 and I Tim. 2:11-15, which reflect the practice of the Greco-Roman culture or perpetuate the synagogue tradition of not admitting women to roles of public leadership or witness. However, other statements of the New Testament, e.g., Gal. 3:27-28, indicate that in the new age inaugurated by the resurrection of Jesus new possibilities are open to women and men in their relationship to each other and in ministries within the eschatological community. The Gospels indicate that Jesus related to women in a new way (Luke 7:36-50;Luke 10:38-42;Mark 14:3-9;Matt. 26:6-13;John 4:4-42;John 20:1, 11-18) and that from Easter onwards, whether as witnesses to the resurrec-

tion of Jesus or as participants in the orders of widows, deacons, prophets, teachers, and apostles, women exercised significant ministry in and for the church. In Christ the alienations and oppressions related to gender are overcome. The differences within the documents of the New Testament point to the observation that Gal. 3:28 identifies the *agenda* for the community of the new age: "There is neither Jew nor Greek, there is neither slave nor free, there is neither male nor female; for you are all one in Christ Jesus." The Church is called to wrestle with the implementation of this agenda against the powers of the "old age." The New Testament documents are themselves evidence that the struggle of the "new age" in Christ against slavery and economic oppression, against ethnic and racial oppression, against sexism and gender oppression has not always, perhaps not often, been successful. But it remains the agenda.

61. Although Jesus appointed men to the Twelve, their ministry to Israel was an eschatological sign (cf. par. 39, above). The New Testament, however, does not identify the function of the Twelve in terms of presiding at the Eucharist nor does it identify Christ's maleness as a quality which is necessary for those who preside at the Eucharist. Jesus identifies his own ministry as the Christ with the decision to be servant, not master (Mark 10:45 and parallels), and with the determination to offer himself sacrificially. The presence and presidency of Christ in the Eucharist has to do with the grace, forgiveness, and sacrificial servant love which frees his community to enter into his way of being in the world. Such presence and presidency is not about gender, much less the domination and oppression which has often been associated with gender.

62. We are mindful of the fact that long centuries of tradition have excluded women from ordained ministry. While the churches provided women with opportunities not generally available to them in other areas of society, it is also true that the history of the church is replete with evidence of the denigration of women in the church (e.g., the accusation that women are the original and continuing cause of sin[11]) and of the domination and oppression of women by men. As churches that have participated in the conservative reformation of the 16th century, we bear witness to the concern that what we have inherited ought not be arbitrarily rejected. But we are also convinced that the historical antiquity of a practice is no guarantee of its validity and that no practice is beyond challenge and reform. We believe that the practice of ordaining only men must be challenged in the name of the gospel, that it is part of the brokenness of the church in history to have excluded women from ordained ministry. We believe that whenever women have been included in the ordained ministries of the church it represents a significant development in the church's struggle against the powers of the "old age." It

is an act of fidelity to the tradition of the *imago Dei* as comprehending both "male and female" (Gen. 1:26-28).

63. Our attempt to discern the implications for polity of the gospel of the reign of God is part of our effort to manifest our visible unity through full communion. We do not yet know whether or how this might take place between churches with and without the historic episcopate. In addition to the example of the early church and the major reform action described above we have before us helpful ecumenical suggestions such as the final paragraphs of *Baptism, Eucharist and Ministry* (pars. 51-55), and the significant proposal of the Roman Catholic/Lutheran Joint Commission, *Facing Unity*. Our current agreement commits us to the quest for full communion. It is clear that the quest will ask of *all* members of our churches just that "lowliness and meekness," that patience and forebearing of one another in love, for which the author of Ephesians begs.

### E. The Church's Doctrine Serves Its Proclamation of the Gospel

64. Doctrine means all teaching that is authentically Christian. Doctrinal formulations can function either descriptively ("This is what Christians, in fact, teach") or prescriptively ("This is what Christians ought to teach"). Throughout the centuries of Christian history both functions have been fraught with problems. Prescriptive doctrine has been experienced as oppressive, obscurantist, stagnating, inhibiting. It has been the occasion for purges, trials, executions, wars. In our churches the very concept of prescriptive doctrine evokes different emotional responses. Lutherans have developed an ethos in which there is considerable doctrinal and theological homogeneity, in which there is significant affirmation of prescriptive doctrine. Episcopalians have developed an ethos in which there is considerable doctrinal and theological variety, in which there is less sense of prescriptive doctrinal tradition, but a greater importance attached to the role of descriptive doctrine. In the face of both historical difficulties and differences in ethos we must proceed carefully so that what we can and must affirm is both clear and persuasive.

65. We can and must affirm the concept of normative doctrine because what is at stake is the authenticity of the church's proclamation, that is, the authenticity of the church's gospel. What is being proclaimed as gospel in the church dare not automatically be identified with what *ought* to be proclaimed as gospel. Hence the concept of normative doctrine requires the church to struggle with the question of the authenticity of its gospel and the quality or faithfulness of its proclamation. The church is called to be the witness in word and deed to God's own vision for the world, God's promise to

the world, God's ultimate gift to the world. The purpose of normative doctrine is not to be the guardian of institutional ideology. The purpose is rather to evaluate the quality and consequence of the church's proclamation. Are the church's words good news for the poor, liberation to captives, light for those who sit in darkness, life for those whose existence is overshadowed by death? When speaking about the normative doctrine of the gospel, the key words are *normative* and *gospel*. There *is* a gospel, hence there is *normative* doctrine; but it is *gospel*, hence anything said or done in the name of the gospel which is death dealing, oppressive, defensive, victimizing, or denigrating is a denial and contradiction of the gospel. Whatever in the church's proclamation does not liberate from the bondage of sin and death, enkindle the vision of the reign of God, promise the final gift of life everlasting, offer ultimate hope and comfort, or give courage for faithful witness, is not the gospel.

66. The church's call is to witness to God's future for the world, to be the bearer of God's promises for the world. The church is therefore the community of living proclamation. The revision of the church's lectionary, especially the expansion into a three-year cycle for Sundays and Festivals and the addition of a reading from the Old Testament to the lessons for the Eucharist, promises more extensive encounter with the Scriptures than has ever been available in the church's liturgy. However, even this more comprehensive lectionary cannot be a substitute for the living proclamation of the word of God. The Scriptures come to us from the past with a narrative of God's interaction with Israel and God's final redemption in Jesus, the Christ, which we confess to be the Word of God. But the word of God is not and cannot be only a narrative from the past. It is a narrative into which we can and must enter so that it becomes God's present address of judgment and promise here and now. The present word of God is always rooted in and normed by the biblical word; but just as there is no substitute for the normative word of Holy Scripture, so there is no substitute for its contemporary proclamation. The church is called, indeed commanded, to speak God's judgment and promise today (Luke 10:16;2 Cor. 5:20;Acts 4:20). It cannot simply read the lessons and hope that the congregation will consider itself addressed. The church must make the address explicit. It must also aid the hearers to discriminate, to understand the words of Scripture through which they are being addressed. It is the task of the sermon to show how these words are to be understood and to be applied in the light of Christ and in the context of our situation. It is in living proclamation that Christians are to hear both a discriminating and an empowering word. The ritual rhetoric of the Christian community is the language by which the community's story is retold so that God's everlasting promises are proclaimed, God's present judgments are announced, and God's saving deeds are remembered and made present. Faith

must have Someone to believe. What faith believes is the promise contained in the living Word of God, rooted in the scriptural witness to Jesus as the Christ, preached here and now in the midst of the congregation.

67. The Holy Scriptures are the norm for the church's proclamation of the gospel. That the gospel was at stake is evident from both the liturgical and the polemical contexts for the formulation of the biblical canon. With the death of the apostolic generation and the gathering of oral traditions about Jesus into Gospel codices, a body of documents became available for reading in Christian communities gathered for worship. The documents which authenticated themselves in worship were authorized for public use in Eucharistic assemblies. The process of reception by the church, which lasted a number of centuries, also at times involved the heat of controversy. The Marcionite practice of circulating lists of approved documents, excluding not only the Scriptures of Israel (Old Testament) but also many of the documents from the apostolic era (New Testament) was one of the major factors that caused bishops and theologians late in the 2nd century C.E. to begin identifying canonical lists. The church early acknowledged its matrix in Israel and its confession that Jesus is Messiah by including the Scriptures of Israel in its canon of authoritative Scripture. This was a decision about the gospel with far-reaching implications for Israel as well as for those who confess that Jesus is Messiah (see above, par. 42). To the Scriptures of Israel the church added documents with a variety of perspectives on the gospel. But what is even more important, it *excluded* documents. In order to understand fully and authentically what gospel the church means to confess on the basis of its canonical writings, it is equally important to know what "gospel" or what versions of the gospel are being rejected and excluded. To be sure, not every document that was excluded is antithetical to the gospel of the canonical documents. But what is most important is that the canon of the Scriptures has to do with the gospel. Only the Scriptures of the church gives us normative access to the authentic gospel. Only the gospel gives the canonical Scriptures its proper and appropriate authority.

68. Like the canon of the Scriptures, dogma came into being at those points in the church's life where alternatives threatened the gospel itself. The creedal affirmation of the world as creation and God as creator was directed against the Gnostic denial of the goodness of the world. At stake is the proclamation of the reign of God and its affirmation of the world's future, its proclamation that life, not death, will have the final word in the consummation of history. Arising out of the Arian and post-Nicean controversies, the christological and trinitarian dogmas identify the God of the gospel with the person and history of Jesus (see above, Section 2). In the Pelagian controversy the church recognized the universal guilt, the bondage of self-justification or self-hatred, which come with our origin. At stake was the comfort and lib-

eration that is conferred by the grace of the gospel. Born in the fires of controversy, dogma identifies the mandatory content of the church's teaching and proclamation, that is, it identifies what *must* be said if the gospel is to continue to be proclaimed.

69. In the 16th century leading reformers both on the European continent and in the British Isles were persuaded that the proclamation of the gospel was in danger of losing its quality as unconditional promise and that therefore the church's proclamation could no longer evoke the faith which alone receives the gospel as comfort and liberation. Among these reformers the doctrine of "justification by faith" functioned as a hermeneutical test for church proclamation. The promise of the gospel was to be so unconditionally proclaimed ("We are accounted righteous before God, only for the merit of our Lord and Savior Jesus Christ by Faith, and not for our own works or derservings." Article II, Articles of Religion, *Book of Common Prayer*, p. 870) that faith in the promise, not works of self-justification, would be the appropriate response. Our churches still acknowledge the validity of the insights of our Reformation ancestors, but we do so in different ways. The proclamation and teaching of Lutheran clergy and parishes must be measured by the standard of the documents contained in the *Book of Concord* of 1580, especially the catholic creeds, the Augsburg Confession of 1530, and the Small Catechism of Martin Luther. In Episcopal parishes the use of the *Book of Common Prayer* is mandated by canon law. The rites and liturgical materials prescribed by the *Book of Common Prayer* function as a standard by which worship, including the administration of the sacraments, as well as doctrine itself, must be measured. Each church can and should ask significant questions of the other and indeed of itself. How, if at all, does the *Book of Concord* shape the worship, including administration of the sacraments, in Lutheran parishes? How, if at all, does the *Book of Common Prayer* shape proclamation and teaching in Episcopal parishes? What is significant in the very asking of these questions is the fact that both churches want to be held accountable for the authenticity of the gospel in the life of the church.

70. This area of the church's life and mission in faithfulness to the gospel provides ample opportunity for the exercise of humility. The relationship between church and the reign of God is not one of identity. By the church's own confession of faith God is Lord of history as well as of the church (Rev. 11:15). The redeeming reign of God can manifest itself in the world, and as a witness to that reign the church is called to discern and acknowledge the fact. This has important implications for the style of evangelization employed by the church. The living Word of God, Jesus Christ, is not imported by Christians or the church into persons or cultures from which God's witness is absent; but, rather, what is surely there inchoately, unclearly, and/or in distorted form is to be brought by true evangelism into com-

pleteness, clarity, and/or authenticity in those persons or cultures to whom the church proclaims the gospel (e.g., Acts 14:8-18). The recognition that the reign of God is larger than the church dare not immobilize the church or inhibit its witness. As the explicit bearer of the gospel and its principal implication in history, the church is called in every time and place faithfully to fulfill its life and mission. The world, with all the questions that it poses for church and gospel, is the locus as well as the object of the church's witness to the reign of God.

## IV. THE *WORLD* AND THE GOSPEL

### A. The Contemporary World

71. The term *world* has been troublesome because it has a variety of meanings in the New Testament, most notably in the Gospel of John. There it means at times all that is hostile to the Christ (e.g., John 15:18-19) and therefore the antithesis to Christ's way of being (e.g., John 18:36-37); or, at other times, it means the object of God's love (e.g., John 3:16-17) and Christian witness (John 17:21-23). Sometimes *world* is simply a neutral designation for the universe or whatever exists (e.g., John 1:10; 9:32). We have at times used the term *world* as a synonym for the universe; but most often we have used it to refer to the "cultural context" within which the church exists and which it is called to address. One major dimension of the world as cultural context is the post-Enlightenment phenomenon known as "secularity." While secularity is complex and has taken on many forms, including hostility to religion and persecution of religious communities, the form or facet of secularity which must be of particular concern to Western Christians is the way it has called into question the public meaningfulness of religious language. This is especially important for churches in the United States of America.

72. Although religious institutions have persisted in the United States and, in contrast to other Western countries, even experienced remarkable growth since the end of World War II, religion is regarded by many as an essentially private or "personal" experience. The central terms and themes of religion, *God, revelation*, and *salvation*, are no longer public terms giving thematic expression to common ways of experiencing the world. As language for individual or subgroup experiences, the terms are relativized ("what God means to me"). Although its institutions are thriving, a relativized religion is a contradiction in terms since the term *God* means, at the very least, whoever or whatever can make a universal and unconditional

claim upon us. Secularity as the privatization of religion thus challenges the church's very ability to address the world meaningfully with a public word.

73. The global consciousness which modern travel and communication have made possible and the interdependence which modern business and industry necessitate have made Western Christians more aware of world religions and greatly complicated our way of relating to world religions. The statistics from the *World Christian Encyclopedia*, edited by David B. Barrett (Oxford University Press, 1982) are striking: In the past 50 years Christianity has increased numerically by more than 50%, to more than one and a quarter billion Christians. But its proportion of the world's population has *decreased* from about 33% to less than 26%. The great non-Christian world religions meanwhile have doubled in size (Islam has actually tripled) and have maintained their proportion of the world's population, about 42%.

74. At the beginning of this century Christians had an uncomplicated strategy for relating to non-Christians: service and evangelism. Western Christians also had ready access to most countries of the world. However, with the Russian revolution at the end of World War I, and the end of the colonial empire together with the establishment of a marxist-socialist government in the People's Republic of China at the end of World War II, Western missionary activity has been banned or severely restricted in many parts of Asia and Africa. Western Christians have increasingly come to ask whether and how the gospel can be addressed to a post-colonial world, and in the midst of resurgent, vital world religions.

75. Meanwhile Western secular culture has experienced a phenomenon often called "the return of enchantment," a reaction to the sterile rationalism of scientific and technological modernity. Fantasy, myth, and magic have regained popularity. Astrology, occultism, cults, new religions, and variations of old religions have won new adherents and have gained new visibility in publishing, entertainment, the media, and public consciousness. The increasing popularity of religious and quasi-religious phenomena, the increasing interest in the transcendental and the supernatural, both confirm some Christian claims and insights about the religious character of human beings and challenge contemporary Christianity's capacity to respond to the religious dimension. In this area Christian discernment is required. A "baptized imagination" (C.S. Lewis) enriches theological reflection, whereas uncritical use of imagination in theology and religion can lead to superstition or sentimentality.

76. Christian churches, including our own, have experienced new movements and the renewal of earlier movements. Liturgical renewal, interest in "spiritual direction," small group gatherings for home Bible study, liberation movements, and attention to peace and justice issues have proliferated in the churches. Three movements have been especially prominent among

Christians in the United States. Renewed Evangelicalism has surfaced in televised revivals, large metropolitan "crusades," and home visitation evangelism programs. Renewed Fundamentalism has advanced its own political agenda and pressed for legislation in such areas as school prayer, censorship, sexual behavior, and the teaching of "scientific creationism." The Charismatic movement has stressed the miraculous response to prayer, a direct and ecstatic experience of the Holy Spirit, direct divine guidance for life decisions, and spiritual renewal of the church.

77. The paradoxical consequence of these latter three movements has been both negative and positive. Many aspects of modern learning have been rejected, often to the point of establishing militantly separatistic educational institutions, and all too often it has seemed that these movements do little more than provide simplistic justifications for a rather shallow nationalism as well as a rather narrow orientation towards this-worldly success in business and politics. On the other hand, it cannot be denied that these movements have spread at least one version of the Christian message, have brought many outsiders to some acquaintance with Jesus, have stimulated interest in the words of Holy Scripture, and have given to many persons a newfound life in the Spirit of Christ.

78. It is the conviction of the churches represented by this document that the church has both the call and the capacity to address the world. The gospel is the proclamation of God's inbreaking future, an alternative to other anticipations of the future, whether secular or religious. The gospel is a vision of God's goal for history which is grounded in Jesus, the Christ. Attention to the grounding of the gospel in the biblical witness to Jesus (Section 1), to the gospel's God characterized by the person and history of Jesus (Section 2), and to the church as the eschatological community called to witness to the reign of God (Section 3), articulates an understanding of the gospel which has three consequences. First, it can be meaningful and intelligible in the context of a secular worldview. Second, it calls human beings to an authentic spirituality. Third, it aids Christians in discriminating among strategies for relating to the universe. It is the task of the following paragraphs to describe a strategy for addressing the world which we believe to be both faithful and meaningful.

## B. The Gospel Vision: The World as Creation

79. The term *creation* as used in Christian theology is neither a philosophical nor a scientific term. Rather, it is a theological statement, that is, a statement about the universe in relation to God, the creator. It is a theological assertion grounded in the gospel, a way of saying that God the creator brings

order out of chaos, light out of darkness, life out of death. When the gospel asserts that the universe is creation, it identifies the Christian doctrine of creation as a major implication of the gospel. Israel's experience and remembrance of the Exodus deliverance are the basis for the way it regards the universe, confesses the universe as belonging to God, and rejoices in the goodness of the universe (e.g., Deut. 26:1-11). The prophet of exile proclaims that the God who comforts and forgives Israel is the creator of the universe (Isa. 40:1-31; 45:1-19). The people of God who have experienced renewal and redemption in Jesus, the Christ, confess him as the Logos through whom "all things were made" (John 1:3), as the "image of the invisible God" through whom and for whom "all things were created" and in whom "all things hold together" (Col. 1:15-18). The Christian good news is neither a negation of the world nor an attempt to escape the world. It is an affirmation of the world.

80. The God proclaimed as Savior in Jesus, the Christ, is a God of sovereign freedom. But God's freedom is not freedom *from* the universe, i.e., a God unaffected by time and space. Rather, God's freedom is freedom to be *for* the universe. Hence the universe is not an unintended emanation from God's being. Rather, it is *creation*, that is, that which is intended by God's love, by God's being as love. By confessing God as creator the church is affirming about God's relationship to space what it already believes about God's relationship to time on the basis of its encounter with Jesus: God loves life and wills into existence that which is not God. As contingent being the world as creation exists *vis-à-vis* God. It is both dependent upon and other than God.

81. By confessing the universe as creation Christians affirm its goodness, it fecundity, its variety, its processes of development and inner creativity, its pleasures, and the natural happiness it affords. Christians confess that human beings have the potential to share in God's creative freedom. Their ability to transcend the instinctual necessities of organic and animal life gives them the capacity to understand, shape, and transform the world. That this potential and capacity has often gone disastrously awry is self-evident. The gospel grounding of the Christian doctrine of creation calls human beings to the freedom of stewardship in relation to the universe, the freedom to bring creation into existence out of our universe. The freedom to "name" other creatures (Gen. 2:19) is the gift of understanding, using, and serving the universe with a steward's care. The universe awaits and benefits from the eschatological salvation of humanity (Rom. 8:18-25).

## C. The Gospel and Evil

82. The Christian doctrine of creation means that the gospel must be proclaimed in the face of evil. A contingent universe includes death as well

as life, disease and pain as well as pleasure and happiness, destructive as well as creative forces. In addition to natural or biological distortion, suffering, and death, there is the perversion of human freedom and stewardship into waste, corruption, oppression, torture, and murder. The reality of evil involves those who confess God as creator and the world as creation in a seeming dilemma: a goodness lacks either power or reality; that is, goodness either cannot or will not triumph.

83. The Christian gospel makes three assertions in the face of evil. First, the freedom of God's creative love means that God accepts the consequences of calling into existence that which is not God. That is always the risk of love. The final freedom of love is the freedom to be hurt by, to suffer through the object of one's love. The freedom to create the universe and to make creation out of the universe is finally the freedom to be vulnerable.

84. Second, God does in fact suffer. That is a theme which is found in the prophetic Scriptures of Israel. That is also the heart of the apostolic Scriptures and the church's dogma: Jesus is the ultimate, the final way God suffers. Here is an alternative to understanding God either as absolute power or absolute indifference. The alternative is that God chooses to be involved as victim. Indeed, salvation or forgiveness occurs in no other way. The God who suffers and dies is available as companion, comfort, and Savior to all who experience the pain of suffering and the dread of death. The people of God believe the good news of God's redemptive suffering as an alternative to despair in the face of evil (I Peter 2:18-25).

85. Third, in the resurrection of Jesus from death the church recognizes God's affirmation of the cross as the way God's love triumphs over evil. Jesus is the firstborn of a redeemed humanity. He has overcome evil by being its victim. The people of God witness to that by forgiving enemies, suffering with hope, identifying with victims, seeking to liberate oppressors and oppressed alike, supporting nonviolent resistance to evil, working to control and contain the use of violence (see the "just war" doctrine common to most Christian churches which requires that governmental use of violence be accountable and limited, that it be understood as the lesser of evils). The promise of the gospel leaves us neither helpless nor hopeless in the face of evil. That is why Christian martyrdom is the ultimate witness (*martyria*) to the gospel.

## D. The Gospel and Human Sin

86. Everything is known more profoundly, known for what it really is, in the light of the gospel. Because of the gospel the church recognizes both the power and the reality of sin. Because sin is fundamentally a theological

reality, because it is against God and the reign of God, therefore it is not adequately recognized and confessed apart from the gospel. Its recognition and
confession belong to the implications of the gospel.

87. Humanity is alienated from the reign of God, from God's call and
vision for us as creation. Humanity has fallen from the freedom for love to
the bondage of self-absorption or self-hatred. Humanity has fallen prey to the
reign of death. The powers that serve death drive us to self-protection at
whatever cost to others or to self-hatred at the cost of distortion of the self.
We serve the powers of death also and not least in our drive/quest for "prosperity" (cf. The Great Litany, *Book of Common Prayer*, p. 149, *Lutheran
Book of Worship*, p. 170). Humanity is captive to false gods, heteronomous
powers, religious or secular; or it is captive to equally false autonomy, seeking to be a law unto itself. The church recognizes that in the last analysis sin
is not so much misbehavior as it is misbelief, faith, and trust directed toward
that which is other than God's redeeming reign, resulting in both groundless
arrogance or groundless despair. Such misbelief or misdirected orientation
means that the whole of our existence, not just individual acts, is guilty existence, existence under condemnation.

88. The good news of the gospel is that God has not abandoned the
world. Rather, the Father gave up the Son, and the Son gave himself up to
death, and thus God made a final irrevocable commitment to the world. Even
God's judgment is a sign that God cares about and cares for the world. Every
uncovering of human sin and evil is a prophetic "word of God." Unexpected
as well as expected voices of God's judgment proclaim the ways in which
humans pervert and deny the goodness of God's world, oppress others, cling
to unwarranted privilege and power at the expense of justice. Recognition of
the justice of God's judgment (Ps. 119:75, "I know, O Lord, that thy judgments are right, and that in faithfulness thou hast afflicted me") is a fundamental implication of the gospel.

89. To be grasped by the gospel of the redeeming reign of God is to be
free to make God's verdict our own. That is the meaning of repentance: to
see matters with a renewed mind; to see matters from the perspective of the
gospel rather than to see them from the false perspective of self-preservation
or self-hatred (Mark 8:35 and parallels). The meaning of confession is to
give up the moralities, legitimations, and self-justifications through which
we seek to protect ourselves before God, others, and our own consciences,
and equally to give up our unrelenting self-accusation and perfectionism.
Confession means to say the same thing (*homologein*) to God that God
knows and says to us: that we are sinners. We dare to give up, to confess,
because the new repentant mind knows what the old unrepentant mind does
not: that God's judgment is penultimate, not ultimate, that God's last word is
the forgiving and ennobling yes.

90. The good news that God reigns is the costly way of the cross. It is costly for God, who does not give up on the world but gives up for the world. Jesus is the way, the truth, and the life because he gave "his life as a ransom for many" (Mark 10:45 and parallels). Forgiveness is always costly for the forgiver for it means bearing the pain of that which is forgiven. It is costly for the sinner as well, for it means conversion from the old age to the new, from serving the powers of death to serving the power of life, from self-hatred to self-affirmation, from self-preservation to self-offering. That is the path opened by Baptism, the sacrament of justification. The sinner is plunged into the affirming death and resurrection of Jesus and thus is liberated to undergo the sinner's own death and resurrection. That is also the path celebrated in our Eucharist. We are united with the "once-for-all-time" sacrifice of Jesus so that we become part of God's sacrificial mission for the world.

## E. The Gospel as Alternative Vision for the Future of the World

91. Jesus, the Christ, is the grounding of God's future for the world, the future of God's redemptive reign. The author of Ephesians (1:16-23) describes it as follows:

> I do not cease to give thanks for you, remembering you in my prayers, that the God of our Lord Jesus Christ, the Father of glory, may give you a spirit of wisdom and revelation in the knowledge of him, having the eyes of your hearts enlightened, that you may know what is the hope to which he has called you, what are the riches of his glorious inheritance in the saints, and what is the immeasurable greatness of his power in us who believe, according to the working of his great might which he accomplished in Christ when he raised him from the dead and made him sit at his right hand in the heavenly places, far above all rule and authority and power and dominion, and above every name that is named, not only in this age but also in that which is to come; and he has put all things under his feet and has made him the head over all things for the church, which is his body, the fullness of him who fills all in all.

That is the "mystery" from which and for which the people of God live. That is the "secret" of the future of the world: the Christ of suffering and vulnerable love is above "all rule and authority and power and dominion."

92. To proclaim in word, in rite, and in deed the good news of that future already present in the world is the meaning and function of apostolic ministry. We hear it again in the words of St. Paul.

Therefore, if any one is in Christ, he is a new creation; the old has passed away, behold, the new has come. All this is from God, who through Christ reconciled us to himself and gave us the ministry of reconciliation; that is, in Christ God was reconciling the world to himself, not counting their trespasses against them, and entrusting to us the message of reconciliation. So we are ambassadors for Christ, God making his appeal through us. We beseech you on behalf of Christ, be reconciled to God. For our sake he made him to be sin who knew no sin, so that in him we might become the righteousness of God. Working together with him, then, we entreat you not to accept the grace of God in vain...We put no obstacle in any one's way, so that no fault may be found with our ministry, but as servants of God we commend ourselves in every way: through great endurance, in afflictions, hardships, calamities, beatings, imprisonments, tumults, labors, watching, hunger; by purity, knowledge, forbearance, kindness, the Holy Spirit, genuine love, truthful speech, and the power of God; with the weapons of righteousness for the right hand and of the left; in honor and dishonor, in ill repute and good repute. We are treated as impostors, and yet are true; as unknown, and yet well known, as dying, and behold we live, as punished and yet not killed; as sorrowful, and yet always rejoicing; as poor, yet making many rich; as having nothing, and yet possessing everything. (2 Cor. 5:17-6:10)

What is promised to the world is not a cataclysmic future, not a self-indulgent future, not an otherworldly future of individualistic salvation, but the final future of God's reconciling reign. What is promised to the world is not the triumph of the American revolution, nor the triumph of the Russian revolution, but the final triumph of the Lamb of God whose servant life and death created a reconciled priesthood from "every tribe and tongue and people and nation" (Rev. 5:9-10), a priesthood whose joy and mission and fulfillment witness to God's reign.

## V. THE *MISSION* OF THE GOSPEL

### A. The Lord's Prayer as the Prayer of Mission

93. Mission is the implication of the gospel *par excellence*. To believe and confess that Jesus is the Christ is to be caught up in his mission, the mission of the reign of God (Matt. 7:21-27;Luke 6:46-49). The people of God struggle with the concrete action which the mission of the reign of God entails when they engage in intercessory prayer in the name of Jesus. To pray in the name of Jesus means nothing else than to be identified with and

shaped by his mission and ministry and its promises. That is the significance of the prayer formula known as the Lord's Prayer which Jesus gave to his disciples (Luke 11:1-4;Matt. 6:9-13). When the disciples asked Jesus to teach them to pray (Luke 11:1), they were asking for that kind of prayer formula which a rabbi frequently gave his disciples and which then became an identifying mark of their group. Jesus gave his disciples such an identifying prayer. It is at the same time "the clearest and the richest summary of Jesus' proclamation which we possess."[12] Since the content of Jesus' proclamation and ministry is the breaking in of the reign of God, those who use the Lord's Prayer are being shaped for and taken up into his ministry.

94. He teaches his disciples, his community, to call upon his "Abba," his Father. That was the way he addressed the one who had sent him, the one with whose mission in history he is utterly identified (Matt. 11:25-27;Luke 10:21-22;John 5:17, 36;John 6:57;John 13:3;John 20:21). The use of this name by Jesus is the antithesis of partriarchalism and oppression. Matthew contains a decisive saying about this:

> But you are not to be called rabbi, for you have one teacher, and you are all brethren. And call no man your father on earth, for you have one Father, who is in heaven. Neither be called masters; for you have one master, the Christ. He who is greatest among you shall be your servant; whoever exalts himself will be humbled, and whoever humbles himself will be exalted. (Matt. 23:8-12)

To be given the "Abba" name is to be called into the *mission* of Jesus and his "Abba," the mission of the reign of God in which and through which alienations and oppressions are overcome.

95. The petitions asking that the name of God be made holy and the kingdom of God come were part of the daily prayer of the synagogue. They were petitions of messianic hope. Jesus now sets them into the context of the fulfillment taking place in his own messianic mission. They are prayed as a cry from the depths by those who know that God's name is profaned and dishonored wherever there is abuse and oppression of people, wherever there are acts of terror and reprisal, wherever there is injustice and hopelessness, wherever there is inequity between the needs of the poor and the means of the rich. To pray these petitions is to recognize the powers of greed and cruelty and vengeance arrayed against God's name and reign. But to pray these petitions also means that we take God's promise seriously, the promise that we live in the time when the turning point has already begun.

96. The proleptic presence of the reign of God is given special expression in the petitions regarding bread and forgiveness. The messianic age will be the triumph of life over death. Jesus often refers to that age in terms of a

banquet in his parables and elsewhere (e.g., Matt. 8:11-12), following the imagery of Isa. 25:6-8. The messianic age finds a special focus in the giving and receiving of the food which nourishes and sustains life. That such sharing of food by the people of God is grounded in the Lord's Supper is self-evident (1 Cor. 11:17-34), for in the Lord's Supper we are anticipating the messianic banquet here and now. Similarly we forgive enemies as an act of trusting not only that God's forgiveness *will be* the final verdict for us but also as a way of trusting that God's forgiveness *is* already ours here and now. As a conclusion Jesus teaches his community to pray that it will be delivered from and in the midst of all assaults which the community will endure because it participates in the mission of Jesus, because it is engaged in witness to the reign of God.

97. All prayer in the name of Jesus grows out of this prayer. No matter with which hopes and fears, needs and desires we begin, if we are praying in the name of Jesus, if your prayers are shaped by the Lord's Prayer, in the end we will be taken up into the ministry and mission of the reign of God. Our life and work, our past and present, our condition and destiny, all are encompassed by the reign of God. In prayer we offer ourselves and seek to discover how and in what concrete form we will be taken up into the mission of the reign of God, trusting the promise of Jesus:

> Ask, and it will be given you;
> seek, and you will find;
> knock, and it will be opened to you. (Matt. 7:7)

The prayer of the people of God is set into the context of word and sacrament because in worship we receive our identity and mission, the gift of Christ and the vocation of witness. Some concrete dimensions of that mission and witness are here organized around three themes, all of which are equally important and mutually interdependent: ecumenism, evangelism, and ethics.

## B. Mission and Ecumenism

98. Repeatedly Christians have confessed that the unity of the church is given, not achieved. The church can only be one because it is constituted by the gospel in word and sacrament, and there is but one gospel. What Christians are seeking when they engage in the tasks and efforts associated with ecumenism is to discover how the unity they have already been given by the gospel can be manifested faithfully in terms of the church's mission. In the often cited prayer of Jesus from the Gospel of John, the unity of the

disciple community is to be visible so that the world can know and believe the messianic mission of the Father and the Son and thus participate in the future of the Spirit here and now (John 17:20-26). The goal of the Christ is the gathering of Gentiles to Israel "in one body" (Eph. 2:11-22). To manifest visible unity is the fundamental vocation of the people of God.

> I therefore, a prisoner for the Lord, beg you to lead a life worthy of the calling to which you have been called, with all lowliness and meekness, with patience, forbearing one another in love, eager to maintain the unity of the Spirit in the bond of peace. (Eph. 4:1-3)

99. Sociological studies of the church have sometimes indicated that attention to ecumenism, especially in the form of visible manifestations of unity, has often resulted in attenuation of mission. Many faithful Christians have concluded that one must choose between ecumenism and evangelism, and they have not hesitated to assign higher priority to the latter. If our churches must acknowledge the validity of the sociological observations, then one of the concrete and necessary tasks before us is the renewal of our understandings of both unity and mission so that their essential and necessary interdependence is evident in the life of our churches. Whatever Christians can do to manifest that they are indeed "one body" is witness to the presence of the reign of God. Concretely for the Lutheran and Episcopal churches this would mean attention to the following, by no means exhaustive, list of actions.

100. We need to engage in as much common education and shared leadership as possible. Some examples:

a. Might it be possible to share the ministries of staff persons, particularly in the area of parish education, between dioceses of the Episcopal Church and synods of the Evangelical Lutheran Church of America (ELCA)?

b. The formation of the ELCA in 1988 provided for the establishment of nine regional centers for parish life and mission. Is it possible to consider staffing these centers jointly with the Episcopal Church and thus encouraging the use of resources available through such centers to both churches?

c. Might there be provision for a periodic convocation of all bishops from both churches for shared education and mutual consultation?

d. Could we encourage a convocation of seminary deans to arrange for regular exchanges of seminary students and faculty? Perhaps as a beginning visits could be exchanged for periods of as brief as a week. Eventually it might be possible for students and faculty from seminaries of one church to spend whole terms at seminaries of the other church.

e. At the present time there are instances of Lutheran faculty persons teaching at Episcopal seminaries and vice versa. Could this practice be expanded beyond the present instances?

f. Could there be periodic conferences of Lutheran and Episcopal theologians?

g. Could there be joint programs of continuing education for clergy of both churches?

h. Might there be encouragement for the clergy of parishes to organize regular, even weekly, gatherings for purposes of mutual prayer, study, and consultation?

i. Could we encourage more Lutheran and Episcopal *parish* covenants as well as more covenants between dioceses and synods so that promising beginnings in this area are rapidly multiplied?

101. We need to cooperate in maintaining and supporting chaplaincies for hospitals, prisons, the military, higher education, and wherever else chaplaincy services are needed or desired. We also need to encourage the cooperation of parishes in particular contexts, e.g., urban situations, for purposes of shared mission and ministry. We also need to cultivate cooperation in establishing new parishes, encouraging shared life and perhaps the use of shared facilities for existing parishes in areas of population decline, and the referring of communicants to one another's parishes in situations where only one of our churches has a parish.

102. Because we already share liturgical traditions that are similar, we need to encourage familiarity with one another's liturgical materials and hymnody. We need to move toward official consultation and common work whenever the revision of our present rite is contemplated. Since both churches have used the texts prepared by the International Consultation on English Texts (ICET) in their revised rites, we should encourage parishes to use and learn the ICET text for the Lord's Prayer. Learning it together would give English speaking Christians a common text for the Lord's Prayer for the first time since the Reformation of the 16th century.

103. We need to continue work towards a shared ecumenical strategy. Some steps might involve occasional joint meetings of the official commissions responsible for ecumenical relationships, inviting representatives from each other's churches to sit on ecumenical and other appropriate commissions, inviting representatives from each other's churches to attend national conventions, coordinating as much as possible the structures for ecumenical work in our respective dioceses and synods.

104. It would be desirable for both churches to become familiar with each other's histories. Since both churches have a number of commemorations in their respective calendars, it would be helpful to make these calendars available in some way to all clergy and parishes. Eventually we should move toward a common list of commemorations. We can also engage in reg-

ular and disciplined prayer for each other, the more specific the better. Helpful would be the practice of having each parish pray for one parish and its clergy from the other church. We ought to pray by name for bishops from each other's churches, for specific schools and mission communities, for churches from each other's communions in other countries. Most helpful would be offerings of money and time for each other's ministries, for by such concrete steps we would develop knowledge of and interest in one another, support for one another, dependence upon one another.

105. It should be noted that all of these steps can be taken prior to the actual realization of full communion. None of these steps imply that we have resolved all questions related to full communion. However, these steps would insure that the eventual realization of full communion would reflect an actual sharing of life and mission. We are using the term "full communion" as a synonym for "altar and pulpit fellowship" and *communio in sacris* (cf. the mandating resolution for LED III cited in par. 1 above).

## C. Mission and Evangelization

106. The good news of the prophet of the exile was, "Your God reigns" (Isa. 52:7-10). The good news of Jesus was, "The kingdom of God is at hand" (Mark 1:15). The good news of the church can be stated as "Jesus, the crucified one, is the Christ, and the promise of the final triumph of the reign of God cannot be defeated because Jesus has been raised from the dead." The church witnesses to the good news through its words (doctrine, confession, proclamation), worship (liturgy, baptism, eucharist) and deeds (polity, life together, ethic). The church is called to its witness by the living Christ (Luke 24:48;Acts 1:8, *inter alia*) and takes up the task of witness with joy in the midst of suffering (Acts 4:23-31; 5:40-42, *inter alia*). It cannot be stressed strongly enough that the church's responsibility is to give attention to the *urgency and quality of its witness.*

107. The church addressed God's call to people that they be converted from the reign of death and all its implications to the reign of life and all its implications. The reign of death has everything to do with human sin (cf. pars. 15, 87) because it enmeshes us in the violence of self-hating, self-justifying, self-protective, self-aggrandizing existence. It robs us of truth, hope and love. It makes us dangerous and destructive toward ourselves, each other, and our world. The reign of God, the reign of life, is the promise that death will not have the last word. The gift of God is life and freedom. The reign of life makes our self-protective attempts unnecessary as well as exposing them as impossible. But what is at stake in the church's call is *conversion*, nothing less! That is, a being transferred from one reign to

another (Col. 1:13). Jesus repeatedly describes the radical nature of the conversion in terms of not being able to serve two masters (Matt. 6:24), of building on rock or sand (Matt. 7:21-27), of following him instead of fulfilling filial obligations (Matt. 8:21-22), even of division in families and households (Matt. 10:34-39). It is a question of the object of one's final trust, one's ultimate concern.

108. Such radical conversion and transfer from one reign to another is inseparably connected in the church's life with the baptism it administers (cf. pars. 12-15). The church baptized persons into the name of the God of the gospel (cf. Section 2), that is, into the reign of life. It baptizes persons into the community of the gospel (Section 3), that is, into the community that lives from and witnesses to the reign of life. It baptizes persons into the lifelong struggle to become and reflect in their lives what they are in fact by virtue of their baptism; the sons and daughters of God and the heirs of the promise of life (cf. pars. 114-123 below). All the baptized share in the eucharistic life and mission of the community of the reign of life. That is, witness to the reign of life is the calling of the baptized community as a whole as well as of each individual member in a manner appropriate to that member's age, experience, calling, and station in life.

109. The church needs to integrate sacramental life, ethics, and ecumenism into a unified understanding and practice of evangelization. Because our churches have a shared understanding of the meaning of baptism, because we recognize fully each other's baptisms, because we have similar rituals of baptism, and because we are striving to effect similar reforms in the administration of baptism, it is appropriate for our churches to give common attention to an understanding and practice of evangelization which has its focus in baptism. Indeed, in this document we are attempting to bear witness to a shared understanding of evangel not so that we may test or prove one another's orthodoxy, but rather so that the mission implications of the gospel (evangelization) may become part of our shared life and ministry.

110. We can here do little more than identify some components of an approach to evangelization when the church's baptism is its central focus. In theology and liturgy the church must be continuously attentive to the necessary connection between baptism and the content and character of the gospel: the eschatological reign of God has begun and is grounded in the life, death, and resurrection of Jesus of Nazareth. Therefore the call and witness of the church is: Be reconciled to God (2 Cor. 5:17-21), that is, be set free by the reign of life from the bondage of the reign of death.

111. The rite of baptism must reflect the radical character of justification by faith for the conversion taking place. The transfer from death to life is the "dying" to the reign of death and the being raised to the reign of life. Therefore our present baptismal rites require of candidates appropriate

renunciations as well as affirmations. The Episcopal Church has canonical provision (*Book of Common Prayer*, p. 312) for renewal of the practice of administering baptism at select times during the Christian year; the Easter Vigil, Pentecost Day, All Saints Day or Sunday, and the Baptism of Jesus (First Sunday After the Epiphany). The *Minister's Desk Edition for the Lutheran Book of Worship* (p. 30) calls for the same practice. The purposes of such reform and renewal include the use of such occasions for teaching about baptism, the appropriate involvement of the congregation in the baptismal rite, the reaffirmation of their baptism by the baptized, and the opportunity for disciplined preparation of candidates for baptism. While all baptisms can hardly be limited to a few occasions in the life of the parish, the calendar focus for the administration of baptism should be the Easter vigil because it provides a thematic connection with the death and resurrection of Jesus and the candidate's being identified with that death and resurrection so that a death and resurrection of the candidate's own takes place.

112. The church has two components of its present baptismal practice which are in need of renewal and redefinition but which have significant potential for the church's mission of evangelization with a focus on baptism: the catechumenate and sponsorship for baptism. In most contemporary baptismal practice sponsorship is limited to the baptisms of infants and very small children. The role of sponsor is usually taken by family members or family friends. The new baptismal rites of our churches envision sponsors for *all* candidates. Further, the sponsor represents the church in bringing the candidate to baptism. These two factors provide openings for the church's ministry of evangelization. Whoever else functions at the actual baptismal rite, one or more sponsors from the congregation can have already been involved in the call and witness to the adult candidate, in involving the candidate in the catechumenate, in attending the candidate during the catechumenate, and in integrating the person newly baptized into the life and mission of the church. In the case of infants brought to baptism by a parent or parents who are already baptized members of the church, parents and family will be the primary sponsors. But even here they may be assisted by other members of the parish, and there may be a short period of instruction to prepare parents and family for their ministry in relation to a baptized infant. The catechumenate needs to be structured in such a way that it includes initiation into the life, teaching, rites, and ministries of the church with assistance from clergy, catechists, and other members of the church. Such a structured catechumenate would need to be extended over a period of months, not all of which would be spent in formal instruction. In all of this it should be clear that baptismal sponsorship is the way the church *seeks* those who might not otherwise take the initiative, the way the church carries out God's mission of *sending* it into the world.

113. These reforms and approaches are necessary because the church, whether it thinks of itself in this way or not, is in fact in a missionary situation in Western countries no less than in the rest of the world. The massive increases in church membership which occurred in the United States between 1950 and 1970 did not necessarily mean that *conversions* to Christianity took place. Much of that increase in membership involved not a little identification of religion with American cultural values. The fact that areas of the United States with the largest population increase in the past decade (South and West) also have the lowest percentage of church membership is further indication that what happened after World War II was more a cultural trend than a period of Christian conversion. Hence we must be attentive both to the continued and even urgent *need* for evangelization and to the *quality* and faithfulness with which we engage in evangelization. These paragraphs are an attempt to identify the administration of baptism as an opportunity for our churches to develop a common and faithful approach to evangelization and conversion.

## D. Mission and Ethics

114. The church's attention to ethics does not mean that it simply serves the public good by cultivating and encouraging behavior patterns characteristic of responsible citizenship. The Christian ethic does in fact ultimately serve the public good by encouraging honesty, stewardship, compassion, responsibility, education, and attention to peace and justice. But its focus is to ask how the good news of the reign of God in Jesus, the Christ, shapes the character and life of the people of God. The teaching of Jesus and the apostolic exhortation are not intended to be an ethic for the state. They are intended to be part of the witness of the community that believes the gospel. (Cf. Matt. 5:3-16 and Romans 12-16 as two examples from the many that could be adduced.) What is at stake is the relationship of Christian ethics to the breaking in of the reign of God. The life of the people of God as a whole as well as the life of its individual members should reflect faith in the gospel.

115. Christians are not always agreed on concrete strategies for the church's life as witness to the reign of God. Deeply committed German Christians who were passionately opposed to the Nazi regime for reasons of faith and confession disagreed on whether or not to engage in violence against the Nazi regime, to cite but one paradigmatic example from our century. We cannot in this document begin to work toward agreement on concrete ethical implications of the gospel for our churches. We can, however, identify several dimensions of the church's ethical mission.

a. We affirm the necessary connection between the church's teaching of the gospel and administration of the sacraments on the one hand and its ethic on the other hand. While it is true that the church's gospel is the redeeming reign of God in Christ, not the church's life, nevertheless, the gospel has implications for the life of Christians which are inseparably linked to it (e.g., Matt. 5-7;Ephesians 4-6;Romans 12-16).

b. We affirm the necessity of common work on matters of life and the concrete issues of ethics. The magnitude and complexity of the church's attention to issues of peace and war, economic and social justice, compassion and stewardship, culture and life not only require resources for study which may be larger than our individual churches have available. Of equal importance is the fact that we need each other's perspectives.

c. We affirm and identify a list of areas which are in continued need of the church's faithful attention for study guidance for its members, and corporate as well as individual action where appropriate.

116. *Stewardship.* We have already indicated (pars. 79-81) that the Christian teaching on and confession of creation calls those who are grasped by the gospel to stewardship of the universe. Authentic stewardship involves something quite different from contributing to the support of the church, however important that is in itself. Stewardship begins with the offertory prayer with which we "set the table" at the Eucharist. The *Book of Common Prayer* suggests the bidding, "Let us with gladness present the offerings and oblations of our *life* and labor to the Lord" (p. 344). The *Lutheran Book of Worship* directs the congregation to pray: "Through your goodness you have blessed us with these gifts. With them we offer *ourselves* to your service and dedicate our lives to the care and redemption of all that you have made" (p. 68, italics added in both examples). All that we are and have is placed into the service of the reign of God. Our stewardship is nothing less than the concrete exercise of our partnership with the creator in the Christian vision of creation which is characteristic of the gospel. Therefore we need to be appropriately attentive to issues affecting the purity of air and water, management of the resources of water and soil particularly in relation to the use of chemical fertilizers, the cultivation of land only marginally suitable for growing crops, the poisoning or depletion of sub-surface water, and many related concerns. We need to be concerned about our individual and corporate use of renewable and nonrenewable resources. We need attention to issues related to energy, to our care for the nonhuman creatures who inhabit the earth with us, and to the quality and care with which we move into the space beyond our planet.

*Sexuality:*

117. Stewardship in service of the Christian vision of creation involves us in the stewardship of our bodies and especially the sexual dimension of

our bodily existence. Biologically we share many characteristics with animal existence. But our humanity means that we are capable of responsibilities and choices which transcend biology. Hence human sexuality is more than genital. It is part of all human existence. It is a significant part of human decisions, human covenants, and human social order. The gospel provides us with a perspective which shapes our responsibilities and choices in the area of our sexuality.

118. We need attention to the interdependent roles of both celibacy and marriage as *vocations* for individuals in the people of God. We need continually to be recalled to chastity in both marriage and celibacy. We need to ask how the church witnesses to the reign of God in its teaching on celibacy and marriage. We need to ask how the church witnesses to the gospel when it encourages and seeks to minister to the lifelong commitment in marriage. We also need to ask how the church witnesses to the gospel when it engages in ministry to those in troubled marriages and to the divorced. We need attention to parenthood as a vocation in terms of the gospel and to the practice of birth control as a dimension of responsible parenthood.

119. *Homosexuality:*

a. In the context of a larger approach to the area of human sexuality and its relation to the reign of God we must be attentive to the issue of homosexuality. There are few areas of human existence in which the church stands in greater need of both wisdom and love. It would seem to some that the acceptance of homosexual behavior is inconsistent with significant portions of biblical testimony. It seems to others, however, that the Scriptures do not provide clear and consistent comment on homosexual relationships. Increasingly, therefore, Christians are finding it difficult to maintain a negative judgment over against all homosexual behavior, even though the search for a positive position remains equally elusive. A growing number of individuals in our churches raise the following questions not because there are ready answers but because the churches need to express compassion, discern righteousness, stimulate study, and urge the quest for a Christian perspective which can guide clergy and laity alike.

b. Is there any difference between the biblical context and our own which would require reconsideration of the church's traditional position on homosexuality? While the Christian doctrine of creation affirms life and procreation, does the same doctrine require us to affirm what may be involuntary differences in sexual orientation? Is there clear agreement among major authorities that differences in sexual orientation are in fact involuntary or irreversible? Can the condemnation which has frequently characterized the church's relationship to homosexual behavior be reconciled with the unconditional depth of divine grace and the universal breadth of divine love? Is there a faithful third alternative to celibacy and marriage? In view of the church's legitimate condemnation of all sexual promiscuity, which is basically predatory, can the church recognize somehow mutual care and commitment in a homosexual relationship as it does in heterosexual marriage? What insights from psychology, sociology, and anthropology can be helpful to the church in formulating an ethical vision for persons with a homosexual orientation? In its attempt to respond to these questions can the church listen faithfully, sensitively, and patiently in the light of Scripture both to the concerns and commitments of Christian persons with a homosexual orientation and to the whole range of concerns and commitments on the part of all of its members? Can the church be a place of genuine dialogue and reconciliation between individuals, families, and larger groups painfully affected by homosexuality?

c. The church needs to be attentive to this issue and to remind itself that no minority group, no matter how small, is beyond its mission and sensitive concern, that is, beyond the gracious and righteous will of God.

120. The church is required to think about how it engages in pastoral ministry with Christians who must face tragic circumstances which make painful choices necessary, who must deal with the competing claims of equally authentic values. The issue of abortion has evoked the concern of Christians on behalf of those women whose pregnancy is the result of victimization and oppression and on behalf of those parents who are faced with difficult choices when a continued pregnancy threatens the life or health of the mother or the viability and well being of the unborn fetus. Christians have been equally concerned about the fetus whose embryonic humanity has claims upon the compassionate care and protection of the larger society. This is especially true when abortion is used as a form of social engineering or birth control. Attention to the issue raises a number of attendant issues, including how public our instruction on the prevention of pregnancy ought to be, how available alternatives to abortion need to be, how our society ought to support single parents, especially the increasing number of early teen mothers, during the crucial early years of the lives of their children, how the church ought to teach and support the value of chastity in a culture saturated with encouragement of promiscuity, how the church ought to express this concern for the rights and responsibilities of women, and how the church ought to cultivate in the male partner a sense of responsibility for both chastity and paternity. The church's commitment to life, not death, requires it to ask both how life can be wanted and nurtured after birth as well as how it needs to be protected before birth.

121. *Compassion and Vocation.* Our churches have a long and good tradition of engaging in ministries of compassion, attention to the needs of the sick, the suffering, the dying, the bereaved, and attention to providing relief and assistance for the victims of poverty, deprivation, and disaster. We

have little or no difficulty making the connection between this humanitarian activity and the church's witness to the gospel. We need here to ask how we can engage in such compassionate witness together, as part of our growing together in shared life and ministry. We have similar common traditions in cultivating the concept of vocation, viewing the various aspects of our individual lives as callings from God, as ministries of God in and for the world. Indeed this is one of the more positive aspects of our Reformation heritage. We need to ask concretely about how the reign of God is related to vocation and ministry in the world.

122. *Social Justice.* Our churches have an ambiguous record with regard to involvement in issues relating to social justice. Indeed, one of the disagreements within our churches is whether or not the church as church ought to be involved in such issues. We wish to affirm questions of social justice as appropriate and in fact mandatory for the church's attention not because the church seeks to order the life of the state or because Christians have more practical wisdom available to them. Rather, the churches must address the questions of social justice because such questions are related to compassion and vocation and above all because such questions are related to the church's witness to the reign of God. That the community in immediate temporal proximity to the resurrection of Jesus saw a connection between the eschaton, the Eucharist, and the sharing of meals and property is evident from the early chapters of Acts, especially Acts 2:42-46 and Acts 5:1-11. The church's involvement in questions of social justice throughout its history has been expressed in its response to such issues as slavery, sexism, unequal education, racism and the exploitation of labor. The question is not whether the church should be involved, but how. How does the corporate life of the church reflect its gospel, and how does the church serve as a community of guidance and support for its members as they exercise their vocations in the social and economic dimensions of society? In this context, American churches cannot evade the question of economic order. Are all economic systems morally neutral? Attention to such questions belongs to the inescapable implications of the gospel. The reign of God has special implications for cultivating equality of opportunity and education, for the overcoming of racism, sexism, ageism, classism, irrational fear of homosexual persons, totalitarianism, and any other oppressive and prejudicial manifestations of the reign of death. How does the church witness to an alternative future, the future of the reign of life? How does the church serve as the vehicle for the Holy Spirit, the Spirit of freedom and the openness for the future? These are questions with which social ethics must wrestle.

123. *Peace.* The relationship of the gospel to the concern for peace is such a major theme of the Scriptures that it needs no documentation. The vision of the prophets that the messianic age would bring peace with it (e.g.,

Isa. 2:2-4;Micah 4:1-4) was echoed in the teaching of Jesus (e.g., Matt. 5:9-12, 38-48) and the apostles (e.g., Rom. 12:14-21;I Peter 2:18-25; 3:8-22). The questions arise because of the church's flawed and ambiguous witness in this implication of the gospel. We need to ask with urgency and clarity what our witness to the gospel means for Christian participation in the military services. It is not a foregone conclusion that Christians must abstain from military service. Both of our churches can draw on the "justifiable violence" or "just war" traditions as part of their heritage. The question is how these traditions can be clarified in terms of the practice of "total war" and the possession of nuclear weapons. We have the further task of schooling ourselves in our authentic traditions and of developing institutional ways for raising the kind of questions which our traditions require. Since biblical *shalom* is more than the absence of war, we also need to ask how we can be peacemakers through attention to violence in our societies, to meaningful disarmament and the turning of our resources and energies toward peaceful purposes, to the economic needs of the world's poor, and to fostering relationships of understanding, exchange, and cooperation with our enemies, especially the Soviet Union and other Marxist-socialist societies. The basic concern is not how our churches support or change governmental policies, but rather how our own corporate life and the individual vocational ministry of our members witness to the reign of God, the triumph of life over death.

124. The magnitude and complexity of the agenda before us must not be a deterrent. God has given our churches many gifts and resources for attention to this agenda. Above all we must be open to and grateful for the resources of Christian churches other than our own. One of the fruits of ecumenical cooperation today is that we can listen to and learn from the documents, thinking, tradition, and life of churches as diverse as the Roman Catholic and the Mennonite. What must be the responsibility of our churches is the integration in the consciousness and life of all our members of the dimensions of ecumenism, evangelization, and ethics as necessarily interdependent dimensions of the one mission of the church as it witnesses to the gospel of the reign of God.

### CONCLUSION

125. We commend to our respective churches, their parishes, bishops, clergy and members, for study and action this common statement on the implications of the gospel.

126. We commend this document for study because in it we have sought to give common expression to our separate theological and ecclesiological traditions. We have attempted to utilize the eschatological horizon of

the New Testament because this perspective has given the vision and hope of the gospel to Christian churches in a variety of contemporary contexts. We have selected from the richness of the New Testament witness the theme of the redeeming reign of God, a concept which the Gospels of Matthew, Mark, and Luke use to describe the mission and ministry of Jesus. We have spoken of the church as an eschatological community with a mission of witness to the redeeming reign of God. We have sought to provide an integrative focus for various facets of the church's life: its matrix in Israel and the implications this has for the church's commitment to Jews; its need for evangelical and catholic authenticity in worship, proclamation, and polity; its call to participate faithfully in God's mission for the world. We have sought to formulate a statement which will be both edifying and challenging.

127. We commend it for action because our work needs to be accepted or adopted by our respective churches as a further step toward full communion. Equally important are the specific recommendations for action which we have made in the areas of worship, ecumenism, evangelism, and ethics, We call attention here to the paragraph locations and substance of those specific recommendations.

1. Paragraphs 29-31 take up the use of appropriate language for the address of God in prayer and worship, and we advocate the use of both masculine and feminine imagery in speaking about God.

2. Paragraph 42 builds on the identification of the church's matrix in Israel with recommendations for our contemporary relationship to Jews.

3. Paragraph 50 advocates the renewal of the Eucharistic liturgy in the parish through conscious movement toward celebration of the Eucharist every Sunday.

4. Paragraphs 100-104 contain recommendations for cooperative activity between Lutherans and Episcopalians in order to manifest the unity we have been given.

5. Paragraph 112 urges common work in evangelization organized around the administration of holy baptism.

6. Paragraphs 114-124 recommend common attention to the ethical dimensions of the Christian life in the areas of stewardship, sexuality, vocation, social justice, and peace.

None of the specific recommendations are dependent upon full communion. All are able to make our churches more faithful in their life and witness. If undertaken cooperatively, they can be a substantial vehicle for God's gift of unity to our churches.

128. We join our prayers with those of our Lord for faithfulness to the gospel and unity in our witness to it.

# Notes

[The text in which note 1 appears in not included in material presented herein.]

2. Lutheran-Episcopal Dialogue II issued five "Joint Statements," the first of them being a "Joint Statement on Justification" (The *Report of the Lutheran-Episcopal Dialogue, Second Series, 1976-1980*, pp. 22-24). Paragraph "C" of the "Joint Statement" reads as follows: "In the western cultural setting in which our communions, Episcopal and Lutheran, find themselves, the gospel of justification continues to address the needs of human beings alienated from a holy and gracious God. Therefore, it is the task of the church to minister this gospel *with vivid and fresh proclamation* (italics added) and to utilize all available resources for the theological enrichment of this ministry."

We affirm justification by faith alone and not by works in terms of an eschatological understanding of the gospel. The justification of the totality of our existence is disclosed only by the ultimate end (*telos*) of all history. We cannot justify ourselves by means of our efforts or achievements in any sphere because we cannot see, much less determine, the ultimate outcome of history. Indeed, our efforts to justify ourselves in the face of our rebellion against the call to love God and the neighbor are profound expressions of our sinfulness. The gospel is the proclamation that justification is the gift and promise of God. Jesus of Nazareth, crucified and raised from death for sinners, is both the ground and the hope of the ultimate outcome of history. The meaning of our cosmos and of ourselves is in him (Col. 1:13-20). He is the Alpha and Omega, the origin and the outcome. Trusting him as "righteousness" and "justification" means that we are free *for* our lives and our callings. We have no necessity to use them for justification. We are free to confess sins, to hear the truth of admonition, to experience the grace of God, because the meaningfulness and justification of our lives does not derive from our being in the right. The key term is "faith" because our justification derives from that event which is promise: Jesus' death and resurrection as God's judgment on our lives and as the outcome of all history.

3. Cf. Virginia Ramsey Mollenkott, *The Divine Feminine* (New York: Crossroad Publishing Company, 1983), and Caroline Walker Bynum, *Jesus as Mother: Studies in the Spirituality of the High Middle Ages* (Berkeley: University of California Press, 1982).

4. "Israel's deed would be overcome, and the people's path to repentance would once again be open. Those who had ruined their lives through their hardening against Jesus receive from God, freely and without merit, the possibility of new life (in biblical terms, atonement). God transforms the murder of his emissary into a deed of his *faithfulness* to Israel (in biblical terms, covenant); he turns the death of his emissary, planned and brought about by men, into the establishment of *definitive and irrevocable* faithfulness to Israel (in biblical terms, new covenant) and thus preserves his claim on the chosen people of God." Gerhard Lohfink, *Jesus and Community* (Philadelphia: Fortress Press, 1984), p. 25.

5. Gustaf Aulen, *Eucharist as Sacrifice*, (Philadelphia: Muhlenberg Press, 1958), p. 200

6. *The Eucharist as Sacrifice*, Lutheran and Catholics in Dialogue III, pp. 187 198; *Eucharist and Ministry*, Lutherans and Catholics in Dialogue IV. pp. 7-33; *The Final Report*, Anglican-Roman Catholic International Commission, pp. 12-25; *Anglican-Lutheran Dialogue, The Report of The European Commission*, pp. 11-12 and 43-46; and The *Report of the Lutheran-Episcopal Dialogue*, Second Series, 1976 1980, (LED II), pp. 25 29.

7. Massey H. Shepherd Jr., "Ministry, Christian," *The Interpreter's Dictionary of the Bible*, Vol. III (Nashville: Abingdon, 1962), p. 386.

8. Leonhard Goppelt, *Apostolic and Post-apostolic Times* (London: Adam and Charles Black, 1970), p. 177.

9. "To serve means to demonstrate love to mankind out of a faith which forgoes the use of right and power and seeks God's help in Jesus. This love is to be demonstrated for the same purpose as it was by Jesus, to inspire a faith in God and compassion for others." Goppelt, *ibid.*, p. 178.

10. Jerome Quinn concludes his careful study of "Ministry in the New Testament" with the following summary: "The structures of first century Ministry involved leadership both by groups (of two, three, seven, twelve, *apostoloi*, prophets, teachers, *episkopoi, diakonoi, presbyteroi*) and by single individuals even within the groups (Peter; Paul; James; Titus in Crete;

Timothy in Ephesus; the *episkopos*). Though there was development in Ministry in the first century, it was not unilinear. It is historically more exact and eventually more instructive theologically to respect the difference in structuring the Ministry that existed simultaneously in different churches (Jerusalem, Corinth, Ephesus, Rome, etc.)" (*Eucharist and Ministry*, Lutherans and Catholics in Dialogue IV, p. 100).

11. Bernard P. Prusak, "Woman: Seductive Siren and Source of Sin?" *Religion and Sexism,* edited by Rosemary Radford Reuther (New York: Simon and Schuster, 1974), pp. 89-116.

12. Joachim Jeremias, *The Prayers of Jesus* (Philadelphia: Fortress Press, 1978), p. 94.

\* \* \*

## STATEMENT OF THE REPRESENTATIVE OF THE LUITHERAN CHURCH—MISSOURI SYNOD

As this phase of the Lutheran-Episcopal Dialogue comes to an end, we the representatives of the Lutheran Church—Missouri Synod wish to express our gratitude for the privilege of full participation in the discussions of the dialogue. We are especially grateful for the opportunities which the dialogue has provided for joint study of the Word of God on theological issues addressed.

The Lutheran Church—Missouri Synod did not enter the Lutheran—Episcopal Agreement of 1982 which included the establishment of a "relationship of Interim Sharing of the Eucharist" and the authorization of a third series of dialogues to discuss outstanding questions to be resolved before full communion. Since this agreement was the basis for the preparation of the document on "Implications of the Gospel," two representatives of The Lutheran Church—Missouri Synod abstained from voting on the statement, and one representative voted no.

As members of the dialogue, the representatives of The Lutheran Church—Missouri Synod will forward the statement on "Implications of the Gospel" to the President of the Synod, with the recommendation that the Commision on Theology and Church Relations be asked to evaluate the statement and possibly to prepare a response.

LCMS Representatives to LED III
Carl Bornmann
Jerald Joersz
Norman Nagel

# "Toward Full Communion"*

## INTRODUCTION

1. Bilateral dialogue between the Episcopal Church U.S.A. and the Lutheran churches which were members of the Lutheran Council in the U.S.A. at that time (The American Lutheran Church, The Lutheran Church in America, and the Lutheran Church—Missouri Synod) was authorized in 1967. The conversations began on October 14, 1969. The first round of conversations (LED I) concluded on June 1, 1972. The agreements, recommendations, and papers were published at the end of 1972 under the title *Lutheran-Episcopal Dialogue: A Progress Report.* The recommendations included "continuing joint theological study and conversation."[1] A second round of conversations (LED II) began in January, 1976, and concluded in November, 1980. The proceedings were published in 1981 under the title *Lutheran-Episcopal Dialogue: Report and Recommendations.*[2] In September of 1978 a representative of the Association of Evangelical Lutheran Churches joined the dialogue. In September, 1982, the Episcopal Church and three of the Lutheran churches, the American Lutheran Church, the Association of Evangelical Lutheran Churches, and the Lutheran Church in America, approved the Lutheran-Episcopal Agreement as follows:

The Episcopal Church and the Lutheran Churches

1) Welcome and rejoice in the substantial progress of the Lutheran-Episcopal Dialogues (LED) I and II and of the Anglican-Lutheran International Conversations, looking forward to the day when full communion is established between the Anglican and Lutheran Churches;
2) Recognize now the (Episcopal Church/The American Lutheran Church, Lutheran Church in America, Association of Evangelical Lutheran Churches) as Churches in which the Gospel is preached and taught;

*William A. Norgren and William G. Rusch, eds., *"Toward Full Communion" and "Concordat of Agreement."* Lutheran—Episcopal Dialogue, Series III (Minneapolis: Augsburg; Cincinnati: Forward Movement, 1991) 11-116.

3) Encourage the development of common Christian life throughout the respective Churches by such means as the following:

a) Mutual prayer and mutual support, including parochial/congregational and diocesan/synodical covenants or agreements,

6) Common study of the Holy Scriptures, the histories and theological traditions of each Church, and the material of LED I and II,

c) Joint programs of religious education, theological discussion, mission, evangelism, and social action,

d) Joint use of facilities;

4) Affirm now on the basis of studies of LED I and LED II and of the Anglican/Lutheran International Conversations that the basic teaching of each respective Church is consonant with the Gospel and is sufficiently compatible with the teaching of this Church that a relationship of Interim Sharing of the Eucharist is hereby established between these Churches in the U.S.A. under the following guidelines:

a) The Episcopal Church extends a special welcome to members of these three Lutheran Churches to receive Holy Communion in it under the Standard of Occasional Eucharist Sharing of its 1979 General Convention.

or (The Lutheran Churches) Extend a special welcome to members of the Episcopal Church to receive Holy Communion in it under the Statement on Communion Practices adopted in 1978.

This welcome constitutes a mutual recognition of Eucharistic teaching sufficient for Interim Sharing of the Eucharist, although this does not intend to signify that final recognition of each other's Eucharists or ministries has yet been achieved.

b) Bishops of Dioceses of the Episcopal Church and Bishops/Presidents of the Lutheran Districts and Synods may by mutual agreement extend the regulations of Church discipline to permit common, joint celebrations of the Eucharist within their jurisdictions. This is appropriate in particular situations where the said authorities deem that local conditions are appropriate for the sharing of worship jointly by congregations of the respective Churches. The presence of an ordained minister of each participating Church at the altar in this way reflects the presence of two or more Churches expressing unity in faith and baptism as well as the remaining divisions which they seek to overcome; however, this does not imply rejection or final recognition of either Church's Eucharist or ministry. In such circumstances the eucharistic prayer will be one from the *Lutheran Book of Worship* or the *Book of Common Prayer* as authorized jointly by the Bishop of the Episcopal Diocese and the Bishops/Presidents of the corresponding Lutheran Districts/Synods.

c) This resolution and experience of Interim Sharing of the Eucharist will be communicated at regular intervals to other Churches of the Lutheran and Anglican Communions throughout the world, as well as to the various ecumenical dialogues in which Anglicans and Lutherans are engaged, in order that consultation may be fostered, similar experiences encouraged elsewhere, and already existing relationships of full communion respected;

5) Authorize and establish now a third series of Lutheran-Episcopal Dialogues for the discussion of any other outstanding questions that must be resolved before full communion (*communio in sacris*/altar and pulpit fellowship) can be established between the respective Churches, e.g., implications of the Gospel, historic episcopate, and the ordering of ministry (Bishops, Priests, and Deacons) in the total context of apostolicity.[3]

2. Lutherans and Anglicans have been in official conversation since the late nineteenth century.[4] In 1909, the Lambeth Conference, representing in some sense the entire Anglican Communion, and with one American bishop on its committee, began dialogue with the Church of Sweden.[5] Before the onset of World War II the conversation had expanded to include the Churches of Finland, Estonia, and Latvia. In 1947 the conversations expanded again to include the Churches of Norway, Denmark, and Iceland. The gift of unity disclosed and discovered in these early conversations resulted in a significant expansion of contacts and agreements which specified an important degree of intercommunion. The first official conversation in this century involving Anglicans and Lutherans in the U.S.A. took place in December, 1935, between the Episcopal Church and The Augustana Evangelical Lutheran Church, a church with its roots in Sweden. The antipathy of the Lutherans to the historic episcopate as it was then perceived and sometimes advocated as well as commitment to growing unity among Lutherans led to a termination of the official conversation after one meeting, although "the colloquy called for the continuation of its efforts and adjourned in a friendly spirit."[6]

3. The Lutheran-Episcopal Agreement of 1982 advances the relationship between churches of the Lutheran and Anglican communions because it involves churches who live side by side in the same country. These churches have come to a new stage in their relationship, a stage characterized by the phrase, "Interim Sharing of the Eucharist." Christ Jesus, Our Lord, gives to the church the gifts of ministry for building up his body toward maturity and wholeness (Eph. 4:11-16). Every level of maturity which is expressed by Christian unity is an occasion for thanksgiving. Lutheran and Episcopalians are grateful to God not only for the Agreement of 1982, but also, and above all, for the reception of that agreement by the churches. Throughout the U.S.A., Episcopalians and Lutherans have been experiencing in worship and

study, in covenants and cooperation, a growing common life and apostolic mission.

4. Now a third series of dialogues (LED III) has been under way since 1983. In response to the mandate from our churches to address such "outstanding questions" as "implications of the Gospel," LED III has published *Implications of the Gospel* in 1988. This document was commended to both churches by their respective standing committees charged with responsibility of ecumenical affairs. The 1988 General Convention of the Episcopal Church and the 1989 Assembly of the Evangelical Lutheran Church in America encouraged its study by clergy and parishes for report back in 1991 as a contribution to the larger effort of moving toward full communion. Its comprehensive character demonstrates the breadth of theological consensus which exists between our traditions. *Implications of the Gospel*, together with its study guide, also provides theological resources for "joint programs of religious education, theological discussion, mission, evangelism and social action" encouraged in provision 3c of the 1982 Agreement.

5. The goal of LED III, mandated by our churches in 1982, is "full communion." In addition to agreement on *Implications of the Gospel*, the action of 1982 requires attention to the "historic episcopate, and the ordering of ministry (Bishops, Priests, and Deacons) in the total context of apostolicity." Subsequent to the mandate of 1982, the term "full communion" is used to identify the ecumenical goal in reports and actions of the Anglican Consultative Council and the Lutheran World Federation as well as in the working document on ecumenism adopted by the Evangelical Lutheran Church in America in 1989. We cite the following actions and documents as examples of this usage.

a. In the Lutheran World Federation, "*The Executive Committee*, with its Standing Committee on Ecumenical Relations (established 1972), is responsible for the interconfessional dialogs and ecumenical relations."[8] In 1983 the Executive Committee of the Lutheran World Federation and the Anglican Consultative Council convened an Anglican-Lutheran "Joint Working Group" at Cold Ash, England. In its report, this "Joint Working Group" described the then current state of Anglican-Lutheran relationships and formulated a statement on the "Goal of Anglican-Lutheran Dialogue." In 1984 the General Secretary of the Lutheran World Federation reported to the Assembly that the Executive Committee received the Cold Ash Report which "stated the goal of the Anglican-Lutheran dialog: 'We look forward to the day when full communion is established between Anglican and Lutheran churches.'"[9] It "voted to establish a joint Anglican/Lutheran committee, as suggested in the report."[10] At Budapest, in 1984, the 7th Assembly of the Lutheran World Federation received a report which encouraged "member churches living in the same region as Anglican churches...to support the mutual direction toward church fellowship, and in their region to act together according to the recommendations of the international and regional consultations." The Assembly resolved "to recommend to the LWF Executive Committee that the dialogs with...the Anglican churches be conducted as planned, geared to the above-mentioned goals."[11]

b. The Anglican Consultative Council, meeting in 1984, commended the Cold Ash report "to the member Churches," and on its basis recommended "that Anglican Churches should officially encourage the practice of eucharistic hospitality to Lutherans," "that as a further step towards full communion...the churches should consider making provision for appropriate forms of 'interim eucharistic sharing' along the lines of that authorized in the U.S.A.," and endorsed "the proposals for closer collaboration between the ACC and the Lutheran World Federation" as set out in the report.[12]

c. The 1988 Lambeth Conference of the bishops of the Anglican Communion adopted a resolution which included the following provisions:

> 4 Recognizes, on the basis of the high degree of consensus reached in international, regional and national dialogues between Anglicans and Lutherans and in the light of the communion centered around Word and Sacrament that has been experienced in each other's traditions, the presence of the Church of Jesus Christ in the Lutheran Communion as in our own.
> 5 Urges that this recognition and the most recent convergence on apostolic ministry achieved in the *Niagara Report* on the Anglican-Lutheran Consultation on Episcopacy (1987) prompt us to move towards the fullest possible ecclesial recognition and the goal of full communion.[13]

d. The Executive Committee of the Lutheran World Federation, meeting in Geneva, Switzerland, July 31 to August 9, 1989, adopted unanimously a series of recommendations on Lutheran-Anglican relationships for action by the 1990 Assembly of the LWF, including the following:

> 7.1 that the LWF renew its commitment to the goal of full communion (see Report of the Anglican-Lutheran Joint Working Group–Cold Ash Report–1982, paras. 25-27) with the churches of the Anglican Communion, and that it urge LWF member churches to take appropriate steps toward its realization;
> 7.2 that the LWF acknowledge with gratitude the 1988 Resolution on A-L relations of the Lambeth Conference and that it concur with that Conference's recommendations to Anglican and Lutheran churches;
> 7.3 that the LWF note with thanksgiving the steps toward church fellowship with national/regional Anglican counterparts which LWF member

churches have been able to take already and that it encourage them to
proceed;

7.4 that the Anglican-Lutheran International Commission both arrange
for further global studies and reports which may be needed and that
ALIC be prepared to assist Anglican and Lutheran churches in taking
steps toward full communion.[14]

This recommendation was adopted by the 1990 assembly at Curitiba,
Brazil.[15]

e. The 1989 Assembly of the Evangelical Lutheran Church in America
adopted "Ecumenism: The Vision of the Evangelical Lutheran Church in
America" as a "working document," which means that it is "to offer provisional and interim guidance for this church during the 1990-1991 biennium."
The document states:

D. *Goal and Stages of Relationships*
The Evangelical Lutheran Church in America is an active participant in
the ecumenical movement, because of its desire of Christian unity. Its
goal is full communion, i.e. the full or complete realization of unity with
all those churches that confess the Triune God. The Evangelical
Lutheran Church in America, both as a church and as a member of the
wider communion of churches in the Lutheran World Federation, seeks
to reach this goal.

Full communion will be a gift from God and will be founded on faith in
Jesus Christ. It will be a commitment to truth in love and a witness to
God's liberation and reconciliation. Full communion will be visible and
sacramental. It is obviously a goal toward which divided churches,
under God's Spirit, are striving, but which has not been reached. It is
also a goal in need of continuing definition. It will be rooted in agreement on essentials and allow diversity in nonessentials.

However, in most cases the churches will not be able to move immediately from their disunity to a full expression of their God-given unity,
but can expect to experience a movement from disunity to unity that
may include one or more of the following stages of relationships.

1. *Ecumenical Cooperation.* Here the Evangelical Lutheran Church in
America enters into ecumenical relations based on the evangelical and
representative principles.

2. *Bilateral and Multilateral Dialogues.* Here the Evangelical Lutheran
Church in America enters into dialogues, with varying mandates, with
those who agree with the evangelical and representative principles, confess the Triune God, and share a commitment to "ecumenical conversion." This conversion or repentance includes openness to new possibilities under the guidance of God's Spirit.

3. *Preliminary Recognition.* Here the Evangelical Lutheran Church in

America can be involved on a church-to-church basis in eucharistic sharing and cooperation, without exchangeability of ministers.

a. One stage requires 1 and 2 above, plus partial, mutual recognition of church and sacraments with partial agreements in doctrine.

b. A second stage requires 1, 2, and 3a, partial and mutual recognition of ordained ministers and of churches, fuller agreement in doctrine, commitments to work for full communion, and preliminary agreement on lifting of any mutual condemnations.

4. *Full Communion*. At this stage the goal of the involvement of this church in the ecumenical movement has been fully attained. Here the question of the shape and form of full communion needs to be addressed and answered in terms of what will best further the mission of the Church in individual cases.

For the Evangelical Lutheran Church in America, the characteristics of full communion will include at least the following, some of which will exist at earlier stages:

1. a common confessing of the Christian faith;

2. a mutual recognition of Baptism and a sharing of the Lord's Supper, allowing for an exchangeability of members;

3. a mutual recognition and availability of ordained ministers to the service of all members of churches in full communion, subject only but always to the disciplinary regulations of the other churches;

4. a common commitment to evangelism, witness, and service;

5. a means of common decision making on critical common issues of faith and life;

6. a mutual lifting of any condemnations that exist between churches.

This definition of full communion is understood to be consistent with Article VII of the Augsburg Confession, which says, "for the true unity of the church it is enough to agree concerning the teaching of the Gospel and the administration of the sacraments." Agreement in the Gospel can be reached and stated without adopting Lutheran confessional formulations as such.[16]

6. Both of our churches have recognized the gift of unity in the gospel (unity in the faith) which has been given to us. Both of our churches expect us to respond to that gift through our search for appropriate ecclesial structures by which we can give expression to that gift. In the Concordat of Agreement appended to this document we will make recommendations to our churches which will take us from the stage of "Interim Sharing of the Eucharist" to expressions of unity commensurate with the degree of consensus we have reached up to this point, stages which will reflect our growing ability to share ecclesial structures. Full communion will include full interchangeability and reciprocity of ordained ministries "subject only but always to the disciplinary regulations of the other churches,"[17] processes for consul-

tation, shared involvement in mission, and agreement in decision making. Such expressions of communion are based on common understanding of the doctrine of the faith (confession of the gospel), mutual recognition of baptism, and sharing together in the eucharist. It is clear from the mandate given by both our churches that questions involved in the historic episcopate and the ordering of ministry will have to be resolved in order for our churches to be in full communion with each other.

## 1. THE HISTORIC IMPASSE

7. We approach these issues of ministry in sober awareness of the importance and the difficulty of the task. Since the adoption of the Chicago-Lambeth Quadrilateral of 1886-88, the Episcopal Church has been committed to the principle that "the Historic Episcopate, locally adapted in the methods of its administration to the varying needs of the nations and peoples called of God into the Unity of His Church" is one of the four elements (together with the Holy Scriptures, the Apostles' and Nicene Creeds, and the sacraments of baptism and eucharist) that constitute the *terminus a quo*, the irreducible basis for any approach to ecumenical reunion of churches. Although this has been restated in varying formulations by different Lambeth Conferences and different General Conventions over the subsequent decades,[1] yet as recently as 1982 the General Convention of the Episcopal Church specified that the Historic Episcopate of the Chicago-Lambeth Quadrilateral is "central to this apostolic ministry and essential to the reunion of the church."[2] The Anglican participants in the Anglican-Lutheran International Conversation (ALIC) stated in the Pullach Report of 1972 that they could not "foresee full integration of ministries (full communion) apart from the historic episcopate."[3] In LED II, this commitment to the historic episcopate was reaffirmed by Anglicans "as essential in any organic reunion or full communion,"[4] and they added that "acceptance of the historic episcopate remains a pre-condition for full communion and /or organic reunion."[5]

8. Lutherans, on the other hand, have opposed the notion that the historic episcopate is required as a *condition* for full communion. At Pullach the Lutherans stated that "since the particular form of episcope is not a confessional question for Lutherans, the historic episcopate should not become a necessary condition for interchurch relations or church union."[6] In a 1984 report on the historic episcopate, the Lutheran churches in the Lutheran Council in the U.S.A. reaffirmed the traditional Lutheran position "that the historic succession of bishops is not essential for the office of the ministry."[7] In a paper presented during LED I on "Lutheran Conditions for Communion in Holy Things," Professor Robert W. Jenson summarized the Lutheran con-

viction that for the true unity of the church it is enough to proclaim the gospel according to a pure understanding of it and to administer the sacraments according to the Word of God. "If other parties can affirm" this about Lutherans,

> they have no right to demand further uniformities as conditions of communion. Indeed, Lutherans have generally regarded any tendency by another party to make further demands for uniformity as *prima facie* evidence that the gospel is not being preached rightly in that quarter. Here is the place where negotiations between Anglicans and Lutherans have repeatedly broken down around the world. The sticking point has been, of course, the episcopacy.[8]

9. The historic impasse, as we have inherited it, seems simple but irreconcilable. If Anglicans insist on the historic episcopate as an essential dimension of the church's catholicity and therefore as a pre-condition for full communion, then Lutherans insist that something is being added to the gospel; and therefore the gospel itself is being undermined if not actually vitiated. For, according to Lutherans,

> The true unity of the church, which is the unity of the body of Christ and participation in the unity of the Father, Son, and Holy Spirit, is given in and through proclamation of the gospel in Word and sacrament. This unity is expressed as a communion in the common and at the same time, multiform confession of one and the same apostolic faith. It is a communion in holy baptism and in the eucharistic meal, a communion in which the ministries exercised are recognized by all as expressions of the ministry instituted by Christ in his church. It is a communion where diversities contribute to fullness and are no longer barriers to unity. It is a committed fellowship, able to make common decisions and to act in common.[9]

Anglicans are convinced that catholicity is being compromised. Lutherans are convinced that "evangelicity" (the gospel) is being compromised. At the 1987 Niagara Falls Anglican-Lutheran Consultation on "Episcope in Relation to the Mission of the Church Today," from which *The Niagara Report* eventually emerged, Professor Stephen Skyes, then Canon of Ely Cathedral and Regius Professor of Divinity at Cambridge University, prefaced his response to a paper on "Episcope in the New Testament" with "a deeply felt personal word."

> The frustrating character of the historic disagreement between Anglicans and Lutherans—its sheer folly—can be formulated thus.

Anglicans say to Lutherans, "If you have no objection in principle to
episcopal government, then your refusal to adopt it can only be obstinacy." Lutherans say to Anglicans, "Of course we can adopt it, provided
you Anglicans say it is not necessary for us to do so." To which
Anglicans reply. "We haven't got any official theology which says that
it, the episcopate, is of the essence of the Church, but we couldn't possibly say, dogmatically, that it wasn't." This conversation is not merely
frustrating, it is dumb. And our parent bodies ought to demand their
money back from us if in this consultation we cannot show a way out of
this ludicrous impasse. It is my conviction that all the necessary elements of deliverance have been placed by God in our hands. God wants
us to work at it and to think and pray our way to a solution.[10]

This comment not only states the impasse sharply. It also expresses the
conviction that the impasse can be overcome.

10. The impasse is more complex than the foregoing summary would
indicate; but happily, in the analysis of its constituent elements, a resolution
has begun to emerge as the result of more recent theological developments
shared in both churches. Another way of stating the historic impasse on the
topic of ordained ministry that has divided Anglicans and Lutherans in the
past is by the questions of Professor J. Robert Wright, in a paper that was
earlier circulated to the members of LED III:

1) Is it possible to possess the substance (*res*) of apostolicity without the
sign (*signum*) of episcopal succession? Lutherans would say, certainly
yes; Anglicans would be less certain, not unanimous, but would tend to
say no.
2) Is it possible to possess the sign (*signum*) of episcopal succession
without the substance (*res*) of apostolicity? Lutherans would say, certainly, yes: Anglicans again would be less certain but would tend to say
no.

Wright rejected this impasse, however, as no longer helpful, remarking,

Do not these questions also pose the issue too sharply, demanding
answers that are more harsh than helpful, and is it not possible to find a
way forward that does not necessitate judgments upon the past and the
present?[11]

11. One major catalyst, cited by Wright, that has helped the churches
to understand and move beyond the impasse on this point was the 1982 Lima
Statement on Baptism, Eucharist, and Ministry from the Faith and Order
Commission of the World Council of Churches, which (in paragraph 38 of
its Ministry section) described the episcopal succession "as a sign, though

not a guarantee, of the continuity and unity of the Church." The Lima Statement went on (in paragraph 53) to propose, for implementation of this principle in the cause of unity, that "Churches which have preserved the episcopal succession are asked to recognize both the apostolic content of the ordained ministry which exists in churches which have not maintained such succession and also the existence in these churches of a ministry of *episkope* in various forms." The 1985 General Convention of the Episcopal Church endorsed this paragraph from Lima as a way forward for its representatives to pursue in the ecumenical discussions of LED III.[12]

12. From the Lutheran side, clear acknowledgement that this approach sets the impasse in a new perspective and meets traditional Lutheran concerns has been forthcoming from the pen of Professor George Lindbeck:

> What the Reformers objected to was the idea that succession constitutes a guarantee or criterion of apostolic faithfulness, but once one thinks in terms of the sign value of continuity in office, this difficulty vanishes. Signs or symbols express and strengthen the reality they signify, but the sign can be present without the reality, and the reality without the sign (as, for example, is illustrated by the relation of the flag and patriotism). Thus it is apostolicity in faith and life that makes the episcopal sign fruitful, not the other way around, but this ought not be turned into an excuse for neglecting the sign.[13]

If the sign/substance way of understanding the impasse has been resolved by a deeper perception of the category of "sign" such as Lima developed, then this really constitutes (in Lindbeck's words) "a shift in the perception of the diachronic dimension, that is, in the way in which succession and apostolicity are perceived."

13. Still another element of the impasse, functional *versus* ontological, has also been transcended by developments in historical and theological perception that are shared in both churches. The historic episcopal succession has traditionally been seen by "high church" Anglicans as being ontological, even an essential element of the gospel given for all time, whereas "low church" Lutherans have traditionally emphasized that the ordained ministry is strictly functional in character, having no ontological dimension whatsoever, especially insofar as ordination might then be seen as establishing a superior or higher class of Christians within the church. But now, increasingly within both churches, ordination—and even the office of bishop—is being seen by historians, theologians, and others as being functional in origin and ontological upon reflection. Once the historically functional origin is agreed, there can then also be agreement, as is obvious, that the reflection upon ordained ministry—even by the laity of both churches—does indeed posit a

certain "ontological" dimension to it, provided always that it is not accorded a status higher than those whom it serves. Thus Lutheran clergy after ordination, just like clergy of the Episcopal Church, are commonly accorded the title of "The Reverend" in front of their names, indicating some change, but not elevation, of status. Thus it has recently been possible for the Lutheran-United Methodist Dialogue to conclude, on the basis of history, that "a ministry of oversight like that of bishops is a practical necessity."[14] The world "practical" is, of course, a recognition of the functional origin, but the word "necessity," even used in this way, cannot help but posit a certain ontological dimension to the office. It has become possible, therefore, as Lindbeck observes, in view of this shift in perception to use "a functional view of ministry in support of episcopacy (thus reversing the nineteenth century situation when functional arguments were employed almost exclusively by those opposed to episcopacy)."[15]

14. In all these ways, then, the historic impasse has proven to be more complex than had been thought, but in the analysis of its constituent elements a resolution has begun to emerge that now points a way forward.

## 2. THEOLOGICAL CONSENSUS

15. A basis for convergence has been in the process of formation for a number of decades. Many of the factors which make up this basis are the direct consequence of the nearly one hundred years of Lutheran-Anglican dialogue which have taken place in Europe, the U.S.A., and elsewhere. Special progress has been made in the U.S.A dialogues since 1968. Historical and theological factors, some more recently recognized, have also contributed to the convergence of the Lutheran and Anglican traditions. The following chapters of the Report seek to identify these factors, often in considerable detail, because it is necessary to provide as much documentation as possible in order to ground adequately the recommendations of the Concordat of Agreement.

## The Contribution of the More Recent Dialogues in the U.S.A. and Abroad

### A. Theological Consensus on the Gospel

16. From its beginnings the church recognized that consensus in the confession of the apostolic gospel was essential to the communion, the unity, of the church. In one of the earliest documents of the Christian movement, the letter to the Galatians, Paul writes:

I am astonished that you are so quickly deserting him who called you in the grace of Christ and turning to a different gospel—not that there is another gospel, but there are some who trouble you and want to pervert the gospel of Christ. But even if we, or an angel from heaven, should preach to you a gospel contrary to that which we preached to you, let him be accursed. As we have said before, so now I say again, if any one is preaching to you a gospel contrary to that which you received, let him be accursed. (Gal. 1:6-9)

The very existence of a *canon* of the New Testament, with its exclusions as well as its inclusions, testifies to the church's need for and commitment to a standard for orthodoxy in distinction from and in rejection of heresy. The inclusion of four different Gospels in the canon of the New Testament, as well as the inclusion of occasional writings by various authors, testifies to the fact that consensus on the gospel does not require uniformity of expression. However, "the ancient church was never in doubt that unity in doctrine belonged to the conditions for eucharistic communion, and that no teacher of false doctrine might commune with an orthodox congregation."[1]

17. As a matter of historical record, the Lutheran churches and the Anglican churches have not engaged in doctrinal controversy with each other on the nature of the gospel, nor do their doctrinal documents contain any official condemnation of each other's doctrine. The Lutheran-Episcopal Dialogues in the U.S.A. have confirmed that there is, indeed, consensus on the gospel between our churches. The initial dialogue report (LED I) included summary statements on Holy Scripture, Christian Worship, Baptism-Confirmation and Apostolicity.[2] The second dialogue report (LED II) included joint statements on justification, on the gospel, on eucharistic presence, on the authority of Scripture, and on apostolicity.[3] The current dialogue (LED III) has already published a comprehensive theological statement, *Implications of the Gospel*, in which the eschatological perspective of the New Testament is used to give expression to our agreement on the gospel and its implications for the church's dogma, ecclesiology, and mission. The church as witness to the Reign of God in its worship, doctrine, and polity is identified as the primary implication of the gospel. The church's mission in the midst of the life of the world is addressed in terms of ecumenism, evangelization, and ethics.

18. A similar consensus was expressed in the reports of the European and international conversations between Lutherans and Anglicans. The consensus was summarized in *The Niagara Report* (1987), paragraphs 61-70:

61. We accept the authority of the canonical Scriptures of the Old and New Testaments. We read the Scriptures liturgically in the course of the Church's year (LED II, 1980, pp. 30-1; *Pullach Report*, 17-22).
62. We accept the Niceno-Constantinopolitan and Apostles' Creeds and

confess the basic Trinitarian and Christological Dogmas to which these creeds testify. That is, we believe that Jesus of Nazareth is true God and true Man, and that God is authentically identified as Father, Son and Holy Spirit (LED II, p. 38; *Pullach Report*, 23-25).

63. Anglicans and Lutherans use very similar orders of service for the Eucharist, for the Prayer Offices, for the administration of Baptism, for the rites of Marriage, Burial, and Confession and Absolution. We acknowledge in the liturgy both a celebration of salvation through Christ and a significant factor in forming the *consensus fidelium*. We have many hymns, canticles, and collects in common (*Helsinki Report*, 29-31).

64. We believe that baptism with water in the name of the Triune God unites the one baptized with the death and resurrection of Jesus Christ, initiates into the One, Holy, Catholic and Apostolic Church, and confers the gracious gift of new life (*Helsinki Report*, 22-25).

65. We believe that the Body and Blood of Christ are truly present, distributed and received under the forms of bread and wine in the Lord's Supper. We also believe that the grace of divine forgiveness offered in the sacrament is received with the thankful offering of ourselves for God's service (LED II, pp.25-29; *Helsinki Report*, 26-28).

66. We believe and proclaim the gospel, that in Jesus Christ God loves and redeems the world. We 'share a common understanding of God's justifying grace, i.e. that we are accounted righteous and are made righteous before God only by grace through faith because of the merits of our Lord and Saviour Jesus Christ, and not on account of our works or merit. Both our traditions affirm that justification leads and must lead to "good works"; authentic faith issues in love' (*Helsinki Report*, 20; cf. LED II, pp. 22-23).

67. Anglicans and Lutherans believe that the Church is not the creation of individual believers, but that it is constituted and sustained by the Triune God through God's saving action in word and sacraments. We believe that the Church is sent into the world as a sign, instrument and foretaste of the kingdom of God. But we also recognize that the Church stands in constant need of reform and renewal (*Helsinki Report*, 44-51).

68. We believe that all members of the Church are called to participate in its apostolic mission. They are therefore given various ministries by the Holy Spirit. Within the community of the Church the ordained ministry exists to serve the ministry of the whole people of God. We hold the ordained ministry of word and sacrament to be a gift of God to his Church and therefore an office of divine institution (*Helsinki Report*, 32-42).

69. We believe that a ministry of pastoral oversight (*episcope*), exercised in personal, collegial and communal ways, is necessary to witness to and safeguard the unity and apostolicity of the Church (*Pullach Report*, 79).

70. We share a common hope in the final consummation of the kingdom of God and believe that we are compelled to work for the establishment of justice and peace. The obligations of the Kingdom are to govern our life in the Church and our concern for the world. The Christian faith is that God has made peace through Jesus "by the blood of his Cross" (Col. 1:20) so establishing the one valid center for the unity of the whole human family (Anglican-Reformed International Commission 1984: *God's Reign and Our Unity*, 18 and 43; cf. *Pullach Report*, 59).[4]

## B. Emerging Convergence of the Dialogues on the Meaning of Apostolicity, Apostolic Succession, and Historic Episcopate

19. Already in the first dialogue (LED I) representatives of our churches were able to arrive at "five substantive agreements" about apostolicity.

1. We agree that apostolicity belongs to the reality of the one holy catholic church; apostolicity is manifested in various ways in all areas of the church's life, and is guarded especially by common confession and through that function of the church designated as *episcope* (oversight).

2. We agree that both our communions can and should affirm that the Eucharistic celebrations held under the discipline of either communion are true occurrences of the Body of Christ in the world. We agree that both our communions are true ministries of the one church of Christ, that is, that they are apostolic ministries. We agree that mutual recognition of ministries by each of the two traditions could create the conditions by which both communions could enter that sort of relationship in which each would receive gifts from the other for greater service to the Lord and his Gospel.

3. We agree that the identity of our gospel with the apostles' Gospel, and of our church with the apostles' church, is the personal identity of the risen Christ; He is always the one crucified under Pontius Pilate and just so the one whose word is new promise in every new historical occasion. The church is able to remain in conversation with this one Lord, and so to remain itself through the opportunities and temptations of its history, by the mediation of the whole continuous tradition of the Gospel in word and sacrament. The church has, within the providence of God, enacted its responsibility that this succession shall be a succession of the *Gospel*, by means of a canon of Scripture, the use and authority of creeds and confessions, sacramental-liturgical tradition, and the institution of an ordered ministry and succession of ministers.

4. We agree that this substance of apostolic succession must take different forms in differing places and times, if the Gospel is indeed to be heard and received. At the time of the Reformation, one of our communions in its place experienced the continuity of the episcopally ordered ministry as an important means of the succession of the Gospel; in various ways the other in its place was able to take its responsibility of the succession of the Gospel only by a new ordering of its ministry. We agree that by each decision the apostolicity of the ministry in question was preserved, and that each of our communions can and should affirm the decision of the other. Until the Lord of the church grants a new ordering of the church, each communion should respect the right of the other to honor the distinct history which mediates its apostolicity, and to continue that ordering of its ministry which its history has made possible. Within the one church, both the Anglican continuity of the episcopal order, and the Lutheran concentration on doctrine, have been means of preserving the apostolicity of the one church.

5. For the future, we agree that if either communion should be able to receive the gift of the other's particular apostolicity, without unfaithfulness to its own, the future of the church would surely be served. In any future ordering of the one church, there will be a ministry and within that ministry an *episcope*. The functional reality of *episcope* is in flux in both our communions. It we are faithful, we will *together* discover the forms demanded by the church's new opportunities, so that the church may have an *episcope* which will be an *episcope* of the apostolic Gospel. Similarly, any future unity of the church will be a unity of common confession. The functional reality of the common confessions of the past (their contemporary interpretation and use) is in flux in both our communions. Our faithfulness will be that we think and pray together seeking to be ready for a new common confession when the Lord shall give us the apostolic boldness to proclaim the Gospel with the freshness and vigor of our fathers in the faith.[5]

No doubt influenced in part by this agreement reached in the LED I dialogue, and citing previous work done in the Faith and Order Commission of the World Council of Churches, the Episcopal Church's Joint Commission on Ecumenical Relations soon adopted a "working statement" on the same subject which it reported to that Church's 1976 General Convention, subtitled "The Relation of the Historic Episcopate to Apostolic Succession," which took the following position:

The Episcopal Church, through its membership in the Anglican Communion has received and preserved the historic episcopal succession as an effective sign of the continuity of the Church in apostolic faith and mission—manifested in community, doctrine, proclamation, sacraments, liturgy and service.

Any plan for the reunion of the Church should, we insist, preserve a succession in the ordained ministry which assures the fullness of *episcope* as a Gift of God.

We acknowledge, however, that apostolicity has many strands. We see a genuine apostolicity in those churches which, while preserving a continuity in apostolic faith, mission and ministry, have not retained the historic episcopate.

This acknowledgment is based in part on our appreciation that many episcopal functions may be preserved in a church which does not use the title "bishop," provided ordination is always done in it by persons in whom such a church recognizes the authority to transmit ministerial commission.

We believe the importance of the historic episcopate is not diminished by our close association with such a church. On the contrary, insights gained from such associations often enable churches without the historic episcopate to appreciate it as a sign of, and element in, the continuity and unity of the Church.

We rejoice that more and more non-episcopal churches, including those with whom we are having unity consultations, are expressing a willingness to see the historic episcopate as a sign and means of the apostolic succession of the whole Church in faith, life and doctrine, and that it is, as such, something that ought to be striven for when absent.

We affirm the desire of our Church to seek ways to promote continuing and growing fellowship with such churches in our pilgrimage together toward full unity.

The Joint Commission on Ecumenical Relations invited study and response on these two statements, the paragraphs from the World Council Study and the one drafted by JCER itself, looking toward the time when they, or some variation on them, might be

> an acceptable stance for the Episcopal Church to take in unity consultations when we are asked to define the meaning of the fourth provision in the Chicago-Lambeth Quadrilateral.[6]

20. The second dialogue between Lutherans and Episcopalians (LED II) built on the five earlier agreements of LED I. Its achievement was to make explicit the distinction between apostolic succession and the institution of the historic episcopate. It will be sufficient for our purposes to summarize the lengthy "Joint Statement on Apostolicity" with its appendices.[7] In Part One, "Apostolicity: A New Appreciation," apostolicity is defined as "the Church's continuity with Christ and the apostles in its movement through

history." Apostolic succession is "a dynamic, diverse reality" embracing faithfulness to apostolic teaching; participation in baptism, prayer, and the eucharist; "sharing in the Church's common life of mutual edification and caring, served by an ecclesiastically called and recognized pastoral ministry of Word and sacrament"; and "continuing involvement in the apostolic mission" of the church by proclaiming the gospel through word and deed. Apostolic succession is not to be understood "primarily in terms of historic episcopate."

21. Part Two is devoted to a historical description of "Lutheran and Episcopalian Views and Expressions of Apostolic Succession." Part Three contains "An Analysis of the Agreement in Apostolic Succession to be Found in the Lutheran and Episcopal Churches." Both churches agree that apostolic mission means the obedience to the call of Christ to "go into all the world" with the gospel, although the actual obedience of both churches has varied, and both "have had glorious moments and sad declines in this aspect of apostolic succession." Both churches agree in acknowledging the normative character of apostolic Scriptures and the catholic creeds. Both churches agree that apostolic succession includes obedience to Christ's commands to baptize, to forgive sins, and to share in the eucharist.

22. The ordained ministry is recognized as the "most controversial area" between Lutheran and Episcopalians. But even here there is "a great measure of agreement not always found with other communions." There is agreement that the ordained ministry of Word and Sacrament is "of divine institution," that ordination is an unrepeated liturgical act presided over "by those set apart in the Church so to ordain in the Name of God," that succession of ordained ministers in office shows the church's continuity in time and space, and that there is a necessary oversight (*episkope*) "which is embodied in an ordained office." Finally,

> Episcopalians recognize that Lutherans do affirm the full dignity of the pastoral office and are open to the historic episcopate as a valid and proper form of that office. Some Lutheran Churches are ordered in the historic episcopate, There is even a preference for the historic episcopate shown in the Lutheran confessional writing where and when that form could be maintained in accord with the Gospel, i.e., in the context of faithful preaching of the Word and the right administration of the Sacraments. Lutherans do not, however, hold the historic episcopate to be the only legitimate form of *episcopé*.[8]

23. In making the distinction between "apostolic succession" and "historic episcopate" LED II anticipated the formulations of the Lima Statement

on Ministry, Section IV, which deals with "Succession in the Apostolic Tradition." In the Lima document "apostolic tradition" is defined as

> continuity in the permanent characteristics of the Church of the apostles: witness to the apostolic faith, proclamation and fresh interpretation of the Gospel, celebration of baptism and the eucharist, the transmission of ministerial responsibilities, communion in prayer, love, joy and suffering, service to the sick and the needy, unity among the local churches and sharing the gifts which the Lord has given to each. (BEM, Ministry, Par. 34)

"Apostolic succession" or "apostolicity" is then understood in terms of Christ's *mission*, and it is defined as "an expression of the permanence and, therefore, of the continuity of Christ's own mission in which the Church participates." (Par. 35)

24. These insights were given further expression in *The Niagara Report*. The life of the early church as it comes to expression in the documents of the New Testament indicates that succession in ministerial office cannot be regarded "as the sole criterion of faithfulness to the apostolic commission." (*The Niagara Report*, Par. 20) The church's "apostolicity" here refers to the church's "mission."

> For apostolicity means that the Church is sent by Jesus to *be* for the world, to participate in his mission and therefore in the mission of the One who sent Jesus, to participate in the mission of the Father and the Son through the dynamic of the Holy Spirit. (Par 21)

Continuity and succession are, therefore, testimony to God's faithfulness in the midst of the church's sin, ambiguity, and unfaithfulness (Paras. 28-30), an accent by which *The Niagara Report* "avoids the triumphalism that too often accompanies...descriptions of the church in ecumenical documents."[9]

## C. Mutual Understanding of Unity

25. LED II already demonstrated the broad areas of agreement between Lutherans and Episcopalians on the doctrine of ministry. Attention to a growing consensus on the doctrine of ministry continued in LED III. This can perhaps be best illustrated by summarizing several papers which were presented early in the dialogue (sessions 2 and 3) and to which the dialogue returned later (session 11). In June, 1984, Professor L. William Countryman

(Episcopalian) presented a paper on "The Gospel and the Institutions of the Church With Particular Reference to the Historic Episcopate."[10] In this paper Countryman pointed out that the *goal* of salvation is, in the language of John 17, "the communion of perfect love within God and among God and humanity." In the New Testament writings generally, the gift and goal is not only to be fully realized in the *eschaton*. Unity is the calling and objective of the Christian community here and now, being a centuries-long process of shaping institutions which could sustain unity in the community. These institutions had their roots in the New Testament era, but they achieved classical form—the form they retained for centuries thereafter—only in the second to tenth centuries. Four such institutions arose: 1) the ritual complex centered on the sacraments of baptism and the eucharist (in classical form by the mid-second century); 2) the threefold ministry (widespread by the late second century); 3) summary statements of Christian belief (taking on familiar form in the late second and the third centuries); and 4) the New Testament canon (largely solidified in the third and fourth centuries). Each of these "institutions" had a particular *use* in the service of the gospel, and each of them was also subject to abuse. "No one institution, however venerable, can be understood to be of the *esse* of the church; only the gospel is that."[11] The church can be and function without any or all of these institutions, including the threefold ministry. But by looking at the actual ordination rites of *The Apostolic Tradition* of Hippolytus, the earliest such rites in the church's history (ca. 210 C.E.), Countryman observed that the symbolic function of the various ordinations, and therefore of the ministries of bishop, presbyter, and deacon, is "to point to the ministerial nature of the whole body, to its articulation of its own life in the present and to its continuity with Christ through the long chain of people who have heard and then proclaimed the Gospel." Countryman said that in the context of the continental Reformation, it was necessary to break the episcopal succession for the sake of the gospel. He further said, and LED III agrees, that it is not necessary to call that decision into question. "Let it be taken for granted that it was the right course at those places and times."[12] Instead, in his view, the succession was transferred to presbyters, so that now we have two different kinds of succession in the two churches, Anglican and Lutheran, neither of which accomplishes the same symbolic purpose, but neither of them *antithetical* to the other. Countryman's conclusion:

> The historic episcopate contains an element of the proclamation of the Gospel not contained in the Reformation successions—*and vice versa*. The historic episcopate declares to us that the Gospel is not only an idea or a proposition or a proclamation, but the animating force of a living community communicated over and over again from one person to

another. The bishop, in this succession, is thus a living image of the unity of the faithful in and with God, a unity yet to be consummated but already at work in us across the barriers of time and space. The Reformation successions also have a message for us: that the Gospel is always transcendent and never merely identical with any of the institutions to which it has given rise among us; if the institutions fail, that does not mean that the gospel has failed nor that the church has ceased. God is perfectly free to make new beginnings with the people.[13]

The two successions are neither identical nor antithetical. Since we believe that the Spirit has given utterance to both, the challenge is "to find ways of sharing and preserving both messages."[14]

26. In his response, Professor Paul Berge (Lutheran) expressed the importance for the dialogue to come to an understanding of God's gift of ministry to the Christian church:

The biblical traditions do not present one understanding of how ministry is to be carried out. Therefore, it is incumbent upon us to recognize this and to realize that not one position on ministry is right—or even more righteous—than the other. The interrelationship of the tradition centering on the Word of God and the tradition of a more highly developed ecclesiastical structure for that Word has been with us since the beginnings of the fledgling Christian communities in the first and second centuries. Likewise, our common heritage from the 16th century is too intertwined and important to the church catholic to even pose the possibility that something is missing in either tradition.[15]

In identifying the concern of LED III for both churches, Berge goes on to say:

Lutheran-Episcopal Dialogues I and II have left for us the task of coming to an understanding on the issue of ministry. But can it be settled by asking the questions, what do you want of us, or what do we want of you? If "adoption" into historic episcopal succession is what you will require of Lutherans on the basis of the Fourth Quadrilateral, then, this will divide us, not unify us. It can be no other, given our tradition. If Anglicans perceive that we are not convinced that they are clear about the gospel, then what does this mean for your church and ministry? The truth of the gospel and its ministry is that the church is not ours to negotiate, but we are one in God's mission in the world—*missio Dei*.[16]

Drawing upon a theology of the Word of God in the Old Testament and Johannine traditions, Berge concluded that "the tradition of the Fourth Gospel and the tradition of Lutheranism are centered in the living voice of the Word of God."[17] The ministry can neither take precedence nor preside over the Gospel. On this issue Countryman and Berge are in fundamental agreement. Berge says, "the lesson Lutherans and Anglicans have learned from history is that when the ecclesiastical system is unwilling to reform, the only word capable of conveying the call for reform is the external truth of the gospel—the Word of God."[18] Hence there can be no creation of an artificial reconciliation of ministries through negotiation. Because we are one in the truth of the gospel we cannot require something of each other which is not essential for salvation. The center for both Lutherans and Episcopalians "is the gospel and its ministry."[19] Countryman would agree, as a later discussion revealed.

27. The dialogue took up both papers again after five years, at Session 11 in June, 1989. Countryman added some "further reflections" which deal even more pointedly with Lutheran concerns as expressed earlier by Berge. He said that we cannot "substitute the ministry of either group for that of the other." But since "our ministries are one way of telling the world who we are," it is necessary for us to think of how our ministries might evolve into something which, in the end, might be "recognizably common." We must re-understand the entire process of ordination, beginning with candidacy and issuing in the actual functioning of ministry, "as a kind of gestural language in which our communities announce, for themselves and each other, who they understand themselves, by God's grace, to be." Ordination can no more be defined simply by the mechanical act of laying on of hands than the eucharist can be defined simply by the mechanical act of reciting the words of institution over the bread and cup. Ordination involves the call and consent of the people of God because it has as much to do with their ministry as with that of the ordained. Hence the symbolic gestures. Countryman summarizes:

> To ordain a bishop, three other bishops must lay on hands. Since these will have had to come from neighboring cities, they were, in effect, bringing the new bishop into a larger network and reaffirming the local community's communion with the larger church. The bishop alone laid hands on deacons to indicate that deacons functioned as extensions of the bishop in serving the church. The intimate connection between the two reemphasized the intimate connection between leadership and servanthood that comes down to us as part of Jesus' teaching. On the other hand, from our earliest records onward, other presbyters share in the laying on of hands when a presbyter is ordained, for the college of presbyters has its own integrity in the local church. While it must function in relation to the larger church, as represented by the bishop, this college also served as the council of elders whose advice could guide and

restrain the bishop on behalf of the local community—in effect, an enlarged voice for that community in the deliberations of its leaders.[20]

All of this can become idolatrous, but *abusus non tollit usum*. The point of the symbolic actions was to proclaim that the Christian community receives its identity from the gospel. We can, of course, become so concerned about abuses that we invoke the kind of "purity" concerns which Jesus and his disciples rejected as criteria for the new community of the messianic age (Mark 7:1-13;Rom. 14:14). Countryman applied his insights to both traditions. Episcopalians need to understand that they do not lose the historic episcopate by acknowledging the existing ministry of the ELCA as a true, gospel ministry. Lutherans need to understand that they can revise their ordination rites *for the future* without any hint that the integrity of their present ministries is being challenged or that their continuity with their Reformation heritage is being broken.[21]

### D. Continuity and Adaptation of Basic Ecclesial Institutions

28. The basic institutions, canon of Holy Scripture, creed, sacraments, and ministry, which have long defined the life of the church, have their roots in the New Testament. Yet in their classic forms they are clearly the result of development and adaptation beyond their biblical roots. Our churches have neither repudiated that development nor avoided the necessity for adaptation in the light of the gospel. Our churches share a respect for tradition which is not slavery to the past and an openness to judicious development which is not addiction to novelty.

29. *The canon of scripture* is both oldest and youngest of the four institutions. It is oldest, in that Israel was already developing a canon, which emerging Christianity adopted piecemeal. Most early Christians seem to have preferred the scriptures of Israel in their Greek dress rather than the Hebrew-Aramaic version we now treat as standard; and there were differences as to where the precise boundaries of the canon lay. Still, canon was a given for the early Christians. By the time when 2 Peter was written (perhaps mid-second century), Christians were beginning to develop a canon of their own around writings of Paul (2 Pet. 3:15-16). The canon of four Gospels was broadly (but not universally) accepted among Greek-speaking Christians by the late second century. From the fourth century onward there was growing agreement on the canon of the New Testament, although some debate continued for centuries afterward. To this day the canon of Scripture remains a matter of historical and theological judgment.

30. While there are no developed creeds in the New Testament itself,

doctrinal formularies existed from very early times. Paul preserves one, apparently antedating his own ministry, concerned with the meaning of baptism: it declared that baptism abolished social distinctions of ethnicity, sex, and class status (e.g., Gal. 3:27-29). Such formulae as this combined with liturgical expressions of praise (such as "Jesus Christ is Lord") to produce a distinctive, Christian way of speaking about God and Christ. Creedal formulae also arose when intra-Christian conflict made it necessary to defend one theological perspective against another. One example might be the summary of the Pauline theology of grace in Titus 3:4-7. Examples more determinative for the future appeared in the late second century when debates with Gnosticism produced "rules of faith" (Tertullian) or "yardsticks of truth" (Irenaeus)—patterns of instruction (rather than exact verbal prescriptions) designed to rule out any separation between the God of Jesus and the Creator of this world. The basis of the second article of the Apostles' Creed seems to lie in the kerygmatic proclamation evident in the epistles of Paul and the sermons of Acts.[22] Finally in the late third century we find the beginnings of creeds in the classic sense: precise compositions meant to be memorized word-for-word and recited by catechumens. Such creeds arose from liturgical use in baptism, and were further developed in settling doctrinal controversies at the councils of Nicaea and Constantinople.[23]

31. The earliest of the church's institutions to reach classic shape were the *sacraments*, baptism and the eucharist. Baptism was the doorway into the Christian community from earliest times. Paul speaks of it often (e.g., I Cor. 1:13-17;Rom. 6:1-11) and Matthew says that the risen Lord commanded its use (Matt. 28:19). We know little about details of practice in the first century; but there may well have been some variation of formula (baptism in the name of Jesus or in that of the Trinity). The narratives of Acts suggest that there was little catechesis preceding it. In the second and third centuries, with the writings of Justin Martyr and Hippolytus, we get a glimpse of more highly developed catechesis and rites. At some point the baptism of infants became more usual than the baptism of adults. Eventually, in the Western Church, confirmation was separated from baptism, a development which is coming under increasing criticism today.[24]

The eucharist reached its classic shape in the second century. The narrative of institution in Paul (I Cor. 11:23-26) and in the synoptic accounts of the Last Supper shows a eucharist still embedded in the community meal. It is difficult to say exactly when the ceremonies of bread and wine were detached from the meal and made a separate rite; but it happened before the time of Justin Martyr (mid-second century). By then, the sacramental rite had not only been separated from the community meal, but also combined with a kind of synagogue service made up of scripture reading, preaching, and prayer. Accommodations to the era of massive persecution and then to the legalization of Christianity produced the great liturgies of the fourth century, foundations of subsequent Christian worship. We still use them, in revisions made by the reformers and by leaders of the modern liturgical movement.[25]

32. Jesus committed his message to people, not books. Therefore *ministry*, as proclamation of the oral gospel and its truth (I Cor. 1:23-24;Gal. 2:5, 14), was integral to Christianity from the first. This called forth an apostolic (missionary) leadership which could call communities of the faithful into being and hand the message on. The new communities required leaders of their own. Early on, Paul urged respect for and obedience to local leaders who devoted themselves to the service of the community. (I Thess. 5:12-13;I Cor. 16:15-16;Rom. 16:1-2, Phoebe). He addressed the Philippians as a community with "bishops and deacons" (Phil. 1:1). In late New Testament documents, such as the Pastoral Epistles, we find an ongoing concern for the tradition of gospel teaching (e.g., I Tim. 1:3-11, 6:20;2 Tim. 1:12, 2:2) joined with a relatively newer concern for the regularization of local ministerial succession. These letters envisage several orders of ministry (e.g., presbyters, bishops, deacons, widows; cf. I Tim. 3:1-13, 5:3-22;Titus 1:5-9). By the early second century, as the letters of Ignatius show, the threefold ministry of bishop, presbyter, and deacon was establishing itself in the provinces of Syria and Asia. By the late second century, it was also found in Gaul and, beginning at least with Victor (end of the second century), in the relatively conservative church at Rome.[26] In time, this threefold ministry became normative in most of Christendom.[27]

33. Both the New Testament grounding of these fundamental institutions of church life and their openness to subsequent development are important. That these have come to be known in classic forms which have served the church well is hereby gratefully acknowledged. Both Lutherans and Anglicans respect tradition. That these institutions have been subject to abuse and misuse, also, but not only, by Lutherans and Anglicans, must be confessed. Both Lutherans and Anglicans join other Christians in recognizing the normative doctrinal character of the canon of Scripture. Both Lutherans and Anglicans join other Christians in recognizing the normative doctrinal authority of the Apostles' and Nicene creeds. Both Lutherans and Anglicans insist that the sacraments of baptism and the Lord's Supper be administered "with unfailing use of Christ's words of institution, and of the elements ordained by Him"[28] even though both churches as well as most other Western churches have recently reformed the rites of administration and envision future reform. Finally, both Lutherans and Anglicans recognize that the ordained ministry in its various developed forms, including the historic episcopate, is a gift of God to the church. And both of us agree that the historic episcopate can be "locally adapted in the methods of its administration to the varying needs of the nations and peoples called of God into the

Unity of His Church."[29] The two subsequent chapters of this report will indicate, among other things, the way in which our two churches have "locally adapted" the episcopate.

## 3. THE LUTHERAN CHURCHES AND EPISCOPAL MINISTRY

### A. Developments Within the History of Lutheran Churches

34. The introduction of the Lutheran reforms in various principalities and free cities of the German empire and in various countries of Northern Europe produced different forms of oversight for the churches, each standing in greater or lesser continuity with the inherited traditions and polities of the medieval church.[1] The situation in Germany proved to be the most radical break with the existing church structure, although the temporal authorities appealed "to late medieval precedents" when they "took over functions that belonged to the bishops."[2] In 1520 Martin Luther rejected the medieval sacramental interpretation of ordination,[3] a position that later was closely reflected in Article XXV of the Thirty Nine Articles of Religion.[4] By 1523 Luther had urged the Bohemians "to forego papal ordinations" because no one should be set over a congregation without the knowledge and election of the people.[5] Beginning in 1525 there were non-episcopal ordinations in several territories.[6] The complex history of developments within Germany included the fact that some dioceses and territories did have bishops from the Lutheran movement for a time: Naumburg, 1542-1547; Schleswig-Holstein, 1542-1551; Merseburg, 1544-1550; and Kammin, 1545-1556.[7] It is helpful to note that all of these bishops were installed before Luther's death, three of them in Saxony (Naumburg, Merseburg, and Kammin), and at least Naumburg with his active participation.[8] By the time of the Religious Peace of Augsburg in 1555, the civil authorities were more or less firmly in charge of the administration of church affairs in the principalities where the reformation had been introduced.[9] For although the Religious Peace of Augsburg merely suspended the authority of the traditional bishops, "the leaders in the Protestant territories viewed this proviso rather quickly as the transferral of the episcopal authority to the territorial princes...(and) the territorial prince was looked upon at the same time as being the bishop of his territorial Church."[10] The civil authorities discharged their episcopal responsibilities through consistories, superintendents, and other institutions which often bore a greater resemblance to civil than to ecclesiastical government.[11]

> Wuerttemberg enacted a "church order" (*Kirchenordnung*) that established a consistory consisting of theologians responsible for the exami-

nation of ordinands and political councilors responsible for legal and financial affairs. A superintendent was appointed by the duke. Superintendents were soon divided into three ranks: special superintendents, who had local jurisdiction; four regional superintendents to exercise general supervision; and a "dean" to supervise the other superintendents. This form of episcopacy became the model for many German territories, although the titles sometimes changed.[12]

The end of the German monarchy in 1918 brought with it the end of church government by the civil authorities. Many of the territorial churches chose to give the title *Landesbischof* to the elected leader of the church. The *Landesbischof* functioned more like an archbishop even when others who shared in the ministry of oversight in a given territorial church did not use or were not given the title of "bishop."[13]

35. In Denmark, Norway, and Iceland, all ruled by the Danish king at the time of the reformation, the reformation was introduced by Christian III (1503-1559), who had been attracted to the reformation as a result of his studies at Wittenberg, and who became king in 1536 after a two-year civil war. He promptly deposed and imprisoned all the Danish bishops because they had opposed him in the civil war, brought John Bugenhagen, pastor of Wittenberg, to Denmark as his advisor, and had Bugenhagen consecrate seven new bishops on September 2, 1537. There is no evidence at the time that there was any attempt made to prevent it.[14] In Sweden there was no conflict between the king and the church on the matter of introducing the reformation. As a result the historic episcopate continued in Sweden,[15] and Sweden was determinative for the restoration of the historic episcopate in Finland and the Baltic states. None of these countries, however, thought that their relationship with Lutheran churches which did not have the historic episcopate was compromised by the difference.

36. The development of leadership patterns and practices in the Lutheran churches of the United States of America was generally uniform. Until well after the end of the Second World War, all Lutheran churches in the U.S.A. exercised oversight through elected leaders who were given the title "president." In 1970 the American Lutheran Church took the decision to make the title "bishop" an optional use for those leaders who had been serving as presidents of its eighteen regional districts. In 1980 the Lutheran Church in America decided to use the title "bishop" for those leaders who had been serving as presidents of its thirty-three regional synods. When the Association of Evangelical Lutheran Churches came into existence a short time later, it subsequently adopted the title "bishop" for its regional and national leaders. At the time that the title "bishop" was introduced, the intention was that this would mean no change in status, function, or understanding

of the office from that which obtained under the title "president."[16] Bishops were elected to specific terms and did not become a separate order of ministry. Nevertheless, it is obvious in all three churches that a development occurred in the office and in the expectations of it as a direct result of the change in title. There was greater regard for the pastoral character of the office and for its function as a symbol of unity. When the Evangelical Lutheran Church in America came into being in 1988 the title of bishop was continued almost without debate.[17] In presiding over and giving leadership to their own synods the synod bishops were given a somewhat enhanced pastoral role, even as their role in the national governing structures of the Evangelical Lutheran Church in America was somewhat reduced in comparison to their role in the former Lutheran Church in America. The constitution of the Evangelical Lutheran Church in America provides for a "Conference of Bishops" with its own staff. The "Conference of Bishops" is recognized as having a "special relationship" with the Evangelical Lutheran Church in America's Division for Ministry and with the Office for Ecumenical Affairs. There are signs that the office of bishop continues to evolve in the Evangelical Lutheran Church in America.

## B. The Lutheran Confessional Heritage

37. The interpretation of the Lutheran confessional writings contained in the Book of Concord has been the subject of renewed disagreement, especially with regard to the historical meaning of articles of the Augsburg Confession dealing with ministry and episcopacy.[18] The issue is familiar to most of the churches whose history included the Reformation of the 16th century, namely, whether the Reformation is to be understood as a *corrective* of errors and abuses in the medieval Western church or as *constitutive* of a new and autonomous ecclesial tradition. The argument in favor of a constitutive understanding of the reformation stresses Luther's opposition to the bishops of Germany, virtually none of whom ultimately came to support the Reformation as well as the fact that autonomous territorial churches were already coming into being at the time that the Augsburg Confession was being formulated, presented, and defended. The most thorough and exhaustive discussion of the historical circumstances surrounding the Augsburg Confession, including the attitudes and intentions of Martin Luther and Philipp Melanchthon, is by Wilhelm Maurer.[19] Because Article XXVIII of the Augsburg Confession is of primary importance in determining what kind of polity the Lutheran reformation permits, it is necessary to summarize briefly the historical circumstances as described by Maurer.

38. Luther's early rejection of the medieval understanding of ordina-

tion included a rejection of the necessity for episcopal ordination.[20] Already in 1520 Luther, in his interpretation of one school of medieval theology, thought of bishops and pastors as having virtually interchangeable offices.[21] Writing to the Bohemians in 1523, Luther attacked the ordination of bishops because "they ordain priests to sacrifice rather than to serve the Word, thus perverting the Sacrament." Hence, the right to ordain belongs to the whole church, "especially in cases of emergency when papal bishops refuse to appoint servants of the Word."[22] However, says Maurer, "the emergency situation in Bohemia should not lead one to deduce a general rejection of the historic episcopate." Although there were strong tendencies toward secularization of bishoprics on the part of all parties in Germany, "Luther did not simply condemn the late medieval episcopacy." In 1528 Luther

> retraced the visiting function of the archbishop and bishop, rediscovering traces of it in canonical law, and using the later decline to show the necessity for this function. He saw the visitations set up by the elector as the beginning of such a restoration. Nevertheless, in no way did he consider this action, and the ecclesiastical offices it created, to substitute for the historic office of bishop.[23]

39. When the emperor summoned the estates to Augsburg in 1530 in order to settle the religious dispute in the empire, the preparations began with proposals for what eventually became Article 28. The proposal presupposed "the continued existence of the medieval hierarchy," and offered a compromise: the reforming territories would recognize again the jurisdiction of the bishops, which had in effect already been lost, if the bishops would not require celibacy and the renunciation of evangelical doctrine by prospective ordinands.[24] Melanchthon won Luther to this compromise by the time the Wittenberg party arrived at Coburg in April of 1530. Luther's commitment to the compromise was the background for his "Exhortation to All Clergy Assembled at Augsburg,"[25] written by early June. "A pact between Lutheran Reformation and the bishops is still possible," wrote Maurer, and that, indeed, was Luther's "top priority" as with "stern love (he) sketches the portrait of a proper Christian bishop."[26]

40. At the heart of Article 28 is "the doctrine of the two ways of governing (two kingdoms)." It is the most fundamental statement on the subject in all of the Lutheran confessional writings. The starting point for the discussion of the spiritual authority of bishops (in contrast to temporal or secular authority) is "the power of the keys, that is, the spiritual authority which is at work in the liturgical events of confession and absolution." The authority of bishops is grounded in the Word of God, that is, the gospel. It is "concentrated in the liturgical events of an ordered church." Rejected as contrary to the

proper exercise of episcopal office is all coercion, which is appropriate only to temporal or secular authority.[27]

41. Nothing came of the compromise proposal at Augsburg. The final draft of the *Confutation*, prepared by John Eck and supported by the traditional party, did not refer to the compromise directly. But in the first draft there was summary rejection of everything initiated by visitations in 1528 of the parishes in Saxony "as in conflict with apostolic ordinances."[28] Meanwhile, in July, Luther continued his apparent attack on the bishops. His blistering *Propositiones adversus totam synagogam Sathanae et universas portas inferorum*[29] contained "the outlines of ordered church reform that would span all of Christendom." In it Luther defined an appropriate relationship between congregation and bishop which provided for

> the agreement of both parties... The pastor has the right and duty to propose new ordinances and to recommend the amendment or abolition of surviving ones—all of this, however, only with the concurrence of the congregation...It is assumed that all the baptized who believe belong to the congregation. The jurisdiction of the pastor can just as well encompass a province as a city, or even the world; there is room for division into bishoprics, and even for a reformed papacy.[30]

By 1531, Maurer believes, Luther and Melanchthon were once again agreed in support of the compromise proposal. For although Melanchthon was disappointed that the compromise was rejected in Augsburg,

> he stated his continued readiness to retain episcopal authority, the polity of the church. In an opinion issued jointly by Melanchthon and Luther at the end of May 1531, the latter basically approved of his friend's standpoint. From the perspective of suffering obedience, Luther was willing to accept the jurisdiction of bishops, even if they "were wolves and our enemies"—"because they still possess the office and sit in the place of the apostles"—as long as pure doctrine would be guaranteed.[31]

42. On the basis of the historical perspective provided by Wilhelm Maurer it is evident that the Lutheran confessional documents of the 16th century, normative for the Evangelical Lutheran Church in America,[32] endorse the historic episcopate in principle. The Lutheran view, according to these documents, is that an understanding of ministerial offices within the one divinely instituted ministry of Word and Sacraments is important, and these offices are useful to the extent that they serve the ministry of Word and Sacraments.[33] This means that, while Lutherans regard structures of *episkope* as in one sense "adiaphora," they do not consider them unimportant. They are, in fact, no less important than the theological insights of Martin Luther

and the documents of the *Book of Concord*, which are also regarded as in one sense "adiaphora."[34] In the Lutheran confessional documents, Lutherans articulated a vision which looks toward a reformed catholic episcopate existing under the gospel and serving the gospel. It is useful to cite at some length the material from the Lutheran confessional writings because the summaries which have appeared elsewhere[35] do not always convey fully the confessional position.

43. The princes and cities which presented their confession to Emperor Charles V at the Imperial Diet of Augsburg in 1530 did so in order that the contending parties could resolve the dispute over reform which had been taking place in Germany so that "all of us embrace and adhere to a single, true religion and live together in unity and in one fellowship and church, even as we are all enlisted under one Christ" (Preface to the Augsburg Confession,4).[36] One cannot simply begin with Article XIV, "Order in the Church," even though in his Apology Melanchthon accepted the interpretation of the phrase "regular call" as *ordinatione canonica* (canonical ordination) on which the opponents had insisted.[37] The "regular call" simply means that "one cannot place oneself in the pastoral office." One is dependent for office on whatever lawful authorities place one into office.[38] It is necessary to begin with Article XXVIII on "The Power of Bishops" which contains the compromise proposal of the evangelical party. At its heart is the attempt to define the authentic spiritual authority of bishops. "Some have improperly confused the power of bishops with the temporal sword" (CA XXVIII,G,1). But "according to the Gospel the power of keys or the power of bishops is a power and command of God to preach the Gospel, to forgive and retain sins, and to administer and distribute the sacraments" (CA XXVIII,G,5).

> This power of keys or of bishops is used and exercised only by teaching and preaching the Word of God and by administering the sacraments (to many persons or to individuals, depending on one's calling). In this way are imparted not bodily but eternal things and gifts, namely, eternal righteousness, the Holy Spirit, and eternal life. These gifts cannot be obtained except through the office of preaching and of administering the holy sacraments, for St. Paul says, "The gospel is the power of God for salvation to everyone who has faith." Inasmuch as the power of the church or of bishops bestows eternal gifts and is used and exercised only through the office of preaching, it does not interfere at all with government or temporal authority. Temporal authority is concerned with matters altogether different from the Gospel (CA XXVIII,G,8-10).

The desire to distinguish political power from the office of bishop was especially necessary in Germany, where many bishops were also secular rulers of the territories included in their dioceses. That this distinction does not imply rejection of episcopacy becomes evident in the conclusion.

> Thus our teacher distinguish the two authorities and the functions of the two powers, directing that both be held in honor as the highest gifts of God on earth (CA XXVIII,G,18).

Insofar as the ministry of bishops is a ministry of the gospel they function by "divine right."

> According to divine right,[39] therefore, it is the office of the bishop to preach the Gospel, forgive sins, judge doctrine and condemn doctrine that is contrary to the Gospel, and exclude from the Christian community the ungodly whose wicked conduct is manifest. All this is to be done not by human power but by God's Word alone. On this account parish ministers and churches are bound to be obedient to the bishops according to the saying of Christ in Luke 10:16, "He who hears you hears me" (CA XXVIII,G,21-22).

However, it is not necessary to obey bishops if they teach or institute anything contrary to the gospel.[40] Article XXVIII now seeks to assign responsibility for the threatening schism to the bishops. The Lutheran reform movement is not seeking to create a new church or institute a new polity.[41] They claim an ancient right to refuse obedience to bishops who teach and issue commands contrary to the gospel.

> St. Augustine also writes in his reply to the letters of Petilian that one should not obey even regularly elected bishops if they err or if they teach or command something contrary to the divine Holy Scriptures. Whatever other power and jurisdiction bishops may have in various matters (for example, in matrimonial cases and in tithes), they have these by virtue of human right (CA XXVIII,G,28-29).

> What are we to say, then, about Sunday and other similar church ordinances and ceremonies? To this our teachers reply that bishops or pastors may make regulations so that everything in the churches is done in good order, but not as a means of obtaining God's grace or making satisfaction for sins, nor in order to bind men's consciences by considering these things necessary services of God and counting it a sin to omit their observance even when this is done without offense...It is proper for the Christian assembly to keep such ordinances for the sake of love and peace, to be obedient to the bishops and parish ministers in such matters, and to observe the regulations in such a way that one does not give

offense to another and so that there may be no disorder or unbecoming conduct in the church (CA XXVIII,G,53-55).

The bishops might easily retain the obedience of men if they did not insist on the observance of regulations which cannot be kept without sin. Now, however, they administer the sacrament in one kind and prohibit administration in both kinds. Again, they forbid clergymen [*Geistlichen*] to marry and admit no one to the ministry unless he first swears an oath that he will not preach this doctrine, although there is no doubt that it is in accord with the holy Gospel. Our churches do not ask that the bishops should restore peace and unity at the expense of their honor and dignity (though it is incumbent on the bishops to do this, too, in case of need), but they ask only that the bishops relax certain unreasonable burdens which did not exist in the church in former times and which were introduced contrary to the custom of the universal Christian church (CA XXVIII,G,69-72).

St. Peter forbids the bishops to exercise lordship as if they had power to coerce the churches according to their will. It is not our intention to find ways of reducing the bishops' power, but we desire and pray that they may not coerce our consciences to sin (CA XXVIII,G,76-77).

The final paragraph was quoted according to the official German text. Here it is important to quote also the official Latin text.

Peter forbids the bishops to be domineering and to coerce the churches. It is not our intention that the bishops give up their power to govern, but we ask for this one thing, that they allow the Gospel to be taught purely and that they relax some few observances which cannot be kept without sin.

The German text concludes:

If they are unwilling to do this and ignore our petition, let them consider how they will answer for it in God's sight, inasmuch as by their obstinacy they offer occasion for division and schism, which they should in truth help to prevent (CA XXVIII,G,78).

44. In his defense of the Augsburg Confession, Philip Melanchthon reiterates the concerns adduced above, and adds this paragraph.

In the Confession we have said what power the Gospel grants to bishops. Those who are now bishops do not perform the duties of bishops according to the Gospel, though they may well be bishops according to canonical polity, *to which we do not object* [*quam non reprehendimus*]. But we are talking about a bishop according to the Gospel. We like the old division of power into the power of the order and the power of jurisdiction [*potestas ordinis, potestas jurisdictionis*]. Therefore a bishop has the power of the order [*Habet igitur episcopus potestatem ordinis*], namely, *the ministry of Word and sacraments.* He also has the power of jurisdiction, namely, the authority to excommunicate those who are guilty of public offenses or to absolve them if they are converted and ask for absolution. A bishop does not have the power of a tyrant to act without a definite law, nor that of a king to act above the law. But he has a definite command, a definite Word of God, which he ought to teach and according to which he ought to exercise his jurisdiction. Therefore it does not follow that since they have a certain jurisdiction bishops may institute new acts of the Word, they have the command about when they should exercise their jurisdiction, namely, when anyone does something contrary to that Word which they have received from Christ.

In the Confession we nevertheless added the extent to which it is legitimate for them to create traditions, namely, that they must not be necessary acts of worship but a means for preserving order in the church, for the sake of peace (Apol. XXVIII,12-15)

Earlier, in his commentary on and defense of Article XIV, on Ecclesiastical Order, Melanchthon both reaffirms the Lutheran commitment to the traditional polity and explains why it has been lost in Germany.

With the proviso that we employ canonical ordination, they accept Article XIV, where we say that no one should be allowed to administer the Word and the sacraments in the church unless he is duly called. *On this matter we have given frequent testimony in the assembly to our deep desire to maintain the church polity and various ranks of the ecclesiastical hierarchy*, although they were created by human authority. We know that the Fathers had good and useful reasons for instituting the ecclesiastical discipline in the manner described by the ancient canons. But the bishops either force our priests to forsake and condemn the sort of doctrine we have confessed, or else, in their unheard of cruelty, they kill the unfortunate and innocent men. This keeps our priests from acknowledging such bishops. *Thus the cruelty of the bishops is the reason for the abolition of canonical government [canonica politia] in some places, despite our earnest desire to keep it.* Let them see to it how they will answer to God for disrupting the church.

In this issue our consciences are clear and we dare not approve the cruelty of those who persecute this teaching, for we know that our confession is true, godly, and catholic. We know that the church is present among those who rightly teach the Word of God and rightly administer the sacraments. It is not present among those who seek to destroy the Word of God with their edicts, who even butcher anyone who teaches what is right and true, though the canons themselves are gentler with those who violate them. *Furthermore, we want at this point to declare our willingness to keep the ecclesiastical and canonical polity*, provided that the bishops stop raging against our churches. This willingness will be our defense, both before God and among all nations, present and future, against the charge that we have undermined the authority of the bishops (Apol. XIV, 1-5. Emphasis added).

The emphasis has been added to point to the fact that churches which accept the doctrinal authority of the *Book of Concord*, as the Evangelical Lutheran Church in America does, are committed in principle to a preference for "the ecclesiastical and canonical polity" with its "various ranks of the ecclesiastical hierarchy."[42] The loss of such "ranks" is here ascribed by Melanchthon to "the cruelty of the bishops," not to outright rejection of bishops, presbyters, and other orders of ministry in the church as a matter of principle or intention.

45. Studies of Martin Luther's understanding of ministry abound,[43] sometimes with emphasis on and interpretations of his antipathy to bishops at certain times in his life. But his views have official standing in the Evangelical Lutheran Church in America only in those writings of which were taken up into the *Book of Concord*. Luther does not deal with the subject of bishops in either of the catechisms which he prepared in 1529. But in the Smalcald Articles of 1537, prepared in anticipation of an ecumenical council, Luther gives expression to his vision of ministry of bishops in terms of how he views his church's history and what he would like to see in a reformed church.

> Consequently the church cannot be *better* governed and maintained than by having all of us live under one head, Christ, and by having all the bishops equal in office (however they may differ in gifts) and diligently joined together in unity of doctrine, faith, sacraments, prayer, works of love, etc. So St. Jerome writes that the priests of Alexandria governed the churches together and in common. The apostles did the same, and after them all the bishops throughout Christendom, until the pope raised his head over them all (SA, Part II, Article IV,9. Emphasis added).

Later Luther both indicates his willingness to accept the ministry of bishops "for the sake of love and unity" and affirms his conviction, almost from despair, that episcopal ordination is not a necessary feature of church polity.

If the bishops were true bishops and were concerned about the church and the Gospel, they might be permitted (for the sake of love and unity, but not of necessity [*nicht aus Not*]) to ordain and confirm us and our preachers, provided this could be done without pretense, humbug, and unchristian ostentation [*alle Larven und Gespenste unchristliches Wesens und Gepraenges*]. However, they neither are nor wish to be true bishops. They are temporal lords and princes who are unwilling to preach or teach or baptize or administer Communion or discharge any office or work in the church. More than that, they expel, persecute, and condemn those who have been called to do these things. Yet the church must not be deprived of ministers on their account.

Accordingly, as we are taught by the examples of the ancient churches and Fathers, we shall and ought ourselves ordain suitable persons to this office. The papists have no right to forbid or prevent us, not even according to their own laws, for their laws state that those who are ordained by heretics shall also be regarded as ordained and remain so. St. Jerome, too, wrote concerning the church in Alexandria that it was originally governed without bishops by priests and preachers in common (SA, Part III, Article X,1-3).

Although Luther here conflates several quotations from St. Jerome, whom he cites from memory, the Roman Catholic participants in the U.S.A. Lutheran-Catholic Dialogue supported Luther's basic conviction:

40. When the episcopate and the presbyterate had become a general pattern in the church, the historical picture still presents uncertainties that affect judgment on the Minister of the eucharist. For instance, is the difference between a bishop and a priest of divine ordination? St. Jerome maintained that it was not; and the Council of Trent, wishing to respect Jerome's opinion, did not undertake to define that the preeminence of the bishop over presbyters was by divine law. If the difference is not of divine ordination, the reservation to the bishop of the power of ordaining Ministers of the eucharist would be a church decision. In fact, in the history of the church there are instances of priests (i.e., presbyters) ordaining other priests, and there is evidence that the church accepted and recognized the Ministry of priests so ordained.[44]

46. The theologians assembled in Smalcald in 1537 did not officially adopt Luther's articles, although they eventually gained official status when they were incorporated into the Book of Concord. The theologians did, however, adopt the "Treatise on the Power and Primacy of the Pope" as a confession of faith and intended it as a "supplement to the Augsburg Confession."[45] The fundamental thrust of the treatise is to contest the primacy of the bishop

of Rome by divine right, and to contest especially his right to "elect, ordain, confirm, and depose all bishops." During the course of making its case the treatise has much to say about episcopacy. It adduces as "Testimony from History" the following:

> 5. The Council of Nicaea decided that the bishop of Alexandria should administer the churches in the East and the bishop of Rome should administer the suburban churches, that is, those that were in the Roman provinces in the West...(TR,12).

> 6. Again, the Council of Nicaea decided that bishops should be elected by their own churches in the presence of one or more neighboring bishops. This was also observed in the West and in the Latin churches, as Cyprian and Augustine testify...(TR,13).

Then the treatise takes up "The Power of Jurisdiction of Bishops."

> In the Confession [Augsburg Confession] and in the Apology we have set forth in general terms what we have to say about ecclesiastical power.

> The Gospel requires of those who preside over the churches that they preach the Gospel, remit sins, administer the sacraments, and, in addition, exercise jurisdiction, that is, excommunicate those who are guilty of notorious crimes and absolve those who repent. By the confession of all, even our adversaries, it is evident that this power belongs by divine right to all who preside over the churches, whether they are called pastors, presbyters, or bishops. Accordingly Jerome teaches clearly that in the apostolic letters all who preside over the church are both bishops and presbyters...And Jerome observes: "One man was chosen over the rest to prevent schism, lest several persons, by gathering separate followings around themselves, rend the church of Christ. For in Alexandria, from the time of Mark the Evangelist to the time of Bishops Heracles and Dionysius, the presbyters always chose one of their number, set him in a higher place, and called him bishop. Moreover, in the same way in which an army might select a commander for itself, the deacons may choose from their number one who is known to be active and name him archdeacon. For, apart from ordination, what does a bishop do that a presbyter does not do?" Jerome therefore teaches that the distinction between the grades of bishop and presbyter (or pastor) is by human authority...Afterwards one thing made a distinction between bishops and pastors, and this was ordination, for it was decided that one bishop should ordain the ministers in a number of churches. But since the distinction between bishop and pastor is not by divine right, it is manifest that ordination administered by a pastor in his own church is valid by divine right. Consequently, when the regular bishops become enemies

of the Gospel and are unwilling to administer ordination, the churches retain the right to ordain for themselves. For whenever the church exists, the right to administer the Gospel also exists (TR,60-66).

47. It is clear from these extensive citations that during the "confessional phase" (1528-1537) of the reforming movement, before there were separated evangelical churches no longer under the jurisdiction of Rome,[46] there are consistent statements of commitment to the church's traditional polity, which includes both the historic episcopate and "ranks" in the hierarchy. It is also clear that Lutherans regarded the ministry of bishops to be a ministry of the gospel, that is, a gospel of preaching the Word and administering the Sacraments. This ministry, like that of pastors, is by divine right and institution. In common with the Western catholic tradition, prior to the patristic rediscoveries of the 17th century, they regarded the distinction between bishops and presbyters, and especially the episcopal ministry of ordination, to be of human origin.[47] They did not reject either the distinction or the episcopal ministry of ordination. It is important to stress, however, that the Lutheran reformers believed that one ministerial office as such had been instituted by God: the pastoral office of proclamation of the Word of God and the administration of the sacraments. Because they believed that both bishops and presbyters had identical divine authorization, they considered their own ordinations to be valid wherever the canonical bishops refuse to ordain clergy for the churches of the reform movement. It must be stressed that for the Lutheran confessional tradition, historical succession of laying-on-of-hands in the ministerial office was not theologically primary. The confessional tradition believes that the divine institution of the ministerial office is evidenced by its faithfulness to and continuity in the apostolic Word and Sacraments as heard and received in the church throughout the centuries.[48] Thus, Lutherans believe, it is the content, and not the form, of ministry that ultimately authenticates it.[49]

## C. The Historic Episcopate in Lutheran-Episcopal Dialogue

48. Lutherans have given unanimous and consistent expression to their confessional heritage on the subject of the historic episcopate in Lutheran-Episcopal Dialogue. At the conclusion of LED I, representatives of each church agreed that the other had preserved "the succession of the Gospel" at the time of the Reformation, although each did so in a different way. This agreement, already cited above in Par. 19, stated:

> One of our communions in its place experienced the continuity of the episcopally ordered ministry as an important means of the succession of

the Gospel; in various ways the other in its place was able to take its responsibility for the succession of the Gospel only by a new ordering of its ministry. We agree that by each decision the apostolicity of the ministry in question was preserved, and that each of our communions can and should affirm the decision of the other...Within the one church, both the Anglican continuity of the episcopal order, and the Lutheran concentration on doctrine, have been means of preserving the apostolicity of the one church.[50]

The Lutherans were able to join the Episcopalians in a vision for the future fully consistent with Lutheran openness to the traditional polity and the ministry of the historic episcopate. Together, as cited above in Par. 19, they said:

For the future, we agree that if either communion should be able to receive the gift of the other's particular apostolicity, without unfaithfulness to its own, the future of the church would surely be served. In any future ordering of the one church, there will be a ministry and within that ministry an *episcope*. The functional reality of *episcope* is in flux in both our communions. If we are faithful, we will *together* discover the forms demanded by the church's new opportunities, so that the church may have an *episcope* which will be an *episcope* of the apostolic Gospel.[51]

As cited earlier, Professor Robert Jenson stated in a concluding essay:

The Lutheran position means that so long as the episcopacy—or any other "ceremony"—is not made an *antecedent condition* of communion, Lutherans are committed to limitless openness thereafter, both in investigating the inadequacy of their own previous arrangements and in achieving new arrangements for future forms of the church. The explicit recognition of "episcope" as an intrinsic function in the church has not been characteristic of Lutheranism; but it in no way violates Lutheran principle, and merely makes up a rather obvious *lacuna* in our thought.[52]

The International Anglican-Lutheran "Pullach Report," as quoted in LED I, states

Since the particular form of episcope is not a confessional question for Lutherans, the historic episcopate should not become a necessary condition for interchurch relations or church union. *On the other hand, those Lutheran churches which have not retained the historic episcopate are free to accept it where it serves the growing unity of the church in obedience to the gospel.*[53]

Gunnar Hultgren, archbishop of Uppsala and Lutheran co-chair of the international dialogue, raised an important question in a personal note attached to the "Pullach Report." While affirming the traditional Lutheran position that "the only necessary condition to full church fellowship is agreement on the truth of the gospel (CA VII)," he asked Lutheran churches whether this necessarily means "that all forms of church order equally serve the church's witness to the truth of the gospel?" In a pointed reformulation, he continued, "Is the absence of the historic episcopate in some Lutheran churches only motivated by faithfulness to the gospel, or have other motives been at work?"[54] Finally, at the end of LED II in 1980, the Lutheran participants in a unanimous "Statement by Lutherans to Lutherans" reached the following conclusion:

> Because of what episcopal succession has meant to the church throughout much of its history, and because of its ecumenical significance today, we recommend that the Lutheran Churches in America begin an internal study of the historic episcopate to determine whether it is a viable form of ministry for our Churches. Our report notes that the Lutheran Confessions show a preference for the historic episcopate where and when that ministry can be maintained in the service of the gospel. We are also aware that the Lutheran Churches in Sweden, Finland, and some Lutheran Churches in Africa have bishops in the historic succession. Indeed, the current President of the Lutheran World Federation, Bishop Josiah Kibira of the Northwest Diocese of the Evangelical Lutheran Church in Tanzania, is ordained into the historic episcopate. We are convinced that our willingness to deal seriously with this issue would be regarded as a most positive sign by our Episcopalian brothers and sisters, could serve the cause of church unity, and might redound to our own blessing.[55]

49. The openness to the "historic episcopate" on the part of Lutherans in the Pullach Report of 1972 has been echoed in subsequent international and other national dialogues with Anglicans. At Helsinki in 1982, the Anglican-Lutheran European Regional Commission (ALERC) reported that in the matter of the "historical succession of bishops"

> there still remains a difference between us because, while Anglicans cannot envisage any form of organic church union without the historic episcopate, Lutheran churches are not able to contribute to the historic episcopate the same significance for organic church union.

At the same time, even though Lutherans

cannot accept any suggestion that the ministry exercised in their own tradition should be invalid until the moment that it enters into an existing line of episcopal succession...Lutheran theologians and Churches are increasingly prepared to appreciate episcopal succession, in the words of the Faith and Order text (BEM), "as a sign of the apostolicity of the life of the whole Church."[56]

## D. Additional Developments

50. In 1984 the Lutheran member churches of the Lutheran Council in the U.S.A. completed a two-year study of the historic episcopate and published a report. The report can well serve as a summary of the openness of Lutheran churches in the U.S.A. to the possibility of the historic episcopate. The study was occasioned both by the introduction of the title "bishop" for regional leaders elected to the ministry of "oversight" and by the attention being given to the historic episcopate in ecumenical dialogues. After summarizing the results of historical study and the teaching of the Lutheran Confessions, the study concludes as follows:

> Some are urging Lutheran churches to adopt the historic episcopate. The "historic episcopate" is variously understood by various churches at the present time, but it usually includes views on the historic succession of bishops. When the "historic episcopate" faithfully proclaims the gospel and administers the sacraments, it may be accepted as a symbol of the church's unity and continuity throughout the centuries provided that it is not viewed as a necessity for the validity of the church's ministry. American Lutheranism is free to create under the guidance of the Spirit forms of leadership that embody *episcopé* and hold ecumenical promise.[57]

In a special appendix on the definition of the historic episcopate, the study, repeating for emphasis, concludes:

> When the "historic episcopate" faithfully proclaims the gospel and administers the sacraments, it may be accepted as a symbol of the church's unity and continuity throughout the centuries provided that it is not viewed as a necessity for the validity of the church's ministry.[58]

The importance of this conclusion for the task of this dialogue and the future reconciliation of Lutheran and Episcopal ministries ought to be self-evident.

51. The 1982 adoption of *Baptism, Eucharist and Ministry* by the Faith

and Order Commission of the World Council of Churches gave encouragement to the developments in Lutheran churches reported above. Despite reservations, there are many features of BEM to which the American Lutheran churches resonated: the "thoroughly theological character of the document, and the seriousness with which it deals with theological issues"; beginning the section on ministry "with an affirmation about the calling and ministry of the whole people of God"; the description of ordained ministry in Paragraph 13; "the description of the authority of the ministry as being derived from the authority of Christ,"[59] the grounding of the ordained ministry in the gospel; the concept of apostolicity; and "the adherence to specific forms of the Tradition."[60] Particularly significant for subsequent developments within the Evangelical Lutheran Church in America is the several-times repeated commendation in *Baptism, Eucharist and Ministry* of the threefold ministry of bishop, presbyter, and deacon as well as commendation of the historic episcopate.[61] For in order to address the issues of ministry left unresolved at the time of the founding, the constitution of the Evangelical Lutheran Church in America contained the following provision:

> During the...period of 1988-1994, this church shall engage in an intensive study of the nature of ministry, leading to decisions regarding appropriate forms of ministry that will enable this church to fulfill its mission. During the course of such study, special attention shall be given to:
> 1) the tradition of the Lutheran church;
> 2) the possibility of articulating a Lutheran understanding and adaptation of the threefold ministerial office of bishop, pastor, and deacon and its ecumenical implication; and
> 3) the appropriate forms of lay ministries to be officially recognized and certified by this church, including criteria for certification, relation to synods, and discipline.[62]

A Task Force on the Study of Ministry, established by the Evangelical Lutheran Church in America in 1988, is now at work under this mandate.

## 4. THE EPISCOPAL CHURCH AND THE MINISTRY OF THE HISTORIC EPISCOPATE

### A. The Legacy of the Church of England

52. It is well known that during the reformations of the 16th century the Church of England maintained the threefold order of the ordained ministry with the episcopate at its heart. Under Henry VIII the royal supremacy

replaced papal supremacy and separated England from the jurisdiction of the bishop of Rome. An Act Restraining the Payment of Annates (1534) took for granted the threefold order focused in the episcopate and ordered that from henceforth the king, in his role as Supreme Head of the Church in England, should nominate to the proper electing body the person to be elected archbishop or bishop.[1] In the reign of King Edward VI an ordinal was devised and published in 1550 with the title, "The forme and maner of makynge and consecratyng of Archebishoppes, Bishoppes, Priestes and Deacons." It was revised and bound up with the 1552 Book of Common Prayer and is to be found in subsequent prayer books. The preface to the Ordinal stated "that from the Apostles' time there hath been these orders of Ministers in Christ's Church,"[2] and this was seen as sufficient reason for the continuance of the threefold order.

53. After the brief and troublesome reign of the Roman Catholic Queen Mary, during which doctrinal reforms were reversed and papal jurisdiction reintroduced for a short time, Queen Elizabeth came to the throne, Parliament restored royal supremacy, and the historic episcopate was again set free from the jurisdiction of the bishop of Rome. Elizabeth did not seek the restoration of the Edwardian legislation (repealed under Mary) that had directed the crown appoint bishops by letters patent rather than following the traditional canonical procedures. She did clarify the supremacy, claiming rather less than did her father, Henry VIII, preferring to be known as "Governor" rather than "Head" of the church, firmly stating that she did not take to herself any authority other than that provided by law, would not tamper with inherited doctrine or ceremony, and would not claim any "function belonging to any ecclesiastical person being a minister of the Word and Sacraments of the Church."[3] She would, so she signified, maintain the historic order of the Church's ministry and its essential integrity. And yet, although the ancient threefold pattern of the ordained ministry was thus retained under reformation, one significant change from the years of Edward VI may be noted as surviving the tumultuous events of that century: bishops, priests, and deacons were permitted to marry.[4]

54. Anglican attitudes toward the episcopate and understandings of its meaning and functions developed during the 16th and 17th centuries. At the outset there were those who continued to regard bishops as primarily servants of the state. On the other hand there were bishops such as John Hooper who labored diligently in his diocese to provide learned clergy and to correct the faults of those perceived to be in error, chiefly through the ecclesiastical courts.[5] The expectation of bishops' attendance at court, necessitating long absences from their dioceses, declined markedly under Elizabeth. John Jewel, Queen Elizabeth's first bishop of Salisbury, reflected the Reformation point of view, stating: "Those oily, shaven, portly hypocrites, we have sent

back to Rome from whence we first appointed them: for we require our bishops to be pastors, labourers, and watchmen."[6] Although in the early years of Queen Elizabeth's reign there were those who did not take a high view of episcopacy, the dominant attitude of that time was probably expressed by the final Elizabethan archbishop of Canterbury, John Whitgift, who believed that episcopacy best suited monarchial government which, incidentally, he regarded as the best form of government. But where the civil government was oligarchical, he considered, the ecclesiastical government might appropriately be presbyteral,[7] and thus foreigners ordained abroad only by presbyters were allowed to minister in England. But none were to be ordained in England save by bishops. The evidence thus suggests that in the sixteenth and early seventeenth centuries the prevalent theological opinion in the Church of England was that where episcopal ordination was available, it should be retained; but in cases of necessity where this was not possible, such as on the continent, then presbyteral ordination might suffice. Richard Hooker expressed the Anglican understanding this way:

> When the exigence of necessity doth constrain to leave the usual ways of the church, which otherwise we would willingly keep, where the church must needs have some ordained and neither hath nor can have possibly a bishop to ordain, in case of such necessity, the ordinary institution of God hath given oftentimes, and may give, place. And therefore we are not simply without exception to urge a lineal descent of power from the Apostles by continued succession of bishops in every effectual ordination. These cases of inevitable necessity excepted, none may ordain but only bishops: by the imposition of their hands it is, that the church giveth power of order, both unto presbyters and deacons.[8]

55. Nonetheless, there was pressure of invective from Rome and from Puritans and Separatists in England. Some of the more militant Puritans sought to replace episcopal government with presbyterian government, such as that of Calvin's Geneva, regarding bishops not as "pastors, labourers, and watchmen," but as "that swinishe rabble," as "pettie Antichrists, proud prelates, intolerable withstanders of reformation, enemies of the gospel, and most covetous wretched priests."[9] Indeed, episcopacy was altogether suppressed in the Church of England following the Civil War during the Commonwealth period (1649-1660), but it was restored after the Interregnum. The result of all this controversy, however, was that, rather than merely accepting the threefold order as an historic given, there were now those who began to argue that the historic episcopate was of divine origin and necessary, somewhat in imitation of the Puritans who argued that presbyterian government was of divine origin and necessary. Richard Hooker

had argued that the first "institution of bishops could be traced back to Christ himself, through the Apostles," but he was careful to qualify this argument by insisting that episcopacy was a matter of "positive law." Bishops thus owed "their continued existence in the church since the death of the Apostles to the authority of the church that had chosen to retain them, rather than to any immutable command of divine law."[10] There would be those in the future who would hearken back to Hooker's judicious understanding, but there would also be those who took a simpler view: Christ instituted bishops, so there must be bishops. The bishops after the Interregnum of the 17th century insisted on ordaining (or re-ordaining) all ministers previously not episcopally ordained during the Commonwealth period, and the Ordinal of the 1662 Book of Common Prayer as well as the Act of Uniformity in the same year now insisted that episcopal ordination was necessary for the holding of ecclesiastical benefice or admission to the pastoral ministry of the Church of England. Henceforth no one would "be accounted or taken to be a lawful Bishop, Priest, or Deacon" unless he were admitted "according to the form hereafter following, or hath had formerly Episcopal Consecration or Ordination." This requirement applied to ministers from all non-episcopal churches, whether in England or elsewhere. The traditional attitude of the Church of England was nevertheless maintained toward reformed churches elsewhere: they were true churches, whose ministries, though irregular and anomalous, were real and effective.[11] But a clear boundary had been set for the limits of Anglican comprehensiveness that has survived even in the latest (1979) Book of Common Prayer of the Episcopal Church in the United States:

> No persons are allowed to exercise the offices of bishop, priest, or deacon in this Church unless they are so ordained [by "the laying on of episcopal hands"], or have already received such ordination with the laying on of hands by bishops who are themselves duly qualified to confer Holy Orders (preface to the Ordinal, page 510).

56. During the latter half of the 17th century there was thus a shift of theological emphasis in Anglican understandings of episcopacy. Partly this shift was due to the exigencies of polemics, as noted above. It was also stimulated, however, by the rediscovery and authentication of certain patristic texts, especially the first epistle of Clement and the letters of Ignatius. The texts dealt with matters of church order and seemed to indicate a separate and distinct episcopal order from early times.[12] Hence, the episcopal ordering of the church began to be envisaged, in some quarters, not only as historically normative or of divine approbation and apostolic origin (though certainly not as necessary to salvation), but as a divine gift that defines the sphere of

covenanted grace and as an apostolic office which is the basis for the
Church's authority and identity independent of civil society. One example of
this tendency is the bishop of Chester, John Pearson (1673-1686), active in
the process of authenticating the genuine letters of Ignatius of Antioch, who
became "sure that there can be no power of absolution or authority to consecrate the elements in the Lord's Supper on the part of one who has not been
episcopally ordained."[13]

57. After this shift in theological emphasis, three ways of understanding episcopacy came to the fore in the following centuries. First were those
for whom episcopacy was still a secondary matter. Among many latitudinari-
ans, episcopacy remained a convenient and traditional manner of ordering
the ministry. Emerging eighteenth-century Anglican evangelicals largely
shared this view with their latitudinarian adversaries. The other two ways of
understanding episcopacy, however, accorded it greater theological significance.

58. The second of these understandings made episcopacy primary.
When confronted with latitudinarian theological understandings combined
with whig political views of ecclesiastical reformation, the shift of emphasis
resulted in the assertion of the Tractarian Movement (1833-1845) that not
only was episcopacy of apostolic foundation, but it was necessary to authentic ecclesial life. Appealing to the example and teaching of the early church
fathers, such as Cyprian of Carthage, emphasis was placed on the church's
self-governance through the episcopate. In Tract 74, for example, it was
asserted that non-episcopal forms of ministry, "men thus sending themselves,
or sent by we know not whom," have no authority to administer the
Sacraments. John Henry Newman (1801-1890) considered bishops to be of
the *esse* of the church and urged "the clergy to remember 'the real ground'
on which their authority was built, their 'apostolical descent.'" He called
upon them "to join with the bishops, and support them in their battle to
defend the Church."[14]

59. A third way of understanding episcopacy, broader but not entirely
dissimilar, represents a more comprehensive view resulting from the revolu-
tionary challenges to Christianity coming with the 19th century, yet stemming from the shift in emphasis noted above, and was encouraged by the
thought of F.D. Maurice (1805-1872). He commended the institution of the
episcopate as "one of the appointed and indispensable signs of a spiritual and
universal society,"[15] and he also held that "the main constituent of the
Church's polity is the episcopate. Bishops have the direct commission of
Christ, as much as did the original holders of the apostolic office."[16] In the
case of the Tractarian and Maurician ways of understanding episcopacy,
though, the shift of attitude corresponds to a shift in the position of the
church in state and society and, as such, informs contemporary discussions

of the episcopate that have been stimulated in part also by the ecumenical movement.

## B. Anglicanism in the American Cultural Context

60. It is remarkable that after the American Revolution colonial Anglicanism survived in the newly founded Protestant Episcopal Church, the first autonomous Anglican Church outside the British Isles but now independent of the civil society. Anglicanism was associated with the tyranny of the British crown, and it might have perished in the United States with the end of British rule. It is also remarkable that the episcopate survived in the new world. There were no resident bishops in colonial Anglicanism and the colonists on the whole had opposed any suggestion of episcopacy, regarding bishops as "proud prelates." The 1789 founding convention of the Episcopal Church met in Philadelphia facing the necessity of resolving widespread differences, principally between those who believed that there could be no discussion of church government without bishops being present and in charge and those who had been prepared to go forward without bishops if for a time the proper consecrations could not be procured, insisting that in this new land it was the faithful people who mattered most. The result was that the historic threefold order of the ordained ministry was continued, though the bishops were elected by both clergy and laity, who were to share in the government of the church in diocesan conventions and in the General Convention.

61. Although Samuel Seabury, the first bishop of the Episcopal Church in America, and some others like him, maintained a high-church estimation of the vital necessity of episcopacy not only to the church but also to Christian life and salvation, and would have preferred for bishops a greater degree of authority,[17] it was nonetheless determined at the insistence of William White, first bishop of Pennsylvania, that laity were also to participate in every level of church government and even in the selection of those to be ordained. Though reminiscent of conciliar patterns in the early church, such changes in the structure, practice, and understanding of the episcopate were influenced by American colonial experience as well as by the history of the English convocations of Canterbury and York and by a positive theological evaluation of American governmental philosophy and practice, the Articles of Confederation being of particular influence. Collectively, these arrangements in the Episcopal Church have come to be known as "the constitutional episcopate." The bishop continued to be understood to fulfill a particular and historic ministry within the community of the faithful, but not apart from it.

62. As a result of their new situation, Anglicans in the United States were given further opportunity to explicate their understanding of the historic episcopate. A case in point is the famous Memorial presented to the 1853 General Convention by, among others, William Augustus Muhlenberg, an Episcopal priest whose great-grandfather was the famous Lutheran "patriarch," Henry Melchior Muhlenberg. It petitioned the House of Bishops to take an initiative by ordaining ministers of other traditions (especially on the frontier) without binding them to the Thirty Nine Articles of Religion and the rubrics of the Book of Common Prayer. While the Memorial met with some enthusiasm, no practical action resulted.[18]

## C. New Understandings from the Ecumenical Movement

63. Yet as the 19th century progressed, the existence of many competing communions in the U.S.A. caused leaders such as William Reed Huntington to address the issue of church unity. In 1886 the Bishops of the Episcopal Church, meeting in Chicago, appealed to "principles of unity exemplified by the undivided Catholic Church during the first ages of its existence," which they understood to be "essential to the restoration of unity among the divided branches of Christendom." The Chicago-Lambeth Quadrilateral, as it came to be known after it had been affirmed by the 1888 Lambeth Conference (in a slightly amended form), identified four principles "as a basis for an approach to reunion":

a) The Holy Scriptures of the Old and New Testament, as "containing all things necessary to salvation," and as being the rule and ultimate standard of faith.
b) The Apostles' Creed, as the Baptismal Symbol; and the Nicene Creed, as the sufficient statement of the Christian faith.
c) The two Sacraments ordained by Christ Himself—Baptism and the Supper of the Lord—ministered with unfailing use of Christ's words of Institution, and of the elements ordained by Him.
d) The Historic Episcopate, locally adapted in the methods of its administration to the varying needs of the nations and peoples called of God into the Unity of His Church.[19]

64. It remained for the 20th century ecumenical movement to multiply conferences and dialogues on matters standing in the way of visible unity. At times the very instruments of unity have appeared to some as barriers, not least the historic episcopate. The bishops of the 1920 Lambeth Conference sought to break the impasse with "An Appeal to All Christian People":

The vision which rises before us is that of a Church, genuinely Catholic, loyal to all truth, and gathering into its fellowship all "who profess and call themselves Christians," within whose visible unity all the treasures of faith and order, bequeathed as a heritage by the past to the present, shall be possessed in common, and made serviceable to the whole Body of Christ. Within this unity Christian Communions now separated from one another would retain much that has long been distinctive in their methods of worship and service. It is through a rich diversity of life and devotion that the unity of the whole fellowship will be fulfilled.[20]

The Appeal was to "an adventure of goodwill and still more of faith, for nothing less is required than a new discovery of the creative resources of God." The four principles of unity in the Chicago-Lambeth Quadrilateral were reworded as follows:

The Holy Scriptures, as the record of God's revelation of Himself to man, and as being the rule and ultimate standard of faith; and the Creed commonly called Nicene, as the sufficient statement of the Christian faith, and either it or the Apostles' Creed as the Baptismal confession of belief;

The divinely instituted sacraments of Baptism and the Holy Communion, as expressing for all the corporate life of the whole fellowship in and with Christ;

A ministry acknowledged by every part of the Church as possessing not only the inward call of the Spirit, but also the commission of Christ and the authority of the whole body.[21]

The Appeal addressed the reality of the ordained ministries of communions without the historic episcopate:

May we not reasonably claim that the Episcopate is the one means of providing such a ministry? It is not that we call in question for a moment the spiritual reality of the ministries of those Communions which do not possess the Episcopate. On the contrary we thankfully acknowledge that these ministries have been manifestly blessed and owned by the Holy Spirit as effective means of grace. But we submit that considerations alike of history and of present experience justify the claim which we make on behalf of the Episcopate. Moreover, we would urge that it is now and will prove to be in the future the best instrument of maintaining the unity and continuity of the Church. But we greatly desire that the office of a Bishop should be everywhere exercised in a representative and constitutional manner...

We believe that for all, the truly equitable approach to union is by way of mutual deference to one another's consciences. To this end, we who send forth this appeal would say that if the authorities of other Communions should so desire, we are persuaded that, terms of union having been otherwise satisfactorily adjusted, Bishops and clergy of our Communion would willingly accept from these authorities a form of commission or recognition which would commend our ministry to their congregations as having its place in the one family life...

It is our hope that the same motive would lead ministers who have not received it to accept a commission through episcopal ordination, as obtaining for them a ministry throughout the whole fellowship.

In so acting no one of us could possibly be taken to repudiate his past ministry. God forbid that any man should repudiate a past experience rich in spiritual blessings for himself and others. Nor would any of us be dishonoring the Holy Spirit of God, Whose call led us all to our several ministries, and Whose power enabled us to perform them. We shall be publicly and formally seeking additional recognition of a new call to wider service in a reunited church, and imploring for ourselves God's grace and strength to fulfill the same.[22]

Thus we have a moving admission of the impoverishment of all ordained ministries by the fact that they are not in communion with each other.

65. Responses to this Appeal and to like messages from other communions have been deliberate but steady. Notable examples are the unions of Anglican dioceses with Christians of other traditions in the Churches of South India, North India, Pakistan, and Bangladesh. Discussions have continued in the World Council of Churches Commission on Faith and Order and between communions in many parts of the world, including the Anglican-Lutheran dialogues. Reflection on the experience of steadily widening dialogue, as well as on that of full-communion concordats with the Old Catholic Churches of Europe, has led the Episcopal Church to an understanding of the goal of visible unity as "one eucharistic fellowship...a communion of Communions."[23] The work of the Consultation on Church Union in the U.S.A. with churches of the Reformed and Methodist traditions has produced a proposal in light of this goal statement which seeks to incorporate the historic episcopate.[24]

66. The Anglican-Reformed International Commission has produced the report *God's Reign and Our Unity*, which is rich in material concerning the reconciliation of ordained ministries. On the issue of continuity of succession, it declares:

We have been led to acknowledge...the reality of one another's churchly life. But this gives us no ground for concluding that the historic continuity of ordinations is an irrelevance. On the contrary it is an element in
the proper visible form of the Church's unity in space and time, to the
end of the age and the ends of the earth. We therefore affirm that the
ways by which our separated churches are brought into unity must be
such as to ensure (a) that the reality of God's gift of ministry to the
churches in their separation is unambiguously acknowledged; and (b)
that the continuity of succession in ordination with the undivided
Church is—so far as lies in our power—visibly restored and maintained.[25]

67. The Standing Commission on Ecumenical Relations of the
Episcopal Church reassessed the relation of the historic episcopate to apostolic succession in light of the ecumenical dialogues, and in 1976 produced
what it called a "working statement" which acknowledged that "apostolicity
has many strands."[26] This general approach was then formally approved
when the 1982 General Convention adopted a resolution on "Principles of
Unity" which reaffirmed the Chicago-Lambeth Quadrilateral and in explication thereof broadened the fourth point to embrace the concept of apostolicity:

Apostolicity is evidenced in continuity with the teaching, the ministry,
and the mission of the apostles. Apostolic teaching must, under the
guidance of the Holy Spirit, be founded upon the Holy Scriptures and
the ancient fathers and creeds, making its proclamation of Jesus Christ
and his Gospel for each new age consistent with those sources, not
merely reproducing them in a transmission of verbal identity. Apostolic
ministry exists to promote, safeguard and serve apostolic teaching. All
Christians are called to this ministry by their Baptism. In order to serve,
lead and enable this ministry, some are set apart and ordained in the historic orders of Bishop, Presbyter, and Deacon. We understand the historic episcopate as central to this apostolic ministry and essential to the
reunion of the Church, even as we acknowledge "the spiritual reality of
the ministries of those Communions which do not possess the
Episcopate" (Lambeth Appeal 1920, Section 7). Apostolic mission is
itself a succession of apostolic teaching and ministry inherited from the
past and carried into the present and future. Bishops in apostolic succession are, therefore, the focus and personal symbols of this inheritance
and mission as they preach and teach the Gospel and summon the people of God to their mission of worship and service.[27]

68. The 1985 General Convention directed Episcopal participants in
Lutheran-Episcopal Dialogue III to advocate paragraph 53(a) of *Baptism,*

*Eucharist and Ministry* as "a way forward" toward the mutual recognition of the ordained ministries of our respective churches:

> Churches which have preserved the episcopal succession are asked to recognize both the apostolic content of the ordained ministry which exists in churches which have not maintained such succession and also the existence in these churches of a ministry of *episkope* in various forms.

## D. The Prayer Book Teaching on the Episcopate

69. This review of the ministry of the historic episcopate in the Episcopal Church as a Province of the Anglican Communion may conclude with statements on the meaning of the episcopate taken from the *Book of Common Prayer* (U.S.A.,1979). "An Outline of the Faith," after identifying the ministers of the Church as "lay persons, bishops, priests, and deacons," each of whom represent Christ in a particular way within the unity of the one Body, describes the ministry of the bishop:

> The ministry of a bishop is to represent Christ and his Church, particularly as apostle, chief priest, and pastor of a diocese; to guard the faith, unity, and discipline of the whole Church; to proclaim the Word of God; to act in Christ's name for the reconciliation of the world and the building up of the Church; and to ordain others to continue Christ's ministry.[28]

In the rite for "The Ordination of a Bishop" the presiding bishop addresses the bishop-elect with this description of the episcopal office during the examination before the consecration:

> ...The people have chosen you and have affirmed their trust in you by acclaiming your election. A bishop in God's holy Church is called to be one with the apostles in proclaiming Christ's resurrection and interpreting the Gospel, and to testify to Christ's sovereignty as Lord of lords and King of kings.
>
> You are called to guard the faith, unity, and discipline of the bishop; to celebrate and to provide for the administration of the sacraments of the New Covenant; to ordain priests and deacons and to join in ordaining bishops; and to be in all things a faithful pastor and wholesome example for the entire flock of Christ.

With your fellow bishops you will share in the leadership of the Church throughout the world. Your heritage is the faith of patriarchs, prophets, apostles, and martyrs, and those of every generation who have looked to God in hope. Your joy will be to follow him who came, not to be served, but to serve, and to give his life a ransom for many.[29]

During the Prayer of Consecration the presiding bishop and other bishops lay their hands upon the head of the bishop-elect and say together:

Therefore, Father, make N. a bishop in your Church. Pour out upon him the power of your princely Spirit, whom you bestowed upon your beloved Son Jesus Christ, with whom he endowed the apostles, and by whom your Church is built up in every place, to the glory and unceasing praise of your Name.[30]

The "Preface to the Ordination Rites" states the intention and purpose of this church to maintain and continue the threefold ministry;

The Holy Scriptures and ancient Christian writers make it clear that from the apostles' time, there have been different ministries within the Church. In particular, since the time of the New Testament, three distinct orders of ordained ministers have been characteristic of Christ's holy catholic Church. First, there is the order of bishops who carry on the apostolic work of leading, supervising, and uniting the Church. Secondly, associated with them are the presbyters, or ordained elders, in subsequent times generally known as priests. Together with the bishops, they take part in the governance of the Church, in the carrying out of its missionary and pastoral work, and in the preaching of the Word of God and administering his holy Sacraments. Thirdly, there are deacons who assist bishops and priests in all of this work. It is also a special responsibility of deacons to minister in Christ's name to the poor, the sick, the suffering, and the helpless.

The persons who are chosen and recognized by the Church as being called by God to the ordained ministry are admitted to these sacred orders by solemn prayer and the laying on of episcopal hands. It has been, and is, the intention and purpose of this Church to maintain and continue these three orders; and for this purpose these services of ordination and consecration are appointed. No persons are allowed to exercise the offices of bishop, priest, or deacon in this Church unless they are so ordained, or have already received such ordination with the laying on of hands by bishops who are themselves duly qualified to confer Holy Orders.

It is also recognized and affirmed that the threefold ministry is not the exclusive property of this portion of Christ's catholic Church, but is a gift from God for the nurture of his people and the proclamation of his Gospel everywhere. Accordingly, the manner of ordaining in this Church is to be such as has been, and is, most generally recognized by Christian people as suitable for the conferring of the sacred orders of bishop, priest, and deacon.[31]

## 5. THE GIFT OF FULL COMMUNION

### A. Concordat of Agreement

70. In Chapter 1 we described the historic impasse which has thus far proven to be an impediment to full communion between Lutherans and Anglicans. In Chapter 2 we identified the theological consensus on the gospel, on apostolicity, and on the unity given us in Christ. Chapters 3 and 4 are surveys of Lutheran and Anglican history for the past 450 years. The dialogues have revealed that there have been profound similarities in our 16th century experience, in the type of reforms introduced in different countries associated with our two traditions, in the theological perspectives shared by our 16th century documents. Our studies of these similarities during the three rounds of dialogue over a period of more than two decades have led us to a deepened appreciation for each other's traditions. Dialogues during a great many years, at every level—national, regional, international—have disclosed that our distinctive emphases are complementary: Lutherans with an emphasis on doctrine, Anglicans with an emphasis on worship. We are now ready to propose a Concordat of Agreement between the Episcopal Church and the Evangelical Lutheran Church in America. It is our fervent prayer that the actions proposed in the Concordat of Agreement can be the means by which the Holy Spirit gives both our churches the gift of full communion.

71. The mandate given to our dialogue is "the discussion of any other outstanding questions that must be resolved before full communion can be established between" our churches. We are using for purposes of the Concordat of Agreement the definition of "full communion" which has been formulated by the Anglican-Lutheran Joint Working Group, meeting in Cold Ash, Berkshire, England, in 1983.[1] "Full Communion" means that "members of one body may receive the sacraments of the other"; that bishops from each church participate in consecrations of bishops from the other church, "thus acknowledging the duty of mutual care and concern"; that clergy from each church "may exercise liturgical functions in a congregation of the other"; and

that there be organs of consultation "to express and strengthen the fellowship and enable common witness, life and service." We cannot emphasize strongly enough the following three convictions with regard to "full communion."

72. (1) The unity which is expressed by the term "full communion" is not something we achieve by processes of dialogue or by legislative agreements. It is a gift which we receive in and from Christ, who has reconciled all of humanity to God "in one body through the cross" (Eph. 2:16), who has made us one through our baptism into him (Gal. 3:26-28). "The unity of the church is given, not achieved. The church can only be one because it is constituted by the gospel in word and sacrament, and there is but one gospel" *(Implications of the Gospel,* Par. 98).

73. (2) The unity which is expressed by the term "full communion" is not intended merely to facilitate the convenience of communicants and clergy. It is intended above all to express the fully shared life and mission of our churches. When the church hears together the one gospel and feasts together at the one table of the Messiah, it is given the gift of life and mission. In the midst of the debilitating and destructive sense of fragmentation and homelessness which often accompanies a pluralistic and rootless culture, every experience of unity which Christ gives his disciple community is a witness. Moreover, the unity of Christ's disciples is received in the midst of as well as for the sake of his mission in the world. Hence both unity and mission are given in and with the gospel.

> The *gift* of Christ is that he sends his disciples as he has been sent (John 20:21), that they are to witness to God's forgiving judgement and verdict by setting at liberty all who are in the bondage of sin, that they are to witness to God's confounding and defeat of evil by unmasking the demonic powers and joining the struggle against them...In Christ the Church is called to be a sign, an instrument and a foretaste of the kingdom of God. The Church awakens to the astonishing discovery that its mission is a gift, that it has indeed been given the pearl of great price, the treasure hidden in a field (Mat. 13:44-46) and that this discovery is the reason for gathering others in order to participate in the joy (Luke 15:8-10).[2]

74. (3) The unity which is expressed by the term "full communion" is, in part, received and expressed in the interchangeability and reciprocity of ordained ministries. "I planted, Apollos watered, but God gave the growth. So neither he who plants nor he who waters is anything, but only God who gives the growth. He who plants and he who waters are equal..." (I Cor. 3:6-8;cf. Gal. 2:7-10). The church which becomes visible when it is gathered by the gospel in Word and Sacrament requires the gift of ministries for the proclamation of the Word and the administration of the Sacraments. Such

ministries have been given by Christ for building up his body "until we all attain to the unity of the faith" (Eph. 4:11-13). The collegiality of the ordained ministries of the church is given in and for the sake of the unity and mission of the gospel (I Cor. 12:4-14:33).

75. We are aware of the fact that our churches have had different histories with regard to ordained ministries since the differing reforms of the 16th century and the differing experiences of our churches in the United States.[3] We are also aware that within each of our churches there are differences of both interpretations and tradition with regard to many aspects of the ordained ministry. We do not believe that "full communion" means the elimination of all of these differences. Both of our churches live with internal diversity of traditions. At Cold Ash, the Anglican-Lutheran Joint Working Group agreed that

> to be in full communion means that churches become interdependent while remaining autonomous. One is not elevated to be the judge of the other nor can it remain insensitive to the other, neither is each body committed to every secondary feature of the tradition of the other...Full communion should not imply the suppressing of ethnic, cultural or ecclesial characteristics of traditions which may in fact be maintained and developed by diverse institutions within one communion.[4]

The purpose of the Concordat of Agreement which we are proposing to our churches is to commit ourselves to the cultivation of just those common forms which will facilitate the maximum reciprocity and interchangeability of ordained ministry.

76. In drafting the Concordat of Agreement which we are proposing to our churches we have been assisted by *The Niagara Report* of the Anglican-Lutheran International Continuation Committee (ALICC). In 1983, the Anglican-Lutheran Joint Working Group, authorized by the Anglican Consultative Council and Lutheran World Federation, recommended the establishment of a permanent international Continuation Committee. This committee was given as its first mandate the convening of an international Anglican-Lutheran consultation on *episkope*. The consultation took place at Niagara Falls, Ontario, in September, 1987. The Continuation Committee then issued a report with a series of recommendations to Anglican and Lutheran churches which grew out of the consultation. The recommendation addressed to churches of the Anglican Communion was as follows:

> Anglican Churches should make the necessary canonical revisions so that they can acknowledge and recognize the full authenticity of the existing ministries of Lutheran Churches.[5]

The 1988 Lambeth Conference welcomed *The Niagara Report*, and commended it "to the member Churches of the Anglican Communion for study and synodical reception." Lambeth also asked the Continuation Committee (now the Anglican-Lutheran International Commission) "to explore more thoroughly the theological and canonical requirements that are necessary in both Churches to acknowledge and recognize the full authenticity of existing ministries." Member Churches of the Anglican Communion are urged "to move towards the fullest possible ecclesial recognition and the goal of full communion" with Lutheran churches.[6] Likewise the Eighth Assembly of the Lutheran World Federation, meeting in Curitiba, Brazil, from January 30 to February 8, 1990, "expressed its joy" at this action taken by the 1988 Lambeth Conference, and resolved that the Lutheran World Federation should "renew its commitment to the goal of full communion with the churches of the Anglican Communion; and...urge LWF member Churches to take appropriate steps toward its realization." At the heart of *The Niagara Report* is an action proposed to each church. If the Episcopal Church can respond positively to the Lambeth resolution which recognizes "the presence of the Church of Jesus Christ in the Lutheran Communion as in our own" and take the canonical steps necessary to recognize the full authenticity of existing ministries of the Evangelical Lutheran Church in America, then the way is open for the Evangelical Lutheran Church in America *simultaneously* to take the equally significant steps to return to the traditional polity (the "historic episcopate") which is affirmed in its confessional documents (cf. paras. 36-41 above), to accept the sign of historic succession for its bishops in the future. Both churches have reason to remember the statement of Archbishop Robert Runcie that "it is dangerous to pray for unity because God is answering our prayers. Doors are opened and we stand wondering if we should enter."[7]

77. We believe that our two churches can enter into the Concordat of Agreement which we propose because of the common confession of the gospel which we share and which we have sought to express in all of our previous dialogue reports. We have also discovered that we share a sufficient common understanding of episcopal ministry, both in future vision[8] and in the past histories of our separate churches, over which we have not officially disagreed nor exchanged invective in the past. Each of us has been and is engaged in extensive dialogue on ordained ministry with other churches with whom we have disagreed about it, such as with the Roman Catholic Church and (in and outside the Consultation on Church Union) with the Methodist churches and with churches of the Reformed tradition. Much progress has been made in the overcoming of past disputes on this point in these dialogues, and we are resolved that they shall continue and that any measure of unity we achieve among ourselves shall also serve as a vehicle for rap-

prochement with them.[9] In our proposed Concordat of Agreement we agree to respect the full communion (pulpit and altar fellowship) with those churches which each of our churches already has. We look forward to possible joint dialogues with other churches in the future. But to our two particular churches, Lutheran and Anglican, the freedom for reconciliation of ministry in mission is being given now.

78. We wish to make clear at this point what will take place if our churches enter into the proposed Concordat of Agreement and some of the meaning of what will take place. As an expression of our communion, all persons newly elected to the office of bishop in both churches will be jointly consecrated by at least three bishops from each of our churches. No bishops already in office will be re-consecrated or re-ordained. Nor will any ordained presbyters (priests/pastors) from either church be re-ordained. Both churches agree to recognize the full authenticity of existing ministries. Nothing will be done which calls into question the authenticity of present ordinations and ministries and sacraments. Lutherans also need to understand that the future joint consecrations do not mean that Lutheran bishops will have greater authority, for the gospel of God's promise confers all the authority which the church and its ministers have or need. Nor will future Lutheran bishops have powers which they do not now have. They will continue to exercise *episkope* on the basis of the framework of constitutional accountability which currently obtains in the Evangelical Lutheran Church in America. Canon law in the Episcopal Church and synodical constitutions in the Evangelical Lutheran Church in America will continue to set terms of office and procedures for the election of bishops. But the Concordat of Agreement envisions those changes which will eventuate in a common *collegium* of bishops. The meaning of the joint consecrations of future bishops is that the bishop is to serve as sign and means of unity between the local and the universal dimensions of the church. The meaning of episcopal succession is that the bishop is to serve as a sign and means of unity between the church in the present and its continuity with the church of the past and the future.[10]

79. We believe that our churches are free to consider and to make the changes called for in the proposed Concordat of Agreement because of the authority of the gospel itself. The authority of the gospel is identified early in the synoptic Gospels. There the authority of Jesus is contrasted with that of the scribes (cf. Mark 1:22 and parallels). Jesus' authority was eschatological, that is, it was based on the present and future Reign of God. He was crucified in an intended negative judgment upon his implicit and explicit messianic claims. The resurrection of Jesus implies a dramatic reversal of this judgment. Indeed, because he can no longer be inhibited by death, the risen Messiah of Matthew's Gospel can make a sweeping and powerful

claim: "All authority in heaven and on earth had been given to me" (Matt. 28:18).

80. Thus Jesus, himself, distinguished between authority which comes from the gospel's promise and authority which comes only from fidelity to the way things are and have been (Mark 2:27-28; 7:1-23;Matt, 8:20-29). Authority which comes only from the past is slavishly dependent upon precedent and is bound to the *status quo*. It serves those who already have power, those who already have a stake in the way things are. But authority which comes from the gospel's promise creates new opportunities, gives new hope to those who are otherwise hopeless, to those who are excluded from the future by oppression and evil, by sickness and sin. The authority of the gospel's promise is grounded in the eschatological life, death, and resurrection of Jesus.[11] It is thus shaped by the history of Jesus which reveals both the way and the destiny of the church. Faith in the gospel involves the church in risks when it acts on the basis of Jesus' promise. For its authority to worship and to witness is the authority of what will finally be when the Kingdom of God is consummated. It is the authority which comes from anticipating the future because Jesus alone has the power to determine the destiny of the world and of all of humanity.[12] It is this authority of promise which gives authority to the Bible, the catholic creeds, and the confessional and liturgical books of the church, as well as to all structures and offices of ministry in the church. This authority is able to reform and renew the church as well as to give life to the dead and to call into existence that which does not exist (e.g., Romans 4:13-25).

81. This understanding of authority has contributed to the ability of our churches to ordain women to the presbyterate/pastorate and to the episcopate. This is evidence that Episcopalians take seriously the provision of the Lambeth Quadrilateral that the historic episcopate can be "locally adapted" from the perspective of the gospel. It is also evidence that the Evangelical Lutheran Church in America is willing and able to understand the episcopate as subject to the gospel, a point also endorsed by Episcopalians. On this basis of authority, our churches are also able to take the responsible risks through which we will be given full communion with each other. We will be able to live with reasonable anomalies and ambiguities for some short time as we await the consummation or complete realization of the gift of full communion. For the gospel of the Kingdom of God calls the churches to risk all the gifts they have been given in answer to God's call to discipleship (cf. Matthew 25:14-30), to risk all the gifts they have been given in response to God's call to unity (John 17:14-16). The church is called here and now to anticipate, in its very being the coming and promised ideal of the Kingdom of God.[13]

## B. Toward Full Communion

82. In the period since the Episcopal Church and the Evangelical Lutheran Church in America have entered into the Agreement of 1982 our churches have built upon our recognition of each other as "Churches in which the Gospel is preached and taught." Our churches have begun to discover that in each other's churches there exists a sustained and serious commitment to the apostolic mission of the Church. We have begun to cultivate the common discipleship to which we have been called in one body, by one Spirit, through one baptism, thankful to one Lord, our Savior Jesus Christ, in whom we have received one faith, one hope, "one God and Father of us all, who is above all and through all and in all" (Eph. 4:3-6). In the eucharists jointly celebrated under the provisions of Interim Sharing of the Eucharist we have already begun to experience that unity and *koinonia* of eschatological promise which is anticipated in every celebration of the eucharist.[14]

83. We are grateful to God for the gift of *episkope* which has been given to each of our churches, although in different forms. We acknowledge in each other's ministries of *episkope* the fruits of the presence of Jesus Christ and the activity of the Holy Spirit; the offering of sacrifices of praise and thanksgiving, the reflection of the faithful love of God towards the world, care for the nurture and growth of all the faithful, commitment to the breaking in of the Kingdom of God in justice and peace for the whole earth.

84. We recognize, however, that the ministries of *episkope* which we have received in each of our churches do not incontestably link our churches to the *koinonia* of the wider Church of God on earth throughout time and place. We confess to God, to each other, and to all Christian people how far, in our discharge of the ministry of *episkope*, our Churches have fallen short of the unity and continuity of the apostolic commission to which we are called. We ask of each other forgiveness for our disregard of each other's gifts, for our lack of humility, and for our past toleration of our division.

85. We earnestly desire to remove those barriers which prevent the life of our churches from reflecting the unity of heart and mind which is God's gift to the people of God. We commit ourselves to whatever is required of us to reach a common mind as to how the mission of the people of God can most fruitfully be served in every place, so that there may be united witness to the gospel, in word and deed, and a common enjoyment of the means of grace. We intend thereby also to promote the unity of all churches with whom we are seeking, or have already discovered, agreement in the one faith of the church catholic.

86. We rejoice in rediscovering in each other our common inheritance of faith and of life. We rejoice in our unity in the One, Holy, Catholic, and Apostolic Church. "Praise be to the God and Father of our Lord Jesus Christ,

who has bestowed on us in Christ every spiritual blessing in the heavenly realms" (Eph. 1:3).

87. We are agreed that the unity and mission of the gospel frees us for more than a simplistic recognition of each other's ministries of diocesan/synodical and parochial/congregational leadership. Authentic recognition involves the interaction and integration of leadership, especially that of *episkope*, for purposes of common life and mission. Such interaction and integration for purposes of life and mission means receiving the gift of comparable, compatible, and interchangeable forms of *episkope*. As this Report demonstrates, both of our churches have already experienced change and development in the forms and understanding of *episkope* throughout our respective histories. Now new developments are being given to both of us. We cannot, therefore, commend uncritically either the appropriation of the historic episcopate as it has developed in the Episcopal Church or the perpetuation of the exercise of *episkope* as it has developed in the Evangelical Lutheran Church in America.[15]

88. Neither of our churches claims such a degree of faithfulness to our calling by the apostolic gospel, that is, a continuity in either doctrine or order as would enable either to sit in judgment on the other. Nevertheless both of our churches have been given by God such faithfulness to the apostolic gospel that today we can recognize each other as sister churches.

89. The Episcopal Church and the Evangelical Lutheran Church in America have received, and can affirm together, as gifts for unity, the canonical Scriptures, the creeds and conciliar decisions of the ancient church, the reforms of the 16th century (especially in confessional writings such as *The Book of Concord*), the liturgical tradition of the church (especially the Book of Common Prayer), and the continuity of the ordained ministry through which the Word of God has been preached and the sacraments and other rites of the Church have been administered. The question of the historic episcopate through which clergy have been ordained, something which has been divisive between us, we believe we have transcended in the Concordat of Agreement attached to this report.

90. Formal recognition of each other's ministries so that our churches acknowledge a relationship of full communion between them cannot simply mean that neither church changes. Nor can it mean that either church changes merely to meet the expectations and requirements of the other. Rather both of our churches are being called to acknowledge that the experience and practice of full communion will involve us both *simultaneously* in changes and commitment to reforms. The simultaneity of the actions of our churches means that we trust each other as churches, that neither church requires prior conditions of the other, and that both churches are willing to make changes for the sake of unity.

91. The *simultaneous* actions which our churches offer each other can facilitate the continuing renewal of the episcopate as a pastoral office engaged in transmitting effectively the apostolic faith, in leading the church in its mission, and furthering the worldwide restoration of church unity on a basis that is ecumenical, evangelical, and catholic.

The Epiphany of Our Lord
January 6, 1991

## Notes

### Introduction

1. *Lutheran-Episcopal Dialogue: A Progress Report* (Cincinnati: Forward Movement Publications, 1972), p. 24.

2. *Lutheran-Episcopal Dialogue: Report and Recommendations* (Cincinnati: Forward Movement Publications, 1981). Reprinted in William A. Norgren, editor, *What Can We Share? A Lutheran-Episcopal Resource and Study Guide* (Cincinnati: Forward Movement Publications, 1985), pp. 38-59.

3. *Journal of the General Convention, The Episcopal Church, 1982*, pp. C-47-C-48. *Report of the Convention of the Lutheran Church in America, 1982*, pp. 182 and 266; *Report of the Convention of the American Lutheran Church, 1982*, pp. 975-976; *Proceedings of the Fourth Delegate Assembly of the Association of Evangelical Lutheran Churches*, September 7-9, 1982, pp. 15-16. Cf. Norgren, *What Can We Share?* pp. 6-8. There are some variations in the use of capital letters between the resolution adopted by the Episcopal Church and the resolutions adopted by the three Lutheran churches. This resolution was reaffirmed at the constituting convention of The Evangelical Lutheran Church in America, uniting the American Lutheran Church, The Association of Evangelical Lutheran Churches, and the Lutheran Church in America in 1987. Cf. *Minutes;* Evangelical Lutheran Church in America Constituting Convention, April 30-May 3, 1987, Resolutions ELCA 87.30.17 and ELCA 87.30.19, pp. 28-30.

4. D.S. Armentrout, "Lutheran-Episcopal Conversations in the Nineteenth Century," *Historical Magazine of the Protestant Episcopal Church,* Vol. 44, No.2 (1975), pp. 167-187, esp. pp. 181ff.

5. Louis A. Haselmayer, "The Church of Sweden and the Anglican Communion," *The Holy Cross Magazine,* Vol. 60, No. 8 (August 1949), pp. 213-222. See also *The Church of England and the Church of Sweden Report of the Commission Appointed by the Archbishop of Canterbury* (Mowbray, 1911); "The Reply of the Bishops of the Church of Sweden to the Resolutions of the Lambeth Conference of 1920. April 1922," in *Documents on Christian Unity* 1920-4, edited by G.K.A. Bell, 1924; *The Church of England and the Church of Finland: A Summary of the Proceedings at the Conferences held in 1933 and 1934* (S.P.C.K., 1934); also reprinted in *Documents on Christian Unity*, 1930-1948, edited by G.K.A. Bell; *Record of a Conference between the Commission of Comity of the Evangelical Lutheran Augustana Synod and the Sub-Committee of the Joint Commission for Conference on Church Unity of the Protestant Episcopal Church, held at Evanston, Illinois, December 3-4, 1935*, typewritten manuscript in the libraries of the General Theological Seminary, New York City, and Nashotah House, Nashotah, Wisconsin (Evanston, 1936); *Conferences between Representatives Appointed by the Archbishop of Canterbury on Behalf of the Church of England and Representatives of the Evangelical Lutheran Churches of Latvia and Estonia (S.P.C.K., 1938); and The Church of England and the Churches of Norway, Denmark, and Iceland: Report of a Committee Appointed by the Archbishop of Canterbury in 1951* (S.P.C.K., 1952).

6.Todd W. Nichol, "The Augustana Synod and Episcopacy," *Lutheran Quarterly,* Vol. III, No. 2 (Summer 1989), pp. 156-159.

7. Available through Augsburg Fortress, Publishers, Minneapolis, and Forward Movement Publications, Cincinnati.

8. From *Dar es Salaam to Budapest 1977-1984,* LWF Report No. 17/18 (April 1984), p. 22, Cf. p. 211.

9. The text of the Cold Ash Report is in William A. Norgren, editor, *What Can We Share?,* *op.cit.,* pp. 85-94.

10. *Ibid.,* pp. 26-27.

11. *Budapest 1984, Proceedings of the Seventh Assembly,* "In Christ--Hope for the World," LWF Report No. 19/20 (February 1985), p. 216.

12. *Bonds of Affection: Proceedings of the Anglican Consultative Council—6, Badagry, Nigeria, 1984,* p. 101

13. *The Truth Shall Make You Free: The Lambeth Conference 1988,* pp. 204-206.

14. Minutes of the Executive Committee, The Lutheran World Federation, July 31-August 9, 1989, p. 21.

15. *Proceedings of the Eighth Assembly of the Lutheran World Federation,* LWF Report No. 28/29 (December 1990), p. 107.

16. *Many Voices One Song, 1989 Churchwide Assembly, Evangelical Lutheran Church in America,* Reports and Records, Vol. 2, pp. 423, 432-433.

17. *Ecumenism: The Vision of the Evangelical Lutheran Church in America* (Chicago: Office for Ecumenical Affairs, ELCA, 1989), p. 14. This is from No.3 of the listing of some of the characteristics of full communion.

## Chapter 1· The Historic Impasse

1. For a survey of these see J. Robert Wright, editor, *Quadrilateral at One Hundred* (Cincinnati: Forward Movement Publications, 1988), pp. 8-46.

2. Texts and references in Wright, *op.cit.,* pp. 41-42.

3. *LED I* (1972), p. 161, Par. 87.

4. *LED II* (1981), p. 16.

5. *Ibid.,* p. 21.

6. *LED I,* p. 162, Par. 89.

7. Report on "The Historic Episcopate," Division of Theological Studies, LCUSA (New York, 1984), p. 6.

8. *LED I,* pp. 135-136. It is most important to add that the paper continued with the following paragraph:

I do not see that the matter should be hopeless. As to the theology of the matter, it seems to me we have some progress. If the understanding arrived at in our last meeting is indeed satisfactory to both denominations, Lutherans should be happy. For the Lutheran position means that so long as the episcopacy—or any other "ceremony"—is not made an antecedent condition of communion, Lutherans are committed to limitless openness thereafter, both in investigating the inadequacy of their own previous arrangements and in achieving new arrangements for future forms of the church. The explicit recognition of "episcope" as an intrinsic function in the church has not been characteristic of Lutheranism; but it in no way violates Lutheran principle, and merely makes up a rather obvious lacuna in our thought. If some such statements as those achieved in our previous meeting could be adopted by an authoritative entity in each denomination, we would be past the point theologically sticky for Lutherans. Nor need Lutherans demand that this be the *only* statement on episcopacy in force in either denomination.

9. Statement on "The Unity We Seek," adopted by the Lutheran World Federation Assembly at Budapest in 1984. See Budapest 1984, p. 175. The entire statement is quoted in the ELCA statement, "Ecumenism: The Vision of the Evangelical Lutheran Church in America," reprinted in *A Commentary on "Ecumenism: The Vision of the ELCA"* (Minneapolis: Augsburg, 1990). See pp. 40-41.

10. *Papers of the Consultation;* Background for *The Niagara Report,* Geneva, 1987, p. 16.

11. J. Robert Wright, "Martin Luther: An Anglican Ecumenical Appreciation," *Anglican and Episcopal History*, Vol. 56, No.3 (September 1987), especially pp. 325-326.

12. Full text in *Journal of the General Convention, The Episcopal Church*, 1958, p. 445, and in *Ecumenical Bulletin* No.71 (May-June 1985), p. 35.

13. George A. Lindbeck, "Episcopacy and the Unification of the Churches; Two Approaches," in *Promoting Unity*, edited by H. George Anderson and James R. Crumley Jr. (Minneapolis: Augsburg, 1989), pp. 53-54.

14. Paragraph 28. Full text in *Ecumenical Trends*, Vol. 17, No.9 (October 1988), pp. 137-143.

15. Lindbeck, *op.cit.*, p. 52.


## Chapter 2: Theological Consensus

1. Werner Elert, *Abendmahl und Kirchengemeinschaft in der alten Kirche hauptsaechlich des Ostens* (Berlin: Lutherisches Verlagshaus, 1954), p. 90. Cf. the translation by N.E. Nagel, *Eucharist and Church Fellowship in the First Four Centuries* (St. Louis: Concordia Publishing House, 1966), p. 109, and the summary of Elert's classic analysis in Eugene Brand, *Toward a Lutheran Communion: Pulpit and Altar Fellowship*, LWF Report No.26 (Geneva: The Lutheran World Federation, 1988), pp. 17-19. Other literature on the subject includes F.J. Hort, *The Christian Ecclesia* (London and New York: MacMillian and Co., 1897), John Knox, *The Early Church and the Coming Great Church* (London: Epworth Press, 1957), Stephen Benko, *The Meaning of Sanctorum Communio* (Naperville: Alex R. Allenson, 1964), Jerome Hamer, O.P., *The Church Is a Communion* (London: Geoffrey Chapman, 1964), Hans von Campenhausen, *Ecclesiastical Authority and Spiritual Power in the Church of the First Three Centuries* (Stanford: Stanford University Press, 1969), Ludwig Hertling, S.J., *Communion; Church and Papacy in Early Christianity*, transl. Jared Wicks, S.J. (Chicago: Loyola University Press, 1972), Kenneth Hein, *Eucharist and Excommunication: A Study in Early Christian Doctrine and Discipline* (Frankfurt: Peter Lang, 1973), and Maurice Wiles, "Sacramental Unity in the Early Church," in *Church Membership and Intercommunion*, edited by John Kent and Robert Murray (London: Darton, Longman and Todd, 1973).

2. *LED I* (1972), pp. 14-22.

3. *LED II* (1981), pp. 22-43.

4. A similar summary appears in the bilingual Meissen Statement (1988) adopted by the Church of England and the Evangelical Church of Germany, *Auf dem Weg zu sichtbarer Einheit (On the Way to Visible Unity)*, pp. 16-19.

5. *LED I* (1972) pp. 20-22.

6. Full text in *Journal of the General Convention, The Episcopal Church*, 1976, pp. AA-75-AA-76, in *Ecumenical Bulletin* 17 (May-June 1976) pp. 8-11, and in *Ecumenical Trends* Vol. 5, No.10 (November 1976), pp. 154-156.

7. *LED II* (1981), pp. 31-53.

8. *Ibid.*, p. 40.

9. Michael Root, *"The Niagara Report:* A Possible Lutheran-Anglican Future?" *Dialog*, Vol. 28, No.4 (Autumn 1989), p. 300.

10. L. William Countryman, "The Holy Spirit and the Institutions of the Church With Particular Reference to the Historic Episcopate," *Anglican Theological Review*, Vol. LXVI, No.4 (1984), pp. 402-415.

11. *Ibid.*, p. 412.

12. Richard Norris regards this attitude as the first phase in the development of Anglican thought and practice with regard to churches *outside of England* whose ministries were not episcopally ordained. Prior to 1662, he writes, "the legitimacy of non-episcopal orders in foreign Churches was conceded on the precise ground of 'necessity', that is, on the ground that such Churches had in practice been compelled to make a choice—between reformation according to scriptural norms of doctrine and practice on the one hand, and, on the other, retention of episcopacy...Hence (the Anglican divines of the seventeenth century) commanded episcopal ordering of the Church at home (for domestic dissenters could make no claim of 'necessity') and commended it abroad, acknowledging their fellowship with Reformed Churches overseas." Richard

A. Norris, "Episcopacy," in *The Study of Anglicanism,* edited by Stephen Sykes and John Booty (Philadelphia: Fortress Press, 1988), p. 304. See also Norman Sykes, *Old Priest and New Presbyter* (Cambridge, 1956), and Paul F. Bradshaw, *The Anglican Ordinal* (London, 1971), Chapter 6.

13. *Ibid.,* p. 414.

14. *Ibid.*

15. Paul Berge, "A Response to Bill Countryman's paper, 'The Gospel and the Institutions of the Church'" (Unpublished Paper, Lutheran-Episcopal Dialogue III, June 10-13, 1984) p.1

16. *Ibid.,* p. 2.

17. *Ibid.,* p. 5.

18. *Ibid.*

19. *Ibid.,* p. 6.

20. William Countryman, "The Historic Episcopate: Further Reflections," Unpublished Paper, Lutheran-Episcopal Dialogue, June 1989, pp. 5-6.

21. "For Lutherans, the preservation of the Reformation heritage is vital. Anglicans have no objection to this; indeed, we see it as embodied in our existing ministry. If Lutherans feel it is insufficiently evident, they should help us see how to make it more so. For Lutherans themselves,the main issue may be how to ensure against any impression that existing orders are being abandoned in favor of something called 'historic episcopate'. Such abandonment might raise questions about the integrity of church life in the past, which would be a betrayal of blessings received and must surely be rejected. Accordingly, it is vital that any change in Lutheran rites of ordination should emphasize that continuity with the Reformation successions is not being broken. This could be done partly with a preface to the ordinal, identifying the distinct strands of succession that are being brought together, partly by bringing in the historic episcopate from Lutheran sources rather than or in addition to Anglican ones, partly by clearly limiting the new ordinal to use for new ordinations. Lutherans already have asserted, in the *Confessio Augustana,* the right of a gospel ministry of word and sacrament to ignore or circumvent those bishops who oppose its work. This, too, would act to preserve a Reformation perspective on the relativity of bishops." Countryman, *Ibid.,* pp. 7-8

22. J.N.D. Kelly, *Early Christian Creeds* (New York: David McKay Company, Inc., 1960), pp. 10-13.

23. Cf. L. William Countryman, "Tertullian and the Regula Fidei," *The Second Century* 2 (1982), pp. 208-227; see also J.N.D. Kelly, *op.cit.,* pp. 62-99, 205-230, and 368-397.

24. Robert Jenson, "Baptism," in Carl Braaten and Robert Jenson, editors, *Christian Dogmatics,* Vol. 2 (Philadelphia: Fortress Press, 1984), pp. 326-333.

25. This has come to be the standard account of the development of our liturgies. See such textbooks as *The Study of Liturgy,* ed. by Cheslyn Jones, Goeffrey Wainwright, and Edward Yarnold (New York: Oxford University Press, 1978), pp. 147-208.

26. Cf. Hans von Campenhausen, *Ecclesiastical Authority and Spiritual Power in the Church of the First Three Centuries* (London: Adam and Charles Black, 1969), pp. 149-177;Robert M. Grant, *Augustus to Constantine* (New York: Harper and Row, 1970), pp. 63-68, 145-160.

27. *Baptism, Eucharist and Ministry,* Faith and Order Paper 111 (Geneva: World Council of Churches, 1982), M. 19-20.

28. "The Chicago-Lambeth Quadrilateral of 1886-88," *Book of Common Prayer,* p. 878. Cf. "Formula of Concord," VII, 74-84, *Book of Concord,* pp. 583-584.

29. "The Chicago-Lambeth Quadrilateral of 1886-88," *op.cit.,* Cf. Chapter III,B, below, for the Lutheran version of episcopacy "locally adapted."

## Chapter 3: The Lutheran Churches and Episcopal Ministry

1. The regional histories are presented in Ivar Asheim and Victor Gold, editors, *Episcopacy in the Lutheran Church?* (Philadelphia: Fortress Press, 1970). For an Anglican evaluation of the continental development cf. J. Robert Wright, "Martin Luther: An Anglican Ecumenical Appreciation," *op.cit.,* pp. 323-325.

2. Wilhelm Maurer, *Historical Commentary on the Augsburg Confession,* tr. by H. George Anderson (Philadelphia: Fortress Press, 1986), p. 15.

3. "The Babylonian Captivity of the Church," *Luther's Works,* American Edition (hereafter cited as LW), Vol. 36 (Philadelphia: Fortress Press, 1959), pp. 106-117. "Therefore this 'sacrament' of ordination, if it is anything at all, is nothing else than a certain rite whereby one is called to the ministry of the church. Furthermore, the priesthood is properly nothing but the ministry of the Word—the Word, I say; not the law, but the gospel. And the diaconate is the ministry, not of reading the Gospel or the Epistle, as is the present practice, but of distributing the church's aid to the poor, so that the priests may be relieved of the burden of temporal matters and may give themselves more freely to prayer and the Word...Whoever, therefore, does not know or preach the gospel is not only no priest or bishop, but he is a kind of pest to the church." Page 116. See however Apology XIII:11-12, which states, "If ordination is interpreted in relation to the ministry of the Word, we have no objection to calling ordination a sacrament. The ministry of the Word has God's command and glorious promises...If ordination is interpreted this way, we shall not object either to calling the laying on of hands a sacrament."

4. The 1979 Book of Common Prayer, p. 872. Article XXV reads in part: "Those five commonly called sacraments, that is to say, Confirmation, Penance, Orders, Matrimony, and Extreme Unction, are not to be counted for Sacraments of the Gospel, being such as have grown partly of the corrupt following of the Apostles, partly are states of life allowed in the Scriptures; but yet have not like nature of Sacraments with Baptism, and the Lord's Supper, for that they have not any visible sign or ceremony ordained of God." This is cited simply to indicate that Martin Luther's views were widely shared by other reforming traditions in the 16th century.

5. LW, Vol. 40, p. 11. "For the time being I will concede the papal ordinations whereby those whom they call priests are anointed and appointed by the authority of the bishop alone without any consent or election by the people over whom they are to be placed."

6. Cf. Robert Goeser, "Word, Ministry, and Episcopacy according to the Confessions," *The Lutheran Quarterly,* Vol. IV, No.1 (Spring 1990), p. 51.

7. Eric Gritsch, "Episcopacy: The Legacy of the Lutheran Confessions," Unpublished Paper, Lutheran-Episcopal Dialogue III, June 17-20, 1990, p. 20.

8. Cf. Peter Brunner, *Nikolaus von Amsdorf als Bischof von Naumburg* (Guetersloh: Guetersloher Verlagshaus Gerd Mohn, 1961).

9. This is similar to the role of the "godly prince" in England described by Richard Norris, "Episcopacy," *op.cit.,* p. 297.

10. *Episcopacy in the Lutheran Church?,* p. 65.

11. Richard Norris describes the problems and distortions attendant upon similar development in England. The life of the church "was openly subjected to the secular, civil authority of Parliament; and its bishops, whose votes in the House of Lords had become necessary to the continuance in office of any government, were becoming political figures, whose attention to pastoral duties, even given the best intentions, had to be severely limited." "Episcopacy," *op.cit.,* p. 305. Cf. also the final paragraph on p. 308.

12. Gritsch, *op.cit.,* p. 20.

13. Cf. *The Niagara Report,* pp. 66-67, for a listing of titles in use in German territorial churches.

14. Svend Borregaard, "The Post-Reformation Developments of the Episcopacy in Denmark, Norway, and Iceland," in Asheim and Gold, editors, *op.cit.,* pp. 116-124.

15. In 1575 "the medieval ritual of episcopal consecration with anointing was used. Among the participants was Bishop Juusten of Turku about whose own earlier consecration there is no doubt. But it cannot be stated with certainty whether or not it was the intention to restore the apostolic succession through the participation of Juusten in the rite of consecration of the new bishop. Scholars are uncertain about this. Sven Kjoellerstroem for instance considers the succession definitely to have been broken during the sixteenth century. (See footnote 14, pp. 239-240.) But it is evident that during the latter part of the sixteenth century there was a clear desire to restore the traditional episcopate." Martii Parvio, "The Post-Reformation Developments of the Episcopacy in Sweden, Finland, and the Baltic States," in Asheim and Gold, editors, op.cit., p. 129.

16. John Reumann, *Ministries Examined* (Minneapolis: Augsburg, 1987), pp. 140-164, especially pp. 156-157.

17. John Reumann, *ibid.,* pp. 199-223, has a description of the debate on ministry in the process which led to the formation of the ELCA.

18. Cf. Avery Dulles and George A. Lindbeck, "Bishops and the Ministry of the Gospel," in George W. Forell and James F. McCue, editors, *Confessing One Faith* (Minneapolis: Augsburg, 1982), pp. 147-172; Robert Goeser, "The Historic Episcopate and the Lutheran Confessions," *Lutheran Quarterly,* Vol. 1, No.2 (Summer 1987), pp. 214-232; Michael Root, "The Augsburg Confession as Ecumenical Proposal: Episcopacy, Luther and Wilhelm Maurer," *Dialog,* Vol. 28, No.3 (Summer 1989), pp. 223-232; William Lazareth, "Evangelical Episcopate," *Lutheran Forum,* Vol. 22, No.4 (November 1988), pp. 13-17; Robert Goeser, "Word, Ministry, and Episcopacy according to the Confessions," *Lutheran Quarterly* 4 (1990) pp. 45-59.

19. Wilhelm Maurer, *op.cit.,* esp. pp. 59-89 and 174-236.

20. *Ibid.,* p. 81. Cf. "Address to the Christian Nobility," of 1520. LW, Vol. 44, p. 127.

21. *Ibid.,* p. 82. Cf. "The Babylonian Captivity of the Church," LW, Vol. 36, pp. 106, 111, 113.

22. *Ibid.,* p. 83. Cf. "Concerning the Ministry," LW, Vol. 40, pp. 13, 37, 40.

23. *Ibid.,* p. 84. Cf. "Instructions for the Visitors of Parish Pastors in Electoral Saxony," LW, Vol. 40, pp. 269-273. In "On War Against the Turk," of 1529, LW, Vol. 46, p. 165, Luther writes that "if the pope and the bishops were involved in the war, they would bring the greatest shame and dishonor to Christ's name because they are called to fight against the devil with the word of God and with prayer, and they would be deserting their calling and office to fight with the sword against flesh and blood."

24. *Ibid.,* p. 59.

25. LW, Vol. 34, pp. 9-61.

26. Maurer, *op.cit.,* p. 71.

27. *Ibid.,* pp. 69-70.

28. *Ibid.,* p. 79.

29. Weimar edition, Vol. 30, Part 2. Cf. the summary in Maurer, *op.cit.,* pp. 225-230.

30. Maurer, *op.cit.,* p. 228.

31. *Ibid.,* p. 80.

32. The constitution of the ELCA states, in Chapter 2, "Confession of Faith," Paragraph 2.05: This church accepts the Unaltered Augsburg Confession as a true witness to the Gospel, acknowledging as one with it in faith and doctrine all churches that likewise accept the teaching of the Unaltered Augsburg Confession, and in Paragraph 2.06: This church accepts the other confessional writings in the Book of Concord, namely, the Apology of the Augsburg Confession, the Smalcald Articles and the Treatise, the Small Catechism, the Large Catechism, and the Formula of Concord, as further valid interpretations of the faith of the Church.

33. It is not necessary here to present a full doctrine of ministry in the Lutheran Confessions. For such a full doctrine see Arthur Carl Piepkorn, "The Sacred Ministry and Holy Ordination in the Symbolical Books of the Lutheran Church," in *Eucharist, and Ministry,* Lutherans and Catholics in Dialogue IV (1970), pp. 101-119, and George A. Lindbeck, "The Lutheran Doctrine of the Ministry: Catholic and Reformed," *Theological Studies* 30:4 (December 1969), pp. 588-612. The most careful analysis of the doctrine of ministry in the Lutheran Confessions to come out of the 19th century debate on the subject is Theodosius Harnack, *Die Kirche, Ihr Amt, Ihr Regiment* (Nuremberg, 1862). Foundational for 20th century study of the Lutheran Confessions is Werner Elert, *Morphologie des Luthertums,* Vol. 1 (Munich: C.H. Beck Publisher, 1931), pp. 297-335. (The English translation is by Walter Hanson, *The Structure of Lutheranism,* published in St. Louis by Concordia Publishing House in 1962. See pp. 339-385 for the discussion on ministry.) Among the most widely recognized works on the Lutheran Confessions are Edmund Schlink, *Theology of the Lutheran Confessions* (first German edition, 1940) (Philadelphia: Muhlenberg Press, 1961), pp. 226-269; Friedrich Brunstaed, *Theologie der Lutherischen Bekenntnisschriften* (Guetersloh: C. Bertelsmann Verlag, 1951), pp. 114-134, 198-212; Leif Grane, *The Augsburg Confession: A Commentary* (first published in 1959) (Minneapolis: Augsburg, 1987), pp. 151-158; Holsten Fagerberg, *A New Look at the Lutheran Confessions* (first published in Sweden in the 1960s) (St. Louis: Concordia Publishing House,

1972), pp. 226-250; and Erich Gritsch and Robert Jenson, *Lutheranism: The Theological Movement and Its Confessional Writings* (Philadelphia: Fortress Press, 1976), pp. 110-123.

34. Cf. George Lindbeck, "Episcopacy," in *Promoting Unity, op.cit.,* pp. 52-53. Lindbeck states, "All three of these elements of traditional episcopal polity (viz. that there be individual persons specially charged with oversight, and they be ordaining and ordained) are more than *adiaphora,* more than matters of indifference. Other things being equal, they are positively desirable. The statement of the *Apology* regarding 'our deep desire to maintain the church polity' should be interpreted as an expression of theological principle rather than as a historically outworn response to sixteenth century circumstances."

35. E.g., *Lutheran-Episcopal Dialogue*(LED II), p. 35; and *Lutherans and Catholics in Dialogue,* Vol. IV ("Eucharist and Ministry"), pp. 106-107, 110.

36. All quotations from the Lutheran Confessional Documents are from *The Book of Concord,* edited by Theodore G. Tappert (Philadelphia, Muhlenberg Press, 1959). The sources are identified in parentheses in the text by the initials of the documents (CA for the Augsburg Confession, Apol. for the Apology of the Augsburg Confession, SA for the Smalcald Articles of 1537, and TR for the Treatise on the Power and Primacy of the Pope), followed by the number of the article in Latin numerals (where applicable) and the number of the paragraph in arabic numerals. Because the translation is from 1959 there is no attention to the use of gender-inclusive language. Because both the Latin and the German texts of the Augsburg Confession are equally official, the Tappert edition translates both, the German text at the top of each page, the Latin text below it. The letter "G" will indicate that the translation of the German text is being quoted. The letter "L" will indicate that the translation of the Latin text is being quoted. The critical edition of the texts of the Lutheran confessional writings is *Die Bekenntnisschriften der evangelisch-lutherischen Kirche,* 2nd edition (Goettingen: Vandenhoeck and Ruprecht, 1952).

37. Herbert Immenkoetter, *Der Reichstag zu Augsburg und die Confutatio* (Muenster: Aschendorf, 1979), p. 59.

38. Maurer, *op.cit.,* pp. 188-204, esp. pp. 191-197.

39. This translation follows the official German text of the Augsburg Confession which reads simply, "Derhalben ist da bishoflich Ambt nach gottlichen Rechten das Evangelium predigen," etc. The official Latin text contains a slight variation: "Proinde secundum evangelium seu, ut loquuntur, de jure divino haec jurisdictio competit episcopis ut episcopis," etc. J. Michael Miller, *The Divine Right of the Papacy in Recent Ecumenical Theology* (Analecta Gregoriana Vol. 218; Rome: Universita Gregoriana Editrice, 1980), Part II, pp. 69-134, shows that both Lutherans and Anglicans have a similar concept of "divine right."

40. Walter Kasper gives additional citations from Irenaeus and Augustine up to Thomas Aquinas which state not only that individual bishops can repudiate the *traditio* and therefore fall from the *communio,* but also that one does not owe them obedience. "Therefore, the ancient and the medieval church know repeated instances of the deposition and condemnation of bishops and even popes. There are instances of whole synods teaching heterodoxy and whose teaching is therefore not to be received. There are times when it is not the bishops, but the faithful, who hand on the true faith." (Unofficial translation from the German original, p. 337) Cf. Walter Kasper, "Die apostolische Sukzession als oekumenisches Problem," *Lehrverurteilungen—Kirchentrennend?* III. Materialien zur Lehre von den Sakramenten und vom kirchlichen Amt. (Freiburg: Herder Verlag, 1990), pp. 329-349, especially p. 337.

41. Grane, *The Augsburg Confession, op.cit.,* p. 152: "The perspective applied here to the division in the church is worthy of note, because it was the perspective of the reformers as a whole. True, the formulation of the CA is shaped by the church-political situation in 1530 in many ways, but its general aim—to demonstrate that the Lutheran Reformation has nothing to do with the formulations of a new church, but is the result of the hierarchy's falling away—has nothing to do with church political tactics." Cf. also pp. 157-158, where Grane concludes: "Precisely because the Lutheran reformers do not consider themselves church founders, it is logical that the AC regards the office of bishop as being normal in the church."

42. Cf. Maurer, *op.cit.,* pp. 194-195: "Commitment to tradition, however, does not prevent rejection of ordination as a sacrament nor openness to new legal forms for the call and ordering of the office. Luther, as we have already seen in his Confession of 1528, recognized a threefold

preaching office. He did not simply equate the office of bishop with that of pastor; instead, he allowed the higher office of oversight (*antistites*) to continue. Its incumbents are 'to oversee all offices, so that the teachers exercise their office and do not neglect it, the deacons distribute goods properly and do not become weary; to punish sinners and invoke the ban promptly so that every office is conducted rightly.'

"Luther's renewal of the diaconate is little known and did not last long in Lutheranism. The reason doubtless lies in the fact that CA 14 does not mention this office or a call to it....He himself had a clear picture of the ancient church's practice: the deacon is, as servant of the bishop, likewise servant of the congregation...

"Occasional statements of Luther then, indicate that he adopted the traditional threefold division of the pastoral office...One thing is clear: these offices derived from the pastoral office—the bishop on a higher level and the preacher on a lower one—serve the truth and the effectiveness of the gospel."

43. See the extensive bibliography in Gert Haendler, *Luther on Ministerial Office and Congregational Function* (Philadelphia: Fortress Press, 1981), pp. 103-110.

44. *Lutherans and Catholics in Dialogue,* Vol. IV, "Eucharist and Ministry," p. 25.

45. The information comes from the introduction to the Treatise in the *Book of Concord,* p. 319. Cf. *Die Bekenntnisschriften der evangelisch-lutherischen Kirche,* p. XXVI.

46. That is, before the Religious Peace of Augsburg of 1555.

47. Walter Kasper, *op.cit.,* p. 339, points out that in Cologne (and there were similar occurrences elsewhere) more than one archbishop had not been consecrated bishop at all. Further, there are numerous instances in the Middle Ages of individual priests who received from popes the authority to ordain.

48. The church "is the mother that begets and bears every Christian through the Word of God," Martin Luther, Large Catechism, Creed, Par. 42.

49. Cf. Lindbeck, "The Lutheran Doctrine of the Ministry: Catholic and Reformed," *op.cit.,* pp. 593-594. Article XXI of the Augsburg Confession concludes: "This is about the sum of our teaching. As can be seen, there is nothing here that departs from scriptures or the catholic church or the church of Rome, insofar as the ancient church is known to us from its writers." Cf. the Evangelical Lutheran Church in America's provisional statement on "Ecumenism" and its definition of "catholic": "To be *catholic* means to be committed to the fullness of the apostolic faith and its creedal, doctrinal articulation for the entire world (Rom. 10:8b-15, 18b;Mark 13:10;Matt. 28:19 20). This word 'catholic' declares that the church is a community, rooted in the Christ event, extending through all places and time. It acknowledges that God has gathered a people, and continues to do so, into a community made holy in the Gospel, which it receives and proclaims. This community, a people under Christ, shares the catholic faith in the Triune God, honors and relies upon the Holy Scriptures as authoritative source and norm of the church's proclamation, receives Holy Baptism and celebrates the Lord's Supper, includes an ordained ministry and professes one, holy, catholic, and apostolic Church." *A Commentary on "Ecumenism: The Vision of the ELCA,"* *op.cit.,* p. 66.

50. LED I, p. 21.

51. LED I, p. 22.

52. LED I, p. 136. Emphasis added. See page 15, footnote 25.

53. "Pullach Report," Par. 89, quoted in LED I, p. 162. Emphasis added.

54. LED I, pp. 172-73.

55. LED II, p. 63.

56. ALERC Report, 1982, Par. 43, quoted in Norgren, *What Can We Share?,* p. 70.

57. "The Historic Episcopate," published by the Division of Theological Studies, Lutheran Council in the USA, 1984, p. 7.

58. *Ibid.,* p. 10.

59. These positive responses are contained in the response of the American Lutheran Church to BEM published in Max Thurian, editor, *Churches Respond to BEM,* Vol. II (Geneva: World Council of Churches, 1986), pp. 80-84. It should also be added that the response of the Standing Committee on Inter-Church Relations of the American Lutheran Church, adopted by the Church Council of the American Lutheran Church, was generally critical of BEM's advocacy of the

threefold ministry of bishop, presbyter, and deacon. Cf. Michael Root, "'Do Not Grow Weary in Well-Doing': Lutheran Responses to the BEM Ministry Document," *Dialog*, Vol. 27, No.1 (Winter 1988), pp. 23-30. Root concludes (p. 29): "As the survey conducted here should make clear, to affirm the agenda-setting function of BEM is not to deny the significant problems in its Ministry text. Nevertheless, simply to reject the BEM Ministry text is to reject the mainstream of Lutheran ecumenism around the world. The Lutheran judgment is that this text provides the appropriate springboard for the continuing ecumenical discussion of ministry."

Cf. also Michael Seils, *Lutheran Convergence?*, LWF Report No.25, September 1988, which is "an analysis of the Lutheran responses to the convergence document *Baptism, Eucharist and Ministry.*"

60. In addition to affirming the same features of BEM as those previously ascribed to the response of the American Lutheran Church, the response of the Lutheran Church in America affirms the features listed subsequently. They are cited in Max Thurian, editor, *Churches Respond to BEM*, Vol. I (Geneva: World Council of Churches, 1986), pp. 33-37. The response of the Lutheran Church in America is open to BEM's advocacy of the threefold ministry of bishop, presbyter, and deacon.

61. Note Paras. 25, 38, and 53 of Section III, "Ministry," in *Baptism, Eucharist and Ministry*.

62. Constitution of the Evangelical Lutheran Church in America, 10.11.A87.

## Chapter 4: The Episcopal Church and the Ministry of the Historic Episcopate

1. G.R. Elton, *The Tudor Constitution* (Cambridge: University Press, 1960), p. 350.

2. Cf. Paul F. Bradshaw, *op.cit.,* Chapter 2.

3. "A Declaration of the Queen's Proceedings Since Her Reign," in W.E. Collins, *Queen Elizabeth's Defense of Her Proceedings in Church and State* (London: S.P.C.K., 1963), p. 45.

4. Cf. Richard Spielmann, "The Beginning of Clerical Marriage in the English Reformation: The Reigns of Edward and Mary," *Anglican and Episcopal History*, Vol. 56, No.3 (September 1987), pp. 251-263.

5. F.D. Price, "Gloucester Diocese under Bishop Hooper," *Transactions of the Bristol and Gloucester Archeological Society* 60:51-151.

6. Cited in J. Booty, *John Jewel as Apologist of the Church of England* (London: S.P.C.K., 1963), p. 23.

7. Cf. P.M. Dawley, *John Whitgift and the English Reformation* (New York: Charles Scribner's Sons, 1954), pp. 140ff.

8. Richard Hooker, *Ecclesiastical Polity*, Book VII, chapter xiv,11: *The Works of that Learned and Judicious Divine, Mr. Richard Hooker*, ed. John Keble, sixth edition, Vol. III, pp. 231-232; punctuation modernized.

9. Cited in Leland H. Carlson, *Martin Marprelate, Gentlemen; Master Job Throckmorton Laid Open in His Colors* (San Marino: Huntington Library, 1981), p. 9.

10. W.D.J. Cargill Thompson, "The Philosopher of the 'Politic Society': Richard Hooker as a Political Thinker," in *Studies in Richard Hooker*, ed. W. Speed Hill (Cleveland and London: Case Western Reserve University, 1972), p. 57.

11. Cf. especially LED II, *op.cit.,* p. 42, note 1; also Norman Sykes, *op.cit.,* and Richard Norris, Episcopacy, *op.cit.,* pp. 304-305.

12. Manuscripts of these patristic texts, which had been lost to the medieval Western church, were rediscovered in the 17th century and led to authoritative editions in England: The First Epistle of Clement (1633), and the Letters of Ignatius of Antioch (1644, 1672).

13. Norris, "Episcopacy," *op.cit.,* p. 305.

14. Desmond Bowen, *The Idea of the Victorian Church; A Study of the Church of England, 1830-1889* (Montreal: McGill University Press, 1968), p. 51 and see p. 87 (citing Tract 1). Also E.R. Fairweather, *The Oxford Movement* (New York: Oxford University Press, 1964), pp. 55-59.

15. Frederick Denison Maurice, *The Kingdom of Christ* (1838; reprinted London: S.C.M. Press, 1958, ed. A.R. Vidler), Vol. II, p. 106.

16. Maurice's view as summarized in B.M.G. Reardon, *From Coleridge to Gore: A Century of Religious Thought in Britain* (London: Longman, 1971), pp. 180-181.

17. Cf. Frederick V. Mills, Sr., *Bishops by Ballot: An Eighteenth Century Ecclesiastical Revolution* (New York: Oxford University Press, 1978).

18. Robert Goeser and William H. Petersen, *Traditions Transplanted: The Story of Anglican and Lutheran Churches in America* (Cincinnati: Forward Movement Publications, 1981), p. 36.

19. Book of Common Prayer (U.S.A., 1979), p. 877.

20. *Conference of Bishops of the Anglican Communion holden at Lambeth Place, July 5 to August 7, 1920* (London: S.P.C.K., 1920), pp. 27-28.

21. *Ibid.,* p. 28.

22. *Ibid.,* p. 28-29.

23. *Journal of the General Convention, 1979,* p. C-46. Cf. J. Robert Wright, editor, *A Communion of Communions: One Eucharistic Fellowship* (New York: Seabury Press, 1979), pp. 3-29, and especially pp. 23-24 for application to Lutheran-Episcopal dialogue, and pp. 185-211 for the essay on "The Concordat Relationships."

24. *The COCU Consensus: In Quest of a Church of Christ Uniting,* edited by Gerald F. Moede (1984), pp. 48-50.

25. *God's Reign and Our Unity:* The Report of the Anglican-Reformed International Commission 1984 (London: S.P.C.K., 1984), p. 57, Par. 90.

26. See Chapter 11, Paragraph 19, above for the full text of this section of the report.

27. *Journal of the General Convention 1982,* pp. C-56-C-57. On the Anglican understanding of apostolicity, see also *Anglican-Orthodox Dialogue: The Dublin Agreed Statement 1984* (St. Vladimir's Seminary Press, 1985), pp. 13-14.

28. Book of Common Prayer (U.S.A., 1979), p. 855 ("An Outline of the Faith").

29. *Ibid.,* p. 517. In the emphases of Irenaeus, Ignatius, and Cyprian, respectively, each of these three paragraphs is mirrored in the writings of the early church.

30. *Ibid.,* p. 521. Much of this wording is paraphrased from the earliest prayer for the ordination of a bishop, *The Apostolic Tradition* of Hippolytus, dating from the early third century.

31. *Ibid.,* p. 510.

## Chapter 5: The Gift of Full Communion

1. Norgren, *What Can We Share?*, pp. 90-92.

2. *The Niagara Report,* Paras. 25-26.

3. Cf. Paras. 41-59 of T*he Niagara Report,* for a brief survey of the history of ministerial structure in the life of the church, and "Ministry," Paras. 19-25, in *Baptism, Eucharist and Ministry* for a similar brief survey. Cf. Also William H. Petersen and Robert Goeser, *Traditions Transplanted: The Story of Anglican and Lutheran Churches in America* (Cincinnati: Forward Movement Publications, 1981).

4. Norgren, *What Can We Share?,* Paras. 26-27, pp. 91-92.

5. *The Niagara Report,* Par. 94.

6. *The Truth Shall Make You Free,* p. 204.

7. Quoted in *Consensus:* A Canadian Lutheran Journal of Theology, Vol. 12, Nos. 1-2 (1986), p. 15.

8. Cf. Mary Tanner, "The Goal of Unity in Theological Dialogues Involving Anglicans," *Einheit der Kirche,* edited by Gunther Gassman and Peder Norgaard Hojen (Frankfurt: Verlag Otto Lembeck, 1988) pp. 69-78.

9. Cf. Michael Root, "Full Communion Between Episcopalians and Lutherans in North America: What Would It Look Like?" Unpublished Paper, Lutheran-Episcopal Dialogue III, June 17-20, 1990, p.14.

10. Michael Root, "Bishops as Points of Unity and Continuity," Unpublished Paper, Lutheran-United Methodist Dialogue, May 1986.

11. Cf. Letty M. Russell, *Household of Freedom: Authority in Feminist Theology* (Philadelphia: Westminster Press, 1987), pp. 17-25.

12. Cf. John D. Zizioulas, *Being as Communion* (St. Vladimir's Seminary Press: 1985), pp. 171-208.

13. An example of this call is the remark of St. Thomas More in *Utopia* (Baltimore: Penguin Books, 1965), p. 124, "Male priests are allowed to marry—for there's nothing to stop a woman from becoming a priest." It should also be noted that More wrote *Utopia* in 1516, before the controversies of the Reformation broke out. He later modified his position.

14. Much of the text which follows is indebted to portions of *The Niagara Report*, Pars. 75-87.

15. *The Niagara Report*, Pars. 100-109, identifies a series of questions which can appropriately be addressed to the current form of the historic episcopate.

# "Concordat of Agreement"

## PREFACE

The Lutheran-Episcopal Dialogue, Series III, proposes this Concordat of Agreement to its sponsoring bodies for consideration and action by The General Convention of the Episcopal Church and the Churchwide Assembly of the Evangelical Lutheran Church in America in implementation of the goal mandated by the Lutheran-Epicsopal Agreement of 1982. That agreement identified the goal as "full communion (*communio in sacris*/altar and pulpit fellowship)."[1] As the meaning of "full communion" for purposes of this Concordat of Agreement both churches endorse in principle the definitions agreed to by the (international) Anglican-Lutheran Joint Working Group at Cold Ash, Berkshire, England, in 1983,[2] which they deem to be in full accord with their own definitions given in the Evangelical Lutheran Church in America's working document, "Ecumenism: The Vision of the ELCA" (1989), and given in the "Declaration on Unity" of the Episcopal Church, General Convention of 1979. During the process of consideration of the Concordat of Agreement it is expected that our churches will consult with sister churches in our respective communions (through, for example, the Anglican Consultative Council and the Lutheran World Federation) as well as those with whom we are currently engaged in dialogue.

## CONCORDAT OF AGREEMENT

1. The Episcopal Church hereby agrees that in its General Convention, and the Evangelical Lutheran Church in America hereby agrees that in its Churchwide Assembly, there shall be one vote to accept or reject, as a matter of verbal content as well as in principle, and without separate amendment, the full set of agreements to follow. If they are adopted by both churches, each church agrees to make those legislative, canonical, constitutional, and liturgical changes that are necessary and appropriate for the full communion between the churches which these agreements are designed to implement

325

without further vote on the Concordat of Agreement by either the General
Convention or the Churchwide Assembly.


## A. Actions of Both Churches

*Agreement in the Doctrine of the Faith*
    2. The Evangelical Lutheran Church in America and the Episcopal
Church hereby recognize in each other the essentials of the one catholic and
apostolic faith as it is witnessed in the unaltered Augsburg Confession (CA),
the Small Catechism, and The Book of Common Prayer of 1979 (including
the "Episcopal Services" and "An Outline of the Faith"), and as it is summarized in part in *Implications of the Gospel* and *Toward Full Communion
between the Episcopal Church and the Evangelical Lutheran Church in
America,* the reports of Lutheran-Episcopal Dialogue III,[3] and as it has been
examined in both the papers and fourteen official conversations of Series III.[4]
Each church also promises to require its ordination candidates to study each
other's basic documents.

*Joint Participation in the Consecration of Bishops*
    3. In the course of history many and various terms have been used to
describe the rite by which a person becomes a bishop. In the English language these terms include: ordaining, consecrating, ordering, making, con-
fecting, constituting, installing.
    What is involved is a setting apart with prayer and the laying-on-of-
hands by other bishops of a person for the distinct ministry of bishop within
the one ministry of Word and Sacrament. As a result of their agreement in
faith, both churches hereby pledge themselves, beginning at the time that this
agreement is accepted by the General Convention of the Episcopal Church
and the Churchwide Assembly of the Evangelical Lutheran Church in
America, to the common joint ordinations of all future bishops as apostolic
missionaries in the historic episcopate for the sake of common mission.[5]
    Each church hereby promises to invite and include on an invariable
basis at least three bishops of the other church, as well as three of its own, to
participate in the laying-on-of-hands at the ordination of its own bishops.[6]
Such a participation is the liturgical form by which the church recognizes
that the bishop serves the local or regional church through ties of collegiality
and consultation whose purpose is to provide links with the universal
church.[7] Inasmuch as both churches agree that a ministry of *episkope* is necessary to witness to, promote, and safeguard the unity and apostolicity of the
church and its continuity in doctrine and mission across time and space,[8] this
participation is understood as a call for mutual planning, consultation, and

interaction in *episkope*, mission, teaching, and pastoral care as well as a liturgical expression of the full communion that is being initiated by this Concordat of Agreement. Each church understands that the bishops in this action are representatives of their own churches in fidelity to the teaching and mission of the apostles. Their participation in this way embodies the historical continuity of each bishop and the diocese or synod with the apostolic church and ministry through the ages.[9]

## B. Actions of the Episcopal Church

4. In light of the agreement that the threefold ministry of bishops, presbyters, and deacons in historic succession will be the future pattern of the one ordained ministry of Word and Sacrament in both churches as they begin to live in full communion,[10] the Episcopal Church hereby recognizes now the full authenticity of the ordained ministries presently existing within the Evangelical Lutheran Church in America. The Episcopal Church acknowledges the pastors and bishops of the Evangelical Lutheran Church in America as priests within the Evangelical Lutheran Church in America and the bishops of the Evangelical Lutheran Church in America as chief pastors exercising a ministry of *episkope* over the jurisdictional areas of the Evangelical Lutheran Church in America in which they preside.[11]

5. To enable the full communion that is coming into being by means of the Concordat of Agreement, the Episcopal Church hereby pledges, at the same time that this Concordat of Agreement is accepted by its General Convention and by the Churchwide Assembly of the Evangelical Lutheran Church in America, to begin the process for enacting a temporary suspension, in this case only, of the 17th century restriction that "no persons are allowed to exercise the offices of bishop, priest, or deacon in this Church unless they are so ordained, or have already received such ordination with the laying on of hands by bishops who are themselves duly qualified to confer Holy Orders."[12] The purpose of this action will be to permit the full interchangeability and reciprocity of all Evangelical Lutheran Church in America pastors as priests or presbyters and all Evangelical Lutheran Church in America deacons as deacons in the Episcopal Church without any further ordination or re-ordination or supplemental ordination whatsoever, subject always to canonically or constitutionally approved invitation (see pars. 14, 15, and 16 below). The purpose of temporarily suspending this restriction, which has been a constant requirement in Anglican polity since the Ordinal of 1662,[13] is precisely in order to secure the future implementation of the ordinals' same principle within the eventually fully integrated ministries. It is for this reason that the Episcopal Church can feel confident in taking this

unprecedented step with regard to the Evangelical Lutheran Church in America.

6. The Episcopal Church hereby endorses the Lutheran affirmation that the historic catholic episcopate under the Word of God must always serve the gospel,[14] and that the ultimate authority under which bishops preach and teach is the gospel itself.[15] In testimony and implementation thereof, the Episcopal Church agrees to establish and welcome, either by itself or jointly with the Evangelical Lutheran Church in America, structures for collegial and periodic review of its episcopal ministry, as well as that of the Evangelical Lutheran Church in America, with a view to evaluation, adaptation, improvement, and continual reform in the service of the gospel.[16]

## C. Actions of the Evangelical Lutheran Church in America

7. The Evangelical Lutheran Church in America agrees that all its bishops will be understood as ordained, like other pastors, for life service of the gospel in the pastoral ministry of the historic episcopate,[17] even though tenure in office of the churchwide bishop and synodical bishops may be terminated by retirement, resignation, or conclusion of term however constitutionally ordered. The Evangelical Lutheran Church in America further agrees to revise its rite for the "Installation of a Bishop"[18] to reflect this understanding. In keeping with these principles the Evangelical Lutheran Church in America also agrees to revise its constitution (e.g., 16.51.41.) so that all bishops, including those no longer active, shall be regular members of the Conference of Bishops.[19]

8. As regards ordained ministry, the Evangelical Lutheran Church in America affirms, in the context of its confessional heritage, the teaching of the Augsburg Confession that Lutherans do not intend to depart from the historic faith and practice of catholic Christianity.[20] The Evangelical Lutheran Church in America therefore agrees to make constitutional and liturgical provision that only bishops shall ordain all clergy. Presbyters shall continue to participate in the laying-on-of-hands at all ordinations of presbyters. It is further understood that episcopal and presbyteral office in the church is to be understood and exercised as servant ministry, and not for domination or arbitrary control.[21] Appropriate liturgical expression of these understandings will be made.[22] Both churches acknowledge that the diaconate, including its place within the threefold ministerial office, is in need of continued study and reform, which they pledge themselves to undertake in consultation with one another.[23]

9. In light of the above agreements and of the actions of the Episcopal Church, the Evangelical Lutheran Church in America hereby recognizes now

the full authenticity of the ordained ministries presently existing within the Episcopal Church, acknowledging the bishops, priests, and deacons of the Episcopal Church all as pastors in their respective orders within the Episcopal Church and the bishops of the Episcopal Church as chief pastors in the historic succession exercising a ministry of *episkope* over the jurisdictional areas of the Episcopal Church in which they preside. In preparation for the full communion that is coming into being by means of this Concordat of Agreement, the Evangelical Lutheran Church in America also pledges, at the time that this Concordat of Agreement is accepted by the Churchwide Assembly of the Evangelical Lutheran Church in America and the General Convention of the Episcopal Church, to begin the process for enacting a dispensation for ordinands of the Episcopal Church from its ordination requirement of subscription to the unaltered Augsburg Confession (Constitution of the Evangelical Lutheran Church in America 10:21) in order to permit the full interchangeability and reciprocity of all Episcopal Church bishops as bishops, of all Episcopal Church priests as pastors, and of all Episcopal Church deacons as may be determined (see Par. 8 above), within the Evangelical Lutheran Church in America without any supplemental oath or subscription, subject always to canonically or constitutionally approved invitation (see Pars. 14, 15, and 16 below). The purpose of this dispensation, which heretofore has not been made by the Evangelical Lutheran Church in America for the clergy of any other church, is precisely in order to serve the future implementation, in the full communion that will follow, of the agreement in the doctrine of the faith identified in Paragraph 2 (above) of this Concordat of Agreement.

## D. Actions of Both Churches

*Joint Commission*

10. Both churches hereby authorize the establishment of a joint ecumenical/doctrinal/liturgical commission to moderate the details of these changes, to assist joint planning for mission, to facilitate consultation and common decision making through appropriate channels in fundamental matters that the churches may face together in the future, to enable the process of new consecrations/ordinations of bishops in both churches as they occur, and to issue guidelines as requested and as may seem appropriate. It will prepare a national service that will celebrate the inauguration of this Concordat of Agreement as a common obedience to Christ in mission. At this service the mutual recognition of faith will be celebrated and, if possible, new bishops from each church will be consecrated/ordained for the synods or dioceses that have elected them, initiating the provisions hereby agreed upon.

*Wider Context*

11. In thus moving to establish one ordained ministry in geographically overlapping episcopates, open to women as well as to men, to married persons as well as to single persons, both churches agree that the historic catholic episcopate, which they embrace, can be locally adapted and reformed in the service of the gospel. In this spirit they offer this Concordat of Agreement and growth toward full communion for serious consideration among the churches of the Reformation as well as among the Orthodox and Roman Catholic churches. They pledge widespread consultation during the process at all stages. Each church promises to issue no official commentary on this text that has not been approved by the joint commission as a legitimate interpretation thereof.

*Existing Relationships*

12. Each church agrees that the other church will continue to live in communion with all the churches with whom the latter is now in communion. Each church also pledges prior consultation about this Concordat of Agreement with those churches. The Evangelical Lutheran Church in America continues to be in full communion (pulpit and altar fellowship) with all member churches of the Lutheran World Federation. This Concordat of Agreement with the Episcopal Church does not imply or inaugurate any automatic communion between the Episcopal Church and the other member churches of the Lutheran World Federation. The Episcopal Church continues to be in full communion with all of the provinces of the Anglican Communion, and with Old Catholic Churches of Europe, with the united churches of the Indian sub-continent, with the Mar Thoma Church, and with the Philippine Independent Church. This Concordat of Agreement with the Evangelical Lutheran Church in America does not imply or inaugurate an automatic communion between the Evangelical Lutheran Church in America and the other provinces of the Anglican Communion or any other churches with whom the Episcopal Church is in full communion.

*Other Dialogues*

13. Both churches agree that each will continue to engage in dialogue with other churches and traditions. Both churches agree to take each other and this Concordat of Agreement into account at every stage in their dialogues with other churches and traditions. Where appropriate, both churches will seek to engage in joint dialogues. On the basis of this Concordat of Agreement, both churches pledge that they will not enter into formal agreements with other churches and traditions without prior consultation with each other. At the same time both churches pledge that they will not impede the

development of relationships and agreements with other churches and traditions with whom they have been in dialogue.

## E. Full Communion

14. Of all the historical processes involved in realizing full communion between the Episcopal Church and the Evangelical Lutheran Church in America, the achieving of full interchangeability of ordained ministries from the beginning of the process, the creation of a common, and therefore fully interchangeable, ministry will occur with the full incorporation of all active bishops in the historic episcopate by common joint ordinations and the continuing process of collegial consultation in matters of Christian faith and life. Full communion will also include the activities of the joint commission (Par. 10 above), as well as the establishment of "recognized organs of regular consultation and communication, including episcopal collegiality, to express and strengthen the fellowship and enable common witness, life and service."[24] Thereby the churches are permanently committed to common mission and ministry on the basis of agreement in faith, recognizing each other fully as churches in which the gospel is preached and the holy Sacraments administered. All provisions specified above will continue in effect.

15. On the basis of this Concordat of Agreement, at a given date recommended by the joint commission, the Evangelical Lutheran Church in America and the Episcopal Church will announce the completion of the process by which they enjoy full communion with each other. They will share one ministry in two churches that are in full communion, still autonomous in structure yet interdependent in doctrine, mission, and ministry.

16. Consequent to the acknowledgment of full communion and respecting always the internal discipline of each church, both churches now accept in principle the full interchangeability and reciprocity of their ordained ministries, recognizing bishops as bishops, pastors as priests and presbyters and *vice versa*, and deacons as deacons. In consequence of our mutual pledge to a future already anticipated in Christ and the church of the early centuries,[25] each church will make such necessary revisions of canons and constitution so that ordained clergy can, upon canonically or constitutionally approved invitation, function as clergy in corresponding situations within either church. The churches will authorize such celebrations of the Eucharist as will accord full recognition to each other's episcopal ministries and sacramental services. All future necessary legislative, canonical, constitutional, and liturgical changes will be coordinated by the joint ecumenical/doctrinal/liturgical commission hereby established.

## CONCLUSION

We receive with thanksgiving the gift of unity which is already given in Christ.

> He is the image of the invisible God, the first-born of all creation; for in him all things were created, in heaven and on earth, visible and invisible, whether thrones or dominions or principalities or authorities—all things were created through him and for him. He is before all things, and in him all things hold together. He is the head of the body, the church; he is the beginning, the first-born from the dead, that in everything he might be pre-eminent. For in him all the fullness of God was pleased to dwell, and through him to reconcile to himself all things, whether on earth or in heaven, making peace by the blood of his cross (Col. 1:15-20).

> Repeatedly Christians have confessed that the unity of the church is given, not achieved. The church can only be one because it is constituted by the gospel in word and sacrament, and there is but one gospel. What Christians are seeking when they engage in the tasks and efforts associated with ecumenism is to discover how the unity they have already been given by the gospel can be manifested faithfully in terms of the church's mission.[26]

We do not know to what new, recovered, or continuing tasks of mission this proposed Concordat of Agreement will lead our churches, but we give thanks to God for leading us to this point. We entrust ourselves to that leading in the future, confident that our full communion will be a witness to the gift and goal already present in Christ, "that God may be everything to every one" (I Cor. 15:28). It is the gift of Christ that we are sent as he has been sent (John 17:17-26), that our unity will be received and perceived as we participate in the mission of the Son in obedience to the Father through the power and presence of the Holy Spirit.[27]

> Now to the one who by the power at work within us is able to do far more abundantly than all that we ask or think, to God be glory in the church and in Christ Jesus to all generations, for ever and ever. Amen. (Eph. 3:20-21)

The Epiphany of Our Lord
January 6, 1991

## Notes

1. Cf. the complete text of the 1982 Agreement in paragraph 1 of the report *Toward Full Communion* which accompanies this proposed Concordat of Agreement.

2. *Anglican-Lutheran Relations: Report of the Anglican-Lutheran Joint Working Group, Cold Ash, Berkshire, England--1983*, in William A. Norgren, *What Can We Share?* (Cincinnati: Forward Movement Publications, 1985), pp. 90-92. The relevant portion of the report reads as follows:

> By full communion we here understand a relationship between two distinct churches or communions. Each maintains its own autonomy and recognizes the catholicity and apostolicity of the other, and each believes the other to hold the essentials of the Christian faith:
> a) subject to such safeguards as ecclesial discipline may properly require, members of one body may receive the sacraments of the other;
> b) subject to local invitation, bishops of one church may take part in the consecration of the bishops of the other, thus acknowledging the duty of mutual care and concern;
> c) subject to church regulation, a bishop, pastor/priest or deacon of one ecclesial body may exercise liturgical functions in a congregation of the other body if invited to do so and also, when requested, pastoral care of the other's members;
> d) it is also a necessary addition and complement that there should be recog nized organs of regular consultation and communication, including episcopal collegiality, to express and strengthen the fellowship and enable common witness, life and service.
> To be in full communion means that churches become interdependent while remaining autonomous. One is not elevated to be the judge of the other nor can it remain insensitive to the other; neither is each body committed to every secondary feature of the tradition of the other. Thus the corporate strength of the churches is enhanced in love, and an isolated independence is restrained.
> Full communion should not imply the suppressing of ethnic, cultural or ecclesial characteristics of traditions which may in fact be maintained and developed by diverse institutions within one communion.

3. Cf. the working document, "Ecumenism: The Vision of the Evangelical Lutheran Church in America," D,1 and 2, adopted by the Evangelical Lutheran Church in America on August 25, 1989, "to offer provisional and interim guidance for this church during the 1990-1991 biennium"; and the "Declaration on Unity" adopted by the 1979 General Convention of the Episcopal Church.

4. Lutheran-Episcopal Dialogue III has held the following meetings,
1) December 4-7, 1983, Techny, Illinois
2) June 10-13, 1984, New York, New York
3) January 27-30, 1985, Techny, Illinois
4) June 2-5, 1985, Erlanger, Kentucky
5) January 26-29, 1986, Techny, Illinois
6) June 8-11, 1986, Cincinnati, Ohio
7. January 11-14, 1987, Techny, Illinois
8) June 7-11, 1987, Techny, Illinois
9) January 3-6, 1988, Techny, Illinois
10) January 5-8, 1989, Delray Beach, Florida
11) June 4-7, 1989, Burlingame, California
12) January 4-7, 1990, Delray Beach, Florida
13) June 17-20, 1990, New Orleans, Louisiana

14) January 3-6, 1991, Delray Beach, Florida

5. Cf. Richard Grein, "The Bishop as Chief Missionary," in Charles R. Henery, editor, *Beyond the Horizon: Frontiers for Mission* (Cincinnati: Forward Movement Publications, 1986), pp. 64-80.

6. *The Niagara Report* (London: Church House Publishing, 1988), Pars. 91 and 96; The Council of Nicaea, Canon 4.

7. Michael Root, "Full Communion Between Episcopalians and Lutherans in North America: What Would It Look Like?" (Unpublished Paper, LED III, June 1990), pp. 10-16. Cf. Michael Root, "Bishops as Points of Unity and Continuity" (Unpublished Paper, Lutheran-United Methodist Dialogue, May 1986).

8. *The Niagara Report*, Par. 69; The Pullach Report, Par. 79; The Lutheran-United Methodist Common Statement on Episcopacy, Par. 28.

9. Cf. Resolutions of the 1979 and 1985 General Conventions of the Episcopal Church, the Canterbury Statement, Par. 16, of the Anglican-Roman Catholic International Commission, and the Evangelical Lutheran Church in America's provisional statement, "Ecumenism: The Vision of the Evangelical Lutheran Church in America," D.3.

10. Chicago-Lambeth Quadrilateral 4.

11. *The Niagara Report*, Par. 94. Cf. Raymond E. Brown, *Priest and Bishop: Biblical Reflections* (New York: Paulist Press, 1970), pp. 83-85.

12. Preface to the Ordinal, The Book of Common Prayer, p. 510.

13. Cf. *The Study of Anglicanism*, ed. Stephen Sykes and John Booty (London/Philadelphia: SPCK/Fortress, 1988), pp. 149, 151, 238, 290, 304-305; Paul F. Bradshaw, *The Anglican Ordinal* (London: SPCK, 1971), Chapter 6.

14. *The Niagara Report*, Par. 91, Augsburg Confession Article 7, Article 28.

15. Cf. Joseph A. Burgess, "An Evangelical Episcopate?" in Todd Nichol and Marc Kolden, editors, *Called and Ordained* (Minneapolis: Fortress Press, 1990) p. 147.

16. Cf. *The Niagara Report*, Pars. 90, 95, and especially 100-110 as examples of the questions and concerns involved in such evaluation. Cf. also *Baptism, Eucharist and Ministry*, Par. 38.

17. Cf. *The Niagara Report*, Par. 90.

18. *Occasional Services*, (Minneapolis: Augsburg Publishing House, 1982), pp. 218-223.

19. We understand the term "regular" to mean "according to constitutionally regulated provisions." A revised constitution of the Evangelical Lutheran Church in America may, for example, give voice but not vote in the Conference of Bishops to bishops who are no longer actively functioning in the office of bishop by reason of retirement, resignation to accept another call, or conclusion of term.

20. Augsburg Confession, Article 21 (Tappert, page 47); Cf. Treatise on the Power and Primacy of the Pope, Par. 66 (Tappert, p. 331).

21. Cf. II Cor. 10:8; also *Anglican-Orthodox Dialogue: The Dublin Agreed Statement 1984* (St. Vladimir's Seminary Press, 1985), pp. 13-14, and ARCIC, *The Final Report* (London: SPCK and Catholic Truth Society, 1982) pp. 83 and 89.

22. Cf. *The Niagara Report*, Par. 92.

23. *Baptism, Eucharist and Ministry*, Ministry Par. 24. Cf. James M. Barnett, *The Diaconate; A Full and Equal Order* (New York; The Seabury Press, 1981), pp. 133-197; John E. Booty, *The Servant Church: Diaconal Ministry and the Episcopal Church* (Wilton, CT: Morehouse-Barlow, 1982); and J. Robert Wright, "The Emergence of the Diaconate: Biblical and Patristic Sources," *Liturgy*, Vol. 2, No.4 (Fall 1982), pp. 17-23, 67-71.

24. The Cold Ash report, par. d. See footnote 2, above.

25. Cf. John D. Zizioulas, *Being as Communion* (New York: St. Vladimir's Seminary Press, 1985), pp. 171-208.

26. *Implications of the Gospel*, Par. 98.

27. *The Niagara Report*, Pars. 25-26.

\* \* \*

### The Dissenting Report of the Lutheran-Episcopal Dialogue, Series III

The undersigned have voted against the report "Toward Full Communion Between the Episcopal Church and the Evangelical Lutheran Church in America" and the proposed "Concordat of Agreement."

We believe that Scripture and the Augsburg Confession clearly teach that the Word of God rightly preached and rightly administered in the sacraments of Baptism and the Lord's Supper constitutes the sole and sufficient basis for the true unity of the Christian church. This unity Lutherans and Episcopalians already share in Christ. In this "Concordat," however, the historic episcopate is made to be a necessity for church fellowship and thus essential to the unity of the church. Under the terms of this "Concordat," the process toward "full communion" will thus not be realized until there is complete interchangeability of ordained ministries on the basis of the joint ordinations of all active bishops of the ELCA—ordained as bishops after the acceptance of the "Concordat"—into the historic episcopacy through the Anglican succession. We believe such provisions for the ministry of the church belong to the realm of the *adiaphora* (things often important but never essential to the unity of the church). To introduce the historic episcopate into the ELCA under the terms of this "Concordat" is to make an *adiaphoron* into a matter of necessity.

We believe that the present context calls for a clear witness to the central insights of the Reformation and a commitment to unassuming servanthood on behalf of Christ's mission in the world. We believe that Christian ecumenism best serves the apostolic mission of the church when it provides for the speaking of God's Word and the administration of the Sacraments in a multitude of ways appropriate to a variety of times and places.

We cherish the fellowship now existing between the Episcopal Church and the ELCA. We look forward to the maturation of this friendship and the engagement of both churches in broader ecumenical ventures as well. We believe that to introduce the historic episcopate into the ELCA under the terms of the "Concordat" could needlessly jeopardize a treasured friendship as well as endanger the collaboration in the gospel and table fellowship we now enjoy. We believe that it could also provoke controversy and division among the congregations and ministers of the ELCA.

Robert J. Goeser
Paul S. Berge

### The Assenting Report of Lutheran-Episcopal Dialogue, Series III

(At the concluding session of the dialogue, the participants authorized the co-chairpersons of the dialogue to release a response to the Dissenting, or Minority Report if they deemed this appropriate.)

We, the undersigned ELCA members of the Lutheran-Episcopal Dialogue, Series III, respect the right of our dissenting colleagues to *interpret* the report and the agreement for full communion as they choose. However, we cannot recognize their interpretation as correct. The initiative of the Episcopal members of the dialogue has been to recognize the existing pastoral ministry of the Evangelical Lutheran Church in America as authentic and to propose a temporary suspension of the preface to the ordinal so that pastors of the ELCA can be invited to function in place of priests of the Episcopal Church. That initiative had made it *possible*, not necessary, for us to propose simultaneously and in concert with our Episcopal colleagues the joint consecrations of *future* bishops resulting in the future participation of ELCA bishops in the historic episcopal succession. In this we have simply been free to propose the restoration of the traditional polity which the Lutheran *Book of Concord* espouses (Pars. 42-47 of the Report). To be given this freedom is in no way "to make an *adiaphoron* into a matter of necessity."

We regret the fact that our colleagues could not endorse the mandate of our churches in which we were directed to move beyond present level of fellowship toward full communion. We regret the fact that they could not endorse the definition of full communion approved by the Anglican and Lutheran world communions, which calls for the bishops of one church to "take part in the consecrations of the bishops of the other, thus acknowledging the duty of mutual care and concern."

We regret the fact that they no longer endorse the conclusion of the Lutheran Council in the U.S.A. report on "The Historic Episcopate," which both of them helped to formulate in 1984, and in which they stated:

> When the "historic episcopate" faithfully proclaims the gospel and administers the sacraments, it may be accepted as a symbol of the church's unity and continuity throughout the centuries provided that it is not viewed as a necessity for the *validity* (our emphasis) of the church's ministry.

We regret the fact that our colleagues cannot endorse the full position of the Lutheran "Formula of Concord" on *adiaphora*, namely, that the church has the "liberty to avail itself" of elements of the tradition which it might have to resist if required of it under persecution or duress (Epitome, Article X, p. 494). Our churches are able to invite bishops to participate in each other's *future* episcopal consecrations (Concordat of Agreement, Par. 3) *because* both churches do now recognize the full authenticity of each other's ministries without the imposition of any demands or further conditions (Concordat of Agreement, Pars. 4 and 9).

We fully agree with our colleagues

that Christian ecumenism best serves the apostolic mission of the church when it provides for the speaking of God's Word and the administration of the Sacraments in a multitude of ways appropriate to a variety of times and places.

because we support the provision of the Lambeth Quadrilateral that the historic episcopate can be "locally adapted in the methods of its administration to the varying needs of the nations and peoples called of God into the Unity of His Church" (Report, Par. 33).

We pray that the controversy and division which our colleagues fear not be incited by those who are determined in advance to resist full communion between our churches and to oppose full collegiality among our bishops.

> The Rev. Dr. Paul Erickson
> The Rev. Dr. Walter R. Bouman
> The Rev. Dr. William G. Rusch
> The Rev. Wayne E. Weissenbuehler, Bishop
> The Rev. Cyril Wismar, Sr.

\* \* \*

## Statement of Lutheran Church-Missouri Synod Participants

Representatives of the Lutheran Church—Missouri Synod have been full participants in all three rounds of the Lutheran-Episcopal Dialogue. The LCMS representatives to these discussions have welcomed with appreciation this opportunity to engage in interconfessional dialogue with brothers and sisters in Christ. The Synod's participation in such discussions reflects its longstanding commitment to the biblical mandate that Christians seek to manifest externally the unity already given to them in the body of Christ and to do so on the basis of agreement in their confession of the gospel "In all its articles (FC SD X,31)."

The Representatives of the LCMS have recognized that due to agreements reached among the other representatives of the dialogue, and in particular, the Lutheran/Episcopal Interim Sharing of the Eucharist Agreement adopted by the non-LCMS participant churches in 1982, the aim of the third round of dialogue has shifted to focus on the achieving of full communion (altar and pulpit fellowship) between the Episcopal Church and the Evangelical Lutheran Church in America. In response to a specific invitation, the LCMS has continued to send representatives as full participants in LED III, even while it has not been a part of the 1982 Agreement, nor the efforts to reach full communion. Although Missouri Synod participation has been limited by these circumstances the LCMS representatives wish to express their gratitude to all the members of the dialogue for welcoming LCMS participation in this phase of dialogue. The LCMS participants remain committed to the value of the discussions themselves as vehicles to achieve greater understanding of and agreement in "the truth as it is taught in the Scriptures and confessed in the Lutheran symbols" ("Guidelines for Participation in Ecumenical Dialogs," prepared by the Commission on Theology and Church Relations, 1975).

We, the LCMS representatives of LED III, ask our gracious God to bless the efforts of our friends and colleagues on the dialogue to achieve a common witness to the gospel of Jesus Christ. We express our best wishes to all present and past members of the dialogue and thank God for the friendships we have come to enjoy and the commonalities we share. And, we look forward to future opportunities to address together differences in doctrine and practice which continue to divide the church.

The Rev. Carl Bornmann  
The Rev. Dr. Norman E. Nagel  
The Rev. Jerald C. Joersz

# Anglican–Orthodox Dialogue

# Agreed Statement on Christian Initiation

**Anglican-Orthodox Theological Consultation in the United States**
**The Feast of St. Cyril of Jerusalem, 1983***

In our understanding, the process of Christian Initiation in both the Orthodox and the Episcopal Churches includes the sacraments of Baptism, Confirmation/Chrismation, and Holy Communion, as well as the catechesis of the Church. Owing to the emphasis on adult baptism in the early Church, yet acknowledging the propriety of the infant baptism, our Churches still employ the theology and liturgy of Christian Initiation used in the early Church.

Baptism is a spiritual birth and passage into the mystical body of Christ, which is the Church. The various types, e.g. passover, water, the Red Sea crossing, dying and rising, new creation, and others, all symbolize the new direction and life for Christians given in Baptism by the work of Christ. Baptism is the one unrepeatable rite of entry into the Church. Confirmation/ Chrismation is a distinct sacrament: the seal of the gift of the Holy Spirit freely given and received in the redemptive process; the empowerment of the neophyte to fulfill a life of grace and service; and the seal of entry into the Church accomplished in Baptism.

1) The usual Orthodox practice of Christian Initiation is to include all three sacraments in one, indivisible rite, normally administered by the priest. The usual Episcopal practice is to separate Baptism (and increasingly First Holy Communion) from Confirmation, which is administered by the Bishop generally at a later time. Thus, the Orthodox Church continues the ancient practice of completing the initiation in one service. The Episcopal Church, by administering the sacrament of Confirmation only after instruction, continues the ancient Christian practice of catechetical preparation prior to initiation.

*Introduction on the Orthodox Church, *BU,* 325. *Ecumenical Bulletin* 62 (November/ December 1983) 22-23.

2) The institution of sponsorship, based on early Christian practice, is an attempt by both churches to meet the problem of adequate preparation of the initiate. The catechumenate is practically absent in Orthodoxy; still, Christian nurture obviously *follows* Baptism/Chrismation. There is no clearly defined liturgical rite of passage at adolescence in the Orthodox Church, such as First Communion, or Confirmation as in the Episcopal Church.

3) The Orthodox practice of Chrismation by the priest involves the Bishop as celebrant indirectly, through the application of the *myrrh* consecrated by episcopal action, as distinct from another oil used earlier in the baptismal rite. Although the Episcopal Prayer Book provides for the blessing of oil by the Bishop which may be used in Baptism (by the Bishop or Priest), this is distinct from the sacrament of Confirmation, which involves the laying on of hands (and may include the use of chrism) only by the Bishop.

4) Both Churches follow the biblical requirements of Baptism "by water and the Holy Spirit," and the use of a trinitarian formula. Both insist on a correspondence between the outward sign and the inward meaning. The Orthodox baptize by triple immersion; Episcopalians usually baptize with a triple pouring of water, although immersion may be used.

5) There are several means of receiving converts (and/or of reconciling) into our respective Churches. Chrismation and a Confession of Faith are the means by which Episcopalians are normally received into the Orthodox Church, validating their Christian baptism by the seal of the gift of the Holy Spirit and thus completing it. Orthodox becoming Episcopalians are, after a Confession of Faith, "received" into the communion of that Church by the local bishop, but are not normally reconfirmed.

6) As a national Anglican-Orthodox Theological Consultation, we commend these statements to our people for further study, comment, and response.

# Agreed Statement on Christian Initiation

**Anglican-Orthodox Theological Consultation in the United States**
**January 1986\***

1. We, the members of the Anglican-Orthodox Consultation in the United States, have been studying the doctrine, liturgy, and pastoral implications of Christian initiation in our respective churches for several years. We find that in all these areas we are in fundamental agreement.

2. We have perceived this agreement in both (a) the liturgical texts in use in our churches and (b) the responses of our churches to the Faith and Order Commission document on *Baptism, Eucharist and Ministry* (henceforth BEM).

*(a) Liturgical texts*

3. In both our churches, Baptism is administered with water in the name of the Father and the Son and the Holy Spirit. It is understood to be the one unrepeatable rite of entry into the Church, a spiritual birth and incorporation into the body of Christ. The scriptural images so prominent in our liturgies, e.g. Passover, the Red Sea crossing, dying and rising, new creation, all symbolize the new direction and life for Christians given in Baptism. The images are many but the reality is one.

4. In the rites of both our churches, the washing in water is immediately followed by actions and words witnessing to the action of the Holy Spirit. In the Episcopal *Book of Common Prayer*, we find: "N., you are sealed by the Holy Spirit in Baptism and marked as Christ's own for ever." In the Orthodox Churches, the following formula is employed: "Seal of the gift of the Holy Spirit."

5. In view of the theological richness and high level of agreement which we see in our liturgical texts, we would encourage their closer study by our congregations, when possible in common.

*Ecumenical Bulletin* 67 (May/June 1986) 25-26.

*(b) Responses to BEM*

6. Both our churches, in their responses to BEM, have commended the general direction and approach taken in the section on Baptism. Indeed, our consultation believes that it would be possible to express our own common agreement on Baptism along the lines of BEM. Even our churches' reservations with regard to the Baptism section of BEM are for the most part held in common:

    i. We emphasize that Baptism is given by God and not dependent upon human response in the way that BEM might suggest.

    ii. We do not accept the distinction which BEM makes between infant Baptism and "believers' Baptism," a term which we in our traditions do not use.

    iii. We stress that the need for repentance does not end with the act of Baptism but continues throughout the Christian life.

    iv. We think that BEM does not adequately treat the ecclesial context of Baptism nor probe its implications sufficiently.

7. In the theological reflection of our consultation we have perceived not only these areas of fundamental agreement but also certain points of difference or divergence which, in our view, need further exploration:

    (a) The way in which the Orthodox understand the significance of the use of myrrh/chrism in Christian initiation and in other rites.

    (b) The way in which Episcopalians understand the significance of the "pastoral office" of episcopal confirmation and its relation to Christian initiation.

    (c) The ecclesiological implications of our respective ways of receiving converts.

8. Because of the high level of agreement which we do discern, we would encourage our churches:

    (a) To promote occasions on all levels for common study of Baptism and reflection upon its significance for the Christian life;

    (b) To call to the attention of the international Anglican-Orthodox Joint Doctrinal Commission the need for consideration of the points of difference or divergence enumerated above.

# Agreed Statement on the Eucharist

**Anglican-Orthodox Theological Consultation in the United States**
**New York, January 16, 1988***

1. We, the members of the Anglican-Orthodox Theological Consultation in the United States, for several years have been studying the doctrine, liturgy and pastoral implications of the Eucharist in our respective churches. Our attention has focused on the Moscow and Dublin Agreed Statements of the international Anglican-Orthodox dialogue (1976 and 1984 respectively), but we have also taken into consideration (a) the World Council of Churches' document on *Baptism, Eucharist and Ministry* (the "Lima Document," hereafter BEM) and our churches' responses to it; and (b) the several bilateral statements of which our churches have been party, such as the Anglican-Roman Catholic statements incorporated in the Anglican-Roman Catholic International Commission's Final Report (1981) and the Orthodox-Roman Catholic International Consultation's statement on "The Church, the Eucharist, and the Trinity" (The "Munich Statement," 1982). We find that we are in fundamental agreement with the conclusions reached in Moscow and Dublin but also that we are able to go beyond them at several points.

## The Church as Eucharistic Community

2. Baptism in the name of the Father and of the Son and of the Holy Spirit is, as many ecumenical statements, including our own on Christian Initiation (January, 1986), have affirmed, the unrepeatable means of our rebirth and incorporation into the body of Christ through the action of the Holy Spirit. It is in the Eucharist that this new life in Christ is nourished and strengthened by the continuing action of the same Spirit. As both Moscow (paragraph 24) and Dublin (paragraph 109) affirm, "the Eucharist actualizes the Church." The Eucharist makes the Church what it is called to be. It both

*Ecumenical Bulletin* 90 (July/August 1988) 15-18.

manifests and constitutes the Church as the Body of Christ, fashioned by the Spirit and called to participation in the very life of God. In the words of the Moscow Statement (paragraph 24), "The Church celebrating the Eucharist becomes fully itself; that is, *koinonia*, fellowship—communion."

3. This emphasis on the ecclesial significance of the Eucharist is not unique to Anglican and Orthodox agreed statements. Increasingly in bilateral and multilateral ecumenical dialogue, the Eucharist is coming to be understood not only as a means of grace duly administered by the Church for the spiritual benefit of the faithful but as expressive of the very nature of the Church. In it the Church's unity is actualized, her apostolic faith expressed, her catholicity manifested, her holiness given. At the same time, such affirmations pose a question: In practice, is the Eucharist truly that source and criterion for church life which ecumenical statements have claimed it to be?

4. Here we would observe that for both Orthodox and Anglicans today the Eucharist is "the principal act of Christian worship on the Lord's Day and other major Feasts" (1979 *Book of Common Prayer*, p. 13), and frequent communion is widely encouraged and practiced (cf. the recommendations in BEM's statement on the Eucharist, paragraph 31).

5. Yet we must also confess that we have not always lived out the implications of our understanding of the Eucharist. "In the Eucharist, the End breaks into our midst, bringing the judgment and hope of the New Age." We become witnesses to the "cosmic transfiguration" of the eschaton. Yet we have not always responded appropriately, in "mission and service to the world" (Moscow, paragraph 28; cf. BEM's very forceful presentation of "The Eucharist as Communion of the Faithful" and "The Eucharist as Meal of the Kingdom," in the statement on the Eucharist, paragraphs 19-26). Our consultation hopes to address this urgent issue in the near future, for we believe that the Church as a eucharistic community is essentially a missionary community, committed to announcing and conveying to the world that which it has received and experienced in the Eucharist (cf. Moscow, paragraph 28).

6. In addition, we must candidly acknowledge that Anglicans and Orthodox disagree at certain points regarding the implications of the Eucharist for church life.

7. (a) For example, we have certain differences concerning the relationship of the Eucharist and church unity. (See Dublin, paragraph 101; "With this [viz. disagreement concerning 'our view of the relationship between the Church's basic unity and the present state of division between Christians,' paragraph 100] is linked a further disagreement concerning communion and intercommunion. The Anglican tradition accepts as legitimate, in certain situations, the use of intercommunion as a means towards the attainment of full organic unity. The Orthodox reject the notion of intercom-

munion, and believe that there can be communion only between local churches that have a unity of faith, ministry and sacraments." (Cf. Dublin, paragraphs 19-20.) Such differences reflect basic ecclesiological issues which have yet to be discussed and resolved. These too we hope to address in our future work, recognizing the concern and pain which they cause among our brothers and sisters.

8. (b) Also serious, in our estimation, is disagreement concerning qualifications for ordination to the priesthood and, by extension, for presiding at the Eucharist. The Orthodox affirms that ordination of women to the priesthood is impossible, while many Anglicans believe that it is possible and even desirable (Dublin, paragraph 103). Clearly the entire subject of the relationship of Eucharist and ministry must be discussed in greater depth.

### The Eucharist as Anamnesis—Sacrifice

9. The Dublin Statement refers in passing to the Eucharist as "anamnesis and participation in the death and resurrection of Christ" (paragraphs 58, 108), but it does not develop this theme further. Had it done so, it might have been able to address an issue which it leaves untouched: "how far the Eucharist may be regarded as a sacrifice" (Dublin, paragraph 111).

10. Recent patristic and liturgical scholarship, reflected in BEM as well as in a number of bilateral ecumenical statements, has shown how the notion of anamnesis—the making effective in the present of a past event—can open the way to a clearer understanding of the relationship between Christ's sacrifice and the Eucharist. The Eucharist is a sacrifice because it is a memorial (anamnesis) of the unique sacrifice of Christ. This memorial does not merely "remind" us of the sacrifice of Christ; it makes this sacrifice truly present for us. At the same time, this sacrifice can properly be described as the Church's sacrifice: In the celebration of the anamnesis, the Church, by the power of the Holy Spirit, enters into Christ's perfect self-sacrifice.

### The True Presence of Christ in the Eucharist

11. Neither of our churches has committed itself unreservedly to a specific philosophical theory which would explain the mode of Christ's presence in the Eucharist. Our reticence on this point in large part is the product of our respective histories. Over the centuries the Orthodox have been suspicious of any practice or teaching which might call into question the reality of Christ's humanity or imply that it is somehow different from our own humanity—a humanity nourished by bread and wine. Anglicans, influenced

by the debates of the 16th century, have sought to avoid a materialistic understanding which might suggest that the change occurs in accordance with the laws of physics and chemistry. For such reasons, both Orthodox and Anglicans maintain that the eucharistic elements do not cease to be bodily nourishment.

12. At the same time, both our churches affirm that in the Eucharist the bread and wine truly become the body and blood of our Lord and Savior Jesus Christ. To be sure, as both the Moscow and the Dublin Statements immediately go on to affirm, this is "in such a way that the faithful people of God receiving Christ may feed upon him in the sacrament" (Moscow, paragraph 25, repeated in Dublin, Paragraph 111), in order "to give us the forgiveness of sins, the new creation, and eternal life" (Moscow, paragraph 26). Yet such qualifications should not be taken as a denial of the change in the elements which takes place in the Eucharist.

13. We affirm that the presence of Christ in the Eucharist does not depend upon our own faith or disposition. By the faith which the power of the Holy Spirit arouses in us, we apprehend Christ's presence in the Eucharist, and our participation in it becomes fruitful, but the presence itself does not depend upon this apprehension and participation.

14. We also affirm that in the Eucharist the bread and wine remain the body and blood of Christ, permitting us to reserve the sacrament, the sign and pledge of his permanent identification with our human condition.


**The Epiclesis of the Holy Spirit**

15. The Moscow Statement (especially paragraphs 29-32), followed by the Dublin Statement (especially paragraph 110), forcefully insisted that "the operation of the Holy Spirit is essential to the Eucharist whether it is explicitly addressed or not" (paragraph 29). At the same time, it cautioned against looking for a "moment" or "formula" of consecration, whether the Words of Institution or the epiclesis, asserting rather that "the consecration of the bread and the wine results from the whole sacramental liturgy" (paragraph 30). Here we see a resurgence of the idea of blessing or thanksgiving underlying the ancient eucharistic prayers of the Church: In the eucharistic prayer we bless God for His promise to make the bread and wine means of receiving the body and blood of Christ through the action of the Spirit.

16. The epiclesis, then, is not only an invocation for the sacramental change of the bread and wine. It is above all a prayer for the fruitful communion of the faithful: for their unity with God in Christ. The Moscow Statement—followed by BEM and a number of bilateral statements—thus

can refer to the epiclesis as a "double invocation" of the Holy Spirit, an invocation upon the eucharistic offering and upon the community (paragraph 31).

17. Here we would also like to take note of the very fruitful way in which the understanding of the epiclesis has been used in the Orthodox-Roman Catholic "Munich Statement" to elucidate the distinct but inseparable operation of the Son and the Spirit not only in the Eucharist but in the entire mystery of our redemption (II.6). We believe that further exploration of this subject by Orthodox and Anglicans can only serve to broaden and deepen the agreement which we already have reached concerning the question of the *Filioque* (Moscow, paragraphs 19-21).

## Concluding Observation and Additional Recommendation

18. Our study of the various agreed statements, bilateral and multilateral, to which our churches have been party has indicated that there is a growing tendency to formulate agreements—and also disagreements—in terms which transcend traditional points of contention. We would encourage our churches continually to review our earlier statements—including the Moscow and Dublin Agreed Statements—in the light of this tendency.

# Joint Reflections on the Nature and Unity of the Church

**Anglican-Orthodox Consultation in the United States**
**Washington, D.C., January 18, 1990, The Confession of St. Peter**

1. The Anglican–Orthodox Theological Consultation in the United States has undertaken to pursue the discussions which led to its agreed statements on Christian Initiation (January 1986) and the Eucharist (January 1988) in the direction of a broader Church. It is our intention to pursue these discussions by taking up once again the issues outstanding in the Moscow (1976) and Dublin (1984) Agreed Statements, as well as keeping in view their treatment in other bilateral statements to which Anglicans and Orthodox have been parties, and in the World Council of Churches' Faith and Order document *Baptism, Eucharist and Ministry* (the "Lima document," or BEM).

2. In proceeding in this way, we recall that at the end of our Agreed Statement on the Eucharist, we noted that "bilateral and multilateral agreements to which our churches have been parties" show "a growing tendency to formulate agreements—and also disagreements—in terms which transcend traditional points of contention," and encouraged our churches "continually to review our earlier statements—including the Moscow and Dublin Agreed Statements—in the light of this tendency" (para. 18). It is our intention here to take our own advice as we begin to explore the nature and unity of the Church.

3. The fundamentally ecclesiological character of Dublin is evident from the opening paragraphs of the document. We are at once reminded that "we live in a deeply divided world" in which the divisions and separations of Christians belie the message of reconciliation with which the Church has been entrusted (Dublin I.2). Dublin here strikes the basic note of the need to elucidate our understanding of the unity of the Church, having always in mind the mission to which the Church is called in the plan of salvation.

4. After noting that "the mystery of the Church cannot be defined or fully described," Dublin observes that the Church, which is "sent into the

world as a sign, instrument and first-fruits of the Kingdom of God," is spoken of in the New Testament "primarily in images" (Dublin I.3). Through this imagery Dublin calls attention to the goal of the Christian life: to be conformed to [Christ's] true humanity, filled with his divinity, and made 'partakers of the divine nature' (*theosis*)" (Dublin I.4 quoting II Peter 1:4). Dublin concentrates on four images: the body of Christ, the messianic gathering, the holy temple of God, and the bride of Christ.

5. We wish now to elaborate the dynamic character of the rich imagery found in the Bible and the Fathers. These images do not suggest that the perfection of the Church is already achieved but rather direct our attention to the continual need for repentance and renewal. To accentuate this the proleptic or eschatological character of the Church—one, holy, catholic, and apostolic—should be further explored. This in turn would allow more fruitful and concrete discussion of our present divisions. God's "plan for the fullness of time, to unite all things in Christ" (Eph. 1:10) is indeed revealed in the Church, but in anticipation of the completion of that plan and the manifestation of that fullness still to come. Christians are indeed "those on whom the end of the ages has come" (I Cor. 10:11) but not in the sense that its completion is now manifest. Christians are those who, in baptism and eucharist "have been enlightened, have tasted the heavenly gift, and have become partakers of the Holy Spirit, and have tasted the goodness of the word of God and the powers of the age to come" (Hebr. 6:4) but they remain, as the context of these words shows only too clearly, beset by the powers of the present age.

6. When discussing the present relationship of our churches, Dublin asserts that "our divisions do not destroy but they damage the basic unity we have in Christ" (Dublin I.9). In this connection, it is further asserted, "Anglicans are accustomed to seeing our divisions as within the Church: they do not believe that they alone are the one true Church, but they believe that they belong to it," while the Orthodox "believe that the Orthodox Church is the one true Church of Christ, which as His Body is not and cannot be divided," but that "they see Anglicans as brothers and sisters in Christ who are seeking with them the union of all Christians in the one Church" (Dublin I.9; cf. Epilogue IV,100e and 99d). Closer attention to the proleptic or eschatological aspect of the Church may make possible the formulation of a more adequate theological framework for explaining such apparent contradictions. By proceeding in that way false dichotomies will be avoided, and the real differences between the positions of our churches will be perceived.

7. Similar problems arise in the discussion of schism and heresy in relation to catholicity. The distinction between schism and heresy is an ancient and legitimate one: the Church through the centuries has recognized

that separation has arisen from various causes and has had various expressions. As Dublin uses these terms, however, it is not always clear what application they have to our own present circumstances. Moreover, Dublin's contrasting description of catholicity as shown in the "multiplicity of local churches, each of which, being in communion with all the other local churches, manifests in its own place and time the one Catholic Church," and whose diversity, "so long as their witness to the one faith remains unimpaired...[is] not a deficiency or cause of division" but "a mark of the fullness of the one Spirit" (I.12c) seems too loosely worded to serve its purpose of distinguishing schismatical and heretical bodies from those in communion with one another, much less to shed light on the earlier statement that our unity is "damaged but not destroyed."

8. In our own discussions, we have come to the conclusion that, by using terms like schism and heresy, i.e., by distinguishing the forms which separation can take, both Anglicans and Orthodox are implicitly recognizing and accepting the existence of a normative orthodoxy in matters of faith and order. Disagreement between us exists not so much over the existence of such a normative orthodoxy but in our understanding of how this is held and expressed: the Orthodox believe that this normative orthodoxy is held and expressed uniquely in their Church, while Anglicans believe it to be held and expressed also in their own and in certain others as well.

9. Dublin's treatment of disunity in contrast to unity and of schism and heresy in contrast to catholicity leads naturally to an attempt to identify differences between Anglicans and Orthodox on the subject of "communion." Here Dublin stated that "Anglicans have come to recognize different stages in which churches stand in a progressively close relationship to each other, with a corresponding and consequent degree of eucharistic sharing..." though they distinguish such "Intercommunion" from "Full or Organic Communion." Correspondingly, Dublin states that "for the Orthodox, 'communion' involves a mystical and sanctifying unity created by the Body and Blood of Christ, which makes them 'one body and one blood with Christ,' and therefore they can have no differences of faith," adding also that "there can be 'communion' only between local churches which have a unity of faith, ministry, and sacraments," so that "the concept of Intercommunion has no place in Orthodox ecclesiology" (Dublin I.19-20).

10. While this may have seemed a fair digest of the two positions as they existed at the time when the Dublin agreement was formulated, it may be doubted that it is such at the present time. Here again, we would caution against setting up a false dichotomy. Among Anglicans it is now common to speak of "organic union" as appropriate to the life of the "local church" in its diocesan or provincial manifestation, and of "communion" or "full communion" as descriptive of the relation of families or bodies of autonomous

Churches professing the same faith and order, accepting the ministrations of one another's ministries, and committed to regular consultation among themselves (*The Truth Shall Make You Free*: The Lambeth Conference 1988, Ecumenical Relations, paras. 66-106; cf. *The Declaration on Unity*, General Convention 1979). It would seem, therefore, that with this terminological clarification Anglicans and Orthodox are in general agreement on what is involved in "organic union" and "full communion."

11. We believe, however, that a more wide-ranging discussion of the meaning of "communion (*koinonia*)" would be useful in clarifying all the issues which we have touched upon thus far. This subject has been examined with precision and sensitivity by modern scholars and has proved useful in ecumenical discussion, including other bilateral dialogues to which our churches have been party. As such work has shown, Christian *koinonia* has a human dimension which is at once tangible and spiritual, but it is ultimately a communion with God given by God. It is grounded in the divine life itself, reflecting and participating in the very life of God who has freely communicated himself to us through his Son by the power of the Holy Spirit.

12. Seen within this larger context, it is clear that "communion" or "intercommunion" is not simply a matter of eucharistic sharing. While Christian *koinonia*, initiated in baptism, is epitomized in eucharistic fellowship, it is not limited to it. Christian *koinonia* expresses itself in many ways: in the bearing of one another's sufferings, in the sharing of material resources, in common concern, in co-responsibility. It is evident to us at least that some aspects of *koinonia* may embrace even those excluded from eucharistic participation, as was anciently the case with catechumens and penitents. It is therefore possible and fully appropriate for both Orthodox and Anglicans to speak of "degrees of communion (*koinonia*)" in which they stand in relation to other bodies of Christians with whom they do not now have "full communion" or "organic union."

13. Consideration of this subject challenges us to strengthen and extend the *koinonia* which we are already privileged to enjoy even in the absence of eucharistic fellowship. We believe that mutual edification is possible even in our present state of separation. In our discussions we have noted several ways in which this is already taking place (e.g., in the deepening of our understanding of the mystery of the Trinity which was initially provoked by bitter disagreement over the *filioque*). We believe that we shall similarly benefit from discussion of such important issues as conciliarity and primacy. Anglicans, we believe, will benefit from Orthodox reflection upon such issues as the role of the Patriarch of Constantinople within the communion of the Orthodox churches: Orthodox will benefit as Anglicans consider new problems of mutual accountability and responsibility which are emerging among the churches of the Anglican communion. Here we both would do

well to heed the hopeful admonition of Metropolitan John (Zizioulas) of Pergamon to the Lambeth Conference 1988: "No Christian can or does any longer act or speak, or even think and debate—I *dare* also say decide—in isolation....We all have to take *seriously* into account the views of others, and we all have to think, act and decide on the basis not of what *we* want, but of what the world demands and really needs in order to have that future promised by God eschatologically in Christ" (*The Truth Shall Make You Free*, 283-4).

# The New Man*

*John Meyendorff and Joseph McLelland, eds., *The New Man: An Orthodox and Reformed Dialogue* (New Brunswick: Standard Press, 1973) 162-65.

## Orthodox-Reformed Dialogues (1968-70)

At the end of each of the three sessions of the Consultation, a brief Summary was signed by the Chairmen, drawing the main conclusions of the discussions. The texts do not represent formal agreements. By choosing deliberately to be descriptive, rather than seeking verbal consensus, the Consultation remained faithful to the spirit of openness and informality which characterized its work from the beginning. The participants felt that small bilateral consultations can best contribute to the ecumenical movement by opening new avenues of thought, rather than by pretending to reach final conclusions. They were unanimous in feeling that several such avenues were discovered and may be used by others.

Here are the three "Summaries":

I. *First Consultation, Princeton Theological Seminary*, May 2-3, 1968.

"Our first meeting has been an important occasion for us. We have discussed mainly the role of creeds and confessions in the life of our churches, as a starting-point for dialogue. We have begun discussions that promise light on the relationship between our churches and on their mutual task in the modern world.

"We believe that America provides an unprecedented opportunity for discussions because many of the historical and cultural obstacles to mutual understanding between our churches have been removed.

"For these reasons we judge further meetings to be in order. We propose to examine certain key issues that confront us together. We have discovered as fruitful areas of discussion the following: God's revelation and the historical process, the nature of catholicity, reconciliation, the significance of Christian hope, questions of authority and freedom in the faith and life of the Church."

II. *Second Consultation, Hellenic College, Brookline, Mass., Apr.* 18-19, 1969.

The topic of our discussion was "God's Revelation and History," based on papers by Father John Meyendorff and Professor Samuel Calian. We are happy to report a genuine agreement concerning the ultimate authority of the Holy Spirit in the Church, as witnessed by such signs as scripture, order and sacraments. The eschatological note of "the Eighth Day" emphasized the Spirit's activity as presence and promise. We believe that the Spirit is the authority that secures the freedom of Christian life in the Community of faith.

Our agreement, however, does not extend to the question of intercommunion. The consequences for the Christian community of the presence and authority of the Holy Spirit are interpreted differently by our respective groups. The Reformed hold that intercommunion is both possible and desirable on the basis of our common baptism and a mutual witness to the Christ present in the Eucharist. The Orthodox, on the other hand, consider intercommunion neither possible nor desirable, without a genuine commitment to one faith and one visible Church (which would of course preserve diversity in form in expressing this same faith).

Accordingly, we seek to pursue further conversations that should cast light on this central issue. We propose to discuss two topics at our next meeting: the Christian community in the second century, and Theosis and Sanctification. The first represents a key period in our common history which is variously interpreted by us, and the second an area of apparent divergence concerning Christian life.

III. *Third Consultation, Princeton Theological Seminary, May* 13-14, 1970.

(1) Discussion of the paper on "the Christian Community in the Second Century" revealed widespread agreement both that the distinction between Body of Christ and *ekklesia* in Paul's thought had not been established (or at least was overdrawn), and that it was indeed true that only in the second century did Christian thought elaborate a theology of the church as a cosmic reality. Orthodox participants regarded the emphasis on hearing and obedience as failing to do justice to *ekklesia* as the locus of sacramental participation in the Body of Christ. One could have wished for fuller discussion of the topics proposed in the last two sections of the paper.

(2) The exchange occasioned by the presentation of the Orthodox teaching of divinization (*theosis*) and the Reformed teaching on sanctification produced extensive preliminary agreement, particularly on the primacy of God's initiative in man's salvation, the role of the life and teaching of Jesus Christ, and the necessity for a proper appreciation of divinization—sanctification. God has objectively established the conditions for our salvation in Christ. Men must live in Christ, must share in his glorified humanity, in a personal and responsible way, in order to appropriate his work. Cooperation (synergy) is implied here between God's grace and man's fallen condition in order that his proper end might be reached. To live the divine life, to share in the life of God by grace and faith, through Christ and the Holy Spirit, does not compromise the essential sovereignty or unknowability of God, since man cannot transcend his essential human created nature. Divinization-sanctification means the fulfillment of man's potentiality and calling by grace.

In fact, during the three meetings, the Consultation followed the logics of the ecumenical development since the beginnings of the century. It started with "comparative ecclesiology," putting side by side the formal positions of the two sides. The comparison led to the pleasant discovery that "America provides an unprecedented opportunity for discussions because many of the historical and cultural obstacles to mutual understanding between our churches have been removed" (Summary I).

The "opportunity"—whose real ecumenical significance should indeed be widely realized—was put to use at the next meeting, not as an occasion for smiling doctrinal relativism, but as a call for a better understanding of the Christian Gospel itself. In spite of its intrinsic pluralism, the contemporary American situation, of which we are all parties, is a powerful factor of unification. It breaks the historical, linguistic, cultural and ideological walls which, for centuries, were separating Eastern and Western Christians from each other. By thus removing the incidentals, it must contribute to focusing the dialogue on the essentials.

Among the essentials, the very nature of our *ecclesial experience* is certainly most important. During the second and third meetings a "genuine" and "widespread" agreement was reached in defining the Holy Spirit as the ultimate authority in the Church and, also, in seeing the Church as the locus where participation in Christ's life becomes a reality, and not so much as a human institution, where the Word is only "heard" and where "obedience" is required, but, in fact, never fully realized in the Body of Christ. The relations between God and man cease to be extrinsic; they are a living communion. In the Orthodox tradition, the realization of this communion is seen primarily in the Eucharistic mystery. This is the point made by Dr. Zizioulas, whose paper was not actually presented at the Consultation, but was added to this symposium in order to present a fuller and more balanced view of the Orthodox position.

A further discussion of the meaning and, particularly, the implications of the Eucharistic communion would perhaps be the best follow-up of the results already reached in our dialogue. A clear disagreement on this point was recorded in summary II, and a further dialogue, on the basis of premises laid by Zizioulas, is obviously needed—a dialogue which recurs inevitably at all levels of the ecumenical movement, where the Orthodox are involved. It involves the Orthodox contention that the Eucharist is neither an end in itself nor a means for achieving unity, but rather an ultimate sign of man's accepting (if not yet fully conforming to) the fullness of God's Truth and Life, in continuity and communion with all the past, present, and the future of the Church.

A really extraordinary consensus was reached during the third and last meeting. Hearing their Reformed colleagues accepting to speak in terms of "synergy" and "divinization" (*theosis*), the Orthodox were seriously shattered in their preconceived notions about Calvinist predestinationism! Here again, the value of a serious bi-lateral dialogue was seen by all, inasmuch as it alone was able to clarify terms and provoke a breakthrough of understanding.

It was a common conviction of the group that bi-lateral conversations, giving full credit to the various ecclesial traditions of Christendom and confronting them with each other, are in no way outdated. They represent a necessary dimension of contemporary ecumenism, a level of debate which otherwise cannot be safeguarded. Multi-confessional encounters, even when they define the right problems, often lack a common starting point for solutions. It was agreed that our progress on the long and painful path of ecumenism can only profit from these two complementary forms of encounter and dialogue.

# Common Statement: Christ "In Us" and Christ "For Us" in Lutheran and Orthodox Theology*

## INTRODUCTION

According to an ancient tradition of the church, the task of theology is to express what is "befitting God "(*theoprepes*). Seldom has this meant coining new words. The primary vehicle of theology has always been the language of the Bible. Even in the most sophisticated theological debates, for example in the disputes over the person of Christ in the fifth century, theologians seldom strayed far from the words and images of the Holy Scriptures. On occasion, non-biblical terms were employed in dogmatic formulation, e.g., *homoousios* (of one essence) in the creed adopted at the Council of Nicaea in A.D. 325, or the four adverbs in the decree of the Council of Chalcedon in A.D. 451, "without confusion, without change, without division, without separation." But these non-biblical terms were always surrounded by biblical words and expressions and were understood within the context of the Scriptures. To this day, as is evident in terms such as grace, justification, sanctification, faith, redemption, salvation, and image of God, the native tongue of Christians, for the theological expression as well as for speaking of the Christian life, is the language of the Bible.

The language of the Scriptures is, however, not univocal, and in the course of time biblical terms took on new connotations or overtones (sometimes assuming a life of their own), as they were filtered through Christian experience and thought. For that reason, even though Lutherans and Orthodox read the same Scriptures and share a common spiritual and theological heritage derived from the early church, our different historical experiences have led us to accentuate distinctive features of the biblical tradition. In piety, liturgy, and theology, Lutherans have their roots in the Western Catholic tradition that developed independently of the East for a thousand

*John Meyendorff and Robert Tobias, eds., *Salvation in Christ. A Lutheran-Orthodox Dialogue* (Minneapolis: Augsburg, 1992) 15-33, 171-73.

years before the Reformation. The Eastern Catholic tradition has its roots in Byzantium, the Middle East and the Slavic world. Though Eastern and Western Christians share a common heritage in the Scriptures, the church fathers, and the early ecumenical councils, they have had little contact with each other for more than a thousand years. After the seventh century and the rise of Islam, Orthodoxy was isolated from the west and large sections of Eastern Christianity were destined to exist for centuries under Muslim and Mongol hegemony and later under Ottoman rule—all hostile in varying degrees to Christianity. These historical, cultural, and political experiences have formed the Orthodox churches in ways that are difficult for Western Christians to comprehend. Conversely, the Orthodox have had no firsthand experience with the distinctive religious and theological concerns of the Reformation, an event that took place only in Western Christendom, and one which is formative for the theological and spiritual outlook of the churches of the Augsburg Confession.

In our discussions over the last six years we have had less difficulty understanding each other when we speak of the principal dogmas formulated by the early church, e.g., the doctrine of the Holy Trinity or the doctrine of Christ, than we have when discussing the mystery of salvation and the particulars of the spiritual life. This report highlights some of the difficulties Lutherans and Orthodox encounter as we try to understand each other on the topic of salvation in Christ and some of the areas in which we have found convergence and agreement. We are not ready to say, as Saint Cyril of Alexandria said in A.D. 433, in a letter announcing theological agreement with Bishop John of Antioch, "Let the heavens rejoice and the earth be glad, for the middle wall of partition is broken down."[1] But we are happy to report that the obstacles to understanding seem less formidable than they did when we began to talk to one another six years ago.

In our traditions, differences of understanding have arisen with respect to a number of terms and phrases: "justification and sanctification," *theosis* (deification), "imputed righteousness," "image of God," "free will," "synergism," "sharing the divine nature," "nature," "grace," "sin," "original sin," and other expressions that bear on the Christian understanding of salvation.

## Justification and Sanctification

In the sixteenth century, when the first tentative contacts took place between the reformers and the patriarchs of Constantinople, language was a barrier. It was not that the reformers did not know Greek (Philipp Melanchthon, for example, was a distinguished humanist), but that biblical terms had come to assume different meanings for the two traditions. The term "justify" in the Augsburg Confession was on one occasion translated by "sanctify" in the version sent to the patriarch of Constantinople, Jeremiah II.[2] Of course Orthodox and Lutherans alike, following the Scripture, used the two terms, but each tradition was heir to a different theological heritage, the one shaped by the scholastic debates of medieval Western theology, the other by the theological developments within the churches of the Eastern Christian and Byzantine world.

For the Lutherans "justification" and "sanctification" are two distinct theological categories, one designating God's declaration of righteousness, the other the gradual process of growth in the Christian life. Hence Lutherans interpret the term "justify" by means of texts such as Rom. 3:23-24, "Since all have sinned and fall short of the glory of God, they are now justified by his grace as a gift, through the redemption that is in Christ Jesus." The Orthodox believe that "justification" initiates a change in human beings and begins the process of growth in the Christian life (what Lutherans call "sanctification"). Furthermore, the Orthodox understand "justification" as forgiveness of sins and deliverance from death and "sanctification" as spiritual growth, which is related to the work of the Holy Spirit in us.[3] Hence they see "justification" and "sanctification" as one divine action, as Saint Paul writes in 1 Cor 6:11: "You were washed, you were sanctified, you were justified in the name of the Lord Jesus Christ and in the Spirit of our God." It is easy to understand why "justify" could be translated "sanctify" from the perspective of the Orthodox, yet such a translation confounded the Lutheran view of justification.

### *Theosis* (Deification)

For the Orthodox *theosis* is a central theological and religious idea, as the title of the book by Georgios I. Mantzaridis, *The Deification of Man*, indicates. "In the Orthodox understanding Christianity signifies not merely an adherence to certain dogmas, not merely an exterior imitation of Christ through moral effort, but *direct union* with the living God, the total transformation of the human person by divine grace and glory—what the Greek fathers termed 'deification'...(*theosis*)," writes Bishop Kallistos Ware.[4] Although the term *theosis* does not occur in the Holy Scriptures, the idea of sharing in the divine nature (which *theosis* means) does occur. The locus classicus is 2 Pet. 1:3-4: "His divine power has given us everything needed for life and godliness, through the knowledge of him who called us by his own glory and goodness. Thus he has given us, through these things, his precious and very great promises, so that through them you may escape from the corruption that is in the world because of lust, and may become participants of the divine nature." Although 2 Peter used the term "divine nature," in this passage, according to the Orthodox, it should not be understood to refer to the transcendent divine being (*ousia*), which is incommunicable; here the word nature refers to the communicable attributes of God, the divine energies.[5]

Of course the passage in 2 Peter is not the only place where the idea of deification is expressed in the Scriptures. Similar concepts appear elsewhere. "Beloved, we are God's children now; what we will be has not yet been revealed. What we do know is this: when he is revealed we will be like him..." (I John 3:2). But the passage in 2 Peter is the most explicit statement within the New Testament and it delineates the central feature of the Orthodox conception. Salvation is understood to mean "participation" or "sharing" or "fellowship" with God, or "indwelling" in the words of the Gospel of John. "You know him, because he abides with you, and he will be in you" (John 14:17). As Vladimir Lossky writes:

> Thus the redeeming work of Christ...is seen to be directly related to the ultimate goal of creatures: to know union with God. If this union has been accomplished in the divine person of the Son, who is God become man, it is necessary that each human person, in turn, should become god by grace, or "a partaker of the divine nature," according to Saint Peter's expression.[6]

Deification does not mean that human beings "become God" in a pantheistic sense. Believers enter into a personal relationship with God through Baptism and participate fully in God's life through the sacraments in the church, the body of Christ, [and] the community of the people of God.

2 Peter 1:4 has no such importance in Lutheran thinking or spirituality. Lutherans are more inclined to cite 1 Pet. 2:24 than 2 Peter: "He himself bore our sins in his body on the cross, so that, free from sins, we might die to sin and live for righteousness." Or 1 Peter 3:18: "For Christ also died for sins once for all, the righteous for the unrighteous, that he might bring us to God..." In speaking of salvation, Lutherans have emphasized the language of vicarious atonement, imputation, and forensic justification, rather than the language of participation or communion. Justification is that act by which God removes the sentence of condemnation on human beings, releases them from guilt, and ascribes to them the merit of Christ. Lutherans have more often spoken of Christ "for us" than they have of Christ "in us." In his commentary of Gal. 3:13, Martin Luther wrote: "Christ is a divine and human Person who took sin, the condemnation of the law, and death upon Himself, not for Himself but for us. Therefore the whole emphasis is on the phrase 'for us.'"[7] In the Apology to the Augsburg Confession Philipp Melanchthon said that "the gospel is, strictly speaking, the promise of forgiveness of sins and justification *because of Christ*."[8]

Yet, "Christ for us" was never a rigid scheme within the Lutheran tradition. Occasionally salvation was expressed in the language of union or even as "sharing in the divine nature," especially in sermons and devotional literature. In his sermons on 2 Peter, for example, Luther said that "through the power of faith...we partake of and have association or communion with the divine nature." He observes, however, that the language of 2 Pet. 1:4 is "without parallel in the New and Old Testament." Nevertheless, finding it in harmony with the rest of the Scripture, he says:

> What is the divine nature? It is...eternal truth, righteousness, wisdom, everlasting life, peace, joy, happiness, and whatever can be called good. Now he [or she] who becomes a partaker of the divine nature receives all this, so that he [or she] lives eternally and has everlasting peace, joy and happiness, and is pure, clean, righteous, almighty against the devil, sin, and death.[9]

Martin Luther's interpretation of this passage from 2 Peter is echoed in an important devotional book written by a Lutheran pastor early in the seventeenth century. This is Johann Arndt's *True Christianity*, a work that was read widely by Lutherans until early in this century. Arndt writes:

> By this deep trust and heartfelt assent, a man [or woman] gives his [or her] heart completely and utterly to God, rests in God alone, gives himself [herself] over to God, clings to God alone, unites himself [herself] with God, is a participant of all that which is God and Christ, becomes one spirit with God, receives from God new power, new life, new consolation, peace and joy, rest of soul, righteousness and holiness, and also, from God through faith, one is reborn [p. 45].

Arndt also speaks of salvation as communion with God.

> Since Christ now lives and dwells in you through faith, his indwelling is not a dead work but a living work. As a result, renewal from Christ though faith comes about.
> Grace brings about two things in you: first, faith places Christ in you and makes you his possession; second, it renews you in Christ so that you grow, blossom, and live in him. What is the use of a graft in a stem if it does not grow and bring forth fruit?...The true sanctifying faith renews the whole person, purifies the heart, unites with God (p. 47)...[10]

Furthermore, salvation as sharing in the divine nature is also affirmed in the Formula of Concord. The discussion there centers on matters of Christology, specifically the hypostatic union of the divine and human natures in Christ. The authors of the Formula of Concord draw a parallel between the union of Christ and the believer and the union of the two natures in Christ: "Saint Peter testifies with clear words that even we, in whom Christ dwells only by grace, have in Christ, because of this exalted mystery, become 'partakers of the divine nature.'"[11] If this is so, continues the Formula of Concord, how much more intimate must be the union of God and human beings in Christ when the apostle says, "in him [Christ] the whole fullness of deity dwells bodily" (Col. 2:9).

What can we conclude from this brief discussion of *theosis* and related theological ideas? The term "deification" is commonly employed among Orthodox, but not among Lutherans, and does not have wide currency in Western theology.[12] The Orthodox understanding of "deification," which was developed most fully in the patristic period, however, has its roots in the Scripture passages in 2 Peter and I John, in the images in the Gospel of John that speak of union between Christ and the believer (e.g., the vine and the branches), and in the concept of mutual indwelling (John 1:32; 14:17, et al.). Similarly, Saint Paul says in Gal. 2:20: "It is no longer I who live but it is Christ who lives in me." These biblical expressions build a bridge across the divide that separates us. The Orthodox understand salvation as communion with God and sharing in God's life in the fellowship of the church, the body of Christ, and the temple of the Holy Spirit. These theological expressions are biblical so they also appear from time to time in Lutheran writings, but without the same centrality and degree of consistency. Although Lutherans are wary to speak of the "deification" of human beings, they do speak of "giving one's heart wholly to God," or "clinging to God alone," and of the "union of God and human beings in Christ." And they affirm that communion with God is mediated through the Word and Sacraments within the fellowship of the church.

In the Lutheran understanding, justification is God's gracious declaration of forgiveness. This justifying word comes to the sinner from without by a declaration of God, by imputation. There is no place for human cooperation in justification; it is God's work alone. Justification, however, requires faith, for it is through faith that believers make Christ's redemptive death and resurrection their own. Faith lays hold of God's action in Christ. Abraham believed God, "Therefore his faith 'was reckoned to him as righteousness'" (Rom. 4:22).

In the dialogues between Lutherans and Orthodox in Finland, it was stated that "faith" played a role in Lutheran theology similar to the role of "*theosis*" in Orthodox theology. *In ipsa fide Christus adest.* (In faith itself Christ is present.) Faith is a way of speaking about union between the believer and God, about fellowship with God. Saint Gregory of Nyssa wrote: From the history of Abraham we learn that one cannot "draw near to God unless faith mediates and unites the soul that seeks God to that [divine] nature that is beyond our comprehension."[13] To become "sons and daughters of God" is to enter into intimate communion with God through the Spirit who dwells in us, a union that is nurtured by the Word and Sacraments within the fellowship of the church. The Finnish statement reads:

> It was perceived that aspects of soteriology are not unrelated to each other nor contradictory, but the traditional Lutheran doctrine of justification contains the idea of the deification of [human beings]. Justification and deification are based on the real presence of Christ in the word of God, in the sacraments, and in worship.[14]

The term *theosis*, what appears to be a major point of contention between Lutherans and Orthodox, can be seen as a fruitful point of convergence from another perspective. The teaching about deification expresses a profound biblical truth that the two traditions share. Both Lutherans and Orthodox affirm that the ultimate goal of salvation is communion with the living God. Reconciliation and fellowship with God is made possible only through the act of divine grace in Christ's vicarious death and resurrection. By the initiative that belongs wholly to the triune God, human beings are introduced into a personal relationship of participation in God's life. By grace we share in what God is by nature and become what God intended us to be.

There are differences in the way the two traditions understand righteousness. Both Lutherans and Orthodox insist that sinners are forgiven without any merit of their own; the only merit is the cross of Christ. Whereas the Orthodox see righteousness as the inner transformation toward "God-like-ness" (i.e., sanctification in Lutheran terminology), Lutherans say that righteousness is imputed to humans. But on the fundamental point, that salvation is a gratuitous act by which God draws sinners into a loving relationship with himself, there is no disagreement. In our view one reason for this is that both traditions have continued to employ the language of the Bible as the primary vehicle of theological expression and spiritual understanding.

## Redemption and Triumph Over Death

Just as the reformers were capable of using the idea of "partaking of the divine nature" and not simply the model of vicarious atonement to speak of salvation, so the Orthodox, following the Scriptures, also speak of the vicarious death of Christ, Christ "for us" (*pro nobis*), and affirm the necessity of the sacrificial work of Christ. They insist, however, that the "juridical image of Redemption" must be completed by the "physical image of the triumph over death..."[15] but they do not rule out the Western church's way of conceiving redemption. Nor did the early fathers express the mystery of salvation in only one image. Saint Athanasius writes:

> But since the debt owed by all men had still to be paid, since all...had to die, therefore after the proof of his divinity given by his works, he now on behalf of all men offered the sacrifice and surrendered his own temple to death on behalf of all, in order to make them all guiltless and free from the first transgression, and to reveal himself superior to death, showing his own incorruptible body as first-fruits of the universal resurrection.[16]

Yet, as John Meyendorff observes, the Anselmian idea of "satisfaction" is not commonplace in Orthodoxy. "Byzantine theology did not produce any significant elaboration of the Pauline doctrine of justification expressed in Romans and Galatians. The Greek patristic commentaries on such passages as Gal. 3:13 ("Christ redeemed us from the curse of the law by becoming a curse for us") generally interpret the idea of redemption by substitution in the wider context of victory over death and of sanctification."[17] Lutherans also speak of redemption in terms of Christ's victory over death.

> It was a strange and dreadful strife
> When life and death contended;
> The victory remained with life,
> The reign of death was ended.
> Holy Scripture plainly says
> That death is swallowed up by death,
> Its sting is lost forever.[18]

Nevertheless, here too there is a significant difference of emphasis. Just as Lutherans have been uncomfortable with the idea of "deification," so the Orthodox have been uneasy with medieval Western formulations that conceive of Christ's atonement as a "satisfaction" for sins. How one assesses these differences depends, in large measure, on how much weight one gives to a specific view of atonement. There is no question that Lutherans and Orthodox are drawn to different biblical words and images to express their respective understanding of salvation. Put much too simply, Lutherans emphasize Galatians and Romans, Orthodox emphasize the Gospel of John and First John. What divides us has less to do with the doctrinal heritage of the early church (e.g., the creed of Nicaea, or the christological statement of faith of the Council of Chalcedon), than with the way the two traditions have appropriated different aspects of the Scriptures in preaching and teaching salvation.

## The Image of God

Lutherans and Orthodox make different use of the biblical phrase "image of God." For the Orthodox the image of God is the "great natural prerogative" of human beings, and refers to specific characteristics in them, notably free will and rationality. Saint Gregory of Nyssa writes: "There is in us the possibility for everything good, for all virtue and wisdom, and every better thing that can be conceived; but one thing is preeminent among all, that we are free from necessity, and are not subject to any natural power, but have within ourselves the power to choose what we wish."[19] Saint Gregory's reasoning is that human beings are moral creatures and that virtue would have no meaning if human beings were not free. Furthermore, the Eastern church fathers see the image of God in human beings as a reflection of divine life and especially divine love, in which human beings were called to grow in likeness with God. The failure of human beings to grow in likeness to God deprived them of authentic life, which is impossible without God. However, for the Orthodox at the fall the image of God was tarnished, but not effaced. Lutherans tend to say that in the fall the image of God was "effaced" or "lost." Nevertheless, Lutheran theology has long recognized the distinction between broad and narrow senses of the image of God.

A key to understanding the use of the image of God in the two traditions can be found in different understandings of the scriptural use of the term. One use is found in the locus classicus in Gen. 1:26: "Then God said, 'Let us make humankind in our image, according to our likeness...'" As Saint Gregory (and almost all Christian theologians) understands the passage from Genesis, "image of God" designates those unique gifts that God bestowed on human beings: free will, rationality, speech, and the capacity for communion with God. The other is found in the New Testament texts that speak of the restoration of the image in Christ (such as Col. 1:15; 3:10, and Eph. 5:9), which speak of putting on a new nature "which is being renewed in knowledge according to the image of its creator." Both understandings of the "image of God" can be found in the early fathers. We have already cited Saint Gregory of Nyssa on one sense of the term. A text attributed to his older brother, Saint Basil of Caesarea, uses image of God in its christological sense.

> Human beings were created according to the image and likeness of God, but sin deformed the beauty of the image, drawing the soul to passionate

desires. But God, who made human beings, is the true life. Whoever has lost the likeness to God, lost fellowship with the light; whatever is without God is not able to share in the blessed light. Let us therefore return to the grace which we possessed from the beginning to which we have become strangers through sin.[20]

In general, Lutherans prefer to speak of the image of God in its christological sense to designate that which was lost in the fall and regained in redemption; Orthodox prefer to speak of the image of God as those distinctively divine qualities reflected in human beings, free will and rationality, which continue to be part of human nature after the fall. However, the Orthodox often make further distinctions between image and likeness (Gen. 1:26). What was lost at the fall was the "likeness" of God, "fellowship with the light," and "communion with God through love." Christ restored this "fallen" image by regaining for us that which we had at the beginning, indeed more than what was bound in Adam; through his incarnation, death, and resurrection Christ once and for all achieved life in communion with God. Neither view, however, excludes the other.

Lutherans believe that human beings retain a basic knowledge of right and wrong, the use of reason in matters of justice, and some sense of God's existence through natural knowledge. As the Lutheran theologian John Gerhard expressed it, everything depends on how one defines the image of God. If the image is only "natural prerogatives," it is not lost through the fall. If, however, the image of God is also understood to mean "righteousness and true holiness," then the image of God has been lost in the fall and regained in Christ. Furthermore, what is regained is in Christ more wonderful than was lost: "By the grace of Christ and the Holy Spirit, that image of God, into which we have begun to be remade in this life, will one day shine in us more brightly and more gloriously than it once shone in Adam, for he was able not to die, but we are not able to die."[21]

## Nature and Grace

Like the term "deification" and the phrase "image of God," the terms "nature" and "grace" carry different overtones within Lutheran and Orthodox traditions. Some Lutherans, for example, could say, "we are by nature sinful and unclean," a formulation that Orthodox would not normally employ. On occasion, however, the Eastern Orthodox fathers depict sin in language that is no less vivid than that of the Lutheran reformers. Saint Gregory of Nyssa wrote:

> Because of the guile of him who sowed in us the weeds of disobedience, our nature no longer preserves the stamp of the divine image; it has been transformed and made ugly by sin. Freely our nature chose to act in accord with the evil one. For this reason human nature has become a member of the evil family of the father of sin.[22]

Lutheran theology has never asserted that human beings are "by nature" sinful. If they are, there could be no redemption. The term "nature" in the phrase "by nature sinful" is a metaphorical expression to express the corrupting power of sin in the lives of human beings. The Lutheran position is more clearly expressed in statements such as:

> We believe, teach, and confess that there is a distinction between human nature and original sin, not only in the beginning when God created human beings pure and holy and without sin, but also as we now have our nature after the Fall. Even after the Fall our nature is and remains a creation of God. The distinction between our nature and original sin is as great as the difference between God's Work and the devil's work.[23]

The Orthodox speak of sin as "fallenness." Humanity strayed from the path of communion with God and now finds itself in a "fallen state." This state is defined in terms of morality (since there is no authentic life apart from God) and distorted priorities, not by expressions such as "natural corruption" or "inherited guilt" as among Lutherans. Sin, which is living out of communion with God, is the lack of true humanness. Therefore it is said that the image of God, the sign of true humanness, has been tarnished. For this reason Christ could become fully human yet remain without sin. In the fallen state human beings are dominated by the "flesh" which, instead of leading nature toward God and to communion with him, turns it away from God.

### Free Will

Lutherans believe that human beings were created good, and that the fall into sin did not destroy the possibility for this goodness to be restored. Yet they embrace a more pessimistic view of human beings than the Orthodox. Lutherans do not speak of "synergy" (cooperation with God) with respect to justification. "Free will," then, is another concept that has different connotations for Lutherans and Orthodox. In an early treatise Martin Luther wrote: "After the fall of Adam, free will is a mere expression; whenever it acts in character, it commits mortal sin."[24] Not all of Luther's utterances are normative for Lutherans, yet statements such as this, and the experience that underlies it, have shaped Lutheran attitudes toward nature, grace, and free will.

In the case of "free will" it is apparent that different historical experiences and different memories have shaped Orthodox and Lutheran views. Early Christian debates with pagan philosophers over "free will" still inform Orthodox thinking: Lutherans bring a distinctly medieval, Western agenda to the discussion. In the ancient world, freedom of choice (freedom of the will) was seen as a necessary doctrine if there was to be any sense of moral responsibility. How could it be said that one was responsible for one's action, i.e., that moral acts were possible, unless one could "choose" one course over another? Without freedom of the will all human actions are determined by external causes. For this reason, "free will" became a foundational teaching of the Christian church and was affirmed by all the early fathers, East and West, including Saint Augustine, especially in his earlier writings.[25]

For the Orthodox the teaching on free will has not led to the belief that humans can save themselves by their own works or efforts. This is what has been referred to as the Pelagian error that the church repudiated in the fifth and sixth centuries. On the contrary, free will was a way of asserting human freedom, and the possibility of fellowship with God and love, for "where there is no freedom there can be no love."[26] Saint Paul says: "Work out your own salvation with fear and trembling; for it is God who is at work in you, enabling you both to will and to work for his good pleasure" (Phil. 2:12-13). In the Orthodox view there can be no contradiction between grace and free will, or between nature and grace. As John Chrysostom wrote: "Human will is not sufficient, unless one receives aid from above; on the other hand we gain nothing by aid from above if there is no willingness."[27] No one has a "natural power" to earn salvation, yet God allows humans to cooperate with grace to embark on the path toward fellowship with God (*theosis*). Fellowship with God does not mean participation in the divine essence (*ousia*) but in the divine attributes or qualities (energies) that God shares with human beings.

On this point the differences between Lutherans and the Orthodox are noteworthy. Each affirms the "freedom of the will" but restricts the arena in which the will is active. Here the Lutheran distinction between "justification" and "sanctification" must be kept in mind. In justification the will is powerless and cannot cooperate with God's grace. "For this reason the mind that is set on the flesh is hostile to God; it does not submit to God's laws—indeed it cannot, and those who are in the flesh cannot please God" (Rom. 8:7). After regeneration, however, the will of the believer, nourished by the Word and Sacraments, learns to desire the good and to work with the Holy Spirit in achieving holiness. Once liberated by "God's power and activity," the human will "becomes an instrument and means of God the Holy Spirit, so that human beings not only lay hold on grace but also cooperate with the Holy Spirit in the works that follow."[28]

We do not wish to minimize our differences on this matter, but it may be helpful to observe on this question, as on others, that the way the two traditions have appropriated the Scriptures has shaped the way that they have understood the mystery of salvation and sanctification. The Orthodox think of one continuous process, whereas the Lutherans distinguish the initial act of justification and regeneration from the process of sanctification. As we have already observed, the different emphases can be traced back to different biblical metaphors. If the metaphor for salvation is communion or participation, then it is natural and inevitable that one speaks of cooperation, of willing, and of love as ways in which fellowship with God is deepened and strengthened. Many texts from the Scriptures speak of salvation in these terms. If, however, the primary biblical metaphor is that of a vicarious death, Christ "for us," and God's saving action takes place independent of us, the idea of cooperation in justification is unnecessary and misleading. Once the sinner is justified, however, then the biblical images of communion, indwelling, and cooperation come into play and it is possible to speak about working out "your own salvation with fear and trembling" (Phil. 2:12).

## The Spiritual Life

Finally, because of their different ways of conceiving of salvation, Lutherans and Orthodox understand the spiritual life differently. Lutherans generally do not speak about "penultimate" goals, of gradual growth in perfection, or of a progressive acquisition of righteousness. The Lutheran concept of *simul justus et peccator* (at the same time justified and sinner) opposes ideas of guaranteed sequential moral improvement. The Orthodox believe that "as we became not apparently but really sinful because of Adam, so through Christ, the Second Adam, we became really justified."[29] The Orthodox speak about the quest for "holiness" as a process based on divine-human cooperation. God's Holy Spirit, the "source of sanctification," bestows upon each human person the life of holiness made available in Christ, in the human nature he assumed for us. In a dynamic process, working "from within," the Holy Spirit leads human persons in the church "from strength to strength, power to power, and glory to glory." Although the Lutheran accent on grace *extra nos* (from the outside) avoids the anxieties of spiritual pulse-taking, the Orthodox find such talk of grace outside of us puzzling. If grace is only outside us and does not bring about a change in the life of the believer, justification can become a fiction that does not touch the substance of life and experience. Lutherans are uncomfortable with talk of growth in perfection and divine-human cooperation because it appears to have Pelagian overtones. In our discussions, however, it became clear that the Orthodox understand human cooperation as the work of the Holy Spirit. The initiative belongs uniquely to God who through the Spirit fills our hearts with the love of the Father. Without our active receptivity, however, God's work would come to nothing. Divine initiative must be met by a moral response on the part of the believer if the work of sanctification is to proceed.

In answer to questions from the Orthodox as to how grace can be "external," Lutherans affirm that faith is a divine work "in us" as well as "for us" and that it changes us. In Lutheran language this is the meaning of sanctification. God does not simply declare the sinner righteous; God also desires that the work of salvation be brought to fulfillment, that human beings become actually perfected. Saint Paul writes: "Not that I have already obtained this or have already reached the goal; but I press on to make it my own, because Christ Jesus has made me his own" (Phil. 3:12).

The question remains: Grace changes us in what way and to what degree? There can be no doubt that Lutherans and Orthodox view the life of faith and the quest for holiness quite differently. For the Orthodox genuine asceticism is an indispensable element in the Christian life. Asceticism has played a very small part in Lutheran life and spirituality. Nevertheless, Lutherans and Orthodox agree that in "working out our own salvation with fear and trembling" it is God who "is at work in you [us] enabling you [us] both to will and to work for his good pleasure" (Phil. 2:13). Only through the word of the gospel, the life of prayer and worship, and participation in the sacraments can the faithful enjoy fellowship with God and be empowered to become "like him."

The Christian life is never inert and static; it is a life lived to God, a life of perpetual growth, in which we are being "changed into the same image [the Lord's] from one degree of glory to another" (2 Cor. 3:18). Christians live in hope of the day when we will see God face to face, and God will be all in all. As Saint Gregory, patriarch of Constantinople, put it in one of his "theological orations": On that day when God will be all in all, we will no longer be captive to our sinful passions, but "will be entirely like God, ready to receive into our hearts the whole God and God alone. This is the perfection to which we press on."[29]

## The Communion of Saints

For both Lutheran and Orthodox, spiritual growth encompasses prayer, the study of the Scriptures, and participation in the sacramental and liturgical life of the church. We are never apart from the fullness of the communion of saints, living and dead, who join with us in praising and glorifying God the Father, Son, and Holy Spirit. In the words of the Te Deum: "The glorious company of apostles praise you. The noble fellowship of prophets praise you. The white-robed army of martyrs praise you. Throughout the world the holy Church acclaims you." Growth in the Spirit, then, is never individualistic, it always takes place in the unity of the body of Christ and is dependent on the growth of all.

### Common Roots and Unity

By the power of the Holy Spirit, we have found ourselves drawn together in Christ on those topics that we had anticipated greatest disagreement. If Lutherans can begin to understand and appreciate the Orthodox emphasis on deification (*theosis*) as communion with God, and the Orthodox can begin to understand and appreciate the Lutheran emphasis on the proclamation of "justification by grace through faith," as we have done in this dialogue,then we have taken a significant step toward breaking down the wall of partition that divides us. Then we can more readily approach other differences that keep us apart, including those concerning the nature of the church.

We have shared different perspectives and emphases, both within and between our traditions, which are often complementary, mutually challenging and informative, and on which we anticipate continuing reflection, cooperation, and convergence.

In future dialogues, the Lutherans and Orthodox hope to continue, in humility and respect, the exploration of our common roots within the Holy Scriptures and the early church. As we have jointly studied the Scriptures, the church fathers, and the reformers, we have learned to recognize our similarities and respect our differences, as well as to rejoice in our unity in Christ and our common confession of the one God, Father, Son, and Holy Spirit, to whom be glory now and forever.

## Notes

1. An English translation of Cyril's letter to John can be found in T. Herbert Bindley, *The Oecumenical Documents of the Faith* (London: Methuen & Co., 1925), 272-78.

2. See Ernst Benz, *Wittenberg und Byzanz*. Zur Begegnung und Auseinandersetzung der Reformation und der oestlich-orthodoxen Kirche (Marburg: N.G. Elwert Verlag, 1949), 114. The translation of the Latin *justificari* is not consistent. At a number of places it is rendered by terms formed from the root *dikaios*, at least in the 1730 edition. See *Augustana Confessio Germanica et Latina cum versione Graeca Pauli Dolsci* ed. M.C. Reineccius (Leipzig: 1730). On this point see Wayne James Jorgenson, "The Augustana Graeca and the Correspondence Between the Tübingen Lutherans and Patriarch Jeremias: Scripture and Tradition in Theological Methodology" (University Microfilms, Dissertation, Boston University, 1979).

3. See Bishop Maximos Aghiorgoussis, "Orthodox Soteriology" in John Meyendorff and Robert Tobias, eds., *Salvation in Christ* (Minneapolis: Augsburg, 1992), 35-58.

4. Bishop Kallistos Ware's remark occurs in the foreword to Georgios I. Mantzaridis, *The Deification of Man* (Crestwood, NY: St. Vladimir's Press, 1984), 7.

5. For the theological significance of "energies" in Orthodox theology, see Christos Yannaras, "The Distinction Between Essence and Energies and Its Importance for Theology," *Saint Vladimir's Theological Quarterly* 19 (1975): 232-45.

6. Vladimir Lossky, *In the Image and Likeness of God* (Crestwood, NY: Saint Vladimir's Press, 1958), 98.

7. "Lectures on Galatians 1535," in American Edition of *Luther's Works*, vol. 26, trans. Jaroslav Pelikan (Saint Louis: Concordia Publishing House, 1963), 287.

8. Apology to the Augsburg Confession 4.43 in *The Book of Concord*, ed. Theodore G. Tappert (Philadelphia: Fortress Press, 1959), 113.

9. "Sermons on the Second Epistle of Saint Peter" at 1.4, in American Edition of *Luther's Works, The Catholic Epistles*, trans. Martin H. Bertram (Saint Louis: Concordia Publishing House, 1967), 30:155.

10. Johann Arndt, *True Christianity*, introduction and trans. Peter Erb (New York: Paulist Press, 1979), 45-46. It is significant that Arndt's writings were popular with leading representatives of Orthodox spirituality, e.g., Saint Tikhon of Zadonsk. cf. Elisabeth Behrsigel "Hesychasm and the Western Impact in Russia: St. Tikhon of Zadonsk (1724-1783)" in Lonis Dupré and Don E. Saliers, eds., in cooperation with John Meyendorff, *Christian Spirituality* III Post-Reformation and Modern (New York: Crossroad, 1989), pp. 432-445.

11. Formula of Concord 8.34, BC, 597.

12. For a discussion of patristic ideas of *theosis* from the perspective of the Reformation debates, see William Rusch, "How the Eastern Fathers Understood what the Western Meant by Justification" in L/RC 7:131-42. See also Henry Edwards, "Justification, Sanctification and the Eastern Orthodox Concept of 'Theosis'" in *Consensus: A Canadian Lutheran Journal of Theology* 14 (1988): 65-80. G.L. Bray, "Justification and the Eastern Orthodox Churches" in *Here We Stand: Justification by Faith Today*, ed. David Field (London: Hodder and Stoughton, 1986), 103-19.

13. Gregory of Nyssa, in *Gregorii Nysseni Opera, Contra Eunomium Libri* (2.91), vol. 1, ed. Werner Jaeger (Leiden: E.J. Brill, 1960), 253.

14. *Dialogue Between Neighbours: The Theological Conversations Between the Evangelical-Lutheran Church of Finland and the Russian Orthodox Church 1970-1986*, ed. Hannu T. Kamppuri, Publication of the Luther-Agricola Society, B 17 (Helsinki, 1986): 19. Tuomo Mannermaa, "Das Verhältnis von Glaube und Liebe in der Theologie Luthers," *Luther in Finnland*, ed. M. Ruokanen, Schriften der Luther-Agricola Gesellschaft A 22 (Helsinki: Vammalan Kirjapaino Oy, 1984) 99-110.

15. Lossky, *In the Image*, 99-100.

16. Athanasius, *Contra Gentes* and *De Incarnatione*, ed. Robert W. Thompson (Oxford: Clarendon Press, 1971), 183.

17. John Meyendorff, *Byzantine Theology* (New York: Fordham University Press, 1979), 160.

18. "Christ Jesus Lay in Death's Strong Bands" (*Christ Lag in Todesbanden*), *The Lutheran Book of Worship* (Minneapolis: Augsburg, 1978), no. 134.

19. Gregory of Nyssa, "De Hominis Opificio 16." *Patrologia graeca* 44 (1846), col. 184 B.

20. *Basilii Caesareae Cappadocini Opera Omnia*, ed. Julien Garnier (Paris, 1839), vol. 2, 445.

21. John Gerhard, *Locorum Theologicorum*. Tomus Secumdus, ed. J.F. Cotta (Tübingen, 1765). Locus IV, *De Imagine Dei in Homine ante Lapsum* can be found on pages 237-93. The relevant passage is on page 289ff. (9.10.138).

22. "Contra Eunomium Libri," (3.10). vol. 2,293.

23. "Epitome 1 on Original Sin, Thesis 1" FC BC, 466.

24. "Ground and Reason of Articles Unjustly Condemned" (Weimar Ausgabe, vol. 7, 445).

25. See Robert L. Wilken, "Justification by Works: Fate and the Gospel in the Roman Empire," *Concordia Theological Monthly*, 40 (1969), 379-92.

26. Kallistos Ware, *The Orthodox Way* (Crestwood, NY: St. Vladimir's Press, 1979), 75-6.

27. John Chrysostom, "Homilies on Matthew," 82.4 (*Patrologia graeca* 57, col. 742).

28. "Epitome 2 on Free Will, Antithesis 9" *BC*, 466.

29. "Saint Gregory, Patriarch of Constantinople, Theological Orations," 4.6, *Christology of the Later Fathers*, ed. E.B. Hardy and Cyril Richardson (Philadelphia: The Westminster Press, 1954), 181.

# Roman Catholics in Dialogue

# The One Mediator,
# The Saints, and Mary*

## INTRODUCTION

(1) From its outset in 1965 the theological dialogue between Lutherans and Roman Catholics in the United States has concerned itself with doctrines that have united or separated their churches from one another since the sixteenth century. The degree of consensus or convergence that exists on the Nicene Creed, Baptism, the Eucharist, the Ministry, Papal Primacy, and Teaching Authority and Infallibility has been expressed in summaries and joint statements[1] that have become important for relations between our churches and for wider ecumenical discussions.

(2) In 1983 the dialogue completed a common statement on "Justification by Faith," published with background papers in 1985.[2] We agreed "that the good news of what God has done for us in Jesus Christ is the source and center of all Christian life and of the existence and work of the church" (§§4). We share an affirmation that "our entire hope of justification and salvation rests on Christ Jesus and on the gospel..." so that "we do not place our ultimate trust in anything other than God's promise and saving work in Christ" (§§4, 157). We asked our churches and Christians of all traditions to study our declaration together and find in it (§§161-64) an invitation to "the good news of God's justifying action in Jesus Christ" that "stands at the center of Christian faith and life" (§§2, 165).

(3) In setting forth our material convergences on this doctrine and an "incomplete convergence on the use" of it as "a criterion of authenticity for the church's proclamation and practice" (§§150-60), we indicated need for further dialogue (§154), testing the use of this critical principle. A number of possible test issues were noted, including ecclesiastical structures, means of grace, papacy, infallibility, and teachings on Mary and the saints (§§117-20).

*G. Anderson, F. Strafford, J. Burgess, eds., *The One Mediator, The Saints, and Mary* (Lutherans and Catholics in Dialogue VIII; Minneapolis: Augsburg, 1992) 21-132, 339-64.

(4) In light of the sole mediatorship of Christ, which was termed "the correlative" of the principle of justification by faith (§117), the present statement focuses on the saints and Mary, which became a divisive subject in the Reformation period. We shall begin in Part One, on issues and perspectives, with (I) the problem in the sixteenth century. Next we shall turn to (II) the perspectives of our two traditions on the crucial issues.

Then (III) we shall reexamine the problem in the present context, which has changed in some ways from the situation in the sixteenth century. We shall here indicate dimensions of the problem and some resulting divergences, investigate whether they need to be church-dividing, propose church-uniting convergences, and draw a conclusion. In support of these convergences and the steps which we ask our churches to consider, Part Two provides foundations from (I) Scripture, which is normative for both our traditions; (II) the second to the sixteenth centuries, where historical studies show the complexity of the issues; and (III) subsequent periods, including the Second Vatican Council. These foundations undergird the proposals at the conclusion of Part One.

(5) In many instances we are dealing not only with doctrines but also Catholic and Lutheran thought structures as well as expressions of worship and piety. It should be noted, however, that the dialogue did not discuss in any depth, nor do we attempt here to report on, present-day matters of popular and folk religion, aspects in comparative religion or the history of world religions, feminist questions, or a total systematic theology of the saints and Mary. Amid these immense and much debated areas we have dealt only with issues that have divided our churches since the sixteenth century and seem still to be divisive.

## PART ONE: ISSUES AND PERSPECTIVES

### I. THE PROBLEM IN THE SIXTEENTH CENTURY

(6) Late medieval piety was marked by a great emphasis on the intercession of deceased saints and in particular by an intensification of confidence in the power of Mary. The steadily increasing number of saints invoked to remedy human needs and ills, and the long-accustomed role of Mary as mediator between the faithful and Christ, obscured the traditional theological distinction between adoration (*latria*) and veneration (*dulia*).[3] In 1517, when Martin Luther called for an academic disputation on the use of indulgences and their relationship to the sacrament of penance, the cult of the saints and Mary became a related issue.

(7) In 1517-18 Luther had assessed and found seriously wanting a number of practices and institutions that he encountered in the church of his

day. His criticism focused on: a) sacramental confession-absolution; b) indulgences; c) the papacy with its powers of binding-loosing; and d) purgatory as well as prayer for the dead. What concerned him with each of these was the role people thought it played in the forgiveness of post-baptismal sin.

(8) To be specific, the constitution *Omnis Utriusque* of the Fourth Lateran Council (1215) required Christian adults to confess their sins once a year and to their parish priest so as to obtain God's forgiveness.[4] But even after one had received absolution in this manner, the obligation remained to perform works of satisfaction for the sins that had been forgiven; indeed, theologians taught that this was an integral part of the sacrament of penance. Here, however, the church could help by mitigating or eliminating the penalties which sins, though forgiven, still deserved in divine justice. The church did this by having recourse to and applying the superabundant merits of Christ and the saints (indulgences). For the use of this treasure, which was to benefit the whole church, the pope, as Christ's vicar, and bishops were responsible. Those who both needed and could profit from such help included the deceased as well as the living (purgatory and prayer for the dead).[5]

(9) Luther regarded the system of which these elements were parts as claiming to bring the forgiveness that could come only from Christ. His attitude to the saints and Mary was guided by this christocentric view of life which was expressed in the fundamental affirmation of justification by faith alone. Luther had gained this christocentric view in an intense struggle for the biblical meaning of penance and a rethinking of the soteriological implications of the trinitarian dogma, focusing on the incarnation of Christ.[6] Having been steeped in the cult of the saints during his formative years, Luther and other Reformers, notably Andreas Karlstadt, began to criticize the cult.[7] They said that it caused people to have greater confidence in the merits of deceased saints than in Christ. Some Reformers, like Martin Bucer, called for the removal of all Saints' Days in the liturgical calendar, but Luther advocated a more moderate stance towards the saints and Mary.[8]

(10) None of Luther's early opponents sensed his concerns about penance more keenly than did the Dominican theologian Thomas de Vio (Cajetan).[9] In his reaction to Luther in 1518 he understood Luther to a) deny that indulgences derive their efficacy from the fact that in granting them the church mediates the merits of Christ and the saints to assist the baptized in making satisfaction before God after the forgiveness of sins and b) maintain that through indulgences the church relies on the promised power of the keys (Matthew 16:19) so as to loose bonds that it has imposed for infractions of its own (rather than divine) laws. Cajetan countered by saying that these positions were at odds with the presentation of indulgences in the bull *Unigenitus*

of Pope Clement VI. And such documents rank right after the authority of the Scriptures.[10]

(11) More was involved here than a Scholastic's appeal to authority. Cajetan set himself to answering each of Luther's various arguments against indulgences as applying the merits of Christ and the saints. But by introducing papal teaching, he was asking Luther to trust in the church and its self-understanding with regard to the forgiveness of sin and its consequences— this on the basis of Matthew 16:19 (the power of the keys).

(12) There was a difference between the two with regard to trust. What Luther distrusted while holding to the promise of Matthew 16:19, Cajetan trusted and urged him likewise to trust on the basis of that same promise. Should the church be trusted to mediate God's forgiveness, both of sin and its consequences? Here they disagreed. The association of the saints' merits with those of Christ figured centrally in the disagreement.[11]

(13) In the bull *Exsurge Domine* of 1520 views taken from Luther's recent writings were condemned. Those views had to do with the same practices and institutions that Luther had criticized in 1517-18. Forty-one propositions were cited without the contexts in which they had originally appeared. The censures ranged from "heretical" to "seductive of the simple-minded" and "at odds with catholic truth."[12] Which censure or censures applied to which proposition and why each was rejected were not indicated, nor was official clarification forthcoming. After Luther's excommunication in 1521 things remained in that state. For further papal and conciliar teaching one had to wait until Pope Paul III convoked the Council of Trent, which met for the first time in 1545.

(14) Luther's rejection of the cult of the saints and Mary was based on the contention that such practice is not based on divine command and detracts from trust in Christ alone. He declared that instead of relying on deceased saints, whose world is hidden and mysterious, baptized Christians should follow the command of Scripture to care for the weak and needy in the world; these need more attention than the deceased saints.[13] Luther was convinced that the practice of invoking the saints only continued the medieval tendency to transform Christ the "kindly Mediator" into a "dreaded Judge" who is to be placated by the intercession of the saints and Mary, and by a multitude of other rites.[14] Departed saints may be remembered, but invoking them is to be omitted from liturgical celebrations.

(15) Luther's attitude toward deceased saints and Mary was centered in his concept of example. Some Christians, now departed, exemplified bold faith while on earth through their words and deeds. To Luther, the most prominent saints were biblical figures like John the Baptist and Paul and later church teachers like, most notably, Ambrose, Augustine, and Bernard. John

Hus was to him also a prominent saint because God had endowed him with great gifts to renew Christianity.[15]

(16) Although Luther was critical of some collected legends of saints, he advocated the use of other legends for edification, such as Jacob of Voragine's *Golden Legend* (*Legenda aurea*), which contained stories about exemplary saints like Bernard, whom Luther "venerated."[16] He also chose to honor Henry von Zutphen, the first Lutheran martyr, executed in Brussels in 1524, and told his story in the style of ancient martyrologies.[17] He also encouraged one of his students, George Major, to publish a revised version of the *Lives of the Fathers* (*Vitae Patrum*) and, in a preface, recommended it as edifying literature. He thus continued the hagiographic tradition in this sense, but he stressed its exclusively edifying and pedagogical character: Deceased saints may be venerated as examples of faith in Christ, "the saint of saints," from whom all holiness flows.[19] But because all of them have become righteous through Christ alone, no saint is holier than another, according to Luther.

(17) Since little had been defined dogmatically about Mary, Luther felt free to develop his own views on the basis of Scripture and tradition. He accepted the dogma of Mary as "God-bearer" (*Theotokos*) and affirmed her perpetual virginity; he called her Immaculate Conception "a pious and pleasing thought."[20] Consistent with his christocentric stance, Luther contended that such notions should not become official doctrines. He affirmed some festivals involving Mary on a scriptural basis, but rejected two: the Assumption and the Immaculate Conception.[21]

(18) According to Luther, Mary embodied God's unmerited grace which was evidenced in the *Magnificat* (Luke 1:46-55), and as such she typified the church. He contended that the church, like Mary's virginity, would never be destroyed, no matter what the opposition and persecution.[22] Luther affirmed Mary's Assumption into heaven, but considered her Assumption no different than that of others like Abraham, Isaac, and Jacob, who had been promised life with God forever. Thus, according to Luther, Mary points only to Christ, whose ascension would be dishonored if she were invoked.[23]

(19) Luther's hymns, when they refer to Mary, do so in the language of a Marian piety reflecting his views. It is a part of an incarnational Christology informed by biblical and patristic tradition which focuses on the exaltation of Christ and on the Trinity.[24] "Christ alone should be invoked as our Mediator."[25]

(20) The first Lutheran constitutions and liturgies (*Kirchenordnungen*) were normed by Luther's doctrinal concern that neither the saints nor Mary is to be invoked because Christ is the only Mediator and Scripture is silent about such invocation. Saints may be honored as mirroring the grace and mercy of God, but Christ alone is the Mediator who represents the faithful

(I John 2:1;Rom. 8:34).[26] Statements such as these represent a significant contribution in the West toward a dogmatic clarification of the veneration of the saints.[27]

(21) When Emperor Charles V invited the princes and representatives of free cities in the empire to discuss their religious differences at the Diet of Augsburg in 1530, Elector Frederick of Saxony asked the Wittenberg theologians to prepare an account of the beliefs and practices in the churches of his land. Philipp Melanchthon was asked by Luther and other leaders of the reform movement to draft what has become known as the Augsburg Confession, which consisted of two parts: "chief articles of faith," and "articles about matters in dispute, in which an account is given of the abuses which have been corrected." CA 21 is the final article of the first part, and it served as the platform for doctrinal dialogue on "the cult of the saints." It reads (German text):

> It is also taught among us that the saints should be kept in remembrance so that our faith may be strengthened when we see what grace they received and how they were sustained by faith. Moreover, their good works are to be an example for us, each of us in his own calling. So His Imperial Majesty may in salutary and godly fashion imitate the example of David in making war on the Turk, for both are incumbents of a royal office which demands the defense and protection of their subjects. However, it cannot be proved from the Scriptures that we are to invoke saints or seek help from them. "For there is one mediator between God and men, Christ Jesus" (I Tim. 2:5), who is the only saviour, the only high priest, advocate, and intercessor before God (Rom, 8:34). He alone has promised to hear our prayers. Moreover, according to the Scriptures, the highest form of divine service is sincerely to seek and call upon this same Jesus Christ in every time of need. "If anyone sins, we have an advocate with the Father, Jesus Christ the righteous" (I John 2:1).[28]

(22) A Catholic response to the Augsburg Confession was mandated not by the pope in Rome but by the emperor in Augsburg. This initiated a drafting process which in turn included revisions that were made because Charles V desired a less polemical tone. The final text, the *Confutation*, was forthcoming on August 3, 1950.[29] Never having received papal or conciliar approval and lacking the status of official teaching in the Catholic Church, it remains to this day what it was at the time of its composition, the work of a group of theologians speaking in their own name at the Diet. That did not, however, keep it from exerting a great deal of influence.

(23) Charles V not only maintained that the *Confutation* was a refutation of the Augsburg Confession; he expected the Lutheran party at the Diet to acknowledge this. In addition to being denied a copy of the text (which

they had heard read), the Lutherans took offense at the harshness of its tone
and were apprehensive as a result of the negative stance it took with regard
to a number of their own positions.

(24) In its response to CA 21 the *Confutation* expresses surprise at the
lack of vigilance on the part of the princes. They have tolerated an error,
namely, that the memory of saints may be cultivated to promote imitation of
their faith and good works but not for the purpose of invoking them and
seeking their help. The civil authorities should have done something to keep
this view from being spread and acted on in their territories. Given that the
church has repeatedly condemned the position in question—so the
*Confutation* states bluntly[30]—CA 21 is to be completely rejected. The princes
are urged to be of one mind with the church. In particular, as regards the veneration and intercession of the saints, they should believe and confess what
the Christian people everywhere believe and confess and what was observed
in all the churches even at the time of Augustine. For to the widespread cult
of the saints he attested when he wrote:

> The Christian people celebrate with religious solemnity the memory of
> the martyrs so as to imitate the latter as well as to be associated with
> their merits and helped by their prayers.[31]

(25) Since CA 21 had appealed to Scripture, the *Confutation* did likewise. If God will honor those who minister to Christ (John 12:26), why
should not mortals do so as well? And it did not stop with veneration; it went
on to intercession. Job (42:10) had his request granted when he prayed for
his friends. Will not the God who acceded to Job's petition do likewise when
the Virgin Mary makes intercession? And if one objects that Job prayed
while yet alive, in Baruch (3:4) God is asked to hear now the prayer of the
dead of Israel. So the dead do pray for us. To that the Old Testament attests
in its presentations of Onias and Jeremiah in the Second Book of Maccabees
(15:12-14). That angels pray for us one learns from the Scriptures (Zech
1:12ff;Job 33:23ff;Rev 5:8, 8:3). If angels do this, why deny that saints do so
as well? Christ is indeed the sole Mediator of redemption (I Tim 2:5;I John
2:1), but there are many mediators who make intercession. For Moses was a
mediator (Deut 5:5) and prayed for the children of Israel (Exod 17:4; 32:11-
13; 30ff) as Paul would later for those sailing with him (Acts 27:23ff). That
same Paul asks the Romans (Rom 15:30), the Corinthians (2 Cor 1:11), and
the Colossians (Col 4:3) to pray for him, and prayer was made in the church
without stopping for Peter when he was in prison (Acts 12:5). The saints in
heaven are Christ's members (I Cor 12:12, 27;Eph 5:30); their wills are conformed to his; they see their head pray for us; who can doubt that they do
what they see Christ doing?[32]

(26) The *Confutation* thus defended both the veneration and the invocation of the saints. Asserting that Christ is the sole Mediator of redemption, it proposed Mary and the saints as "mediators of intercession."[33] It did not regard invocation as contrary to Scripture but as having a biblical basis. At the same time it did not criticize aberrations in this form of Christian piety. What the *Confutation* did was to call for trust in the church's understanding of itself as a body whose members (deceased as well as living) are empowered by Christ their head to help one another.

(27) Melanchthon responded to the *Confutation*'s criticism of CA 21 in the Apology of the Augsburg Confession (1531). The honor of the saints, he repeated, is in no way denied by Lutherans. "Honoring the saints" included: 1) giving thanks to God for them as examples of God's mercy and of faithfulness; 2) being strengthened in one's faith by God's grace in their lives; and 3) imitating their faith, love, and other virtues. Melanchthon readily conceded that angels and living saints in the church universal on earth and in heaven intercede for believers.[34] What he denounces is the step from intercession to invocation. "Scripture does not teach us to invoke the saints or to ask their help."[35] Invocation of the saints, he submits, has no command or example or promise in the canonical Scriptures and therefore no certainty. In fact, it is a relative novelty not attested in the early church before Pope Gregory the Great (590-604).[36] The Confutators make matters worse by introducing the notion of the merits of the saints being applied to other Christians, thus making the saints propitiators instead of intercessors when they claim that there is "one Mediator of redemption" (*unus mediator redemptionis*) and there are "many mediators of intercession" (*multi mediatores intercessionis*).[37] But a propitiator must have a clear promise that God will hear prayers through him and that his merits will be accepted to make satisfaction for others. Christ has both promises, the saints have neither, despite theological statements to the contrary and the formulae of the liturgy. The saints are not authorized by God to act as mediators of redemption, nor is Mary so authorized. As the Mother of God she is worthy of the highest honors, prays for the church, and is an example of faith and humble obedience. But she never claimed to have the authority which later teaching applied to her when it contrasted her mildness to the image of Christ as the dreaded judge. Such authority belongs to Christ alone. Christians have no grounds for trusting that the saints' merits are transferrable to others.[38] Equally erroneous in Melanchthon's eyes is the notion of specialization among saints, each providing special help for those who call on them. Such teaching is dangerous, indeed pagan.[39] Seeking help and trusting in other mediators besides Christ leads to the collapse of trust and diminishes knowledge of Christ. Melanchthon draws on historical experience for this central assertion: First, there was simple commemoration of the saints in the ancient prayers; then

came the invocations of saints with all its abuses, that were worse than pagan practices, especially in the superstition surrounding images, undergirded by preposterous and fabricated legends. Melanchthon notes that these abuses are not only present in popular piety and practice, but are aided and abetted by the teachers of the church, including the Confutators who do not use their knowledge of doctrine to expose these manifest abuses. To require, as the *Confutation* suggests, the invocation of the saints is tantamount to requiring abuses, and temporal authorities need to exercise their God-given responsibility to protect the consciences of the faithful from abusive ecclesiastical requirements and to defend those who teach sound doctrine.[40]

(28) When Pope Paul III called a General Council to meet in Mantua in 1537, Elector John of Saxony instructed Luther to prepare a statement indicating the articles of faith in which concessions might be made for the sake of peace and the articles in which no concessions could be made. Luther quickly produced a statement as his theological testament in case he should die, since he had become severely ill. The statement was submitted for adoption by the Smalcald League, an alliance of princes, at its meeting at Smalcald on February 8, 1537. Though present, Luther was unable to participate in the discussions because of his illness. The statements was never adopted by the league. But many of the clergy attending the meeting signed what became known as the *Smalcald Articles,* which became part of the *Book of Concord* in 1580.[41]

(29) In the section on "the invocation of the saints," Luther charged that their invocation is in conflict with the chief article, justification by faith, and undermines knowledge of Christ. He also repeated the warning of the *Augsburg Confession* that the invocation of the saints is not commanded in Scripture because "we have everything a thousandfold better in Christ."[42] Luther conceded that the saints in heaven "perhaps" (*vielleicht, fortassis*) pray for those on earth, but it does not follow that the saints in heaven should be invoked. "If such idolatrous honor is withdrawn from angels and dead saints," Luther contended, "the honor that remains will do no harm and will quickly be forgotten."[43]

(30) In 1541 Emperor Charles V persuaded Rome and leading Protestant Reformers to discuss their theological differences during the meetings of the Diet of Regensburg. A papal delegation, led by the papal legates Gasparo Contarini and Giovanni Morone, and a Protestant team, headed by Philipp Melanchthon, discussed the cult of the saints in the context of the doctrine of justification. But both sides were unable to move beyond the positions of the *Confutation* and of CA 21. Catholics asserted the legitimacy of the invocation of the saints as an authentic ecclesiastical tradition; Lutherans opposed the practice because it obscures the sole mediatorship of Christ.[44]

(31) In 1563 a response to the Reformation critique of the cult of saints was forthcoming in the form of conciliar teaching. At the very close of the Council of Trent three decrees were approved dealing with purgatory; the invocation, veneration, and relics of the saints as well as sacred images; and indulgences.[45] Each was written with the intention of providing a mandate for the correction of abuses. For none of these decrees was there time to formulate more than a brief *doctrinal* exposition. The majority of the Council members wished to bring the proceedings to a close. Lengthy debate was out of the question. But to propose no teaching at all on what had been such neuralgic issues would leave the impression that nothing could be said on behalf of the practices in question. What is more, there was general agreement that these practices needed reform.

(32) In dealing with justification, the Council had already described the defective character of the saints' holiness in this life (Mary excluded, they were not exempt from venial sin). Because it felt more was needed, it went on to approve a decree dealing with the invocation, veneration, and relics of the saints as well as with sacred images. The points emphasized in that decree would later be very influential.[46]

(33) The decree expressed concern about the need to teach the Christian people that the saints reigning with Christ pray to God on our behalf. The faithful should be instructed that it is good and useful to invoke the saints as well as to have recourse to their prayers and help in obtaining God's benefits through our one Redeemer and Savior, Jesus Christ. Conversely it is ungodly (*impie sentire*) to deny that saints are to be invoked or to assert that: a) they do not pray for human beings; b) calling on them to pray for our individual needs is idolatry; c) such invocation is at odds with honoring the one Mediator, Jesus Christ; and d) it is foolish to beseech with voice and heart those who reign in heaven.[47]

(34) Attention is then directed to a closely related issue—relics. Because of the doctrines of the Mystical Body, the indwelling of the Holy Spirit, and the hope of future resurrection, the bodies of the martyrs and other saints are to be venerated. In this way, many favors come from God.[48]

(35) As for religious art, the decree stipulates that images of Christ, Mary, and the saints are to be retained in churches. But the grounds for this do not lie in a belief that: a) there is any divinity or power in those images; b) anything is to be sought from them; or c) trust and reliance are to be placed in them as pagans once looked to idols and put their hope in them. Rather, the honor paid to such images is referred to those imaged. Not an innovation, this is said to be the position of earlier councils and in particular that of Nicea II (787) in its struggle with the Iconoclasts. Through images and paintings, people are taught and confirmed in the articles of faith. They are challenged by the benefits and duties that come from Christ as well as by the

miracles God works through the saints and the salutary example of the saints. They are encouraged to thank, love, and adore God; to cultivate piety; and to live their lives in imitation of the saints.[49]

(36) As for abuses, they are to be eliminated. There are to be no images that portray what is dogmatically false or that offer the occasion of dangerous error to the unsophisticated. God cannot be represented so as to be seen by human eyes; people should not be left to think otherwise. In all these matters superstition and avarice are to be eliminated as well as anything that is sexually suggestive. Holiness befits God's house. Celebrations of saints' feasts and the veneration of relics should not be times of revelry. As for the future, episcopal oversight and approval are required if it is a question of introducing sacred images departing from the customary or of acknowledging new miracles or relics.[50]

(37) Pastoral care is to be exercised by bishops both in teaching about the solidarity of Christ's members (living and deceased) as well as in the elimination of abuses. That was the Council's prescription for what was needed in the cult of the saints. This was to become an important part of the agenda of the Counter Reformation.

(38) The Lutheran position remained what Luther had asserted in the SA of 1537.[51] Lutheran response to the Council of Trent is summarized in the massive work of Martin Chemnitz, *Examination of the Council of Trent* (1565-73), which rejects the Tridentine teachings on the invocation of the saints and Mary. Chemnitz contends that neither Scripture nor tradition, as viewed by Luther and the CA, supports such teachings.[52] Normative Lutheran teachings, collated in the *Book of Concord* in 1580, are based on the CA, Ap, and SA, which affirm commemorative veneration of the saints and Mary, but reject any invocation of them. Mary is honored as "the Mother of God" (*mater Dei*) and as "the most blessed virgin" (*laudatissima virgo*) in the context of Christology.[53] One of Luther's disciples, Ludwig Rabus (1524-92), attempted to preserve the intention of the Lutheran Confessions by creating the first massive Lutheran martyrology, portraying saints as models of Christian witness.[54]

## II. PERSPECTIVES ON CRITICAL ISSUES

(39) In the sixteenth century Lutherans and Catholics were at odds as to whether veneration and invocation of Mary and other saints in heaven detracted from the trust, confidence, and hope that should be put in Christ the one Mediator. Today the problem has not vanished. Its continuing character will be clear if one considers how different the perspectives of our two faith communities can still be on the matter. Such a systematic analysis will help

to show how and why each community is consistent in holding the position it does on the saints and Mary.

## A. Lutheran Perspectives

(40) Lutherans prefer to address the complex problem and series of issues narrated above, first of all, in a positive way.

a. They are convinced that Jesus Christ, crucified once for all, is the one Mediator between God and humanity and so is all-sufficient to save.

b. They believe that Jesus Christ as the Risen and Exalted One intercedes for us at God's right hand (Rom 8:34) and that, since we are justified by faith, we have access to God (Rom 5:1-2); we are enjoined therefore to speak in prayer directly to God through Christ.

c. If Lutherans use the term "mediation" at all with reference to the communication of God's grace to us, they speak of it especially in terms of the work of the Spirit and the ministry of word and sacraments as means of grace.

d. Lutherans, following the New Testament, regard all justified believers in Christ as saints and view sanctification both as God's gift, along with justification, through baptism and faith, and as a way of living in a holy manner according to God's will.

e. Lutherans have been willing to speak of the advance not only of the gospel in the world but also of believers in faith (Phil 1:12, 25), and of reflecting or even beholding the glory of God and being transformed or conformed through baptism and the Spirit to the divine image (2 Cor 3:18; 4:6;Rom 8:29), but they are always aware that such advance or conformation is accomplished only by a gracious activity which exposes the depth of sin at the same time as it works to combat such sin. Lutherans have therefore preferred to speak in terms of the "*simul*" of justification/sanctification and sin (*simul justus et peccator*) when describing Christian life, lest growth in grace be confused with human paradigms of progress or human accomplishment. Such growth in grace, for Lutherans, does not come to consummation in this life, but only when the promise which inspires such growth is completely fulfilled in Christ's return.

f. For believers "on the way" in Christ, Lutherans have spoken positively of the exemplary nature of saints, living or dead, and of Mary.

g. In speaking of the Christian dead, Lutherans trust the witness of Scripture and the hope of the resurrection, but do not find scriptural support for encouraging or requiring the invocation of saints who have died or of Mary to intercede for us. Prayer, Lutherans have insisted, must come from faith and faith must rest on promise. Since Scripture makes no explicit promise in this regard, the practice can have no sure basis (Ap 21:10) and could trouble consciences if required.

(41) In many of these interrelated areas Lutherans have had also to respond in the negative to assertions by Catholics that Lutherans regard as unwarranted. Such responses are the reverse side of the positive position presented above and stem ultimately from the criteriological function of the doctrine of justification by faith. In some cases specific differences appear with regard to the extension of the meaning of biblical passages under the church's magisterium. In this way there is a difference over ecclesial authority, in relation to Scripture, for making doctrinal assertions. Lutherans have found the emphasis on "many mediators of intercession" in the *Confutation* confusing and seeming to detract from the unique role of Jesus Christ. Furthermore, the origins and unofficial standing of the *Confutation* add to Lutheran uncertainty about the gravity of this emphasis.

(42) The crucial issue in this dialogue for Lutherans therefore remains that of the sole mediatorship of Christ over against the invocation of the saints and Mary. Although Lutherans do not deny that deceased and living saints join together in praising God—indeed this is affirmed in some eucharistic and other liturgical celebrations—they have difficulties with the customary definition of invocation when it applies to someone other than Christ, namely, as the practice of calling on someone and asking for something for one's benefit. Lutherans believe such practice detracts from the sole mediatorship of Christ because it seems to assume or to imply that Mary and certain deceased saints are somehow more accessible or benevolent than Christ. That is why Lutherans appeal to the doctrine of justification as the norm by which the practice of invoking saints and Mary needs to be judged. Lutherans continue to ask why it is useful, or indeed necessary, to place one's trust not only in Christ but in the saints and in Mary as well. Justifying faith rests on the sufficiency of Christ, who alone is to be trusted as the Mediator through whom God, in the Holy Spirit, pours out the gracious gift of salvation. Thus Lutherans could ask, "Granted that blessed Mary prays for the church, does she receive souls in death, does she overcome death, does she give life? What does Christ do if blessed Mary does all this?" (Ap 21:27).

(43) From a Lutheran perspective the crucial issue here is the nature of Christ's mediation itself. It should be noted that the term "mediator" does not figure prominently in Lutheran Christology. Even though the I Tim 2:5 passage is cited in CA 21, the emphasis is clearly on the fact that however Christ's saving work is described, he is the *only one* who does it. So CA 21 cites the I Timothy passage to emphasize that Christ is the *one* "Mediator," but is quick to add other titles as well that relate to the issues at hand: Christ is "the *only* Savior, the *only* High Priest, Advocate, and Intercessor." The

emphasis is quite obviously not on the concept of mediation as such but on the uniqueness of Christ's work for us before God over against the question of the invocation of saints. As with all christological titles, the meaning and use of "Mediator" is determined by what actually happens in Christ and not by previously given usage. The point is that Christ establishes himself as the one and only "Mediator" through his own person and work. This must be borne in mind in discussions such as the present one where the term gains a prominence not usual in Lutheran theology.

(44) Consequently, we can here put the question sharply: What sort of mediation is it of which Christ is the sole agent? In the Lutheran view, Christ's mediation is such that his life, death, and resurrection authorize and institute a speaking and doing (word and sacrament) through which he *himself* is imparted to create faith. The act of salvation is not, as the word suggests, that of a "go-between" who imparts some "thing" or prior timelessly existing divine favor or "grace."[55] He gives himself. He is what and who is to be given, and the proclamation of his life, death, and resurrection is the giving. His self-giving is such that it can be perpetuated only in the proclamation in word and sacrament. Thus it reaches its goal only in the proclamation of the victory achieved in the concrete event of the cross and the resurrection. Christ enters the world of sin and death, becomes a curse for us, and the outcome hangs in the balance. If the victory is not won, if there is no resurrection, sin and death win the battle and there is no mediation because there is nothing to be proclaimed. Since, however, Christ is raised, he alone is to be proclaimed, and only through faith in him can one stand in the judgment. The only mediation there is occurs in the speaking, the promising, and the sacramental giving engendered by the event itself. For Lutherans Christ alone engenders such speaking and doing, and Christ alone is therefore not only the sole Mediator, but the one who is mediated.

(45) It goes almost without saying, therefore, that the sole mediatorship of Christ does not exclude but rather impels to further "mediation" in the sense of a transmitting through word and sacrament. But Lutherans rarely speak of "mediation" in this connection and prefer rather to speak of the ministry of word and sacrament, the actual doing of the deed in the living present. They confess that this ministry was instituted by God for the sake of the gospel, to instill faith in Christ, the sole source of salvation. Salvation is thus "mediated" or communicated through the gospel, preached and heard as well as sacramentally enacted. Thus the word and the sacraments are sometimes spoken of as "means" (*Mittel, instrumenta*) through which the Holy Spirit gives faith to those who receive the gospel (CA 5). Ministry is thus service impelled by the sole mediatorship of Christ. One may be said to "cooperate" with God when one obeys the commission of the risen Christ to serve as his ambassador and declare him to be the Lord. In other words, one

"cooperates" with God when one lives and acts in the belief that Christ alone is the sole Mediator, trusting that we are saved *sola fide, sola gratia.*

(46) The differing "thought structures" referred to in our dialogue on justification[56] no doubt affect views on mediation and subsequent attitudes toward the practice of invoking saints and Mary. Lutherans fear that a "transformationist model" tends to understand mediation too much as the distribution of "transforming grace" from the "treasury" of the superabundant merits of Christ and the saints through exemplary or properly authorized "intermediaries." The result is to extend mediation ecclesiologically via sacramental ordination, episcopacy, and perhaps speaking of the church as sacrament here on earth and the activity of saints and Mary on behalf of the faithful in heaven. Lutherans, however, think about mediation more in christological than ecclesiological terms: Christ gives himself in word and sacrament, thus continuing to be present to those who receive him in faith through the power of the Holy Spirit. Those who, through the power of the Spirit, in faith receive Christ in word and sacrament experience "mediation" of salvation. Thus Christ himself is the mediation. He takes our sin and gives us his righteousness. In such a view any suggestion that the righteousness of the saints somehow avails before God, even if such righteousness is acquired by the power of grace, will appear to question Christ's sole mediatorship and become cause for turmoil of conscience. Nevertheless, in the Lutheran view, deceased saints may still be exemplary models of faith in Christ alone, but they are not perceived as mediators additional to the Christ communicated in the gospel.

(47) The Lutheran Reformation called for a redefinition of the term "saint" in the light of the gospel of justification by faith alone. A saint is one who is justified by faith alone and who consequently lives and acts on that basis, one who claims and desires nothing for self but lives in the light of divine grace. Implicit in this view of sainthood is a critique of what Lutherans understood to be a theology of merit and the idea that saints were those who because of meritorious service enjoyed the immediate beatific vision and so could share their merits or be invoked. Lutherans held that saints are those who, being justified by faith, are freed to turn their attention toward the living saints, the neighbor, the naked, hungry, thirsty, and poor. Saints who do this in conspicuous fashion are celebrated and held up as examples and encouragement for the life of faith in this world. In other words, they are not viewed as gaining extraordinary status in the afterlife according to a scale of merit, but rather simply as prominent examples of the obedience and perseverance of faith in suffering and trial. This issues in a somewhat different understanding of the "communion of saints." Saints are those who because of faith participate in the sufferings and the joys of brothers and sisters here on earth, identifying with their burdens in order to free

them from such burdens. Saints, therefore, are respected and venerated when their example in the life of faith on earth is followed, not when they are invoked for aid after death or when their merits or works are in some way substituted for the shortcomings of "less-saintly" Christians. The critique of the system of merit means that Lutherans have been more concerned about saints as examples for the service of the living than as possible intercessors beyond death. Lutherans have generally held that since the life of the departed is hidden from us, no affirmations of faith can be based thereon and that attention should be turned to the service of the living.

(48) Lutherans therefore continue to adhere to the Lutheran Confessions, which hold that we should thank God for deceased saints as examples of divine mercy, that they should be viewed as models of faith, and that they should be honored and imitated.[57] Some Lutherans concede that "perhaps" the saints in the church triumphant intercede on behalf of the saints in the church militant.[58] Other Lutherans grant that blessed Mary prays for the church.[59] All remain suspicious of invoking deceased saints, even though Catholics insist that, in a "rightly ordered faith," the practice—though sometimes abused—does not conflict with the sole mediatorship of Christ. Lutherans contend that such an extension of Christ's mediation has no scriptural mandate, provides insufficient spiritual certainty, and tends to encourage abuse in the church's devotional life.

(49) With regard to Mary, Lutherans affirm her as the "God-bearer" (*Theotokos*) and hold her in high esteem as the most praiseworthy of all the saints. In this sense Mary is to Lutherans a symbolic prototype of the church: she is obedient to the mandate of the Holy Spirit, humble in her great calling, and the embodiment of the unmerited grace of God. Luther and Lutherans continue to affirm that she gloried neither in her virginity nor in her humility, but only in the gracious regard God had for her.[60] The Marian dogmas affirming her Immaculate Conception (1854) and her bodily Assumption (1950) have saddened Lutherans because these dogmas have no scriptural basis and were promulgated as infallible truths without consultation with other Christians. Lutherans feel compelled to object to both the method used and the assertions made in these papal definitions because they represent a doctrinal development reflecting specifically Catholic concerns rather than ecumenical ones.[61] Lutherans have, however, preserved and recovered some cherished aspects of Marian devotion, based on the "Magnificat" (Luke 1:46-55): The prophetic proclamation pointing to the power of the unmerited grace of God.

(50) The Lutheran critique of the invocation of the saints and of Mary must be viewed in the light of a Lutheran emphasis on the sanctified life as the proper response to Christ, the sole Mediator of salvation. Lutherans believe that proper praise and glory are given to the work of the one

Redeemer when the saving mercies of the justifying God are reflected in a life of obedient, loving service. Lutherans hold, furthermore, that faith does not mean individualism, but rather a being born anew into the communion of believers, the body of Christ which is the church. As members of the church, believers participate by grace in the divine trinitarian life—in a "mystical union" (*unio mystica*) that anticipates the full future glory of Christ "beheld with an unveiled face" (2 Cor 3:18; cf. 5:1-10 and Rom 8:20-30 in the context of 8:18-39). By the work of the Holy Spirit the ministry of word and sacraments "mediates" the present Christ, to whom the faithful respond with worship, with good works, and with other fruits of the Holy Spirit. Growth in grace, knowledge, love, and hope are the unfailing consequence of justifying faith. The interim between Christ's first coming in Israel and his final return at the end of time is filled with the advance of the gospel and, through the power of the Holy Spirit, response to it. All of Christian life is nurtured and sustained by the Christ who is "mediated" through the gospel and the Holy Spirit.[62] Thus Lutherans speak of God's solidarity (oneness) with creatures, of God "for us" (*pro nobis*) in Christ, and of unmerited salvation "outside us" (*extra nos*).

(51) At several points above the Lutheran emphasis on Scripture and a hesitancy to extend its meaning on the basis of the church's magisterium have been apparent. An example is the citation of James 5:16 with reference to the invocation of saints. The context is discussion of "the prayer of faith." The assurance that "the prayer of a righteous person avails much when set in operation (by God)" or "…in its effects" is not extended by the passage itself to deceased justified or holy ones. Similarly with 2 Thess 1:10[63] God "who is wonderful in his saints," which possibly refers to angels, is in context a reference to the *parousia*, not the invocation of the dead. Such uses of Scripture do not provide the clear basis Lutherans would require to move beyond the Confessional writings.

## B. Catholic Perspectives

(52) "Christ is the Light of the Nations" was the theme with which the Second Vatican Council introduced and set the tone for its teaching about the church. It did so in *Lumen Gentium*,[64] where doctrine about the Lord Jesus and the salvation that Christ brings in the Holy Spirit is determinative for doctrine regarding the church. To be sure, as a result of a deliberate choice made by the Council, its treatments of Mary (chapter 8) and other believers who are now in heaven (e.g., the apostles and Christ's martyrs: chapter 7 and esp. §§49-50) are found in the same document, which deals with God's people and church on earth.[65] But in context this people and church have already

been presented (chapters 1 and 2) as tracing their historical reality and identity to the eternal mystery of the Father's will to save human beings through the Son in the Holy Spirit. Both the incarnation and the mystical body are intimately connected aspects of that same trinitarian mystery of salvation. Each involves faith on the part of human beings, as well as the works that are its fruit. But whether these gifts are found in the Lord's mother, her kinswoman Elizabeth, Anna, Stephen, Paul, or later disciples, their reality and effectiveness result entirely from the unique mediation of Jesus Christ.

(53) But what does it mean to speak of Christ as Mediator? And as for Mary and other disciples of her day or later, how do their faith and its fruits relate to the salvation of which he alone is Mediator? Like other Christians, Catholics ought to regard the answer to the first of these questions as determining the reply to the second.

(54) In answering the first, it is important to recall at the outset that language is being stretched when the term *Mediator* is used of Christ. The starting point is the practice of describing a person as mediating when he or she stands in between two others (whether the latter be individuals or groups) with the purpose of setting up or changing a relationship between them. An essential feature of this conventional usage is that all parties involved are human beings.

(55) The New Testament and later Christian tradition employed the term to describe Jesus in the relationship between human beings and the God whom he called Father. The intent behind this usage was to point to the historical figure who unites in himself the natures of God and humanity and who by his work in the flesh reconciles to God the alienated human family. Clearly some elements that were involved when the mediation was exclusively between human beings could not survive in this theological version. Thus in the New Testament Jesus Christ is not Mediator in the sense that on his initiative something was done which caused both God and human beings to change their stance toward one another. To be more specific, his suffering and death did not require an otherwise unwilling God to be compassionate by granting sinners forgiveness and new life. Everything that Jesus accomplished as Mediator came about because God from eternity chose to love the human race and to save it only through and because of Jesus. Led in his humanity by God's prevenient grace, which was poured out upon him without measure, he freely returned the Father's love, becoming "obedient unto death, even death on the cross" (Phil 2:8). "Therefore," in view of his activity as Mediator, Jesus was exalted as risen Lord and unique head. He is called sole Mediator because no justification, sanctification, grace, or merit can come about except through him and as merited by him.

(56) If the term "mediation" is applied to exemplary believers, angels, priests, or others, this is only in a derivative sense, insofar as the one

Mediator chooses to work through them as instruments or channels. Included in the Mediator's role is the empowering of apostles, prophets, preachers, teachers, and other kinds of disciples for the benefit of those who need to be apprised of God's grace toward all because of Jesus and who must be helped if they are to respond in faith, hope, and charity. But how do the roles of those others relate to his? They neither add to it nor detract from it. They make it real throughout the ages, result from it, and draw on it as an unsurpassable source.

(57) Here recourse to an important text of the Second Vatican Council may be helpful. In chapter 8 of *Lumen Gentium* the subject is Mary, who is described as being invoked in the church under the titles of Advocate (*Advocata*), Aid (*Auxiliatrix*), Helper (*Adjutrix*), and Mediatrix (*Mediatrix*). After noting this, the council adds immediately that the dignity and efficacy of Christ the one Mediator are not thereby threatened. As grounds for this it submits that no creature can ever be numbered along with (*connumeriar potest*) the incarnate Word, the Redeemer. There is no standard of measurement common to Creator and creature. Nevertheless, it goes on, the priesthood of Christ is shared in (*participatur*) both by ordained ministers and by all the baptized. Similarly there is but one divine goodness; nevertheless, it is really diffused (*realiter diffunditur*) in creatures in diverse ways. Then, after the introduction of the analogies of Christ's priesthood and God's goodness, the council moves to make an application:

> So also the sole mediation of the Redeemer does not exclude but rather gives rise to a cooperation (*cooperationem*) that varies on the part of creatures and that is but a sharing (*participatam*) from this one source (*ex unico fonte*).[66]

As Christ's priesthood is shared and God's goodness is really diffused, so Christ's mediation gives rise to derived cooperation on the part of others.

(58) The council thus singled out a role that Mary exercises at the present and in the same context of *Lumen Gentium* described that role as intercession. In saying, then, that Mary is invoked in the church, it meant that her assistance (or intercession) is sought by disciples in need on earth. And concerned to allay the suspicion that this compromises Christ's mediation, it compared her heavenly role at present with the cooperation that it regarded as the hallmark of Christian discipleship on earth. But what does the latter entail?

(59) The New Testament presents individuals who were empowered by God to carry our roles engaging a freedom born of grace and resulting in others being touched by divine favor (e.g., Luke 1:44-45 for Mary and the as-yet unborn John; Acts 16:13-15 for Paul's preaching and Lydia's believing).

These are instances of what *Lumen Gentium* would later describe as cooperation that is both derived from and totally dependent on the one Mediator, Jesus Christ. But the question must still be posed: If faith and its fruits involved cooperation on Mary's part as well as on the part of Paul, if that same faith and its fruits have similar implications for other disciples, how is that cooperation to be understood?

(60) In Catholic teaching it implies that from eternity the Father chooses to save for Christ's sake and in a way that involves the free agency of human beings. By grace the latter conform their wills to the divine and so like Christ seek for others the good which it is God's pleasure to offer. A life of faith despite adversity, service, to one's neighbor with no hope of recompense, unselfish prayer for one's sisters and brothers in Christ—these are examples of such involvement or cooperation. They are effective because: a) the Father grants salvation in the Holy Spirit thanks solely to Jesus Christ; b) the efficacy of this one Mediator is so great as to enable disciples to share freely and actively in his saving work; and c) given the incommensurability of the infinite and the finite, that sharing does not reduce either the Mediator to being a partial source of forgiveness and new life or his disciple's role to doing nothing at all in this regard. As a result, even and especially when they are in spiritual need, followers of Christ can turn for help to sisters and brothers in the Lord who are expected to respond because they are empowered by grace to be of assistance. Seen in this light, reservations regarding Christ's having commissioned disciples to help fellow wayfarers toward salvation would be a limitation of his mediation. Catholic teaching has these presuppositions when it uses *cooperation* to describe the roles of disciples in relation to their Lord's accomplishments.

(61) It is Christology that is decisive. The human obedience of the Word Incarnate was at once the result of grace and the source of grace for others.[67] Because this is so, the cooperative roles that Jesus Christ gives to his disciples on earth through the centuries are the fruit of his mediation and contribute to others' reception of grace he mediates. At times those roles are described as a kind of "derived mediation." But this means only that the New Testament makes Jesus Christ the Mediator in the sense that he alone can and does accomplish the whole of salvation, without his disciples thereby doing nothing of salvific importance. Their cooperation results from his mediation, which transforms sinners into ministers so that it is not simply their human words but rather God's word in theirs that reaches hearers who come to believe (I Thess 2:12-14). Because of his mediation disciples are enabled to suffer with him as a prelude to being glorified with him (Rom 8:17-18); like Paul they are legates on behalf of Christ, with God, as it were, exhorting through them (2 Cor 5:19-20). In the one Spirit they have been baptized into one body where each member lives not merely to share in what

happens to others but to meet the needs of other members (I Cor 12:12-28). Because of this solidarity Christians can accept responsibility for one another; by prayer, by recalling for one another God's promises and claims, by shouldering the burdens of neighbors, by correction as well as example, and by associating themselves with the sufferings of their crucified Lord and Head in works of penance flowing from faith. This is what it means for the Mediator to empower disciples; their total dependence involves sharing actively and freely in his saving work—doing more than nothing on behalf of others in need of salvation.[68]

(62) Hopes and fears enter into Catholics' assessment of the "derived mediation" or creaturely cooperation through which Christ's saving grace reaches human beings. They fear that without it Christ's unique mediation will be made fruitless and sterile. This threat appears realistic to them if every form of piety and worship, function, office, every meaning, truth claim, and type of witness are liable to be suspected of being a pretender seeking to displace the Lord unless it has explicit biblical foundations. This could happen if justification by faith alone were to be made the *sole* norm for judging all churchly discourse and practice. They hope to avoid this and to give God what is God's by stressing the truth of his manifold cooperation to which Christ's mediation gives rise as his grace is brought to those in need.

(63) This dialogue has led to a better understanding of the fears and hopes of Lutherans. They too fear that Christ's unique mediation will be made fruitless and sterile. They fear this especially with regard to what has been called "derived mediation" or creaturely cooperation. Christ has been and is still today displaced at times by forms of piety and worship, offices and functions, meanings, truth claims, and types of witness. Each of these may call for trust that is misplaced because it is grounded in no divine promise or guarantee. Hope in Christ as Mediator requires criticism of "derived mediation"; prime candidates for such criticism are the cult of Mary and canonized saints in Catholic teaching and piety.

(64) Catholics can learn from Lutheran hopes and fears. Even so, Catholics may rightly maintain that the possibility of abuse does not warrant abolition of a teaching or practice. They freely recognize that ethnic, racial, and cultural factors enter into the expression of piety with regard to Mary and canonized saints as well as into its criticism. They know that piety in this form is deeply rooted in the lives of ever so many Catholics throughout the world. But although not all that can be described as an abuse in this matter is so in fact, still where real abuses are found, efforts must be made to direct the piety in question toward Christ the one Mediator. This may at times involve support of church leaders when the latter attempt to determine whether alleged apparitions of Mary or a canonized saint are authentic, only to be characterized as lacking faith for doing so.

(65) Perhaps a further point is worth considering. The two sets of hopes and fears described above and associated with Catholics and Lutherans may express different but not incompatible reactions to the mystery of the coexistence of the triune God and responsible human agents.[69]

(66) Of course Mary and many other of God's holy ones are no longer on earth. But the love of God in Jesus Christ is stronger than death (Rom 8:38-39). And Catholic teaching promotes confidence that death is not strong enough to keep those united with Christ in heaven from continuing to pray for others yet *in via* and from being called on by those others for just that prayer.

(67) The New Testament commends petitions on behalf of all human beings. But is also encourages Christians to turn to their fellow disciples for help and prayer on their behalf. That turning is in no way in conflict with the mediation of Christ, in whom there is ever so much more to be found than in any of his followers. In similar fashion Catholics are not deterred from turning to Mary or other sisters and brothers now in heaven for help and prayer. This is not in their view an affront to Christ or a meaningless gesture. Indeed, in this recourse they are encouraged by the conviction that the prayers of disciples now in heaven will proceed from a charity heightened by personal experience and awareness of the serious plight of wayfarers. One way, among others, of avoiding misdirection of such prayer and consequent abuses in the Catholic Church was by establishing and from time to time reforming the process of beatification and canonization. Neither beatification nor canonization conflicts with the Catholic teaching that all who are justified are holy people and saints. Similarly neither implies that only those beatified and canonized are in heaven now while earthly history continues. Furthermore, neither means that canonized saints have merits which make God bound to do what they request on behalf of clients on earth. But both do account at least in part for the fact that the term *saint* in Catholic parlance more often than not means one recognized by the church as in heaven and so one who can be turned to with trust as a true disciple of Christ.

(68) One may be unable to explain in detail or with apodictic certainty how Mary and canonized saints in heaven know the needs for which they are to pray when asked to by a disciple on earth.[70] Still in their cases as with Paul (Phil 1:23) the end of life on earth led to something much better: being with Christ. Like the repentant thief, they are in paradise today with the Lord, who has entered his kingdom (Luke 23:42-43). They are, however, still his disciples and as such imitate what their Lord does as he makes intercession for us with God (Heb 7:25;Rom 8:34).

(69) From a Catholic point of view, then, honoring Mary and the saints, imitating their example, and calling on them for help can be ways of

attesting vividly to the unique mediation of Jesus Christ as well as to the truth of the gospel.

## III. THE PROBLEM REEXAMINED

### A. Dimensions of the Problem

(70) The problem faced by our dialogue on the one Mediator and the questions about mediation is a complex one. Both our churches are committed to Jesus Christ as Lord, hope, and goal of their existence. Both recognize the importance of the canonical Scriptures, Christian tradition, the ministry of word and sacrament, ecclesial community, and the examples of Christian saints past and present. Both agree on the unique mediatorship of Christ (*solus Christus*) and the justification for sinners (*sola gratia*) that Christ provides; they use this doctrine "as a criterion of authenticity"[71] for the church's practice with regard to the saints and Mary. The problem, however, is how to affirm the unique mediatorship of Christ so that all the "mediations" in his church not only do not detract from, but communicate and extol, his sole mediatorship. However, the very fact that we have come to agree on this form of the question and especially on the priorities that question reflects is for us a cause for joy.

(71) In earlier statements this dialogue has discussed Baptism, the Eucharist, the Ordained Ministry, Papal Primacy, Teaching Authority, and Justification by Faith. In each of these areas, and especially in connection with justification by faith, we have encountered differences related to one aspect of mediation, that is, how Christ's saving work is communicated. We think that we have found further clarity and convergence on that basic issue.

(72) Among the repercussions of this problem of how the Mediator's saving work is communicated are specifically questions about the roles of the saints, including Mary, and about intercession and invocation of the saints and Mary. Both our churches affirm that the risen Christ, through the Holy Spirit, continues to effect salvation in and through the church. Both speak of human sinfulness, the importance of Christ's cross and resurrection, the word of God, and sacraments. Both allow for human agency in proclamation, witnessing, ministry, and the response of faith. It can be said, however, that there is a contrast in our respective understandings of continuity and discontinuity. That "God's word saves by being declared" introduces, into the Lutheran understanding of the life of faith, discontinuity between the old and the new, between the bound will and the liberated will, and between the gravity of sin and the grace of justification, so that the justified are *simul iusti et peccatores.*[72] In contrast, Catholic theology stresses "transformation

or perfecting of the old," including an element of continuity as well as of renewal.[73] The contrast can also be seen in "another critical principle," urged by Catholics, alongside of justification by faith, namely, "to recognize God's grace where it is at work," including its renewing effects already present.[74] The contrast is exhibited in the fact that Catholics tend to use mediation language for the action of human ministers, as well as for the saints and Mary, whereas Lutherans tend to reserve such language for Christ the one Mediator. These differing emphases have had important consequences for piety and devotion. At issue has been how the saints and Mary function in mediation.

(73) The difficult questions in the present round of the dialogue are tied to the criteriological use of justification and of the continuity of grace at work. We have also been aware, however, of a number of further questions, some of which have been touched on in previous rounds of dialogue, some in this round, and others not yet in depth. For example, how should the church and its tradition be subject to Scripture and influence the interpretation of Scripture? Does doctrine develop, and if so, how does one ascertain the legitimacy of such developments? What is the value of the *lex orandi* and of the *sensus fidelium* as sources of dogma? What is the teaching authority and, more specifically, the teaching authority of the hierarchy, particularly the pope? How does the church deal with distortions and abuses as it responds to the call for continuous conversion to the gospel? However, we do not think that these issues have to be dealt with before any real progress can be made on substantive questions concerning Mary and the saints. On the contrary, we dare to hope that the advances which this present round of the dialogue reflects may in time shed light on these other issues as well.

## B. Resulting Divergences

(74) In Section II we have alluded to differences in the ways our two traditions understand the very concept of mediation and apply it to Christ as the one Mediator. Questions can arise, especially about the role of the humanity of Christ in the work of redemption, including the relationship between the two natures in Christ and the sharing of attributes (*communicatio idiomatum*). In what sense does he take on our sins and "become sin" for us (cf. 2 Cor 5:21;Gal 3:13)? How does Christ function as head with respect to his body, the church? Christology and ecclesiology are themes that must constantly be kept in mind.

(75) The present round of discussion raises questions about the relationship between Christians living on earth and those who have passed

beyond the veil of death, and more specifically the relationship with those regarded as saints in heaven, among whom Mary holds a special place in the official Confessions or teaching of both our churches. In this regard we have identified four divergences.

## 1. The Term "Saint"

(76) The first divergence concerns the meaning of the basic term "saint" or "holy one" (*hagios, sanctus*). As applied to human beings, it can be used in at least four senses: (1) All those who have been justified by the grace of Christ, whether living or dead; (2) those who, having been thus justified on earth, have entered into eternal life; (3) particular figures, especially biblical personages, who are examples of holiness; and (4) those of any age or nation whom the church, either through custom or formal canonization, has singled out as members of the church triumphant so that they may be commemorated in public worship. Lutherans tend on the whole to use the term "saint" in its wider, biblical meaning, as including all the justified, whether on earth or in heaven, whereas Catholics tend to use the term in a narrower sense to mean those in heaven, especially those officially "canonized" and proposed as models of holiness.

## 2. Intercession of Saints

(77) An initial question regarding the prayer of saints in heaven for the sake of others (intercession) has to do with our knowledge about the condition of the Christian dead. Do they now live with Christ and, if so, are they aware of the situation and needs of people still on earth? If these questions are answered in the negative, it is more difficult to claim an intercessory role for them and to justify calling upon their help in our prayers.

(78) The Catholic magisterium teaches that some of the deceased are already glorified, beholding "clearly the triune God as he is" (LG 49).[75] As biblical grounds for the intercession of saints, the *Confutation* referred to texts such as Baruch 3:4, 2 Macc 15:12-14 and Rev 5:8 and 8:3-4, but the exegetical difficulties are today recognized. For their confidence in the prayers of the saints in heaven Catholics rely not simply on biblical texts but also, as stated elsewhere,[76] on the sense of the faithful, on ancient and approved liturgical prayers, on the explicit teaching of popes and councils, and on theological reasoning from the biblical data. Thus the dispute comes down in great part to the sources of Christian doctrine and principles of interpretation.

(79) Lutherans point to the paucity of information provided by Holy Scripture concerning the state of the dead between their death and the endtime. Like Catholics, Lutherans confess that God gives life to the dead in Christ. Lutherans grant that the saints in heaven and Mary intercede for the church in general (Ap 21:9) or at least perhaps do so (SA 2:2:26), but in nei-

ther alterative do they find any decisive ground for affirming that the departed are aware of prayers addressed to them (Ap 21:9, 12, 27;SA 2:2:26).

## 3. Invocation

(80) Sharper differences arise concerning the invocations of saints: Should Christians be encouraged or required to ask their prayers and help either in general terms or for certain specific favors? Catholics hold that the practice of invocation is encouraged by the church, which is to be trusted. More specifically, they argue that the invocation of saints, although not explicitly commanded in Scripture, is not forbidden and seems to be a legitimate extension of the biblically approved practice of asking for the intercession of those living on earth (e.g., Rom 15:30-32;2 Cor 1:11;Col 4:3) and the special value attributed in Scripture to the prayer of the righteous (Jas 5:16). The legitimacy of the extension, to be sure, depends on the conviction that those who die in close union with Christ are taken up into eternal life and become outstanding members of the communion of saints. Relying in part on materials that have come to light since the sixteenth century, Catholics point out that the practice goes back to the early centuries and was taught by a number of church fathers in the East and West prior to Gregory I.[77]

(81) The invocation of saints, in the Catholic view, does not attribute to them the power that belongs to God alone because the saints are not addressed as saviors or redeemers but simply as intercessors, in much the same way that fellow human beings on earth are addressed when one asks them to pray for some intention. Far from detracting from the work of Christ, the practice, they believe, provides increased awareness of his work, for Christ is glorified in his saints (cf. *LG* 48 and 50). Prayer to God and invocation of the saints do not stand in a competitive relationship, but in turning to the saints as intercessors one places trust ultimately in God and in Christ to whom all prayer is ultimately directed. No benefits are conferred by the saints that are not conferred by Christ himself. Although Catholics are encouraged to pray directly to God, they may also draw profit from asking the intercession of the saints, in whom God's grace was so effective when they still lived on earth.

(82) In certain periods of history and certain parts of the world the practices of invoking the saints and treasuring their relics were adversely affected by popular superstitions that have somewhat obscured the role of Christ as sole Mediator of redemption. Church authorities have a responsibility to be vigilant in preventing superstition, to the extent that they can effectively control popular religion. In the present ecumenical climate many Catholics would agree that if Christ is faithfully preached, abuses will gradually recede.

(83) Lutherans oppose the invocation of saints, particularly for help on

specific issues, on the twofold ground that it leads to uncertainty in prayer and detracts from the sole mediatorship of Christ. In support of the first objection they assert that the invocation of saints is not commanded or recommended in the canonical Scriptures and therefore rests upon no biblical promise. For the second objection the Lutheran contention has been and is that invocation attributes to the saints honor and power that belongs to God alone; that it obscures the word of Christ; and that it transfers to the creature the trust that should be placed in no one other than God.

### 4. Marian Doctrine

(84) In relation to the theme of the present dialogue, the central question about Mary has to do with her mediatory role. Inspired by the doctrine of the divine motherhood[78] and by biblical texts such as John 2:1-11, Catholic spiritual writers have attributed exceptional power to Mary's intercession with her son. Medieval authors such as Bernard of Clairvaux and Bernadine of Siena viewed her as "mediator with the Mediator." A number of modern popes, such as Pius IX, Leo XIII, Pius X, and John Paul II, in devotional instructions, have applied to Mary the title "Mediatrix." But movements to define the doctrine of Mary as "Mediatrix of all graces" have thus far met with no encouragement from Rome. While noting that Mary is invoked *in* the church as Mediatrix, Vatican II chose deliberately to use this formula rather than assert that she is so invoked *by* the Church (cf. *LG* 62).[79] Without necessarily repudiating the poetic language of hymnody and devotion, many contemporary Catholics hold that it is theologically inappropriate to speak of Mary as Mediatrix because "Mediatrix" is so easily misunderstood in ways that weaken the doctrine of Christ as "sole Mediator."

(85) Lutherans, while conceding that Mary "prays for the church" and is "worthy of the highest honors," have consistently denied that she, or other saints, should be regarded as mediators or propitiatiors, on the ground that reliance on their merits would detract from the sole mediatorship of Christ. They particularly object to the practice of extolling the mercy of Mary as though Christ were "not a propitiator but only a terrible judge and avenger" (Ap 21:28).

(86) The most difficult areas regarding Mary are undoubtedly the two dogmas defined in the Roman Catholic Church since the sixteenth century: the Immaculate Conception and the Assumption. As regards the former, Catholics point out that Mary was in a true sense redeemed by Christ and that her "preservative redemption" is in fact the supreme instance of his redemptive work. The dogma emphasizes the absolute prevenience of grace, inasmuch as Mary was redeemed without prior merits of her own "in view of the merits of Jesus Christ."[80] The definition was an assertion of papal authority but it was preceded by centuries of increasing agreement among Catholic

theologians and among the Catholic people, by numerous petitions for the definition, and by a virtually unanimous consensus of the episcopate in response to the consultation undertaken by Pius IX.[81] The lack of ecumenical consultation in the definition of the Immaculate Conception may today seem regrettable, but such consultation was rarely practiced by popes or councils for their doctrinal decisions prior to Vatican Council II.

(87) Luther himself professed the Immaculate Conception as a pleasing thought though not as an article of faith (and indeed the belief had not attained dogmatic status at that time). The Lutheran Confessions are silent about it. Lutherans overwhelmingly rejected the dogma as defined in 1854. Their objections are based on the normative Confessional assertion that all descendants of Adam and Eve except Christ are "conceived and born in sin" (CA 2:1); that there are no positive biblical testimonies to Mary's exemption from original sin; and that the definition itself was an unwarranted assertion of papal authority, one made after consulting only Roman Catholics.

(88) The dogma of the Assumption (1950) gives rise to similar divergences. Catholics generally agree that neither the Immaculate Conception nor the Assumption is taught as such in Scripture or in early patristic tradition. They see these dogmas as having a limited grounding in certain biblical teachings, such as Mary's being "highly favored" by God and her unique maternal relationship to Jesus. Beyond this, many theologians appeal to various biblical types and figures of Mary as developed in the tradition. These have included the typology of Mary as the "second Eve" and the interpretation of her as the "woman clothed with the sun" in Revelation 12. Modern authors, including Pius XII in his bull of 1950, see a nexus between the Immaculate Conception and the Assumption: it was appropriate for Mary, being preserved from original sin, to be exempted from subjection to the power of death and corruption.[82]

(89) Luther preached on the Assumption and held that not only Mary but several other biblical figures were already taken up into the life of glory. There were early Lutheran pastors who affirmed the Assumption as both evangelical and Lutheran.[83] The Lutheran Confessions do not refer to the Assumption of Mary. Generally Lutherans reject the doctrine as lacking support in the Scriptures and in the early patristic tradition.[84] Like the dogma of the Immaculate Conception, the 1950 promulgation lacked ecumenical consultation.

## C. Need the Divergences Be Church-Dividing?

(90) The goal of ecumenical dialogue is not to eliminate all differences, but to make certain that the remaining differences are consonant with

a fundamental consensus in the apostolic faith and therefore legitimate or at least tolerable. Reconciliation is a process admitting of many degrees, leading up to full fellowship in faith, in sacramental worship, and in a structured ecclesial life.[85] It is therefore important to ascertain what bearing the differences disclosed in the present round of the dialogue have on the kinds of fellowship just mentioned.

## 1. The Term "Saint"

(91) The difference of usage of the term "saint" in our two traditions can make for some difficulty of communication but is not of itself church-divisive, since neither church actually rejects the usage of the other. Lutherans, although they commonly use the term "saint" to include all justified believers, do accord certain individuals, biblical or postbiblical, the title of "saint" and sometimes commemorate such individuals on particular days in their liturgical calendar and name churches or religious groups in their honor. While Catholics tend to reserve the title of saint to particular individuals whose eminent holiness is certified to them by the church, they also use the term in a much broader sense, to include all who have entered into the joy of eternal life, as in the feast of All Saints, or all who are justified and live by their faith in Christ.

## 2. Intercession of Saints

(92) The discrepancy between Catholic and Lutheran teaching on the intercession of saints is not the decisive one. Lutherans do not deny the Catholic doctrine, but question its biblical basis and its certainty. They assert that Christ prays for us, as do saints on earth and perhaps in heaven. Catholic doctrine affirms the intercession of the saints in heaven. This intercession is seen as a presupposition for the doctrine of invocation, which has held a greater place in the controversy. Intercession as a church-dividing issue, therefore, can best be treated below under invocation.

## 3. Invocation

(93) The question of church-divisiveness may be engaged by considering three more specific questions: Does the Catholic Church require its members to invoke saints? Could Lutherans live in union with a church in which this practice was encouraged but not imposed? Could the Catholic Church live in union with Lutherans who preach Christ as sole Mediator with the conviction that the invocation of saints will thereby recede?

(94) The most formal statement of the Catholic Church on the invocation of saints comes from the Council of Trent, which, in its positive teaching, affirmed that it is good and useful to invoke saints and to have recourse

to their prayers and help in obtaining God's benefits through Jesus Christ, "who alone is our Savior and Redeemer."[86] But neither Trent nor any other council or pope has imposed upon the individual Catholic the obligation of venerating saints or of invoking them. Vatican II in *Lumen Gentium* described it as "supremely fitting" (*summopere decet*) to invoke the saints and have recourse to their prayers (*LG* 50).

(95) Although it seems clear that no one is obliged to invoke the saints in private prayer, the question of public prayer is more complex. In the eucharistic liturgies (canons) of the Catholic Church, including those approved by Paul VI, all prayers are addressed to God—none to the saints, even Mary. The invocation of the saints is rare in the official prayers of the church, but it does occur in the first of the penitential rites of the Eucharist and in the Litany of the Saints, which is used in the Easter Vigil and in the rites of baptism and ordination. Mary is, of course, invoked in many approved nonliturgical prayers, such as the second part of the angelic salutation (the "Hail Mary"). Precisely because the church regards the invocation of the saints and Mary as "good and beneficial," the individual Catholic is strongly encouraged to make use of, and participate in, such prayers. Many Catholics continue to respond to this encouragement with enthusiasm. But there is no reason for thinking that a person who refrained from personally invoking saints would forfeit full communion with the Catholic Church. This freedom now enjoyed by Catholics would certainly be enjoyed also by Lutherans should a greater degree of communion between the respective churches be achieved.

(96) In response to the second question above in paragraph 93, it may be noted that in the sixteenth century Lutherans asked for freedom to abstain from the invocation of saints and freedom to preach the doctrine of justification by faith so as to protest against the practice and the abuses which that practice had occasioned. Melanchthon objected to the *Confutation* on the grounds that it presented the invocation of departed saints as "necessary" and condemned the Lutherans because they "do not *require* the invocation of saints" (Ap 21:1; emphasis added). But Melanchthon and others did not refuse to be in communion with a church that did not require them to invoke saints.

(97) This dialogue has not reached agreement on the substantive issue whether invocation of saints is legitimate and beneficial. Catholics deny that the practice in and of itself is idolatrous or injurious to the honor of Christ the one Mediator, even though the practice must be protected against abuses. The Catholics of this dialogue recognize that abuses have occurred and that the doctrine of the sole mediatorship of Christ provides one critical principle for identifying abuses. Other critical norms are given in official Catholic teaching, notably in the apostolic exhortation of Paul VI, *Marialis Cultus*.[87]

The Lutherans of this dialogue are of the opinion that the practice is not church-dividing provided that the sole mediatorship of Christ is clearly safeguarded and that in any close future fellowship members would be free to refrain from the practice.

(98) In response to the third question raised in paragraph 93 above, Catholics could enter into a fellowship with the understanding that their own tradition of worship would be respected and not impugned as idolatrous.

### 4. Marian Doctrine

(99) With regard to the mediatory role of Mary, our dialogue has not revealed any tendency on the part of Catholics to look upon Mary as a propitiator or to consider that her mercy is anything but an expression and reflection of the mercy of Christ himself. Catholics today do not commonly speak of Mary's heavenly "mediation," if they use the term at all, except to express her intercessory role with her son. Understood in this way, the heavenly mediation of Mary differs only in degree from what we have dealt with under the headings of the intercession and invocation of saints.[88]

(100) In an earlier round of dialogue we have already discussed the disagreements between Lutherans and Catholics on the two modern Catholic Marian dogmas, the Immaculate Conception and the Assumption. In our discussions of teaching authority and infallibility in the church the Catholics were asked to what extent the nonacceptance of these two Marian dogmas (as well as the dogma of papal infallibility) would preclude communion and unity. The Catholic members took the position that disagreements regarding these particular dogmas did not "*of themselves* exclude all Eucharistic sharing between the churches."[89] In other words, if there were sufficient doctrinal agreement on other matters (including, for example, the ordained ministry), it might be possible to have limited eucharistic sharing even beyond what is now permitted by canon law.[90] But the Catholics added that in such a relationship of incomplete ecclesial communion Lutherans and Catholics could not ignore the remaining differences. They would have to pray and study these disputed questions and "search for a more shared understanding of the Word of God as it applies to Mary."[91] The Catholic members of the dialogue reassert this position today.

(101) From the Lutheran side, one may recall the honor and devotion paid to the Mother of God by Luther himself, including his own attitude to the Immaculate Conception and the Assumption, which he accepted in some form. The Lutheran Confessions offer high praise for Mary as foremost of all the saints. When confronted with contemporary abuses, however, the Confessions warn of "idolatry" with regard to the saints (LC Ten Commandments 21:*BC* 367;SA 2:2:26;*BC* 297) and express the fear that Mary "in popular estimation...has completely replaced Christ" (Ap

21:28;*BC* 232-33). Lutheran reactions, where voiced, to the dogmas about Mary's Immaculate Conception (1854) and Assumption (1950) were negative. The statements of the Second Vatican Council, however, demonstrate that the sole mediatorship of Christ can be asserted and the role of Mary further interpreted by Roman Catholics in ways that old Lutheran fears can be diminished. The Lutherans of this dialogue are of the opinion that, as long as the sole mediatorship of Christ is clearly safeguarded, these two Marian dogmas need not divide our churches provided that in a closer future fellowship Lutherans as members would be free not to accept these dogmas. But the link between the problem of infallibility and these theological assertions about Mary makes full agreement unattainable at the present time.

(102) In the greater fellowship we envisage between our churches, continuing efforts would have to be made together to apply hermeneutical principles to the Marian dogmas.[92] Lutherans and Catholics would have to try to see together how far decisions since the separation have been stamped with a certain particularization in thought and language, and how they could be reread in the context of the whole tradition and with a deeper understanding of Scripture. In this way it might be possible to transcend differences regarding the definitions of 1854 and 1950 without doing violence to the essential content. Unless and until such agreed reinterpretations can be achieved, the two Marian dogmas must be acknowledged as an obstacle to full fellowship between our churches, though they need not prevent a significant advance in the relationship that already exists.

## D. Church-Uniting Convergences

(103) Although such divergences continue, Lutherans and Catholics in this dialogue can propose together a number of convergences pertinent to our topic which we commend for consideration within our churches and beyond them:

1. We reiterate the basic affirmation that "our entire hope of justification and salvation rests on Christ Jesus and the gospel whereby the good news of God's merciful action in Christ is made known; we do not place our ultimate trust in anything other than God's promise and saving work in Christ" (L/RC 7:4, 157).

2. We now further assert together that Jesus Christ is the sole Mediator in God's plan of salvation (I Tim 2:5). Christ's saving work and role in God's design thus determine not only the content of the gospel and its communication but also all Christian life, including our own and that of Mary and the saints who are now in heaven.

3. As Christ prayed in the days of his flesh (Heb 5:7) for those whom

God had given him (John 17), the risen Christ continues an intercessory role for us at the right hand of God (Rom 8:34;I John 2:1;Heb 7:25).

4. The Holy Spirit both intercedes for us with God (Rom 8:26-27) and is God's advocate with us (John 14:16-17; 15:26; 16:7-15).

5. The grace of Christ the Mediator is mediated to us as ongoing communication of the gospel, through the Spirit, in the ministry of word and sacrament.

6. The Holy Spirit acts in those who minister, as, through the means of grace, sinners are brought to faith, justified, and sanctified in Christ.

7. One specific result of the gospel's communication is thus sanctification or holiness, a gift from God through Christ, experienced by faith, in the Holy Spirit. Granted in baptism, holiness is confirmed, preserved, and deepened by word and sacrament.

8. The term "saint" is used in both our traditions for all those justified by the grace of Christ, and, to one degree or another, for certain individuals among them, marked by holiness, who live the life of faith in devotion toward God and love toward the neighbor in exemplary ways, calling forth praise to God.

9. All those sanctified, together with the One who sanctifies (Heb 2:11), constitute a communion of saints in Jesus Christ.

10. The fellowship of those sanctified, the "holy ones" or saints, includes believers both living and dead. There is thus a solidarity of the church throughout the world with the church triumphant.

11. It is in this community of saints that we are promised through Christ forgiveness, communion with God, and eternal life.

12. This fellowship included the hope of resurrection, Christ being "the first fruits of those who have fallen asleep" (I Cor 15:20).

13. In the fellowship of living and departed saints, believers are inspired by others, as examples of God's grace, to greater faith, to good works, and to thanksgiving for one another.

14. Christians honor saints in at least three ways: by thanking God for them; by having faith strengthened as a result of the saints' response to God's grace; and by imitating in various situations their faith and other virtues.

15. Among the saints who have played a role in God's plan of salvation of humanity, Mary, who bore Christ, is in particular to be honored, as "God-bearer" (*Theotokos*) and as the pure, holy, and "most blessed Virgin" (*laudatissima virgo*).

16. Prayer to God—as doxology and thanksgiving; as confession of sin; as petition and intercession; and as submission to God's will—has divine

command and promise and is an integral part of the Christian life (Luke 18:1; Rom 12:12; I Tim 2:1; John 16:23).

17. Saints on earth ask one another to pray to God for each other through Christ. They are neither commanded nor forbidden to ask departed saints to pray for them.

18. Devotion to the saints and Mary should not be practiced in ways that detract from the ultimate trust that is to be placed in Christ alone as Mediator.

19. Doctrine (*lex credendi*), on the one hand, and liturgy and devotion (*lex orandi*), on the other, belong together and shape each other. While each of our traditions has put that relationship differently at various times and under changing circumstances, what is normative in both our traditions is that doctrine and worship together should promote the unique mediatorship of Christ. Both our traditions are characterized as liturgical churches with concern for piety and devotion.

## E. Next Steps

(104) Building upon our prior consensus about Jesus Christ and the gospel as the source and center of all Christian life, we have in this round of dialogue come to a deeper appreciation of the unique mediatorship of Jesus Christ and its normative role with regard to the issues before us. His sole mediatorship is the ground of our common hope and of the communion of all the faithful, living and dead, in the new life of grace. While united by these bonds, our churches are still separated by differing views on matters such as the invocation of saints and the Immaculate Conception and Assumption of Mary. Notwithstanding these differences, our churches would make greater progress toward fellowship by taking two further steps within the framework of common study and dialogue:

1. if Lutheran churches could acknowledge that the Catholic teaching about the saints and Mary as set forth in the documents of Vatican Council II (cf. §§192-201) does not promote idolatrous belief or practice and is not opposed to the gospel (cf. §101); and

2. if the Catholic Church could acknowledge that, in a closer but still incomplete fellowship, Lutherans, focusing on Christ the one Mediator, as set forth in Scripture, would not be obliged to invoke the saints or to affirm the two Marian dogmas (cf. §§100, 102).

(105) These steps put difficult questions to both our churches, but we believe them to be realistic in view of all that we have said about the existing convergences and the possibilities of dealing with unsurmounted diver-

gences. The steps are further supported, we believe, by the biblical and historical foundations to which we now turn.

## PART TWO: BIBLICAL AND HISTORICAL FOUNDATIONS

### I. SCRIPTURE ON CHRIST, THE SAINTS, AND MARY

(106) The sixteenth-century problem concerning the saints and Mary and the resulting issues between Catholics and Lutherans rest on a long, generally shared history over many prior centuries. The scriptural witness at the outset of Christianity provides a starting point on these subjects in both our traditions. Because of the normative nature of Scripture for Lutherans and Catholics, its teachings can point toward and support agreements and convergences. Anything said about saints or "holy ones" in the Bible must be viewed in the framework provided by the scriptural depiction of the holy God who redeems and creates a people, first in Israel and then through Jesus Christ.

(107) The Old Testament presents as the One God a Lord who had brought Israel out of Egypt and who entered into a covenantal relationship with a people who were to be God's "own possession among all people" and a "holy nation" (Exod 19:4-6). This God, the Holy One, had elected Israel out of love (Deut 7:6-8; 26:18-19) and both promised to dwell in the midst of this people (Exod 29:45-46;Deut 16:6, 11) and called for them to be holy, consecrated to God's will (Lev 11:44-45; 19:2).

(108) In the New Testament, faith finds its center in Christ Jesus who died for our sins and whom God raised from the dead and exalted. God is his "holy Father" (John 17:11), who through the gospel calls Jew and Gentile out of all peoples and tongues and nations into his own kingdom, in Christ (I Thess 2:12;Rev 5:9; 14:6). The God who calls is holy; those called and elect are a holy nation and are to be holy in their conduct (I Peter 1:15-16; cf. 1:2; 2:9). They are washed (baptized), sanctified, and justified (I Cor 6:11); they are God's own possession (I Pet 2:9).

(109) For the New Testament period one can speak of a "communion of saints" (*koinōnia tōn hagiōn, communio sanctorum*), to use a later creedal phrase.[93] For those who believe in Jesus Christ have fellowship with the Father and the Son (I Cor 1:9; 10:16;I John 1:3), participation in the Spirit (Phil 2:1;cf. 2 Cor 13:14) and in Christ's sufferings with the hope of the resurrection (Phil 3:10), and have fellowship also with one another (I John 1:7). Since Christ who died lives now at God's right hand, this communion extends beyond earthly life. A variety of images are employed in the New

Testament to suggest the present state of the dead in Christ; these images will be discussed below.

## A. Christ the Mediator

(110) For this fellowship Jesus the Christ is the pioneer and perfector of faith (Heb 12:2), the One who sanctifies and around whom those who are sanctified gather (Heb 2:10-12), the Holy One (Acts 3:14; 4:27, 30) through whom forgiveness of sins is proclaimed and by whom God exonerates (Acts 13:35-39;Rom 8:29-30, 33-34). The risen Christ intercedes for us (Rom 8:34;Heb 7:25). Among the many titles in the New Testament honoring Jesus Christ for what he is and what he did, one played a particular role in Lutheran-Catholic debate of the sixteenth century—"Mediator."

(111) The Hebrew Scriptures mention intermediaries who act on behalf of Yahweh. These include God's "messengers" (the *mal'āk YHWH,* "the angel of the Lord," and "angels" generally), the spirit, wisdom, and the word. At times the latter figures are personified, even hypostatized in developing Judaism. Priests, prophets, and kings sometimes play intermediary roles in passing on God's will to his people. In particular, Moses, especially at the sea (Exod 14:15-18) and at the mountain (Exod 19:3-6; 24:4-8), carries out such an intermediary function. He is aware of himself as God's archetypal prophet or mouthpiece (Deut 18:15) and is even commissioned to "consecrate" Aaron and his sons to serve as Yahweh's "priesthood" for his people (Exod 28:3, 41, 43, 29:1-44). In yet another way Moses serves in an intermediary role when he "besought the Lord his God" on behalf of the Hebrews who had sacrificed to the golden calf (Exod 32:11). Still other prophets and priests served in a similar intermediary role; in particular, Jeremiah and Ezekiel "addressed the word of the Lord" to Judah or to the exiles (Jer 1:1-3;Ezek 1:1-3). Again, in another sense an intermediary role was played by the Servant of Yahweh when he "made intercession for transgressors" (Isa 53:12). Thus, "though the word [mediator] is not used, mediatorship is at the heart of OT religion."[94]

(112) The Greek word *mesitēs,* "mediator," which occurs six times in the New Testament, is found in the Septuagint only at Job 9:33. The Hebrew of this verse reads: "There is no arbitrator (*môkîah*) between us, [who] will set his hand upon us both." In the Septuagint this is expanded: "Would that there were a mediator for us, even a judge, who also listens in the midst of us" (*eithe ēn ho mesitēs hēmōn kai elenchōn, kai diakouōn ana meson amphoterōn*). Here the Septuagint has introduced a contemporary term for an "umpire, arbitrator, mediator," attested in secular Hellenistic Greek, where it served to express mediation between human and divine beings in many reli-

gions.[95] In Job 9:33, Job begins to depict the God in whom he trusts as an "arbitrator," as he will eventually depict him also as his "witness" (*'ēd*, 16:18) and his "Redeemer" (*gō'ēl*, 19:25; cf. Job 33:23).

(113)Against such a background of intermediaries in the religion of Israel, the New Testament affirmation of Jesus as "the mediator (*mesitēs*) between God and the human race" must be understood. The term occurs in I Timothy 2:5 in a creedal passage, possibly derived from liturgy or catechesis,

> For there is one God.
> There is also one mediator between God
> and the human race,
> Christ Jesus, himself human,
> who gave himself as ransom for all. (NABRNT, I Tim 2:5-6a)

The death of Jesus is testimony (v. 6b) to God's will that all human beings be saved and is the truth (vv. 4, 7) which Paul proclaims. Other New Testament passages speak similarly of Christ's mediation: "the Mediator of a better/new covenant" (Heb 8:6; 9:15; 12:24) or even "the 'surety' (*engyos*) of a better covenant" (7:22). Jesus is not only the Mediator of a better covenant, enacted on better promises (Heb 8:6), but is now also the sole Mediator between God and human beings. I Timothy 2:5 asserts the unique mediatorship of Christ; in him alone, not in Moses (the intermediary between God and Israel, Exod 19:3-6; 24:4-8;Deut 5;27; cf. Gal 3:19-20) or angels (Gal. 3:19;Acts 7:53) or anyone else, is salvation to be found (Acts 4:12).

(114) When the New Testament uses *mesitēs or mesiteuein*, it denotes what God has accomplished for human beings through Christ. It is primarily a movement from God to us. The New Testament, however, also portrays Christ Jesus as an intermediary in other senses: he interceded (*entygchanein*) on our behalf with his heavenly Father (Rom 8:34;Heb 7:25; 9:24), "we have an advocate (*paraklēton*) with the Father, Jesus Christ the righteous" (I John 2:1). In this case the movement is from human beings to the Father through Christ; though an intermediary role is expressed, it is not called "mediation" in the New Testament. Similarly the Spirit functions in both ways, from God to us, and to God on our behalf, the Spirit interceding "for the saints according to the will of God" (Rom 8:27), but *mesitēs* and its cognates are never used of the Spirit (cf. Rom 5:5; 8:26-27,John 14:16-17, 26 [*paraklētos*]).

(115) The exact context in which I Timothy 2:5-6 (cited above in section 113) is found is important and a matter of some dispute. The reference to the one Mediator occurs in an exhortation to prayers of various sorts "for all human beings" (2:1) and "for kings and all who are in high positions, that we may lead a quiet and peaceable life, godly and respectful in every way"

(2:2 RSV; NABRNT "a quiet and tranquil life in all devotion and dignity"). The passage later speaks about the conduct of men at prayer (2:8) and of women in dress, adornment, and deeds (2:9ff.). There is dispute over the word "this" in v.2, "This is good, and it is acceptable in the sight of God…"

a. One view runs thus. Although v.3, "this is good and pleasing to God our Savior," may seem at first to refer to that immediately preceding purpose clause ("that we may lead a quiet and tranquil life…"), in the larger context the demonstrative "this" undoubtedly refers to the prayers "for all human beings" (including kings and other authorities), whom "God wishes to be saved" (v.4). Thus the author exhorts Christians to address their supplications to God that all "may come to the knowledge of the truth" that God is one and that there is "one mediator between God and the human race, Christ Jesus, himself human, who gave himself as a ransom for all" (2:5). Thus the truth of the unique mediatorship of Christ is affirmed in a context in which Christians themselves are urged to supplicate God for the salvation of all. The apostle sees himself as a herald of this truth: "a teacher of the Gentiles in faith and truth" (2:7).

b. The alternative holds that when v.3 says "this is good and pleasing to God…," the reference is to the prayers in v.2b ("that we may lead a quiet and tranquil life"), in the spirit of Jer 29:7 (prayer for the welfare of Babylon). If one takes the reference in the word "this" more broadly and claims that what is "acceptable to God' is the prayers of Christians for everyone (2:1), that all come to "knowledge of the truth" about salvation (2:4), then that interpretation calls for certain distinctions: first, between Christ's unique self-giving as ransom for all and Christians' intercessions. The way to knowledge of the truth is the apostolic preaching (v.7). It requires, second, a distinction between prayers "for everyone" (v.1) to come to the knowledge of truth (4b, in relation to the divine will and work to save them) and prayers "for kings and all in authority" that we may live at peace (v.2). The prayers and supplications for the peace and quiet of the civil and social world of Christians are thus not directly for the conversion of pagan rulers and others.[96]

c. At issue between Lutherans and Catholics have been later theological extensions of themes in this passage with regard to intercession and "mediation" by Christians in relation to Christ as the one Mediator. Aspects of this issue have been seen in Part One, above.

(116) I Timothy 2:1 employs a variety of terms for praying: "supplications, prayers, intercessions, and thanksgivings" (*deēseis, proseuchas, enteuxeis, eucharistias*),[97] For our concerns it is important to note that, just as the New Testament speaks of Christ interceding for us with the Father, so it also recognizes that Christians can intercede for others (1 Tim 2:1, *enteuxeis*, otherwise only at I Tim 4:5, "prayer"). The New Testament, using various

other terms, frequently urges Christians to pray, especially for one another (Eph 6:18;Col 4:3;I Thess 5:17), even if some limits are suggested (John 17:9;I John 5:16). The term "intercessions" occurs in the RSV only at 1 Tim 1:5, with the verb only at Heb 7:25 (*entygchanein*, of Christ; see [114] above) and Isa 53:12 (hiphil of *pagaᶜ*, of the Servant). "Invocation" is reflected in RSV only in the verb at 1 Pet 1:17 (invoke God as Father; Greek *epikaleisthai*, "call upon").[98]

(117) Through his mediatorial death and resurrection Jesus accomplished salvation for human beings and guarantees it. In the Pauline letters there are many ways of expressing this mediation.[99] We may single out two of these here. In the context of his discussion of justification, Paul depicts God setting forth Christ Jesus "as an expiation by his blood, to be received by faith" (Rom 3:25). In 2 Cor 5:18-21 Paul speaks of how God "reconciled us to himself through Christ and gave us the ministry of reconciliation" (v.18). In (or through) Christ God was reconciling the world to himself, not counting their transgressions against them (v.19, cf. 21). "To us" God entrusted "the message of reconciliation" (v.19). "We, therefore, are ambassadors for Christ, God making his appeal through us; on behalf of Christ we make our appeal, 'Be reconciled to God'" (v.20). "For our sake" God made Christ "to be sin who knows no sin, so that in him we might become the righteousness of God" (v.21). In such ways Paul portrays the mediating role of Christ Jesus in the justification and salvation of human beings and the role of Christ's ambassadors in a ministry of reconciliation (v.18), with a message of reconciliation (v.20).

(118) Colossians 1:24 occurs in a passage about reconciliation through Christ (1:22) and Paul as minister and preacher of it (1:23). In the history of interpretation 1:24b has had an important role in that it helped open the way to medieval ideas of a treasury of merits to which saints, by their sufferings, contributed, for the redemption of others. The passage deals with how Paul, by his preaching, proclaims Christ, whose cross reconciles those hostile and estranged (1:21-23, 25-29). In his sufferings during the course of his missionary ministry, the apostle says "I am filling up what is lacking in the affliction of Christ on behalf of his body, which is the church" (NABRNT). Interpretations are numerous, among them the claim that something is lacking in the vicarious sufferings by Christ himself, which is being supplied by Paul (and subsequently others). Hence the view arose that the sufferings of Christ and the saints combine to form the *thesaurus ecclesiae*, each contributing a share. Such "merits" were the target of Reformation critique, though Col 1:24 itself does not enter into the discussion in the *Confutation* or the *Book of Concord*.

(119) Today Catholics and Lutherans can agree that, however the details of 1:24 are understood, there is no disparagement in the passage of

the unique mediation by Christ through the cross. Nor does the "filling up" contradict the reconciliation wrought by God through Christ "in his body of flesh" and solely "by his death," a reconciliation of which the author regards himself a "minister" (1:22-23). One likely interpretation finds here an expression of the sufferings that Paul vicariously endures for the "saints" or the church, sufferings which unite them or it with Christ; the author supplies, in his preaching and suffering, what may still be lacking in the share of sufferings that all are called on to endure in proclaiming of the word of God (cf. 2 Cor 1:4-6). Another interpretation is that Col 1:24 reflects an idea found at least in later Jewish apocalyptic texts, a quota of "woes of the messiah" [100] that must be met.

## B. The "Holy Ones"

(120) It is within the biblical framework of God, Christ, and the believing community of those justified and redeemed that a fuller understanding of "saints" and of Mary must be unfolded. In this discussion the unique mediatorship of Christ himself is assumed and agreed upon.

### 1. Holy Ones or Saints in General

(121) God, the Creator of all things, made a covenant with and gave the law to Israel as his chosen people. The Israelites were called to be dedicated to God's service as "a holy people," 'am gādôš (Greek *ethnos hagion*, Exod 19:6; cf. Lev 19:2).

(122) Not only was Israel as a whole so characterized, but it was inspired by the example and memory of saintly forebears: the "righteous" Noah, "blameless in his generation" (Gen 6:9); Abraham, reckoned as righteous because of his faith (Gen 15:6); the patriarchs Isaac and Jacob; Moses and the judges; kings and prophets. Individuals within this people were further characterized as "holy" because of their dedication to Yahweh or his temple service: Elisha (2 Kgs 4:9), the Levites (2 Chr 35:3), the Nazarite (Num 6:5). In this way the holiness of Yahweh was reflected in his people.

(123) It was also reflected in the heavenly court of angels, often called "holy ones": "Yahweh, your God, will come, and all his holy ones with him" (Zech 14:5; cf. Deut 33:2;Job 5:1). They were associated with Israel's cult (Ps 89:5, 7 [=Hebrew Ps 6,8]) and were believed to assist the people (Dan 10:11-13; 12:1).

(124) In time there emerged in Judaism itself, especially as notions about the afterlife (resurrection, immortality) developed, the remembrance and veneration of holy ancestors. Though Ecclesiastes pessimistically comments, "There is no remembrance of bygone human beings" (1:11), Sirach

records his famous eulogy of Israel's ancestors (44:1-50:24). For him they were "men of piety" (44:1), whose "righteous deeds have not been forgotten" (44:10). That eulogy singles out Moses as "equal in glory to the holy ones" (45:2), records about Elisha that "in his life he performed wonders, and after his death marvelous deeds" (48:14), and utters a prayer for the Minor Prophets, "May their bones return to life from their resting-place" (49:10).

(125) This honoring of the saints of old led to the building of "tombs of the prophets" and "monuments of the righteous" (Matt 23:29). This was a manifestation of popular religion among Palestinian Jews in the last two pre-Christian centuries. It provided, in particular, special honor for those who suffered or died because of their Jewish faith in times of persecution. Thus were venerated the aged scribe Eleazar (2 Macc 6:18-31) and the seven sons of a Jewish mother, tortured and killed because of their refusal to eat pork (2 Macc 7:1-42). These stories, further embellished in 4 Macc 5:4-6:30; 8:3-17:10, even record the epitaph: "Here lie an aged priest, a woman full of years, and her seven sons. Through the violence of a tyrant bent on destroying the Hebrew nation, they vindicated the rights of our people, looking unto God and enduring torments even unto death" (17:9-10).[101]

(126) The term "holy" was applied to Christian disciples in earthly life, now regarded as God's people in an extended sense. I Peter 1:15-16 explicitly quotes Lev 11:44-45 or 19:2 and applies it to Christians. For Paul "saints" becomes the common designation of Christians to whom he writes (Rom 1:7; 15:25;I Cor 1:2;2 Cor 1:1;Phil 1:1). This designation is a mark of their calling, a destiny envisaged also by John 17:17, 19.

(127) Though Paul never calls himself *hagios,* "holy," he does recommend to his Christian readers at times that they "be imitators" of him, as he is "of Christ" (I Cor 11:1; cf. Phil 3:17;I Thess 1:6). He is also aware of the Thessalonians as an example (*typos*) for all believers in Macedonia and Achaia.

(128) "Saints" is a title extended even to those who had fallen asleep and were raised at the time of Jesus' death and appeared in Jerusalem after his resurrection (Matt 27:52-53).

(129) The Epistle to the Hebrews, having defined faith as "the reality of things hoped for, the proof of things that one cannot see" (11:1), goes on to praise Old Testament figures famous for such faith, those who because of it received divine approval (Abel, Enoch, Noah, Abraham, Sarah, Isaac, etc.). "All these, though well attested by their faith, did not receive what was promised, since God had foreseen something better for us, that apart from us they should not be made perfect" (11:39-40). They become, however, "a cloud of witnesses" that surround us (12:1), and the author of Hebrews thus hints at a solidarity existing between his Christian readers and such people of faith in times gone by. Christian leaders are commended as "those who

addressed to you the word of God; contemplate the outcome of their lives and imitate their faith" (13:7).

(130) The Book of Revelation makes use of apocalyptic devices to honor Christians who have died for their faith. They "have come forth from the great tribulation, having washed their robes and made them white in the blood of the Lamb" (8:14). Numberless, from every nation, tribe, people, and tongue, clothed in white, they stand before the enthroned Lamb, for their salvation has been achieved by the Lamb (14:1-12). A beatitude is uttered over them, "Blessed (*makarioi*) are the dead who die in the Lord from now on...that they may rest from their struggles, for their deeds follow them" (14:13). Thus a Christian author has not only adopted a traditional Jewish literary genre, but has also continued the Jewish practice of honoring "saints" who have died for the faith. As was suggested by Heb. 12:1, "the cloud of witnesses" (see [129] above), the author of Revelation implies a corporate relationship of those already put to death for the word of God with others still to suffer that fate. The souls under the altar are told to wait a little longer "until the number of their fellow servants and brethren be filled up, those who were going to be killed as they themselves had been" (6:9-11; cf. Rev 18:20, 24).

(131) The later Pauline letters, however, reflect an ambiguity in the veneration of holy ones, especially when by this is meant "the worship of angels" (Col 2:18). False teaching in Asia Minor churches seemed to exalt "principalities and powers" (2:15; cf. Eph 1:20-23) and to impugn the role of the cosmic Christ, now seated at God's right hand "in the heavenly places, far above every rule, authority, power, or dominion—and above whatever name can be named" (1:21). All these God has put under the risen Christ's feet and "made him the head over all for the church" (1:22). As in other New Testament writings, these letters were insisting that faith in Christ, as the perfect image of the Father (Col 1:15) and the only Redeemer, must be the touchstone of belief and worship among the people of the new Israel.

(132) Just as Old Testament passages speak at times of individual holy persons and recall their faith, so in the New Testament individuals are singled out as holy ones; for example, in the Epistle to the Hebrews (chap. 11, of Old Testament figures). Thus Elizabeth and Zechariah, "upright in God's sight, living blamelessly according to all the commandments and requirements of the Lord" (Luke 1:6); John the Baptist (Luke 1:15); Simeon, "upright and devout," with whom the Holy Spirit was (2:25); Anna, "worshiping day and night with fasting and prayer" (2:37); Joseph of Arimathea, "a disciple of Jesus" (John 19:38), "a good and upright man" (Luke 23:50); and, after Jesus' resurrection, Stephen, "full of faith and the holy Spirit" (Acts 6:5), "full of grace and power" (6:8). Though none of these persons is explicitly proposed in the New Testament for imitation or special reverence,

their exemplary character serves to glorify God and his Christ, with whom they are associated.

## 2. Deceased "Holy Ones"

(133) What of the saints who have departed from this life? The Augsburg Confession cites I Tim 2:5 in a context that states, "It cannot be proved from the Scriptures that we are to invoke saints and seek help from them" (21:1). The Apology (21:9; *BC* 230) insists "there is no passage in Scripture about the dead praying, except for the dream recorded in the Second Book of Maccabees (15:14)," a reference to how Judas Maccabeus encouraged his troops by reporting a vision he had had. In it, Onias the high priest prayed for the Jews, and Jeremiah, the prophet who had died over four hundred years before, appeared and gave Judas a golden sword, thus endorsing self-defense by the Jews on the Sabbath. The *Confutation* also cited Baruch 3:4, "O Lord, Almighty, God of Israel, hear now the prayer of the dead of Israel...," with the comment, "Therefore the dead also pray for us." Underlying any discussion here is the question of the state of Christian (and Jewish) holy ones who have died. If they are not yet raised to life or not yet purged from their sins or they simply "sleep," how can they pray for us? But if they already reign in glory, ought not one invoke them to make petitions for us, with Christ as they are? Lutherans have raised the first question, and Catholics have stressed the second. Our views rest on the same biblical data. We also share certain common influences in the history of the development of the many views that exist on the present status of the dead in Christ. These views sometimes cut across Confessional lines.[102]

(134) For the most part, the Old Testament Scriptures envision after death, at best, a diminished existence, cut off from God, in Sheol, a place of gloom and silence (though not of punishment) in the netherworld (Ps 94:17, 88:10-12;Job 10:21-22; 30:23). Yet Israel's strong sense of divine justice looked at times toward a future righteous balancing of inequities of life, and Israel's long experience of God's redemptive power brought assertions about God's hand reaching even to Sheol (Amos 9:2;Ps 139:8). It is often difficult to tell whether certain verses refer to a real resurrection of individuals who have experienced physical death or to a corporate restoration of the nation.[103] While Ezek 37:1-14;Isa 26:19; 53:10-12; 66:19; and Hos 6:2-3 have all been taken to refer to resurrection of the dead, Dan. 12:2-3 is the clearest reference. Here, as elsewhere, there is an apocalyptic setting about what will happen "at the time," i.e., on the day of the Lord. Since the state of the dead is often described as "sleep" (Job 14:10-12;Dan 12:2;Jer 51:39, 57), resurrection is "awakening," especially for the righteous (Ps 16:10-11;Isa 26:9-19). Occasionally there is reference to a "double resurrection," of both good and

bad, "some to everlasting life, and some to...everlasting contempt" (Dan 12:2).

(135) In the literature of Judaism,[104] often in writings that Protestants count as Apocrypha and the Council of Trent included in its canon, there are further statements of expectation about an afterlife. These are sometimes put in terms of resurrection. In contrast to gloomy pictures of Hades (Sir 14:16; 17:27-28; 22:11; cf. 46:19), there is hope for vindication (cf. Wis 3:7, in light of Dan 12:1-3) and resurrection (Sir 46:12a). The Maccabean martyrs cherished the hope of being raised, but their oppressors would not be raised (2 Macc 7:9, 14; 2 Esdras [Vulgate 4th Esdras] 7:32-38, 47). Benediction 2 in the synagogue prayer *Sh^emoneh 'Esreh* says of God, "Thou quickenest the dead." The Mishnah later denied any share in the world to come to the person "who says that there is no resurrection of the dead [prescribed in the Law]."[105] But not all Jews agreed on the resurrection hope. As is well known, the Sadducees are depicted in the New Testament as denying it, but the Pharisees as embracing it (Mark 12:18 par.; Acts 23:8). The 2 Maccabees 12 passage, about Judas Maccabeus "taking account of the resurrection" (v.43), suggests that some Jews thought that those who fell in battle would not rise; others thought that they would but that "atonement for the dead" was proper.[106] The invocation at Baruch 3:4, that God hear "the prayer of the dead of Israel," likely, however, refers to Israelites in exile in Babylonia or is a mistranslation in the Greek.[107] The evidence in the Dead Sea scrolls from Qumran about a belief in an afterlife is ambiguous.[108] Sometimes hope for an afterlife was expressed in terms of immortality. The latter view is derived from the body-soul dichotomy of Greek thought (Wis 3:1, 4;Philo *Abr.* 258:Josephus, *Jewish Wars* 3.8.5=3.372-75; and rabbinic references).[109]

(136) In the Gospels Jesus affirms the resurrection hope.[110] His announcement of God's imminent kingdom and the overcoming of Satan (Matt 12:28 par. Luke 11:28; cf. Luke 10:18 and the healing miracles, including raising of the dead; and Matt 11:5 par. Luke 7:22) was joined with references to judgment (Matt 12:41-42 par. Luke 11:31-32;Matt 10:28) and apocalyptic expectations about the coming day of the Lord (Matt 8:11-12 par. Luke 13:29-29;Mark 13 par.). In the dispute with the Sadducees (Mark 12:18-27 par.) Jesus answered their question about the resurrection with the claim that by God's power the dead are raised, for God is "the God of the living." A bodily existence is involved in the "life" and "kingdom" one enters (Mark 9:43, 45, 47 par.); so also with the Old Testament patriarchs (Matt 8:11 par.). Jesus' own expectation of vindication for himself included being raised up (Mark 8:31; 9:31; 10:34 par.), and, for the Twelve, exaltation in the "new world" (Matt 19:28 par. Luke 22:28-30).

(137) It is Jesus' own resurrection that is the real starting point for New Testament development of teachings about life after death. The testimo-

ny that "God raised Jesus from the dead " (I Thess 1:10;I Cor 15:15) or
"Christ has been raised/is risen" (I Cor 15:4) or, more rarely, "Jesus rose"
(I Thess 4:14) meant, to those attuned to the Pharisaic-eschatological hope,
God's victory over death, promise of the new age soon to come, and expectations of resurrection/life/the kingdom of God for Jesus' followers. In particular, the fact that Jesus was raised made him the "first fruits" (I Cor 15:20)
pointing to the full harvest that would follow for his disciples.[111]

(138) "Resurrection" is to be distinguished from mere "resuscitation"
out of death, where someone was brought back to natural, terrestrial life for a
time.[112] The New Testament vocabulary for resurrection resulting in eternal
life involves terms meaning "raise (up), cause to stand on one's feet, awak-
en" (*anistēmi, egeirō*), but also "make alive" (*zōopoieō*), "live" (*zaō*), and
even "be vindicated, justified" (*dikaioō*; I Tim 3:15).[113]

(139) The connection between Christ's resurrection and that of believers is clearly made in Paul's letters: because we believe Jesus died and rose,
so too will God raise us up (I Thess 4:14, 16-17) and make us alive (I Cor
15:20-21), through the "Spirit which dwells in" justified believers (Rom
8:11). To present this hope and its implications Paul employed a variety of
images in I Thess 4:13-5:11;I Cor 15;2 Cor 5:1-10;Phil 1:19-26, and elsewhere, some of them cast in apocalyptic terms. Paul "hoped for, preached,
and defended a personal 'resurrection form the dead' not as a radically new
creation out of nothing but as a making alive and transformation of the dead,
earthly 'body,' i.e., the personal, bodily existence" of the individual
believer.[114] There is continuity (not *creatio ex nihilo*), but only by God's creative power can resurrection come about. The "spiritual body" (*sōma pneu-
matikon,* I Cor 15:44)—with the "image" of Christ, the last Adam and life-
giving spirit, vv. 45, 49—is Paul's term to preserve both aspects, continuity
and newness Such divine action is necessitated because of the reign of sin
over all human beings, so that all persons do sin, with death coming in sin's
wake (I Cor 15:21-22;Rom 5:12-21, cf. 3:9, 20, 23). Involved in the human
situation is "eternal" death (Rom 6:16, 21, 23), not merely that we are "dead
in sins" (Rom 7:13, cf. vv. 9-11;Eph 2:1) but also death at the end, as the
"last enemy" (I Cor 15:26); from all this, Christ rescues (I Cor 15:54-56). In
the face of those who would stress present salvation alone, Paul had reservations, for there is a future aspect for the believer. Yet Paul can apply resurrection, new-life language to existence now in Christ (2 Cor 5:17) or for the
(eschatological) "acceptance" of Israel, which is termed "life from the dead"
(Rom 11:15).

(140) The other New Testament writings exhibit in varying degrees the
present and the future sides of redemption. The Fourth Gospel especially
stresses the former, as do Colossians and Ephesians; the Pastoral Epistles and
to a considerable extent Luke-Acts, the latter side. But a certain balance is

maintained throughout.[115] From Luke's depiction of the risen Christ as "flesh and bones" (Luke 24:39) was to develop the later phrase in the Apostles' Creed, "resurrection of the *flesh*," a terminology impossible for Paul (cf. 1 Cor 15:50) and a departure from usual New Testament phraseology, "resurrection of or from *the dead*."[116] The judgment aspect is frequently connected with a future resurrection.[117]

(141) As to when Christians arise, find life, or live, three general ways of speaking can be distinguished, each with scriptural support.[118] These three ways do not necessarily exclude one another. In subsequent centuries there have been various combinations of the three with each other and with the ideas of resurrection and immortality.

a. One way holds that the promised life with God begins immediately after an individual's death, with judgment either at that moment or later.[119] Paul writes, for example, of his desire "to depart and be with Christ" (Phil 1:23; cf. 2 Cor 5:1-10, with mention of "the judgment seat of Christ"). Sayings in Luke support such an expectation ("today you will be with me in Paradise," 23:43; cf. the analogy to Christ, 24:26;Acts 2:32-33). John's Gospel insists that the person who believes in Jesus shall, upon dying, live and never die (11:25). Rev 6:9-11 pictures the "souls" of the slain to be "under the altar" and waiting for the Lord to judge. This view offers great personal consolation: each receives life at his or her own death. It preserves the future aspect in that all is not attained in this life. But it weakens the corporate nature of the New Testament view of the resurrection.

b. Another way is that there will be a general resurrection and judgment at the last day and that, until then, the dead "sleep" or "rest" (cf., e.g., Dan 12, esp. vv. 2-4, 9, 13; or I Thess 4:14-18).[120] The strengths of this view include its corporate emphasis on the people of God coming into eternal life together and a realism about the fact that all is not yet fulfilled and cannot be till all the redeemed live together in God's kingdom. A weakness is the tendency toward apocalyptic scenarios about what happens step by step at the parousia. The future aspect may divert attention from life now in God's world and from awareness of the salvation already achieved in Christ's cross and resurrection.

c. A third way sees the new life of the resurrection to be already present, now, during the believer's days on earth.[121] John's Gospel most clearly presents such a realized eschatology: the believer "does not come into judgment, but has passed from death to life" (5:24-27; 6:35-51). According to Paul, newness of life is available "in Christ," through Jesus our Lord, "who was put to death for our transgressions and raised for our justification" (Rom 4:25-5:2; cf. also Eph 2:5-7; and the hymnic excerpt 5:14, probably connected with baptism, "Awake, O sleeper, and arise from the dead, and Christ shall give you light").[122] This view brings the resurrection life vividly into the present. Its eschatology, however, when one-sided, can lead to the heresy of those "who have swerved from the truth by holding that the resurrection is past already" (2 Tim 2:18; cf. I Cor 15).

(142) These New Testament ways of speaking, using "rise/find life/live," though multivalent, involve for believers the hope of a personal resurrection and a post-mortem, post-parousia eternal life. This life of God's new age will be bodily (though the new body will be "spiritual"), corporate with others, and with Jesus, before God. It is not the result of possessing an "immortal soul,"[123] although a saying of Jesus once refers to "those who kill the body but cannot kill the soul" (Matt 10:28).[124] This life will be a renewed spiritual existence given by God, which is called in I Corinthians "donning immortality" (15:53-54). It involves more than escape from death, for there is also deliverance from sin. Resurrection of the dead is, like justification, dependent on God's promise and saving work in Christ. At times the resurrection hope is depicted as a future fulfillment for all together, at times as individual, and on occasion as already impinging on existence as life now.

### 3. Mary

(143) Against the biblical background about saints in general one has to view the treatment of Mary in the New Testament.[125] Though there may immediately come to mind the words put on her lips by Luke, "From now on all generations will count me blessed" (1:48), that verse must not be torn from its context, for it has to be seen against the various ways in which Mary is pictured in the New Testament.

(144) Whereas "God" is mentioned in every book of the New Testament, and also "Jesus" (Christ)—except for 3 John, Mary is named only in the Synoptic Gospels and Acts. In the Johannine Gospel she is referred to as "the mother of Jesus" or "his mother" (2:1, 3, 5, 12; 19:25-26). In the other twenty-two books indirect allusion to her may appear in Gal. 4:4-5 and Rev. 12:1-17; otherwise no mention is made of her. These other New Testament writings are concerned either with early Christian exhortation, with ad hoc problems, or with an interpretation of the Christ-event and its meaning for humanity; thus mention of her would be uncalled for. Most attention has been devoted to her in the Gospels of Matthew, Luke, and John, whereas she is mentioned but twice in Mark (3:20-35; 6:3) and once in Acts (1:14). Although other terms of praise are used for Mary in the NT, as we shall see, yet at no place in the NT is she called "holy, saint" (*hagia*) or "upright, righteous" (*dikaia*).

(145) In Mark, usually deemed the first Gospel to be written and a source for Matthew and Luke, Mary is mentioned in two passages. (a) Mark 3:20-35 is a literary unit in which vv. 20-22 are related to vv. 31-35.[126] Verses 31-35 clearly concern Jesus' "mother and his brothers" and are understood

by commentators to explain "his own" (*hoi par' autou*) in v. 21. Hence the NAB and the RSV (1971 edition of the New Testament) render v. 21 as "his family" (cf. NABRNT, "his relatives"). This means that Jesus' mother and brothers, who have heard about him, have come out to take him in hand because "he is beside himself" (v. 21).[127] Later, when they stand outside the house crowded with those listening to him and ask for him, Jesus substitutes a spiritual family for his physical, natural family: "Whoever does the will of God is my brother, and sister, and mother." (b) In Mark 6:1-6a Jesus in "his own country" astonishes people in the synagogue: "Where did he get all this?...Is not this the carpenter, the son of Mary, and brother of James, Joses, Judas, and Simon?" Jesus comments: "A prophet is not without honor except in his own country, and among his own relatives, and in his own house." Thus Mary shares in the misunderstanding of Jesus that his own disciples manifest frequently in the Marcan Gospel.[128] In these Marcan passages, though Mary has a carpenter son, she is not said to be part of his spiritual family nor one who understands him or honors him as a prophet.

(146) In the Matthean Gospel two passages parallel the Marcan episodes just discussed. (a) In 12:46-50 those who constitute Jesus's spiritual family are his "disciples," not his physically related mother and brothers. A difference is detected in the omission by Matthew of reference to "his own" who consider him to be "beside himself." (b) In 13:53-58 Matthew omits in v.57 Mark's reference to "his own relatives," and Jesus is now said to be not "the carpenter" but "the son of the carpenter," and his mother "is called Mary." In these ways the Matthean form of these episodes tones down the negative picture of Mary in Mark (reducing it at least to neutrality).

(147) A more pronounced role that accounts for this shift in emphasis is given to Mary in the opening infancy narrative in Matthew. Like other women mentioned in the genealogy of Jesus (1:1-17), Mary is seen as an instrument of divine providence in the messianic plan of God; of her is "begotten Jesus, who is called the Christ." Her virginal conception of him is, according to some source critics, taken over from a pre-Matthean source and clearly set forth in 1:18-25 (*virginitas ante partum*). In chapter 2 she plays little part aside from v.11; she is referred to in the phrase "the child and his mother" in vv.13, 14, 20, and 21. Thus Matthew's opening presentation of Mary singles her out and sets the tone for presenting a less negative picture of her in her two appearance during Jesus' ministry (see §146).

(148) Luke presents the most extensive portrait of Mary in his Gospel and Acts. Though she does not appear in the genealogy (3:23-38) and plays no part in the accounts of his ministry, death, and resurrection, she is indirectly referred to in two episodes (that correspond to the Marcan passages). In the account of the rejection of Jesus at Nazareth (4:16-30), those who listen to him ask, "Is not this the son of Joseph?" (4:22); all reference to the

carpenter, to Mary, and to his brothers and sisters disappears. Jesus' own remark about the reception of a prophet becomes merely, "No prophet is acceptable in his own country" (4:24), with all reference to relatives and house suppressed. Again, whereas Mark and Matthew portrayed Jesus substituting a spiritual family for his physical, natural family, the Lucan Jesus depicts it otherwise: "My mother and my brothers are those who hear the word of God and do it" (8:21).

(149) In still another episode, peculiar to Luke, a woman moved by Jesus' preaching during his ministry utters a beatitude over the mother who bore him and nursed him. Jesus himself counters with a beatitude of his own: "Blessed, rather, are those who hear the word of God and keep it" (11:27-28). Though his reply has often been taken as a corrective (= "No, rather"), it is more likely intended as a modification (= "Yes, but even more"). Thus 11:28 may be related to 8:21. In such episodes of the ministry Luke has sketched Mary far more positively than either Mark or Matthew has done.

(150) Mary's portrait in the Lucan Gospel is most emphatically painted in the infancy narrative. The announcements of the births of John and Jesus and the accounts of their birth, circumcision, and manifestation set forth their origins in antithetical, step-parallelism, which enhances the role of Jesus over John. If John is born by heaven's intervention to barren parents, Jesus is so born to a virgin, Mary. If John is to be great before the Lord and go before him in the power and spirit of Elijah, Jesus will be "great," the heir to David's throne, and Son of God. Mary herself is *kecharitōmenē*, "highly favored woman," chosen by God to bear this extraordinary child through "the power of the Most High"; and to this singular election she responds with her obedient *fiat* (1:26-38; contrast Zechariah's disbelief [1:20]).

(151) In the visitation scene (1:39-56) she is recognized by Elizabeth as "the mother of my Lord" (1:43) and pronounced both "blest" (*eulogēmenē*) in her motherhood and "blessed" (*makaria*) because of her faith in the fulfillment of what has been said to her by the Lord (1:42b, 45). Mary answers with her Magnificat, praising God who "has done great things" for her and who works mightily in behalf of the hungry and those of low degree. In the course of it she explains why from now on all generations will count me blessed" (*makariousin*, 1:48).

(152) Mary gives birth to Jesus in Bethlehem, where she has gone with Joseph who, as a member of the house of David, is to be registered in the census. There her newborn child is identified by a heavenly chorus as "Savior, Messiah, and Lord" (2:11). Mary is said by the evangelist to have "kept all these things in her heart" (2:19, 51), pondering over them. She is depicted in the oracle of Simeon as one through whose soul "a sword shall pierce" (2:35), because her child is "marked for the fall and rise of many in Israel." The implications of that ominous pronouncement over Mary herself

are spelled out, when Jesus as a twelve-year-old is taken to Jerusalem for the Passover and remains behind in the temple when his parents start off for home in Nazareth. When they return and find him, Mary complains, "Child, why have you treated us like this? Look, your father and I have been terribly worried and have been searching for you." Jesus replies, "Why are you searching for me? Did you not know that I had to be in my Father's house?" (2:48-49). Thus the sword of discerning judgment pierces Mary's soul as she begins to learn what sort of son she has borne; her physical motherhood has to yield to another relationship. And Luke depicts that as discipleship, for in Acts 1:14 he portrays her sitting in the upper room in Jerusalem after the passion and death of her son, along with "the women" and "his brothers," praying and awaiting "the promise of the Father" (Luke 24:49; cf. Acts 1:4). In this lengthy Lucan treatment of Mary she is extolled for her motherhood and faith, but tested in her devotion and comprehension.

(153) Mary's role is differently developed in the Fourth Gospel, which has no infancy narrative, never names her, and has no parallels to the Marcan ministry episodes. She appears as "the mother of Jesus" in two episodes peculiar to this Gospel, at the wedding of Cana (2:1-12) and at the foot of the cross (19:25-27). Indirect reference may be made to her in 1:13; 6:42; 7:41-43; 8:41. At Cana Mary indirectly requests of Jesus an intervention to relieve an embarrassing situation, the failure of the wine supply at a joyous wedding celebration. The episode has a primary christological purpose in that the miracle reveals Jesus's power and him as a source of help in time of trouble; what he does is an example of the "greater things" of which he himself spoke in 1:50, and it "manifests his glory" (2:11). But Mary plays an important role in raising the question about the wine and in giving directions to the waiters (vv. 3, 5). She is depicted, it might seem, as having confidence in her son but as initially misunderstanding his "hour" or role (v.4). Yet he acquiesces to her persistence and supplies the wine. The passage has given rise to various interpretations, some affirming Mary's "intercessory" role, others not.

(154) Mary's trust, despite her lack of comprehension, eventually leads to a more profound understanding and solid faith. She remains with Jesus (unlike his brothers, 7:5) and at length appears with other women at the foot of the cross (19:25-27), at "the hour" when he is glorified (17:1). There she becomes a model for those who believe in him. The dying Jesus is then presented as concerned about his mother and entrusts her to the care of the beloved disciple, who has not deserted Jesus (like the other disciples), but who becomes the witness par excellence of Jesus' ministry and death, and who guarantees his community's understanding of Jesus. Mary and this disciple thus symbolize the community of believing disciples that the crucified and dying Jesus leaves behind, the kind of community that comes into being in the post-resurrectional or Pentecostal period in other traditions. The new

mother-son relationship proclaimed by the dying Jesus reflects the replacement of his natural family by a new family of disciples. As in the Lucan writings, the mother of Jesus thus meets the criterion of the spiritual, eschatological family of Jesus. Mary's role is a symbol for other Christians.

(155) Overall, in the New Testament writings, there is a variety of portraits of Mary. Though Mark's picture of her is somewhat negative, Matthew's is less so, Luke changes the picture more dramatically, and John is most positive. As the tradition about her develops from this New Testament matrix, there is a rich and imaginative unfolding of a new body of doctrine in the second and following centuries.[129]

## II. FROM THE SECOND TO THE SIXTEENTH CENTURY

(156) The development in Christian history of the biblical themes sketched in the preceding sections was not only indebted to Jewish sources but was also affected by the common culture of the Greco-Roman world into which the young church carried its message. Recent scholarship has emphasized the fact that the early Christian movement established its own theology and lifestyle in close interaction with the thought forms, conventions, and customs of contemporary people.[130] While the Christian faith shaped much of the ideological and cultural framework of the West from the fourth century on, Christianity itself had not been impervious to the influence of its environment. There can be no doubt, for instance, that the doctrinal formulations of Christology in the early centuries owed much to the dialogue with the popular philosophies of the time, especially Stoicism, Platonism, and various Gnostic systems. A comparable contact with the religious thought of the age must be assumed in the evolution of Christian ideas about mediators and the unique mediatorship of Christ. The belief in angelic and demonic powers between heaven and earth was part of the fundamental convictions of most people, both Jews and pagans, and the idea of a redeemer revealing knowledge from the divine realm to humans and bringing salvation to believers formed the core of the teaching of a number of cults and cultic associations.

(157) Similarly, Christian convictions and practices regarding holy people and martyrs were shaped in an environment which had its own saints. After the Maccabean revolt with its heroes and martyrs, Jewish popular piety intensified the cult of biblical figures and other reputed saints at their tombs, where their memory was celebrated and their intercession sought despite official hesitation. In the Hellenistic world after Alexander the Great (356-323 B.C.), the classical hero worship at local sanctuaries of mythical demigods, kings, or founders had given rise to an official ruler cult which under the Roman Empire became an emperor cult and was extended by

Caligula (37-41 A.D.) and especially Domitian (81-96 A.D.) to the living emperor, finding expression in elaborate symbols and rituals.[131] Veneration of the emperor's image by decoration or coronation, solemn procession, prostration, and other worship gestures customary in the East became an important part of public ceremonial throughout the Empire. Since Augustus, temples and shrines were erected in the emperor's honor, encouraging devotional exercises similar to those which characterized the shrines of popular healing deities such as Asclepios and Sarapis. These practices included pilgrimages, sacrifices, prayers, oracles, votive gifts, incubation (sleeping in the holy precinct in expectation of dreams, revelations, healings), and traffic in charms, amulets, and other mementos. While the civic ritual of the emperor cult and of local deities was resolutely rejected by Christians, nevertheless, parallel devotional phenomena developed in their own cult of martyrs and saints. This paradox is a sign not so much of deliberate borrowing or unconscious imitation but of participation in the religious expressions of an age in which, in the final analysis, both sides gave and received.[132] In the history of the first Christian centuries the task of sorting out what was truly compatible with the centrality of Christ and the uniqueness of his mediatorship in the beliefs and practices surrounding other mediators proved endless. A book such as the *Shepherd of Hermas*, written in Rome in the middle of the second century, shows some of the difficulties.[133] Here, Christology borrows from angelology, and Christ, the Son of God, is associated with heavenly figures such as the Shepherd, the Angel of Repentance, and other angelic spirits and powers.

(158) Of great importance for all subsequent development in this area was the firm insistence of the New Testament on the resurrection of Jesus and of all Christians, even though the term "resurrection" allowed for different ways of reading the biblical data in light of popular convictions about death and the afterlife. The canonical and apocryphal Acts of the Apostles speak of the difficulties encountered by Paul and the early Christian missionaries when they preached the resurrection.[134] The second century seems to have been the age of debates over the resurrection, especially with Gnostics, who, in the perception of many Christians, tried to interpret away the reality of the message.[135] In the later creeds of the church a special accent fell on the "resurrection of the dead and the life of the world to come" (Creed of Nicaea-Constantinople) or, in an ancient phrase fervently defended by Tertullian, "the resurrection of the flesh" (Apostles' Creed), perhaps because of such denials of the promised future life. Internal disputes are recorded in the third century when Christians in Arabia, apparently seeking to preserve aspects of the biblical witness against a doctrine of the soul's immortality, argued that the human soul dies with the body and will be raised together with it. Eusebius testifies that Origen of Alexandria (c. 185-253/54) was

instrumental in having this view rejected.[136] While Origen's own theories about the fate of souls in a cyclical process of salvation remained under suspicion and were censured by the Emperor Justinian in 543,[137] it seems quite clear that by his time the teaching of the immortality of the soul, understood in one way or another, had come to be a widely held, if not the dominant view in Christian theology, often combined, but sometimes also in tension with, the basic assertion of the resurrection of the dead.

(159) For the early generations of Christians the question of the afterlife of those who have died and of their interim state until the general resurrection received added actuality through the persecutions and the ensuing martyrdoms. In the late first century, conviction about the destiny of martyrs after their death is documented in a context where the primary concern is to offer an example that may be imitated. Corinthian Christians, plagued by strife, contention, and envy, are told in the First Letter of Clement that peace will not be restored to their church without faith and the endurance of suffering on their part. They are given Old Testament examples from which they are to draw this conclusion. To the same end they are asked to consider what they may learn from the great Christian "athletes" of their own generation, specifically from the apostles Peter and Paul. Because of jealousy Peter suffered many tribulations; in this way he gave his witness and "went to the glorious place which was his due" (I Clement 5:4). Paul, too, suffered as a result of jealousy and strife. A herald in the East and West, he gained renown for his faith, teaching righteousness to the entire world. Having witnessed before rulers, he passed from this life and went "to the holy place," thus providing the most sterling example of endurance (5:5-7). Finally the Corinthians are reminded of a great host of other Christians (perhaps the *multitudo ingens* that Tacitus says Nero persecuted [*Annales* 15:44]) who were victims of jealousy and became great examples in their endurance of torture (6:1).

(160) Early in the second century Ignatius of Antioch shows his own conviction about what lies in store for him after martyrdom in Rome. He expresses his desire to be killed by the wild beasts quickly so that he may "get to Jesus Christ" (Rom 1:2; 5:3). In line with New Testament texts that suggest an existence with the risen Christ immediately after death for specific believers (I Thess 4:15-17;Luke 23:43), especially those who suffered for his sake (Phil 1:23;Acts 7:54-60;Rev 6:9-11; cf. Luke 16:19-31), it became a common Christian conviction that the martyr's reward included the immediate transition to eternal life with Christ. The Acts of the Martyrs are replete with indications that this very hope emboldened persecuted Christians to face martyrdom with calm.[138]

(161) As the martyrs seemed to join the "great cloud of witnesses" above (Heb 12:1), their remembrance celebrated in rituals such as memorial meals on the anniversary of their martyrdom (*dies natalis*), gatherings and

graffiti at their place of burial, and the erection of funerary monuments assigned them a special place in the body of Christ; their intercessions in heaven for those who were left behind was thought to be especially power-ful.[139] The earliest mention of a memorial cult at the resting place of the bones of a Christian martyr is found in the *Martyrdom of Polycarp* (18:1-3), written shortly after the middle of the second century. Respect for, and ven-eration of, the saints, burial in the vicinity of their tombs, pilgrimages to the places where they had lived and died or were buried, and adoption of a saint as "patron" of a church or town were practices endorsed and even recom-mended by some church fathers.[140] Similar to the conviction of many pagans, the belief that these saints can and do perform miracles on behalf of their devotees was not uncommon. There was less clarity about the fate of other deceased Christians in the interim state. But since Christians believed that all who died in Christ would eventually share in his resurrection, their funerary art could portray the dead as praying in heaven with the community of saints on earth. In the imagination of many, these "souls in peace" formed a great crowd around the martyrs, ascetics, virgins, and widows who were honored for the special holiness of their lives. Thus the understanding of the church of the "saints" (cf. Rom 1:7;I Cor 1:2; 2 Cor 1:1; etc.) was not limited to those fighting here on earth under the banner of Christ, but included those perfect-ed by their death in Christ, a church triumphant such as the visions of Rev 7 describe it.

(162) Early references to Mary, the Mother of Jesus, outside the New Testament are rare. They include, however, several remarks in the letters of Ignatius of Antioch which, in an antidocetic argument, point to the mystery of Jesus' birth by the Virgin.[141] The first clear signs of an independent bio-graphical interest in the person of Mary appear in the literature of the late second century. This interest in the Mother did not develop in competition with the central theological affirmations about the person and work of Christ, but as its natural complement. As the imagination of Christian authors tried to fill what could be perceived as gaps in the accounts of the life of Jesus, apocryphal writings made their appearance, inventing new details, especially in relation to his birth and infancy and the days between his death, resurrec-tion, and ascension. Curiosity about the childhood of Jesus spawned leg-endary tales which tended to heighten the miraculous nature of his birth. Foremost among them was the so-called *Protevangelium of James*, written during the late second century, a fanciful account of Jesus' birth and its pre-history which promoted a high ideal of Christian asceticism by presenting an exalted picture of Mary the Virgin, her noble origins, her early life, and her extraordinary personal sanctity.[142] The interest in the days after Good Friday and Easter directed attention to the eschatological perspective of Christ's ultimate victory over death by describing his descent into the underworld and

his triumphal ascent into heaven. The extracanonical traditions were often linked to secret wisdom presumably communicated to the Apostles and Mary by the risen Lord.[143] Such literature had a considerable impact on popular piety and devotional practices in regard to Mary and the Christian dead. As the apocryphal writings often painted a docetic picture of Christ, magnifying his divine character at the expense of his humanity, the human ties between Mary and her son became important in the theological defense of Christ's coming as a true incarnation: being fully divine, the Word of God was also fully human as the son of a human Mary.

(163) It was the task of the bishops and other Christian leaders to teach the truth of the gospel by making sure that such developments and the piety which accompanied them remained subject to the unique, sufficient, and universal mediation of Christ. They were not always equal to the task. Bishops did try to curb the use of noncanonical gospels, acts, and apocalypses; together with many other similar books, the *Protevangelium* is expressly denounced as "apocryphal," i.e., inauthentic, by the so-called Gelasian Decree (end of the fourth century).[144] But while some early leaders such as Tertullian advocated rigorous standards in rejecting pagan ways and customs, others encouraged "baptizing" all kinds of practices and writings for use among Christians. To check this syncretism and resist the constant pressure of popular piety, which was pursuing goals and interests of its own, would have required a practical and spiritual authority which was beyond the modest means of the average local leadership in the churches. Thus it is easy to discover a great deal of ambiguity about the doctrinal issues involved in the popular devotion to the saints and Mary in the actions and pronouncements of the leaders of the church, and many of the obvious tensions between sound doctrine and pious practice remained unresolved. Nevertheless, official writings like the Acts of the Martyrs[145] stressed the conformity of the saints with Christ as an example of true discipleship for all Christians. By the same token the function of confessors, martyrs, and saintly ascetics who seemed to be "imitators of Christ" in an exceptional way was easily associated with Christ's sole intercession and mediatorship: such saints pray with Christ and can be prayed to.[146] Developments in the doctrine of the Holy Spirit during the trinitarian controversy of the fourth century helped Christians to perceive their martyrs and saints as instruments of God's Spirit, and the precision achieved with regard to the doctrine of the Word of God Incarnate during the christological struggles of subsequent centuries was a clear reminder that the saints must remain subordinate to, and at the service of, Christ the one Mediator.

(164) In the second century Justin and Irenaeus already suggested that, as Christ is the new Adam (cf. Rom 5:11-19;I Cor 15:45), so Mary may be seen as the new Eve.[147] This typology found a significant echo among patris-

tic writers as well as in late Marian piety: "Death came through Eve, life through Mary."[148] As a consequence of the christological debates of the fifth century, the place of Mary in relation to Christ and other saints received further attention. By endorsing the Second Letter of Cyril of Alexandria against Nestorius and taking note of the attached anathemas, the Council of Ephesus in 431 accepted the doctrine of *Theotokos*, i.e., the accuracy of the title "God-bearer" for the mother of Jesus, in order to insist that her son was the Eternal Word made flesh.[149] This decision marked the beginning of an enthusiastic wave of new Marian devotion which swept through all parts of the Empire and expressed itself in many forms, including the dedication of churches in her honor.[150] Like the expressions of the cult of the saints, the expressions of popular devotion to the Virgin Mary had parallels in beliefs and practices of the surrounding culture connected with the veneration of female deities such as Aphrodite, Artemis, Isis, or the "Great Mother" of Asia Minor, but also in the concerns of ascetic movements which extolled virginity and abstinence. The conviction, not explicitly shared and sometimes rejected as unbiblical by writers of earlier centuries, that Mary not only conceived as a virgin (*virginitas ante partum*), but remained a virgin throughout her life (*post partum*), even in the act of giving birth (*in partu*), became now widely shared. It was understood both as affirming the totality of God's action in the incarnation of the Word and as enhancing Mary's role as a model for the church and the faithful, especially Christian virgins.[151] Both doctrines seemed to imply the unique holiness of Mary, although there was never unanimous agreement in the early church as to the implications of her divine motherhood for her own person. Comparison with the martyrs and apostles suggested to a few that she might have died a martyr herself, but the ancient writers were generally silent on this point, ignorant as they were of the time, the place, and the manner of her death.[152] Apocrypha from the Old Syriac, Coptic, and Ethiopic traditions speak of Mary's assumption into heaven at some point after her death.[153] Probably in the early part of the fourth century Mary was mentioned by name as an intercessor in the eucharistic liturgy of Syria where Marian praises in hymnody and panegyrics already flourished.[154] The practice spread from there to other areas, including Rome. Similarly, liturgical feasts of Mary began to be celebrated in the East. We know of a general feast in her honor in Cappadocia in the fourth century, the Feast of the Dormition in Jerusalem c. 430, and of others somewhat later, with the West slowly following suit.[155] Whether or not Mary had a place in private piety during the early centuries is not known; a form of the Marian prayer, *Sub tuum praesidium*, addressed to the *Theotokos*, has been dated to the third or fourth century on paleographical grounds.[156]

(165) The incarnational logic of the christological dogma is reflected in the formulation of the third article of the so-called Apostles' Creed, which

comes from the early fifth century: the Holy Spirit is at work in the church, making it a *communio sanctorum* or community of saints (*sancti/sanctae*) through the sharing in the holy mysteries (*sancta*).[157] By their baptism all the Christian faithful have been made saints. Yet as they experience the reality of divine grace in repentance and forgiveness, they also know themselves to be sinners. By contrast, in the case of the Virgin Mary the work of the Spirit in the incarnation of the Word of God was understood as having rendered the *Theotokos* all-holy (*panagia*).[158] For some fourth and fifth-century Fathers such as Ambrose and Augustine, this meant that the God-Bearer, "full of grace," as the Latin Bible rendered Luke 1:28, could not be considered to be tainted by the same sinfulness as other human beings.[159]

(166) The polemics on original sin and on the nature of grace in which Augustine was involved have a bearing on the role of the saints in his thinking. Echoing Ambrose, Augustine exhorts the faithful that, while they must "worship God alone," they should also "honor the saints," specifically the martyrs.[160] In his sermons Augustine could be quite critical of devotional excesses and superstitions among his people, but he clearly encouraged the cult of the saints, including their invocation. In his eyes these saints are examples of the working of God's grace in sinful human beings, models to imitate as well as intercessors who pray to God for the faithful. An elaborate martyrs' cult, including the regular invocation of the saints, was a common feature of worship life in Africa at his time.[161] In this connection, pondering the old notion of a "cleansing fire" for the purgation of souls in the interim state after death (cf. I Cor 3:11-15), he suggested that belief in post-mortem purgatorial punishments was not impossible.[162] Chiefly in his later years, but already at the time of his conversion when he witnessed Ambrose promoting the cult of saints Gervaise and Protaise in Milan, Augustine admitted that the saints may, in and through Christ's sovereign power, intervene on earth through miracles.[163] Such posthumous miracles were told of Ambrose in a *Life* written at Augustine's request by Paulinus of Milan, who took as his model the famous *Life of Saint Martin of Tours* by Sulpicius Severus.[164] In all the saints, Augustine was convinced, Christ crowns his own gifts in a special way, granting the faithful a foretaste of the age to come and allowing them to see the power of the resurrection at work. Christ's millennial reign with the saints (Rev 20:4) has started already in the baptized here on earth and in the saints in heaven who are commemorated at the altars of the church.[165]

(167) Steeped in the full range of themes of Augustinian piety, Pope Gregory the Great (590-604) took special interest in the fate of the human soul after death. Book IV of his *Dialogues*, in which he answers the questions of Peter the Deacon about this topic, demonstrates that concerns of this kind were very much alive among the faithful of his time. Gregory makes use of legends and hearsay tales of visions, apparitions, and extraordinary

miracles in order to illustrate his teachings about the lively interaction between the saints above and the church on earth and about the interim state of the faithful departed. According to him, the souls of the saints (*sanctorum animae*) or of the righteous go directly to heaven after death. In heaven the saints enjoy different degrees of bliss according to their virtues. Conversely, in hell there is but one fire that burns with different degrees of intensity in proportion to the faults of each sinner.[166] It is necessary to believe also in a purgatorial fire after death whereby minor sins not remitted in this life are purged away. By intercessory prayer the faithful on earth may assist souls in the purgatorial state. Masses said by the living on behalf of the dead can be effective for this purpose. According to one of Gregory's stories, a suffering soul was released from punishment after thirty masses had been said for it on successive days.[167]

(168) At the end of the patristic period the basic soteriological affirmation of Christ's incarnation, death, and resurrection as the only channel of the divine grace bestowed upon the faithful in the Holy Spirit remained unanimous and unchallenged. At the same time, as examples of holy life multiplied through the growth of the monastic movement, the cult of saints and of Mary continued to expand without arousing a sense of danger for, or rivalry to, the unique mediatorship of Christ. But the ambiguity of the competing devotions remained. That Mary was proclaimed in Byzantine oratory as having been raised above all the angels[168] may be seen as a celebration of the divine grace exhibited in the *Theotokos*; in the understanding of others it may have served as a necessary critique of an excessive cult of other heavenly powers. But it may also be seen as having led to an exaltation of Mary which could eventually undermine faith in the unique mediatorship of Christ. All of these views could and did coexist. It was a constant challenge for church leaders, theologians, and the laity to keep all affirmations about the honor and veneration of the angels, the saints, and the Virgin Mary under the judgment of the christological affirmations established by the early church.

(169) The Christology of the early Middle Ages continued that of the Fathers and the great Councils. Yet ongoing debates on adoptionism and the hypostatic union of Christ's two natures as well as the Western addition of the *filioque* to the Creed of Nicaea-Constantinople were part of a religious climate in which new theological interpretations and new forms of piety would develop. Soteriology remained closely tied to Christology. Anselm's satisfaction theory of the atonement provided strong support for the belief in the sole mediatorship of Christ.[169] At the same time a different kind of religious mentality took over as the moralizing tracts of monks and preachers exercised their influence on popular piety and spiritual aspirations. The decrees of the Synod of Orange (529), with their anti-Pelagian intentions, were no longer known among post-Carolingian theologians.[170] An inadequate

revision of Pelagius's *Commentaries on the Pauline Epistles* circulated under the names of orthodox writers.[171] In the predestinarian controversy of the ninth century it became painfully clear that there was no firm agreement on the question of human freedom, cooperation with divine grace, and human capacity in relation to salvation.

(170) Compared with the East, however, the development and expansion of the cult of the saints, especially of the Virgin Mary, was relatively slow in the medieval West, being accompanied by the equally important deepening of a piety focused on the person of Christ, his cross, and his eucharistic presence. To be sure, Western devotion both to the saints and to Mary had strong roots in earlier centuries, partly under the impact of the exuberant rhetoric of the Eastern liturgical tradition, partly in response to tribal and local customs and emphases. There is ample evidence, for example, of a deeply felt veneration for Saint Peter among the Franks and the Anglo-Saxons, and the cult of Saint Martin of Tours in Gaul and in the Germanic territories reached its peak long before the eighth century.[172] The works of Gregory the Great and numerous monastic writers as well as the preaching of the Irish monks on the continent nourished a keen interest in the afterlife, in the benefits of penitential discipline, in purgatory, and in Western saints and their miracles. We find Mary's praise being sung here and there in Marian poetry and in sermons which echo the rich expressions of Eastern hymnody and oratory, and her perpetual virginity being extolled in line with its fervent defense by Western patristic writers, especially Jerome. There were also, however, echoes of a biblical critique of Mary, for example, in the interpretation of the marriage feast at Cana in Galilee (John 2:3-4).[173] It was in the eleventh century that mariological interest started to blossom in a fresh way, reaching new dimensions which perhaps are most clearly reflected in the works of the theologians of Chartres and Anselm of Canterbury.[174]

(171) The Iconoclastic controversy of the eighth century in the East, culminating in the decrees of Nicaea II (787) and the restoration of icons (843), illustrates the different mentalities of the Christian East and West in regard to the saints and Mary.[175] In the East icons of Christ, the *Theotokos*, and the saints had since the fourth century become a deliberate alternative to emperor-worship and popular as pilgrims' mementos.[176] Some images were believed to have been miraculously painted, providing a holy prototype for the iconography of Christ and the Virgin. Theologians carefully distinguished between *latria* or adoration (of God and Christ) and *dulia* or veneration (of Mary, the saints, and the icons). Nevertheless, they taught that images participate ontologically in the depicted subject, for they generally embraced a symbolic view of the world informed by a platonic understanding of reality. In the *Libri Carolini*, however, Charlemagne's theologians argued—following Gregory the Great—that holy images had their lawful use

in the Christian church as educational tools only.[177] They rejected the notion of participation as applied to the icons and (wrongly) accused the Council Fathers of confusing veneration and adoration and of idolizing the saints. Their intention was to keep the material and spiritual realms separate and to follow the literal meaning of Scripture. Veneration, they claimed, was appropriate only for the cross, the elements of the Eucharist, and the relics of the saints—because the bones of holy persons will share materially in the resurrection. Several concerns seem to converge in this theology. The obvious fear of idolatry reflected an interest in preserving the theocentricity of Christian worship. A christological and soteriological motive was operative in the conviction that veneration of the saints and their relics was justified by the saints' presence in heaven, and in view of the future resurrection of the body. There was also a philosophical motive in that it was the immortal soul that was understood to be saved from eternal death, the body becoming associated with salvation in the future resurrection.[178]

(172) It has been suggested that the Frankish theologians exhibited a polemical attitude against any independent value given to the saints and their images which is not unlike that of the Protestant Reformers; the argumentation of Agobard of Lyons and Claudius of Turin is especially impressive in this regard.[179] Yet this critical attitude did not prevail. The decrees of Nicaea II were received and endorsed by the popes.[180] Platonic and Neoplatonic thought, already present in the Augustinian tradition, was greatly favored in the work of John Scotus Erigena (c. 815-c. 880) and later by the school of Chartres. Through John the writings of Pseudo-Dionysius the Areopagite became known and were much appreciated. Moreover, the cult of relics which had been endorsed by the *Libri Carolini* was of great importance for the functioning of feudal society. Relics were sold, traded, and stolen.[181] Pilgrimages to the shrines of particular saints contributed to local pride and wealth. Monastic piety, which gave prominence to saints as founders, patrons, and protectors, served as a model for popular devotion. It fostered among the laity a fervent concern for personal virtue and meritorious works which was open to Pelagian distortions and tended to underplay the christocentric motif of *imitatio Christi*. The eschatological orientation toward final salvation provided a framework for moral efforts in which the saints had an important place as helpers and intercessors along the way. The prayer routine of the monasteries includes the public celebration of the memory of the saints; the sanctoral cycle mushroomed. The elaborate liturgies popularized by Cluny gave the saints a prominent place, and there was a private flowering of Marian hymnody from the eleventh century on.[182] Lay piety, which largely followed monastic ideals, was instructed by preachers who urged the people on to do pious works, In all this the religious mentality of the people

was nourished by ancestral customs, interest in local cults, concern for one's fate in the afterlife, and the conception of saints as ideals and heroes.

(173) During the following centuries Mary emerged among the saints as the object of special veneration.[183] Both the laity and the monasteries contributed to this development. The laity was sensitive to the chivalresque ideal of the lady honored by her knight and to the image of the queen of heaven in the splendor of her feudal court. Clearly, popular pressure pushed toward more extensive Marian devotions. From the twelfth century on, many churches were dedicated to the Virgin; shrines and pilgrimages in her honor multiplied; miracle stories were told; new feasts honoring Mary were celebrated and requested.[184] The monasteries cultivated the image of Mary as an ideal of purity, virginity, and holiness. Her role in the history of salvation was lifted up for contemplation. Christolgically she was seen as the Mother of God, soteriologically as the most obedient actor in the process of salvation. Praises of Mary in hymns and antiphons were introduced into the liturgical hours;[185] votive masses were dedicated to her. New Marian titles appeared in poetry and art, often inspired by biblical images and types.[186] New prayers such as the *Ave Maria*, the *Angelus*, and the *Salve Regina* gained great popularity. The Theophilus legend, which came from the East and told of a sinner's dramatic rescue from the devil through the Virgin's intervention, was eagerly peddled and had a significant influence on the invocation of Mary as intercessor.[187]

(174) Both the monastic and the Scholastic authors of the Middle Ages provide ample evidence of the increasing importance of Mary in the piety of the age. Anselm of Canterbury, Bernard of Clairvaux, Bonaventure, and Thomas Aquinas were highly devout and eloquent in their extolling of Mary's virtues. Hugh of St. Cher, a Dominican theologian, and his confrere Albert the Great distinguished the *dulia* or veneration of the saints from *hyperdulia*, a higher veneration appropriate to the Virgin. The idea of Mary as the image of the church spread. The Song of Songs, which had been interpreted as dialogue between Christ and the church or the soul in the earlier tradition, received a mariological interpretation in biblical commentaries from the early twelfth century on.[188] As monastic and lay piety urged each other on, lay devotees used monastic Marian devotions such as the "Little Hours of the Blessed Virgin Mary," just as monks sublimated the cruder forms of popular piety into a more reflective spiritual mood. There was a spiral of excesses exemplified by such projects as the rewriting of the biblical psalms into a "Psalter of the Virgin," or the adaptation of the traditional *Te Deum* to the praise of Mary.[189] From Mary's womb "as from a kind of ocean of the divinity have flowed the streams and rivers of all graces."[190] Mary's praise at times outshone that of Christ.

(175) Theologically one can also discern the continuation of a moder-

ate line, a kind of *via media*, in the medieval attitude toward the veneration of the saints and Mary. Theologians whose personal Marian piety was emphatic remained nevertheless traditional and cautious in their teaching. The traditional christological context of the consideration of Mary in the history of salvation made them shun independently developed Marian doctrines. The references to Mary in Anselm's *Cur Deus Homo* and his other theological treatises are clearly restricted to the christological context.[191] Bernard of Clairvaux pioneered a new affective approach to Marian piety in his sermons while at the same time objecting to the new feast of Mary's Conception.[192] Bonaventure saw the sum of all perfection in Mary and preached a famous group of sermons on her virtues. Nevertheless, he rejected the doctrine of the Immaculate Conception and made no mention of Mary's bodily Assumption in his *Commentary on the Sentences* even though he endorsed the concept personally.[193] Thomas Aquinas expressed his praise and admiration for Mary's eminent dignity, but he was cautious in his Mariology. He accepted the Assumption but opposed the Immaculate Conception and in his *Summa theologiae* spoke of Mary strictly according to the biblical outline of the life of Christ.[194]

(176) Thomas's famous discussion of the conception of Mary (*S.T.* 3.27) provides clear evidence that new aspects were entering the discussion of the problem of the human soul during the Scholastic age. As a purely spiritual creature, the soul was believed to be immortal by its very nature. Under the influence of Aristotle's metaphysics it was regarded as the "form" of its "matter," the body, form, and matter being interdependent.[195] Thus the separation of the soul from its body results in an abnormal situation. This interpretation served to underscore the urgency of the issue of the interim state, which now posed itself as the question of the fate of the separated soul between death and the resurrection of the body. Concern for the interim state was instrumental in spreading the liturgical commemoration of all the faithful departed on All Souls' Day (November 2), one day after All Saints (November 1).[196] The personal piety embodied in the liturgy of the dead and powerfully illustrated by the thirteenth-century sequence *Dies Irae* obviously appealed to the popular imagination.[197] For many Christians the threat of the Last Judgment was very real, even though the image of Christ as the stern judge of souls, whose deeds are weighed by the archangel Michael, was balanced by that of Christ's gift of grace and mercy as epitomized in the holiness of the Virgin Mary, "advocate of sinners." The old theme of Mary as the new Eve who had reversed *Eva* into *Ave* was featured in sermons and hymns. Yet theological speculation about the interim state remained sober. The theologians generally affirmed the survival of the immortal soul, its waiting for the resurrection of the body and the final judgment, the legitimacy of prayers for the dead and that their sins may be forgiven, and the availability of assis-

tance for the souls suffering punishment. The nature of the interim state became a point of contention between the Byzantine East and the Latin West for Eastern theologians did not find the term "purgatory" in their tradition and refused to speak of a material cleansing fire.[198] The Second Council of Lyons in 1274 endeavored to obtain a consensus between the Latin bishops and the envoys of Emperor Michael Palaeologos. The confession of faith accepted by the emperor dealt explicitly with the fate of the dead prior to the end of the world. It included the statement that the living can assist the dead "through supplications, the sacrifices of masses, prayers, almsgiving, and other acts of piety."[199]

(177) The question, however, was not allowed to rest there. In several sermons preached in the years 1331-32, Pope John XXII proposed that until the Last Judgment the saints remaining "under the altar" (Rev 6:9) enjoy the vision of Christ's humanity but not the vision of God.[200] Yet later he had to retract this opinion and described the lot of the saints with the biblical images of the kingdom of heaven, paradise, or being with Christ; the saints see God and the divine essence clearly face to face, at least insofar as the condition of a bodiless soul permits it.[201] John's successor, Benedict XII, tried to clarify the state of the saints before the final resurrection further in his constitution *Benedictus Deus* (1336); after the passion of Christ the souls of all the saints who had died earlier as well as of all the faithful departed— those in whom "nothing needed to be cleansed," and those who "have been cleansed after dying"—are in heaven with Christ. They see the divine essence "in an intuitive vision face to face," without the mediation of any- thing created.[202] The same issue was considered again by the Council of Florence in 1439, which endorsed the teachings of Lyons and of Benedict XII. The Council also stated that the saints see the Holy Trinity and that, in keeping with their respective merits, the bliss of one saint may surpass that of another. Without using the noun "purgatory," it taught that the soul after death is "cleansed in purgatorial pains" and endorsed the formula of Michael Palaeologos regarding assistance of the dead by the living.[203]

(178) On the eve of the Reformation an elaborate penitential system with contrition, confession, absolution, and satisfaction by pious works as the constitutive elements of the sacrament of penance was in place and func- tioning, designed to assure everyone of the opportunity to obtain forgiveness of postbaptismal sins. Yet the widespread presence of frightful threats to per- sonal health and safety together with natural disasters and intense fear of death tended to increase concern for the state of the departed soul. Life itself was often seen as a penance in preparation for that state. In this situation the concept of the "treasury of merits" acquired prominence.[204] The church, it was believed, had at its disposal a wealth of merits from the saints and Mary as well as from Christ for the relief of temporal and purgatorial punishments.

The widespread demand for indulgences in the fourteenth and fifteenth centuries was based on this understanding.[205] Spiritual writers tried to keep a balance between the concerns of the fearful conscience and the loving intimacy which the faithful are called to enjoy with Christ, the saints, and the Virgin Mary. John Duns Scotus and the theologians of the *via moderna* distinguished between God's omnipotence ("absolute power") and self-chosen immanence to his creatures ("regulated power"). This distinction allowed them to emphasize that God's freedom is inscrutable and beyond all human norms and at the same time that God's mercy is fully and reliably accessible for the forgiveness of sins through Christ, the church, the sacraments, the saints, and the Virgin Mary.

(179) The history of the fourteenth and fifteenth centuries demonstrates that, despite considerable expansion in practice, there was hesitation and ambiguity in the church's official stance toward the veneration of saints. Local, diocesan, and national interest favored the proliferation of shrines, feasts, and pilgrimages. Yet official caution was often a retarding factor. New cults were less frequently accepted at random.[206] The earlier informal canonizations of saints by popular acclaim were replaced by formal and regular procedures.[207] The christological and soteriological principles inherited from the early church demanded attention, making it difficult to accommodate innovative developments in regard to the saints theologically. Attempts by preachers and theologians to push ahead and find a basis in Scripture or tradition for such views led at times to questionable readings of these authorities or mere arguments of "fittingness" and from there to a dubious "theology" of purgatory or indulgences. The invocation of saints could be justified in principle by age-old customs relating to the cult of the martyrs and by appeal to the solidarity of the "communion of saints" in the Creed. But from the veneration of saints as the *Libri Carolini* envisioned it, medieval piety had progressed to their invocation as a focus of personal devotion. Moderate in the public liturgy of the church where the saints were chiefly asked to "pray for us" (as in the litanies of the saints and the confession of sins in the Mass), this invocation developed increasingly bizarre forms in extraliturgical piety, as when particular saints were claimed as patrons by families, guilds, and nations in competition with each other, or when the "fourteen auxiliary saints," popular in Southern Germany, were believed to have special areas of competence in answering prayer requests.[208]

(180) Similar ambiguities marked the official attitudes toward Marian piety in the Middle Ages. Bishops and popes often encouraged new steps in the devotion to Mary, yet they also experienced the need of having to curb excesses. Frequently local cults, new feasts, and enthusiastic titles for Mary were actively promoted despite initial hesitation. These titles included Mary as Queen of Heaven, crowned by the Father and her Son, and Mary as *auxili-*

*atrix* or *mediatrix*.[209] A feast of Mary's conception had been celebrated in the West since the eleventh century in many places (earlier in the East), and her sanctification in her mother's womb was generally acknowledged. At the Council of Basel in 1439 her conception was proclaimed to have been "immaculate"; the Council called this assertion "a pious doctrine in conformity with the church's worship, the Catholic faith, right reason, and sacred scripture."[210] Yet the session of the Council at which the proclamation took place was not recognized as ecumenical by pope or church, and the statement was therefore not received. In spite of vivid popular interest in reports of miracles and apparitions, bishops and popes demanded evidence to substantiate claims concerning such phenomena; they sometimes restricted local cults; they sought to verify claims of the Virgin's supernatural interventions. Above all, they did not formulate or proclaim Marian dogmas, despite the progress of theological support for the Immaculate Conception along the lines proposed by John Duns Scotus and considerable pressure from the secular powers at times.[211]

(181) Today both Protestant and Catholic historians would agree that late medieval developments in regard to the theological and popular concern for the departed souls, the saints, and Mary were closely tied to the situation that resulted from the peculiar shape of a system in which the sacrament of penance, with the ensuing stress on satisfaction and the recourse to indulgences, had become a focus of popular attention and therefore of pastoral care. Doctrinally the christological framework of salvation was retained. Yet the weight of the assurance of salvation was shifting to human works and efforts for which the zeal of the faithful found a wide range of opportunities in practices and ideas connected with the cult of the saints and Mary. Undoubtedly these developments were perceived by many as abuses; there was theological resistance at many points, and calls for reform were commonplace. But the momentum seemed unstoppable. As a consequence, the christological foundation of soteriology and the biblical understanding of the justification of sinners were obscured.

### III. FROM THE REFORMATION TO THE PRESENT

(182) In the post-Reformation period, to which we now turn, Lutheran and Catholic attitudes toward the saints and Mary disclose increasing divergences and a hardening of lines most apparent after the promulgation of the two Marian dogmas, the dogmas of the Immaculate Conception (1854) and the Assumption (1950). Guided by the Council of Trent, Catholic piety and reflection continued to give a significant place to the saints and Mary, illustrated by many canonizations, additions of saints' feasts, and a renewal of

devotion to Mary as one of the best ways to counter the influence of the Reformation. Lutherans viewed these developments with a mixture of suspicion and benign neglect before 1854, but then reacted with sharp polemics.

(183) Post-Tridentine Catholicism, anxious to offset the influence of the Reformation, emphasized specifically Catholic doctrines and forms of worship. Apologists and church leaders encouraged veneration of the saints and Mary, along with emphasis on the papacy and the Blessed Sacrament, as badges of Catholic identity. Peter Canisius,[212] Francis Suarez,[213] and Robert Bellarmine,[214] among others, responded to Protestant objections to the invocation of saints, the cult of relics, and the veneration of images. Canisius (1521-1597) composed a major treatise on Mary, *De Maria Virgine incomparabili*,[215] which ran through four editions in eight years. Polemical in tone, it defended traditional Catholic language about Mary and argued for the suitability of veneration of the Mother of God. The actual term "Mariology" seems to have been introduced in 1602 by Nicholas Nigido in his systemic work *Summa sacrae Mariologiae*.[216]

(184) In the sixteenth and seventeenth centuries, as dogmatic theology became increasingly abstract and as liturgy became more formalized, popular piety tended to become less theological and less liturgical. In the baroque period the Mass often took the form of a splendid celebration with a minimum of congregational participation. At the same time the devotion of the people found expression in extraliturgical forms such as novenas, often in honor of the saints, pilgrimages, and visits to the Blessed Sacrament. The rosary received its definitive form in the sixteenth century, and in 1573 Pius V instituted the Feast of the Holy Rosary. In 1563 Johannes Leunis, S.J., established the first Sodality of Our Lady,[217] an increasingly popular lay movement that by 1576 had thirty thousand members and enjoyed rapid growth.[218] Canonizations of new saints took place in increasing numbers, including many founders and members of the religious orders.[219]

(185) Church official were aware of the need to keep enthusiasm within bounds. Sixtus V in 1588 and Urban VIII in 1642 enacted new regulations for beatification and canonization. Subsequently Prosper Lambertini, as an official of the Congregation of Rites, wrote a voluminous treatise *De servorum Dei beatificatione et beatorum canonizatione* (1734-36), in which he laid down norms for the recognition of miracles and sanctity.[220] In 1748, as Pope Benedict XIV, Lambertini defended the historian Ludovico Muratori's work, *De ingeniorum moderatione in religionis negotio* (1714), which had criticized certain exaggerations in piety toward the saints and Mary. The Bollandists, founded by Jean Bolland, S.J. (1596-1665), introduced critical principles of historiography into the study of the lives of the saints.[221]

(186) Theologians of the French school, following Cardinal Pierre de Bérulle (1575-1629), while promoting religious sentiment, sought to focus

devotion primarily on the person of the Incarnate Word. Within this framework Marian piety flourished.[222] A typical representative of the French school, Jean Eudes (1601-80), in his *Le Coeur admirable de la très sainte Mère de Dieu,* exalted the immense dignity of the heart of Mary, beating near the heart of Jesus in her womb.[223] Louis Grignion de Montfort (1673-1716), also of the French school, composed a *Traité de le vraie dévotion,*[224] in which he argued that, since grace comes to us from Christ through Mary, we should return to Christ through her. By cultivating devotion to Mary, the individual receives the influence of the Holy Spirit, who overshadowed Mary at Nazareth so that Christ is formed in the soul. On its first publication in 1842 this book gave rise to the practice of renewing one's baptismal vows by making an act of personal consecration to Mary. The most popular of all books on Mary, appearing in close to a thousand editions since 1750, was *Le glorie di Maria* by Alphonsus Liguori, an Italian Redemptorist (1699-1787).[225] More devotional than theological, this work teaches that all grace passes through the hands of Mary, to whom Christ has surrendered all the riches of his mercy.

(187) The Romanticism of the early nineteenth century brought with it a new wave of enthusiasm for medieval practices and a distaste for the rationalism of the Enlightenment. Marian piety was intensified by a whole series of apparitions, beginning with the visions of Catherine Laboure at Paris in 1830. The apparitions to Bernadette Soubirous at Lourdes in 1858 and the miracles worked at that site were taken by many Catholics as signs of approval of the dogma of 1854, since the Lady there was reported to have said, "I am the Immaculate Conception." Marian devotion was further stimulated by the apparitions at Fatima in 1917. New lay associations were founded, attracting millions of members, for example, the *Militia Immaculatae* founded by the Polish priest Maximilian Kolbe in 1917 and the Legion of Mary founded by the Irish layman Frank Duff in 1921.

(188) Devotion to the saints and to Mary spread in the English-speaking world with the help of two distinguished converts to Roman Catholicism, Frederick William Faber (1814-63) and John Henry Newman (1801-90). Faber attempted to popularize devotions in a radical Italian baroque style,[226] whereas Newman preferred a more sober English style. In his response to Pusey's *Eirenicon,*[227] Newman in 1865 was able to take as agreed points, accepted by his Anglican opponent, that the invocation of saints is, as the Council of Trent had put it, "good and useful" and that favors are obtained through their intercession. In this same response Newman presented a clearly christocentric view of the *Theotokos*, reemphasizing the image of Mary as the new Eve, first propounded by Justin, Irenaeus, and Tertullian. He insisted that Mary "is nothing more than Advocate, not a source of mercy."[228]

(189) Seeking to integrate Mariology into the total system of Catholic

dogmatics, Matthias Joseph Scheeben (1835-88) in his final masterwork, *Handbuch der katholischen Dogmatik*, situated the theology of Mary between the treatises on Christ and on the church. He singled out as the fundamental principle of Mariology the divine motherhood, understanding by this term not simply Mary's physical maternity but also her association with her son's redemptive work.[229] Subsequent treatises on Mariology gave close attention to the question of the fundamental principle of Mariology, which was variously identified as the divine motherhood, spiritual motherhood, close association with Jesus, and the mission to represent humanity or the church.[230] Marian privileges such as the Immaculate Conception, the Assumption, and Heavenly Queenship were studied in great detail. A number of Marian theologians sought to pave the way for dogmatic definitions of new Marian titles, such as Coredemptrix and Mediatrix of all graces.[231] By the mid-twentieth century periodicals entirely devoted to Marian research were being published in several languages. In addition, regional, national, and international Marian congresses published volumes of their proceedings. The theological literature on Mary in this period is so vast that to date only a superficial survey has been attempted (e.g., at least 5,758 titles in 1952-57).[232]

(190) From Pius IX (1846-78) to Pius XII (1939-58) papal teaching and preaching carried forward theological reflection on Mary and devotion to her. Ranging in style from formal encyclicals to informal allocutions to pilgrimage groups, these papal pronouncements were enormously influential in furthering Catholic interest in Mary. Calling attention to the literary genre of these pronouncements, René Laurentin has cautioned:

> The most widely misunderstood consideration is this: the Marian documents issued by the papal magisterium in the last century had, for the most part, a devotional objective, notably the rosary. Although they include important doctrinal considerations destined to guide the piety of the faithful, they are not, for all that, dogmatic constitutions. They seek less to define a body of doctrine than to bring forward considerations for the nurture and guidance of fervor. For this reason they belong more to the homiletical genre. Moreover, their language is by choice oratorical, full of images, sometimes more generous than rigorous. They intend to stir up and excite emotions, not to promote opinions or solve academic disputes. It would be bad method to try to set up these suggestive expressions as dogmatic theses.[233]

In spite of that *caveat*, there can be no doubt that over a century of public papal encouragement of Marian piety left its mark on Catholic attitudes.

(191) The culmination of these Marian trends in popular, theological,

and papal activity was the official definition of two Marian dogmas. The doctrine of the Immaculate Conception had been discussed for centuries. Opposed by theologians of the caliber of Bernard of Clairvaux and Thomas Aquinas,[234] it nevertheless slowly gained ground, especially after Duns Scotus responded to the objection that it makes Christ's redemption unnecessary in the case of Mary. For Scotus, Mary in her Immaculate Conception was redeemed because Christ's merits preserved her from original sin, which she would have otherwise contracted.[235] In 1854, having consulted the episcopate and been given a response that was ninety percent affirmative, Pius IX issued the decree *Ineffabilis Deus*. After giving a history of this doctrine and showing the close link between it and Mary's dignity as Mother of God, the decree states:

> The doctrine that maintains that the most Blessed Virgin Mary in the first instant of her conception, by a unique grace and privilege of the omnipotent God and in consideration of the merits of Jesus Christ, the Savior of the human race, was preserved from all stain of original sin, is a doctrine revealed by God and therefore must be firmly and constantly held by all the faithful.[236]

With acceptance of the definition in the Catholic world, studies on the subject multiplied. The apparitions at Lourdes seemed to affirm the dogma and linked it with a deep well of piety. Churches, cities, schools, and countries (including the United States of America) were dedicated to Mary under the title of the Immaculate Conception.

(192) Almost a century later Pius XII consulted the episcopate regarding the doctrine of the Assumption and received a similarly positive response. Leaving open the disputed question of whether or not Mary actually died, he declared as divinely revealed dogma that:

> The Immaculate Mother of God, Mary ever Virgin, when the course of her earthly life was finished, was assumed body and soul to the glory of heaven.[237]

This dogma, too, was, with some exceptions, well received by Roman Catholics.

(193) Lutherans paid little attention to these Catholic developments since Trent. Seventeenth-century Lutheran Orthodoxy in its dogmatic formulations either defended the position of the Lutheran Confessions or ignored the saints and Mary. For example, John Gerhard, an influential theologian, spoke of Mary's virginity in the chapter on original sin and viewed deceased saints as examples for strengthening character, thus disclosing the commu-

nion between the church militant and the church triumphant.[238] Conrad Dannhauer, a popular preacher and theologian (1603-66), expressed fears that Jesuit Marian spirituality would "end up in Mariosophy."[239] When Lutherans in Germany and Scandinavia began to stress individual piety in addition to and over against doctrinal purity, the saints and Mary played no significant role. The rationalistic tendencies of the Enlightenment only increased Lutheran disinterest in a veneration of the saints and Mary. Typical is the attitude of Johann Salomo Semler, a leading theologian (1725-91), who emphatically rejected any veneration of Mary and regarded it as part of Catholic superstition.[240]

(194) Under the influence of the Romantic movement, Mary became a popular symbol of the eternal mother, expressed by the poet Friedrich von Hardenberg, known as "Novalis" (1772-1801): "Mother, who thee once has seen, wholly lost hath never been."[241] The nineteenth-century revival of Lutheran Confessionalism, with its emphasis on the sixteenth-century Confessions, on liturgy, and on sacraments, also awakened interest in deceased saints as models of faith. Thus Wilhelm Löhe (1808-72), a leader of this movement, advocated a virgourous catechesis which was to depict deceased saints as models of faith, with Luther as the central figure.[242] Regarding Mary, influential theologians like Friedrich Schleiermacher summed up the sentiments of many Lutherans when in 1806 he declared in his reflections on Christmas that "every mother can be called Mary."[243] Some, like Paul de Lagarde, a German intellectual and a critic of a "Jewish" Paulinism (1872-91), even advocated the transformation of the Madonna cult into a symbolic expression of "German religion."[244]

(195) The dogma of the Immaculate Conception of Mary (1854) drew bitter criticism from Lutherans. The Lutheran king of Prussia, Frederick William IV, set out to organize an international protest which, however, failed because of disagreements among the parties involved. Popular Lutheran theological handbooks and massive tomes condemned the dogma as a betrayal of everything found "in Scripture, the Fathers, and reason."[245] Even those few Lutherans who had favored some rapprochement with Rome could not accept the dogma. The only Lutheran "mariologist" at the time who faintly praised the dogma, Pastor W.O. Dietlein, could not accept its infallibility.[246] The prevailing Lutheran attitude was repudiation of the dogma.

(196) Lutherans, however, were involved in many ecumenical trends. In the latter half of the nineteenth century a liturgical movement advocated a veneration of the saints and Mary based on the Lutheran Confessions. The head of the German deaconess house Kaiserwerth, Theodor Fliedner, continued the concerns of Wilhelm Löhe by compiling a massive work (1849-59) on martyrs and other witnesses of the "evangelical church." Friedrich Heiler

(1892-1967), a Marburg professor and a convert from Roman Catholicism,[247] promoted a "high church" mentality by calling for Marian devotions, but without any sympathy for the Marian dogmas of 1854 and 1950. The "St. Michael's Brotherhood" (which grew out of the "Berneuchener Circle") was founded in Marburg in 1931 to promote liturgical reforms that included some Marian devotion and a Lutheran calendar of saints. The Brotherhood, though small in number, had considerable influence through prominent liturgiologists and journals.[248] Between World Wars I and II some individual theologians, such as Hans Asmussen (1898-1968), created renewed theological interest in Mary.[249]

(197) The 1950 papal definition of Mary's Assumption revived anti-Catholic polemics among Lutherans. Shortly before the promulgation of the dogma, the Heidelberg Evangelical Theological Faculty transmitted an "opinion" (*Gutachten*) to Rome, leveling severe criticisms against Catholic Mariology. The "opinion" noted that there is no scriptural or early patristic evidence in favor of the dogma and its promulgation would have the effect of a "painful estrangement" in ecumenical relations.[250] After the promulgation of the dogma, prominent Protestant leaders and bishops of the international ecumenical movement deplored this latest development in Catholicism. Walter Künneth, a Lutheran theologian, even charged that the new dogma created a "*status confessionis*" for Lutherans: it threatens the gospel itself.[251] The "Evangelical League" (*Evangelischer Bund*), which had been formed in 1866 to combat Catholic renewal in Germany, engaged in polemics on a popular level. Many Lutherans spoke of the paganization of the gospel through the elevation of Mary by this dogma; and the international journal of the *Una Sancta* movement, *Ökumenische Einheit*, identified the doctrine of Mary's assumption as a Gnostic legend.[252] Even Hans Asmussen, who had tried to revive Marian devotions in Lutheranism, deplored the promulgation of the dogma as an undesirable form of "Marianism."[253]

(198) Despite such polemics against the two Marian dogmas, an ecumenical appreciation of Mary and the saints existed among some Lutheran groups which were linked to the liturgical and confessional renewals of the nineteenth century. After 1945 there were numerous experiments in communal living, stressing the veneration of the saints and Mary. Among these experiments are the "Sisters of Mary" (*Marienschwesterschaft*) in Darmstadt led by Klara Schlink, the sister of Professor Edmund Schlink. Many Lutherans were also influenced by the ecumenical community of Taizé, whose Marian devotions became widely known through Max Thurian's promotion of Mary as daughter of Zion and image of the church.[254] The veneration of the saints received particular attention through Max Lackmann, a German theologian, who argued in 1958 that deceased "saints" (*Heilige*) relate to "the holy" (*das Heilige*) in the Eucharist.[255] But on the whole all

these groups and individuals promote veneration rather than an invocation of the saints and Mary and as such reflect the limitations set by the Lutheran Confessions.

(199) The Lutheran liturgical tradition, especially in eucharistic prefaces, acknowledges a doxological link between living and deceased Christians.[256] Funeral liturgies include prayers for the dead commending them to God's care.[257] There are Lutheran calendars of saints in which one finds a great variety of names associated with "commemorations," e.g., Albert Schweitzer (September 4) and Dag Hammarskjöld (September 18).[258]

(200) In some Catholic circles the definition of the Assumption raised hopes that new Marian privileges, such as her role as Coredemptrix or as Mediatrix of all graces, would soon be defined. But tendencies in this direction were countered by the biblical, patristic, liturgical, and catechetical renewals, all of which, in combination with the ecumenical movement, favored restraint with regard to the saints and Mary. Focusing in fresh ways on the centrality of Christ, these movements prepared for the shift of emphasis that was to come at Vatican Council II (1962-65).

(201) Vatican II witnessed a certain clash of mentalities. The conservative minority (as it came to be labeled) pressed for continued Marian development in the directions pursued by Pius IX and Pius XII. Thus the Preparatory Theological Commission drew up a schema *De beata virgine Maria matre Dei et matre hominum* and presented it in 1962, strongly defending the title *"gratiarum Mediatrix"* and explaining that her universal mediation "in Christ" was totally dependent on the unique mediation ascribed by Holy Scripture to Christ himself (I Tim 2:6). As the Council focused attention primarily on the mystery of the church, the schema was revised and put forward under the title, "On the Blessed Virgin Mary, Mother of the Church." In the fall of 1963 a debate took place on the question whether the schema on Mary should stand as an independent document or be incorporated into the *Dogmatic Constitution on the Church*. By a close vote on October 29 the latter alternative prevailed.[259]

(202) Vatican II attempted to deal with Christ, the saints, and Mary with sensitivity to Protestant concerns. Thus this teaching is contained chiefly in its Dogmatic Constitution on the Church (*Lumen Gentium*).[260] The very structure of this constitution provides a hermeneutical key to the relationship it asserts among Christ, the saints, and Mary. The first chapter on "The Mystery of the Church" opens with the definition: "Christ is the light of all nations" (§1). In the radiance of his light the church itself is brightened and, by proclaiming the gospel to every creature, helps to shed on all people the light of Christ. This, then, is the relationship: Christ the sole Redeemer, and the church as the assembly of all those who believe in him and witness to him to the world.

(203) The reality of the church is not exhausted in those who are still alive, for the bonds which unite believers to Christ are strong enough to perdure even through death. Therefore in chapter seven the *Constitution* turns its attention to the dead who are with Christ, those "friends and fellow heirs of Jesus Christ" (§50) with whom the living form one communion. This it does in tandem with consideration of the eschatological nature of the pilgrim church. It is within this context of those believers who are definitively with Christ (whom Catholics generally refer to as "saints") that chapter 8 considers the role of the Blessed Virgin Mary, Mother of God and preeminent member of the church. (§53).

(204) In an age of individualism the *Constitution* thought it important to clarify both the fact and the foundation of the *koinonia* of all disciples. This lies in the truth that

> in various ways and degrees we all partake in the same love for God and neighbor, and all sing the same hymn of glory to our God. For all who belong to Christ, having his Spirit, form one church and cleave together in him (§49).

This is not a new belief. Historically, the church from its beginning centuries has always believed that the apostles and martyrs, as well as Mary and other holy people, are closely united with those living in Christ and "has always venerated them" in special ways (§50). The church, the Council continues, has believed that they are inseparably united with Christ; in this relationship they contribute to the upbuilding of the church on earth through their holiness and their prayer, offered in and with him. The benefits which come to the living by remembering the saints are many. Our faith is inspired by theirs, our way is made more sure by their example, and the communion of the whole church is strengthened. Indeed,

> in the lives of those who shared in our humanity and yet were transformed into especially successful images of Christ (2 Cor 3:18), God vividly manifests to human beings his presence and his face. He speaks to us in them, and gives us a sign of his kingdom, to which we are powerfully drawn, surrounded as we are by so many witnesses (Heb 12:1) (§50).

The proper response of living disciples is to love these friends of Christ, to thank God for them, to praise God in their company (particularly during the eucharistic liturgy), to imitate them when appropriate, and (with reference to the Council of Trent) to invoke their intercession, which means to ask for their prayers. In the vision of the *Constitution* each one of these actions terminates through Christ in God, who is wonderful in his saints (cf. 2 Thess 1:10).

(205) Concerned that veneration of the saints has not always hewn to the proper christocentric/theocentric pattern, the *Constitution* calls for prevention and correction of "any abuses, excesses, or defects which may have crept in here and there" (§51). The faithful should be taught that authentic veneration of the saints consists not so much in external acts, but rather in the intensity of love; communion with those in heaven, provided that it is understood in "the more adequate light of faith," serves only to enrich the worship given to God through Christ in the Spirit.

(206) The eighth chapter of the *Constitution* does not aim at presenting a complete doctrine about Mary. Within the context of teaching concerning the church, it aims at describing both the role of Mary in the mystery of Christ and the church, and the proper cultivation of her memory (§§52, 54). The tone is set by the assertion that Mary at the Annunciation "received the Word of God in her heart and in her body, and gave life to the world" (§53). Thus Mary is identified as the one who in a singular way "heard and kept the Word of God" (§58; cf. Luke 11:27-28). If certain trends of the Marian era had tended to imagine Mary in a kind of privileged and splendid isolation, the Council makes clear that she is to be connected firmly and in differing ways to Christ and to the church. As a preeminent and singular member of the church, she is related both to Christ and to us. Indeed, while her great dignity stems from her role as Mother of the Son of God, she is at the same time a daughter of Adam and, as such, one with all human beings in the need for salvation (§53).

(207) By means of a running commentary on scriptural and patristic texts, the *Constitution* tells the story of Mary's life in relation to the saving events of the life of Jesus Christ. What is emphasized throughout is the faith through which she responded to the call of God in different situations. With reference to the Annunciation, for example, the interpretation is made that,

> Embracing God's saving will with a full heart and impeded by no sin, she devoted herself totally as a handmaid of the Lord to the person and work of her Son. In subordination to him and along with him, by the grace of almighty God she served the mystery of redemption (§56).

In summation, her life is described as a "pilgrimage of faith" (§58) which led her all the way to the cross and to the subsequent waiting in the midst of the community of disciples for the outpouring of the Spirit. The reality of Mary's life, then, is intertwined with the great events of the coming of salvation in Jesus Christ.

(208) Recovering the patristic theme of Mary as a model of the church

in faith, charity, and perfect union with Christ (Ambrose), the Council reflects on how Mary shines forth to the whole community as an exemplar of integral faith, firm hope, and sincere charity. It further develops this idea of Mary as *typos* of the church with reference to maternity and virginity. By accepting God's word in faith, the church too becomes a mother, bringing forth new children of God through preaching and baptism; the church is also a virgin in full-hearted fidelity to Christ (§§65, 66). As the *Constitution on the Sacred Liturgy* was to phrase the same idea, in Mary the church

> holds up and admires the most excellent fruit of the redemption, and joyfully contemplates, as in a faultless model, that which she herself wholly desires and hopes to be (§103).

(209) Within this framework the question of Mary's mediation is dealt with (§§60-62). This crucial section begins with the confession that there is but one Mediator between God and human beings, the human being Jesus Christ, who gave himself as a ransom for all (I Tim 2:5-6). In this context Mary is described as praying for wayfarers who are beset with difficulties. For this reason she is called upon in prayer in the church (not by the church, as some had wished to say) under many titles, including Mediatrix.[261] This, however, is to be understood in such a way that it neither adds to nor detracts from the dignity and efficacy of Christ the one Mediator. Mary's agency arises

> not from some inner necessity but from the divine pleasure. It flows forth from the superabundance of the merits of Christ, rests on his mediation, depends entirely on it, and draws all power from it (§60).

As a participation in Christ mediation, Mary's "mediation," then, shows the power of Christ.

(210) The *Constitution* gives attention to the special reverence with which believers should venerate Mary. Differing from the adoration due to God alone, this veneration has taken diverse forms in various times and places and is to be encouraged. But the Council "earnestly exhorts" preachers and theologians to avoid excesses both of exaggeration and minimalism, and urges ecumenical sensitivity. The document ends by noting that, in glory with Christ, Mary is an image of the church as it will be in the age to come; as such, she is a sign of hope and solace for the pilgrim people of God.

(211) The theology of Mary developed and taught by Vatican II is integrated with major themes of Christian faith. Rooted in Scripture and the patristic tradition, it attempts to be christological, ecclesiological, ecumenical, and eschatological in perspective, presenting Mary in connection with

the events of salvation history and the ongoing presence of Christ in the church. Mary in the midst of the community of saints in heaven; the saints as sharing the *koinonia* of all the people of God; and the whole church itself reflecting the light of Christ as the moon does that of the sun—such is the relationship set by Vatican II among the one Mediator, the saints, and Mary.

(212) During and after Vatican II the liturgical year was modified so as to give greater emphasis to the sequence of feasts pertaining to Christ and the mystery of salvation. As a result, the feast days of the saints were reduced in emphasis and numbers.[262] On the other hand, the multitude of beatifications and canonizations has increased especially under Pope John Paul II.[263] The processes of beatification and canonization were simplified by Pope Paul VI in 1969 and again by John Paul II in 1983.[264] About thirty new causes come to the Congregation for the Causes of Saints each year. About a thousand causes are at present under study.[265]

(213) A decade after the Council Paul VI wrote an apostolic exhortation on *Devotion to the Blessed Virgin Mary (Marialis Cultus)*.[266] After reviewing the Marian feasts and texts of the renewed liturgy of the Roman rite and mediating on Mary as a model of the church at worship, the pope concentrates on directives for the renewal of Marian devotion in the contemporary world. Conscious that some forms of piety show the "ravages of time" (§24) and need renewal, he calls for creative effort to revise pious expressions in keeping with recent theological and conciliar developments. To that end, theological principles and practical guidelines are pointed out as criteria for proper Marian devotion (§§25-37).

(214) The first and most detailed criterion is theological: Pious practices directed toward the Virgin Mary should clearly express a trinitarian and especially a christological focus; they should take note of the Holy Spirit and of the newer emphasis on the intrinsic ecclesiological content of Marian devotion. Next, such devotions should have a biblical imprint, being imbued with the great themes of the Christian message. They should, in addition, harmonize with liturgical prayer, be in some way derived from it, and lead back to it. Equally important, they should be ecumenical in tone, careful to avoid any exaggeration which could mislead other Christians about the true doctrine of the Catholic Church. Finally, they should be anthropologically sensitive, taking note of contemporary culture and life-style, especially the emergence of women into the public arena. It is in connection with the last-mentioned criterion that the pope, wishing to offset the alienation that increasingly arises when the domesticity of Mary of Nazareth is offered as an example to women today, observes that

the Virgin Mary has always been proposed to the faithful by the church as an example to be imitated not precisely in the type of life she

led...She is held up as an example rather for the way in which, in her
own particular life, she fully and responsibly accepted God's Will (Lk.
1:38), because she heard the Word of God and acted upon it, and
because charity and a spirit of service were the driving force of her
actions. She is worthy of imitation because she was the first and most
perfect of Christ's disciples (§35).

(215) Throughout this document, in conformity with the Council, there
are repeated calls for correcting abuses—vain credulity, ephemeral sentimentality, errors and deviations, legends and falsity, self-seeking, one-sided-
ness—all of which separate Marian devotion from its proper doctrinal content. Only by removing these errors can the ultimate purpose of such devotion show itself, namely, to glorify God and lead Christians to commit themselves absolutely to the divine will. As examples of pious practices which are
governed by the five principles, the pope describes the Angelus and the
Rosary. These are practices that should be fostered, and new ones should be
created.

(216) The conciliar stress on the relation of Mary to Christ and to the
church is carried out here with attention to practical matters. Mary is venerated because of her singular dignity as Mother of the Son of God. At the same
time she is "truly our sister, who as a poor and humble woman fully shared
our lot" (§56). Her prayer, her example, and the divine grace which is victorious in her encourage us to follow Christ, who alone is the way, the truth,
and the life (John 14:4-11). Thus did Paul VI envision the renewal of a proper postconciliar devotion to Mary.

(217) A few months before Paul VI published *Marialis Cultus*, the
United States Catholic bishops had issued a pastoral letter, *Behold Your
Mother: Woman of Faith*, in which many of the same emphases are found.[267]
The central idea is that of Mary as model and exemplar of the church, and in
that context the Immaculate Conception and the Assumption are explained as
typifying the election and eventual glorification of the church. Dealing at
some length with the biblical roots, this letter portrays Mary as a perfect disciple who heard and courageously followed the word of God, thus making
herself "the model of all real feminine freedom." With a view to restraining
excesses of enthusiasm, the bishops warn that the private revelations given
even to canonized saints are never to be accepted as matters of Christian
faith. The place of Mary in any sound ecumenism is adroitly treated.

(218) The same concentration on the twofold bond which unites Mary
to Christ and to the church both structures and permeates John Paul II's
encyclical *Mother of the Redeemer (Redemptoris Mater)*[268] written to herald
the opening of a Marian year (1987-88). Most particularly he concentrates on
Mary's life story as a pilgrimage of faith. Her pilgrimage, which made her

blessed, is of significance not just for herself but for the whole people of God. While devotional in tone, this letter does not propose any new devotions. Rather, it limits the meaning of Mary's faith in the mystery of Christ and of the church in order to encourage all in the church to live the life of faith more intensely. Vatican II and subsequent Catholic teaching[269] have thus sought to present the interrelationship of Christ the one Mediator, the saints, and Mary in more biblical and christological perspectives.

(219) In retrospect: Several difficulties have become manifest in our discussion of the one Mediator, the saints, and Mary. The doctrines in question are experienced through traditional forms and customs of piety that long usage has made venerable. But practices of devotion may be inspired by a variety of motivations (psychological, ethnic, national, etc.), which call for caution in the use of the axiom, *lex orandi lex credendi*. While such forms of piety are subject to judgment based on doctrine, the people who have found spiritual consolation in them should also be treated with pastoral prudence.

In addition, theological reflection cannot place all these doctrines and devotions on the same level. Some of them are close to the center of the gospel because they are directly implied in the incarnation (e.g., that Jesus Christ is the one Mediator, that Mary is the *Theotokos*). Others are more distant from this center (e.g., that Mary always remained a virgin, that saints may be venerated), while some are matters of speculation (e.g., how the saints in heaven pray, how they hear prayers addressed to them).

It remains our hope that the present report will contribute to a clarification of the matters we have examined and will help our churches to remove the remaining obstacles on the way to ecumenical reconciliation.

## CATHOLIC REFLECTIONS

(1) The sessions together have made clear to us as Catholics that our intellectual and dogmatic differences over "Christ the One Mediator, the Saints, and Mary" are rooted in part in deeply felt patterns of life and spirituality. After almost five centuries of living separately, Lutherans and Catholics have come to embody different ways of living out the gospel.

(2) One basic theological and liturgical conviction which has carried the Catholic tradition holds that Jesus Christ alone is never merely alone. He is always found in the company of a whole range of his friends, both living and dead. It is a basic Catholic experience that when recognized and appealed to within a rightly ordered faith, these friends of Jesus Christ strengthen one's own sense of communion with Christ. It's all in the family, we might say; we are part of a people. Saints show us how the grace of God may work in a life; they give us bright patterns of holiness; they pray for us.

Keeping company with the saints in the Spirit of Christ encourages our faith. It is simply part of what it means to be Catholic, bonded with millions of other people not only throughout space in countries around the world, but also throughout time. Those who have gone before us in faith are still living members of the body of Christ and in some unimaginable way we are all connected. Within a rightly ordered faith, both liturgical and private honoring of all the saints, of one saint, or of St. Mary serves to keep our feet on the gospel path.

(3) *Within a rightly ordered faith.* There is the rub. For in the course of our history and even today some devotional practices operate within a disordered faith. This means that by the way they are structured they invite a person to transfer ultimate trust away from Jesus Christ and toward Mary or the saints. In time, the friends of Christ come to substitute for the saving Redeemer in the life of an individual or community. Such practices of piety are expressions of fruitless and passing emotion, vain credulity or exaggeration, to use the words of Vatican II;[1] they deserve critique.

(4) Popes and councils have frequently acted to restrain popular excesses, but at certain times, as in the late Middle Ages, have acted less vigorously than they should. Yet there are limits to what church authorities can do without destroying proper freedom or undermining the faith of believers. In this connection some authors appeal to texts such as Matt 13:29 (on not uprooting the wheat with the weeds).[2] In a secular age perhaps an immature sense of the transcendent is preferable to no faith at all. Yet it is far from the ideal.

(5) Pope John Paul II, aware of these dangers, has called for "the evangelization of popular piety." Pastors, he has said, must see to it that devotion to the saints, expressed in patronal feasts, pilgrimages, processions, and other forms of piety, "should not sink to the level of a mere search of protection for material goods or for bodily health. Rather, the saints should be presented to the faithful as models of life and of imitation of Christ, as the sure way that leads to him."[3]

(6) The purification of popular devotions is well addressed by the apostolic exhortation *Marialis Cultus* which Paul VI issued ten years after the council to guide the renewal of Marian devotion in the postconciliar church.[4] While its subject is the special saint Mary, the principles and guidelines which it proposes are just as applicable to devotion to any or all of the saints, and it is in that comprehensive light that we consider this pastoral teaching.

(7) The theological principles that serve as criteria for the proper honoring of the saints and Mary are trinitarian, christological, pneumatological, and ecclesial truths. These criteria stem from basic creedal faith. There is only one God, who is Father, Son, and Holy Spirit. There is only one merci-

ful Savior, one Mediator between God and human beings, himself human, Jesus Christ. All the gifts of grace given to human beings show forth the working of the Spirit. In the church all the members are bonded together and concerned with each other's welfare; in a special way Mary typifies what the church is called to be and ultimately hopes to be. Each of these theological principles should be at home, at least implicitly, in any proper devotional practice. Any such practice, therefore, which would overshadow the triune God, impugn the mercy and effective mediatorship of Jesus Christ, neglect the sanctifying power of the Holy Spirit, or isolate a particular church member or saint from the whole body is to be judged "out of order."

(8) In addition to these global theological principles, there are four practical guidelines which should norm devotion to the saints and Mary. These are drawn from the biblical, liturgical, ecumenical, and anthropological areas coming anew into consciousness since the Council. Devotional practices should be imbued with the Scriptures, not just a text or symbol here or there, but the great biblical themes of salvation history. Since the liturgy is the golden norm of Christian piety, these devotions should harmonize with its spirit, its themes, its seasons. In this ecumenical age care should be taken lest a wrong impression be given to members of other Christian churches, even unintentionally, especially with regard to Christ's unique role in salvation. Finally, devotional practices should accord with the cultural mores of the people engaging in them, for the church is not bound to the specific anthropological ideas of any period. In this regard, for example, given the emergence of women into all fields of public life, Mary need not be presented in a way that contemporary people might find timidly submissive or repellently pious, but rather as one who fully and responsibly heard the word of God and acted upon it. Thus she, and the other saints, can be held up as examples for believers today. These guidelines should function in the judgment of the adequacy of traditional devotional practices or the formation of new ones. Any such practice, therefore, which ignores biblical themes, does not accord with the dynamism of liturgical prayer, gives ecumenical offense especially with regard to the perceived role of Christ, or is out of tune with cultural advances is to be judged "out of order."

(9) With the experience of this dialogue clearly before us, we strongly recommend that our bishops, priests, pastoral leaders, preachers, teachers, and catechists disseminate these theological principles and practical guidelines and use them to judge the adequacy and inadequacy—even the danger—of preaching and devotional practices now in use. For example, the rather common idea that Mary or one of the other saints has a particular power over God or Christ and, if prayed to correctly, can obtain a benefit for the petitioner from an otherwise unwilling Almighty—this "friends in high places" model of devotion—needs to be shifted toward a proper understand-

ing of God's providential care and our solidarity in community. In this and other instances the integrity of the faith would be well served by good pastoral application of these norms. Taken together, they insure that honoring the memory of Mary, as well as other saints, remains coherent with the vital structure of Christian belief.

(10) One phenomenon of popular religion deserves special mention in these reflections, namely, apparitions or appearances of Mary or, less often, some other saint. These are puzzling phenomena to explain in ecumenical dialogue; even to many Catholics their status is not clear.

(11) The first key to their interpretation is the theological distinction between public and private revelation. What is named public revelation transpired in and through the person of Jesus Christ and the early generations of disciples who wrote the Christian Scriptures. It is this view which undergirds the axiom that revelation closed with the death of the last apostle. Subsequent to that death, the church hands on in a living tradition all that it has received, interpreting it anew in every age but not adding to the essential message. Private revelation, on the other hand, is insight granted to an individual person in the course of time. Private revelation when received by the church can be seen as a gift for the church, but it does not demand belief or allegiance as does public revelation.

(12) Different methods are used to investigate the claims of an individual to have received a private communication from heaven; all have in common that they are under episcopal direction. A very small percentage of apparitions or other such communications have ever been granted official approval by the church. When approval is given, what it signifies is simply this: the message and practices associated with the happening are in accord with the gospel. This message can be trusted, and participating in these practices will not lead a person astray. Prayer, penance, service to others—these are gospel values and characterize the message of those apparitions that have received official approval. But church approval does not oblige any church member to direct devotion toward the apparition or even to interest oneself in its story, for such matters belong to the sphere of private revelation and are not binding on the whole church.

(13) In a pastoral letter on Mary, the United States Catholic Bishops consider authenticated appearances such as at Lourdes or Fatima to be "providential happenings [that] serve as reminders to us of the basic Christian themes: prayer, penance, and the necessity of the sacraments." In the context of this affirmation these happenings are then put into proper perspective:

> Even when a private revelation has spread to the entire world, as in the case of Our Lady of Lourdes, and has been recognized in the liturgical calendar, the Church does not make mandatory the acceptance either of

the original story or of the particular forms of piety springing from it. With the Vatican Council we remind true lovers of Our Lady of the danger of superficial sentiment and vain credulity. Our faith does not seek new gospels, but leads us to know the excellence of the Mother of God and moves us to a filial love toward our Mother and to the imitation of her virtues.[5]

What is important is the gospel of Jesus Christ, not a new invention. In the case of Mary genuine honor is expressed by love which shows itself in following her example. These cautions are necessary in the light of the tendency toward substitutions.

(14) There is no definitive church teaching about what actually happens during an appearance, and theologians interpret the phenomenon in various ways. Such an occurrence is a manifestation of the charismatic element in the church, a freely given moment in which the Spirit of God inspires the memory and imagination of a person to receive a message from God (Rahner). Or again, it may be interpreted as a hermeneutic of the nearness of God to people who feel themselves to be outside the normal official channels of access to divine power, such as the poor, the young, the nonordained, the uneducated, or rural women (Schillebeeckx). In particular circumstances, such a happening may be interpreted as a sign of God's compassionate solidarity with defeated people, unleashing a new power of hope and human dignity (Elizondo on Guadalupe).[6]

(15) In any event, these phenomena are in the domain of private, not public revelation, and as with other devotional matters the individual is free to participate or not, as the Spirit moves. Prudence would dictate that in the case of current happenings on which the church has not yet given final judgment, great care and caution be exercised.

(16) In addition to the falsity of exaggeration on the one hand, Vatican II also exhorted that we equally avoid the excess of narrow-mindedness on the other. In our country and in the countries of the North Atlantic generally, a number of traditional practices of veneration have diminished in importance in the postconciliar church. Thus, in addition to vigilance against abuses, there is need for creativity in doing for this age what our forebears in the faith did for theirs, namely, to renew inherited practices of devotion and shape new ones suitable to the temper of the times. Biblical prayer vigils, reflective reading of Scripture, preaching, litanies, the rosary, pilgrimages, and personal meditation have all been adapted in ways that cohere with the theological principles and practical guidelines of *Marialis Cultus*. These could well be encouraged, for within a rightly ordered faith they serve to enhance the life of the church.

(17) As our dialogue sessions have made clear and as the preceding

considerations reflect, the most neuralgic difficulty over the issue of the "One Mediator, the Saints, and Mary" lies especially in the area of piety. Our different mentalities have interpreted "Christ alone" in different thought patterns, and this has had practical consequences in shaping pious practices. We have come to realize why certain Catholic practices appear so problematic to Lutherans. In embracing the criterion of justification by faith alone, Lutherans have developed a yardstick with which to measure deviations from adherence to the singular role of Jesus Christ in salvation. Both historically and theologically Lutheran sensitivity in this area is acute. We have come to appreciate the profound christocentric belief and piety which undergirds this stance.

(18) Futhermore, it has been encouraging to discover that we do share some common ground for honoring the saints and Mary. Scripture and patristic tradition are appreciated by both communions. In addition, Martin Luther's hymns and meditations, for example, his "Commentary on the Magnificat," and the Lutheran Confessions in part are also compatible with Catholic sensibility. Apology 21, in addition to criticizing the practice of invoking the saints, also gives a positive direction to honoring the saints: We may thank God for them, take courage from their faith, and follow their example where appropriate, elements that foreshadow *Lumen Gentium*, chapter 7. In trying to deal with the unfinished business of the sixteenth century, we have recognized that in spite of our real differences we are not as far apart as it seemed at first glance. From a common basis of belief Catholics challenge Lutherans to give clearer expression in ecclesial practice to the *koinonia* of saints which includes the living and the dead in Christ. At the same time Lutherans challenge Catholics to give clearer expression to the sole mediatorship of Christ in the devotional practices involving the saints and Mary in which we engage. It is this challenge which we call to the attention of our church.

(19) The steps proposed in our common statement (Part I, Section III) may call for some elucidation. They are based on the supposition that the Catholic Church aspires to full communion (or fellowship, as it may also be called) with all Christians, including Lutherans. One obstacle to full communion is the suspicion sometimes voiced by Lutherans and others that the invocation of saints and the honor paid to Mary in the Catholic Church are idolatrous and injurious to the honor that belongs to God alone (cf. SA 2-3:26; *BC* 297). We believe that in light of the teaching of Vatican II, reinforced by many statements of Paul VI and John Paul II, it may now be possible for Lutherans to declare that such accusations are today unwarranted. We are gratified that the Lutherans of this dialogue join us in recommending that their church authorities make an acknowledgment to this effect.

(20) The second step envisages that Catholic church authorities agree that in an ecclesial communion Lutheran churches and their members might be left free not to profess belief in the Marian dogmas of 1854 and 1950 and

not to invoke saints in their prayer. To prevent misunderstanding, three points should be kept in mind. First, we are in no sense maintaining these disagreements are unimportant. Within the closer fellowship we envisage these issues would continue to be seriously discussed. *Full* ecclesial communion would involve agreement with regard to all truths that either church holds to be binding in faith or inseparable from the gospel. Second, these divergences from Catholic belief and practice certainly do not preclude *all* communion, for it is Catholic teaching that a measure of communion already exists between the Catholic and Lutheran churches.[7] Third, if there is sufficient convergence—involving, presumably, mutual recognition of ordained ministries—it may be possible to have reciprocal eucharistic sharing between Catholics and Lutherans.[8]

(21) In the midst of the difficulties of this age, the Catholic tradition of the saints and Mary is a great resource for developing habits of the heart which cherish community, especially needed in contemporary Western culture which so emphasizes the individual. Our consciousness of participation in the life given in Christ expands as we acknowledge the graced lives of the great cloud of witnesses from times past, thank God for them, and receive benefit in their company on the road of discipleship. In the words of praise to God in the Preface for Holy Men and Women:

> You are glorified in your saints,
> for their glory is the crowning of your gifts.
> In their lives on earth
> you give us an example.
> In our communion with them
> you give us their friendship.
> In their prayer for the Church
> you give us strength and protection.
> This great company of witnesses spurs us
> on to victory, to share their prize of
> everlasting glory through Jesus Christ our Lord.
> With angels and archangels
> and the whole company of saints
> we sing our unending hymn of praise:
> Holy, holy, holy…[9]

## Lutheran Reflections

(1) What does this Common Statement mean for actual life in Lutheran churches? Very much indeed. In summary fashion, it is possible to see we

have much in common with Roman Catholics on the subject of the sole mediatorship of Christ, the saints, and Mary.

(a) *The sole mediatorship of Christ:* Together with the Roman Catholics we confess Christ as the one Mediator (1 Tim 2:5-6a) who "determines not only the content of the gospel and its communication but also all Christian life, including our own and that of Mary and the saints who are now in heaven" (CS § 103.2).

(b) *The saints:* We have become more aware of the doxological dimension of the church, i.e., the unity of the church militant on earth with the church triumphant in heaven. We affirm, along with Roman Catholics, the importance of honoring the saints as examples of Christian life and faith. (Cf. CA 21:1; *BS* 83b; *BC* 46; Ap 21:4-7; *BS* 317-18; *BC* 229-30.)

(c) *Mary:* We have become more aware of the place of Mary in the New Testament (CS §§ 143-55); of Luther's high view of Mary, notably his Christmas meditations on Mary and his exposition of the Magnificat where he extols the virgin who, faced with the incomprehensible role of bearing the Son of God, lived by faith alone (CS §§ 18-19); and of Mary in the Lutheran Confessions, in which statements are made that Mary is the "Mother of God" (*mater Dei*; cf. *theotokos*, "God-bearer"), the "most blessed Virgin" (*laudatissima virgo*), and "perpetual Virgin" (*semper virgo*) (CS §§ 17, 38).[1]

Faced with a secularized world in which the spiritual is neglected or distorted, we rejoice that we are able to spell out another aspect of our common Lutheran and Roman Catholic witness to Christ and the doxological dimension of his church.

(2) What problems remain ecumenically? Lutherans and Roman Catholics encounter each other more and more and with heightened awareness at funerals, inter-Christian weddings, inter-Christian families, and the like. None can help sensing differences in style and practice. Differences may even be perceived as abuses. Here, too, ecumenical progress is evident.

(3) Spirituality does not have to be homogenized, Lutherans have learned in this dialogue. In some cases differences in piety and worship are merely differences in taste. Styles vary with the times as well as among groups. Present-day Roman Catholic spirituality, itself not unified, is the product of a long and complex development Lutherans know little about. We have learned that Roman Catholics made a serious distinction between worship (*latria*, for God) and veneration (*dulia*, for saints; *hyperdulia*, for Mary) and that they have a long tradition of fighting against abuses in worship and piety. (Cf. CS §§6, 82, 171, 174, 185, 204, 209, 214, as well as the Catholic Reflections.) We have also learned in this dialogue how incorrect it is for Lutherans to disdain Roman Catholic piety regarding the saints and Mary and simply condemn it as idolatry. (Cf. CS §§101, 104.1; SA 2:3:26; *BS* 425; *BC* 297.)

(4) It is just as incorrect, on the other hand, to disdain Lutheran worship and piety because it is said to lack elements found in another style of spirituality. Lutherans have a rich tradition of spirituality, of Bible reading, hymns, public worship, prayer meetings, family devotions, biblical and missionary heroes, and reading devotional literature. With all of its complexities, the interaction between Orthodoxy and Pietism in the seventeenth and eighteenth centuries produced a deep spirituality largely unaffected by Rationalism.[2] This spirituality continued in the nineteenth century. In recent times Lutherans have profited from Roman Catholic liturgical renewal beginning in the last part of the nineteenth century and continuing up to the present as an increasingly ecumenical process. (Cf. CS §§195, 197-98.)

(5) But what of abuses? Abuses exist, of course. How are they to be discerned? Once again we can point to significant convergence between Lutherans and Roman Catholics. In our previous series of dialogue we were able to affirm together that "our entire hope of justification and salvation rests on Christ Jesus and on the gospel..." so that "we do not place our ultimate trust in anything other than God's promise and saving work in Christ" (L/RC 7:4, 157). Our "fuller material convergence" on justification by faith (L/RC 7:155, cf. 152) has as "its counterpart" *solus Christus*: "He alone is to be ultimately trusted as the one mediator" (L/RC 7:160, cf. 117).

(6) Our dialogue was able to affirm "a significant though lesser convergence" on the "use" of this doctrine "as a criterion of authenticity for the church's proclamation and practice" (L/RC 7:152, cf. 121). It is a "lesser convergence" in that Lutherans hold to justification by faith alone in Christ alone as "the" criterion, "the" *articulus stantis et cadentis ecclesiae* (cf. L/RC 7:88-93, 117, 121, 154); Roman Catholics, in contrast, hold that our "ultimate trust" (L/RC 7:4, 157) is, to be sure, in Christ alone for salvation, but that the "alone" in the Lutheran "by faith alone" does not allow for "the traditional Catholic position that the grace-wrought transformation of sinners is a necessary preparation for that salvation" (L/RC 7:157); then justification is only "an" *articulus stantis et cadentis ecclesiae* (L/RC 7:155; cf. CS §62), along with the sole mediatorship of Christ, among "[o]ther critical norms" (CS §97) for judging doctrine and practice. Recognizing that we as Lutherans also face abuses in both worship and piety, we welcome the convergence we have discovered in these critical norms as criteria for judging all doctrine and practice.

(7) We do, however, disagree over whether there is one criterion or there are many criteria. The topic of the "saints and Mary" is a means of testing the extent and nature of our agreement as well as a possible model for dealing with other outstanding topics between Lutherans and Roman Catholics (L/RC 7:116, 119, 153-54; CS §§3-4).

(8) Why this Lutheran insistence on the sole criterion, justification by

faith alone in the sole Mediator? Because only such faith can be the assured faith (*certitudo*) that the sinner requires. *Certitudo* is not a psychological category, i.e., a kind of feeling. What produces such *certitudo* is solely faith in Christ, in contrast to *securitas*, i.e., a false faith based on any person or thing other than faith alone in the sole Mediator. By this Lutherans discern what is or is not abuse or error. The question of *securitas* is not for Lutherans basically a matter of spirituality. It is intrinsic to the working of the gospel. Here "gospel" is not a vague, general concept, but salvation solely by faith in Christ (SA 2:1:5; BS 145; BC 292). Where this gospel is not proclaimed and the sacraments are not celebrated according to this gospel, Lutherans ask whether abuse or error has crept in (cf. CA 7; *BS* 61; *BC* 32). As we examine such a topic as the "saints and Mary," it is crucial that Lutherans see how this criterion functions.

(9) 1. *Proper understanding of the saints and Mary.* Because Lutherans emphasize doctrine, we all too readily make proper understanding the criterion for doctrine and practice. Proper understanding of the "saints and Mary" is important and has its place. Things need to be put in context, and we need to be challenged by different spiritualities and conceptualities. This does not mean, however, that to understand all is to accept all. The fundamental question is: Does spirituality involving the saints and Mary in any way undermine assured faith?

> It becomes necessary to make a careful distinction between faith as trust in the divine promises and those aspects of the faith of the Church which are responses to the divine promise through confession, action, teaching, and doctrinal formulations. These responses are necessary: the gospel (the promise of God) does indeed have a specifiable "knowledge" content. But the authority of this content, Lutherans believe, is established by its power to convict of sin and convince of grace through the work of the Holy Spirit and is not enhanced by saying that the teaching office or doctrinal formulations are themselves infallible. (L/RC 6:III, §10, p.63)

(10) 2. *Extension of Biblical Passages on the Saints*

a) Because the church militant and church triumphant are one (and here Lutherans do not disagree; see above [1][b]), Roman Catholics go on to hold that invoking departed saints is a legitimate extension of asking living saints to intercede (Rom 15:30-32; 2 Cor 1:11; Eph 4:19; Col 4:3) and of the prayer of the righteous (Jas 5:16) (CS §§51, 80).

b) Roman Catholics appeal to tradition, including the extension of certain biblical passages in the tradition as well as other tradition established by the magisterium (CS §§67, 68, 78) as the basis for holding that the departed are aware of prayers addressed to them. On this point the biblical evidence is mixed (CS §§133-42), and some Roman Catholic theologians have asked whether departed saints are aware of what we who remain on earth are concretely asking and doing.[3]

c) Roman Catholics hold "that those who die in close union with Christ are taken up into eternal life and become outstanding members of the communion of saints" (CS §80). Those dying in an imperfect union with Christ are in purgatory and lack the beatific vision. (Purgatory is a topic involving biblical extension and magisterial tradition.) Those dying "in close union" have "a charity heightened by personal experience and awareness of the serious plight of wayfarers" (CS §67; cf. "so effective," §81) and, in the case of Mary, "exceptional power" in her intercession because of her divine motherhood (CS §84). Thus it is said to be "supremely fitting" (*summopere decet*) to invoke the saints (LG 50). The Marian dogmas of the Immaculate Conception (1854) and the Assumption (1950) are also based on biblical extension and magisterial tradition (CS §§84, 86, 88).

(11) To rehearse this material is to make evident that the use of Scripture remains controversial between Lutherans and Roman Catholics.

a) As Lutherans, we grant that the angels and "perhaps" the saints pray for us (Zech 1:12; Ap 21:10; *BS* 318; *BC* 230), yet even this needs to be kept within the perspective of the assured faith found only by faith in the sole Mediator. Prayer for the dead has not been frequent in Lutheran piety; funeral liturgies may include prayers that commend the deceased to God.[4] But there is no biblical promise that our intercessions can affect the situation of those already dead. Even if infrequent, such intercessions must be only by faith in Christ. Further, Lutherans should examine intercession by "living saints" to see if this is thought to be efficacious because it is intensive, because many intercessors are involved, or more "spiritual" Christians take part, rather than only because of faith in Christ.

b) Because the biblical evidence for the sort of awareness departed saints have is mixed and thus the Lutheran Confessions do not find "any decisive ground for affirming that the departed are aware of prayers addressed to them" (CS §79), Lutherans ask how one can be confident that prayers are heard.

c) The New Testament speaks of all believers, e.g., in Corinth, as "saints" or "holy ones" in Christ. All saints, living or departed, are equal because all are justified only by faith in Christ. While recognizing that "reward" language is found in the New Testament, Lutherans hold that these are rewards in a very different sense (cf. L/RC 7: pp. 94-110). Whatever the case may be, "rewarded" saints are not therefore more accessible or benevolent. Moreover, although Lutherans are very familiar with making both living and departed saints into spiritual examples of the faith, we are also very familiar with possible abuses. In Luther's exposition of the Magnificat he exalts Mary because she faces her situation by faith alone. An attempt to use Mary or another Christian to extol any other "virtue" than faith raises the question of undermining living only by faith in Christ. [5]

(12) When dealing with the issue of biblical extension, however, it is important to keep a wide focus. What is ultimately at stake is not a wooden approach to Scripture or endless delay while settling exegetical disputes. For Lutherans hold that "the scriptural witness to the gospel remains the ultimate norm" (L/RC 6:III, §11, p. 63), and this gospel is the gospel of God's unconditional mercy in Jesus Christ to which the biblical writings are the primary witness (L/RC 6:III, §7, p. 62).

(13) 3. *Invoking the saints and Mary*. Lutherans have been assured that the *Confutation*, although interpreted correctly by Melanchthon in the *Apology* as requiring invocation of the saints, was written in and for its own time and is not to be considered part of the official teaching of the Roman Catholic Church (CS §22). Thus what was a major problem for the Lutheran Confessors has been eliminated. And our present dialogue partners assure us that "in any closer future fellowship members would be free to refrain" from invoking the saints (CS §97), just as this freedom is presently enjoyed by Roman Catholics today (CS §94). What remains unclear is what would be required of Lutheran participation that is not just personal in official rites, such as baptism and ordination, where the saints are invoked.

(14) More importantly, whatever invocation might be as an ideal in and of itself, the Confessors held that it lacks a divine promise, produces insufficient spiritual certainty, and leads to abuses in devotional life, even though saints are to be honored (CS §83). Further, if "there is no expectation of return," the saints "will quickly be forgotten" (SA 2:3:28; *BS* 425; *BC* 297), and this actually happened.

(15) These are all, however, negatives. The positive, as the present dialogue has put it, is the freedom to proclaim the sole mediatorship of Christ clearly (CS §98). Then everything else will fall into place, including discerning abuses and errors, because everything will be only by faith.

(16) Once again, it is important to keep a wide focus. What the Lutheran Confessions meant and mean will be disputed, perhaps endlessly. Lutherans look to their Confessions for guidance concerning the invocation of the saints and Mary, yet we are aware of the fact that doctrinal formulations for Lutherans are, on the one hand, confessions and doxologies rather than promulgations of infallible dogma; and, on the other, they function as guides for the proper proclamation of the gospel, the administration of the sacraments, and the right praise of God rather than as statements which are themselves objects of faith. (L/RC 6:III, 11, p. §63).

(17) 4. *Intent, experience, and the saints and Mary*. The criterion for

judging doctrine and practice is not the intent of the believer, for example, that the believer intends the good or "feels good" concerning the saints and Mary. That would mean that assured faith depends on the individual and is individualistic. We do not judge the heart; we cannot even judge our own hearts (cf. 1 John 3:20). The same is true for experience, intuition, conscience, speaking in tongues, and private revelations. These all have their proper place, but they are not final criteria for right doctrine and practice. The criterion remains whatever is discerned solely by faith in Christ.

(18) A correlate is the problem of "communion" whenever the comfort of human solidarity is confused with the comfort we have *sub contrario* because we live in brokenness, finally dying, and the cross is our hope and comfort (*sola cruce*). In Christ we may be abased and we may abound. What is decisive is not our experience in all its brokenness and exaltedness, but whether our *communio* is solely by faith in Christ or is by another gospel.

(19) Therefore in any future fellowship with the Roman Catholic Church the freedom Lutherans would have clearly to proclaim the sole mediatorship of Jesus Christ would mean that at all levels of the church Lutherans would always be free to discern whether invoking of the saints and Mary is carried out in such a way that it produces assured faith (*certitudo*) because it is the proclamation (*usus*) of justification by faith alone in the sole Mediator, Jesus Christ. This methodology would be applicable to similar issues that still divide our churches, for example, indulgences and any proposal that the Marian dogmas be "accepted in some form" (cf. CS §101 and CS §17, n. 20).[6]

(20) We are alert to the fact that the question of Scripture and tradition lies behind much of what still separates Lutherans and Roman Catholics concerning the saints and Mary. We already signaled the importance of this question in our first round of dialogue (L/RC 1: p. 32). It was fundamental for our dialogue on Teaching Authority and Infallibility in the Church (L/RC 6). In the present round of dialogue on the saints and Mary we have again discovered the need to investigate biblical extension and magisterial tradition (Lutheran Reflections, §§10-12; CS §100).

(21) Lutherans take the appeal to church history seriously, as is shown by our appeal to a lack of early testimony to invocation of the saints (Ap 21; BS 81-82; BC 46-47), even though there is now further evidence on the matter, as has been noted above (CS §80; cf. §88, on the Marian dogmas). We know that reception is integral to the life of the church (cf. L/RC 6:III, §14, p. 65: "interpreted by the community of faith"), and we are alert to the fact of development, particularly the development of the biblical canon. Our Confessional writings appeal to the teachings of the Fathers of the church: "This teaching is grounded clearly on the Holy Scriptures and is not contrary or opposed to those of the church catholic or even the church of Rome inso-

far as its teachings are reflected in the writings of the Fathers." [7] Thus, even while holding firmly to the fact that "the scriptural witness to the gospel remains the ultimate norm" (L/RC 6:III, §11, P. 63), we also believe that "the unfailing guidance of the Holy Spirit" (L/RC 6:III, §14, p. 65) leads the church. We therefore rejoice in what we as Lutherans have been able to say together with Roman Catholics and look to the Lord of the church to bring us to unity as well as to guide us into all truth.

## Notes

### Common Statement: The One Mediator, the Saints, and Mary

### Introduction

1. Lutherans and Catholics in Dialogue, 6 vols. 1. *The Status of the Nicene Creed as Dogma of the Church* (1965); 2. *One Baptism for the Remission of Sins* (1966); 3. *The Eucharist as Sacrifice* (1967); 4. *Eucharist and Ministry* (1970); 5. *Papal Primacy and the Universal Church* (Minneapolis: Augsburg, 1974); 6. *Teaching Authority and Infallibility in the Church* (Minneapolis: Augsburg, 1980). Vols. 1-4 were originally published by the Bishops' Committee for Ecumenical and Interreligious Affairs, Washington, D.C., and the U.S.A. National Committee of the Lutheran World Federation, New York, N.Y. Vols. 1-3 have been reprinted together in one volume by Augsburg Publishing House (n.d.), as has vol.4 (1979).

2. *Origins* 13:17 (Oct. 6, 1983) 277, 279-304 (preliminary text); L/RC 7 (final, official text).

### Part One: Issues and Perspectives

### I. The Problem in the Sixteenth Century

3. See the historical sketch by Karl Hausberger, "Heilige/Heiligenverehrung. Abendlandisches Mittelalter," TRE 14 (1985) 652. The Greek terms *"latreia"* and *"douleia,"* Latinized as *latria* and *dulia,* referred, respectively, to the fullness of divine worship accorded to God alone and the reverence which may be paid to the saints. The term *"hyperdouleia"* (Latin: *hyperdulia*) was used with reference to Mary.

4. DS 812-14.

5. For church teachings on indulgences during the Middle Ages, cf. DS 819, 868, 1025-27, 1447-49.

6. Erich W. Gritsch, "The Origin of the Lutheran Teaching on Justification," L/RC 7; pp. 164-67.

7. Andreas Bodenstein of Karlstadt, dean of Wittenberg University, was an iconoclast who succeeded in establishing a new "church order" in Wittenberg in 1521. Luther modified this order in 1523. See James H. Preus, *Carlstadt's Ordinances and Luther's Liberty* (Cambridge MA: Harvard University Press, 1974).

8. One example of Luther's modification of tradition is his *Fourteen Consolations*, 1520. WA 6:104-34;LW 42:119-66. On Martin Bucer, see Frieder Schulz, TRE 14 (1985) 664.

9. Thomas de Vio of Gaeta (known as Cajetan), general of the Dominican order and cardinal, conducted the first hearing of Luther in Augsburg in 1518.

10. Thomas de Vio Cardinal Cajetan, *Opuscula Omnia. Tractatus de Indulgentiis* (Venice: Apud Haeredem Hieronymi Scoti, 1580) q.1, 51, v, 1 G.

11. See Carl J. Peter, "The Church's Treasures (*Thesauri Ecclesiae*) Then and Now," *Theological Studies* 7 (1986) 251-72.

12. DS 1492.

13. *Sermon on the Birth of Mary*, 1552. WA 10/3:317, 4-318, 7. See also Luther's critique in the context of his view of *communio sanctorum* in Paul Althaus, *The Theology of Martin Luther* (tr. Robert c. Schultz; Philadelphia: Fortress, 1966) 298-300. Luther's movement toward rejection of the cult of the saints has been analyzed by Lennart Pinomaa, "Luther's Weg zur Verwerfung des Heiligendienstes," *Lutherjahrbuch* 29 (1962) 35-43. See also *idem, Die Heiligen bei Luther* (Helsinki: Luther-Agricola-Gesellschaft, 1977). Very helpful is also the detailed analysis of Luther's view by Peter Manns, "Luther und die Heiligen," *Reformatio Ecclesiae. Beiträge zu kirchlichen Reformbemühungen von der Alten Kirche bis zur Neuzeit* (FS. E. Iserloh; ed. R. Bäumer; Paderborn, Munich, Vienna, Zurich: Schöningh, 1980) 535-80; cf. Horst Gorski, *Die Niedrigkeit seiner Magd.* Darstellung und theologische Analyse der Marientheologie Luthers als Beiträg zum̄ gegenwärtigen lutherisch/romish-katholischēn Gesprach (Europäische Hochschulschriften 23: Berlin, New York: Lanning, 1987).

14. *The Bondage of the Will*, 1525. WA 18:778, 8-13; LW 33:280.

15. *Concerning Rebaptism*, 1520. WA 26:168, 12-16; LW 40:256. Luther's concept of example is closely related to Augustine's concept of *sacramentum et exemplum*; cf. Kenneth Hagen, *A Theology of Testament in the Young Luther. The Lectures on Hebrews* (Studies in Medieval and Reformation Thought 12; Leiden: Brill, 1974) 114-15.

16. *Lectures on Genesis*, 1539. WA 43:108, 24-31; LW 3:325. On *Divum Bernardum veneror, see Leipzig Disputation*, WA 59:445, 410 44; cf. Franz Posset, "Bernard of Clairvaux as Luther's Source; Reading Bernard with Luther's 'Spectacles,'" *Concordia Theological Quarterly* 54 (1990) 281-304.

17. *The Burning of Brother Henry*, 1525. WA 18:224-40;LW 32:265-86. How Luther and other reformers continued the patristic and medieval martyriological tradition has been demonstrated by Robert Kolb, *For All the Saints. Changing Perceptions of Martyrdom and Sainthood in the Lutheran Reformation* (Macon GA: Mercer University Press, 1987); on Henry of Zutphen, 21, 66.

18. *Vorrede...*, 1544. WA 54:109-11.

19. Sermon on May 13, 1526. WA 20:390, 6-8. Sermon on June 17, 1526. WA 20:444, 1-2. Wilhelm Maurer, *Historical Commentary on the Augsburg Confession* (tr. H. G. Anderson; Philadelphia: Fortress, 1986) 371-75, has shown how Luther linked the veneration of saints to Christ and the "Word." Maurer concludes that CA 21 disclosed Melanchthon's concern about abuses more than the depth of Luther's thought (ibid., 375).

20. With regard to the Immaculate Conception, Luther taught that Mary had been conceived in sin but her soul had been purified by infusion after conception. *Sermon on the Feast of the Immaculate Conception*, 1527. Festival Postil (*Festpostille*). WA 17/2:288, 17-34. In 1518 Luther declared that, even though the Immaculate Conception of Mary was an opinion asserted by the Council of Basel (1431-49), a contrary opinion need not be considered heretical unless it is disproved. *Explanations of the Ninety-Five Theses*, 1518. WA 1;583, 8-12;LW 31:173. See also Hans Düfel, *Luthers Stellung zur Marienverehrung* (Kirche und Konfession, Veröffentlichungen des konfessionskundlichen Instituts des Evangelischen Bundes 13; Göttingen: Vandenhoeck and Ruprecht, 1968) 169-70. That Christ should be born of a virgin who was "immaculate" is "a pious and pleasing thought" (*haec pia cogitatio et placet*) which need not be imposed on the faithful (*Exposition of the Ninth Chapter of Isaiah*, 1543/44. WA 40/3:680, 31-32). Luther taught that Mary remained a virgin before the birth of Christ (*ante partum*), at the birth (*in partu*), and after his birth (*post partum*) (*That Jesus Was Born a Jew*, 1523. WA 11:320, 1-6;LW 45:206). Further evidence in William J. Cole, "Was Luther a Devotee of Mary?" *Marian Studies* 21 (1970) 119-20; on the Immaculate Conception, ibid., 120-23.

21. In the sixteenth century most Lutheran territories celebrated the Marian festivals of the

Purification (February 2), of the Annunciation (March 25), and of the Visitation (July 2). See Walter Delius, "Luther und die Marienverehrung." *Theologische Literaturzeitung* 79 (1954) 414.

22. "Like Mary's virginity, the church will not be destroyed (*vertilgt*)" (*Sermon on the Sunday After Christmas on Luke 2:23-40*. Church Postil [*Kirchenpostille*], 1522. WA 10/1/1:405, 13-16). Luther interpreted Luke 1:48b ("All generations call me blessed"): "Not *she* is praised thereby, but God's *grace* towards her" (WA 7:568,4;LW 21:321). Here he learned from, and resonated to, Nicholas of Lyra; see Kenneth Hagen, "Lyra and Luther on Luke 1:26-55," p. 3 (unpublished; Sept. 1983); see also Eric W. Gritsch, "Embodiment of Unmerited Grace. The Virgin Mary According to Martin Luther and Lutheranism" in *Mary's Place in Christian Dialogue* (ed. A. Stacpoole; Wilten CN: Morehouse-Barlow, 1983) 133-41. On "*typus ecclesiae*," see Heiko A. Oberman, "The Virgin Mary in Evangelical Perspective," *Journal of Ecumenical Studies* I (1964) 13; reprinted in Facet Books, Historical Series 20; Philadelphia: Fortress, 1971).

23. *Sermon on the Festival of the Assumption*, August 15, 1522. WA 10/3:269, 12-13; also the sermon on August 15, 1544. WA 52:681, 27-31.

24. Most of Luther's hymns originated in 1523 and 1524. (Thirty-six hymns are listed in WA 35:411-73; English translations in LW 53:211-309.) It is mostly the festival hymns that refer to Mary, especially Advent and Christmas hymns. See Karlfried Froehlich, "Mary in the Hymns of Martin Luther" (unpublished; Sept. 1983).

25. *Confession Concerning Christ's Supper*, 1528. WA 26:508, 14-15;LW 37:370.

26. *Instructions for the Visitors of Parish Pastors in Electoral Saxony*, 1528. WA 26:224, 26-31;LW 40:300.

27. The significance of this step is stressed by George Kretschmar and René Laurentin. "The Cult of the Saints," *Confessing One Faith. A Joint Commentary on the Augsburg Confession by Lutheran and Catholic Theologians* (ed. G.W. Forell and J.F. McCue; tr. R. Gehrke; Minneapolis: Augsburg, 1982) 276; recall as well the teachings of the Second Council of Nicaea (DS 600-601).

28. CA 21:2;BS 83b-c;*BC* 47.

29. Reference will be to the German and Latin text as found in Herbert Immenkötter, *Die Confutatio der Augustana vom 3. August 1530* (Corpus Catholicorum 33; Münster: Aschendorff, 1979); English translation in J.M. Reu (ed.), *The Augsburg Confession: A Collection of Sources with an Historical Introduction* (Chicago: Wartburg Publishing House, 1930; reprinted, St. Louis: Concordia Seminary Press, 1966).

30. *Die Confutatio* 21:124, 11-12 (German); 125, 10 (Latin).

31. *Contra Faustum* 20:21; CSEL 25:562, 8-10.

32. *Die Confutatio* 21:130, 3-4 (German); 131, 304 (Latin).

33. *Die Confutatio*, 21:129, 14-16: "Nam etsi fatetur unum esse mediatorem redemptionis Caesarea majestas cum tota ecclesia, tamen multi sunt mediatores intercessionis" (Reu 361).

34. Ap 21:8-9, *BS* 318; BC 230.

35. Ap 21:10; *BS* 318; BC 230.

36. Ap 21:3; *BS* 317; BC 229.

37. *Die Confutatio*, 21:129, 14-16 (Reu 361).

38. Ap 21:29; *BS* 322; *BC* 233.

39. Ap 21:17-32; *BS* 320-23; *BC* 231-33.

40. Ap 21:38-44; *BS* 325-28; *BC* 234-36.

41. See Kenneth Hagen, "The Historical Context of the Smalcald Articles," *Concordia Theological Quarterly* 51 (1987) 245-53.

42. SA 2:25; *BS* 424; *BC* 297.

43. SA 2:28; *BS* 425; *BC* 297.

44. CR 4:369-70.

45. For the complete texts, C.O.D. 75-52; 772-73; see also Carl J. Peter, "The Communion of Saints in the Final Days of the Council of Trent" in L/RC 8:219-34.

46. *LG* 50-51.

47. C.O.D., 750-51.

48. C.O.D., 751; DS 1822.

49. C.O.D., 751.

50. C.O.D., 751-52.

51. See above, CS §§28-29.

52. Martin Chemnitz, *Examination of the Council of Trent* (tr. Fred Kramer; St. Louis: Concordia, 1986) 2:353-507.

53. FC Ep 8:12; *BS* 806; *BC* 488; *FC SD* 8:24; *BS* 1024; *BC* 595.

54. Rabus's work has been analyzed and evaluated by Kolb (n.17 above).

## II. Perspectives on Critical Issues

### A. Lutheran Perspectives

55. See Robert Bertram, "Luther on Christ as the Sole Mediator" L/RC 8:pp. 249-62.

56. L/RC 7:24-25; 24:25; 70:154.

57. Ap 21:4-7; *BS* 317-18; *BC* 229-30.

58. SA 2:3:26; *BS* 425; *BC* 297.

59. Ap 21:27; BS 322; BC 232.

60. The Magnificat, 1521. WA 7:561; LW 21:314.

61. Cf. Arthur C. Piepkorn, "Mary's Place within the People of God according to non-Roman Catholics," *Marian Studies* 18 (1967) 46-86, esp. 73-78.

62. CA 1-17; *BS* 50-73; *BC* 27-39.

63. Cited in a note in *LG* 50.

### B. Catholic Perspectives

64. *LG* 1.

65. For the background regarding the conciliar debate leading up to this decision, see Carl J. Peter, "The Eschatology of *Lumen Gentium*" and S.C. Napiorkowski, "Marie dans la piété Catholique," *Collectanea Theologica* 56 (1986) 69-84.

66. *LG* 61.

67. Augustine, *De Praedestinatione Sanctorum* 15:30-31;PL 44:981-82; Aquinas, *Super Epistolam ad Romanos*, I Lect. 3, 48-49.

68. *The Church's Confession of Faith: A Catechism for Adults* (ed. M. Jordan; tr. S. Arndt; San Francisco: Ignatius, 1987) 348.

69. Carl J. Peter, "A Moment of Truth for Lutheran-Catholic Dialogue," *Origins* 17 (1988) 541; reprinted, *One in Christ* 24 (1988) 151.

70. Medieval theologians rather commonly held that in seeing the eternal God, to whom all is present, the saints in heaven see as well whatever is of legitimate concern and interest to them on earth. For Thomas Aquinas, cf. *In IV Sent.*, d. 45, 1.3, a,1, sol. and S.T. III, q.10, a.2, c. Melanchthon referred to a dispute that had arisen precisely because this was taken as a given (Ap 21:11).

## III. The Problem Reexamined

### A. Dimensions of the Problem

71. L/RC 7:152; cf. 121.

72. L/RC 7:91.

73. Ibid.

74. Carl J. Peter, "The Need of Another Principle," L/RC 7: p. 309; cf. 314; also L/RC 7:118, 154.

## B. Resulting Divergences

75. Vatican II is here quoting the *"Decretum pro Graecis"* of the Council of Florence (DS 1305).

76. CS §§159, 165, 166, and 177; also 50 and 51.

77. For some evidence, see Robert Eno, *St. Augustine and the Saints* (The Saint Augustine Lecture for 1985; Philadelphia: Villanova University Press, 1989) 29-48.

78. For an example of how the term "divine motherhood" took on a more-than-physical meaning, see the work of Scheeben as summarized in CS §189.

79. On the debate about Mary as Mediatrix at Vatican II, see the literature cited in n.261; also Elizabeth A. Johnson, "Mary as Mediatrix," L/RC 8: pp. 311-26. In the 1962 schema *De beata Maria Virgine matre Dei et matre hominum*, no.3, it had been stated that "the most blessed Virgin is not undeservedly called Mediatrix of graces." Note that in the final text the only mention of Mary as Mediatrix, made in passing, is in the context of her maternal intercession in heaven. For further discussion, see Guilherme Barauna, "Le très sainte Vierge au service de l'economie du salut," *L'Eglise de Vatican II* (Unam Sanctum 51c; ed. G. Baraúna; Paris: Cerf, 1966) 1226-30.

80. Pius IX, *Ineffabilis Deus* (December 8, 1954), DS 2803.

81. See Frederick M. Jelly, "The Roman Catholic Dogma of Mary's Immaculate Conception," L/RC 8: pp. 263-78.

82. In the apostolic constitution, *Munificentissimus Deus* (November 1, 1950), Pius XII, defining the dogma, pointed out that many Scholastic theologians made the connection between Mary's absolute sinlessness and her Assumption. Summarizing the theological arguments, the pope presented the Assumption as the crowning privilege that follows upon, and is the appropriate complement to, four other privileges: Mary's connection with Christ in one and the same decree of predestination; her Immaculate Conception; her virginal motherhood; and her intimate association with Christ's redemptive work. In this connection the text speaks explicitly of Mary's having been "preserved from the corruption of the tomb," though the concluding paragraph containing the binding definition states only that Mary, "having completed the course of her earthly life, was assumed body and soul into heavenly glory." See the text of the bull in *Papal Documents on Mary* (ed. W.J. Doheny and J.P. Kelly; Boston: St. Paul Editions, 1981) 200-320, esp. 318, corresponding to DS 3902; also Avery Dulles, "The Dogma of the Assumption," L/RC 8:pp. 279-94.

83. Valerius Herberger, "Am Tage Mariae Himmelfahrt," *Evangelische Herz-Postilla*, Ander Theil (reprinted Leipzig: Gleditsch, 1687) 200-204.

84. In some instances Lutherans contended that the Assumption had its roots in pagan polytheism and raised Mary to quasi-divine status; see Eric W. Gritsch, "The Views of Luther and Lutheranism on the Veneration of Mary," L/RC 8:pp. 235-48.

## C. Need the Divergences Be Church-Dividing?

85. Cf. *Facing Unity: Models, Forms and Phases of Catholic-Lutheran Fellowship* (Geneva: Lutheran World Federation, 1985) §§47-49.

86. DS 1821. For discussion see Carl J. Peter, "The Communion of Saints in the Final Days of the Council of Trent," L/RC 8: esp. 230-31. For a more general statement on the obligation of invoking saints, see Karl Rahner and Johann B. Metz, *The Courage to Pray* (New York: Crossroad, 1981) 33-34.

87. The five principles set forth by Paul VI to guide proper Marian devotion (§§25-37 of the text AAS 64 [1974]) are discussed in detail in the Roman Catholic Reflections, 451-57 below.

88. See the quotations from Karl Rahner and other contemporary Catholic theologians in Elizabeth A. Johnson, "Mary as Mediatrix," L/RC 8:pp. 324-26. On Vatican II, see n.79 above.

89. L/RC 6:50; emphasis added; consult also the further clarifications in "Observations on the Critique Submitted by the Committee on Doctrine of the National Conference of Catholic Bishops," *Lutheran Quarterly*, ns 1 (1987) 137-58.

90. The conditions under which eucharistic sharing with Protestants may be permitted are spelled out in the *Code of Canon Law* (1983), canon 844, which permits Catholic ministers under some circumstances to administer Holy Communion to Protestants. Canon 908 forbids

concelebration of the Eucharist with ministers of churches not in full communion with the Catholic Church.

91. L/RC 6:50.

92. In *Christian Unity and Christian Diversity* (Philadelphia: Westminster, 1975) 90-96, John Macquarrie proposed an ecumenical reinterpretation of the dogma of the Immaculate Conception. Joseph Ratzinger, *Church, Ecumenism and Politics* (New York: Crossroad, 1988) 82-83, speaks of a "hermeneutics of unity" for dogmas defined in separation. For discussion of Ratzinger's position in light of similar proposals by Yves Congar and others, see Avery Dulles, *The Reshaping of Catholicism* (San Francisco: Harper & Row, 1988) 238-41.

## Part Two: Biblical and Historical Foundations

# I. Scripture on Christ, the Saints, and Mary

93. Cf. Josef Hainz *Koinonia: "Kirche" als Gemeinschaft bei Paulus* (Biblische Untersuchungen 16; Regensburg: Pustet, 1982) 232-72, for ecumenical development of the term in Roman Catholic, Reformation, and Orthodox Churches.

94. A. Oepke, *TWNT* 4 (1942) 618: *TDNT* 4 (1967) 614.

95. Thus Mithra, the mediator between Persian Ahuramazda and Ahriman (Plutarch, *Is. et Os.* 46 [2.369e]), and various cosmic beings and spirits.

96. For exegetical details on a and b, see respectively the papers by J.A. Fitzmyer, "Biblical Data on the Veneration, Intercession, and Invocation of Holy People," L/RC 8:pp.135-47; and J. Reumann, "How Do We Interpret 1 Timothy 2:5 (and Related Passages)?", L/RC 8: pp. 149-57.

97. Other Greek nouns for prayer in the New Testament include *aitēma* ("request," Phil 4:4); *hikēteria* ("supplication," Heb.5:7); and *eperōtēma* ("appeal," 1 Pet 3:21), not to mention the related verbs.

98. The verb *epikaleisthai*, "call upon," is also used in this sense at Rom 10:12, 13, 14; 1 Cor 1:2; 2 Cor 2:23; 2 Tim 2:22; Acts 2:21; 9:14, 21; 22:16; believers are "those who call on the name of the Lord"; cf. also Heb 11:20 and 1 Chron 16:4 (to invoke, thank, and praise the Lord; hiphil *zakar*). In the Latin Vulgate *invoco* is employed for *epikaleisthai* in all the above New Testament passages, but *invocatio* only at 2 Macc 8:15 ("on account of invocation of [the Lord's] holy and magnificent name over them").

99. L/RC 7:132

100. Understood as a translation of the Hebrew, *heblo šel-māšîah*, "the travail of the messiah," the phrase would refer to woes such as rebellion, war, pestilence, drought, crop failure, inflation, penury, apostasy, and cosmic cataclysms, expected to precede the end-time when God will send an appointed agent to deliver his people.

101. The Luther Bible includes Sirach (Ecclesiasticus or The Wisdom of Jesus the Son of Sirach) and 2 Maccabees in the Apocrypha, with the comment "good and useful for reading" but not on a par with the canonical books for the purposes of doctrine. The Council of Trent included them as part of its listing of the canon of holy Scriptures; they are sometimes termed by Catholics "deuterocanonical." 4 Maccabees, though in important Greek manuscripts of the Bible and revered in Eastern churches, has never been canonized. All three books are in the RSV Apocrypha, Expanded Edition, 1977.

102. For surveys of the biblical data, see J. Reumann "Death," and Osmo Tiililae, "Resurrection," in *The Encyclopedia of the Lutheran Church* (ed. J. Bodensieck; Philadelphia: Fortress; Minneapolis: Augsburg, 1965) 1:667-71 and 3:2048-50; P. Benoit and R. Murphy (eds.), *Immortality and Resurrection* (Concilium 60: New York: Herder and Herder, 1970); Gunter Kegel, *Auferstehung Jesu-Auferstehung der Toten: Eine traditionsgeschichtliche Untersuchung zum Neuen Testament* (Gütersloh: Gütersloher Verlagshaus Gerd Mohn 1970); L. Coenen and C. Brown, "Resurrection," *NIDNTT* 3 (1978)259-309; G. Stemberger and P. Hoffmann, "Auferstehung der Toten 1/2. Judentum," 1/3. Neues Testament," "Auferstehung

Jesu Christi 11/1. Neues Testamentum," *TRE* 4(1979) 443-67,478-513; H. C. Cavallin, "Leben nach dem Tode im Spätjudentum und in frühen Christentum," *Aufstieg und Niedergang der römischen Welt* II 19/1 (1979)240-345; P. Hoffmann, *Die Toten in Christus: eine religionsgeschichtliche und exegetische Untersuchung zur paulinischen Eschatologie*, Neutestamentliche Abhandlungen, Neue Folge 2; (Münster: Aschendorff, 1966); Pheme Perkins, Resurrection: *New Testament Witness and Contemporary Reflection* (Garden City: Doubleday, 1964); R. Martin-Achard, "Resurrection (A.T. Judaisme)," *Dictionnaire de la Bible*, Supplement 10 (1985) 437-87; Gisbert Greshake and Jacob Kremer, *Resurrectio Mortuorum: Zum theologischen Verständnis der leiblichen Auferstehung* (Darmstadt: Wissenschaftliche Buchgesellschaft, 1986); Julien Ries, "Immortality," and Helmer Ringgren, "Resurrection," ER 7:123-45; 12:344-50.

103. Cf. Isa 25:8 Hos: 6:1-3; Job 19:26; Ps 49:15; 73:23-38; Isa 65:17; 66:22-24. J.L. McKenzie, *JBC* 77:168, has written, "It is generally held by scholars that no hope of individual survival after death is expressed in the OT before some of its latest passages, which were probably written in the 2nd century B.C." M. Dahood, *Psalms I* (AB 16; Garden City, NY: Doubleday & Co., 1966) vi and passim, has, however, on the basis of Canaanite motifs in the Psalter, argued for references to resurrection and even "Elysian Fields" there.

104. See especially A.M. Dubarle in *Concilium* 60:34-45 (n. 102 above); G. Stemberger, *TRE* 4:446-51 (n. 102 above); Cavallin (n. 102 above); Martin-Achard (n.102 above); George W.E. Nickelsburg, *Resurrection, Immortality, and Eternal Life in Intertestamental Judaism* (Harvard Theological Studies 26: Cambridge: Harvard University Press, 1972); Kremer, *Resurrectio*, 60-76 (n. 102 above).

105. For the Eighteen Benedictions (*Sh*ᵉ*moneh 'Esreh*) see Simeon Singer, *The Authorized Daily Prayer Book of the United Hebrew Congregations of the British Empire* (15th ed. rev.; London: Eyre & Spottiswoode, 1935) 158-64; further, C.G. Montefiore and H. Loewe, *A Rabbinic Anthology* (Cleveland and New York: World Publishing Company; and Philadelphia: Jewish Publication Society of America, 1960), "Life to Come: Resurrection and Judgement," 580-608, esp. 599-600. For *m. Sanhedrin* 10.1a, see Herbert Danby, *The Mishnah* (Oxford: Clarendon, 1933) 397; the bracketed phrase is lacking in some texts. For resurrection, in addition to passages already cited in 2 Maccabees and 2 Esdras, see 2 Macc 12:43-45; 1 (Ethiopic) Enoch 22;51;91;10;92:3 (Syriac Apocalypse of) Baruch 21:23-24; 42:7-8; 50:2; 2 Esdras 7:88-99 [v. 97, cf. Dan 12:3]; and Pseudo-Philo, *Biblical Antiquities* 3.10; 19.12; 32.13. For Enoch references, see *Old Testament Pseudepigrapha* (ed. J.H. Charlesworth; Garden City NY: Doubleday & Co., 1983-85) 1:24-24, 36-37, 72, 74; 2 Baruch, ibid. 1:628, 634, 638; for the *Liber Antiquitatum Biblicarum*, ibid. 2:307, 328, 346-47; Kremer, *Resurrectio*, 60-70 (n. 102 above).

106. 2 Macc 12:39-45 describes how it was discovered that all the Jews who died in a battle had amulets of idols under their tunics. Supplication was made that this sin might be blotted out, and Judas took up a collection for an expiatory sacrifice at the Jerusalem temple, that "they might be delivered from their sin." Vv. 44 and 45 seek to justify Judas's belief in the resurrection: "if he were not expecting that those who had fallen would rise again, it would have been superfluous and foolish to pray for the dead. But if he was looking to the splendid reward that is laid up for those who fall asleep in godliness, it was a holy and pious thought." T. Corbishley, S.J., in *A New Catholic Commentary on Holy Scripture* (London: Thomas Nelson, 1969) 599d (p. 758) sees here "a clear-cut and confident belief in personal immortality and in the value of intercessory prayer for the dead," even though "such an idea is unparalleled in Jewish Literature"; Judas's gesture strengthened the faith presupposed but then under debate among Jews. The note in the NAB views the statement about prayers and sacrifices as made "only for the purpose of proving that Judas believed in the resurrection of the just," the expiation here being "similar to, but not quite the same as, the Catholic doctrine of purgatory." Jonathan A. Goldstein, *II Maccabees* (AB 41A; Garden City: Doubleday, 1983) 449-51, thinks the author "has engaged in a complicated piece of logical gymnastics to prove that Judas believed in the resurrection of the dead." Judas and his soldiers were probably following Lev 4:13-21, about a sin that taints the community; there one sin offering, a bull, is called for, to take away the corporate guilt in the surviving community, not offerings for each dead soldier (in rabbinic law, "sac-

rifices do not secure expiation for the dead"). G. Stemberger, in *TRE* 4 (1979) 447, suggests one early scribe wrote in the margin that to pray for the dead is foolish, but another that atonement for the dead is good; a copyist harmonized both ideas in vv. 44-45.

107. "The dead of Israel" is explained in 3:10-11 to refer to Israel "in the land of your enemies,...defiled with the dead,...counted among those in Hades"; cf. Isa 59:10; Lam 3:6 in its context of 3:1ff. *A New Catholic Commentary* (n.106 above; 505i, p. 630; P.P. Saydon and T. Hanlon) points out that "a desperate condition is sometimes compared to death; cf. Is 26:19." The NAB takes the Hebrew underlying the Greek tōn tethnēkotōn to be, not mêtê "dead," but m$^e$tê "the few of Israel" (cf. Isa 41:14: [New International Version] "O little Israel"; [Luther] *"du armer Haufe Israel"*).

108. References like 1QH 6.29-30, that the sons of truth "shall awake and the sons of iniquity shall be no more" (cf.6.34), or 7.31, the sons of truth shall be established before God for ever (cf.11.12-14), may simply be metaphors for deliverance from dangers. Belief in immortality and/or resurrection seems to be absent. So Helmer Ringgren, *The Faith of Qumran* (Philadelphia: Fortress, 1963) 148-51; ER 12:346; H. Braun, *Qumran und das Neue Testament* (Tübingen:Mohr [Siebeck], 1966) 2270-72; Kremer, *Resurrectio*, 61-63 (n. 102 above); Stemberger, *TRE* 4 (1979) 447.

109. Cf. David Winston, *The Wisdom of Solomon* (AB 43; Garden City: Doubleday 1979) 25-33 and 125-27 (further references) on "the souls of the just" and "immortality"; this book in the Apocrypha, likely first century B.C., reflects a new emphasis in Jewish sources on a preexistent and immortal soul; cf.2:23-3:9, Kremer, *Resurrectio*, 71-76 (n. 102 above).

110. See esp. F. Mussner, in Concilium 60:46-53 (n. 102 above); P. Hoffmann, *TRE* 4 (1979) 452-54 (n. 102 above); Perkins, *Resurrection*, 71-112 (n. 102 above); today we distinguish "levels of meaning"—the evangelist, the source, and Jesus, respectively—Christians until the nineteenth century by and large took all gospel accounts as historical fact, on the "Jesus level."

111. B. van Iersel, in *Concilium* 60:54-67 (n. 102 above); *NIDNTT* 3:276-77, 281-302 (n. 102 above); Perkins, *Resurrection*, 113-292 (n. 102 above); E. Käsemann, "The Beginnings of Christian Theology," *New Testament Questions of Today* (Philadelphia: Fortress, 1969) 82-107 ("in post-Easter apocalyptic" there was "a new theological start," 102).

112. See the examples wrought by Elijah (1 Kings 17:17-24), Elisha (2 Kings 4:18-37), Jesus (Mark 5:35-43; John 11) or the apostles (Acts 9:36-42;20:9-12).

113. Examples: "make alive" (*zōopoieō*) John 5:21; Rom. 8:11; 1 Pet 3:18; "live" (*zaō*), Rom 14:9 RSV "Christ died and lived again"; 2 Cor 13:4; John 6:51 "live forever"; Rom 1:17, the person who is "righteous by faith will have life." In addition to the older articles in the *TDNT* on all these terms, see also J. Kremer, *"anastasis*, etc." and *"egeirō"* in *EWNT* 1 (1980) 210-21 and 899-910. 114. Kremer, *Resurrectio*, 42 (n. 102 above).

114. Kremer, *Resurrectio*, 42 (n. 102 above).

115. Ibid. 43-50 on these letters and the rest of the New Testament. The later (deutero-) Pauline writings incline more to the present side of redemption, but even here the future aspect of fulfillment when Christ comes is not lost (Col 33:1-4; Eph 2:5-6, cf. 1:13-14, 4:30 and 6:11-15), though the emphasis is on "the presence of the future" in the church (cf. M. Barth, *Ephesians* [AB 34; Garden City: Doubleday, 1974] 115). The Pastoral Epistles emphasize more emphatically the future appearing of Christ (1 Tim 6:14; 2 Tim 1:18; 4:1, 8, yet *epiphaneia* is used also of Christ's past appearing, 1:10). In Hebrews, resurrection of the dead is regarded as one of the "elementary doctrines" (6:2), already known to Abraham (11:19) and to women in the Elijah, Elisha, and Maccabees stories (11:35). In John "eternal life," as is well known, becomes a present gift (e.g., 5:24-27, cf. 3:15-16), but the future aspect at the resurrection of the dead is preserved in the final form of the Fourth Gospel (e.g., 5:28-29; 6:39-40). Luke uses Jesus' resurrection to ground a teaching for his Gentile audience about the general resurrection (cf. Acts 26:23; 5:31; 3:15), in contrast to the Jewish, Pharisaic expectation of a general resurrection as the initial, significant exemplar (cf. P. Hoffmann, *TRE* 4 [1979] 463-64 [n. 102 above]; Kegel, *Auferstehung Jesu*, 81-100 [n. 102 above]).

116. Ibid 464; E. Earle Ellis, *Eschatology in Luke* (Facet Books. Biblical Series 30: Philadelphia: Fortress, 1972) 9 n. 16.

117. See Acts 10:42;24:15; John 5:28-29; cf. also vv. 24 and 27; Matt 19:28; 25:31-46; Heb 9:27.

118. Cf. the literature cited in n.102, especially in *The Encyclopedia of the Lutheran Church;* Concilium 60; Perkins; and Kremer, *Resurrectio.*

119. In addition to references cited above, see also 2 Esdras 7:88-89 ("when they shall be separated from their mortal body," v. 88; "they hasten to behold the face of" God, v.98), and the martyr Eleazer in 4 Macc 7:13, 19. Jesus' words to the Sadducees suggest the patriarchs were each already alive and with God (Mark 12:18-27 par.).

120. See also Isa 26:19 in the context of 26:1 and 27:1, 2, and 6. For Paul, see 1 Cor 15:23-28, 49-55; 2 Cor 4:14; Phil 3:20-21. Further, Col 3:3-4, Eph 4:30; John 5:28-29; 6:39, 40, 44, 54; 1 John 3:2.

121. If, as the Hebrew Scriptures say, the Lord "kills and brings to life" or "brings down to Sheol and raises up," God may then do this already in one's present existence; cf. Deut 5:2-3; Ps 68:20; or passages where God's kingship is regarded as already in place over all the world (Ps 47); perhaps also 2 Macc 7:36. The connection may be made via conversion, faith, or baptism: now the person "lives".

122. For Paul, see Rom 6:4; 8:1, 11; 2 Cor 5:15, 17. Cf. further Col 2:11-13; 3:1-2, 4.

123. Cf. Kremer, *Resurrectio*, 158-61 (n. 102 above): The New Testament provides no basis for notions of a bodiless soul or an immortal soul (159, 161, and passim). See also P. Benoit, "Resurrection: At the End of Time or Immediately after Death?" *Concilium* 60:103-14 (n. 102 above). T. Francis Glasson, *Greek Influence in Jewish Eschatology* (SPCK Biblical Monographs 1: London: SPCK, 1961),1 argued however, for reincarnation as well as immortality of the soul as a Greek influence in Jewish apocalypses and pseudepigraphs (28-32, 38-45, 82-83).

Though the idea of an "immortal soul" and the expression *psyche athanatos* appear in Greek literature as early as Plato (*Phaedo* 28 [80b]; *Meno* 81b; Ep. 7 [335a]), the expression occurs in the LXX only in the apocryphal 4 Macc 14:6 and possibly 18:23 (with a variant in ms. S). It is not found in the New Testament. *Athanasia*, "immortality," begins to surface in the deutero-canonical Book of Wisdom (3:4; 4:1; 8:13, 17; 15:3) and in the apocryphal 4 Macc (14:5; 16:13)—along with a denial of it: "a son of man is not immortal" (Sir 17:30). In 1 Cor 15:53-54, "What is mortal" (*to thnēton*) is said to "don immortality" (*endysasthai athanasian*), "at the last trumpet," when "the dead will be raised imperishable," but it is not stated how this is to be understood.

124. In Matt 10:28 Jesus warns his disciples about persecution: "Do not fear those who kill the body, but cannot kill the soul; fear rather him who can destroy both soul and body in gehenna." Apropos of this saying, three things should be noted.

(1) Scholars usually view it as derived from "Q," and its Lucan form runs: "To you my friends I say, Do not fear those who kill the body and afterward can do no more. I shall show you whom you should fear: Fear him who after killing has authority to hurl you into gehenna" (12:4-5). Though M.J. Lagrange (*Evangile selon Saint Matthieu* [3d ed; Paris: Gabalda, 1927] 208) regards the phrase "kill the soul" as "surely original"; the Hellenistic dualism of *sōma* and *psychē* would argue against its originality. Matthew, who uses it also in 6:25, has adopted the distinction here (so J.P. Meier, *Matthew* [New Testament Monographs 3: Wilmington: Glazier, 1980] 112), possibly under the influence of the Hellenistic synagogue (W. Grundmann, *Das Evangelium nach Matthäus* [Theologischer Handkommentar zum Neuen Testament 1;5th ed.; Berlin: Evangelische Verlagsanstalt, 1981] 297).

(2) "Fear rather him who can destroy both soul and body in gehenna" (10:28b) is to be understood neither of Satan or the Evil One (so Meier, ibid.; K. Stendahl, "Matthew," *Peake's Commentary on the Bible* [ed. M. Black and H.H. Rowley; London: Nelson, 1962] 783) nor of an avenging angel (Rev 9:11), but of God himself, as did many church fathers and as do the majority of modern commentators (Allen [see below, n.124,§3]; John C. Fenton, *The Gospel of St. Matthew* [Baltimore: Penguin Books, 1963]; Floyd V. Filson, *A Commentary on the Gospel according to St. Matthew* [Black's New Testament Commentary; 2d ed.; London: A. & C. Black, 1971]; M.J. Lagrange [see above, n. 124, §1]; Leopold Sabourin, *The Gospel According to St. Matthew* [2 vols.; Bandra (Bombay, India): St. Paul Publications, 1962]; Eduard Schweizer, *The Good News according to Matthew* [tr. D.E. Green; Atlanta: Knox, 1975];

Wansbrough [see below, n. 124, §3]). Disciples sent forth to preach the gospel are not to fear human persecutors, but rather God himself, who can subject the whole person of the faithless disciple to the destruction of gehenna.

(3) Commentators disagree about whether 10:28a adopts the "Hellenistic" distinction between body and soul not present in the Lucan parallel. Among those who find the Hellenistic position in this text are J.L. McKenzie (*JBC* 43:70, "unusual in the NT"), Benedict Viviano (*NJBC* 42:70, "seems Hellenistic"). and J. Meier (*Matthew*, 112). These commentators do not deny that in 10:28a, "the seeming opposition is between the body and the whole person (*nepes*, translated into Gr.*psuche*)" (H.Wansbrough, "St. Matthew," *New Catholic Commentary on Holy Scripture* [ed. R.C. Fuller *et al*; London: Nelson, 1969]). Cf.*NJBC* 33:12, 13,28, and 77:66. Hence the sense of "life" is preferred by some for *psychē*, as at Luke 21:19 (RSV, JB) on the grounds that it is "dangerous…for the understanding of Old Testament psychology to translate *nepes* as 'soul' *tout court*. First and foremost the word means 'life,'…*life bound up with a body*" (W. Eichrodt, *Theology of the Old Testament* [Philadelphia: Westminster, 1967] 2:135). Indeed according to E. Schweizer ("*Psychē*…,"*TWNT* 9 [1937] 645;*TDNT* 9 [1974] 646), "the reference to God's power to destroy the *psychē* and *sōma* in Hades is opposed to the idea of the immortality of the soul." Though BAGD (893) lists Matt 10:28 under *psychē* meaning "the soul as seat and center of life that transcends the earthly," it comments further: "Men cannot injure it, but God can hand it over to destruction." A classic commentator, W.C. Allen, paraphrases: "'In your work of making my teaching public you will meet with persecution. Fear not physical death. But fear the wrath of God against unfaithfulness to Him, for He can destroy soul and body together in Gehenna'" (*A Critical and Exegetical Commentary on the Gospel according to S. Matthew* [International Critical Commentary; New York: Scribner, 1907] 109).

Once the idea of *psychē athanatos* became rooted in the Christian tradition, the Matthean phrase "cannot kill the soul" was explained in terms of that idea. Indeed, it may be a legitimate conclusion from that Matthean phrase, but it is not yet explicit in Matt 10:28. Since we are dealing with texts that are on the borderline between the implicit and the formal expression of the "immortality of the soul," there is the danger of reading back into the Matthean formulation an interpretation that eventually enters the tradition. It is precisely this borderline situation that commentators on Matthew have been trying to respect.

125. For further treatment see the study prepared previously for this dialogue, *Mary in the New Testament: A Collaborative Assessment by Protestant and Roman Catholic Scholars* (ed. R.E. Brown, K.P. Donfried, J.A. Fitzmyer, and J. Reumann; Philadelphia: Fortress, New York. Paulist, 1978).

126. The technique is sometimes called "sandwiching," to begin one story, tell another, and then return to the first one. See further 4:21-22 (4:23) 4:24-25; 5:21-24 (5:25-34) 5:35-43; 6:6b-13 (6:14-29) 6:30-34; 11:2-14 (11:15-19) 11:20-21; 14:53-54 (14:55-65) 14:66-72. Others speak of a chiastic structure in 3:20-35; see John McHugh, *The Mother of Jesus in the New Testament* (Garden City: Doubleday, 1975) 235-39, especially n.3. See further Rudolf Pesch, *Das Markusevangelium, I. Teil* (Herders Theologischer Kommentar zum Neuen Testament II/I; Freiburg: Herder, 1976) 209-25, esp. n.4.

127. Instead of *akousantes hoi par autou*, "his own having heard" (3:21), mss. D and W and the Old Latin version read rather *akousantes peri autou hoi grammateis kai hoi loipoi*, "the scribes and the others, hearing about him, came out…" But this reading cannot be preferred to that of the best Greek mss. (used above) since it is clearly the correction of a later Christian copyist who sought to tone down the pejorative connotation of v. 21 ("He is beside himself") and to dissociate Jesus' family (mother and brothers) from it.

128. See 6:6b-8:21; 8:23-33; 9:32-37; 10:35-45. E. Best, *Disciples and Discipleship: Studies in the Gospel according to Mark* (Edinburgh: Clark, 1986); cf. *Following Jesus: Discipleship in the Gospel of Mark* (Journal for the Study of the New Testament, Supplement 4; Sheffield: Journal for the Study of the Old Testament, 1981). Other commentators interpret Mary in Mark's Gospel in more positive terms.

129. *Mary in the NT*, 241-82. See CS §§162, 164.

## II. From the Second to the Sixteenth Century

130. E.g., Robin Lane Fox, *Pagans and Christians* (New York: Knopf, 1987); R.A. Markus, *Christianity in the Roman World* (London: Scribner, 1974); S. Benko and J.J. O'Rourke, (eds.,) *The Catacombs and the Colosseum* (Valley Forge: Judson Press, 1971)l; with reference to the cult of saints: Peter Brown, *The Cult of the Saints: Its Rise and Function in Latin Christianity* (Chicago: Chicago University Press, 1981). Relevant work is carried on by the Franz-Josef-Dölger Institute for the Study of Early Christianity at the University of Bonn under whose auspices one of the major tools in the field is being published: *Reallexikon für Antike und Christentum* (ed. by T. Klauser *et al.*; vol. 1-13 ["Heilgötter"]; Stuttgart: Hiersemann, 1950-1986).

131. See H. Koester, *Introduction to the New Testament History, Culture, and Religion of the Hellenistic Age* (Philadelphia: Fortress, 1982) 1:32-36 and 366-71.

132. The degree of Christian borrowing, and especially the evaluation of the phenomenon as licit or illicit, is much debated. Robert Eno, *St. Augustine and the Saints* (The Saint Augustine Lecture for 1985; Philadelphia: Villanova University Press, 1989) 1-10, surveys the scholarly debate about the roots of the Christian devotion to the saints since Lucius and Anrich. His summary remarks emphasize that, while being much closer to each other today in their assessment of the literary and archeological evidence, Protestant and Catholic scholars still view the same phenomena with a different agenda in mind and with very different value judgments.

133. Greek-English in *The Apostolic Fathers* (LCL; ed. and tr. K. Lake; London: Heinemann: Cambridge: Harvard University Press, 1965 [1913]) 2:6-305. The subject of mediating powers in the Shepherd is discussed by J. Danielou, *The Theology of Jewish Christianity* (Philadelphia: Westminster, 1964) 37-38; 119-27, esp. 122 (Sim. 9.12:7-8, the son as sole Mediator, in "an attack on the cult of angels"), and 125 (Michael the Word); cf. Test. Div. 6.2 "the angel that intercedes for you, for he is a mediation between God and man." Cf. also H. Moxnes, "God and His Angel in the Shepherd of Hermas," *Studia Theologica* (Oslo) 28 (1974) 49-56.

134. Acts 17:32; Acts of Paul and Thecla 5, 12, 14; III Cor 24; Martyrdom of Paul 2, 4; Acts of Peter 7-8. See *New Testament Apocrypha* (ed. W. Schneemelcher; English ed. R. McL. Wilson; Philadelphia: Westminster, 1963-64) 2:354, 356, 35;376; 384; 288-90.

135. W.C. Van Unnik, "The Newly Discovered Gnostic 'Epistle to Rheginos' on the Resurrection," *Journal of Ecclesiastical History* 15 (1964) 141-52; 153-67; esp. 141-43; 153-55; Perkins, *Resurrection*, 331-90 (n. 102 above).

136. Eusebius, *Church History* 6.37. Origen discusses the topic in his "Dialogue with Heraclides," which was discovered among the Toura papyri in 1941; English translation: *Alexandrian Christianity* (Library of Christian Classics; tr. J.E.C. Oulton and H. Chadwick; Philadelphia: Westminster, 1954) 2:437-55. The discussion focuses here on the interpretation of Lev 17:11; Deu 12:23; and Luke 23:46.

137. DS 403-11.

138. Acts of the Scillitan Martyrs 15 (ed. H. Musurillo [see below, note 145] 86-89); Tertullian, *De resurrectione* 23; Cyprian, *Epist* 31:3; Ps. Cyprian, *De laude martyrii* 14. See Eno, *St. Augustine* 11; 16-17 (n. 132 above).

139. See Eno, ibid. 20-24.

140. Eno, ibid., 25-27. Many of these practices are described in the *Carmina natalicia* celebrating St. Felix, the patron saint of Nola, written in 410/30 by Paulinus of Nola. See Eno, ibid., 29-35.

141. Smyrn 1:1;l Trall 9:1; Eph 7:2; 18:2; 19:1.

142. English translation: *New Testament Apocrypha*, 1:370-88 (see n. 134 above); M. R. James, *The Apocryphal New Testament* (Oxford: Clarendon, 1953) 38-49. Commentary: H.R. Smid, *Protevangelium Jacobi, A Commentary* (Assen: Van Gorcum, 1963). See also *Mary in the New Testament*, 247-49; 258-61.

143. Cf. the apocryphal Apocalypses of Peter, Paul, John, James, and the "Questions of Bartholomew," as well as several Gnostic writings found among the Nag Hammadi codices. James, *The Apocryphal New Testament* 563-64 (n. 142 above), reports on two forms of an

Apocalypse of Mary; on these and other Marian apocalypses, see A. Wenger, "Marie, mère de miséricorde; les apocalypses de la Vierge," in *Maria, Etudes sur la sainte Vierge* (ed. H. du Manoir; Paris, 1961) 5:956-62. On the traditions concerning Christ's decent into hell, see E. Koch, "Höllenfahrt Christi," *TRE* 15 (1986) 455-61 (bibliography).

144. Erwin Preuschen, *Analecta: Kürzere Texte zur Geschichte der Alten Kirche und des Kanons.* 2: *Zur Kanonsgeschichte* (2d ed. Tübingen: Mohr, 1910) 59 no, 15: "Liber de natiuitate saluatoris et de Maria uel obstetrice, apocryphus, "*New Testament Apocrypha* 1:22 (see n. 134 above); see also Jerome's sharp criticism: *Adversus Helvidium* 8(PL 23:192).

145. "Acts" or "Deeds" of the Martyrs constituted a literary genre in which the suffering and triumph of the Christian martyrs were told in a form suitable for congregational reading. Such "Acts" were often based on court records, eyewitness reports, and other contemporary sources. The standard edition by H. Musurillo, *The Acts of the Christian Martyrs* (Oxford: Clarendon Press, 1972), gives texts and English translations of twenty-eight such documents from the second and third centuries.

146. Origen, *On Prayer* 11.1. A prayer to the three young men in the fiery furnace found in Hippolytus's *Commentary on Daniel*, II. 30 (GCS Hippolyt 1; ed. N. Bonwetsch and H. Achelis; Leipzig: Hinrich, 1897) 98:21-22, is sometimes regarded as the first literary instance of an "invocation" of saints; see Eno, *St. Augustine*, 20-25 (n. 132 above).

147. Justin Martyr, *Dialogue with Trypho the Jew* 100.4f. *Die altesten christlichen Apologeten* (ed. E.J. Goodspeed; Göttingen: Vandenhoeck & Ruprecht, 1914) 215; Irenaeus, *Adversus Haereses* III.22.4; 32:1; V.19.l; *Demonstr.*33; cf. Tertullian, *De carne Christi* 7. A sentence in the *Epistle to Diognetus* 12:7 is sometimes thought to be the first occurrence of the theme: "Then Eve is not seduced, and the virgin is trusted," but the date of the writing is uncertain (*Mary in the New Testament*, 255, notes 563-64). On the comparison between Eve and Mary and the theme of the "New Eve" in patristic times, see W. Burghardt, in: *Mariology* (ed. J.B. Carol; Milwaukee: Bruce) 1(1955) 110-17; 2(1957) 88-100

148. Jerome, *Epistula* 22.21 (CSEL 154:173), quoted in LG 56, note 180. The Early Syrian tradition seems to have been particularly fond of this theme; see R. Murray, "Mary the Second Eve in the Early Syrian Fathers," *Eastern Churches Quarterly* 3 (1970-71) 372-95.

149. C.O.D. 39:2; 48:1; cf.DS 252. While the church historian Socrates (early fifth century) says that Origen already used the term *Theotokos* (7.32), and a fragment of Hippolytus (c. A.D. 220) has been adduced for its earlier occurrence (H. Rahner, "Hippolyt von Rom als Zeuge fur den Ausdruck *Theotokos*," *Zeitschrift fur katholische Theologie* 59 [1935] 73-81; cf. also H. Vorgrimler, "*Theotokos,*" *LThK* [2d ed.; Freiburg: Herder, 1965] 10:95), the first undisputed literary occurrence is in the letter of Bishop Alexander of Alexandria to Alexander of Thessalonica 1.12 (GCS 44 [19] 23; PG 18: 568C), written in A.D. 324; cf. also n. 156 below.

150. The earliest literary and archeological evidence for churches dedicated to the Virgin Mary in Palestine and Constantinople is discussed by M. Jugie, *La mort* (see n. 152 below), 89-95. According to contemporary sources, the Council of 431 met in the main church of the city which was named after "John the Theologian" and: "the Virgin *Theotokos*, Saint Mary"; it is not known whether this designation was in use prior to the Council or was result of it (Jugie, 96-98 [n.152 below]).

151. On these traditions, see *Mary in the New Testament*, 267-78; R. Eno ("Mary and Her Role in Patristic Theology," L/RC 8:pp. 159-76) discusses the evidence for dissenting opinions in Origen and Tertullian.

152. See W. Burghardt, *The Testimony of the Patristic Age Concerning Mary's Death* (Westminster MD: Newman, 1957). The most comprehensive treatment of this question is found in the historical part of M. Jugie's book, *La mort et l'Assomption de la Sainte Vierge: Etude historico-doctrinale* (Studi e Testi 114; Vatican City: Biblioteca Apostolica Vaticana, 1944), which contributed significantly to the papal decision to define the dogma of the Assumption in 1950. The suggestion of a violent death was put forward as a possibility by Epiphanius, *Panarion* 78.11 (PG 42:716) on the basis of the mention of the "sword" in Luke 2:35; it was explicitly rejected by Ambrose, *Commentary on the Gospel of Luke* 11.61. For a brief report on the modern controversy about Mary's death in connection with the papal definition, see Michael O'Carroll, *Theotokos* (rev. ed.; Wilmington DE: Glazier, 1983) 17-118 ("Death of Mary").

153. The most common delay is three days, but the Coptic and Ethiopic tradition also reckons with a much longer time span. For an informative survey of the *"transitus"* literature, see the article on "Assumption Apocrypha" in O'Carroll, *Theotokos*, 58-61 (with literature) (n. 152 above).

154. "Anaphora Syriaca XII Apostolorum," *Anaphorae Syriacae* (ed. A. Raes; Vatican City: Pontifical Institute of Oriental Studies, 1939-44) 222. G. Frenaut, "De intercessione B.V. Mariae in Canone Missae Romanae et in Anaphoris Liturgiarum Orientalium ante VII saec.," in *De primordiis cultus mariani. Acta congressus mariologici-mariani in Lusitania anno 1967 celebrati* (Rome: Academia Mariana Internationalis, 1970) 2:459-62, interpreted this instance as "invocation." On Mary in early Syrian poetry see K. McVey, Introduction to *Ephrem the Syrian; Hymns* (Classics of Western Spirituality; New York: Paulist Press, 1989) 30-34.

155. For a survey of the development of Marian feasts in the early and medieval church, see O'Carroll, *Theotokos*, 220-24 (n. 152 above). Also K. McDonnell, "The Marian Liturgical Tradition," L/RC 8: pp.177-91.

156. "God-bearer, [hear] my supplications; do not allow us [to be] in adversity, but deliver us from danger. Thou alone..." The text is found on a papyrus fragment now in the John Rylands Library in Manchester and first published in 1938. On the debate concerning the date, see O. Stegmüller, "Sub Tuum Praesidium. Bemerkungen zur ältesten Uberlieferung," *Zeitschrift für katholische Theologie* 74 (1952) 76-82.

157. On the options in interpreting the meaning of the phrase "communion of *sancti/sancta,*' see J.P. Kirsch, *The Doctrine of the Communion of Saints in the Ancient Church* (London: Sands, 1910); A. Michel, "La communion des saints," *Doctor Communis* 9 (1956) 1-125. Sharply critical of the tendency to minimize the difference: Ernst Wolf, "Sanctorum Communio. Erwägungen zur Romantisierung des Kirchenbegriffs," *Peregrinatio* (2d ed.; Munich: Kaiser, 1962) 1:279-301.

158. As a title for Mary, the term seems to occur for the first time in Origen's *Homilies on the Gospel of Luke*, Hom. 6 and 7 (GCS 35, Origenes Bd. 9; ed. M. Rauer, 1930) 44 and 50. It was generally accepted in Byzantine theology from the sixth century on. See W. Burghardt, "Our Lady's Holiness," in *Mariology*, 2:125-139 (n. 147 above).

159. Augustine, *De natura et gratia* 36.42 (CSEL 60:263f.); but cf. *Opus imperfectum contra Iulianum* 4.122 (PL 45:1418). See also Ch. Boyer, "La controverse sur l'opinion de s. Augustin touchant la conception de la Vierge," in: Virgo *Immaculata, Acta congressus mariologici-mariani, Romae anno 1954 celebrati* (Rome: Academia Mariana Internationalis, 1955) 4:48-60. Eno ("Mary and Her Role in Patristic Theology," L/RC 8: pp.159-76") is more cautious in his conclusions.

160. Veneramini martyres,...Deum martyrum colite" *Sermo* 273.9 (PL 38:1252B). For other texts see Eno, *St. Augustine and the Saints*, 29-48 (n. 132 above).

161. See Guy Lapointe, *La célébration des martyrs en Afrique d'après les sermons de saint Augustin* (Cahiers de communauté chrétienne 8; Montreal: Communauté chrétienne, 1972).

162. The central texts come from the later works: *Enchiridion* 18.68-69; *De civitate Dei* 21.26f. Augustine, however, polemicized in these instances against the notion that there is *only* a purgatorial, that is, a temporary fire and not also an eternal one. To him such a Christian "universalism" seemed dangerous because it might lead to a lack of pious zeal in this life. On the development of Augustine's thought on this theme and earlier notions of a cleansing fire, see R. Eno, "The Fathers and the Cleansing Fire," *Irish Theological Quarterly* 53 (1987) 184-202. Jacques Le Goff, *The Birth of Purgatory* (Chicago: Chicago University Press, 1984) 62-85, quotes the relevant passages at length. See also below, n. 196.

163. *De civitate Dei* 22.10. The theme became prominent with the arrival of the relics of St. Stephen at Hippo: cf. Eno, *St. Augustin* (n. 132 above) 74-82. On the miracles connected with the discovery of the bones of Saints Gervase and Protase at Milan, see the *Confessiones* 9.7.16.

164. *Vita sancti Ambrosii* 10.48-11.56 (ed. Sister M.S. Kaniecka; Patristic Studies 16; Washington DC: Catholic University Press, 1928) 93-101.

165. *De civitate Dei* 20.9 and 13.

166. Gregory the Great, *Dialogues* 4.29.1; 45.1-2 (SC 265; ed. de Vogue and Antin; Paris: Cerf, 1980) 99; 169-71. Also *Moralia in Job*, 9.98 (CCL, 143; Turnhout: Brepols, 1979) 526-27.

167. Gregory the Great, *Dialogues* 4.40 .13; 41.3-4; 57.1-17 (SC 265:147, 149, 185-95). Regarding Gregory's views on the afterlife see G.R. Evans, *The Thought of Gregory the Great* (Cambridge, England: Cambridge University Press, 1986) 13-15; Le Goff (above, note 162), 88-95.

168. A well-known text is the *megalynarion*, a brief praise of Mary sung by the choir in the Divine Liturgy after the censing of the gifts and elsewhere: "More honorable than the cherubim and infinitely more glorious than the seraphim, who didst bear the Word of God without stain, true *Theotokos*, we magnify Thee" (Isabel F. Hapgood, *Service Book* [5th ed.; Englewood, NJ: Antiochian Orthodox Christian Archdiocese of New York and All North America, 1975] 14; 108).

169. J. Pelikan, *The Growth of Medieval Theology* (600-1300) (The Christian Tradition 3; Chicago: Chicago University Press, 1978) 116-19 and 133-44.

170. See A.E. McGrath, *Iustitia Dei: A History of the Christian Doctrine of Justification. 1. Beginnings to 1500* (Cambridge, England: Cambridge University Press, 1986) 74f., who refers to the discovery of this curious fact by H. Bouillard, *Conversion et grâce chez S. Thomas d'Aquin* (Paris: Aubier, 1944) 90-133.

171. The revision was undertaken at Vivarium in the sixth century by Cassiodorus and his pupils. It was known under the names of Jerome (*PL* 30:669-746) and, in a different version, Primasius of Hadrumetum (*PL* 68:413-686).

172. Th. Zwoelfer, *Sankt Peter, Apostelfürst und Himmelspförtner: Seine Verehrung bei den Angelsachsen und Franken* (Stuttgart: Kohlhammer, 1929); J. van den Bosch, *Capa, basilica, monasterium et le culte de Saint Martin de Tours* (Nijmegen: Dekker & Van de Vegt, 1959).

173. Rupert of Deutz interpreted Jesus' word, "O woman, what have you to do with me?" (v.4), as a rebuke of the mother who did not yet understand. The patristic precedents are described in A. Smitmans, *Das Weinwunder von Kana* (Beiträge zur Geschichte der biblischen Exegese 6; Tubingen: Mohr, 1966) 97-124.

174. On Anselm's Mariology, see J. Bruder, *The Mariology of St. Anselm of Canterbury* (Dayton OH: Mount St. John's Press, 1939), and several articles in the work: *De cultu Mariano saeculi VI-XI. Acta congressus mariologici-mariani in Croatia anno 1971 celebrati* (Rome: Academia Mariana Internationalis, 1972) 3:597-664. The Cathedral of Chartres housed a celebrated Marian relic, the tunic of the Virgin, which had been given to the bishop by King Charles the Bald (840-77).

175. DS 600-603; C.O.D. 111-13.

176. See H.G. Thummel, "Builder, V.l. Byzanz," *TRE* 6 (1980) 532.

177. The text of the *Libri Carolini* is found in the *Monumenta Germaniae Historica, Legum Sectio III, Concilia II, Supplementum* (ed. H. Bastgen; Hannover and Leipzig: Hahnsche Buchhandlung, 1924); the two letters of Gregory the Great to Serenus of Marseille in: *Gregorii Magni Registrum Epistularum Libri VII-XIV* (CCL 140A; ed.D. Norberg; Turnhout: Brepols, 1982), 768 (9.209) and 873-76 (11.10). See K. Froehlich, "The *Libri Carolini* and the Lessons of the Iconoclastic Controversy," L/RC 8: pp. 193-208.

178. This accusation was probably grounded in a faulty Latin translation of the original Greek terms employed at Nicaea II.

179. Agobard of Lyon, *Liber de imaginibus sanctorum* (PL 104:199-228). Agobard's central point is that, whatever they represent, pictures and statues are only the works of human hands. Claudius, a Spaniard who became bishop of Turin, rejected the cult of relics and the invocation of saints as well as the veneration of images; his *Apologeticum atque rescriptum adversus Theodemirum abbatem,* written in 823, is known chiefly through long quotations in a refutation by Jonas of Orleans, *De cultu imaginum* (PL 106:306-88); the beginning of Claudius's book is in PL 104:615-20. The attitude of the Frankish theologians was not unlike that of many of the Protestant reformers.

180. Already Hadrian I (772-795) formally endorsed Nicaea II, rejecting the doctrine of the *Libri Carolini: Epistola ad Carolum Regem de imaginibus* (PL 98:1247-92). This attitude prevailed under his successors as well; none of them showed sympathy for the Frankish theologians. On the attitudes of Eugenius II, Nicholas I, and especially John VIII, see G. Haendler,

*Epochen karolingischer Theologie* (Theologishe Arbeiten 10; Berlin: Evangelische Verlagsanstalt, 1958).

181. K. McDonnell, "The Liturgical Veneration of the Saints. A Note" (unpublished). See also R. Kieckhefer, "Major Currents in Late Medieval Devotion," *Christian Spirituality, High Middle Ages and Reformation* (ed. J.Raitt; New York: Crossroad, 1987) 93-96; Patrick Geary, *Furta Sacra: Thefts of Relics in the Central Middle Ages* (Princeton: Princeton University Press, 1978).

182. See, e.g., the collection of Marian poetry made by Alphonsus X the Wise, King of Castile and Leon, *Cantigas de Maria*, on the model of the popular *Cantigas de amiga* that were sung by the troubadours. The collection contains more than four hundred *cantigas* for the Virgin; these are of two kinds: some forty *cantigas de loor* (of praise), all the others being *cantigas de miragros* (of miracles). See P. Droncke, *The Medieval Lyric* (2d ed.; New York: Cambridge University Press, 1977) 70-72.

183. Elizabeth Johnson, "Marian Devotion in the Western Church," *Christian Spirituality*, 392-414 (n. 181 above).

184. On the emergence of the important collections of Marian miracles, see Benedicta Ward, *Miracles and Medieval Mind* (Philadelphia: University of Pennsylvania Press, 1982) 132-65.

185. See K. McDonnell, "The Liturgical Veneration of the Saints, A Note," and "Extended Memo on the Veneration of the Saints" (unpublished).

186. Elizabeth Johnson (n.183 above); see the prayer of St. Francis of Assisi in G. Tavard, *The Forthbringer of God. St. Bonaventure on the Virgin Mary* (Chicago: Franciscan Herald Press, 1989) 149-50. Theologians often invented new Marian titles; Alan of Lille invoked Mary, among other titles, *virtutum gazophylacium*, "treasure-keeper of the virtues" (*In Cantica Canticorum elucidatio*, PL 210:53). Enthusiastic Marian titles abound in the sermons of St. Bonaventure.

187. Elizabeth Johnson, 403 (n. 183 above).

188. Among the first commentators who identified Mary as the bride of the Son of Songs were Rupert of Deutz (d.1130), *In Cantica Canticorum de incarnatione Domini commentarium* (PL 168:839-962), and Alan of Lille (PL 210:51-110). According to Alan the Song refers *specialiter et spiritualiter* to the church, *specialissime et spiritualissime* to the glorious Virgin (PL 210:53). In the fifteenth century Dionysius the Carthusian (d. 1471) explained in his *Enarratio in Cantica Canticorum Salomonis* that each verse of the Song of Songs refers to the bridegroom's *sponsa generalis*, which is the church, to his *sponsa specialis*, which is the faithful soul, and to his *sponsa singularis*, the Virgin Mary. A detailed account of the new mariological commentaries is given by H. Riedlinger, *Die Makellosigkeit der Kirche in den lateinischen Hoheliedkommentaren des Mittelalters* (Beiträge zur Geschichte der Philosphie und Theologie des Mittelalters 38.3; Münster: Aschendorff, 1958) 202-33.

189. Quoted by Elizabeth Johnson, 408 (n. 183 above).

190. "Virgo de cuius utero quasi de quodam diuinitatis oceano rivi et flumina emanabant omnium gratiarum,:" St. Bernardine of Siena, *Sermo* 61.8, *Opera Omnia* (Quaracchi: Collegia S. Bonaventura, 1950) 2:378.

191. John Johnson, "Anselm on the Virgin Birth. A Reflection on Mary" (unpublished).

192. Elizabeth Johnson, 397 (n. 183 above).

193. Tavard, "Bonaventure" (n. 186 above).

194. He agreed with [Ps.] Augustine that the Assumption can be reasonably argued even though it cannot be derived from Scripture: *S.T.* III, q.27, a.i,c; on the Immaculate Conception: a.2.

195. That the soul is the "form" of the body was even the object of a decree at the Council of Vienne in 1312; the opposite opinion was declared to be heretical (DS 902; C.O.D. 336-37). This declaration was solemnly repeated by the Fifth Lateran Council in 1513 (DS 1440; C.O.D., 581). Albert Lang, in his study, "Der Bedeutungswandel der Begriffe 'fides' und 'haeresis' und die dogmatische Wertung der Konzilsentscheidungen von Vienne und Trient," *Münchener Theologische Zeitschrift* 4 (1953) 133-46, shows that medieval councils did not use terms such as "de fide," "anathema," "heretical" in the sense of a dogmatic definition as understood after the First Vatican Council.

196. In his *Vita Odilonis* St. Peter Damian records that Abbot Odilo of Cluny (962-1049) ordered all Cluniac monks to devote November 2, the day after the feast of All Saints, to prayers for the dead; this was done around 1030 at the request of a hermit in Sicily who had told the abbot that he could hear the cries of the souls being tormented in a nearby volcano (PL 144:935-37); from Cluny the custom spread to the whole Western church. There were antecedents. Amalarius of Metz had devoted three chapters of his *De ecclesiasticis officiis libri* IV to the liturgical care of the dead (Book II,2 ch. 44: *De missa pro mortuis* [PL 105:1161-64]; Book IV, ch. 41: *De exsequiis mortuorum* [PL 105:1236-38]; ch. 42: *De officiis mortuorum* [PL 105:1238-40]). Among other points he explained that it is proper *orare et sacrificare pro mortuis* every day, but especially on the third day (for the three aspects of the soul: *ex toto corde, ex toto anima, et ex toto virtutue*), on the seventh (for the four elements of the body, three plus four being seven), and on the thirtieth (for this is the end of the month and the month represents *curriculum praesentis vitae, ut ex statu lunae facile dignoscitur*) [PL 105:1162]; in this way Gregory the Great's series of thirty Masses for the deceased was justified. A liturgical commemoration of all the dead is featured in many places in the ninth and tenth centuries, though at varying dates in the calendar (*Dictionnaire d'Archéologie et de Liturgie* [Paris: Letouzey, 1953] 15/2:2677-823). Peter Damian himself reports someone else's claim that Mount Vesuvius is one place where the souls are tormented by demons; popes and bishops are among them, notably Benedict (presumably Benedict VIII [1012-24], since Peter reports an alleged message from him addressed to his successor, John XIX [1024-32]). Some of these souls may be seen in the late afternoon on Saturdays in the shape of birds (*Opusculum XIX: De abdicatione episcopatus ad Nicolaum II; PL* 145:427-30).

197. The poem *Dies irae* was composed in Italy in the twelfth or thirteenth century; see Pierre Adnes, "Liturgie de la mort," in *Dictionnaire de Spiritualité* (Paris: Beauchesne, 1980) 10:1773-74. Numerous confraternities were devoted to preparing their members for a good death (Kieckhefer, 77 [n.181 above]). At the end of the Middle Ages, a new literary genre of "guides for dying" (*Ars Moriendi*) had considerable success. Much of its inspiration derived from the writings of the Paris chancellor Jean Gerson, especially his *Opus tripartitum de praeceptis decalogi, de confessione, et de arte moriendi, Opera Onmia* (2d ed.; ed. E.L. DuPin; Hagae Comitum: apud Petrum De Hondt, 1728) 425-30. See Mary Catherine O'Connor, *The Art of Dying Well: The Development of the Ars Moriendi* (Columbia Studies in English and Comparative Literature 156; New York; Columbia University Press, 1942).

198. The word, *purgatorius*, was first used as an adjective, with the meaning of "purgatorial, cleansing," in such expressions as *ignis purgatorius*; in the Profession of Faith of Emperor Michael Palaeologus it was equivalent to *catharterius* (καθαρτήριος): DS 856. In the neuter form, *purgatorium*, it was used later as a substantive, meaning "purgatory." The first use of the noun seems to go back to Odo of Soissons (d.1171) or Peter Comestor (d.1178/79) in a *Sermo* 85 formerly attributed to Hildebert of Mans (PL 171:739); see J. Le Goff, *The Birth of Purgatory* (n. 162 above), 158-59, and Appendix II, 362-66. In papal documents the substantive appears for the first time in a letter of Pope Innocent IV to his legate in Constantinople. Innocent urges the legate to impose this term on the Greeks *iuxta traditiones et auctoritates sanctorum patrum* in spite of the Greeks' objection that the word has not been received from their own doctors (*ex eorum doctoribus*): DS 838.

199. DS 856-59. This Confession of Faith had been proposed to the Emperor by Pope Clement IV in 1267. It was read at the fourth session of the Council in the presence of Pope Gregory X, though it was not included in a conciliar decree., The Confession of Faith distinguishes among three categories of souls: first, those that still need to be cleansed because they did not fully satisfy the divine justice in this life; second, those that need no cleansing, either because they died just after baptism, or because, although they have sinned, they have also "repented and been cleansed, in this life or in the next"; third, those "who die in sin, whether this is original sin or mortal sin." The first go to the place of "purgatorial pains," the second to heaven, the third to hell. All of them will stand before Christ in their risen bodies on the Day of Judgment.

200. See M. Dykmans, *Les sermons de Jean XXII sur la vision béatifique* (Rome: Gregorian University Press, 1973). The second sermon lays out the authorities from Scripture and tradition.

Before preaching these sermons John XXII had endorsed the doctrine of the Confession of Faith of Michael Palaeologus on the three categories of souls; see his letter, *Nequaquam sine dolore* to the Armenians, dated 1321 (DS 925-26). The contradiction between this and the view expressed in his later sermons did cause some consternation and occasioned the polemic that led to the pope's retraction.

201. See the retraction in DS 990-91.

202. DS 1000-1001.

203. Session VI, "Decree for the Greeks": DS 1304-1306; cf. C.O.D. 503-504.

204. C. Peter, "The Communion of Saints in the Final Days of the Council of Trent," L/RC 8: pp. 219-33.

205. Elizabeth Johnson, "Mary as Mediatrix," L/RC 8; pp.311-26.

206. K. McDonnell, "Liturgical Veneration" (n. 181 above). On the critical attitude of the Holy See before alleged miracles, see André Vauchez, *La sainteté en occident aux derniers siècles du moyen age, d'après les procès de canonisation et les documents hagiographiques* (Rome: Ecole française, Palais Farnese, 1981) 559-82.

207. The institutionalization of the process for the canonization of saints began in the tenth century; the first official canonization by "regular procedure" was that of Bishop Ulrich of Augsburg on January 31, 993 (Vauchez, *La sainteté*, 39-120).

208. Devotion to the "fourteen auxiliary saints" was based on fifteenth-century legend. Luther drew on it by way of contrast in his booklet *Fourteen Consolations*; see G. Tavard, "Luther's Teaching on Prayer," *Lutheran Theological Seminary Bulletin*, Gettysburg PA, 67 (1987) 7-8.

209. Elizabeth Johnson, "Mary as Mediatrix," L/RC 8: pp. 311-26.

210. Text in Hyacinthus Ameri, O.F.M., *Doctrina Theologorum de Immaculata B.V. Mariae Conceptione Tempore Concilii Basiliensis* (Bibliotheca Immaculatae Conceptionis; Rome: Academia Mariana Internationalis, 1954) 4:216-17, n. 6.

211. See Tavard, *Bonaventure* (n. 186 above); F. Jelly, "The Roman Catholic Dogma of Mary's Immaculate Conception," L/RC 8: pp. 263-78. King Alphonse V of Aragon (1416-58) made it an official Spanish policy to promote the doctrine of the Immaculate Conception (see n. 210 above).

## III. From the Reformation to the Present

212. In his *Catechismus maior seu summa doctrinae christianae* (1556), Peter Canisius insists that the communion of saints includes not only members of the pilgrim church on earth but also the pious souls in purgatory and the blessed who are with Christ in heaven (chapter 1, art. 18). In his explanation of the angelic salutation, he holds that Gabriel provides a model for the way Christians should greet Mary; he adds a series of testimonies to the holiness of Mary from the Greek and Latin Fathers (chapter 2, part 2); see P. Canisius, *Catechismi Latini* (Rome: Gregorian University, 1933) 1:89, 95-97.

213. In his *De virtute et statu religionis, Tractatus* I and III, Suarez explains the distinction between the adoration (*latria*) due to God and the honor (*dulia*) due to the saints. While defending the veneration of the saints, he holds that it would sacrilegious to adore them. See F. Suarez, *Opera omnia* (Paris: Vives, 1853) 13:10-14, 616-19.

214. Robert Bellarmine has a very thorough discussion of the veneration and invocation of saints in *Disputationes de controversiis christianae fidei*, Controversy III, *De Ecclesia triumphante*, Book I, 141-97. He holds that the saints are not immediate intercessors with God, but that whatever they ask from God they ask through Christ (179). In Book II he has a full discussion of the relics and images of the saints (199-266). See Robert Bellarmine, *Opera omnia* (Paris: Vives, 1870), vol. 3.

215. Ingolstadt: excudebat David Sartorius, 1577.

216. Cf. René Laurentin, *Maria, Ecclesia, Sacerdotium* (Paris: Nouvelles Editions Latines, 1953) 211. For a history of Mariology see Hilda C. Graef, *Mary, A History of Doctrine and*

*Devotion* (2 vols.; New York: Sheed & Ward, 1963); reprint, Westminster, MD: Christian Classics, 1985.

217. The purpose of the Sodality was the practice of devotion to Our Lady, which was accomplished by the pursuit of personal perfection according to the Sodality's way of life, and by engaging in apostolic works. Cf. Elder Mullan, *The Sodality of Our Lady Studied in the Documents* (New York: P.J. Kenedy and Sons, 1912) 9. A detailed description of the history, goals, and the rules of the Sodality can be found in this work.

218. Cf. William V. Bangert, *A History of the Society of Jesus* (St. Louis: The Institute of Jesuit Sources, 1972) 56. For further information on the spread of the Sodality, cf., ibid., 106-107.

219. For statistics see Pierre Delooz, *Sociologie et canonisations* (The Hague: M. Nijhoff, 1969). For canonizations by pontifical power prior to 1662 he lists eighty-eight religious, twenty diocesan clergy, eleven laity, and six of unknown status. For canonizations by formal procedures before the Congregation of Rites since 1662 (to 1967) he lists: 129 religious men (including twenty-four founders), forty religious women, fifteen diocesan clergy, and fifty-six laity.

220. Accessible in Benedict XIV, *Omnia Opera* (Prati: Aldina, 1839-47), vols. 1-7.

221. Their work is found in *Acta Sanctorum* (Paris: Victor Palmé, 1863ff.). For an account of the Bollandist movement, cf. Hippolyte Delehaye, *A travers trois siècles, l'oeuvre des Bollandistes* (Brussels: Bureaux de la Sociétés Bollandistes, 1920); English tr. *The Work of the Bollandists through Three Centuries,* 1615-1915 (Princeton: Princeton University Press, 1922).

222. For detailed references and more extensive coverage of the Mariology of this period, see René Laurentin, *Queen of Heaven* (tr. G. Smith; London: Burns, Oates & Washbourne, 1956); and Hilda Graef, *Mary: A History of Doctrine and Devotion* (New York: Sheed and Ward, 1965), vol. 2.

223. *The Admirable Heart of Mary* (tr. C. DiTargiani and R. Hauser; New York: P.J. Kenedy & Sons, 1948).

224. *A Treatise on the True Devotion to the Blessed Virgin* (tr. R.W. Faber; London: Burns & Oates, Limited, 1888).

225. English tr. *The Glories of Mary* (Baltimore/Dublin: Helicon, 1963; New York: P.J. Kenedy & Sons, 1948).

226. F.W. Faber, who had edited a controversial series of lives of English saints as a Tractarian in 1844, undertook as a Catholic in 1846 to publish a series of lives of the modern saints, translated from other languages. The first biographies, which appeared in 1847, were criticized by some Catholics as unsuited for English readers. Thereupon Newman, as Faber's religious superior, wrote to him communicating the decision that the series should be suspended. But in the following year, 1849, the series was resumed with Newman's agreement, and in 1851 Cardinal Wiseman approved and sanctioned the series; see John E. Bowden, *The Life and Letters of Father William Faber* (London: Burns and Oates, 1969).

227. J.H. Newman, "A Letter Addressed to the Reverend E.B. Pusey, D.D. on the Occasion of His Eirenicon," reprinted in *Certain Difficulties Felt by Anglicans in Catholic Teaching* (Vol. 2; London: Longmans, Green, 1907).

228. Ibid., 101.

229. Cf. vol. 5, reprinted Freiburg: Herder, 1954.

230. E.g., Karl Rahner, "Le Principe fondamental de la théologie mariale," *Recherches de science religieuse* 42 (1954) 481-522.

231. See Elizabeth Johnson, "Mary as Mediatrix," L/RC 8: pp. 311-26.

232. Cf. Giuseppe M. Besutti, *Bibliografia Mariana,* Vol. 3 (1952-57) (Rome: Edizioni "Marianum," 1959). Besutti has compiled five other volumes of Marian bibliographical information; these span the years 1948-77.

233. *La Question Mariale* (Paris: Editions du Seuil, 1963), 117-18. *Mary's Place in the Church* (tr. I. Pidoux; New York: Holt, Rinehart and Winston, 1965) 99; translation adapted.

234. See above, CS §175, nn. 192-94.

235. See George Tavard, "John Duns Scotus and the Immaculate Conception," L/RC 8: pp. 209-17.

236. DS 2803.

237. *Munificentissimus Deus*, 1950; DS 3903.

238. Gottfried Maron, "Mary in Protestant Theology" in: *Mary in the Churches* (ed. H. Küng and Jürgen Moltmann; Marcus Lefebure [English ed.]; *Concilium* 168; Edinburgh: Clark; New York: Seabury, 1986) 42. Maron refers to Gerhard's *Confessio Catholica* (1634-37). Pertinent text in *TRE* 14 (1985) 664.

239. Quoted in Maron, 42 (n. 238 above).

240. Ibid., 43.

241. Quoted in Maron, 43 (n. 238 above).

242. Frieder Schulz, "Heilige/Heilgenverehrung," VII: "Die protestantischen Kirchen," *TRE* 14 (1985) 664.

243. Ibid; quoted from Schleiermacher's *Weihnachtsfeier* (1806).

244. Maron, 43 (n. 238 above).

245. The sharpest Lutheran reaction came from the theologian Eduard Preuss *Die römische Lehre von der unbefleckten Empfängnis aus den Quellen dargestellt und aus Gottes Wort widerlegt* (Berlin: Schlawitz, 1865). See also Eric W. Gritsch, "The Views of Luther and Lutheranism on the Veneration of Mary," L/RC 8: pp. 235-48.

246. Wilhelm O. Dietlein, *Evangelisches Ave Maria, Ein Beitrag zur Lehre von der selig zu preisenden Jungfrau* (Halle: Fricke, 1863). The work is summarized in Walter Delius, *Geschichte der Marienverehrung* (Munich and Basel: Reinhardt, 1963) 302-303.

247. When Heiler received communion at the Lord's Supper at Vadstena, Sweden, in 1919, he was given assurances by his host, Archbishop Söderblom, that no formal repudiation of Catholicism would be required of him. "As entries in his diary indicate, he himself saw it less as a conversion (*Übertritt*) than as an ecumenical act" (Günther Lanckowski, "Friedrich Heiler," *TRE* 14 [1976] 539). Annemarie Schimmel speaks of "Heiler's double allegiance to the Catholic church and his new Lutheran affiliation" as "never resolved" (Friedrich Heiler," *ER* 6 [1987] 250). Instead, he became "a wanderer between two worlds, Catholic and Protestant, fully at home in neither in their present state, but living out a vocation in aid of their eventually coming to terms with one another" (Paul Misner, "*Religio Eruditi*: Some Letters of Friedrich Heiler," *Journal of the American Academy of Religion* 45 [1977] 842).

248. See Karlfried Froehlich, "Report: Modern Liturgical Movements, The Saints, and Mary in Protestantism (Germany Only)" 1-2 (unpublished; February 1986).

249. Hans Asmussen, *Maria die Mutter Gottes* (Stuttgart: Evangelisches Verlagswerk, 1950).

250. *Evangelisches Gutachten zur Dogmatisierung der leiblichen Himmelfahrt Mariens* (Munich: Kaiser, 1950). See also the summary and discussion of this *Gutachten* in "Zur Dogmatisierung der Assumptio Mariae. Ein Gutachten evangelischer Theologen," *Theologische Literaturzeitung* 75 (1950) 578-85.

251. Walter Künneth, *Christus oder Maria?: Ein evangelisches Wort zum Mariendogma* (Berlin: Wichern: 1950) 10.

252. The Transitus legend. See "Das neue Mariendogma im Lichte der Geschichte und im Urteil der Ökumene," *Ökumenische Einheit* 2 (1950), Fascicles 2 and 3. These and other reactions to the dogma of 1950 are summarized in Friedrich Heiler, "*Assumptio*. Zur Dogmatisierung der leiblichen Himmelfahrt Marias," *Theologische Literaturzeitung* 79 (1954) 45.

253. Hans Asmussen, *The Unfinished Reformation* (tr. R.J. Olsen; Notre Dame: Fides, 1961) 127.

254. Max Thurian, *Mary, Mother of All Christians* (tr. N.B. Cryer; New York: Herder and Herder, 1963). Thurian is a Reformed theologian who converted to Catholicism.

255. Max Lackmann, *Verehrung der Heiligen, Versuch einer lutherischen Lehre der Heiligen* (Stuttgart: Schwabenverlag, 1958). Although his position was widely rejected, it was cautiously supported by some. See Adolf Köberle and Reinhard Mumm, *Wir gedenken der Entschafenen* (Kassdel: Staude, 1981) 63-67.

256. The Prefaces end with "And so with the Church on earth and the hosts of heaven, we praise your name and join their unending hymn...." "See, for example, *LBW, Ministers Desk Edition* (1983) 208-20.

257. For example, "Into your hands, O merciful Savior, we commend your servant, _____ name _____. Receive *him/her* into the arms of your mercy, and into the glorious company of the saints in light," Service for the "Burial of the Dead," *LBW* (1978) 211.

258. *LBW. Ministers Desk Edition* (1983) 44.

259. For background history of the chapter on Mary, cf. René Laurentin, *La Vierge au Concile* (Paris: Lethielleux, 1965) 8-50. *Marian Studies* 37 (1986) is also devoted to this chapter and contains much material on textual evolution; contributing authors include: Frederick M. Jelly, James T. O'Connor, Charles W. Newman, George F. Kirwin, and Eamon T. Carroll.

260. Translations in the main taken from *The Documents of Vatican II* (ed. W.M. Abbott; New York: America Press, 1966); Arabic numbers in the text of this paper refer to articles of the Dogmatic Constitution on the Church.

261. According to the *Relatio* of November 14,1964, "132 Fathers propose that, instead of 'Propterea B. Maria *in* Ecclesia...'[the text] should say 'Propterea B. Maria *ab* Ecclesia...,' for these titles [advocata, auxiliatrix, adiutrix, mediatrix], they say, occur very frequently, even in pontifical documents." But since difficulties were raised also from the other side, with sixty-one Fathers requesting the deletion of the title"mediatrix," the Theological Commission retained the reading "in Ecclesia" as representing a middle path, likely to win acceptance by a larger group. See A.V.S. (1976) 2:8:163-64. The whole debate is thoroughly described in Michael O'Carroll, "Vatican II and Our Lady's Mediation," *Irish Theological Quarterly* 37 (1970) 24-55, esp. for the present question at 49-52.

262. See *Sacrosanctum Concilium* 108 and 111. See also *Documents on the Liturgy* 1963-1979: *Conciliar, Papal, and Curial Texts* (Collegeville: Liturgical Press, 1982).

263. Statistics in *Index ac status causarum* published by the Sacred Congregation for the Causes of the Saints, editions of 1975, 1985, and 1988.

264. Apostolic Constitution, *Divinus perfectionis magister,* of January 23,1983, AAS 75 (1983), and Norms published by the Congregation for the Causes of the Saints, February 7, 1983, AAS 75 (1983) 396-404.

265. Yvon Beaudoin, "Le Processus de canonisation dans l'Eglise Catholique Romaine," a paper on "Saints and Models" presented at the 21st International Ecumenical Seminar, Institute for Ecumenical Research, Strasbourg, 1987.

266. AAS 64 (1974); English tr., Washington, D.C.: United States Catholic Conference, 1974.

267. Text in *Catholic Mind* 72 (1974) 26-64; *Behold Your Mother: Woman of Faith* (Washington D.C.: United States Catholic Conference, 1973).

268. AAS 69 (1987) 361-433; English tr. *Origins* 16 (1987) 745-66.

269. Stephano de Fiores, "Mary in Postconciliar Theology," *Vatican II: Assessment and Perspectives* (Vol. 1; ed. R. Latourelle; New York: Paulist, 1988) 469-539.

## Catholic Reflections

1. LG 67.

2. Such reservations on the suppression of superstitions are eloquently expressed by John Henry Newman in his 1877 Preface to *The Via Media of the Anglican Church* (Vol. 1; new ed.; London: Longmans Green & Co., 1897) lii to lxxvi.

3. John Paul II, *Ad Limina* address to the Bishops of the Episcopal Conference of Abruzzo and Molise (Italy), April 24, 1986, *L'Osservatore Romano* (Weekly Edition), May 12, 1986, 8-9.

4. The Apostolic Exhortation *Marialis Cultus,* issued Feb. 2, 1974; English tr., *True Devotion to the Blessed Virgin Mary* (Washington DC;: United States Catholic Conference, 1974); for what follows, see especially 25-39.

5. In the pastoral letter *Behold Your Mother: Woman of Faith, Catholic Mind* 72 (1974) 26-64; §100.

6. Karl Rahner, *Visions and Prophecies* (tr. E. Henkey and R. Strachan; New York: Herder

and Herder, 1963); Edward Schillebeeckx, *Mary, Mother of the Redemption* (tr. N.D. Smith; New York: Sheed & Ward, 1964) 131-75; Virgil Elizondo, "Our Lady of Guadalupe as a Cultural Symbol: The Power of the Powerless," *Liturgy and Cultural Religious Traditions* (ed. H. Schmidt and D. Power; New York: Seabury, 1977) 25-33.

7. See Vatican Council II, Decree on Ecumenism, no.3; cf. Extraordinary Synod of Bishops, 1985, Final Report,II C 7; *LG* 15; we take this as applying to the Lutheran churches.

8. This possibility was discussed in the Catholic Reflections in our earlier volume on teaching authority, with some explanations that apply to the present recommendation; L/RC 6:II, §§42-50; cf. CS §100 above.

9. *Lectionary for Mass.* Translation of the Roman Missal by the International Committee on English in the Liturgy (Washington DC: United States Catholic Conference, 1969).

## Lutheran Reflections

1. That Mary was "always virgin" (*semper virgine*; SA 1:4; *BS* 414; *BC* 292), though not directly asserted in the biblical canon, was often an aspect of sixtenth-century spirituality.

2. Cf. John Stroup, *The Struggle for Identity in the Clerical Estate* (Studies in the History of Christian Thought 33; Leiden: Brill, 1984).

3. Cf. Karl Rahner, "The Church of the Saints," *Theological Investigations* (Baltimore: Helicon, 1967) 3:100, n. 6; *idem*, "Why and How Can We Venerate the Saints?" *Theological Investigations* (New York: Herder and Herder, 1971) 8:23; *idem*, "The Life of the Dead," *Theological Investigations* (Baltimore: Helicon, 1966) 4:352; cf. *idem*, "Gebet. IV. Dogmatisch," *LThK* (2d ed.; 1960) 4:545.

4. Luther accepted the practice as a "free devotion" to be done "once or twice" apart from funerals. See "Confession Concerning Christ"s Supper" (1528), WA 26:508; *LW* 37:369. The Lutheran Confessions honor such prayer as an ancient custom that need not be forbidden as long as the Lord's Supper is not transferred to the dead (Ap 24:94, 96; *BS* 375, 376; *BC* 267). See also *LBW*, 211, Commendation (18).

5. The faith of the saints is to be imitated, as are "their other virtues" (Latin text only) in accordance with one's calling (Ap 21:6; *BS* 318; *BC* 230). But faith "which takes hold of Christ" is the only "virtue that justifies" (Ap 4:227; *BS* 203; *BC* 138).

6. Typical for Lutherans in this process of discernment is that we avoid making infallible pronouncements because we find the language of infallibility "dangerously misleading" (L/RC 6:III, §16, p. 65); cf. the cases of Richard Baumann and Paul Schulz, where the German regional churches refused to make decisions about dogma ("Entsheid des Spruchkollegiums in Lehrzuchverfahren betreffend Pfarrer i. W. Richard Baumann. Erlass des Ev. Oberkirchenrats vom 7. August, 1953, Nr. A 9609," *Amtsblatt der Evangelischen Landeskirche in Württemberg* 35, Nr. 36 [1953] 445-54, esp. 453; *Nachdruck der Niederschrift über das Festellungsverfahren nach dem Kirchengesetz der Vereignten Ev. Luth. Kirche Deutschlands über das Verfahren bei Lehrbeanstandungen gegen Pastor Dr. Paul Schulz, Hamburg* [ed. Lutherisches Kirchenamt, Hannover; Hamburg: Lutherisches Verlagshaus, 1979] passim).

7. *CA* Conclusion of Pt 1:1; *BS* 83d; *BC* 47; *CA* Conclusion of Pt 2:5; *BS* 134; *BC* 95; cf. Martin Chemnitz, *Examination of the Council of Trent* (tr. F. Kramer; St. Louis: Concordia, 1971) 1:215-307; David Hollaz, *Examen Theologicum Acroamaticum* (ed. R. Teller; Leipzig: Kiesewetter, 1750), De Sacra Scriptura, q. 51; 177-82.

# Orthodox–Roman Catholic Dialogue

## Agreed Statement on the Holy Eucharist*

**Worcester, MA**
**December 13, 1969**
**Fifth Meeting**

We, the members of the Orthodox-Catholic Consultation, have met and discussed our understanding of the Holy Eucharist. After a dialogue, based on separately prepared papers, we affirm our remarkable and fundamental agreement on the following:

1. The Holy Eucharist is the memorial of the history of salvation, especially the life, death, resurrection, and glorification of Jesus Christ.

2. In this eucharistic meal, according to the promise of Christ, the Father sends the Spirit to consecrate the elements to be the body and blood of Jesus Christ and to sanctify the faithful.

3. The eucharistic sacrifice involves the active presence of Christ, the High Priest, acting through the Christian community, drawing it into his saving worship. Through celebration of the Eucharist the redemptive blessings are bestowed on the living and the dead for whom intercession is made.

4. Through the eating of the eucharistic body and drinking of the eucharistic blood, the faithful, who through Baptism became adopted sons of the Father, are nourished as the one body of Christ, and are built up as temples of the Holy Spirit.

5. In the eucharistic celebration we not only commend ourselves and each other and all our lives unto Christ, but at the same time accept the mandate of service of the Gospel of Jesus Christ to mediate salvation to the world.

*Edward Kilmartin, *Toward Reunion: The Orthodox and Roman Catholic Churches* (New York: Paulist Press, 1979) 73-74.

6. Through the Eucharist the believer is transformed into the glory of the Lord and in this the transfiguration of the whole cosmos is anticipated. Therefore the faithful have the mission to witness to this transforming activity of the Spirit.

Recognizing the importance of this consensus, we are aware that serious differences exist in our understanding of the church, eucharistic discipline, and pastoral practice which now prevent us from communicating in one another's churches. Our task should consist in exploring further how these differences are related to the agreement stated above and how they can be resolved.

# The Pastoral Office: A Joint Statement*

## Washington, DC
## May 19, 1976
## Fourteenth Meeting

### Introduction

1. Both the Orthodox and the Roman Catholic Churches acknowledge that the pastoral office, exercised by bishops and priests, is an essential element of the structure of the church founded by Jesus Christ.

The members of this dialogue, while recognizing this fact, also understand that certain changes have taken place in the exercise and in the understanding of this office both in the early church and later in the separated churches.

2. In the interest of furthering the mutual recognition of the pastoral office exercised in each of our churches this Consultation has judged it useful:

> (a) To record the results of its discussions of the understanding and function of pastoral office in the history of the Orthodox and the Roman Catholic Churches;
>
> (b) To formulate a statement concerning important elements of our common understanding of pastoral office;
>
> (c) To single out recent discussions on the subject of pastoral office which seem to require the serious attention of both churches.

### I. Historical Considerations

According to the New Testament, the witnesses to the resurrection formed the original church on the basis of their common faith in Christ. Within this group, chosen witnesses were given special authority by the risen

---

*Edward Kilmartin, *Toward Reunion: The Orthodox and Roman Catholic Churches* (New York: Paulist Press, 1979) 79-85.

Lord to exercise pastoral leadership. While this leadership seems to have been exercised in a variety of concrete ways in the New Testament period, the tendency towards a presbyteral form of government, presided over by a bishop, was apparently more common.

At the outset of the second century this movement towards a more monoepiscopal form of local church government continues to develop. In the course of the second and third centuries the bishop gradually emerges everywhere as the center of unity of his own local church and the visible point of contact with other local churches. He is responsible for faith and order locally.

During this period the presbyterate comes to share in the exercise of more aspects of the pastoral office in subordination to the bishop. This subordinate role is seen especially in presbyteral ordination, which is reserved to bishops.

In accord with the development whereby the presbyterate is explicitly included in the pastoral office of the bishop under virtually all aspects, the presbyter is viewed as having the same relationship to Christ as the bishop. Both are seen directly to represent Christ before the community and, at the same time, to represent the church, as confessing believers, in their official acts.

However, the tendency in the West towards the dissociation of pastoral office from its ecclesial context provided a difference of perspective on the conditions for the valid exercise of the functions of pastoral office. Thus, while Orthodoxy never accepted in principle the concept of "absolute ordination," this notion did find acceptance in the West in the late Middle Ages.

However, the Second Vatican Council's stress on the pastoral dimension of priestly office corrected the weakness of western theology of priesthood. Furthermore, the fathers of the council refocused attention on two major traditional themes; (a) the sacramental nature of episcopal consecration; and (b) the collegial or corporate character of each of these orders, a theme which harmonizes with the traditional Orthodox perspective.

## II. Our Common Understanding of the Pastoral Office in the Orthodox and Catholic Traditions

Although the historical perspective points out many divergent practices through the centuries, the members of the consultation recognize the following as important elements towards the development of a consensus.

1. In the rites of ordination of bishop and presbyter a commission is bestowed by the Holy Spirit to build up the church (Eph. 4:12) on the cornerstone of Christ and the foundation of the apostles (Eph. 2:20).

2. Presiding at the Eucharist belongs to those ordained to pastoral

office: bishops and presbyters. This exclusive connection between ordination to the pastoral office is realized most directly in this celebration of the faith. In the Eucharist the Lord builds up his church by uniting it with his saving worship and communicating his personal presence through his sacramental body and blood (I Cor. 10:16-17).

3. The offices of bishop and presbyter are different realizations of the sacrament of order. The different rites for ordination of bishop and presbyter show that a sacramental conferral of office takes place by the laying on of hands with the ordination prayer which expresses the particular significance of each office.

4. While both bishop and presbyter share the one ministry of Christ, the bishop exercises authoritative leadership over the whole community. The presbyter shares in the pastoral office under the bishop.

5. Ordination in apostolic succession is required for the bestowal of pastoral office because pastoral office is an essential element of the sacramental reality of the church: Ordination effectively proclaims that pastoral office is founded on Christ and the Spirit who give the grace to accomplish the task of exercising the ministry of the apostles.

6. The fundamental reason why pastoral office is required for the celebration of the Eucharist lies in the relationship of pastoral office to church and the relationship of Eucharist to church. Pastoral office is a constitutive element of the structure of church and the Eucharist is the place where the church most perfectly expresses and realizes itself. Consequently, the requirement of correspondence between the comprehensive ecclesial reality and the Eucharist dictates the exercise of pastoral office.

7. Bishops and presbyters can only represent Christ as bishops and presbyters when they exercise the pastoral office of the church. Therefore, the church can recognize only an ordination which involves a bishop with a pastoral office and a candidate with a concrete title of service.

8. We have a common understanding of these effects of sacramental ordination: (a) the ordained is claimed permanently for the service of the church and so cannot be reordained; (b) in the exercise of his office, he is distinct but not separated from the community; (c) he is not dependent merely on his subjective capabilities for the exercise of his service, since he receives the special bestowal of the Spirit in ordination.

Catholic theologians have explained these elements in terms of *character*, priestly *character*. Similar elements are included in Orthodox understanding of priesthood as a *charisma*. Both character and charisma stress the relationship of the ordained to the gift of the Holy Spirit on which the exercise of his ministry in service to the community depends.

## III. Recent Trends and Disputed Questions in Both Traditions

Roman Catholic and Orthodox theologians today have addressed themselves to several major topics related to the theology of pastoral office.

1. Some Roman Catholic theologians are challenging the traditional presentation of the pastoral office as direct representation of Christ. They interpret pastoral office as directly representing the faith of the church and consequently, Christ who is the living source of the faith. From this viewpoint the peculiarity of pastoral office is situated in the public guardianship of the common matter of all believers: the mission of Christ.

2. The traditional exclusion of women from ordination to the pastoral office affects both Catholic and Orthodox theologians, but in a differing way. Concerning this issue, Catholic theologians are examining biblical data, traditional practice, theological and anthropological data. Since they have not reached a consensus, the question remains disputed among them.

Some Catholic theologians share the position of those Orthodox theologians who reaffirm the traditional practice of excluding women from the pastoral office and base this on the necessity of the iconic representation of Christ in the person of bishops and presbyters.

3. Two of the issues touching the life-style of those called to pastoral office come under serious consideration in both traditions: (a) the compatibility of ordination with occupations which are not directly part of the pastoral office, and (b) the existing practice of celibacy.

   (a) Both Catholic and Orthodox theologians see a long tradition of ordained persons exercising certain occupations compatible with the pastoral office which are also seen to serve the sanctification of society.

   (b) In the Orthodox Church questions are raised concerning a married episcopate and marriage after ordination. Among Catholics of the Latin rite the celibacy issue focuses on the possibility of also committing the pastoral office to a married clergy.

4. Faced with the important issue of mutual recognition of ministries, both Orthodox and Roman Catholic theologians are searching for criteria leading to such a goal.

## Conclusion

The members of the Consultation draw the following conclusions: despite differing emphases, both churches agree on the nature and forms of pastoral office; theologians of both traditions perceive that they have common as well as distinct questions to be resolved.

# Primacy and Conciliarity*

## Orthodox-Roman Catholic Consultation
## October 26-28, 1989
## St. John's Seminary, Brighton, MA

For the past three years, the Orthodox-Roman Catholic Consultation in the United States of America has been studying questions related to the theology and practice of councils and to the exercise of primacy in our churches. Our papers and discussions prompted the following reflections, which we now offer in the hope that they will advance the work of the international Orthodox-Roman Catholic dialogue and the wider relations among the churches as they have advanced our own understanding of these issues.

1. In both Orthodox and Roman Catholic theology, the church is the mystery of God-given unity among human beings, who are bound together by their faith in the risen Lord and by the transforming gift of the Holy Spirit into the divine and human fellowship (*koinonia*) we call the body of Christ (1 Cor. 12:13). Joined by the Holy Spirit to the Son in his loving obedience to the Father's will, the church manifests redeemed creation within the embrace of the triune reality of God, calling God, "Abba! Father!" by the gift of the Spirit of his Son (Gal. 4:6), as it strives toward the fullness of his kingdom.

2. Individual human persons become sharers in this mystery through sharing in the church's profession of the apostolic faith and through baptism "in the name of the Father and of the Son and of the Holy Spirit" (Mt. 28:19). "Born" there into the church's life "by water and the Holy Spirit" (Jn. 3:5), they may now "consider themselves dead to sin and alive to God in Christ Jesus" (Rom. 6:11). So the church, in its most extensive and inclusive sense, genuinely comprises all those who profess the apostolic faith and are baptized in the name of the Holy Trinity, recognizing them as "fellow citizens with the saints and members of the household of God" (Eph. 2:19).

*"Primacy and Conciliarity," *Origins* 19(1989) 469, 471-72.

3. When it gathers under the life-giving impulse of the Holy Spirit to celebrate in the eucharist the Son's "obedience unto death" (Phil. 2:8) and to be nourished by participation in his risen life, the church most fully express-es what in God's order of salvation it is: an assembly of faithful human per-sons who are brought into communion by and with the persons of the Holy Trinity, and who look forward to the fulfillment of that communion in eter-nal glory. So the clearest human reflection of the church's divine vocation is the Christian community united to celebrate the eucharist, gathered by its common faith in all its variety of persons and functions around a single table, under a single president (*proestos*), to hear the Gospel proclaimed and to share in the sacramental reality of the Lord's flesh and blood (Ignatius, Eph. 5:2-3; Philad. 4), and so to manifest those gathered there as "partakers of the divine nature" (2 Pt. 1:4). "If you are the body of Christ and his members," proclaims St. Augustine, "your divine mystery is set on the table of the Lord: you receive your own mystery...Be what you see and receive what you are" (Serm. 272).

4. The mystery of Christ's church, in its fullness, is therefore most directly and clearly encountered in the eucharistic community. Each local church, recognized in its celebration of the eucharist, is a full sacramental realization of the one church of Christ, provided it remains within the full apostolic faith and is bound in love and mutual recognition to the other com-munities who profess that faith. The church in each place expresses its par-ticipation in the universal church through its celebration of the one eucharist and in its concern for the worldwide spread of the Gospel and for the welfare and right faith of its sister communities, as well as in its prayer for their needs and the needs of the world.

5. United with Christ and within itself by the divine gifts of faith and love and by the other charisms and sacramental events which enliven it, the church is also "set in order," as St. Basil reminds us, "by the Holy Spirit" ("On the Holy Spirit," 39). This ordering of charisms within the community is the basis of the church's structure and the reason why permanent offices of leadership have been divinely established within the eucharistic body since apostolic times as a service of love and a safeguard of unity in faith and life. Thus the same Spirit who unites the church in a single universal body also manifests his presence in the institutions which keep local communities in an ordered and loving communion with one another.

6. The two institutions, mutually dependent and mutually limiting, which have exercised the strongest influence on maintaining the ordered communion of the churches since apostolic times have been the gathering of bishops and other appointed local leaders in synods and the primacy or rec-ognized preeminence of one bishop among his episcopal colleagues.

a) Synods—whether held at the provincial, national or universal level, whether standing bodies (such as the *synodos endemousa* of the ecumenical patriarchate), regularly convened gatherings or extraordinary meetings called to meet some historic crisis—are the faithful community's chief expression of the "care of all the churches" which is central to every bishop's pastoral responsibility, and of the mutual complementarity of all the body's members.

b) Primacy—whether that of the metropolitan within his province or that of a patriarch or presiding hierarch within a larger region—is a service of leadership that has taken many forms throughout Christian history, but that always should be seen as complementary to the function of synods. It is the primate (*protos*) who convenes the synod, presides over its activities and seeks, together with his colleagues, to assure its continuity in faith and discipline with the apostolic church; yet it is the synod which, together with the primate, gives voice and definition to the apostolic tradition. It is also the synod which in most churches elects the primate, assists him in his leadership and holds him to account for his ministry in the name of the whole church (Apostolic Canons, 34).

7. The particular form of primacy among the churches exercised by the bishops of Rome has been and remains the chief point of dispute between Orthodox and Roman Catholic churches and their chief obstacle to full ecclesial communion with each other. Disagreement has often centered on the way in which the leadership exercised by Peter in expressing and confirming the faith of the other disciples (Mt. 16:17f;Lk. 22:32;Jn. 21:15-19) is to be realized in church life. The Orthodox have emphasized that the role of Peter within the apostolic college is reflected principally in the role of the bishop within the local church. Roman Catholics have claimed for the bishops of Rome, since the fourth century, not only the first place in honor among their episcopal colleagues but also the "Petrine" role of proclaiming the church's apostolic tradition and of ensuring the observation of canonical practices.

As our consultation has suggested in its earlier statement, "Apostolicity as God's Gift in the Life of the Church" (1986; par. 12), "There is no intrinsic opposition between these two approaches." The Orthodox do accept the notion of universal primacy, speaking of it as a "primacy of honor" accorded to a *primus inter pares*; at the same time, they cannot accept an understanding of the role of the primate which excludes the collegiality and interdependence of the whole body of bishops and in consequence continue to reject the formulation of papal primacy found in Vatican I's constitution *Pastor Aeternus*. Engaged since the Second Vatican Council in further development of the doctrine of papal primacy within the context of a collegially responsible episcopate (see especially *Lumen Gentium*, 22-23), the Roman Catholic Church is presently seeking new forms of synodal leadership which will be compatible with its tradition of effective universal unity in faith and practice, under the headship of the bishop of Rome.

8. The fullest synodal expression of the church's universal reality is the gathering of bishops from various parts of the world in "ecumenical council" to deal with questions of urgent and universal importance by clarifying and defining the "ecumenical" faith and practice of the apostolic tradition (see the statement of the International Dialogue Between the Roman Catholic Church and the Orthodox Church, "The Sacrament of Order in the Sacramental Structure of the Church" [New Valamo, 1988] 54). The Orthodox and Roman Catholic churches agree in recognizing the seven great councils of the early church as ecumenical in character and import. Because the circumstances of their convocation, their preparation and membership, and the process of their subsequent recognition by the churches vary, history offers us no single juridical model of conciliar structure as normative. Still, the acceptance of the binding authority of certain councils by the apostolic churches in worldwide communion—however and whenever that acceptance becomes clear—constitutes for the whole body of Christ an event of charismatic unity at the highest level. It is in the reception of a common faith, especially as that faith is formulated by the ecumenical councils, that the churches experience most authentically the unity in the Lord that is the foundation of eucharistic communion.

# Joint Statement on Ministry

## Roman Catholic-Orthodox Bishops*

At their last two meetings (Milwaukee, November 10-11, 1987 and Boston, September 6-8, 1988), members of the Joint Committee of Orthodox and Roman Catholic Bishops have heard presentations and discussed in several sessions the perpetuity of the effects of Ordination. They also reviewed the recently released statement of the Joint International Commission for Theological Dialogue between the Roman Catholic Church and the Orthodox Church—"The Sacrament of Order in the Sacramental Structure of the Church with Particular Reference to the Importance of Apostolic Succession for the Sanctification and Unity of the People of God." The Joint Committee of Orthodox and Roman Catholic Bishops now issues this summary of its discussions:

Three general points of agreement on Orders were noted: 1) the three sacred orders of Diaconate, Presbyterate, and Episcopate have a sacramental nature; 2) these orders are exclusively conferred by Bishops with unquestionable apostolic succession; and 3) Ordination implies a setting apart. Roman Catholic theology has emphasized an indelible sacramental character to explain this distinctive status as a special configuration to Christ the High Priest. Thus the Sacrament of Orders adds an essential specification to the indelible characters resulting form Baptism and Confirmation—Sacraments more recently described as relating all the faithful to the mission and witness of Christ.

From the Orthodox point of view, the distinctive status resulting from Ordination is intended to last permanently. A cleric, however, may be the subject of deposition because of serious sin which creates a permanent

*The Joint Committee of Orthodox and Roman Catholic Bishops includes U.S. bishops of Greek, Serbian, Ukrainian, Carpatho-Russian jurisdictions, and the Orthodox Church in America as well as Catholic bishops.

Metropolitan Silas of the Greek Orthodox Diocese of New Jersey and Catholic Archbishop Rembert C. Weakland of Milwaukee, Chairpersons of the Joint Committee of Orthodox and Roman Catholic Bishops, issued this statement.

canonical hindrance to performing his sacred function. In such a case, even though he may be penitent, he cannot be restored to clerical status. On the other hand, there are some offenses of a canonical nature for which the penalty of deposition is foreseen but that are not necessarily an obstacle to canonical reintegration to Holy Orders, if they are not an impediment to Ordination itself.

With either the Roman Catholic understanding of character or the Orthodox understanding of the creation of a permanent hindrance due to sin, "reordination" is impossible. Even in cases when a Roman Catholic cleric may lose clerical status either through cause or petition, the sacred Ordination never becomes invalid. For both Orthodox Christians and Roman Catholics, when a member of the clergy who has been ordained in a church that shares with them an understanding of the Priesthood and by a Bishop in an unquestionable apostolic succession is received into either the Orthodox or the Roman Catholic Church, his Ordination should be recognized. It should be noted, however, that until such time when the practice of the Orthodox Church will be unified, these cases will be decided by each Autocephalous Orthodox Church.

# A Pastoral Statement on Marriage

## Joint Committee of Orthodox and Roman Catholic Bishops in the United States
## October 3-5, 1990, Johnstown, PA

### Introduction

A growing trust and a spirit of cooperation have developed between the Orthodox Church and the Roman Catholic Church during the last twenty-five years, not only in the United States but also in other parts of the world. Under the inspiration of the Holy Spirit, our churches have been led to recognize more profoundly the need to manifest our unity in Christ and to pray for healing the wounds of centuries-old estrangement.

As bishops of these two churches, we hail this progress in mutual commitment to Church unity. We recognize that the Orthodox Church has expressed its seriousness in working for unity in the Church of Christ in this century through encyclicals and gestures of reconciliation. The Pan-Orthodox conferences held at Rhodes and preparations underway for convening a Great and Holy Synod are tangible signs of hope. We also recognize that the Roman Catholic Church, especially at the Second Vatican Council (1962-1965), committed itself to the cause of Christian unity and recognized its close ties with the Orthodox Church. The creation of the Vatican Secretariat (now Pontifical Council) for Promoting Christian Unity is one sign of its dedication to restoring visible unity. Both our churches welcomed the establishment in 1975 of the official Joint International Commission for Theological Dialogue. Notwithstanding the difficulties this commission has encountered and no doubt will continue to encounter, we rejoice in the work which it has already accomplished.

In the United States, under the sponsorship of the Standing Conference of Canonical Orthodox Bishops in America (SCOBA) and the National Conference of Catholic Bishops (NCCB), a fruitful series of theological consultations has been continuing since 1965. Twice each year members of the

U.S. Orthodox/Roman Catholic Consultation meet to discuss common doctrinal and pastoral concerns of our two churches. Already this Consultation has met forty times and has published thirteen agreed statements on important religious concerns. It has also shared its work with the Joint International Commission for Theological Dialogue.

A Joint Committee of Orthodox and Roman Catholic Bishops was formed in the United States in 1981 at the suggestion of His Eminence Archbishop Iakovos, Primate of the Greek Orthodox Archdiocese of North and South America, especially to address common pastoral concerns. Foremost among these concerns was the marriage between members of the Roman Catholic and Orthodox churches.

In this present statement, we, as members of this joint committee, wish to share a number of conclusions from our recent discussions, and to propose recommendations that could be implemented in our churches in this country without delay.

To prepare for this statement we have reflected on earlier texts regarding Christian marriage produced by the U.S. Orthodox/Roman Catholic Consultation: three agreed statements on (1) Mixed Marriages (May 20, 1970); (2) the Sanctity of Marriage (December 8, 1978); (3) the Spiritual Formation of Children of Marriages between Orthodox and Roman Catholics (October 11, 1980); and (4) a reaction to an agreement concluded in Boston between Cardinal Medeiros and Bishop Antimos (April 8, 1981) on ways of regularizing non-canonical marriages between an Orthodox and a Roman Catholic spouse (May 29, 1982). Also submitted to us for comment was a document of the Metropolitan New York/New Jersey Orthodox/Roman Catholic Dialogue, an "Agreed Statement on Orthodox-Roman Catholic Marriages" (January 6, 1986). Our own Joint Committee provided a response to its practical suggestions on March 23, 1989. At our previous meetings in 1988 and 1989, we also consulted scholars of Sacred Scripture regarding New Testament perspectives on the indissolubility of marriage.

Meeting now from October 3 to 5, 1990, in Johnstown, Pennsylvania, we wish to make this joint statement about Christian marriage and to offer recommendations which, if implemented, could assist Roman Catholic and Orthodox couples to fulfill more responsibly the requirements of their churches regarding the marriage ceremony, married life in Christ, and the spiritual formation of children.

## The Sacredness of Marriage

At a time when the sacredness of married life is seriously threatened by contrary views and "lifestyles," we wish to reaffirm our common faith in the profound reality of married life in Christ. We regard Christian marriage as a vocation from God in which the liberating effect of divine love, a gift of Holy Spirit, is experienced through human love. This human love expresses itself in permanent commitment to mutual fidelity and support in all aspects of life, spiritual as well as physical. It also expresses itself in the generation of new life, that is, in the procreation and nurturing of children on both the spiritual and physical levels. A primary responsibility of parents is the spiritual formation of their children, a task not limited to assuring church membership and providing for formal religious education but extending to all aspects of Christian living.

We regard Christian marriage as having a social dimension which extends beyond the partners and their relatives. Through marriage, husband and wife assume new roles in the church community. Consequently, just as marriage partners have a responsibility for the building up of the Church, so too the church community has a responsibility to help each Christian family foster its life of faith. In particular the church community shares in the parents' responsibility for the spiritual formation of children.

## The Sacramentality of Marriage

We share a common faith and conviction that, for Christians in both the Orthodox and Roman Catholic churches, marriage is a sacrament of Jesus Christ. We profess the presence of Christ in the Holy Spirit through the prayers and actions of our wedding liturgies. We express our belief that it is Christ who unites the spouses in a life of mutual love. Hence, in this holy union, both are seen as being called by Christ not only to live and work together, but also to share their Christian lives so that each spouse, under grace and with the aid of the other, may grow in holiness and Christian perfection. According to our shared belief, this relationship between husband and wife has been established and sanctified by the Lord. Marriage, as a sacred vocation, mirrors the union of Christ with the Church (Eph 5:23).

The Gospels record that Jesus affirmed the profound significance of marriage. Christian tradition, building upon the teaching of Jesus, continues to proclaim the sanctity of marriage. It is a fundamental relationship in which man and woman, by total sharing with each other, seek their own growth in holiness and that of their children, and show forth the presence of God's Kingdom. Having God's love poured in their hearts by the Holy Spirit, husband and wife exemplify and reflect in their lives together the mystery of love which unites the three persons of the Holy Trinity. Thus, marriage becomes a dynamic relationship which challenges the spouses to live according to the high standards of divine love.

In the teaching of our churches, a sacramental marriage requires both the mutual consent of the believing Christian partners and God's blessing imparted through the official ministry of the Church. At the present time, there are differences in the ways by which this ministry is exercised in order to fulfill the theological and canonical norms for marriage in our churches. The Orthodox Church, as a rule, accepts as sacramental only those marriages of Christians baptized in the name of the Holy Trinity which are sanctified in the Church's liturgy through the blessing of an Orthodox bishop or priest. The Catholic Church accepts as sacramental those marriages of Christians baptized in the name of Holy Trinity which are witnessed by a Catholic bishop or priest (or, in more recent discipline, a deacon), but it also envisages some exceptional cases in which, whether by law or by dispensation, Catholics may enter into a sacramental marriage in the absence of a bishop, priest or deacon. There are also differences in our theological explanations of this diversity. As older presentations of sacramental theology indicated, Orthodox theologians often have insisted that the priest is the proper "minister of the sacrament," whereas Roman Catholic theologians more often have spoken of the couple as "ministering the sacrament to each other."

We do not wish to underestimate the seriousness of these differences in practice and theological explanation. We consider their further study to be desirable. At the same time, we wish to emphasize our fundamental agreement. Both our churches have always agreed that ecclesial context is constitutive of the Christian sacrament of marriage. Within this fundamental agreement, history has shown various possibilities of realization so that no one particular form of expressing this ecclesial context may be considered absolutely normative in all circumstances for both churches. In our judgment, our recent differences of practice and theology concerning the required ecclesial context for marriage pertain to the level of secondary theological reflection rather than to the level of dogma.

## The Enduring Nature of Marriage

The common teaching of our churches follows Sacred Scripture in affirming the enduring nature of marriage. Already the Old Testament used marriage to describe the covenantal relationship between God and God's people (Hosea). The Epistle to the Ephesians saw marriage as the type of the relationship which exists between Christ and the Church (Eph 5:31-33). Jesus spoke of marriage as established "from the beginning of creation." He also taught: "and the two shall become one. So they are no longer two but one. What therefore God has joined together, let no man put asunder" (Mk 10:6, 8-9;Mt 19:4-6).

A number of scholars of Sacred Scripture in our churches consider it likely that Jesus' teaching about the indissolubility of marriage may have already been interpreted and adjusted by New Testament writers, moved by the Holy Spirit, to respond to new circumstances and pastoral problems (cf. Mt 5:32 and I Cor 7:15). Hence they ask, if Matthew, under the inspiration of the Holy Spirit, could have been moved to add an exceptive phrase to Jesus' saying about divorce, or if Paul, similarly inspired, could have introduced an exception on his own authority, then would it be possible for those exercising authoritative pastoral decision-making in today's Church to explore the examination of exceptions?

Our churches have expressed their conviction concerning the enduring nature of Christian marriage in diverse ways. In the canonical discipline of the Orthodox Church, for example, perpetual monogamy is upheld as the norm of marriage, so that those entering upon a second or subsequent marriage are subject to penance even in the case of widows and widowers. In the Roman Catholic Church the enduring nature of marriage has been emphasized especially in the absolute prohibition of divorce.

Our churches have also responded in diverse ways to the tragedies which can beset marriage in our fallen world. The Orthodox Church, following Mt 19:9 ("whoever divorces his wife *except for unchastity*, and marries another, commits adultery"), permits divorce under certain circumstances, not only in the case of adultery but also of other serious assaults on the moral and spiritual foundation of marriage (secret abortion, endangering the life of the spouse, forcing the spouse to prostitution and similar abusive situations). Out of pastoral consideration and in order better to serve the spiritual needs of the faithful, the Orthodox Church tolerates remarriage of divorced persons under certain specific circumstances as it permits the remarriage of widows and widowers under certain specific circumstances. The Roman Catholic Church has responded in other ways to such difficult situations. In order to resolve the personal and pastoral issues of failed consummated marriages, it undertakes inquiries to establish whether there may have existed some initial defect in the marriage covenant which provides grounds for the Church to make a declaration of nullity, that is, a decision attesting that the marriage lacked validity. It also recognizes the possibility of dissolving sacramental non-consummated marriages through papal dispensation. While it is true that the Roman Catholic Church does not grant dissolution of the bond of a consummated sacramental marriage, it remains a question among theologians whether this is founded on a prudential judgment or on the Church's perception that it lacks the power to dissolve such a bond.

Study of the history of our various traditions has led us to conclude that some at times may raise a particular theological explanation of relatively recent origin to the level of unchangeable doctrine. The Second Vatican

Council's "Pastoral Constitution on the Church in the Modern World" stated that there was need for a renewal of the Roman Catholic Church's understanding and approach to its teaching on marriage. That council implicitly recognized that teaching on marriage had frequently proceeded from a biological and juridical point of view rather than from an interpersonal and existential one.

## Spiritual Formation of Children

We also share a common conviction that in marriages in which one spouse is Catholic and the other is Orthodox both should take an active role in every aspect of their children's spiritual formation. Our priests are expected to counsel parents and children against indifference in religious matters. But since unity in Christ through the Holy Spirit is the ultimate goal of family life, all family members should be willing in a spirit of love, trust and freedom to learn more about their Christian faith. They are expected to pray, study, discuss and seek unity in Christ and to express their commitment to this unity in all aspects of their lives.

In marriages in which our two churches are involved, decisions, including the initial one of the children's church membership, rest with both husband and wife. The decisions should take into account the good of the children, the strength of the religious convictions of the parents and other relatives, the demands of parents' consciences, the unity and stability of the family, and other specific contexts. In some cases, when it appears highly probable that only one of the partners will fulfill his or her responsibility, it seems desirable that children should be raised in that partner's church. In other cases, the children's spiritual formation may include a fuller participation in the life and traditions of both churches, respecting always each church's canonical order. In these cases, the decision regarding the children's church membership is more difficult to make. Yet we are convinced that it is possible to make this decision in good conscience because of the proximity of our churches' doctrine and practice which enables each, to a high degree, to see the other precisely as Church, as the locus for the communion of the faithful with God and with each other through Jesus Christ in the Holy Spirit.

## Recommendations

In the light of our discussion together, we submit to our churches the following recommendations which we judge will greatly contribute to promoting Christian charity and honesty in our two sister churches in regard to marriages between our faithful.

(1) We urge that SCOBA and the NCCB establish and sponsor a joint committee to prepare for publication our common teaching regarding Christian marriage, family life, and the spiritual formation of children. Such an ecumenical publication would be produced in common for the guidance of our clergy and the use of all involved in marriages between Orthodox and Roman Catholics. Such material would reflect the profound spirit of love and commitment to Christian unity that has marked our churches in recent times. Such a publication would indicate that our common faith leads to the recognition of the sacramentality of marriage in each other's church.

We recommend that, in this jointly prepared material, pastors and couples be offered up-to-date information about the recent and persistent efforts to foster a closer relationship between our two churches. It would encourage Orthodox-Catholic families to draw deeply from the spiritual wealth of both churches. It would urge them to safeguard the richness and integrity of each tradition by cautioning against attempts to absorb one partner into the other's church.

We also recommend that this material include sensitive and accurate presentation of the present canonical discipline of our churches with regard to marriage in order to aid pastors in counseling couples in a responsible manner, especially if there has been a previous marriage.

(2) We recommend that when an Orthodox and a Catholic marry there be only one liturgical ceremony in which either one or both priests are present, with the rite being that of the officiating priest. The guest priest, normally dressed in cassock, would be invited to greet the bride and groom and to offer a prayer toward the end of the ceremony. We recommend that such marriages be recorded in the registries of both churches.

We recommend that in the case of marriages celebrated in the past, if it should be decided that some supplementary liturgical action is needed for a member to be readmitted to full eucharistic communion in one's church, care should be taken that this liturgical celebration avoid the impression of being another marriage ceremony thereby implying that what had already taken place was not a marriage.

We earnestly submit these recommendations to the NCCB and SCOBA for adoption and rapid implementation by our churches.

While recognizing the integrity of the canonical and pastoral practices and procedures in both our churches which seek to provide for the faithful whose marriages have failed, we also note the major differences which exist between our practices and procedures. We therefore would also encourage further serious and specific study by canonists and others in a common effort to understand and, insofar as possible, resolve these differences of practice and procedure to move toward a commonly accepted declaration of freedom to marry. Our own Joint Committee, with the assistance of the U.S. Orthodox/Roman Catholic Consultation, and of specialists in canon law, church history, and sacramental theology, hopes to pursue this ongoing task.

We realize that this undertaking, as well as the many others that lie before us, is of such magnitude that it cannot be accomplished easily or quickly. Yet, relying on the Holy Spirit, we are confident that it can be achieved, given the spirit of trust and cooperation which exists in our churches and which we have experienced in our own deliberations.

# Anglican Orders: A Report on the Evolving Context of Their Evaluation in the Roman Catholic Church*

## ARC/USA July 6, 1990

### Introduction

The Anglican-Roman Catholic Consultation in the United States has since 1986 addressed the question of the evaluation by the Holy See of Anglican orders. In 1985 Cardinal Jan Willebrands, using a phrase taken from the Anglican-Roman Catholic International Commission's Final Report, had recognized that "a new context" is now affecting the discussion of Anglican orders within the Roman Catholic Church because of the development of the thinking in the two communions regarding the nature of the eucharist and ordained ministry. It has been the purpose of ARC/USA to discuss and to outline the positive dimensions of this "new context."

We wish to underline at the outset the limits of this study. We have focused our attention on factors that seem most to encourage the reconciliation of our two communions. Other observers may point to additional features of Anglican-Roman Catholic relationships in the last century such as an interpretation of *Apostolicae Curae* as an infallible pronouncement of the Holy See, the encyclical *Mortalium Animos* of 1928 or the reluctance of some Anglicans to move toward belief in the eucharistic celebration as a sacrifice.

And there are recent developments which have been omitted from consideration in this statement such as the ordination of women to the priesthood and episcopate within the Anglican Communion. No realistic observer can exclude these events from "the new context." Yet we have acted on the suggestion of Cardinal Willebrands in his 1985 letter that it is the negative judg-

*Origins 20 (1990) 136-46.

ment of Pope Leo XIII in *Apostolicae Curae* (1896) against the validity of Anglican ordinations that is still "the most fundamental" issue that hinders the mutual recognition of ministries between the Roman Catholic Church and the Anglican Communion. Here we stress only the manner in which the themes addressed in *Apostolicae Curae* have been a point of departure for dialogue and debate between our two communions for almost a century, and we record the progress made on these issues.

## 1. Overview

The question of the validity of orders conferred according to the Anglican ordinal has come up occasionally in Roman Catholic theology since the period of the Reformation. In 1550 the archbishop of Canterbury, Thomas Cranmer, issued a new ritual of ordination that was destined to replace the medieval rituals hitherto in use in England, of which the rite of Sarum (Salisbury) was the most widespread. When Cardinal Reginald Pole, under Queen Mary, tried to restore the old religion in England, he received instructions from Popes Julius III and Paul IV regarding the mode of reconciliation of schismatic priests and bishops. Nonetheless, the exact meaning and scope of these instructions, as well as the actual decisions of Reginald Pole, have been a matter of scholarly debate.

In the late 19th century, Pope Leo XIII, acceding to urgent pleading from some unofficial groups of Anglicans and from a few Roman Catholics, commissioned a team of scholars to examine the problem. This resulted in the pope's apostolic letter *Apostolicae Curae* (1896), in which Leo XIII concluded that the orders conferred with the use of the Anglican ordinal were not valid according to the standards of the Roman Catholic Church.

And yet the aspiration of Christian unity between Anglicans and Roman Catholics did not come to an end in 1896. Almost immediately, this aspiration found expression in private talks, mutual friendships and scholarly exchanges which bore witness to a slow and gradual convergence. This quiet convergence was nurtured by theological renewal, and it was reinforced in both communions by somewhat similar liturgical reforms derived from a wider knowledge of early Christian worship. Gradually there was official recognition of an evolution toward a new context quite different from the one of 1896. On the Anglican side the Lambeth Conferences of 1908, 1920, 1930, 1968 and 1988 gave official voice to this movement, and on the Roman Catholic side the Second Vatican Council (1962-1965) was the most important event that signaled a new context.

Following Vatican Council II, developing ecumenical relations between the Anglican Communion and the Roman Catholic Church have called attention again to the question of Anglican orders. The conditions of our times have become quite different from what they were in 1896. Theology and style of leadership have evolved in the two churches. It is now not uncommon to think that the position of the problem of Anglican orders is no longer what it was under Pope Leo. A fresh examination of the data has shed new light on the subject.

## 2. How the Question Was Raised at the End of Vatican Council II

The question of Anglican orders was brought to the attention of Pope Paul VI on Nov. 20, 1965, before the Secretariat for Christian Unity, that was still occupied by the work of Vatican Council II and busy with the composition of the Ecumenical Directory and the preparation of international bilateral dialogues, was able to face the problem. This was in a private audience with the bishop of Huron, Ont., George Luxton, of the Anglican Church of Canada.

According to the bishop, the pope invited him "to add to our personal conversation." This was done in a long letter to Paul VI that the bishop released to the public in English and Latin in February 1966. The letter begins with a summary of the papal audience. In their meeting the bishop of Huron gave information on projects of reunion between Anglicans and other Christians in Nigeria, Ghana, East Africa, Sri Lanka, North India, Pakistan and Canada. The pope asked if these would be "new" churches. The bishop answered that there would be continuity of ministry in "the historic episcopate." As the bishop of Huron reminds Pope Paul in his letter, "you mentioned the bull of Leo XIII as a definitive statement of your church on Anglican orders and noted that it was given after a careful study of historical events and related documents."

One may note the word *definitive*. What is the implication of this term in the context of a private conversation? It comes naturally to the mind of a Roman Catholic referring to a solemn statement made by a pope. It seems to fit naturally in a reference made by Paul VI to a decision taken by his predecessor Leo XIII. But the use of term does not amount to a doctrinal declaration that the decision in question, while it was definitive in the mind of Leo XIII, must always remain definitive.

The bishop of Huron then "expressed the hope that these same events and documents, when studied in the new climate of our inter-church relationships, might possibly allow other interpretations than those that were apparent at the close of the 19th century. It was then that you expressed yourself as willing to receive from me and to consider any related material that I might be able to send."

The bishop also included three requests in his letter: 1) that a review of Anglican orders be made, 2) that Pius V's sentence of excommunication on Queen Elizabeth be revoked, on the model of the recent decision concerning the excommunication of the patriarch of Constantinople, and 3) that, as a long-range project, there be envisaged an eventual "intermingling of the orders of the Roman Catholic Church with our own orders and with the orders of other communions which are in full intercommunion with us."

The first request deserves to be quoted at length:

"That you ask one of your commissions to review the matter of Anglican orders, to compare afresh the Anglican ordinal with the early ordinals, with the Roman one described by Hippolytus...; the Eastern rite of St. Serapion...; the later Byzantine rite, the Gregorian and the Gelasian Sacramentaries, as well as the Spanish Mozarabic rite. *In all these the matter and form are very close to that of the English Reformation ordinal.* Also the commission might review the whole of the English ordinal through phases of development for a further testing of its intention to continue (as the Preface declares) 'the orders of ministers...etc.'

"When this new study which I am requesting is set in our present climate of theological dialogue, we believe that your commission would arrive at different conclusions. Our conviction in this matter is strengthened by the fact that in recent years new interpretations of the doctrine of eucharistic sacrifice have been proposed by distinguished scholars in the Roman Catholic Church (reference to Eugene Masure, Maurice de la Taille and Abbot Anscar Vonier). Since the heart of the argument in *Apostolicae Curae* turns on the understanding of eucharistic sacrifice by the English Reformers, these new interpretations of your theologians seem to call for a reconsideration of the earlier verdict of 70 years ago."

At the end of his letter, the bishop of Huron recalls that in their conversation Paul VI "noted that the intermingling of Anglican orders with theirs (those of the Old Catholics of Europe) is relevant to any modern review of Anglican orders." Further, the bishop remembers that "the possibility" of "the participation" of Roman Catholic bishops "as co-consecrators" in Anglican ordinations "came to your mind at the close of my November audience with you, and that you mentioned having heard it under discussion."[1]

### 3. Apostolicae Curae

Pope Leo's letter of 1896 is at the heart of this 1966 exchange because it laid out the doctrinal basis for the offical Roman Catholic rejection of the validity of Anglican ordained ministry. The ultimate judgment of Pope Leo XIII is that Anglican orders are "absolutely null and utterly void." Leo XIII asserts that the Roman See has always treated Anglican orders as null and void whenever the question has arisen in practice and that this policy of non-recognition could be traced back without break to the period of the Marian restoration of the Roman Catholic Church in England, 1553-1558. *Apostolicae Curae* interprets the instructions sent by Popes Julius III and Paul IV to the Roman legate in England, Cardinal Pole, as stating explicitly that those ordained in the Church of England must be absolutely reordained to become Roman Catholic priests.[2]

*Apostolicae Curae* presents a theological defense of this tradition of Vatican rejection of the validity of Anglican orders. It is based on the argument that the Church of England ordinal was defective in "intention" and "form." By "defect of intention" Leo XIII meant that by the omissions of any reference to the eucharist as a sacrifice and to a sacrificing priesthood in the ordination ritual of the 1552 Book of Common Prayer, the Church of England intended to introduce a radically new rite into England, one markedly different from those approved by the Roman Catholic Church. By "defect of form" Leo XIII meant that the words of the Anglican ordination prayer, "Receive the Holy Ghost," did not signify definitely the order of the Catholic priesthood with its power to consecrate and offer the body and blood of Christ in the eucharistic sacrifice.

This is the position of *Apostolicae Curae* in 1896: The exclusion of the concept of sacrifice from eucharistic worship in 1552 signified that the Church of England did not intend to ordain bishops and priests in the way that such ordinations had taken place before the Reformation in the Catholic Church in England. The exclusion of a sacrificing priesthood nullified any Anglican intention to do what the Catholic Church does at an ordination.

One key element in the new context for the evaluation of Anglican orders today is that in 1978 the Vatican archives were opened through the year 1903. This has brought to light documents that show that the decisions of *Apostolicae Curae* were arrived at through a more complex process than we had previously imagined. The process, it must be admitted, is not so important as the conclusion. However, it is helpful to observe the process. The documents now available to scholars definitely confirm the existence of two distinct groups among the eight members of an apostolic commission appointed by Leo XIII in January 1896 to re-examine the validity of Anglican orders. Leo's commission was divided, and four members of the commission believed that a "historic continuity" with the medieval church in England could be traced in modern Anglicanism. In 1896 Vatican opinion on the invalidity of Anglican orders was not as solidly negative as we once imagined prior to 1978. It would not be to our purpose to comment on the opinions of the four members who were in favor of invalidity because these arguments found their way into *Apostolicae Curae*. Almost unknown today are the positions of the papal commissioners who concluded positively in favor of the orders.[3]

For example, one member of the papal commission, Louis Duchesne, believed that the practice of regarding Anglican orders as null and void did not derive from "an ecclesiastical sentence" given in full knowledge of all the facts in the case. For a second commission member, Pietro Gasparri, the material succession of Anglican orders was intact. A third member, Emilio de Augustinis, held that the ordination rite of the 1552 Book of Common Prayer safeguarded the substance of the sacrament of order and that the formula *"accipe Spiritum Sanctum,"* contained in the 1552 book, was a valid form of Catholic ordination. A fourth member, T.B. Scannell, believed approvingly that "true Roman caution" had prevented the papacy from making a definitive negative judgment on Anglican orders in the 16th century.[4]

Today we can study these conclusions for ourselves: 1) Rome in the 16th century did not state categorically and explicitly that all orders conferred with the Anglican ordinal of 1552 were null and void; and Anglican orders were not consistently rejected by the Roman See during the Marian restoration in England of 1553 to 1558. 2) The vague nature of the instructions sent to Reginald Pole, the Roman Catholic legate in England during that period, suggests that reordination was not the only means of reconciliation of ministries in the 16th century. This conclusion is amplified by the fact that Pole himself was not a priest until March 1556. In any case, whatever conclusions one may reach today about the 16th century, we do have much more information about the background of the papal decision of 1896. This has made enough historical facts available to us to justify new investigation and appraisal.[5]

Why did Leo XIII reject the historical arguments of four members of his commission? The recently opened documents in the Vatican inform us that Pope Leo XIII apparently decided that the issue of reconciliation with the Church of England was not a matter of historical continuity alone. More important, to the pope validity was a matter of sacramentology and of ecclesiology. The new documents suggest this interpretation of *Apostolicae Curae*: Greater weight must be given to theological and institutional unity between Rome and Canterbury than to the proof of historical and sacramental continuity.

Leo XIII thus decided that historical proof of a continuation of sacramental validity within the Church of England was not the central question between Anglicanism and Roman Catholicism. History is not the question. Theology is the question. For there to be sacramental validity within the Church of England from the perspective of Rome, Anglicans and Roman Catholics must be in one institutional community of faith, which implies agreement about the theology of sacraments and ministry, and some Anglican recognition of the papacy.[6]

From this standpoint, Leo XIII was not saying no to Anglicanism. Today we can read letters in the Vatican archives in which Leo XIII and his secretary of state, Cardinal Rampolla, wished to encourage further contacts and discussion with Anglicans after the promulgation of *Apostolicae Curae.* They urge Anglicans and Roman Catholics to move toward unity in faith before the issue of sacramental validity is resolved. In the light of new historical documents, *Apostolicae Curae* did not end a process of dialogue. It began a process of dialogue. The Vatican response was theological, not political. It set out clear theological conditions for validity. Could this not imply that, given theological development, there could be some *future* discernment of substantial agreement between Anglicans and Roman Catholics on sacraments and ministry which could sustain a positive judgment of *future* ordinations in the mind of Rome?

This does not mean that we doubt the intention of Leo XIII in 1896 "to settle definitively the grave question about Anglican ordination," as he later wrote the archbishop of Paris. But the documentation in the Vatican archives suggests that this decision on the precise technical point of Anglican orders was not meant to end contact between the two communions.

After 1896 Cardinal Rampolla supported informal visits, meetings, correspondence and prayer in order to "maintain good relations with the Anglicans" and to encourage Anglicans to continue to persevere in "positive sympathies toward the Roman church." In a similar manner, the chief Anglican protagonist of 1896, Lord Halifax, also believed that dialogue would continue. He wrote: "We have failed for the moment...but God means to do the work himself... The matter is as certain as it ever was."[7]

### 4. From *Saepius Officio* (1897) to the Anglican-Roman Catholic Preparatory Commission (1967)

The next stages of this process of dialogue were *Saepius Officio* and the Malines Conversations. Anglican prelates and the Vatican continued a private dialogue through correspondence, and then in March 1897 the archbishops of Canterbury and York replied to *Apostolicae Curae* in the encyclical letter *Saepius Officio.* The document derived considerable authority from the fact that it was addressed on behalf of the Anglican Communion to all the bishops of Christendom. Here the Anglican archbishops argued that the Anglican Church makes it clear that she intends to confer the office of priesthood instituted by Christ and all that it contains. Canterbury and York contended the Church of England teaches the doctrine of the eucharistic sacrifice in terms at least as explicit as those of the canon of the Roman Mass: "Further we truly teach the doctrine of eucharistic sacrifice and do not believe it to be a 'nude commemoration of the sacrifice of the cross,' an opinion which seems to be attributed to us... We think it sufficient in the liturgy which we use in celebrating the holy eucharist...to signify the sacrifice which is offered at that point of the service in such terms as these." Finally, the archbishops pointed out that the words and acts required by the pope in 1896 are not found in the earliest Roman ordinals, so that if their omission renders an ordination invalid, the orders of the Church of Rome are on no surer footing than those of the Church of England.

The archbishops were making two essential responses to the arguments of Rome: 1) "We plead and represent before the Father the sacrifice of the cross." 2) "The whole action...we are accustomed to call the eucharistic sacrifice." Their summary of the Anglican understanding of the eucharistic sacrifice deserves to be quoted in some detail:

"The matter is indeed one full of mystery and fitted to draw onward the minds of men by strong feelings of love and piety to high and deep thoughts. But, inasmuch as it ought to be treated with the highest reverence and to be considered a bond of Christian charity rather than an occasion for subtle disputations, too precise definitions of the manner of the sacrifice of the eternal priest and the sacrifice of the church, which in some way certainly are one, ought in our opinion to be avoided rather than pressed into prominence."

The general tone of the letter is also important because it assumes that the bishops of the Anglican Communion are engaged in an ongoing debate with "our venerable brother," the pope. It was even understood that the outcome of this debate might be positive. The archbishops wrote: "God grant that, even from this controversy may grow fuller knowledge of the truth, greater patience and a broader desire for peace in the church of Christ." In the same hope of eventual resolution of these matters with Rome, the Lambeth Conference of 1908 proclaimed that there could be no fulfillment of the purpose of God in any scheme of reunion that "does not ultimately include the great Latin church of the West."[8] And the dialogue continued in this sense: The Vatican responded to *Saepius Officio*, restating its conclusions of the 1896 investigation in a French and Latin letter to the archbishops of Canterbury and York of June 1897 (letter No. 38245 in the Vatican archives), and inviting a continuing study of the doctrinal issues between the two churches.

The document *Saepius Officio* argued that there is a continuity of Anglican belief in the eucharistic sacrifice stretching from the 16th to the 19th century and, since *Saepius Officio* was formally endorsed by the Lambeth Conference in 1930, into the 20th century. At the 1930 Lambeth

Conference a delegation of Orthodox bishops asked what Anglicanism teaches on the eucharistic sacrifice. The answer given by the Lambeth committee in charge quoted the passage from *Saepius Officio* mentioned here, and this passage was endorsed by the whole Lambeth Conference in its Resolution 33.

Further, the Malines Conversations, meetings of a group of Anglican and Roman Catholic theologians held in Belgium between 1921 and 1925 under the presidency of Cardinal D.J. Mercier, did stimulate movement for greater unity in sacramental theology and ecclesiology. It was informally agreed by Anglicans and Roman Catholics at Malines that the pope should be given a primacy of honor, that the body and blood of Christ are indeed taken in the eucharist, that the sacrifice of the eucharist is a true sacrifice, but after a mystical manner, and that episcopacy is by divine law.

The impression has been left that the Malines Conversations "ran into the sands and got nowhere"; and yet Pope Paul VI said in 1966 that these conversations were "epoch-making." Why was this so?

First, Malines may be seen as a new start continuing the debate that had begun at the time of *Apostolicae Curae*. Pius XI had no objection to what Cardinal Mercier was doing, and the pope was urged in this direction by his secretary of state, Cardinal Gasparri. This was the same Pietro Gasparri who had been one of the papal commissioners in 1896; his judgment had been that Anglican orders were at the least doubtfully valid.

Second, two key figures at Malines, Lord Halifax and Fernand Portal, had also been key figures in 1896. Malines built on the talks, discussions, lectures and private friendships that Halifax and Portal had kept alive for the 25 years since *Apostolicae Curae*. And there was a real advance from 1896: In 1896 Anglican orders had been considered by a commission that included only Roman Catholics. Malines was a mixed conference with theologians from both sides meeting on basis of equality.

Finally, by 1925 the Anglican group at Malines expressed conclusions on the eucharistic sacrifice that moved a step closer to the position of Leo XIII in *Apostolicae Curae*. A memorial written on behalf of the Anglicans by Lord Halifax on May 21, 1925, defined the distinctive priesthood of the ordained ministry in such a way that there is a marked connection to the sacrificial character of the eucharist. The priest is defined as one who offers up the sacrifice of the cross by prayers and a commemorating rite. The faith of Halifax in the eventual triumph of reunion was so strong that even when the Malines conversations came to an end with the death of Cardinal Mercier, Halifax, then in his 90th year, was said to have uttered: "Now for a new departure."[9]

## 5. The Preparatory Commission for Dialogue Between the Anglican Communion and the Roman Catholic Church (1967)

Despite the attempts at Malines and individual contacts between scholars and members of religious orders of the two churches, polarization is the word that best describes the debate on Anglican orders down to the 1960s.

*Apostolicae Curae* produced an enormous amount of literature, Roman Catholic authors generally explaining and defending the papal decision, Anglicans affirming the effective transmission of valid orders in England through the turmoils of the Reformation.[10]

A significant shift in this polarization took place in the context of the Anglican-Roman Catholic Preparatory Commission that was established by Pope Paul VI and Archbishop Michael Ramsey. At the first meeting of this commission (Gazzada, Italy, January 1967), the documentation from the bishop of Huron was made available to the members. At the second meeting (Huntercombe Manor, England, August-September 1967), the preparatory commission invited two of its members, Canons Findlow and Purdy, to "make a preliminary report on the question of the advisability and/or procedure to be followed in reconsideration of the problem of orders."

The Findlow-Purdy report was presented at the last meeting (Mosta, Malta, December 1967-January 1968). It was based in part on a brief memorandum that Canon Findlow had prepared "with the archbishop of Canterbury's knowledge." The memorandum evoked the past (*Apostolicae Curae* and the bull of Paul IV, *Praeclara Carissimi*). It looked at the present (the contemporary approach to sacramentality, *Unitatis Redintegratio*, the Lambeth Appeal to All Christian People of 1920, the Church of England-Methodist Proposals). It discarded several suggestions: concentration on the Irish line of Anglican succession or on the work of Archbishop de Dominis, or increasing the Old Catholic participation in Anglican consecrations or making retrospective applications of the apostolic constitution of Pius XII on the matter and form of sacred orders (1948) "as a possible means of validating the invalid." It recognized that "the concept and understanding of the church has developed, as it must, and is developing still." Turning to the future, the memorandum noted that the time has "not quite yet" come for "a reopening of the old question of Anglican orders in the wider context of the whole church on earth, its faith, its ministry and its sacraments." It suggested that a special commission be given the task of outlining a *modus discutiendi* rather than a*gendi*

The Findlow-Purdy report also drew on considerations contained in two papers by Archbishop Henry McAdoo and Bishop Christopher Butler. These papers, however, treated the question of orders only incidentally. The report included a rather lengthy survey of recent literature: J.J. Hughes' books on *Apostolicae Curae*, articles by Daniel O'Hanlon and Franz Josef van Beeck in favor of some recognition of all Protestant ministries, other articles by Harry McSorley and Gregory Baum.

The report concluded by outlining two possible courses of action. First, there could be a joint inquiry by a pair of scholars into *Apostolicae Curae;* this could take account of various criticisms that have been made of the decision of Leo XIII and "consider what aspects of the problem were ignored." Second, another pair of scholars could investigate "the possibility of, and formulae for, a commission or recognition (Lambeth 1920)." In other words, it recommended that a search be initiated for an acceptable form of what is now called the reconciliation of ministries. "This," the report concluded, "is likely to produce quicker results."

As it examined the Findlow-Purdy report, the preparatory commission had in hand a mimeographed essay by a Dominican, Father J. Smith. This is essentially an examination of the then-recent volumes by Francis Clark (*Anglican Orders and Defect of Intention* 1956) and J.J. Hughes (*Absolutely Null and Utterly Void,* 1969, and *Stewards of the Lord,* 1970). Smith's judgment is that J.J. Hughes has succeeded "in his main endeavor to bring forth solid arguments to show the validity of Anglican orders." Smith also provides a convenient summary of several suggestions made in modern Roman Catholic theology in favor of the recognition of Anglican orders.

There is "an approach in terms of matter, form and intention" that is inspired by *Apostolicae Curae* but reaches opposite conclusions. In addition, Smith mentions "an approach through the concept:

–"Of reception *in voto* (Küng).
–"Of extraordinary ministers (van Beeck).
–"Of a wider understanding of apostolic succession and an application of the principle of *ecclesia supplet* along the lines of the Orthodox 'economy' (Villain, Tavard)."

Toward the end of his essay, Smith explains these suggestions further, and he adds some others:

1. After making "a special study of the teaching of councils and popes about the legitimacy of ministers of the eucharist from Innocent III to Vatican I, McSorley believes that it is within the Roman Catholic Church's power of the keys to declare valid and legitimate ministries she has formerly called invalid or illegitimate."

2. "Kilian McDonnell...favors an understanding of Reformation ministries as a set of charismatic ministries standing in a different way in the apostolic succession alongside episcopal orders, and believes that they

should be acknowledged by the Roman Catholic Church on the principle of *ecclesia supplet* and the working of the 'economy.'"

3. Father Coventry draws attention to two meanings of validity: recognition by the (Roman Catholic) Church, and "strength, authenticity, full value," and raises the question of the relationship between these two meanings; this leads him to the view that orders should be "recognized as orders insofar as a church is recognized as church, and not vice versa."

Father Smith's own conclusion is the following:

"It is evident how much the new argument, in all its versions, depends upon the renewal of theology taking place under the stimulus of Vatican II...The coinherence of church and sacrament is no longer to be understood in a way that makes church character ('ecclesiality') and the sacraments a possession of the Roman Catholic Church that must be jealously guarded and kept to herself alone."

## 6. The Malta Report (1968)

The recommendation of the preparatory commission was embodied in the Malta Report. This report is the first document issued from an official commission of the two communions that illustrates the emergence of the new context for the evaluation of Anglican orders by the Roman Catholic Church.

After examining the documents at its disposal, the preparatory commission included a specific recommendation. Although this Malta Report does not discuss the substance of the question, it notes that the contemporary desire for "intercommunion" points to the urgency of the matter. And it sets the question in the broad context of ecclesiology:

"19. We are agreed that among the conditions required for intercommunion are a true sharing in faith and the mutual recognition of ministry. The latter presents a particular difficulty in regard to Anglican orders according to the  traditional judgment of the Roman church. We believe that the present *growing together of our two communions* and the needs of the future require of us a very serious consideration of this question *in the light of modern theology*. The theology of the ministry forms *part of the theology of the church* and must be considered as such. It is only when sufficient agreement has been reached as to the *nature of the priesthood and the meaning attached in this context to the word "validity"* that we could proceed, working always jointly, to the application of this doctrine to the Anglican ministry of today. We would wish to *re-examine historical events* and past documents only to the extent that they can throw light upon the facts of the present situation" (emphasis added).[11]

The points underlined contain the outline of an approach to the matter of Anglican orders. The question should be re-examined 1) in the light of modern theology, 2) and in the context of an ecclesiology of "communion"; 3) the process should include an agreement on the nature of the priesthood, 4) and on the meaning of sacramental validity; 5) but it need not return to the debates concerning the events of the 16th century except if and when this may be necessary to throw light on the modern situation. The contemporary question deals with the advisability of taking a step forward toward the reconciliation of the churches by recognizing Anglican orders today, whatever may have been the problems of the past.

## 7. The Work of ARCIC I (1970 to 1981): The Formulation of a "Substantial Agreement"

The recommendation of the Malta Report became part of the project of ARCIC I. How this first commission that had charge of the international dialogue between the two communions acted on the recommendation of the Malta Report further illustrates the growth of the new context for the evaluations of Anglican orders.

Not all the work proposed by the preparatory commission was attempted. ARCIC I arrived at what it identified as a "substantial agreement" on the sacrament of the eucharist (Windsor Statement, 1971, with the Elucidations of 1979), and on ministry and ordination (Canterbury Statement, 1973, with the Elucidations of 1979). It formulated the beginning of a substantial agreement on authority in the church (Venice Statement, 1976, with the Elucidations of 1981, and the second Windsor Statement, 1981).

The agreed statement on authority in the church included the principle of the primacy of the bishop of Rome in the college of bishops, but not all the range of authority that the Roman Catholic tradition has come to recognize in the primate. Four questions were left open in 1976:

1) The meaning and relevance of the Petrine texts of the New Testament.

2) The question of the divine right (*jus divinum*) that is attributed in the Roman Catholic Church to the Roman primacy and that is seen in the agreed statement as resulting from the divine providence by which God guides the church in its history.

3) The nature and extent of this primatial jurisdiction of the bishop of Rome.

4) The doctrine of papal infallibility as defined at Vatican I and as reformulated at Vatican II.

By 1981 and the publication of the Final Report, substantial agreement was reached on the first two points. Some progress was made on the last two. But the agreement registered was neither complete nor final.

Following the lead of the Malta Report, ARCIC-I did not delve into such historical questions as Cranmer's sacramental theology, the ordination of Matthew Parker as archbishop of Canterbury, the meaning of the bulls of Julius III and Paul IV. It did not investigate what is meant by the validity of sacraments and specifically of the sacrament of orders.

## 8. ARCIC I and the "Koinonia Ecclesiology"

ARCIC I went beyond what was explicitly foreseen by the preparatory commission regarding ecclesiology, although the Malta Report contained a hint of it. The introduction to the Final Report was itself discussed, composed and endorsed by ARCIC as an agreed statement. It drew attention to the ecclesiology that was at work in the documents of ARCIC and that underlay its claim of having arrived at substantial agreements in matters of doctrine. This ecclesiology was focused on "the concept of *koinonia* (communion)." This concept draws on the close relationship that exists between eucharistic communion and the church as the community that gathers for the eucharistic celebration. It identifies the church precisely as the eucharistic community. Or, in the formula that was used by Pope John Paul II and Archbishop Runcie, in their common declaration of Oct. 3, 1989, "the church is a sign and sacrament of the communion in Christ which God wills for the whole of creation."

ARCIC I saw the notion of communion as the key to the images of the church in the New Testament (No. 4). It embodies the principle of the believers' relationship to God and Christ in the Holy Spirit and to one another in Christ (No. 5). It is related to the eucharist, to ministerial *episcope* and to the primacy (No. 6), to the visibility of the church (No. 7), to the spiritual life of the community of Christians (No. 8) and to the unity that Christ wills for his church (No. 9). It is therefore in the light of its eucharistic doctrine and practice that the continuation of orders in the Anglican Communion is to be assessed. The insight of ARCIC I on the church as communion was in line with a previous study by (the future) Cardinal Jerome Hamer. It has been echoed in much recent writing.[12] In an address given at Great St. Mary's in Cambridge, on Jan. 18, 1970, Cardinal Jan Willebrands described the church of the future in which Anglicans and Roman Catholics will be reconciled. To do so, he drew on an essay in which Dom Emmanual Lanne had shown that the universal church is not only a communion of communions, but a communion of diverse types of communions. In the universal communion, therefore, several *typoi* of the church must be at home:

"When there is a long coherent tradition, commanding men's love and loyalty, creating and sustaining a harmonious and organic whole of complementary elements, each of which supports and strengthens the others, you have the reality of a *typos*.

"Such complementary elements are many. A characteristc theological method and approach...a spiritual and devotional tradition...a characteristic canonical discipline, the fruit also of experience and psychology...

"Through the combination of all these, a *typos* can be specified."[13]

This trend of thought leads evidently to the idea that contemporary Anglicanism, with its liturgies, its spirituality, its episcopal organization and its customary mode of authority, qualifies as an ecclesial *typos* which would have its proper place in the reconciled universal church. If a *typos* of the church is understood to be eucharistic community standing in apostolic succession, teaching the Catholic faith and practicing its mode of worship and government within the oneness of the universal church, then the Anglican Communion throughout the world would be such a *typos*.

## 9. The Notion of "Sister Churches"

The question of the transmission of apostolic succession by way of episcopal ordination is not a matter of sacramental theology only. Since it is in the church that priests and bishops fulfill their tasks, the sacraments are to be seen on the background of ecclesiology. Precisely, Pope Paul VI raised the question of the ecclesial status of the Anglican Communion as he envisaged the future reconciliation of the Anglican and the Roman Catholic churches.

On Oct. 25, 1970, at the canonization of the 40 martyrs of England and Wales, victims of the Reformation, the pope included this passage in his homily:

"There will be no seeking to lessen the legitimate prestige and the worthy patrimony of piety and usage proper to the Anglican Church when the Roman Catholic Church—this 'humble servant of the servants of God'—is able to embrace her ever beloved sister in the one authentic communion of the family of Christ, a communion of origin and of faith, a communion of priesthood and of rule, a communion of the saints in the freedom of love of the Spirit of Jesus. Perhaps we shall have to go on waiting and watching in prayer in order to deserve that blessed day. But already we are stengthened in this hope by the heavenly friendship of the 40 martyrs of England and Wales who are canonized today."[14]

Pope Paul did not call the Anglican Communion a "sister church." Yet by evoking a future embrace of it as the Roman Catholic Church's "ever beloved sister," he implicitly suggested that it has the making of a sister church. In this case, ecclesial sisterhood is virtual. It needs to be elicited and actualized. In other words, Pope Paul proposed a model for the work that should lead to a reconciliation of the two churches.

Precisely, the ecumenical climate is affected by images and symbols, no less than by clear formulations and attitudes. The warmth that is implied in the expressions used by Paul VI contributes to the new context for the evaluation of Anglican orders.

## 10. Vatican II and the Sacramentality of the Episcopate

The new context for the evaluation of Anglican orders results in part from the orientation given by Vatican Council II to sacramental theology. In the Western Middle Ages the scholastic understanding of episcopal ordination differed widely from that which was suggested in the early patristic writings of St. Ignatius of Antioch. For the scholastics, episcopal ordination is simply the solemn granting of wider responsibility and authority to a person who has already received the fullness of the sacrament of orders in sacerdotal ordination. Episcopacy as such was not thought to be a sacrament: The sacrament was the priesthood. In the 16th century, however, the reform of the English ordinal was made on the principle that the ordination of a bishop is as sacramental as that of a priest. Accordingly, the sacramentality of the episcopate has been the common teaching of Anglican theologians.

There was an additional discrepancy in the 16th century between the Roman Catholic and the Anglican understanding of ordination. When Pope Paul IV denied the value of the ordination of Matthew Parker (Dec. 17, 1559), this was due to the fact that the Anglican ordinal included an explicit denial of papal authority. For the pope understood that episcopal ordination, while it does not give sacramental grace, signifies the grant of episcopal jurisdiction by the bishop of Rome.

On these two counts, Vatican II returned to the patristic tradition. In the first place, the constitution *Lumen Gentium* adopted a view of episcopacy that had been increasingly accepted among Catholic theologians, though it had not yet been endorsed magisterially: Being the highest form of the sacrament of orders, the episcopate is itself a sacrament. The conciliar text runs as follows:

"The holy synod teaches that the fullness of the sacrament of orders is conferred by episcopal consecration, that fullness, namely, which both in the liturgical tradition of the church and in the language of the fathers of the church is called the high priesthood, the acme of the sacred ministry... In fact, from the tradition, which is expressed especially in the liturgical rites and customs of both the Eastern and the Western church, it is abundantly clear that by the imposition of hands and through the words of consecration, the grace of the Holy Spirit is given and a sacred character is imprinted" (No. 21).

In the second place, Vatican II taught that the sacramental ordination of bishops introduces them into the episcopal college. From the perspective of Vatican II, hierarchical communion is also needed for incorporation into the episcopal college. The bishops' jurisdiction therefore pertains to them as "vicars and legates of Christ," not as "vicars of the Roman pontiff" (*Lumen Gentium*, 27).

These reforms of the Catholic theology of the episcopate contributed to the new context for the evaluation of Anglican orders. This is all the more striking as they were followed by a reform of the ritual of ordination.

### 11. The Reform of the Sacrament of Orders by Pius XII (1947) and Paul VI (1972)

Already Pope Pius XII, in the apostolic constitution *Sacramentum Ordinis* (Nov. 30, 1947) explicitly excluded the "porrection" of instruments from the "matter" of ordination. In this ceremony of medieval origin the ordinand touches a chalice that is presented by the ordaining bishop. This gesture, the pope declared, was not required "by the will of our Lord Jesus Christ for the substance and validity of the sacrament." Furthermore, "if it was at one time made necessary to (the sacrament's) value by the church's will and statute, all know that the church can change and abrogate its statutes.". The matter of the sacrament is simply the laying on of hands, that is of biblical origin. For the priesthood, it is "the first laying on of hands, that is done in silence"; for episcopacy, it is "the laying on of hands that is done by the consecrator." As to the form, it is in both cases contained in the "preface."

The logical consequence was drawn by Pope Paul VI. Through a series of *motu proprio* documents, Pope Paul reformed the sacrament of orders. In *Sacrum Diaconatus Ordinem* (June 18, 1968), he re-established the permanent diaconate. In *Pontificalis Romani Recognitio* (June 18, 1968), the Latin rite for the ordination of bishops came closer to the Oriental rite; in the ordination of priests he "brought closer unity to the rite," doing away with the porrection of instruments. For the three sacred orders, Pope Paul specified which "words of the consecratory prayer...belong to the essential nature (of the sacrament), so that they are required for the validity of the action."[15] These are for the priesthood:

"*Da, quaesumus, omnipotens Pater, his famulis tuis presbyterii digni-*

*tatem; innova in visceribus eorum Spiritum sanctitatis: acceptum a te, Deus,*
*secundi meriti munus obtineant, censuramque morum exemplo suae conver-*
*sationis insinuent.*" (Almighty Father, grant to these servants of yours the
dignity of the priesthood. Renew within them the Spirit of holiness. As co-
workers with the order of bishops may they be faithful to the ministry that
they received from you, Lord God, and be to others a model of right conduct.)

For the episcopate, the words are:

"*Et nunc effunde super hunc electum eam virtutem, quae a te est,*
*Spiritum principalem, quem dedisti dilecto Filio tuo Jesu Christo, quem ipse*
*donavit sanctis apostolis, qui constituerunt ecclesiam per singula loca ut*
*sanctuarium tuum, in gloriam et laudem indeficientem nominis tui.*" (So now
pour out upon this chosen one that power which is from you, the governing
Spirit whom you gave to your beloved Son Jesus Christ, the Spirit given by
him to the holy apostles, who founded the church in every place to be your
temple for the unceasing glory and praise of your name.)

In *Ministeria Quaedam* (Aug. 15, 1972), Paul VI abolished the minor
orders of porter and exorcist and the subdiaconate (keeping the ministries of
lector and acolyte). In *Ad Pascendum* (same date), he established norms for
the permanent diaconate and for admission of candidates to the priesthood.

The chief thrust of this reform was to simplify and clarify the ritual of
ordination. Unlike the reform of the ordinal that was effected in the 16th
century by Archbishop Cranmer, the reform of Paul VI was not tied to a shift
in the theology of the church or of the sacraments. Paul VI himself formulated his principle: to keep close to the patristic rites and to those of the
Oriental church. Yet by so doing, he also narrowed the gap between the
Anglican ordinal and the pontifical. Thus the Roman reform of the ritual of
ordination helped to shape the new context for the evaluation of Anglican
orders.

## 12. The Letter of Cardinal Willebrands on Apostolicae Curae (1985)

In the conclusion of the Canterbury Statement on ministry, ARCIC I
recognized the emergence of a new context:

"17. We are fully aware of the issues raised by the judgment of the
Roman Catholic Church on Anglican orders. The development of the thinking in our two communions regarding the nature of the church and of the
ordained ministry as represented in our statement has, we consider, put these
issues in a new context. Agreement on the nature of ministry is prior to the
consideration of the mutual recognition of ministries. What we have to say

represented the consensus of the commission on essential matters where it considers that doctrine admits no divergence... Nevertheless we consider that our consensus, on questions where agreement is indispensable for unity, offers a positive contribution to the reconciliation of our churches and of their ministries."

The nature of this new context was explored in a letter addressed by Cardinal Willebrands to the co-chairs of ARCIC I (July 13, 1985). The president of the Pontifical Council for Promoting Christian Unity recognized that a "new context" is now affecting the discussion of Anglican orders. He approved the principle that a study of the question "cannot be a purely historical one." The cardinal summed up *Apostolicae Curae*: Leo XIII's decision rested on the belief that the Anglican ordinal betrays a *nativa indoles ac spiritus*, a "natural character and spirit," that was judged unacceptable by the pope. This *nativa indoles* was found in "the deliberate omission of all references to some of the principle axes of Catholic teaching concerning the relationship of the eucharist to the sacrifice of Christ and to the consequence of this for an understanding of the nature of the Christian priesthood."

In the light of the liturgical renewal, the cardinal drew the conclusion that the doctrinal agreements of ARCIC I, once endorsed by the proper authorities of the Anglican Communion in a solemn "profession of faith," could remove what Leo XIII perceived as the Anglican *nativa indoles*. This in turn could "lead to a new evaluation of the sufficiency of these Anglican rites as far as concerns future ordinations." Such a study could prescind "at this stage from the question of the continuity in the apostolic succession of the ordaining bishop."[16]

Thus the new context that is now in the making may make it possible to reach a decision for the future without passing judgment on the past.

## 13. The Response of the Lambeth Conference (1988)

One of the conditions of Cardinal Willebrands has now been met by the Anglicans at the 1988 Lambeth Conference, which officially recognized the agreed statements of ARCIC on eucharistic doctrine, ministry and ordination, and their elucidations as "consonant in substance with the faith of Anglicans." These statements can now be used pastorally and academically as examples of the doctrinal teaching of the Anglican Communion, and they point to a convergence in theology of ministry and eucharist which brings to an end the era of polarization.

Lambeth voted that such an agreement on eucharist and ministry offers a sufficient basis for taking "the next step forward" toward the reconciliation of ministries of the two churches grounded in this agreement in faith. The willingness expressed in Lambeth Resolution 7 to explore even more seriously with Roman Catholics "the concept of a universal primacy in conjunction with collegiality" is related to the need for a "personal focus" of unity and affection and the realization that such a universal primacy would symbolize and strengthen in new ways the fundamental unit of the human family.

In preparing for Lambeth 1988, the provinces of the Anglican Communion also gave a clear yes to Lambeth on both the statement on eucharistic doctrine and the statement on ministry of ARCIC I. No province rejected the statement in the Final Report that "the eucharist is a sacrifice in the sacramental sense," and many were extremely positive that the Final Report is "a helpful clarification" that "sufficiently expresses Anglican understanding." The provinces also reacted in a positive manner to this statement of the Final Report: "Because the eucharist is the memorial of the sacrifice of Christ, the action of the presiding minister in reciting again the words of Christ at the Last Supper and distributing to the assembly the holy gifts is seen to stand in a sacramental relation to what Christ himself did in offering his own sacrifice." The provinces saw such a statement as giving help "to further the reconciliation of ministries and growth toward full communion."

In the light of the debate since *Apostolicae Curae*, the Lambeth Conference resolutions on ARCIC I assume historic proportions. And further, not only the Lambeth Conference, but now also 25 of the 27 provinces of the Anglican Communion have accepted the eucharistic doctrine and ministry sections of the Final Report. One may ask if the prevailing mind of the Anglican Communion is still as contrary to the Roman Catholic understanding of eucharist, priesthood and ordination as Pope Leo XIII believed it was.[17]

## 14. Significant Gestures

The relationships between the Anglican Communion and the Roman Catholic Church are now evolving in a context that is marked not only by an ecumenical shift in doctrine and liturgy, but also by a growing number of ecumenical events that have allowed the archbishops of Canterbury and the bishops of Rome to know each other personally.

Archbishop Fisher was received by John XXIII on a private "visit of courtesy" on Dec. 2, 1960. Archbishop Ramsey paid an official visit to Paul VI on March 1966. On this occasion, the two bishops joined in leading a prayer service at St. Paul-Outside-The-Walls. Pope Paul called this "not yet a visit of perfect unity, but...a visit of friendship placing us on the way to unity."[18] In an unusual symbolic gesture, he passed his own episcopal ring from his finger to that of the archbishop of Canterbury. Archbishop Coggan was received by Paul VI in April 1977, and they jointly presided at a liturgy of the word in the Sistine Chapel.

John Paul II paid an official visit to the cathedral of Canterbury, where he was received by Archbishop Runcie (May 1982). This visit was returned when Archbishop Runcie came to Rome in September-October 1989. On this occasion the two prelates worshiped together at the Church of St. Gregory, from which Gregory the Great had sent Augustine to England to preach the Gospel to the Anglo-Saxons.

It is apparent that such symbolic gestures can be diversely assessed. By themselves, they do not imply that the difficulties faced by Leo XIII are no longer operative. Yet their cumulative effect reinforces the impression that relations between the two communions have entered a phase marked by serenity and cordiality. This is a feature of the new context for the evaluation of Anglican orders.

## 15. Conclusion

The purpose of the present survey has been to draw attention to the changing climate between the Anglican and the Roman Catholic communions since the condemnation of Anglican orders by Leo XIII. There has been a growth in understanding and friendship between members of the two churches. Vatican Council II marked a point of no return. With the creation of the Pontifical Council for Promoting Christian Unity, the wish to substitute dialogue for polemic was given an institutional instrument. The movement of rapprochement has begun to bear fruit in the work of ARCIC I, ARCIC II, and a number of regional and national joint commissions.

A new context for the resolution of pending problems between the churches is thus in the making. This context is now posing new questions. Among them there is that of a possible revaluation of Anglican orders by the Roman Catholic magisterium. To what extent the new context allows for new approaches to the apostolic letter *Apostolicae Curae* and to its conclusion is a question that deserves discussion. To what extent this context has also been negatively affected by the ordination of women in the Anglican Communion is itself a point that should receive careful examination.

At the conclusion of the present report, ARC/USA invites theologians of their two churches to assess anew the past and present climate of their relationships as well as this report and to suggest possible ways forward to preserve and promote the ecumenical impact of Vatican II and of the recent dialogues, even in the face of whatever serious difficulties still exist.

ARC/USA trusts that its own efforts will contribute to the clarification

of at least some of the issues involved in the assessment of the new context
in which the churches now live.

## Notes

1. The bishop of Huron had his correspondence with Pope Paul printed and distributed widely: *A Local Item in the Roman Catholic-Anglican Dialogue...1965-1966,* 7 pages.

2. The definitive Latin text of *Apostolicae Curae* is in Leonis XIII, *Acta,* Vol. XVI, Rome,
1897, pp. 258-275. In G. Rambaldi, "A proposito della Bolla *Apostolicae Curae* di Leone XIII,"
*Gregorianum* (61, 4, 1980), pp. 677-743, Rambaldi provides the entire text of the first scheme
of an Italian draft by Cardinal Camillo Mazzella, the first Latin text and the final text. For an
English edition see *Apostolicae Curae,* trans. by G.D. Smith (London: Catholic Truth Society,
1956) and *Anglican Orders* (English) (London: SPCK, 1957).

3. The foundation of any new look at *Apostolicae Curae* has to be the new material now
open to us in the Vatican archives. This consists primarily of four dossiers: 1. Segreteria di
Stato, Anno 1901, Rubrica 66, Fasc. 1, 2, 3; 2. Epistola ad Principe, 142; 3. Lettere Latine,
1896; 4. Spoglia Rampolla, pacco 3.

These materials add new information to our understanding of the preparation and meaning of
*Apostolicae Curae* in the following ways:

1. Here we find the previously unpublished positive *Vota* of Louis Duchesne and Emilio de
Augustinis with negative hand-written comments in English, perhaps expressing the views of
the negative papal commissioners. Spoglia Rampolla contains the manuscript of a positive evaluation by Baron Friedrich von Hügel, "Memoire, addressé par ordre à son Eminence le Cardinal
Rampolla sur les Rapports entre les Catholiques Anglais et les Anglicans," dated December
1895.

2. Here we find the various drafts of *Apostolicae Curae* from the first scheme of a full Italian
draft by Cardinal Camillo Mazzella, prefect of the Papal Palace, through the definitive Latin
text. The various drafts contain changes and notations in Leo XIII's hand, so that we can see
how the pope shaped the final versions of the document and came to his own conclusions on the
issue of Anglican orders.

3. In addition, there are many letters of Cardinal Mariano Rampolla del Tindaro (1843-
1913), the papal secretary of state, who maintained an extensive correspondence with the
Anglican hierarchy and with Lord Halifax, the president of the English Church Union, W.E.
Gladstone, the prime minister of Great Britain, Fernand Portal, the French priest who had
worked closely with Lord Halifax, the scholars Louis Duchesne, Peitro Gasparri, Emilio de
Augustinis, Friedrich von Hügel and Luigi Tosti, the abbot of Monte Cassino. Rampolla
emerges as the Vatican figure who is the leading advocate of reconciliation with the Anglicans.
There are also reports from the future Cardinal Raphael Merry del Val, an opponent of reconciliation with the Anglicans, building a case against the validity of the Anglican orders, as well as
letters from the English, Irish and Scottish Roman Catholic hierarchy urging no recognition of
validity.

4. Recent publications in Italian and French make the positions of all the papal commissioners available to us today. 1) Louis Duchesne, of the Institute Catholique in Paris - G. Rambaldi,
"La memoria di Mg. L. Duchesne sulle Ordinazioni Anglicane ed un suo esame critico contem-
poraneo," *Gregorianum* (62, 4, 1981), pp. 681-746. Here Rambaldi provides the entire French
text of Duchesne's positive evaluation of Anglican orders, "Memoire sur les ordinations
Anglicanes," with a historical introduction which shows how Duchesne was involved by Leo
XIII and Cardinal Rampolla in the project. More on Duchesne's position is contained in G.
Rambaldi, "Leone XIII e la memoria di L. Duchesne sulle Ordinazioni Anglicane." *Archivum
Historiae Pontificiae* (19, 1981), pp. 333-345. 2) Emilio de Augustinis, rector of the Gregorian
University in Rome—G. Rambaldi, "Il Voto del Padre Emilio de Augustinis sulle Ordinazioni
Anglicane," *Archivum Historicum Societatis Jesu* (50, 1981), pp. 48-75. Here Rambaldi pro-
vides the entire Italian text of de Augustinis' positive evaluation of Anglican orders, "Sulla

Validita delle Ordinazioni Anglicane," with a historical introduction. More on de Augustinis' position in relation to the constitution *Sacramentum Ordinis* of Pius XII and the 1985 letter of Cardinal Willebrands on *Apostolicae Curae* can be found in G. Rambaldi, "La Sostanza del Sacramento dell Ordine e la validita delle ordinazioni Anglicane secondo E. De Augustinis, S.J.," *Gregorianum* (70, 1, 1989), pp. 47-91. 3) Pietro Gasparri of the Institut Catholique in Paris -Pietro Gasparri, *De la valeur des Ordinations Anglicanes* (Paris, 1895). 4) T.B. Scannell, an English Roman Catholic parish priest from Kent. His position and that of his three colleagues are analyzed and contrasted with the negative opinion, in G. Rambaldi, "La bolla *Apostolicae Curae* di Leone XIII sulle Ordinazioni Anglicane—I," *Gregorianum* (64, 4, 1983), pp. 631-667, and "La bolla *Apostolicae Curae* di Leone XIII sulle Ordinazioni Anglicane—II," *Gregorianum* (66, 1, 1985), pp. 53-88. The substance of Scannell's position can be found in three letters to the *Tablet*: Aug. 24, 1895; Oct. 19, 1895; Nov. 9, 1895.

5. For analysis in English of the new historical materials in the Vatican archives see three articles of R.W. Franklin, "The Historic Episcopate and the Roman Church: From Huntington's Quadrilateral to 1988," in *Quadrilateral at One Hundred*, ed. by J. Robert Wright (London, Oxford and Cincinnati: Mowbray and Forward Movement, 1988), pp. 98-110, "*Apostolicae Curae* of 1896 Reconsidered: Cardinal Willebrands' Letter to ARCIC II," *Ecumenical Trends* (15, 5, 1986), pp. 80-82; "The Historical Foundations of *Apostolicae Curae*," *Ecumenical Trends* (16, 2, 1987), pp. 24-29. See George Tavard, *A Review of Anglican Orders: The Problem and the Solution* (Collegeville, MN: The Liturgical Press, 1990).

6. G. Rambaldi reconstructs the stages of the pope's thinking from the response to the positive commissioners through the various drafts and schemata of *Apostolicae Curae* in two articles, "A proposito della Bolla *Apostolicae Curae* di Leone XIII," *Gregorianum* (61, 4, 1980), pp. 677-743; "Relazione e voto del Raffaele Pierotti, O.P., Maestro del S. Palazzo Apostolico sulle Ordinazioni Anglicane," *Archivum Historiae Pontificae* (20, 1982), pp. 337-388.

7. The letter of Leo XIII to the archbishop is found in the *Acta Sanctae Sedis* (29, 1896-1897), future evaluation of Anglican orders was underlined by James O'Connor in a paper on *Apostolicae Curae* presented to ARC/USA in July 1987. The larger context of the sentence is discussed by G. Rambaldi, "Una Lettera del Cardinale Richard sulla Fine della 'Revue Anglo-Romaine,'" *Archivum Historiae Pontificae* (18, 1980), pp. 403-410. The encouraging letters of Cardinal Rampolla quoted here are to Cardinal Domenic Ferrata, pro-nuncio in Paris, Sept. 24, 1986 (33180 in Vatican archives) and to Abbot Luigi Tosti of Monte Cassino, Oct. 9, 1896 (33468 in Vatican archives). Other letters encouraging dialogue and contact were sent by Cardinal Rampolla to Lord Halifax on March 15, 1897 (36409) and to Frederick Temple, archbishop of Canterbury on June 21, 1897 (38245). The Vatican initative toward Anglicanism in the 1890's and the complex understanding of reconcilation within the Curia are discussd by G. Rambaldi in two articls, "Un Documento Ineditio sull' Origine della Lettera di Leone XIII 'Ad Anglos,'" *Archivum Historiae Pontificae* (24, 1986), pp. 405-414; "Verso 1' Incontro tra Cattolici e Anglicani negli Anni 1894-1896," *Archivum Historiae Pontificae* (25, 1987), pp. 365-410. The sentiments of Halifax are quoted in Roger Greenacre, *Lord Halifax* (London: Church Literature Association, 1983) p.17. See also Regis Ladous: *L'Abbé Portal et la Campagne Anglo-Romaine, 1890-1912* (Lyon: Université de Lyon, 1973).

8. *Saepius Officio* (London: The Church Literature Association, 1977), pp. 13-16, 38-39. For a more complete analysis of *Saepius Officio* see E.R. Hardy, "Priesthood and Sacrifice in the English Church," *The Holy Cross Magazine* (July 1943), pp. 1-10. Other important Anglican letters to Rome after *Apostolicae Curae* encouraging dialogue and found in the Vatican archives are W.E. Gladstone to Abbot Luigi Tosti, Sept. 23, 1896 (33468), Lord Halifax to Cardinal Rampolla, March 5, 1897 (36409) and March 20, 1897 (36681), Frederick Temple, archbishop of Canterbury, to Leo XIII, April 4, 1897 (38245) and to Cardinal Rampolla April 1, 1897 (38245). *The Lambeth Conferences: 1867-1948* (London, 1948), p. 128.

9. Leo XIII, in the French and Latin response to *Saepius Officio* (Letter 38245 in Vatican archives) argues that despite "the preservation of Catholic traditions in England...the doctrine discussed in your brochure on ordination and on the priesthood as well as on the sacrifice of the Mass show that your doctrine is not that of the Roman Catholic Church." For new documentation on Malines see John A. Dick, *The Malines Conversations Revisited* (Louvain: Louvain

University Press, 1990). Paul VI is quoted by Owen Chadwick in the *Tablet* (Feb. 17, 1990), p. 216. Excerpts from the memorial of Halifax can be found in G.K.A. Bell, *Documents on Christian Unity: Second Series* (London, 1930), pp. 36-37. Halifax is quoted in Margot Mayne, "Catholic Reunion: The Noble Cause," *Church Observer* (Spring 1984), p. 14.

10. The most complete bibliography through 1968 is given in John Jay Hughes, *Absolutely Null and Utterly Void* (Washington and Cleveland: Corpus Books, 1968), pp. 309-342.

11. Alan C. Clark and Colin Davey, *Anglican/Roman Catholic Dialogue. The Work of the Preparatory Commission* (London: Oxford University Press, 1974), pp. 112-113. This is reprinted in Anglican-Roman Catholic International Commission, *The Final Report* (London: CTS/SPCK 1982), pp. 114-115.

12. See Jerome Hamer, *The Church Is a Communion* (New York: Sheed and Ward, 1964); Jean-Marie Tillard, *Eglise d'Eglises. L'ecclésiologie de communion* (Paris: Le Cerf, 1987).

13. Secretariat for Christian Unity, *Information Bulletin* (March 11, 1970), p. 14.

14. Quoted in Robert Hale, *Canterbury and Rome, Sister Churches* (New York: Paulist Press, 1982), p. 16.

15. These texts are quoted from *La Documentation Catholique* (Paris, July 7, 1968, n. 1520, col. 1169), and the English translation is taken from *The Rites of the Catholic Church as Revised by Decree of the Second Vatican Ecumenical Council and Published by Authority of Pope Paul VI* vol. 2 (New York: Pueblo Publishing Company, 1980), pp. 83 and 95.

16. *Origins* (1987), pp. 662-663. The phrase *nativa ordinalis indoles ac spiritus* first appears in *Apostolicae Curae* on p. 270 (736-737). Not all recent letters from Rome on Anglican relations have had the positive tone of Cardinal Willebrands'. An important critique of The Final Report has come from the prefect of the Congregation of the Doctrine of Faith, Cardinal Joseph Ratzinger, "Observations on the Final Report of ARCIC," *Enchiridion Vaticanum*, vol. 8 (Bologna: Edizioni Dehoniane, 1984). For Cardinal Ratzinger, the Final Report "does not yet constitute a substantial and explicit agreement on some essential elements of Catholic faith." Similarly, the Committee on Doctrine of the U.S. National Conference of Catholic Bishops, in its "Evaluation of the ARCIC Final Report," *Origins* (14:25, 1984), pp. 409-413, found that "an unfinished agenda precludes our saying at present that this doctrinal agreement in faith includes all that is essential for full communion between the two churches." Some recent Roman Catholic publications have defended the conclusions of *Apostolicae Curae* on Anglican orders. See Christopher Monckton, *Anglican Orders: Null and Void?* (Canterbury: Family History Books, 1987); and Brian W. Harrison, "The Vatican and Anglican Orders," *Homiletic and Pastoral Review* (89:1, 1988), pp. 10-19.

17. The full texts of the Lambeth resolutions may be found in the *Ecumenical Bulletin* (November-December 1988), pp. 19-21; the Final Report, pp. 20, 35; see also on these points Emmanuel Sullivan, "The 1988 Lambeth Conference and Ecumenism," *Ecumenical Trends* (17:10, 1988), pp. 145-148; and Thomas Ryan, "The 1988 Lambeth Conference," *America* (Sept. 24, 1988), pp. 162-164.

18. *La Documentation Catholique* (April 17, 1966, n. 1469, col. 673, note 1). See also Edward Yarnold, *Anglican Orders—A Way Forward?* (London: Catholic Truth Society, 1977).

# Holy Living, Holy Dying*

## (1986-88)
## Roman Catholic-United Methodist Dialogue

### Introduction

For three years, as representatives of The United Methodist Church and of the Roman Catholic Church in the USA, we have carried on a dialogue on ethical issues in the Christian care of the dying. Early in our discussions we agreed to base our conversations on four sources: Scripture, Tradition, experience and reason. Foremost among these is Scripture which provides us with the primary revelation of faith and with the nature and character of holy living and holy dying in light of that faith. Tradition provides us with a history of the theological, ethical and pastoral concerns of the Church that must be considered when treating the issue of care for the dying. Experience narrates the concrete human situation where persons encounter the issue of dying and the need for merciful and just care. Reason, as a source, provides us with the wisdom of the human arts and sciences which are so important in our efforts to understand and love the dying in our age. It enables us to integrate all of the other sources into a coherent whole. Having used this approach, we now offer the following theological and ethical principles which we consider crucial to any consideration of the subject of our dialogue.

### PART I: THEOLOGICAL AND ETHICAL PRINCIPLES

#### Affirmation of Human Life

*We affirm all human life as the gift of God.* Distinct from other creatures, we are created male and female in God's image with intellect and free

*Joseph Dalaney and Benjamin Oliphint, eds., *Holy Living and Holy Dying* (Cincinnati: General Board of Global Ministries, 1988) 14-18.

will. Thus endowed with the capacities for knowledge, freedom, and personal relationships, we are called in community to realize the divine purpose of living which is to love God and one another. As Christians we believe that God reaffirms the value of all human life through the incarnation of Jesus Christ and through the empowering presence of the Holy Spirit.

### Stewardship of Human Life

*Life is given to us in trust:* not that we "might be as gods" (Gen. 3:5) in absolute autonomy, but that we might exercise stewardship over life while seeking the purposes for which God made us. In this life we are called by God to develop and use the arts, sciences, technologies and other sources within ethical limits defined by respect for human dignity, the creation of community, and the realization of love.

### The Human Condition

*Humanity in its actual condition is subject to disease and the inevitability of death.* This situation is exacerbated by our sins of violence, greed, exploitation, and indifference, and by the moral failure engendered by stupidity and narrow-mindedness. As a result we have rendered our earthly environment unhealthy and produced unjust social structures perpetuating poverty and waste. This deprives much of the human family of health; it hastens death, or robs it of dignity.

### The Healing Christ

In the face of the ultimate mystery of why humans suffer and die we affirm two realities: (a) *Through Jesus Christ God enters into our suffering even to the point of dying an agonizing death;* (b) *In the healing ministry and sacrificial death of Jesus Christ we experience God always seeking to turn suffering and death into wholeness and life.* These realities call us to witness to God's presence in the midst of suffering by sharing compassionately in the tasks of healing the sick and comforting the dying.

### Caring

*The Christian community as a whole must be engaged in promoting health, in healing suffering, and in being present with the dying.* Our care of the dying, however, must always be guided by the principle of loving stewardship of life. The direct intentional termination of innocent human life, either of oneself or another, has been generally treated in Christian tradition as contradictory to such stewardship because it is a claim to absolute dominion over human life.

The application of this norm in certain cases, however, has been problematic. Sacrificing one's life for others or ending life in face of irreversible and intractable suffering, or choosing martyrdom, for example, tests this principle. Among the dialogue participants there are those who hold that Tradition provides a norm which must lead one to the unequivocal rejection of suicide and active euthanasia, while others hold that there may be exceptions. In our discussion we noted that the Roman Catholic Church reaffirmed its rejection of suicide and euthanasia in its 1980 "Declaration on Euthanasia."

We affirm that the obligation to employ life-sustaining treatments ceases when the burdens (physical, emotional, financial, or social) for the patient and the caregivers exceed the benefits to the patient. The application of excessive procedures, sometimes encouraged by the ingenuity of modern medical technology, does not reflect good stewardship because it does not serve the purpose for which God gave life. In determining what constitues Christian care we should engage our biblical and doctrinal understanding with the wisdom of new knowledge about human life and with our own experience of the reality of disease and death. This enables us to remain fully open to the reality of God's continuing guidance and to our need to discern God's intentions for us as we minister to those who suffer and die.

## Resurrection

*The ultimate purpose of our life is union with God in the community of the risen Christ.* Then our bodily and spiritual healing will be complete in perfect wholeness and holiness. Only then will the mystery of suffering and death find its complete answer. Until then holy living and holy dying means mutual support among pilgrims on the way.

## Issues for Further Exploration

We have not resolved two issues which both parties to our dialogue acknowledge have elicited differing viewpoints. These are the ethical application of the norm of love and the theological view of human nature. The diversity that has emerged among us can be explained in the following way: in our ethical reflection can it be said that the supreme law of love permits, in certain situations, the direct taking of innocent life, or does it always forbid it? And, in theological understanding, is death to be viewed as part of finite existence, a boundary ordained by God in the ordering of creation, or is it the consequence of our fallen nature and therefore necessarily evil?

## PART II: PASTORAL CARE

### Description of Pastoral Care

Pastoral care implies intentional relationships that empower and engage persons in holy living and holy dying. Such care is an experience of families, the various caregivers and, of course, the sick and dying themselves.

The U.S. Catholic Bishops in their pastoral letter "Health and Health Care" emphasize that pastoral care is offered within a *faith* perspective: "Since the limitations of the human condition impose a degree of suffering and ultimately death for all of us, those involved in the healing mission of Christ render a unique service by bringing a faith dimension to these crucial moments."[1]

Pastoral care to dying persons means engaging in a relationship with them so that they may know the signs of God's presence. This care may come from many sources including the church, family, friends, neighbors, and the healthcare team. Through the pastoral relationship common acts of service are signs of God's disclosure and presence as the basis for hope and the power for healing.

Persons offering pastoral care should manifest solidarity with suffering patients by empathizing with them, understanding the wounds of their lives, and comforting them by pointing beyond their human pain to glimpses of strength and hope. Even in the face of an obviously terminal condition, pastoral carepersons may join the suffering patient in prayer for a cure, but the primary focus of prayer should be on that healing which points to wholeness in the person, whether dying or not. This wholeness comes from love whose sources are relationships with God, with others, and with oneself. It enables the dying person to face death realistically and "wholely." Healing implies the affirmation of the goodness of life and the realization that, while life is a gift, death is not always an enemy.

We believe that through Jesus Christ God enters into human suffering even to the point of dying an agonizing death. In both the healing ministry and in the sacrificial death of Jesus Christ we experience God seeking always to turn suffering and death into wholeness and life. We believe this because the ultimate purpose of our life is union with God in the risen Christ. The healing ministry includes sustaining patients through illness or guiding them through the passage of sickness unto death. It may well include reconciliation whereby one assists a patient in reestablishing broken relationships with God and with others.

## Giving and Receiving Pastoral Care

Pastoral caregivers need to understand both themselves and others through the art of communication and listening. They need to experience the meaning of life and human relationships and, most of all, to experience God through their particular faith tradition.

Suffering and dying persons remain autonomous and have a right to choose the depth of their relationships with the pastoral caregivers. Pastoral care should be extended to families and friends of patients. They need time and a place to share their grief and to be reminded that these feelings are normal. Families congregating at the bedside act according to long-established patterns of relationships. Caring for these families involves seeking the signs of God's presence even in this difficult time.

Pastoral care also occurs within families when members and pastoral carepersons wrestle with difficult questions that have many answers, or none, or which lead to more questions. The supporting community of the church provides the family access to the proclaimed Word of God, specific faith and family traditions, experiences of God, and the freedom to engage in critical thinking and decision-making. The pastoral act helps to develop these relationships.

Another group of people who need pastoral care are healthcare workers themselves. Caregivers are generally expected to do their work without debilitating emotional involvement. However, for those who work regularly with dying people, it is unrealistic to expect emotional detachment. Doctors, and especially nurses, have physical contact with dying people in ways experienced by few others. This interaction, while remaining intense, does demand some emotional distance. Pastoral care with caregivers means helping them to take loving care of themselves as well as their patients.

## Specific Pastoral Concerns

A pressing pastoral concern is communication with the sick or dying person. Pastoral carepersons are trained to help patients clarify their understanding of their illness and its prognosis. While they should normally not communicate medical information to patients, they can assist patients and families in assimilating information provided by medical personnel. Pastoral carepersons are especially needed when illness is terminal and neither patients nor families will discuss this freely. Pastoral caregivers can gently and lovingly facilitate discussion of treatment options, including home and hospice care. Christian faith in life after death may often be at the heart of these discussions.

The complexity of treatment options and requests by physicians for patient and family involvement in life-prolonging decisions require good communication. Pastoral carepersons can bring the insights of Christian values and Christian hope to discussions when decisions are being made. If advance directives for treatment ("living wills") are contemplated or are being interpreted, the pastoral careperson can offer thoughtful and reflective guidance.

Some patients, in their suffering and anguish, may consider suicide as a means to hasten death. Some may even ask caregivers for assistance in taking their lives. We wish to accent the importance of the teaching offices of our churches in preparing clergy and laity to give witness to Christian hope and the dignity of human life in dealing with these complex issues and tragic situations. The appropriate pastoral care response for those patients who contemplate suicide is to assist them in understanding God's gift of life, the human stewardship of life, and the saving action of Christ in his suffering, death, and resurrection.

Passing judgment on the guilt of persons who die by suicide, restricting pastoral services based on such judgments, or stigmatizing survivors are actions that have no place in responsible ministry. The loving presence of Christ as manifested in the church community should surround those contemplating suicide and the survivors of those patients who take their own lives.

Another specific pastoral concern is the donation of organs for transplants or of one's body after death to medical research. The gift of life in organ donation allows survivors to experience positive meaning in the midst of their grief and is an important expression of love in community. Our churches support these practices as long as death is not hastened and is determined by reliable criteria. Pastoral carepersons should be willing to explore these options with patients and their families.

Finally, the major pastoral concern of pastors and chaplains is the spiritual growth of patients, families, and healthcare personnel to whom they minister. This growth can be described as a deepening unity with Christ in the church. The Bible is a primary source of spiritual growth for Christian people. Patients and their loved ones who bring their Bibles to the hospital clearly indicate its role in their lives. Pastoral carepersons who offer prayers and read the Scriptures with patients witness to the Word of grace, comfort, and salvation.

Roman Catholic pastoral practice offers these sacraments as signs and sources of spiritual growth: Reconciliation (Penance), the Anointing of the Sick, and Holy Communion. The fruitful and faith-filled realization of each of them is a major responsibility of those in Catholic pastoral care. Anointing of the forehead and hands can be offered to all who are seriously ill or in frail health. Ideally, the family, close friends and healthcare personnel participate in the sharing of Scripture and in the prayers associated with these sacraments.

In the United Methodist tradition, the process of spiritual growth is enhanced by Holy Communion services, the laying on of hands, and by informal prayers of repentance, reconciliation, and intercession. New rituals are being developed for prayer services in the care of the sick and dying. For example, a ritual of prayer after miscarriage, or after a death in a hospital or nursing home brings comfort and grace to the participants. Rituals developed in connection with a diagnosis of terminal illness, or of welcome to a hospice or nursing home could also enhance spiritual growth.

Pastoral care points us to signs and glimpses of God's presence and work in the world. As the community of faith, we are called to be open to these signs, to engender hope, and to enable the whole people of God to live and die in faith and in holiness.

## Discussion Questions

1. What steps can you or your congregation take to make your ministry to the sick and dying more effective?
2. How can pastoral care be given to and experienced by those who tend the sick and dying (i.e., families, workers in hospitals, nursing homes, hospices)?
3. As a member of the community of faith, how do you understand ministry to those who are suffering and dying? What will help you and others to overcome your anxieties and fears about being with those who are suffering?
4. What is the distinction between curing and healing? What does it mean to pray when a cure seems unlikely?

## PART III: THE SOCIAL DIMENSION

The social context of dying and death decisively affects individual ethical decisions to forgo treatment and to embrace death at the time of terminal illness. "Social" describes the policies and practices emanating from legislative bodies, public agencies, and institutions which may be presumed to reflect, to some degree, a societal consensus. In order that individuals may find alternatives to long, painful, expensive dying, or to a ready, easy euthanasia/suicide, social policies and practices must protect the fundamental values of respect for persons, self-determination, and patient benefit in treatment.

Concern for the social context of dying is consistent with the United Methodist focus on life in community and social activism rooted in seeking a holy life both through individual experience of conversion and sanctification, and through disciplined groups seeking to create communities which promote individual and social good. Concern for the social context of dying is likewise consistent with Roman Catholic social tradition that recognizes the inseparability of mercy and justice and calls for sustained efforts against unjust social structures and institutions.

### Respect for Persons: Dying with Dignity

Dying with dignity calls for care that puts emphasis on compassion, personal interaction between patient and caregivers, respect for the patient as a whole person with social as well as medical needs, and open, honest communication. In dying, as in living, it is in accord with human dignity to participate, in so far as possible, in those activities that are distinctively human: namely, the cognitive and affective activities that enable conscious, loving relationships with others in community. Medical technology supports the preservation of human dignity to the extent that it is used to sustain, support and compensate for human functions. Indeed, medical technology is a gift of our age supported by the will and resources of a society that values life and is willing to apply the measures necessary for extending life when possible.

However, when technology becomes an end in itself, unduly prolonging the dying process, it creates a paradox in which human dignity may be undermined and where the goals of treatment are distorted to accommodate the imperatives of technology. When a person is dying and medical intervention can at best prolong a minimal level of life at great cost to human dignity, structures of care and use of medical technology should focus on maximizing the individual's capacity for awareness, feeling, and relationships with family and community. Decisions that subordinate the humane dying of a terminally ill man or woman to the technological imperative, or personal or institutional self-interest—legal, financial, professional—are not consistent with Christian values and traditions.

### Patient Benefit

All persons, by virtue of their common humanity, deserve the opportunity for meaningful life as they die. Each person should have access to the means necessary for a dignified death, regardless of age, race, social status, lifestyle, communicability of disease, or ability to pay for adequate care. The biblical witness to God's concern for justice, particularly for those most marginalized and powerless in society, demands such commitments.

Equitable allocation of resources will help to assure that the holistic needs of the patient—social, spiritual, emotional, physical—are attended to. Such allocation will also assure that the common good of society is balanced with the right of individuals to be protected in their dying as far as possible from neglect, social isolation, unnecessary pain, unreasonable expense, and from the extremes of premature or delayed termination of treatment.

### Self-Determination

The right of persons to exercise autonomy and to be self-determining is protected in a just society by norms and procedures that involve the patient as an active participant in medical treatment decisions. The Christian community supports such personal rights because it views all persons as created in the image of God, endowed with freedom and called to accountability before God and their covenant community for the decisions they make.

In order to safeguard the right of self-determination at a time when one may lack decision-making capacity due to dementia or unconsciousness, individuals will be encouraged (a) to designate a "proxy," or to appoint an "attorney-in-fact" under a durable power of attorney statute, where this is authorized; and (b) to stipulate, in written advance directives, guidelines for their treatment in terminal illness. Congregations and other church groups can play a particularly important role in helping persons consider such advance directives, choose between alternatives, and find support for carrying them out.

Public support for the exercise of self-determination in illness is enhanced through state legislation that (a) gives expression to societal consensus regarding dying and death; (b) moderates between vagueness and stringency in setting parameters for forgoing treatment; and (c) protects the interests of society traditionally understood as preservation of human life, prevention of suicide, protection of innocent third parties, and upholding the standards of the medical professional.

### Pain and Dying

The withholding or withdrawal of medical interventions of little benefit to the patient compared with the burdens they impose should not be confused with euthanasia or suicide. "Euthanasia," as commonly understood, is the deliberate taking of life with the assistance of another in order to end all suffering. "Suicide" is the intentional and direct taking of one's own life.

Today there seems to be a growing belief that euthanasia and suicide may be the most humane solution for many terminal or irreversible medical conditions. This belief is encouraged by increasing emphasis on the autonomy of the individual, the application of sophisticated medical techniques for sustaining patients who are in the final stages of life, the ethos of the medical profession that impels the use of such technology even when it is inappropriate to a patient's condition, and by the fear of physicians concerning legal liability for failing to use available technology. These factors are exacerbated by efforts to control costs.

The proper application of medical science, as demonstrated by hospice care, can in most cases enable patients to live and die without extreme physical suffering. Provided the intention is not to kill but to relieve pain, such methods of controlling pain, even when they risk or shorten life, can be used for terminally ill patients.

If adequate support by community, family and competent pastoral care-givers is provided, the mental suffering of loneliness, fear and anguish, which is often more painful than physical suffering, can be alleviated. This support is particularly important in those patients who have very slight objective abnormalities or are without any physical pain but who suffer extreme emotional trauma in their knowledge that they are in the early stages of certain diseases; e.g., dementing illness such as Alzheimer's Disease, a slowly progressive but fatal central nervous disorder such as amyotrophic lateral sclerosis, or Huntington's chorea, HIV infection, and the early stages of certain cancers which with present medical knowledge are absolutely incurable.

Here the participants in the dialogue did not reach unanimity. In the situations just described, some of the participants considered that euthanasia, given certain circumstances, might be an ethically permissable action. Other participants disagreed, including the Roman Catholic team, insisting that euthanasia is objectively sinful in any and all circumstances. The Roman Catholic Church has affirmed this exceptionless norm in its "Declaration on Euthanasia."

## Social Constraints

Certain social constraints militate against the ideals of holy dying. A sense of justice and compassion that prompts us to secure for ourselves and loved ones a humane and dignified dying will alert us to the detrimental influence of these constraints.

*Attitudes toward dying*

The attempt to deny death frequently results both in reluctance by individuals to plan ahead for their dying and unwillingness in professionals to "let go" even when a patient is beyond medical help or benefit. This denial is exacerbated by negative attitudes toward old age, poverty, and disability which are most often the perceived circumstances of dying.

*Ethos of the medical profession*

The emphasis on curing, healing and restoration contributes to uneasiness among physicians in making the transition from cure to care when the possibilities of cure are exhausted. Members of the medical profession must accept the legitimacy of medicine oriented toward relief of suffering rather than extension of life for the dying, and they must use their skill in identifying when it is appropriate to discontinue treatment. This is not easily done: there is often a continuum of treatment for life-threatening conditions and a tendency to seek one more procedure that can legitimately prolong a patient's life.

*Failures in distributive justice*

Budget allocations and reimbursement policies for healthcare by both private and governmental health plans give priority to funding technologically sophisticated diagnosis and treatments while denying or minimizing payments for less costly services that are critical for humane and dignified dying.

In addition, healthcare professionals are often constrained in their efforts to implement care plans that have patient benefit as their goal by payment policies of government and insurance companies that dictate the length and modalities of treatment.

A society committed to helping every person die with dignity will reverse these policies and give highest priority to such services as hospice and homecare, social services and pastoral resources.

*Interference by courts in the decision-making process*

The courts have increasingly become the site of medical decisions in a growing number of states. The failure of society to provide effective support systems in healthcare facilities, including the use of ethics committees, leaves individuals and institutions vulnerable to outside interference.

Dying patients become subject to medical practices that are calculated to protect the professional against criminal or civil liability as much as they protect the patient's right to be treated with dignity in the dying process.

Consumers have sought to redress perceived injustices in medical treatment or to resolve difficult cases in the adversarial setting of the court room. The resulting practice of defensive medicine has increased the use of

futile diagnostic and treatment procedures by physicians and the costs of
patients and payers.

*Polarizing movements that seek to institutionalize in law and/or public policy*
*particular moral perspectives on dying*
    While some advocate legislation that would require use of life-sustain-
ing treatment in all circumstances, others promote legalization of assisted
suicide under certain conditions. Open and judicious public dialogue is
imperative on issues of such importance.
    Unfortunately, the polemical nature of the controversy impedes clear
and responsible decision-making among those who are sensitive to the ambiguity involved in life-death decisions.

**Response of the Churches**

    It is not enough to identify and analyze the social dimensions of holy
living and holy dying. Our churches must articulate in ever more creative
and relevant language the themes of the sanctity of human life, the Creator's
dominion, and our stewardship of human life as well as the nature and meaning of death. As communities that attach utmost significance to respect for
persons, self-determination, and patient benefit as norms for holy dying, we
need to work together to overcome the social constraints described above.
    Our intention is to create a context in which we can:
    a. Acknowledge dying as part of human existence, without roman-
       ticizing it. In dying as in living, mercy and justice must shape
       our corporate response to human need and vulnerability.
    b. Accept relief of suffering as a goal for care of the dying rather than
       focusing primarily on cure or prolongation of life. In addition to
       pain control, comfort-giving measures in a setting of communal
       affection and support such as a hospice are within our human and
       financial means if we make this a priority of our society.
    c. Assure equitable access for all to the resources that will relieve
       the dying and their loved ones of anxieties about financial crises
       created by medical expenses while providing holistic care to
       accompany patients through their dying.
    d. Promote effective support systems for healthcare professionals
       who must implement difficult decisions on behalf of the dying
       and their families. Intra-institutional support systems such as
       ethics committees are preferable to the courts or other forums for
       weighing alternatives in the sensitive balance that the circum-
       stances of dying may require.

e. Participate as communities of faith in public dialogue to help shape consensus on treatment of the dying. The insights drawn from the United Methodist and Roman Catholic theological traditions offer valuable contributions to this discussion.

The right of every person to die in dignity, with loving personal care and without efforts to prolong terminal illness, will be defended to the extent that society reaches out in mercy and justice, touching individual persons, but also touching the social conditions that hinder the wholeness which is God's desire for humanity.

## IMPLICATIONS FOR ACTION

In order that the principles and concerns articulated in the document Holy Living and Holy Dying be translated into practical action, the following recommendations are submitted to our churches:

### Recommendations to Congregations and Parishes

a. Encourage United Methodist and Roman Catholic study of this document, jointly where possible.
b. Provide for study and dialogue on issues related to decisions at the end of life, with particular attention to:
   –role of advance directives ("living wills," Durable Power of Attorney for medical decisions),
   –importance of communication with physician, family, and loved ones prior to a medical crisis with emphasis on the rights and responsibilities of the patients,
   –hospice philosophy.
c. Facilitate and cooperate in the formation of support groups and systems for those dealing with terminal illness. Where this can be done on an ecumenical basis, this should be promoted.

### Recommendations to Church Leadership

a. Promote ecumenical dialogue at the national and parish level and with advocacy groups and decision-makers on issues such as allocation of finite healthcare resources and access to healthcare resources needed for holy dying.

b. Encourage the training of pastoral personnel on the issues raised in this study.
c. Promote dialogue and exercise leadership to influence public attitudes and policy on end-of-life decisions.
d. Support public advocacy for adequate funding for hospice, homecare, and similar programs for all persons.

## Recommendations to Healthcare Institutions

a. Provide multi-disciplinary education for community and specialized healthcare personnel on issues related to holy living and holy dying.
b. Encourage the formation of institutional ethics committees for policy advising, discussion of issues, and educational leadership.
c. Encourage the establishment of policies and procedures that support alternatives in terminal care.
d. Assure the presence and availability of persons and programs to:
    —assist in the resolution of doubt and conflict associated with the use of life-sustaining technology.
    —support those who must make and implement the complex decisions that arise at the end of life.

## Recommendations to Seminaries and Other Educational Institutions

a. Promote dialogue among church and academic communities around the issues addressed in this study.
b. Incorporate into the curriculum study and reflection on theological, ethical and pastoral issues related to dying and death.
c. Encourage the study of public policy on the use of healthcare resources and the psycho-social impact of these issues on care and treatment of terminal cases.
d. Foster in all formation programs the development of caring skills toward those facing the end of life in terminal illness.

## Note

1. "Health and Health Care," A Pastoral Letter of the American Catholic Bishops, U.S. Catholic Conference, Washington, D.C. (November 19, 1981).

# Journeying Together in Christ*

## Summary Report of
## the Polish National Catholic–
## Roman Catholic Dialogue (1984-89)

### A Survey of the Findings of the Dialogue Thus Far

When he addressed the dialogue in 1986, Prime Bishop John F. Swantek stated succinctly a conviction which we have held from the start of our sessions and one which has grown still stronger as we have worked together. He said, "The conversations between the Polish National Catholic Church and the Roman Catholic Church are a very important step in ecumenism because they bring two Churches together which have been separated by the events of history, but they have so many common characteristics in faith and liturgical expression." In our dialogue we have carefully studied these common characteristics which forge deep, underlying bonds of communion (*koinonia*) between our Churches, noting both major areas of identity or close similarity between us and, at the same time, areas of difference or

*After a long period of dissatisfaction with Roman Catholic administration and ideology and, in addition, through the strong desire for religious freedom, this body was organized in 1897. The beginning of the division occurred in St. Judwiga's Parish, Chicago, Illinois in 1894. In 1897 a similar polarization between congregation and the Roman Catholic Bishop developed in Sacred Heart parish in Scranton, Pennsylvania. The two groups formed the Polish National Catholic Church, with Polish used in the liturgy, lay participation in governance, and eventually married clergy. Since 1921 there are also Polish National Catholic Churches in Poland as a result of United States missions. In 1970, 165 congregations and 285,000 communicants were reported in the United States. The Polish National Catholic Church is a member of the Old Catholic Union of Utrecht. The earliest friendly contacts between the National Conference of Catholic Bishops and the Polish National Catholic Church occurred in 1965, but the first steps to initiate dialogue occurred in 1981. This document is a summary of conversations between 1984-89. (Cf. Arthur Carl Piepkorn, *Profiles in Belief* [Vol. 1; New York: Harper and Row, 1987] 280-85.)

Text published in: Stanislaus Brzana and Anthony Rysz, eds., *Journeying Together in Christ: The Report of the Polish National Catholic-Roman Catholic Dialogue (1984-1989)* (Huntington, IN: Our Sunday Visitor, Inc., 1990) 13-35.

distinctiveness which are also significant. We began with an extended discussion over a number of sessions focused on the sacramental life of the Church.

## The Sacraments

Both the PNCC and the RCC faithfully regard the sacraments as special gifts of Christ to His Church, outward signs instituted by Him as means of grace, wherein He acts in the power of the Spirit to nourish and strengthen the Church and be present among His faithful. Along with Orthodox Churches and all the Churches of the Union of Utrecht, the PNCC and the RCC hold seven sacraments: baptism, confirmation, penance, Eucharist, anointing of the sick, holy orders and matrimony (cf. *Nasz a Wiara—Our Faith*, by Bishop F. Hodur, Scranton, 1913, page 32).

## Sacraments of Initiation: Baptism and Confirmation

It is the common faith shared by the RCC and the PNCC that "by Baptism persons are grafted into the mystery of Christ; they die with Him, are buried with Him, and rise with Him. They receive the spirit of adoption as children 'in which we cry, Abba, Father' (Rom. 8:15) and thus become true adorers such as the Father seeks." (Vatican II *Constitution on the Divine Liturgy*, n. 6). Together we hold that through baptism, celebrated in our Churches according to the faith handed down to us from the Apostles, we are each made members of the one Mystical Body of Christ. In both our Churches not only adults but also infants are baptized. In both Churches baptism is administered by a bishop, priest or deacon.

In the PNCC, and the RCC, baptism and confirmation are counted as two closely inter-related sacraments. However, both Churches teach that confirmation completes baptism. Both Churches hold that confirmation imparts in a special way the special gift and seal of the Holy Spirit, strengthening the person confirmed to live according to the holy vocation of a Christian, and both typically confer this sacrament on young people at about the age of 12 to 15. In the PNCC as in the Latin rite of the RCC, the bishops are the ordinary ministers of confirmation. However, in both Churches provision is made for priests to administer it when this is necessary or appropriate (e.g. in remote areas which the bishops cannot visit regularly, in the face of large numbers to be confirmed requiring that the bishops have further assistance, on occasion in the course of receiving an adult into membership in the Church, or in danger of death faced by one not yet confirmed).

## The Eucharist

It is evident that the Holy Eucharist holds a place of central importance in the life of both Churches and a great many parallels have been noted in both our past and present practices. The 1889 *Declaration of Utrecht*, article 6, held and taught by the bishops of the PNCC, speaks of it as "the true and central point of Catholic worship" while the Vatican II *Constitution on the Divine Liturgy*, no. 10, speaks of the liturgy culminating in the Eucharist as "the summit toward which the activity of the Church is directed (and) also the fount from which all her power flows."

To appreciate more fully how the eucharistic faith of the Union of Utrecht compares with that of the Roman Catholic Church, it is helpful to see at somewhat greater length the sources just cited. This is a more complete citation from article 6 of the *Declaration of Utrecht*:

> "Considering that the Holy Eucharist has always been the true central point of Catholic worship, we consider it our duty to declare that we maintain with perfect fidelity the ancient Catholic doctrine concerning the Sacrament of the Altar, by believing that we receive the Body and Blood of our Saviour Jesus Christ under the species of bread and wine. The Eucharistic celebration in the Church is neither a continual repetition nor a renewal of the expiatory sacrifice which Jesus offered once for all upon the Cross; but it is a sacrifice because it is the perpetual commemoration of the sacrifice offered upon the Cross, and it is the act by which we represent upon earth and appropriate to ourselves the one offering which Jesus Christ makes in Heaven, according to the Epistle to the Hebrews, 9, 11-12, for the salvation of redeemed humanity, by appearing for us in the presence of God (Heb. 9:24). The character of the Holy Eucharist being thus understood, it is, at the same time, a sacrificial feast, by means of which the faithful in receiving the Body and Blood of our Saviour, enter into communion with one another (1 Cor. 10.17)."

And here follows the statement on the Eucharist from article 47 of the II Vatican Council *Constitution on the Divine Liturgy:*

> "At the Last Supper, on the night he was betrayed, our Savior instituted the eucharistic sacrifice of his Body and Blood. This he did in order to perpetuate the sacrifice of the Cross throughout the ages until he should come again, and so to entrust to his beloved Spouse, the Church, a memorial of his death and resurrection: a sacrament of love, sign of unity, a bond of charity, a paschal banquet in which Christ is consumed, the mind is filled with grace, and a pledge of future glory is given to us."

In reflecting on these texts we find in them a very close correspondence in the faith which each expresses in its own words. Though differences of linguistic usage can be found (e.g. *transsubstantiatio*—Trent, sess. XIII, cap. 4; and *przeistoczenie*—PNCC Catechism, 1944, p. 33) our experience of the lived faith and eucharistic devotion found in our Churches convinces us that ours is a shared belief that Christ in His unbounded love "did institute these holy mysteries in which spiritually and bodily, in His entire being... (He) abides among us" (PNCC *Canon*) under the appearances of bread and wine. Thus together we affirm that "the Holy Eucharist is the true Body and the true Blood of our Lord Jesus under the appearances of bread and wine for the nourishment of mankind for eternal life" (*Katechism*, catechism by Bishop F. Hodur, Scranton, 1920, page 32).

There is indeed a great deal of correspondence in eucharistic practice in our two Churches. Both Churches encourage the active participation of the faithful in the eucharistic liturgy and to this end celebrate the liturgy in the language of the people. In the United States today this is most commonly done in English in both Churches, though Polish is at times used in the PNCC and Latin or other languages in the RCC. Both Churches encourage the faithful to the frequent reception of Holy Communion, having prepared themselves for this with the Sacrament of Penance. In the PNCC children do not make their First Communion until the age of seven, and in the RCC not until they have reached the age of discernment, which is also generally seven. In both Churches children are encouraged to prepare themselves for this by first receiving the Sacrament of Penance. In addition to the requisite dispositions of the soul, the faithful are also enjoined to observe a fast from solid food and alcoholic beverages before receiving the Eucharist (for two hours in the case of the PNCC, for one hour in the case of the RCC). In both Churches the reception of the Eucharist is made available to the faithful not only on Sundays and Holy Days, but daily. Both Churches provide three ways for the reception of the Eucharist: 1) receiving the Sacred Host and the Most Precious Blood separately, 2) receiving by intinction, i.e. the Sacred Host dipped in the Most Precious Blood, or 3) receiving under one species, e.g. only the Sacred Host. In the PNCC, the second form, reception by intinction, is the most common; whereas in the RCC reception in either the first or third form is more often the case.

Besides these commonalities, we have found the following practical differences between us. In the PNCC the minister of Holy Communion is a bishop, priest or deacon, whereas in the RCC it may be one of these or one who, though not ordained, has been commissioned by the Church to serve as a eucharistic minister. The PNCC adminsters the Eucharist only to members of its Church. The RCC as a general rule restricts admission to the sacraments to members of the Roman Catholic Church and to Eastern Orthodox

Christians who ask to be admitted; but in certain circumstances of need will also admit individual Christians of other churches or ecclesial communities who request the sacraments with faith and are properly disposed.

Finally we have found that eucharistic devotion, i.e. the adoration of Christ in the Blessed Sacrament, continues to play an important part in the life of the PNCC, e.g. on the Feast of Corpus Christi, after the principal Mass on the first Sunday of each month, in the Procession of the Sacrament on Easter Morning, after Lenten Services such as the Stations of the Cross, after Penitential Services in Advent and Lent, after May and October devotions to Our Lady and June devotions to the Sacred Heart. Such eucharistic devotions have also been a prominent feature of the practice of the RCC in the past, but have now diminished in frequency because of the greater emphasis liturgical renewal has placed on the eucharistic celebration itself and the greater frequency with which it is celebrated. Thus, as an example, in many parishes the celebration of evening Masses on the days of Lent has taken the place of paraliturgical Lenten devotions such as the Stations of the Cross and the extra eucharistic devotions which accompanied them.

## The Sacrament of Penance

Together the RCC and the PNCC hold that Penance is the sacrament instituted by Jesus Christ in which through confession, sorrow and a strong purpose of amending our lives, sins are forgiven. It is grounded on the words of Christ: "As the Father has sent me so I also send you... Whose sins you shall forgive, they are forgiven them" (Jn. 20:21, 23). With these words we believe Christ gave His Apostles and their lawful successors power and authority to absolve from sin those who sincerely repent of their offenses. On this there is no difference between us.

However, we have found practical differences which are revealed in the forms used by our Churches for the adminstration of this sacrament.

The PNCC uses two forms in its penitential practice. Form I is Auricular (or private) Confession of the individual penitent to the confessor. This form, which may be used by all, is mandatory for children and youth until the age of 16. Form II is General Confession, the form more commonly used by adults. Following this form a penitential service is conducted in which all seeking the sacrament participate and all are absolved in common. This service, distinct from the penitential rite at the beginning of every Mass, consists of the following elements: invitation to repentance, a penitential hymn, prayer invoking the Holy Spirit, exhortation, examination of conscience, the confiteor, the assignment of a penance, and absolution.

The RCC, in contrast, has three forms for the administration of this sacrament. Form I is the Rite for the Reconciliation of Individual Penitents, and it corresponds to Form I of the PNCC. However, the RCC considers this to be the ordinary means of reconciliation with God and with the Church in which there takes  place the healing encounter between our need and God's merciful compassion. Form II is the Rite for the Reconciliation of Several Penitents with Individual Confession and Aboslution. This rite is followed at penitential services which are regularly scheduled by Roman Catholic parishes, especially during Advent and Lent, with a sufficient number of confessors present to hear the confessions and absolve each of those who come forward to receive the sacrament. Form III is the Rite for the Reconciliation of Several Penitents with General Confession and Absolution. This is similar to the PNCC Form II, but with these differences: 1) It is limited to circumstances of serious necessity. 2) It may not be received twice without an intervening individual confession of sins unless a just cause requires this. 3) It should be followed in due course by an individual confession in which each grave sin that has not previously been confessed is confessed. 4) It does not remove the obligation of each Roman Catholic to confess individually at least once a year all grave sins not previously confessed. 5) This third rite may not be publicly scheduled or announced in advance. 6) This third rite may not be used as part of any eucharistic liturgy.

The RCC admits Christians of other churches and ecclesial communities to this sacrament under the same conditions, by way of exception, whereby they are admitted to the Eucharist.

In reviewing these correspondences and practical differences, it was the conclusion of our dialogue that the difference between us is more a difference of form than of underlying intention or understanding of the sacrament itself.

**The Anointing of the Sick**

Our discussion of this sacrament revealed no differences between us in matters of faith. It can be noted, however, that the administration of this sacrament by the RCC and the PNCC has undergone in recent years a notable degree of renewal in its liturgical celebration so that it can be seen more clearly by the faithful as a sacrament of the sick intended for healing and not constricted to the "last rites" for the dying. In certain RCC and PNCC parishes there are now on occasion communal services at which this sacrament is administered. The RCC admits other Christians to this sacrament upon the same conditions whereby they are, by way of exception, admitted to the Eucharist.

## Holy Matrimony

Marriage in Christ is held by both Churches to be a sacrament of the New Law given to us by the Lord. Thus the RCC holds that "The matrimonial covenant, by which a man and a woman establish between themselves a partnership of the whole of life, is by its nature ordered toward the good of spouses and the procreation and education of offspring; this covenant between baptized persons has been raised by Christ the Lord to the dignity of a sacrament" (*Code of Canon Law*, Canon 1055, 1). In the PNCC it is taught that "Matrimony is the Sacrament which makes a Christian man and woman husband and wife, gives them the grace to be faithful to each other, and to bring up their children in love and devotion to God" (Rt. Rev. Thaddeus Zielinski, *A Catechism of the Polish National Catholic Church*, p. 77).

A number of notable points of comparison emerged in the course of the dialogue. In the PNCC the priest who officiates at the wedding is regarded as the minister of the sacrament of matrimony. Marriages entered into without the presence of a priest are seen as legal unions but are not held to be sacramental marriages until the blessing of the priest has been received. In the Latin rite of the Roman Catholic Church the husband and wife are regarded as the ministers of the sacrament of matrimony and the priest is the official witness of the Church. In the 1983 *Code of Canon Law*, baptized Latin rite Catholics who have not formally withdrawn from the Church (i.e. deliberately and knowingly) are obliged to marry in the presence of a priest and two other witnesses. This requirement (known as the "canonical form of marriage") must be observed for the marriage to be recognized as valid by the Roman Catholic Church. Exceptions may be granted only by a dispensation from the Roman Catholic bishop. Roman Catholic priests do confer the "nuptial blessing" at marriages, though this is seen as something distinct from the conferral of the sacrament itself. In times past the nuptial blessing was conferred only at the first marriage of a bride and was also restricted to certain times of the liturgical year, not being conferred during Advent and Lent. It is now conferred more widely.

Both Churches hold to the inviolability of marriage. In 1958 the PNCC determined that each of its dioceses would have a matrimonial court since cases of need were increasing. Before this date rare exceptions depended upon episcopal review of the case and concurrence of the Prime Bishop. Now these courts review cases and make their recommendations; then the bishops of the dioceses instruct their priests as to the direction to be taken. These rules are strictly enforced in the PNCC, and only active members of this Church may appeal to its matrimonial courts. The possible grounds for the annulment of marriage were set down in the guidelines of the 1958 Synod.

The diocesan bishop does not usually take such a direct hand in the matrimonial courts of the Roman Catholic Church. Declarations of nullity are granted only when a case is reviewed by two successive courts and grounds have been established proving the existence of a prior block which impeded a true marriage. This must be satisfactorily proven, for marriage enjoys "the favor of the law" and thus may not be declared null without such proof. While, in the past, formal cases were quite rare in Roman Catholic matrimonial courts, there has been a marked increase in more recent times.

The increase noted by the Churches was seen by the bishops as an indication of the need to convince people of the sanctity of marriage so that they prepare themselves better for it. In the face of secularizing trends, the anonymity of urban life in which people become lost and the serious problem of teenage marriage, both the Church and families have much to do.

Attention was also given to mixed marriages between Polish National Catholics and Roman Catholics. Today both Churches provide for closer contact in preparing couples for such marriages and their celebration. Ideally the priests of both Churches should be called upon to assist in this preparation, though in practice this as yet occurs too rarely. Due to the restrictions observed with respect to sharing the Eucharist together, the celebration of these mixed marriages outside the context of the Eucharist is counseled in many instances. Special notice was made of the promise which the Roman Catholic Church asks of its members entering mixed marriage; namely, to do all that they can to see to the Catholic baptism and upbringing of future children. While it can be explained that this promise is not intended to cancel the religious duties of the PNCC partner, the PNCC bishops pointed out that it continues to constitute a real difficulty for their people. They felt it needed to be understood that a Catholic upbringing is also provided children of the Polish National Catholic Church.

## Holy Orders

It is understood that the RCC and the PNCC similarly maintain the threefold pattern of the ordained ministry, made up of bishops, presbyters and deacons; and further that both Churches regard the apostolic succession of bishops to be integral to the ordained ministry of the Church. Given this, the dialogue turned its attention to the rites which are employed by the two Churches in the ordination of bishops as well as the rites used to ordain priests and deacons. It was the conclusion of the bishops that these rites display an essential similarity. It was noted that the sacramental form used for the ordination of a bishop in the PNCC is nearly an exact Polish rendering of the Latin form used by the Roman Catholic Church prior to the reforms instituted by Pope Paul VI in 1968.

The apostolic succession of bishops as seen in light of the teachings of the II Vatican Council and those of the Polish National Catholic Church were also presented. A good deal of clarity emerged on this matter so that the bishops were able to discern that apostolic succession is not an issue in question between the Churches. It seemed clear to the Roman Catholic participants on the basis of the evidence that the bishops of the Polish National Catholic Church are validly ordained bishops in apostolic succession.

Other matters reviewed and discussed included the procedures followed by the Churches in the selection of candidates for the office and ministry of bishops. And some further questions were raised concerning the manner in which bishops exercise the authority of their office. Principal among these was the collegiality of bishops. We see the need and the desirability of discussing further the collegiality of Roman Catholic bishops with the Bishop of Rome as the head of their college as well as the fraternal links which exist between the bishops of the PNCC and other bishops of the Old Catholic Union of Utrecht.

## The Word of God

There are numerous points on which we find no disagreement between the RCC and the PNCC with respect to the Word of God. Together we hold that "Christ the Lord, in whom the entire revelation of the Most High God is summed up (cf. 2 Cor. 1:20; 3:16; 4:6) commanded the apostles to preach the Gospel" (Vatican II, *Constitution on Divine Revelation*, n.7). Further we concur that "in order that the full and living Gospel might always be preserved in the church the Apostles left bishops as their successors. They gave them 'their own position of teaching authority' (St. Irenaeus, *Adv. Haer.* III, 3, 1:PG 7,848). This sacred Tradition, then, and the sacred Scripture of both Testaments are like the mirror in which the church during its pilgrim journey here on earth contemplates God, from whom she receives everything, until such time as she is brought to see Him face to face as He really is (cf. 1 Jn 3:2)" (Vatican II, *Ibid.*). Also we agree that "the task of giving an authentic interpretation of the Word of God, whether in its written form or in the form of Tradition, has been entrusted to the living teaching office of the Church alone. Its authority in this matter is exercised in the name of Jesus Christ. Yet this Magisterium is not superior to the Word of God, but is its servant. It teaches only what has been handed on to it" (*Ibid.* n. 8).

Prizing the Word of God as one of His greatest gifts, received from Christ with the command that it be proclaimed and preached in His name throughout the world to every person, the PNCC has not hesitated in the past to speak of the Word of God heard and preached in the Church as having sacramental power (*moc sakramentalna*) (Resolution of the Second Synod, 1909; in *Wiara i Wiedza*, Scranton, 1913, page 12).

For its part the RCC does not speak of the Word of God as a sacrament distinct from and along side the seven sacraments which it celebrates. It considers the proclamation of the Word of God to be an integral part of the celebration of all the seven sacraments. The Word of God permeates all the sacramental rites. To ensure that this would be realized in practice the Second Vatican Council provided for a new emphasis on preaching and a new structure for its liturgy. The Council stressed that "two parts which in a sense go to make up the Mass, viz. the liturgy of the word and the eucharistic liturgy, are so closely connected with each other that they form but one single act of worship" (*Constitution on the Sacred Liturgy*, n. 56). Because "access to Sacred Scripture ought to be open wide to the Christian faithful" (*Constitution on Divine Revelation*, n. 22) a new lectionary or book of readings has been developed for a three-year liturgical cycle providing a much wider selection of scriptural readings at Mass than the previous one-year cycle could provide. Further the Council urged that "all clerics, particularly priests of Christ and others who, as deacons or catechists, are officially engaged in the ministry of the word, should immerse themselves in the Scriptures by constant sacred reading and diligent study. For it must not happen that anyone becomes 'an empty preacher of the word to others, not being a bearer of the word in his own heart,' (St. Augustine, *Serm.* 179; *PL* 38,966) when he ought to be sharing the boundless riches of the divine word with the faithful committed to his care, especially in the sacred liturgy" (*Constitution on Divine Revelation*, n. 24).

This having been said, while we recognize a certain difference at least in descriptive terminology used by the PNCC and the RCC, we see as well a deep point of contact beneath this formal difference. For the RCC also holds that in His Holy Word Christ makes himself present to His people with power (*Ibid.* 13, 17) and for this reason "the Church has always venerated the divine Scriptures as she venerated the Body of the Lord, in so far as she never ceases, particularly in the Sacred Liturgy, to partake of the bread of life and to offer it to the faithful from the one table of the Word of God and the Body of Christ" (*Ibid.* n. 21).

Thus while a formal difference remains, one can see in both Churches the same instinct of faith at work, cherishing and reverencing the Sacred Scriptures and acknowledging their power in our lives.

### The Life to Come

After our dialogue on the sacraments a further subject for discussion was the doctrine of the Church concerning God's universal call of all to salvation, and teachings of the Church concerning heaven, hell and purgatory. Our dialogue took into account the teachings of Sacred Scripture, the ancient creeds, the Fathers of the Church (both East and West) as well as subsequent Church tradition.

Discussion was prompted by the fact that in the past some thought there was a difference in the Churches' teachings because of differing emphasis in preaching. The Polish National Catholic Church does not wish to stress the fear of hell and damnation as a motivation for living a Christian life since in the end it could have a demoralizing effect on the people. It was made clear in this dialogue that the Polish National Catholic Church, by its positive homiletic emphasis on God's universal salvific will as well as His gracious assistance and loving mercy toward sinners, does not intend to deny any other element of Christian teaching. The Church's basic teaching may be summed up in the words of the Most Reverend Francis Hodur, the first bishop of the Polish National Catholic Church:

> "I believe in final Divine justice, in future life beyond the grave which will be the further continuation of present life dependent in state and degree of perfection and happiness on our current life but before all else on the state of our soul in the last hour before death.
> "I believe in immortality and happiness in eternity, in the union with God of all people of all generations and times because I believe in the Divine power of love, charity and justice, and I desire nothing other than that it should happen to me according to my faith."

In the dialogue a fundamental agreement by the Churches in their teaching concerning heaven was ascertained. In both Churches the intercession of the saints in heaven is invoked. Further agreement exists on prayers for the deceased, including the celebration of Masses for them. Today both Churches emphasize the compassionate mercy and love of God in preaching without denying the seriousness of hell. God is just, will never punish unjustly, and wills the salvation of all. Both Churches acknowledge that fear of damnation is not the best motive for Christian living, but it is a salutary one.

Having established this much, our dialogue gave close attention to an apparent difference which surfaced in the past. Specifically this has to do with whether hell is eternal. In *A Catechism of the Polish National Catholic Church* published by the Mission Fund PNCC, one finds the question: "What of eternal punishment?" To this the answer is given: "Eternal punishment would be contrary to the wisdom, love and justice of God" (N. 169). A different teaching is found in the *Constitution on the Church* of the Second Vatican Council, where one reads: "Since we know neither the day nor the hour, we should follow the advice of the Lord and watch constantly so that when the single course of our earthly life is completed (cf. Heb. 9:27), we may merit to enter with him into the marriage feast and be numbered among the blessed (cf. Mt. 25:31-46) and not, like the wicked and slothful servants (cf. Mt. 25:36), be ordered to depart into the eternal fire (cf. Mt. 25:41), into the outer darkness where 'there will be weeping and gnashing of teeth' (Mt. 22:13 and 25:30)" (N. 48).

In considering this disparity, three factors should be taken into account. First, the catechism cited, though significant, is not a magisterial document of the PNCC. It does not carry the weight of a citation from the Second Vatican Council, for instance. Second, the dialogue is in receipt of a statement subscribed to be the six current bishops of the PNCC under date of March 1, 1988 which reads: "Maintaining the teachings of the undivided Church, we, the Bishops of the Polish National Catholic Church, in conformity with the *Declaration of Utrecht* (September 24, 1889), affirm the following: 'The Polish National Catholic Church has not taught and does not teach the so-called doctrine of Universal Salvation.'" Third, assurances have been given that catechetical materials in use by the PNCC will be in conformity with this teaching of its bishops.

We recognize that Jesus, as recorded by the New Testament, made use of the language of His time. He spoke both of *Sheol*, the dark abode of all the dead; and *Gehenna*, the postexilic Jewish idea of an eschatological place of punishment for apostate Jews and Gentile sinners where they suffered the pain of everlasting fire. From this basis Christian theology has proceeded through a complex and extended development guided by faith in the resurrection of the dead. Nonetheless, whatever may be implied by the terms "unquenchable fire" and "everlasting fire," they should not be explained away as meaningless. On this we agree, whatever further questions remain before us.

While Roman Catholics do hold to the "fire" of hell, both Churches agree that hell's greatest torment is that of immeasurable loss. Neither Church teaches that individual human beings, even those who might be damned, are annihilated and cease to exist, as some have argued on the basis of Mt. 10:28, "Be afraid of the one who can destroy both the body and the soul in Gehenna." Both Churches appreciate that the so-called "last things" are described in our teaching by eschatological imagery and that much concerning the life beyond remains unavoidably mysterious to us as long as we sojourn in this life.

## Our Dialogue Thus Far

As we look back on the path our dialogue has taken since its beginning in 1984, we find that we have thus far discovered no doctrinal obstacle that would impede the further growth of our Churches toward that unity which we believe is Christ's will (Jn. 17:21). Though we still have more to discuss, we already have much for which to be grateful. We appreciate the words which Cardinal Bernardin addressed to us in 1988:

> The existence and progress of the dialogue between bishops of the Polish National Catholic and Roman Catholic Churches is a real sign of hope and source of joy for all of us. What we witness in your work is a sincere and dedicated effort to heal a division that occurred right within the American Catholic family. Therefore it touches us deeply as Catholics living in America. We know how deeply any family can be hurt by separation among its members. Many painful memories still remain among us, for the sad events which brought us to go separate ways are not long buried in the past. They are within the living memory of many, and truthfully we must admit they still hurt. To this your dialogue is an important healing force. By rekindling our hopes it helps to free us from our sad memories and to be renewed in the promise of Our Lord that through the power of His Spirit He can build up anew our unity with one another. Through the dialogue we grow in the keen realization of how much we share together in faith and in sacramental life. We recognize that together we belong to the great Catholic family. I wholeheartedly agree with what Prime Bishop Swantek said in welcoming you to your session in Buffalo two years ago: "The conversations between the Polish National Catholic Church and Roman Catholic Church are a very important step in ecumenism because they bring together two Churches which have been separated by events of history, but they have so many common characteristics and essentials in faith and liturgical expression..."

In 1986 the General Synod of the Polish National Catholic Church welcomed Cardinal John Krol as the representative of our National Conference of Catholic Bishops. On that occasion His Eminence stressed that our efforts toward unity must be undertaken in a way that is "radically new" and in keeping with the vision of Pope John XXIII which seeks "unity in essentials—not uniformity." In pursuit of "unity with diversity" His Eminence pointed out that the II Vatican Council called upon us to go beyond a mentality seeking "return" or "absorption." He rightly stressed that "The concept of the restoration of unity does not imply inertia and expectancy on the part of the Catholic Church and a denial of their past on the part of other Christians."

"Rather, he said, "it means a dynamic movement toward unity in which each moves toward the other by living more faithfully the valid Christian elements in each's tradition measured against and constantly renewed according to the will of Christ."

It is precisely this "dynamic movement toward unity" to which we believe the people of our Churches are called by Christ.

In behalf of Pope John Paul II, Cardinal Agostino Casaroli, Secretary of State for the Holy See, wrote to Prime Bishop Swantek on January 16, 1988. Speaking for His Holiness, the Cardinal said:

"The Holy Father has deep interest in the dialogue between the Polish National Catholic Church and the Bishops' Committee for Ecumenical and Interreligious Affairs of the U.S. National Conference of Catholic Bishops and prays for its success, so that the communion between us can be deepened. He was happy therefore to hear of your positive assessment of that dialogue, and the progress toward understanding and unity that is being made.

Many steps must be taken for the goal of unity to be reached and these must be properly discerned as we move forward. But the conviction of His Holiness is that our ecumenical goal must be nothing less than the achievement of full ecclesiastical communion; it is toward this that the Spirit is leading us. For divisions among Christians are an obstacle to the mission of preaching the Gospel and bringing to others the saving mysteries of Christ.

We cannot go back to those fateful days, decades ago, and change the difficult events which led to separation between our people. But today's new ecumenical atmosphere allows us both to see those tragic events in a new perspective, and above all to be open to the promptings of the Spirit who alone can lead us into all truth (cf. Jn. 15:26).

The new millennium that is approaching is a special Christian moment, a special time of grace. With God's help we can make use of this opportunity to focus together on Christ, and the unity of his followers for which he prayed (cf. Jn 17:21).

It remains our hope that this dialogue, which from the beginning we have entrusted to the care and protection of the Holy Mother of God, may contribute to the progress of all our people toward the great goal of unity. We commend this report to their study and reflection and ask their prayers that God may open before us the path He intends us to follow.

# How We Agree/How We Differ*

## Roman Catholic—Southern Baptist
## The Scholars' Dialogue
## (1986-88)

### Introduction

In our discussions over the past decade, we have come to realize that despite the different vocabularies we use in presenting and explaining our beliefs and despite very real differences which remain, we do share a basic understanding of what it means to be a follower of Jesus Christ by the grace of God. We do not claim to speak either for all Southern Baptists or for all Roman Catholics, nor do we attempt to cover all aspects of our respective beliefs. We recognize that considerable diversity of thought exists within both communions. We reflect the discussions held over the past decade on issues which we felt are important for Christian witness today. We have seen how the gift of faith and the experience of God's grace have shaped our personal lives and the lives of people in our churches. Though we list below primarily doctrinal points of agreement and divergence, the most profound experience of unity occurred in those times when we told the stories of our journeys in faith and when we gathered to hear the word proclaimed and to offer our prayers to a loving God. We not only confessed but experienced "One Lord, one faith, and one baptism" (Ephesians 4:5). Our hopes and prayers are that the gifts of mutual understanding and respect, along with love and friendship, which we received in a decade of dialogue may be shared by other Southern Baptists and Roman Catholics.

### On Scripture

We Roman Catholics and Southern Baptists agree that the ultimate authority and object of faith is the triune God and that the primary source of our knowledge of God is in the revelation of God in Scripture. We concur

*To Understand Each Other: Roman Catholics and Southern Baptists, The Theological Educator, #39 (1989) 97-107.

that the self-disclosure of God in Scripture is to effect a redemptive relation-ship between God and creation (both humanity and nature). We both affirm that the Bible is the inspired Word of God authoritative for faith and practice, and that the Bible is to be at the center of public worship and of the spiritual life of individual believers.

We also value tradition and heritage as an interpretative and shaping source for understanding Scripture. Southern Baptists, while recognizing the implicit authority of tradition, affirm that all tradition must be tested against the explicit authority of Scripture, and hold to the right of individual inter-pretation of Scripture. Roman Catholics affirm the necessity of individual appropriation of Scripture but affirm that any interpretation of Scripture must be measured against the manner in which Scripture has been proclaimed and lived by the whole church in its tradition and teaching.

## On Salvation

Both Southern Baptists and Roman Catholics agree that salvation is God's free gift of grace, unmerited by any human works or righteousness, and that this salvation was accomplished for all through the life, teaching, suffering, death, and resurrection of Jesus Christ, the Son of God. We also agree that the proclamation of the offer of salvation to all peoples is the prime mission of the church. Southern Baptists stress the experience of sal-vation when, in faith, a person accepts Jesus as his or her personal Saviour. Catholics tend to emphasize the work of Christ and the way in which the effect of the redemption by Christ is made available to the faithful through faith and the sacraments in the church.

## On Spirituality

The gift of salvation is expressed in Christian life. Roman Catholics and Southern Baptists describe this in different ways: "spirituality," "disci-pleship," "spiritual growth," "growth in holiness," "sanctification," "devo-tional life," and "Christian witness." We both set the highest priority on seeking a conscious relationship with God in this life and on striving for the ultimate goal of living in glory with God in heaven, and we affirm that our love for God is best achieved in a close relationship with Jesus, coupled with a Christ-like love of neighbor.

Catholic practice places great emphasis on communal participation in and celebration of the sacraments. While Southern Baptists stress the com-plete sufficiency of a direct and personal but non-sacramental relationship to

God, their spirituality is also church-related with a stress on face-to-face fellowship in the local church.

The Bible has always been at the center of Southern Baptist life. Since the Second Vatican Council, Catholic spirituality has also become strongly biblical. The proclamation and exposition of the Scriptures are central to the Sunday liturgies, and the celebration of every sacrament is to be accompanied by reading from the Bible. Reading, prayer, and study of the Bible are central to both Roman Catholic and Southern Baptist practice.

Over the centuries devotion to Mary and the saints has been a source of division and misunderstanding between Roman Catholics and Southern Baptists. While Roman Catholics affirm with Baptists the sole mediatorship of Christ, they also honor the Virgin Mary as the Mother of God and affirm with the Second Vatican Council that she is "inseparably linked with her Son's saving work" ("Constitution on the Sacred Liturgy," 103, in *The Documents of Vatican II*). They invoke or pray to Mary and to the canonized saints as an aspect of their belief in the communion of the saints (heavenly, earthly, and in purgatory). Southern Baptists honor Mary as the mother of Jesus Christ and emphasize the communion of saints as primarily a present reality among Christians, but they do not address prayer to Mary or to deceased Christians lest such infringe the sole mediatorship of Jesus Christ.

Since Vatican II, devotion to Mary has undergone significant changes among Roman Catholics. Mary is described in more biblical terms as the model disciple whose life is one of devotion to Jesus and who stands at his cross. Mary is seen also as an advocate of the poor and oppressed when she rejoices in a God who exalts the lowly and puts down the mighty from their thrones (Luke 1:46-55). Devotion to Mary and the saints is an area where significant differences between Baptists and Catholics remain, but where great progress has been made in mutual understanding and respect. Catholics have come to appreciate the sincere problems Southern Baptists have with Marian devotion, and Southern Baptists have come to feel the depth of devotion and affection for Mary among Roman Catholics.

Because of theological, historical, and cultural factors, Catholic and Southern Baptist experiences of communal worship differ significantly in tone and style. Catholic worship centers on the Sunday Eucharist and the liturgical seasons. Various devotional practices also play a part. The texture of Catholic experience is shaped as well by the use of statuary, art, and other religious symbols such as incense, holy water, oil, and liturgical vestments. Southern Baptist Sunday worship centers on preaching, choral singing, communal prayer, and the study of Scripture. Church architecture is usually characterized by simplicity; use of religious symbols is restrained. Both Southern Baptists and Catholics share a strong commitment to communal worship and to the importance of deep religious experience within the context of public worship.

Although our two communions differ significantly in their approaches to worship, there are significant convergences in fundamental attitudes. Both groups have a strong sense both of human sinfulness and of God's love even amid our sins and failings; both stress strong family life and sexual morality; both stress active engagement in church life.

## On Church and Ministry

We both affirm that the church is at the heart of the New Testament and of Christian life. In the New Testament the church is a community of people bound to Jesus Christ and to one another with the bonds of faith and love, acceptance and commitment. One major image found there is that of the church as the people of God (Hebrews 4:9; 11:25; 1 Peter 2:10) which describes an understanding of church in both our communities. As Jesus called disciples to follow him, so people today are divinely called to the church. We both affirm that the church must be obedient to the Word of God in Scripture and proclaim and witness to it in its daily life.

Most distinctive of Southern Baptist theology is the stress that "the visible church" is "a congregation of baptized believers, associated by covenant in the faith and fellowship of the Gospel" (from The Philadelphia Confession of 1742). Both Southern Baptists and Roman Catholics affirm with the New Testament that the church is the body of Christ and includes the redeemed of all the ages. For Southern Baptists the primary meaning of church is the local congregation. Southern Baptists stress fellowship in this congregation as a manifestation of that faith which leads to baptism and joining the church.

Roman Catholic theology describes the church in several different ways, for example, as "people of God," "the mystical body of Christ," "the household of God in the Spirit" (Ephesians 2:19-22; see also the "Dogmatic Constitution on the Church," 6, in *The Documents of Vatican II*), and a visible society or institution. Most fundamentally the church is a mystery comprising the union of God with men and women in community effected by the saving work of Christ, and the union of the members among themselves through baptism. Catholics affirm that just as Christ is at work in the celebration of the sacraments he is also at work in the church, which is often called the fundamental sacrament of the divine-human encounter. For Catholics the local congregation, called a parish, is one community which, with others, makes up a diocese. Catholics use the phrase "local church" to refer to a diocese headed by a bishop in communion with all other bishops under the leadership of the Bishop of Rome.

Both Southern Baptists and Roman Catholics recognize the multiplicity of ministries that characterized the church of the New Testament. On the basis of the New Testament, both communions also recognize a clear distinction between ordained and non-ordained persons. In practice, the ministry of a Baptist pastor and a Roman Catholic pastor exhibit many similarities, although they are not identical. For Roman Catholics, the primary functions of the priest/pastor, often assisted by permanent deacons, are preaching the Word of God, presiding at the celebration of the Eucharist and administering the other sacraments of the church, and pastoral care and administration. For Southern Baptists the preaching task of the pastor is central, especially the role of evangelist. No less important, however, is the day-by-day pastoral care of the congregation and the administration of the church as an organization.

While Southern Baptists recognize an important difference between ordained and non-ordained persons, they also emphasize the ministry of the laity. There is an increasing emphasis on the ministry of the laity in the Catholic Church, where there are emerging ministries of lay people acting as campus ministers and chaplains (in hospitals and other institutional settings such as prisons) and pastoral associates (assistants officially appointed for the direction of a parish). One becomes a pastor in a Southern Baptist church by virtue of an invitation or call by the congregation. Tenure is at the pleasure of the congregation. In Catholicism, a priest is ordained by a bishop and receives his assignment to a parish or other ministry from a bishop or other church authorities.

## On Grace

We Roman Catholics and Southern Baptists agree upon the normative role of the Holy Scriptures in coming to an understanding of grace. Even so, in both our traditions we acknowledge post-biblical influences affecting our language and doctrine respecting grace.

Among Roman Catholics there is a tendency to connect the grace of God with the goodness of creation as well as with salvation-history, whereas among Southern Baptists there is a tendency to understand grace primarily in relation to human salvation from and divine forgiveness of sin.

We stand in the heritage of the grace/favor of God which was manifest to the people of Israel, and we affirm together that the supreme manifestation of God's grace occurred in the birth, life, teaching, healing, suffering, death, resurrection, and ascension of Jesus Christ, the Son of God.

We agree on the universality of sin and on God's gracious provision through the atoning sacrifice of his Son for the remission/forgiveness of human sins. Whereas Southern Baptists tend to emphasize the individual and personal aspect of sin and grace and Roman Catholics tend to stress the ecclesial and social dimension, both groups struggle to maintain a balance between the two. Roman Catholics, unlike Southern Baptists, teach that the Virgin Mary was without sin through the grace of her Son Jesus Christ.

For Roman Catholics the grace of God in Jesus Christ is normally mediated to human beings through the church and the sacraments. For Southern Baptists the grace of God in Jesus Christ is normally mediated through the experience of repentance, faith, regeneration, justification, forgiveness, and so on. Roman Catholics do not deny the personal reception of grace, and Southern Baptists do not deny that grace is normally received through Scripture, church, preaching, and witness.

Both Roman Catholics and Southern Baptists agree that the Christian baptism of believing persons testifies to the grace of God and that it is God's grace that leads one to faith and baptism. Roman Catholics believe that baptism, which is to be performed only once, is a sacrament and means of grace which unites the believer to the passion, death, and resurrection of Christ. It may be administered in different ways (immersion, affusion, aspersion) to infants as well as to adult converts. The present "Rite of Christian Initiation of Adults" notes that the initiation of adult converts into the faith provides the norm for a Catholic understanding of baptism. Southern Baptists baptize only professed believers, by immersion only, and believe that baptism is a symbol of Christ's death, burial, and resurrection and also a testimony that God's grace has been received by the baptized.

Both Roman Catholics and Southern Baptists agree that the Eucharist or Lord's Supper is a memorial of Jesus' passion and death and an anticipation of his return for the gathering of the faithful into glory. Roman Catholics believe that the Eucharist is the sacrament wherein, by the words of institution and the power of the Holy Spirit, the body and blood of Jesus Christ become really present under the form of bread and wine. Thus Jesus is uniquely present to the recipients and invites them to offer themselves in union with him. Southern Baptists believe that the Lord's Supper was ordained by Jesus as both obedient testimony to and proclamation of his death and an occasion of communion, following self-examination, with him and with fellow Christians.

Both Roman Catholics and Southern Baptists agree upon the obligation and significance of discipleship in the life of grace. With variant patterns of Christian obedience and of spirituality, they nevertheless can together emphasize the personal commitment essential to discipleship and explore the greater usefulness of the term "community of disciples" as an ecclesiological theme.

Both Roman Catholics and Southern Baptists believe in God's graciousness and base their hope for salvation upon it. Southern Baptists believe that once a sinner has received the grace of God through repentance and faith, there is normally certain assurance of this gift, and, therefore, they express their confidence in "being saved." They also believe that through the promises, faithfulness, and keeping power of God, and despite the doubts, temptations, and backslidings of genuine believers, the latter will certainly attain final salvation. Roman Catholics, while trusting in God's grace to help them to persevere, believe that it is still possible to fall from grace through serious sin and that only when God moves the sinner to repent is it possible for grace to be restored. They therefore tend to speak with less assurance about "being saved."

## On Mission and Missions

Both Roman Catholics and Southern Baptists speak of the mission of the church in the sense of the vocation of the church to witness to the saving love of God and to proclaim God's redemption in Jesus Christ in order that men and women may experience grace and salvation. We also use "mission" and "missions" in the sense of the fulfilling the command of Jesus "to preach the gospel to all peoples" (Mark 13:10) and to "make disciples of all nations" (Matthew 28:19).

Roman Catholics use the term "evangelization" for that dimension and activity of the church's mission of proclamation which presses to offer every person the valid opportunity to be directly challenged by the explicit gospel of faith in Jesus Christ. Southern Baptists prefer the term "evangelism" for proclaiming the gospel and leading people to a decision of faith in Jesus. Among Christian denominations Roman Catholics and Southern Baptists have been notable especially in the nineteenth and twentieth centuries for missionary activity among peoples who have not yet heard the gospel. Both Southern Baptists and Roman Catholics have combined explicit proclamation of the gospel with other works of charity such as healthcare and education.

Roman Catholics and Southern Baptists agree upon the ecclesial and Christian mandate to proclaim the gospel of God's grace to all peoples and all nations, but Roman Catholics tend to be more confident than Southern Baptists in affirming that God's saving grace may be efficacious apart from specific confession of the name of the incarnate, crucified, and risen Jesus. Catholics also speak of the "evangelization of culture" or of a "mission to social structures" and in some areas practice Christian presence rather than explicit proclamation.

In practice Southern Baptists have stressed the importance of doing missions through and under the direction of the denomination rather than through outside or parachurch missionary organizations. The intent of the missionary activity has been to establish independent indigenous churches in mission areas. Roman Catholics also stress the responsibility of the local diocese for both home and foreign mission, but they understand that no local church is completely independent but is always in communion with all other local churches, which have similar missionary responsibilities. For Roman Catholics, the whole church is in mission through all the local churches in mission.

Both Roman Catholics and Southern Baptists reject a distorted witness or proselytism which involves improper attitudes and behavior in the practice of Christian witness and does not respect the right of the human person, Christian or non-Christian, to be free from external coercion in religious matters. We also recognize the tensions in attempting to be faithful witnesses of the gospel and in proclaiming the gospel to others. In predominantly Roman Catholic countries, Southern Baptist missionaries and local Baptists have sometimes suffered legal and social discrimination. At times, Southern Baptist missionaries have labored among Roman Catholics without respecting their faith and beliefs. When competition and conflict emerge in missionary activity, our efforts to share the gospel which we proclaim and which sustains our lives can become a stumbling block to those who have not heard the gospel.

## On Eschatology

In Roman Catholic theology the term "eschatology" has traditionally referred to teaching about "the four last things," namely, death, judgment, heaven, and hell. Under the impact of recent biblical studies it has taken on the richer meaning of teaching about the destiny of human history and its relation to the kingdom proclaimed and enacted by Jesus.

Roman Catholics affirm that those individuals who die in a state of friendship and union with God (the state of grace) will be happy with God for all eternity. Catholic theology strongly affirms the existence of hell and that an individual who freely rejects God's offer of love and grace and chooses to live in conscious enmity to God and hatred of the neighbor can lose eternal salvation. While Catholics await the second coming of Jesus and the general judgment, they affirm the judgment of the individual soul after death. Purgatory, or the stage of purification from the effects of earthly sinfulness prior to the fullness of happiness with God, is a firm part of Catholic teaching and remains a point on which Catholics and Southern Baptists disagree. In attempting to speak of the end of one's own life and of history as a whole, one stands before the mystery of God and the mysterious relation of time and eternity, so all language is inadequate.

Southern Baptists emphasize the leading themes of Reformation eschatology, that is, death, resurrection, second coming, last judgment, hell, and heaven. Such teaching normally implies a conscious intermediate state, distinct from soul sleeping and from purgatory, and carefully avoids both the belief that all persons will be saved (universalism) and the belief that unbelievers will be annihilated. In the nineteenth century Southern Baptists began to be influenced by pronounced differences regarding the timing and sequence of end time events (especially concerning the thousand-year reign of Christ) and the meaning of the kingdom of God. In the late twentieth century such differences have contributed to denominational tensions.

Roman Catholic doctrine and practice have in general not been open to different forms of millennialism. However, more and more ordinary Catholics are being caught up in contemporary popular apocalyptic movements.

## Conclusion

This chapter is a summary of what we at the Roman Catholic/Southern Baptist Scholars' Dialogue concluded about how we agree and differ. More detailed information about our agreements and differences may be found in other chapters of this book. But this common statement, reviewed and amended in plenary session, gives testimony in a special way, we think, to the fact that Baptists and Christians share many fundamental convictions, including our Christian faith in God the Father, the Son, and the Holy Spirit.

# EVANGELICAL ECUMENICAL DOCUMENTS

# Introduction

The term "evangelical" is rather loosely used to describe a variety of currents, largely rooted in various revival traditions, that tend to stand outside the "ecumenical" circles and movements of the mainstream or tend to take a position of opposition within the "mainline" or "ecumenical" churches. The opposition of "evangelical" to "ecumenical" in the common parlance of our age is unfortunate because such usage tends to obscure the extent to which such groups are often fiercely "ecumenical" within their own circles (in cooperative programs, in common social witness, and in eucharistic celebration) and such usage tends to perpetuate perceptions of polarization rather than facilitate a bridging between traditions.

This situation also creates difficulties in discerning what might constitute an "evangelical ecumenical document." "Evangelical" gatherings that qualify as "ecumenical" are often more informal in sponsorship, speaking to constituencies but often without the ecclesial location or authority more common in the "ecumenical" world. The documents chosen for this section reveal this informal tendency and might better be seen as signs of new sensitivities and openness within the "evangelical" world that promise a new "ecumenical" posture.

"The Declaration of Evangelical Social Concern" (often termed "The Chicago Declaration") was composed during the Thanksgiving holiday of 1973 at a meeting in the modest surroundings of the now closed Chicago YMCA. This meeting was called by Ronald J. Sider and others to bring together the leaders of the older generation of the "neo-evangelical" movement and the leaders of various new socially engaged circles of younger evangelicals that began to emerge in the 1960s and early 1970s. Representing various strands of "evangelicals" (including Pentecostal, Holiness, and various Evangelical groups as well as members of mainline churches), this "declaration" had great influence during the rest of the decade. Billy Graham identified with it, the Christian Holiness Association adopted it as a plenary resolution, and it became the basis of dialogue with officers of the National Council of Churches and precipitated formal dialogue with various denominations—especially with the Lutherans and the

Methodists. Most noteworthy of the formal responses was that of the Unit Committee of the Division of Church and Society of the National Council of Churches. This response is also reprinted here to indicate the extent to which these polarized parties were moving tentatively toward each other during the 1970s as the "renewal of evangelical social concern" helped bridge the gap between the heirs of the "social gospel" and the heirs of an emphasis on the priority of personal conversion.

In 1977 a similar group, including a few participants from the earlier meeting, issued "The Chicago Call," which expressed a renewed appreciation for the classical traditions of Christianity, including an explicit call for visible Christian unity. This statement can be interpreted from many angles, but clearly expressed increasing uneasiness with the dominant low-church ethos of much revivalistic "evangelicalism." Some saw parallels to the "Oxford Movement" of nineteenth century England, and several participants in "The Chicago Call" have played out similar trajectories to identify with Roman Catholic, Orthodox, and Anglican churches. For those who have continued to identify with various "evangelical" currents, the "Chicago Call" signaled a new openness to and appreciation for the more traditional expressions of Christianity—a theme that has continued to gain force in the years since 1977.

## References

Donald W. Dayton, "Yet Another Layer of the Onion: Or, Opening the Ecumenical Door to Let the Riffraff In," *Ecumenical Review* 40 (1988) 87-110.

Ronald J. Sider (ed.), *The Chicago Declaration* (Carol Stream, IL: Creation House, 1974).

Robert Webber and Donald Bloesch (eds.), *The Orthodox Evangelicals* (Nashville: Nelson, 1988).

# A Declaration of
# Evangelical Social Concern

As Evangelical Christians committed to the Lord Jesus Christ and the full authority of the Word of God, we affirm that God lays total claim upon the lives of his people. We cannot, therefore, separate our lives from situations in which God has placed us in the United States and the world.

We confess that we have not acknowledged the complete claims of God on our lives.

We acknowledge that God requires love. But we have not demonstrated the love of God to those suffering social abuses.

We acknowledge that God requires justice. But we have not proclaimed or demonstrated his justice to an unjust American society. Although the Lord calls us to defend the social and economic rights of the poor and the oppressed, we have mostly remained silent. We deplore the historic involvement of the church in America with racism and the conspicuous responsibility of the evangelical community for perpetuating the personal attitudes and institutional structures that have divided the body of Christ along color lines. Further, we have failed to condemn the exploitation of racism at home and abroad by our economic system.

We affirm that God abounds in mercy and that He forgives all who repent and turn from their sins. We call our fellow evangelical Christians to demonstrate repentance in a Christian discipleship that confronts the social and political injustice of our nation.

We must attack the materialism of our culture and the maldistribution of the nation's wealth and services. We recognize that as a nation we play a crucial role in the imbalance and injustice of international trade and development. Before God and a billion hungry neighbors, we must rethink our values regarding our present standard of living and promote more just acquisition and distribution of the world's resources.

We acknowledge our Christian responsibilities of citizenship. Therefore, we must challenge the misplaced trust of the nation in economic and military might—a proud trust that promotes a national pathology of war and violence which victimizes our neighbors at home and abroad. We must resist the temptation to make the nation and its institutions objects of mere religious loyalty.

We acknowledge that we have encouraged men to prideful domination and women to irresponsible passivity. So we call both men and women to mutual submission and active discipleship.

We proclaim no new gospel, but the Gospel of our Lord Jesus Christ who, through the power of the Holy Spirit, frees people from sin so that they might praise God through works of righteousness. By this declaration we endorse no political ideology or party, but call our nation's leaders and people to that righteousness which exalts a nation.

We make this declaration in the biblical hope that Christ is coming to consummate the kingdom and we accept his claim on our total discipleship till he comes.

Chicago, Ill., November 25, 1973.

# A Response to a Declaration of Evangelical Social Concern

Thanksgiving, 1973, a group of evangelical Christians in Chicago drew up a "Declaration of Evangelical Social Concern" which represented an important event for the life of the whole Christian community in this country.

Members of the Division of Church and Society and of other units of the NCC have been impressed with the degree to which that statement lessens the distance that is often assumed to separate "evangelical Christians" from "ecumenical Christians." We deplore the use of such labels as though they were mutually exclusive, and we welcome the Chicago Declaration as an expression of a common concern. We do not suppose those who made it to be any less evangelical for having lifted up afresh the social concern that has always been implicit, and sometimes explicit, in their tradition. In the same sense, we do not relinquish any of our historic concern for social justice by reminding ourselves that we have not sufficiently manifest the evangelical spirit that has always been implicit in the ecumenical movement.

Though the Declaration neither invites nor requires response, we are moved by the Holy Spirit to express a deep feeling of kinship with that statement and with our fellow Christians who issued it. Using the same form and some of the same words, we offer a response in the spirit of humility and seaching, to the end that a new understanding, a new dialogue, and possibly a new reconciliation may emerge.

As people "committed to the Lord Jesus Christ and to the full authority of the Word of God," we too affirm that "God lays total claim upon the lives of the people." We cannot separate our efforts to alleviate the distresses of human society from the urgency to proclaim the Gospel of Christ, which truly saves and frees persons to become what God created them to be.

We acknowledge that we have not adequately expressed or embodied our commitment to the sovereignty of the one God, the Lordship of Christ, and the power of the Holy Spirit. As a result, many have failed to see in us

573

the Christian motivation which compels our work in the world: that we are there at the behest of the Savior for the deliverance of our fellow human beings for whom he died.

"We acknowledge that God requires love." But we have not always shown love to those who have disagreed with us on the need to transform the structures of society. We have been too often inclined to criticize or ignore those who have tended to emphasize the personal rather than the structural.

"We acknowledge that God requires justice," and we have tried to help bring about a more just society. We are aware of shortcomings and defects in the means we have chosen. While we do not in any way recede from our continuing determination to seek justice for all of God's children, we acknowledge that we have not sufficiently shown this determination to be rooted in Christ's Gospel. Though sometimes denounced as "radical," we have not been nearly as genuinely radical as the Gospel calls us to be. We have sometimes forgotten that we are pilgrims and sojourners. We have failed to deal with the structures of the world as instruments of the principalities and powers. We have not proclaimed the full truth of Christ, which brings a more profound diagnosis of the human condition, a farther-reaching cure, and the possibility of real healing and transformation of persons and communities.

"We affirm that God abounds in mercy and that he forgives all who repent and turn from their sins." So we seek a Christian discipleship that is no longer shy or diffident about proclaiming the complete Gospel of Christ, with both its personal and its social implications. We must not only "attack the materialism of our culture and the maldistribution of the nation's wealth and services" and "promote more just acquisition and distribution of the world's resources," but we must offer by word and deed a witness to God's purposes for human life as expressed both in Scripture and in God's mighty acts in history, so that struggling, suffering, despairing people can find personal redemption in Christ that will empower them to liberate themselves and others.

We must not only "resist the temptation to make the nation and its institutions objects of near-religious loyalty," but we must free ourselves from the many captivities of our inherited cultures, West and East. Therefore, we "ecumenical" Christians would like to join other Christians in a faithful pilgrimage beyond the systems and structures of our present bondage into the new ways in which God may lead us, for there is "more light yet to break forth from his holy Word."

*The Unit Committee of the Division of Church and Society,*
*National Council of Churches*

# The Chicago Call:
# An Appeal to Evangelicals*

## (1977)

### Prologue

In every age the Holy Spirit calls the church to examine its faithfulness to God's revelation in Scripture. We recognize with gratitude God's blessing through the evangelical resurgence in the church. Yet at such a time of growth we need to be especially sensitive to our weaknesses. We believe that today evangelicals are hindered from achieving full maturity by a reduction of the historic faith. There is, therefore, a pressing need to reflect upon the substance of the biblical and historic faith and to recover the fullness of this heritage. Without presuming to address all our needs, we have identified eight of the themes to which we as evangelical Christians must give careful theological consideration.

### A Call to Historic Roots and Continuity

We confess that we have often lost the fullness of our Christian heritage, too readily assuming that the Scriptures and the Spirit make us independent of the past. In so doing, we have become theologically shallow, spiritually weak, blind to the work of God in others and married to our cultures.

Therefore we call for a recovery of our full Christian heritage. Throughout the church's history there has existed an evangelical impulse to proclaim the saving, unmerited grace of Christ, and to reform the church

*Robert Webber and Donald Bloesch, eds., *The Orthodox Evangelicals* (Nashville: Nelson, 1988) 11-16.

according to the Scriptures. This impulse appears in the doctrines of the ecumenical councils, the piety of the early fathers, the Augustinian theology of grace, the zeal of the monastic reformers, the devotion of the practical mystics and the scholarly integrity of the Christian humanists. It flowers in the biblical fidelity of the Protestant Reformers and the ethical earnestness of the Radical Reformation. It continues in the efforts of the Puritans and Pietists to complete and perfect the Reformation. It is reaffirmed in the awakening movements of the 18th and 19th centuries which joined Lutheran, Reformed, Wesleyan and other evangelicals in an ecumenical effort to renew the church and to extend its mission in the proclamation and social demonstration of the Gospel. It is present at every point in the history of Christianity where the Gospel has come to expression through the operation of the Holy Spirit: in some of the strivings toward renewal in Eastern Orthodoxy and Roman Catholicism and in biblical insights in forms of Protestantism differing form our own. We dare not move beyond the biblical limits of the Gospel; but we cannot be fully evangelical without recognizing our need to learn from other times and movements concerning the whole meaning of that Gospel.

## A Call to Biblical Fidelity

We deplore our tendency toward individualistic interpretation of Scripture. This undercuts the objective character of biblical truth, and denies the guidance of the Holy Spirit among his people through the ages.

Therefore we affirm that the Bible is to be interpreted in keeping with the best insights of historical and literary study, under the guidance of the Holy Spirit, with respect for the historic understanding of the church.

We affirm that the Scriptures, as the infallible Word of God, are the basis of authority in the church. We acknowledge that God uses the Scriptures to judge and to purify his Body. The church, illumined and guided by the Holy Spirit, must in every age interpret, proclaim and live out the Scriptures.

## A Call to Creedal Identity

We deplore two opposite excesses: a creedal church that merely recites a faith inherited from the past, and a creedless church that languishes in

a doctrinal vacuum. We confess that as evangelicals we are not immune
from these defects.

Therefore we affirm the need in our time for a confessing church that
will boldly witness to its faith before the world, even under threat of persecution. In every age the church must state its faith over against heresy and
paganism. What is needed is a vibrant confession that excludes as well as
includes, and thereby aims to purify faith and practice. Confessional authority is limited by and derived from the authority of Scripture, which alone
remains ultimately and permanently normative. Nevertheless, as the common
insight of those who have been illumined by the Holy Spirit and seek to be
the voice of the "holy catholic church," a confession should serve as a guide
for the interpretation of Scripture.

We affirm the abiding value of the great ecumenical creeds and the
Reformation confessions. Since such statements are historically and cultur-
ally conditioned, however, the church today needs to express its faith
afresh, without defecting from the truths apprehended in the past. We need
to articulate our witness against the idolatries and false ideologies of our
day.

## A Call to Holistic Salvation

We deplore the tendency of evangelicals to understand salvation solely
as an individual, spiritual and otherworldly matter to the neglect of the
corporate, physical and this-worldly implication of God's saving activity.

Therefore we urge evangelicals to recapture a holistic view of salvation. The witness of Scripture is that because of sin our relationships with
God, ourselves, others and creation are broken. Through the atoning work
of Christ on the cross, healing is possible for these broken relationships.

Wherever the church has been faithful to its calling, it has proclaimed
personal salvation; it has been a channel of God's healing to those in physical and emotional need; it has sought justice for the oppressed and disinher-
ited; and it has been a good steward of the natural world.

As evangelicals we acknowledge our frequent failure to reflect this
holistic view of salvation. We therefore call the church to participate fully
in God's saving activity through work and prayer, and to strive for justice
and liberation for the oppressed, looking forward to the culmination of salvation in the new heaven and new earth to come.

## A Call to Sacramental Integrity

We decry the poverty of sacramental understanding among evangelicals. This is largely due to the loss of our continuity with the teaching of many of the Fathers and Reformers and results in the deterioration of sacramental life in our churches. Also, the failure to appreciate the sacramental nature of God's activity in the world often leads us to disregard the sacredness of daily living.

Therefore we call evangelicals to awaken to the sacramental implications of creation and incarnation. For these doctrines the historic church has affirmed that God's activity is mainfested in a material way. We need to recognize that the grace of God is mediated through faith by the operation of the Holy Spirit in a notable way in the sacraments of baptism and the Lord's Supper. Here the church proclaims, celebrates and participates in the death and resurrection of Christ in such a way as to nourish her members throughout their lives in anticipation of the consummation of the kingdom. Also, we should remember our biblical designation as "living epistles," for here the sacramental character of the Christian's daily life is expressed.

## A Call to Spirituality

We suffer from a neglect of authentic spirituality on the one hand, and an excess of undisciiplined spirituality on the other hand. We have too often pursued a superhuman religiosity rather than the biblical model of a true humanity released from bondage to sin and renewed by the Holy Spirit.

Therefore we call for a spirituality which grasps by faith the full content of Christ's redemptive work: freedom from the guilt and power of sin, and newness of life through the indwelling and outpouring of his Spirit. We affirm the centrality of the preaching of the Word of God as a primary means by which his Spirit works to renew the church in its corporate life as well as in the individual lives of believers. A true spirituality will call for identification with the suffering of the world as well as the cultivation of personal piety.

We need to rediscover the devotional resources of the whole church, including the evangelical traditions of Pietism and Puritanism. We call for an exploration of devotional practice in all traditions within the church in order to deepen our relationship both with Christ and with other Christians. Among these resources are such spiritual disciplines as prayer, meditation, silence, fasting, Bible study and spiritual diaries.

## A Call to Church Authority

We deplore our disobedience to the Lordship of Christ as expressed through authority in his church. This has promoted a spirit of autonomy in persons and groups resulting in isolationism and competitiveness, even anarchy, within the body of Christ. We regret that in the absence of godly authority, there have arisen legalistic, domineering leaders on the one hand and indifference to church discipline on the other.

Therefore we affirm that all Christians are to be in practical submission to one another and to designated leaders in a church under the Lordship of Christ. The church, as the people of God, is called to be the visible presence of Christ in the world. Every Christian is called to active priesthood in worship and service through exercising spiritual gifts and ministries. In the church we are in vital union both with Christ and with one another. This calls for community with deep involvement and mutual commitment of time, energy and possessions. Further, church discipline, biblically based and under the direction of the Holy Spirit, is essential to the well-being and ministry of God's people. Moreover, we encourage all Christian organizations to conduct their activities with genuine accountability to the whole church.

## A Call to Church Unity

We deplore the scandalous isolation and separation of Christians from one another. We believe such division is contrary to Christ's explicit desire for unity among his people and impedes the witness of the church in the world. Evangelicalism is too frequently characterized by an ahistorical, sectarian mentality. We fail to appropriate the catholicity of historic Christianity, as well as the breadth of the biblical revelation.

Therefore we call evangelicals to return to the ecumenical concern of the Reformers and the later movements of evangelical renewal. We must humbly and critically scrutinize our respective traditions, renounce sacred shibboleths, and recognize that God works within diverse historical streams. We must resist efforts promoting church union-at-any-cost, but we must also avoid mere spiritualized concepts of church unity. We are convinced that unity in Christ requires visible and concrete expressions. In this belief, we welcome the development of encounter and cooperation within Christ's church. While we seek to avoid doctrinal indifferentism and a false irenicism, we encourage evangelicals to cultivate increased discussion and cooperation, both within and without their respective traditions, earnestly seeking common areas of agreement and understanding.

# FAITH AND ORDER DIALOGUES
# (NATIONAL COUNCIL OF
# CHURCHES)

# Introduction

The documents in this section illustrate various functions of Faith and Order in the National Council of Churches of Christ in the USA.[1] It is to study "the theological implications of…the ecumenical movement," as it has done in "The Ecclesiological Significance of Councils of Churches" (1963). It is to study "questions of faith, order, and worship along with the social, cultural, political, gender, class, racial and other factors as they affect the unity of the church and their current divisions," as it has done in its study of the controversial issue of the application of the Universal Fellowship of Metropolitan Community Churches for membership in the NCCC (1983).[2] It is to encourage "steps being taken by the churches toward closer unity with one another, including bilaterial and multilateral conversations," as it has done in "A Report of the Bilaterals Study Group of the Faith and Order Commission of the National Council of Churches" (1987).

It is to be a partner "in implementing World Council Faith and Order work," as it has done in the remaining three documents. The "Report of the Harlem (1988) Consultation on Unity and Renewal with Black Churches in the USA" demonstrates how a case study in a local context can have universal ecumenical import.[3] The Summary Statement from the *Spirit of Truth* is an attempt by a national group to assist in the "reception" of international dialogue results by evaluating them, bringing in new dialogue partners, and applying the results to particular issues. In this case the classical *filioque* question has been set in the context of other related concerns such as the Pentecostal and Holiness churches, feminism, spirituality, the ethical dimension of ecclesiology, and the like.[4] The Summary Statement of the Faith to Creed Consultation takes up issues particularly developed or important in one culture but possibly not of universal concern at the moment. Here issues that have been church-dividing, such as the differences between credal and non-credal churches, or issues that are dividing the churches today, such as, on the one hand, Brazilian, Pentecostal, or feminist perspectives, and the perspectives of classical North American credal churches, on the other hand, have been looked at through the lens of the fourth century.[5] The NCCCUSA, like other councils around the world, has provided several studies in preparation for the WCC volume, *Confessing One Faith*.[6] Such studies have enabled voices such as those of the Pentecostals, African-American churches, and Anabaptists, sometimes underrepresented in international conversations, to make specific contributions to ecumenical dialogue.[7]

## Notes

1. Jeffrey Gros, "The Vision of Christian Unity: Some Aspects of Faith and Order in the Context of United States Culture," *Mid-Stream* 30 (1991) 1-19.

2. Jeffrey Gros, "The Church, the Churches and the Metropolitan Church," *Ecumenical Review* 36 (1984) 71-81; *idem*, "Faith and Order Commission Report on the Application for Membership in the NCCC of the Universal Fellowship of Metropolitan Community Churches," *Mid-Stream* 22 (1983) 453-67.

3. "Report of the Harlem (1988) Consultation on Unity and Renewal with Black Churches in the USA," *Mid-Stream* 28 (1989) 412-20; cf. *Church and World: The Unity of the Church and the Renewal of Human Community* (Geneva: WCC, 1990); Gennadios Limouris (ed.), *Church Kingdom World: The Church as Mystery and Prophetic Sign* (Geneva: WCC, 1986).

4. Theodore Stylianopoulos and Mark Heim (eds.), *Spirit of Truth: Ecumenical Perspectives on the Holy Spirit* (Brookline: Holy Cross Orthodox Press, 1986); cf. Paul Fries and Tiran Nersoyan (eds.), *Christ in East and West* (Macon: Mercer, 1987); the NCCUSA has also provided a parish study guide for the Nicene Creed: *Confessing One Faith: Grounds for a Common Witness. A Guide for Ecumenical Study* (Cincinnati: Forward Movement, 1988).

5. Mark Heim (ed.), *Faith to Creed* (Grand Rapids: Eerdmans, 1991).

6. Geneva: WCC, 1991.

7. David T. Shannon and Gayraud Wilmore (eds.), *Black Witness to the Apostolic Faith* (Grand Rapids: Eerdmans, 1988); Thaddeus Horgan (ed.), *Apostolic Faith in America* (Grand Rapids: Eerdmans, 1988); Jeffrey Gros, "Expressing the Apostolic Faith: The Peace Churches' Contribution," *Ecumenical Trends* 19 (1990) 92-94; the spring issue of *Pneuma* in 1987 printed the papers and reports of the consultation on "Confessing the Apostolic Faith: Pentecostal Churches and the Ecumenical Movement" as *Pneuma* 9, 1 (1987).

# The Ecclesiological Significance of Councils of Churches

## Preface

The rise and spread of councils of churches in the United States in the twentieth century has been a remarkable phenomenon. The United States was the principal "seedbed" of the modern council of churches movement, for the many voluntary nondenominational organizations and movements in the nineteenth century prepared the way for the erection of official interdenominational agencies in the last decade of the nineteenth century and in the early years of the twentieth. The example of the Federal Council of the Churches of Christ in the U.S.A. (1908-1950) and other interchurch bodies influenced the rise and shape of church federation movements in other parts of the world. The merger of eight major interdenominational agencies to form the National Council of the Churches of Christ in the U.S.A. in 1950 was itself a significant milestone in the history of councils of churches.

For reasons that will be discussed, councils of churches have rarely significantly dealt with theological or ecclesiological questions related to their formation or their operation. In the past few decades, however, currents of theological renewal have been flowing in the churches. Biblical, historical and theological study of the doctrine of the Church has been of great importance. Hence, the timeliness of the North American Conference on Faith and Order, held at Oberlin, Ohio, in 1957, and the appropriateness of its call for "an ongoing study of the ecclesiological significance of local, state, and national councils of churches."[1] A National Study Commission, constituted by the newly established Department of Faith and Order Studies of the National Council of Churches, was the first result. The Commission has sought to understand the remarkable growth of councils of churches, and to study their bearing on the prospects for Christian unity.

While the Commission took its task seriously, its members recognize that not all aspects of the topic have been fully explored. It is hoped that our report will raise many questions and stimulate much further thought and study on the important matters that are here discussed.

Robert T. Handy 1963

## Part I. Historical Perspectives

*The Conciliar Motif in Christian History*

The meeting of representatives of Christian communities for discussion and action on questions of mutual concern is recorded very early in church history. The Council of Jerusalem (Acts 15:1-29) was the first such significant gathering. As the number of Christian communities grew, the value of such meetings in helping to maintain the health and extension of the Christian movement was recognized. In the latter half of the second century, the rise of Montanism made it necessary for the bishops of Asia to meet for deliberation and concerted action. By the third century, the practice of holding such meetings had become widely accepted. Assemblies such as these formed the pattern for the provincial and ecumenical councils which became important features in the life of the Church after its emancipation in the time of Constantine. There were wide variations, however, in the developing patterns of synods and councils. Some of the more local synods and councils met regularly, while national synods were usually occasional and the ecumenical councils were called only to meet particular problems.

Synods and councils were convened for several different purposes, such as the exchange of information and general consultation among neighboring bishops, to pronounce on questions of internal order and discipline, and to examine reports of heresy of individuals and groups. The early councils were understood to be manifestations and guardians of the unity of the Church, and their deliberations and decisions were believed to be in part the result of the working of the Holy Spirit. The phrase with which the members of the Council of Jerusalem announce the decision, "It has seemed right to the Holy Spirit and to us..." (Acts 15:28) is the constant motif of succeeding councils.

As a means for the interpretation of Christian truth and for the guarding of tradition, synods and councils were regarded as one of the elements in the continuous process of the explanation and elucidation of the faith, a process which was recognized as men's understanding of the faith increased from generation to generation. In this respect, for example, a refutation and condemnation of a heresy by a council constituted not only the negative act of condemnation but the positive act of clarifying and strengthening the body of the faith. Thus successive councils were thought of as adding to the accumulated wisdom of the past, both by the testing of new attempts to interpret the truth (e.g., Arianism) and by the new formulation of statements of orthodox faith (e.g., the Definition of the Faith of Chalcedon). The early church was well aware that there were aspects of the original teaching which had not been presented in detail in the Scriptures and so required further study, such as the doctrine of the Trinity. The councils, especially those of ecumenical scope, were thought of as the concerted effort of the Body of Christ to grow in understanding the Gospel. While the outcome of the deliberations of a council summoned to deal with heresy was regulatory, judicial and administrative, the purpose of the meeting was basically theological. Though the councils did not have or need permanent uniform structures, they were understood to have regular and necessary functions in the life of the Church. The first canon of Chalcedon, for example, reaffirms and upholds in force all the canons passed in each council of the Church up to that time. Thus the councils were not isolated, sporadic phenomena, but parts of a continuous process of growth and enlargement.

While there are certain similarities between the synods and councils of the early and medieval church and modern councils of churches, the differences are far greater. The early synods and councils were concerned with the unity and efficiency of the Church and with the clarification of the faith, as are also contemporary councils of churches. The early councils, however, were gatherings within a single ecclesiastical structure, whereas modern councils of churches have been designed to provide means for cooperation among churches which have become separated from one another, and to provide opportunities to move toward fuller manifestations of unity. To be sure, in the early centuries there were differences of opinion and interpretation which led to the appearance of separate bodies (e.g., Montanists, Donatists, Arians, Monophysites, Nestorians); councils sought to define the true faith in the face of what were understood to be heresy and schism, but were instruments of one church and were not meeting places of representatives of separated bodies. Meetings of the latter kind occurred, but were *ad hoc* conferences convened to reconcile separated bodies and were distinguished from the councils. The early councils did not have or need continuing organizational structures as modern councils do, for the regular ecclesiastical structures were sufficient, and carried the responsibility of publicizing the results and continuing appropriate action. In the earlier period councils were called in order to preserve, define and strengthen when there was danger of schism, whereas modern councils of churches are called to show forth the partial unity we have and to seek its fullness.[2] The early councils were a special form of Christian witness giving both general witness to the faith and particular witness to the unity of the Church. The bishops in scheduled provincial synods affirmed the unity of the church simply by meeting for regular and routine deliberation. These routine meetings, not called for special purposes such as trials for heresy, were nearly the only means by which the local churches could step beyond the local bounds of the city and make a display of solidarity beyond the cities.

With respect to their objectives the "reformatory councils" during the so-called "conciliar period," roughly from the mid-fourteenth century to the mid-fifteenth, were more like the present councils of churches.[3] Indeed, the reformatory councils of that period were the last sustained collective attempts at a reconciliation of estranged church bodies and jurisdictions prior to the contemporary ecumenical thrust in its various manifestations. The conciliar movement had to face three sets of problems. First, the state of separation between the Western (Latin) Church and the Churches of the East was addressed. Efforts at reconciliation had to deal with doctrinal, psychological, and political differences. The combined weight of these problems prevented a durable reunion of the churches. Second, the rise of sectarian movements, independent from or in revolt against the hierarchy, had to be faced. Such movements were adjudged to be heretical (e.g., the Petrobrusians, the Arnadists, the Poor Men of Lyons and of Lombardy, the Cathari and Albigensians, condemned by the second, third, and fourth Lateran Councils in the twelfth and thirteenth centuries) and were generally suppressed. Third, the conflicts of jurisdiction and obedience within the Western Church, the so-called "Great Schism," had to be overcome. It was during this conciliar period that extensive systematic attention to the theological significance of the Church as a structure was first given. (It is a striking fact that the great thirteenth century theologians, Bonaventura, Aquinas, Duns Scotus, had, properly speaking, no ecclesiology.) The holding of the reformatory councils (Pisa 1409; Constance 1414-18; Basle, 1431-49; Ferrara-Florence, 1438-45) was accompanied by the rise and development of conciliar theology. Some "Conciliarists," notably Henry of Langenstein, Pierre d'Ailly and Gerson, argued that the Council was an exceptional procedure to be called only when other means of breaking deadlocks failed; they were not primarily interested in discussing in the abstract the respective authority of Popes and Councils. Some, however, like Dietrich of Niem, Francisco Zarabella, and Nicholas of Cusa, theorized that the authority of General Councils, inasmuch as they enjoy the infallible assistance promised by Christ to the Church as whole, was itself superior to the authority of the pope.[4]

In some ways the story of the reformatory councils is relevant to the present situation, for the conciliar movement sought to reform, renew and reunite the Church. However, it sought to do this in large measure by attempting to set limits to the authority of ecclesiastical officials, whereas modern councils of churches seek to do certain things on behalf of the churches and to work for a fuller unity. The reformatory councils did not need to develop permanent organizational structures, but sought to purify the existing structures of the Church. The failure of the conciliar movement confirmed the thesis that a council could properly be called only by the pope. The crystallization of this view tended to check the emergence of a new conciliar movement in the early years of the Reformation—this combined with a remembrance of the way Hus and the Hussites had been treated by the councils of Constance and Basle. But the reformers generally advocated genuinely free councils[5]—i.e., free from papal control and free to respond to the word of God. For example, it is clear that Luther saw the value of churchwide gatherings of ecclesiastical representatives for the purpose of preventing or healing a breach in the Church.[6] He or his representatives attended all meetings of this character and found fault with the Roman hierarchy for not calling such an ecumenical council to consider issues which had been raised by the reformers.

### The Background for the Councils of Churches Movement in the U.S.A.

The modern ecclesiological situation is strikingly different from that of the early centuries, the fourteenth century, or the Reformation era. There are radically different conditions in the Church—the practical acceptance of pluralism—and in the world—the reshaping of patterns of thought and life through science and technology. The contemporary councils of churches movement has illustrated some of the same motifs that have appeared in the council development of the past but reflect also the different conditions in the Church and in the world. Separate communions which have avoided recognizing other Christian bodies as churches or entering into relations with them are today often ready to recognize them as churches, or at least as Christian bodies preserving elements of the Church, and hence are willing to enter into discussion and cooperative activities with them.

Consideration of certain developments in American church history may cast light on the ecclesiological setting in which councils of churches have proliferated. The majority of Christians who came to North American shores in the seventeenth century believed in religious uniformity and in the establishment of the Church by law. They believed that there should be but one church for a given territory, that it should be given a favored if not an exclusive position, and that it should be supported by public funds. Church establishments by New England Congregationalists, New Netherlands Reformed, and Southern Anglicans carried out these ideas. Dissenting groups were viewed as sects and repulsed as vigorously as circumstances allowed. The established churches felt that they had a measure of responsibility for the society of which they were a part, and they sought to fulfill these obligations in fairly direct ways, as through cooperation with legislative and administrative officials of the state. The established churches claimed to be the sole rightful embodiment of the Church in their territory, and hence there were no denominations in the later sense (though perhaps some sects), and no need for councils of churches.

Already in the seventeenth century, however, colonies existed in North America in which there were no religious establishments—Rhode Island, New Jersey, Pennsylvania. In these there was a large measure of religious liberty from the beginning. As other colonies grew much more pluralistic religiously, there was increasing toleration, even in those that had been originally most rigorous in repelling dissenters. Finally, as the consequence of complex developments, religious liberty, implemented by the separation of church and state, was accepted as the newly-independent nation chartered its course after the Revolution. The remaining state establishments presently disappeared. Henceforth, religious liberty is "voluntaryism" in religion.[7] Furthermore, the increasing pluralism of American religion, a pluralism that steadily grew more complex through immigration and the founding of indigenous bodies, meant that in no large area was any one religious group able to retain the loyalty of a majority of the population. With the acceptance by most of the religious bodies of ideas of religious toleration and liberty, claims by given groups to be the sole embodiment of the Church in a particular area were (or had to be) given up. Churches took on some of the aspects of sects, and sects of churches—or, more accurately, both became denominations.

The word "denomination" came into vogue among Protestant bodies during the early years of the Evangelical Revival in England during the eighteenth century. Some Protestant leaders, drawing on the writings of a group of Puritan divines of the previous century, presented a "denominational theory of the Church." Its basic contention was that "the true church is not to be identified in any exclusive sense with any particular ecclesiastical institution."[8] This view contributed to the acceptance and spread of denominationalism in England and America. But immigration, schisms, and the forming of new religious movements brought onto the church scene new denominations which had differing points of view. In modern usage, the word "denomination" can be and is applied to all religious bodies, whatever their understanding of themselves and others.

On the American scene, the denominational system was in full development by the early nineteenth century. With the flowering of religious liberty, separation of church and state, and the denominational system, a quite different relationship on the part of the churches to the society of which they were a part had to be developed. No longer could the relationship be direct and official through the channels of the state. It had to be indirect, primarily through the shaping of public opinion. But this could not be accomplished successfully on a national basis without the cooperation of Christians of many denominations. In an article dealing with the transition from "Church" to "denomination" in New England, James F. Maclear has explained how the church leaders hoped to mold public opinion so as to conform to their understanding of Christian morality:

> To implement this purpose organization was needed. Therefore, coincident with the fall of the New England Establishments, an expansion of interdenominational voluntary societies was undertaken. The Connecticut Moral Society of 1813 was the beginning of many such foundations, spreading from New England to New York and the Middle West. These moral societies were seconded by organizations for allied purposes—tract societies, Bible societies, temperance societies, missionary societies, Sabbath School societies—all striving to extend "that influence which the law could no longer apply."[9]

Only in a few cases were the relationships between denominations in the nineteenth century "official" (the Plan of Union between sister Congregational and Presbyterian churches is one important exception). Normally the voluntary societies were made up of interested individual Christians from many denominations. Among the great national societies were the American Education Society (1815), the American Bible Society (1816), the American Sunday School Union (1817-24), the American Tract Society (1825), the American Temperance Society (1826), and the American Antislavery Society (1883). These societies had overlapping memberships and directorates, and worked closely together in what has been called "the benevolent empire." In the same general pattern were the Y.M.C.A. and Y.W.C.A. (founded in England in 1844 and 1854), which soon were flourishing in America as important nondenominational lay efforts. Such voluntary societies were understood by many Christians to be doing Christian work; they were doing part of the work of the Church. Ecclesiologically, the very appearance of the vast national voluntary societies was an admission that all of the work of the Christian Church could not be done by a denomination—it took many denominations, and some kind of additional agency or agencies also. For a number of reasons, some relating primarily to the intense individualism and great stress on freedom so characteristic of nineteenth-century American life, others stemming more out of the widespread popularity of the evangelical-pietist concept of the church itself as voluntary society, the nondenominational society method of providing the additional agents was satisfactory to most Protestants in the last century.[10] The emergence of the denominational system was accompanied by a network of additional agencies which were recognizably engaged in church work; these were necessitated in order that the churches might deal with some effectiveness with the society of which they were a part.

Many of the agencies developed in the early nineteenth century still survive—missionary societies, Bible societies, etc. But for many reasons they did not prove to be wholly satisfactory. The nineteenth century was a Protestant century in America, for the most part. Protestants could feel that the society was receptive to their interests, and that the state was friendly to their views. In part because of an underlying faith in harmony and progress, it was believed that the many activities of churches and religious societies could be left largely uncoordinated, for they all contributed somehow to the whole Christian cause. Such efforts at coordination as there were were unofficial from the point of view of the churches; the "interlocking directorate" of the "benevolent empire" was one such effort; the Evangelical Alliance was another. These were both cast in the nondenominational, voluntary society pattern.

The later nineteenth century presented new and difficult situations to the Protestant forces. The magnitude and difficulty of the world missionary task, to which the churches were generally committed, became more apparent. The vast flood of immigrants brought many non-Protestants; the Roman Catholic Church especially profited. By mid-century that church was already the largest single religious body numerically, but was generally considered to be an alien enclave in Protestant America. Religious pluralism had been the order of the day in America, but by the time of the twentieth century immigration, pluralism was wider than ever as Catholic, Orthodox, and Jewish minorities grew stronger. By the middle of the twentieth century, the society could no longer be confidently assumed to be Protestant. At the same time, the urbanization of the country was preceding rapidly. The Protestant triumph of the early nineteenth century had been largely a rural and smalltown phenomenon. The burgeoning cities of the new century with their patterns of pluralism and secularism were proving much more difficult. It was no longer easy as it had been to influence public opinion in accordance with the morality of the Gospel. The voluntary society principle seemed no longer to be a fully adequate way for the churches to relate effectively to the general society and to carry out their missionary tasks properly, either at home or abroad. Consequently, new ways had to be sought, and the churches began to reach out to each other to form official agencies of cooperation. Pioneer efforts of this kind were the Foreign Missions Conference of North America, which traces its origin back to 1893, the Missionary Education Movement (1902), the Home Missions Council (1908), and the Sunday School Council of Evangelical Denominations (1910).

Early in the twentieth century, the Federal Council of Churches (1908) and many state and local councils were formed. Under changed conditions, they fulfilled purposes similar to these of the earlier nondenominational societies. Denominations need additional agencies if they are to discharge their responsibilities to the faith and to the society of which they are a part in adequate fashion. The shift from an established church pattern of the seventeenth century to denominational pluralism made the development of agencies of cooperation a needed expedient; the deepening of that pluralism and the increase of secularism necessitated official organs of cooperation or councils of churches. The sovereignty of the denominations, understood chiefly in juridical rather than in theological terms, was carefully safeguarded in the new development. The rise of the councils of churches came at a time when ecclesiological interest was at a low ebb in American churches (except in certain communions which oftentimes were not prominent in the formation of the councils). Concepts which did in part inspire the formation and growth of councils of churches, for example, hope in the coming kingdom of God on earth and belief in progress, put little emphasis on the doctrine of the Church. For these reasons, councils of churches have been slow to enter the field of ecclesiological discussion.

## Renewed Interest in the Doctrine of the Church

The background and context for the present study also involve the resurgence of interest in ecclesiology of the past quarter century. This has been stimulated by numerous forces, including the general theological renewal, the heightened appreciation of the authority of the scriptures, the rapid development of the ecumenical movement, the new situation of Christendom in a world in upheaval, and the growing awareness of need for renewal in the Church. In such a new theological, ecclesiastical and social context the questions of the nature and mission of the Church have had to be raised anew in and for every Christian community, and a vast literature has already resulted from the study of the doctrine of the Church by individuals, by groups within and among denominations, and by theological commissions, particularly of the World Council of Churches. It is out of just such renewal of interest in the doctrine of the Church that the present study has emerged, and questions of the nature of the Church, especially of its unity, have repeatedly emerged in the work of this Commission. We have not sought to arrive at a formal statement of ecclesiology, but our thinking has been informed by this recent discussion and we mention briefly some of its characteristic themes.

A dominant emphasis in the renewed understanding of the Church is its radical dependence on the act and presence of God. The report of the section on "The Universal Church in God's Design" at the first Assembly of the World Council of Churches, which was received by the Assembly and commended to the churches for their serious consideration and appropriate action, contained these significant agreements:

> We all believe that the Church is God's gift to men for the salvation of the world; that the saving acts of God in Jesus Christ brought the Church into being; that the Church persists in continuity throughout history through the presence and power of the Holy Spirit...

> We believe that the Church has a vocation to worship God in His Holiness, to proclaim the Gospel to every creature. She is equipped by God with the various gifts of the Spirit for the building up of the Body of Christ. She has been set apart in holiness to live for the service of all mankind, in faith and love, by the power of the crucified and risen Lord and according to His example. She is composed of forgiven sinners yet partaking already, by faith, in the eternity of the Kingdom of God and waiting for the consummation when Christ shall come again in the fullness of His glory and power.[11]

This implies that the God who calls the Church into being is the triune God, and the Church can be understood only in relation to Him. It is thus "theocentric," "Christocentric," and "pneumatocentric." A trinitarian understanding of the life of the Church requires that the Church be seen in relation to the totality of the work of God, in the whole of creation and history, in the people of Israel before the incarnation, in the world outside the Church, in the consummation of all things. It requires recognition of the inseparability of Christ and the Church, such that it can be called His Body. The Church cannot be said to be simply identical with Christ, though analogies (thus involving contrast as well as similarity) may be drawn between the nature of Christ and the nature of the Church. Apart from His work and presence there is no Church. A trinitarian understanding of the Church further requires recognition of its dependance on the presence and work ot the Holy Spirit, not in separation from but in unity with Father and Son. It is the community which lives by the pouring out of the Spirit, in which the Spirit is the power of life, knowledge and of holiness. All that is truly Christian is inspired by Him and accomplished by the assistance of His grace. By His virtue we are reborn in Jesus Christ as children of the heavenly Father. By Him both form and freedom are given in the Church, in His ordering of the common life and in the variety of His gifts. Finally, the unity of the triune God is the basis of the unity which is given to the Church and which it is called upon to embody. As God is one, as Christ is the unity of God and man, so the source, center and goal of the life of the Church is one.

In recent discussion, other emphases, seeking to reflect the manifoldness and unity of the New Testament images of the Church, flow from and are interrelated with such an understanding of the Church.

a. As the person and work of Christ are inseparable, so that He is what He does and He does what He is, the nature and mission of the Church are inseparable and interdependent. The Church has its existence in its relation to God and the world, as it participates in Christ and His work and as He and the Spirit are active in and through it.

b. The Church is not a collection or contractual association of believers, but an incorporation into membership of the Living Christ and into mutual participation with all other members—an event which of course includes the faithful response of men.

c. The Christ Who is Lord and Head of the Church is also Lord of the world. Thus the line is drawn not only from Christ through the Church to the world but also from Christ through the world to the Church. In faithfulness to its Master, the Church is something in itself in participation in Christ and its *diakonia* in and for the world springs from this.

d. By virtue of the whole work of Christ and the freedom and variety of the gifts of the Holy Spirit, "minimal" descriptions of the essential "marks" of the Church (e.g., word and sacraments; or word, sacrament and ministry; or unity, holiness, catholicity, apostolicity) may not properly be separated from the whole range of the Church's life of testimony and faith, of adoration and proclamation, of suffering and serving, of reconciliation and intercession.

e. As in the incarnation the eternal Word of God took upon Himself the fullness of genuine humanity, so the Church is wrought out of the stuff of human history and society. This treasure is in earthen vessels. The Church is not constituted by man, but by the Triune God, yet in and through humanity. The Holy Spirit does not replace or coerce the human spirit, but releases and engages the freedom of man's spirit. And the response of man in the Church is fraught with contradiction to Christ's presence and work. The mystery of the holiness of the Church is not the same as the sinlessness of Christ. The Church yet requires cleansing from Christ and fulfillment of its hope. It embraces in its life the paradox of the life of the Christian man as at once sinful and justified. In disunion, disbelief and disservice, the response of man in the Church wars against the unity, reconciliation and purity which is given in the Church and to which it is called.

f. The Church is essential and not merely accidental to God's working in the world, a sphere in which Christ and the Holy Spirit are uniquely at work, and yet it lives by mercy and cleansing and looks forward to what God will do in and to it.[12]

A further theme in recent thinking is the awareness that the Church, as the people of God in pilgrimage, participates in the frailty and fragility of all created things. Its history is influenced by international and racial strife, by the characteristics of an industrial and technological society, and by the peculiar anxieties of contemporary life. The ecclesiastical organizations we know are often more effective in shielding people from the God of Jesus Christ than in bringing His judgment and mercy into their lives. Thus, amid the swift historical movements of our time the Church must be open to the possibility of institutional changes that may make some of its future forms as different from those we know as a typical congregation today is different from the Church on the first Pentecost.

While these themes are not presented as conclusions on which the members of our Commission are all agreed, they reflect emphases of pervasive importance which must be taken into account. They, and others equally relevant and not converging necessarily toward a uniform ecclesiology, pose questions for every congregation, every denomination, and every council of churches—questions concerning the adequacy of our response to the divine gift and demand. Is coexistence substituted for reconciliation? Is aggregation substituted for mutual participation? Has self-satisfaction replaced the hope of transformation? Have freedom and variety in the Spirit been made into license for disorder and dissension? Have ecclesiastical structures been forms for Christ's freely ministering through the Spirit or techniques of human aggrandizement and control? Is the unity of the Triune God and of Jesus Christ made manifest or obscured?

Contemporary discussion of the doctrine of the Church requires that the ecclesiological significance of councils of churches be interpreted and understood in the light of such questions, a task to which we turn more specifically in Part III of this report.

## Part II. Some Aspects of the Current Situation

### *The Growth of Councils of Churches in the United States of America*

The twentieth century has seen a remarkable growth in the number and significance of councils of churches at every level: local, state, national, regional, and world. In the United States, the primarily locus of this study, most of the some thousand local and state councils of churches have been formed in the present century.[13] The councils were founded originally in many cases to serve primarily as instruments of cooperation by denominations which had had little direct contact with each other. The leaders of the councils of churches movement often intentionally avoided facing issues of ecclesiology, the study of the nature of the Church. That is, in order to get on with the cooperative tasks at hand, they quite deliberately minimized the importance of theological and ecclesiological questions. Because of the theological position of their churches some were not inclined to emphasise matters of faith and order anyway; others who might normally stress theological matters were willing to let the doctrinal issues be by-passed for the sake of practical cooperation.

The members of this commission found at the outset of the study that it would be helpful to study the self-understanding of councils of churches as revealed in their formal constitutional statements. A survery of the constitutions of local, state and national councils of churches in the United States was undertaken by the Faith and Order staff of the National Council of Churches in the spring of 1961. It revealed that certain recurring positions concerning councils of churches are widely held among the churches which support them. There is fairly widespread acceptance of an "evangelical basis" for councils of churches in the United States. The phrase, "Jesus Christ as Divine Lord and Savior," is generally incorporated in the preamble to the constitution of councils of churches.[14]

Most councils of churches also, implicitly or explicitly, maintain the "representative principle" (voting membership consists of delegates appointed by the churches). Dr. J. Quinter Miller has indicated the import of this in these words: "A councils of churches so constituted is the representative agent of its member congregations."[15] It is generally understood (and often specifically stated) that a council of churches in no way legally or technically modifies the autonomy of its member churches; a council of churches may not legislate for its members.

The constitutions of 105 local councils of churches in the United States were studied.[16] A little over one half (57) of these affirmed the "evangelical basis." Local council memberships are made up largely of churches (congregations); of the 105 studied some (34) also admitted as members organizations having a Christian purpose, while others (15) admitted such organizations as affiliates. The local councils list various objectives; the most frequently recurring objects stated are as follows (the numbers in parentheses indicate the number of councils citing that goal in some way):

> To manifest (evidence, express) more fully oneness in Jesus
>     Christ (49)
> To manifest the common purpose of the churches in carrying out
>     their mission to the world (24)

To do those things which the churches can do more effectively
together (14)

To express the essential unity of the Church (9)

Many functions for these local councils are listed in their constitutions, especially the following:

To carry on such work as the members authorize the council to
undertake on their behalf (service, education, social action,
study, research, conferences, etc.) (99)

To facilitate and encourage mutual counsel, conversation, association (fellowship), and understanding among the members
(67)

To extend fellowship among particular groups of Christians
(clergy, laymen, laywomen, students, etc.) (55)

To assist the members in their task of evangelism (including the
development of means to proclaim the gospel) (47)

To maintain relations with other councils of churches (local,
state, national, regional, world) and with other Christian organizations (missionary, etc.) (46)

To provide a ministry to special groups (migrants, immigrants,
students, construction workers, foreign language groups,
American Indians, etc.) and institutions (29)

To foster and encourage greater cooperative work within the
council and coordination among the members (27)

The constitutions of 43 *state* councils of churches were reviewed. Twenty-five of these defined the council as "an inclusive cooperative agency of the Christian churches." Thirty-six of the state councils have adopted the "evangelical basis" in some form; twelve explicitly state the "representative principle" and eleven the principle of denominational sovereignty. Their memberships are made up for the most part of denominational jurisdictions; some (16) also have councils of churches of lesser geographical areas as members, while a few (8) admit organizations having a Christian purpose. Fifteen admit the latter as affiliates. Ten councils allow in their memberships congregations of which the jurisdictional bodies are not members or which have no suitable jurisdictional connection. The stated objects of the state councils vary, but often listed are the following:

To manifest (evidence, express) more fully oneness in Jesus
Christ (32)

> To manifest the common purpose of the churches in carrying out
> their mission in the world (14)
>
> To do those things which the churches can do more effectively
> together (3)
>
> To express the essential unity of the church (3)

The state councils express their intended functions in a variety of statements,
but the following appear most often:

> To carry on such work as the members authorize the council to
> undertake on their behalf (service, education, social action,
> study, research, conferences, etc.) (40)
>
> To extend fellowship among particular groups of Christians
> (clergy, laymen, laywomen, students, etc.) (30)
>
> To provide a ministry to special groups (migrants, immigrants,
> students, construction workers, foreign language groups,
> American Indians, etc.) and institutions (29)
>
> To facilitate and encourage mutual counsel, conversation, associ-
> ation (fellowship), and understanding among the members
> (28)
>
> To maintain relations with other councils of churches (local,
> state, national, regional, world) and with other Christian orga-
> nizations (missionary, etc.) (24)

The National Council of Churches of Christ in the U.S.A. was organized in 1950 through the merger of eight major interdenominational agencies, including the Federal Council of the Churches of Christ in the U.S.A.
(formed in 1908). It accepts the "evangelical basis," and is predicated upon
the "representative principle" and the principle of denominational sovereignty. The Preamble to its constitution reads in part as follows:

> In the Providence of God, the time has come when it seems fitting more
> fully to manifest oneness in Jesus Christ as Divine Lord and Savior by
> the creation of an inclusive co-operative agency of the Christian church-
> es of the United States of America...

The objectives of the National Council are stated in Article II. This list provides an insight into the common state of mind concerning councils of
churches among the denominations which formed the National Council of
Churches.

> 1. To manifest the common spirit and purpose of the co-operating
> churches in carrying out their mission in the world.

2. To do for the churches such co-operative work as they authorize the council to carry on in their behalf.

3. To continue and extend the work of the interdenominational agencies named in the Preamble of the Constitution, together with such additional objectives and purposes as the churches through their representatives in the Council from time to time agree upon.

4. To encourage study of the Bible and to assist in the spread of the Christian religion.

5. To encourage fellowship and mutual counsel concerning the spiritual life and religious activities of the churches.

6. To foster and encourage co-operation among the churches for the purposes set forth in this Constitution.

7. To promote co-operation among local churches and to further in communities, states, or larger territorial units the development of councils of churches and councils of church women, in agreement with the Preamble of this Consititution.

8. To establish consultative relationships with national councils of churches in other countries of North America.

9. To maintain fellowship and co-operation with similar councils in other areas of the world.

10. To maintain fellowship and co-operation with the World Council of Churches and with other international Christian organizations.

This survery of local, state, and national[17] councils of churches suggests that in America the churches have not dealt significantly with theological or ecclesiological questions in the formation or the operation of the councils of churches. Doctrinal matters have been largely reserved to the communions.

The existence of councils of churches on the American scene actually presupposes a high degree of mutual recognition among the member denominations. The councils exhibit an impressive amount of common service. In this sense they are significant organs of unity. But they also grew up during a period when less attention than is now deemed necessary was paid to certain questions about the true nature of the Church; in many quarters it was often assumed that questions of faith and order could be safely ignored, detoured, or postponed.[18] The churches when in cooperation seem to take the existing church situation somewhat for granted, and to be prepared to work cooperatively within its limits. Hence as explicit organs of unity they have serious limitations, which can perhaps be removed, at least in part, as the ecclesiological issue is more fully discerned.

*The Ecclesiological Significance of Denominations*

In the contemporary highly pluralistic situation, as churches are brought into confrontation with each other, primarily through the ecumenical movement, the question of the ecclesiological significance of the denominations themselves is raised. It has often been observed that in the New Testament the word "church" can be applied to a local congregation or to the universal body of the faithful. Similarly most contemporary doctrines of the Church, based as they are on New Testament images, embrace the local units and the Church Universal with reasonable clarity and definitiveness. But denominations are more difficult to define or defend theologically. Nothing like our denominations existed in the first century. Yet all Christian bodies must attempt to understand themselves ecclesiologically. They must also decide their relationships with other denominations.

Such decisions vary according to the ecclesiology of the denomination making them. The following classification is oversimplified, but it may be helpful for purposes of analysis. (a) Some churches must, if they are to be true to their ecclesiologies, make it perfectly clear that from their point of view no other body is fully and properly the Church of Jesus Christ. Churches of widely variant backgrounds come into this group, for widely variant theological reasons. (b) Other churches, equally convinced of the *given* unity of the Church of Jesus Christ, and equally troubled by the fact of the existence of many denominations, differ from the first in that they do not claim to be "The Holy Catholic Church," but rather to be *part* of it. This position has sometimes been expressed as "the Branch Theory" or "the Invisible Church," but here again theological motivations are varied. (c) Still other churches either have hitherto found it necessary to give theological account of their existence vis-à-vis other denominations, or have found it necessary more recently to consider and reinterpret and perhaps to modify their original ecclesiology due to the development of the ecumenical movement and the councils of churches. But in whichever classification it may be found, no church has remained totally unaffected ecclesiologically by the existence of the ecumenical movement.

In the oft-quoted 1950 Toronto Statement, "The Church, the Churches, and the World Council of Churches: The Ecclesiological Significance of the World Council of Churches," it was said by the Central Committee of the World Council:

> All the Christian Churches, including the Church of Rome, hold that there is no complete identity between the membership of the Church Universal and the membership of their own church. They recognize that there are Church members "extra muros," that these belong "aliquo modo" to the Church, or even that there is an "ecclesia extra ecclesiam."

This recogniztion finds expression in the fact that with very few exceptions the Christian Churches accept the baptism administered by other
Churches as valid.[19]

The existence of the ecumenical movement and of councils of churches
requires all denominations to rethink their own meaning and their relation to
other bodies of Christians. Depending on their conceptions of the Church,
their conceptions of themselves, and their histories, the existing denominations will have varying kinds of difficulties in interpreting councils theologically and in relating themselves to them. Churches in categories (b) and (c)
above will find it less difficult theologically to interpret their participation in
councils of churches. In general, they can affirm that in respect to the unity
which Christ gives to His Church and to which He calls it, councils of
churches are in principle no more difficult to accept than the existence of
separate denominational structures. The councils are not normally viewed by
them as the Church, but insofar as the councils seek to serve Christ and to
press toward a fuller manifestation of the unity of the Church they are understood to be related to it. But churches in category (a) have special *theological*
problems posed by the existence of denominations and hence of councils,
though practically they may be active participants. Such communions are
often most sensitive to the prayer of our Lord that all His followers may be
one (John 17:21, 22). In reality, no church sees itself as absolutely the only
one; all see some reality of Christianity outside any given church. As H.H.
Wolf has put it.

> The fact of the ecumenical movement already means that Christian
> churches with their different historical origins and traditions—whether
> members of the World Council or not—have given up claiming to be
> exclusive, i.e., claiming that their own form of church is the only mani-
> festation of the One Church of Jesus Christ. They cannot deny that other
> churches also represent a form of the Church of Jesus Christ, though
> less fully, and although they may see much to criticize in them.[20]

In councils of churches communions may in various ways work together,
study together and pray together for fuller unity. But it is much easier for
some bodies to do this than others.

## Part III. Ecclesiological Conclusions

Understanding that councils of churches can be said to have ecclesiological significance if they bear significantly the marks of the Church, or if

they are genuinely related to the Church in important ways, we present our conclusions in answer to three questions: (1) To what extent, if at all, is the reality of the Church expressed in Councils of Churches? (2) To what extent, if at all, are Council of Churches instruments which the churches should use in fulfilling their mission? (3) To what extent, if at all, are councils of churches contributing, or capable of contributing, to the realization of the unity of the Church?

## *Is the Reality of the Church Expressed in Councils of Churches?*

In the contemporary ecumenical discussion about the nature of the Church (see Section C), it is emphasized that the presence of the Church may be discerned by such evidences as the following: the activity of the Holy Spirit, right preaching of the Word, due administration of the sacraments, provision for proper church order, the upholding of the faith of the apostles, growth in the grace of holiness, witness to the Lordship of Jesus Christ over the world, service to needy men in the name of God, and the gathering of separated brethren in the unity of reconciliation. This is by no means an exhaustive list; not all Christians would agree that all of these marks are essential to the discernment of the Church; there are many variant interpretations of them. But insofar as some of these realities can be discerned in the life of the councils of churches, the latter then participate in the reality of the Church.

There are convincing signs of the presence and activity of God the Holy Spirit in the council of churches movement. The Holy Spirit moves where He wills; His activities are not bound within our historical institutions nor can they be summoned at our bidding (John 3:8). But many contemporary Christians do bear witness to His Presence in the councils of churches, bringing the fruits of love, joy, peace, patience, kindness, goodness, faithfulness, gentleness, and self-control (Galatians 5:22). Of course, it must be remembered that the Holy Spirit works as He wills outside of as well as within our churches; from His Presence it does not logically follow that a visible church is brought into being. But in another sense, as Irenaeus declared in the second century, "Where the Spirit of God is, there is the Church and all grace."[21] Therefore, insofar as the presence of the Holy Spirit can be discerned in the life and work of the councils of churches, the latter must be judged to be related through Him to His activity in the denominations (insofar as He is at work in *them*), and, with the denominations, through Him they bear a relationship to the One Church. His presence in the work of councils of churches, which can never be guaranteed but which has been convincingly felt, does bring to them ecclesiological significance.

Another way in which the reality of the Church is expressed in councils of churches is their provision of structures through which the denominations may participate in the loving service, *diakonia*, that is essential to the fullness of the Church.[22] There are many areas of service to human beings in need in the modern world, areas especially demanding Christian attention, which could not be opened except through the cooperative efforts of churches in council. When the communions and their individual members through their councils of churches bring food to the hungry, clothing for the naked, medicine to the sick, education to the illiterate, love to the rejected, the Church is surely there in the acts of love and service. When the denominations through the councils contribute to the fairer treatment of those who have known injustice, then the work of the Church is being done.

The councils of churches also share in certain ways in the ministry of the Church. The ministry is a continuing institution in the Christian community from the time when the Lord "appointed twelve, to be with him, and to be sent out to preach and have authority to cast out demons" (Mark 3:14-15). The Christian ministry is the ministry of Christ; there is no Christian priesthood or ministry apart from His priesthood and ministry. Sharing His life, the Church as the Body of Christ has a general ministerial function derived from that of Christ. In this every member has his share, according to his capacities and calling (II Cor. 5:19; I Peter 2:9). In the Book of Acts, the Church is set before us as a body of believers having within it, as its recognized focus of unity and organ of authority, the apostolate. The apostolate was followed by a special, official, or ordained ministry to carry out the liturgical, preaching, teaching, absolving, and pastoral care functions of the Church, although Christians not formally ordained to the ministry could perform some of these functions also, and participate in others. Various theories of the official ministry and differing understandings of the meaning and method of their ordination arose in the long course of church history; some churches emphasizing and some minimizing (or denying) the distinction between clergy and laity. Although today the official ministry of the One Church is neither united nor universally recognized, councils of churches can serve as partial expressions of the general ministry of the whole Church in effective ways. The general ministry, as carried on through councils, does not supplant the special ordained ministry of the churches nor does it represent an emerging new form of that ministry, but it serves as an effective reminder and token that the ministry of Christ is one despite the brokenness of the Church.

In councils of churches, not only churches are brought into association with one another, but also their members are brought into an intimate and sometimes profound relationship with one another in which together they witness to a larger and more inclusive community than exists in any separate church or denomination. Although this larger community does not have all the essential marks of the Church, it is a fellowship in the name of Jesus

Christ; and in its work and worship the participants experience a quality of unity with one another which brings them closer to Him. Here, then, is one manifestation, partial though it may be, of the Church of Christ in its wholeness. Moreover, a change, subtle perhaps, takes place in the attitudes of the participants, because of the participation in a form of Christian community which may be wider and deeper than they have known in their own denominations. Thus this community, which in some measure witnesses to the essential unity of the Church in Jesus Christ, also stirs consciences to strive more vigorously for its fuller expression.

Though the reality of the Church is expressed in certain ways in councils of churches, the councils of churches are not themselves churches. Councils of churches do not normally have creeds or determine theological issues, and do not administer the sacraments or ordain. Nevertheless, as described in the preceding paragraphs, councils of churches may and do have important ecclesiological significance.

### Are Councils of Churches Instruments Which the Churches Should Use in Fulfilling Their Mission?

Congregations and communions can find and have found opportunities to deepen and enrich their own lives through participation in councils of churches. In separation from one another, the denominations can lose sight of important emphases of the Gospel, and can be content with ideas of the Church not fully adequate to the New Testament. In competition with each other, they can magnify certain duties and practices but let others go in the effort to maintain distinctiveness. But through participation with others in councils of churches, they can move toward richer, more adequate understandings of the nature of the Church as they are freely led thereto through the study of the Word of God under the guidance of the Holy Spirit. Councils of churches can help to bring the churches into encounter so that they must witness to each other of what they deem essential to the faith, appealing to the Bible, tradition, history, and the guidance of the Holy Spirit in the mutual and free search for fuller understanding of Christ and His Church. The very way in which a particular body of Christians understands and witnesses to the faith may bring inspiration and guidance to others; it may also painfully confront us with our own inadequacies and need to recover the fullness of the faith and of the Church. Congregations and communions may find their own lives deepened and renewed as they think and work with other Christians in councils of churches. Church renewal movements, in our times, have often been stimulated and extended by councils of churches.

There is great emphasis in contemporary Christian literature on the importance of the missionary and evangelistic tasks of the Church—an emphasis which is richly sustained in New Testament study. In the face of the difficulties and complexities before congregations and denominations in carrying out these tasks, councils of churches can help to make the efforts and contributions of individual bodies more effective.[23] By providing means through which the churches can eliminate duplication of effort, and by securing and sharing relevant information, the councils of churches can help congregations and communions do their work of witness better. From this point of view, councils of churches are instruments of the churches which help them do their proper churchly tasks more effectively and relevantly. They are also a testimony, though incomplete and confused, that God has given one Gospel to one Church for the sake of one world.

The way in which councils of churches share in the reality of the Church through acts of Christian service, through *diakonia*, has already been mentioned (Para. 33). A further point is now appropriate. In this day of vast human and social needs, part of the proper work of every congregation and denomination can be done better through the pooling of resources and competencies in cooperative action than alone. Given the situation of a deeply divided Church facing vast human needs, cooperation in councils of churches would seem to be the least that could be done in order that Christian *diakonia* be maintained on a scale in any way commensurate with the needs of the world. *Diakonia* should not be understood as flowing only from church to world, however. For it is also important within the life of the Church; indeed, in the New Testament the emphasis is on *diakonia* in the Church. This has been forcefully expressed by Nikos A. Nissiotis:

> The division of the Church as a mystery hidden in the incomprehensible nature of God is not primarily either the result of hatred among the Churches, or of disagreement on fundamental views concerning Christian dogma. One is led by historical events to believe that at the root of the schisms in the Church there is one fundamental cause: the lack of care of the local churches for one another, the absence of *koinonia* between them, without which the vertical communion with God, though not broken, becomes a further power of alienation and isolation...Among the main reasons for the Church heresies, schisms and divisions is the lack of this inner power of mutual service, of mutual interdependent existence. The greatest sin of the people of God is that they have neglected to perceive the theological vertical dimension of *diakonia* in the ecclesiological, horizontal one.[24]

Councils of churches provide ways for churches to exercise such mutual service, to the glory of God and the enrichment of the people of God.

Part of the work of every Christian congregation and communion is to make more manifest the unity of the Church. As it was said at the Oberlin Conference, "Concern for unity is not an option open to those who happen to be interested in ecumenical affairs."[25] It is for all Christians. Section 1 at the Oberlin Conference, considering "Imperatives and Motivations" for the quest for unity, stated the case for unitive concern by every Christian, congregation, and communion in strong terms:

> The unity of the Church is both a gift and a demand. The Church is one as Christ is One (I Cor. 1:12-13). In a variety of images this unity is portrayed in the New Testament. The true vine has many branches but it is one vine (John 15:5). The One Shepherd has many sheep but they belong to one flock (John 10:16). The Church is the household of God, in which the members of God's family are at home (Eph. 2:19). It is the Israel of God, the heirs of the promises and responsibilities of the chosen people of the old covenant (I Peter 2:9-10). An outstanding description of the Church's unity is the figure of the Body of Christ (I Cor. 12:12-31). It is by *One* Spirit that men are incorporated into One Body. Within the Body there are many members, but all are coordinated by Christ who is the Head. There are diversities of gifts and ways of service, but under the guidance of the Spirit these are enhanced by the supreme spiritual gift of love and contribute to the upbuilding of the Body. As a physical body is animated by the spirit, so the Church is a visible community in which the Risen Christ is present in the midst of his people in life-giving and unifying love.
>
> Thus the imperative to manifest our unity concretely and visibly in the world is based on the truth that God has made us one in Christ. Christ's sacrifice, which displays the infinite love and undeserved grace of God, places us under obligation to love one another, even as He has loved us (I John 4:17-21). Any form of disunity that prevents the fullest expression of love in community and which promotes strife, jealousy, or factionalism is a denial of the full meaning of the Gospel.[26]

Councils of churches provide readily available channels for the churches to fulfill the clear imperatives to seek unity. They are important means for bearing witness to the unity we have and enlarging our concepts about the unity we seek. They are structures by which congregations and denominations join together in the quest for Christian unity. The report of the section dealing with "The Role of the Councils in the Quest for Unity" at the world's first Faith and Order conference on an area basis (The Pacific Northwest) well said:

> ...We earnestly look for the day when a congregation will count service in the local council part of its mission and the pastor will accept leadership as part of his ministry.[27]

Councils of churches help congregations and denominations fulfill their own God-given tasks of seeking to make more fully manifest the unity of the Church.

## *Are Councils of Churches Contributing to the Unity of the Church?*

The council of churches has its most dramatic ecclesiological significance in the fact that in it the churches labor together for the fullest possible manifestation of the unity of the Church. The very existence of the councils implies a continuing call for the overcoming of divisions in all areas of the life of the churches. The councils have taken seriously—perhaps at times too seriously—that they are councils of *churches*, and that they represent the churches. Councils of churches have not sought nor have they been asked or called upon to negotiate church unions They have often been content to be agencies of cooperation—a significant role indeed. But even so, are they not called to become active agents of reconciliation? They can and should show an unceasing concern for feasible and Christian steps toward the larger unity of the Church. They can work in suitable ways toward the unity Christ wills as set forth, for example, in the Report of the Section on Unity at the Third Assembly of the World Council of Churches at New Delhi:

> The love of the Father and the Son in the unity of the Holy Spirit is the source and goal of the unity which the Triune God wills for all men and creation. We believe that we share in this unity in the Church of Jesus Christ, Who is before all things and in Whom all things hold together. in Him alone, given by the Father to be Head of the Body, the Church has its true unity. The reality of this unity was manifest at Pentecost in the gift of the Holy Spirit, through Whom we know in this present age the first fruits of that perfect union of the Son with His Father, which will be known in its fullness only when all things are consummated by Christ in His glory. The Lord Who is bringing all things into full unity at the last is He Who constrains us to seek the unity which He wills for His Church on earth here and now.
>
> We believe that the unity which is both God's will and His gift to His Church is being made visible as all in each place who are baptized into Jesus Christ and confess Him as Lord and Savior are brought by the Holy Spirit into ONE fully committed fellowship, holding the one apostolic faith, preaching the one Gospel, breaking the one bread, joining in common prayer, and having a corporate life reaching out in witness and service to all and who at the same time are united with the whole Christian fellowship in all places and ages in such wise that ministry and

members are accepted by all, and that all can act and speak together as occasion requires for the tasks to which God calls his people.

It is for such unity that we believe we must pray and work.[28]

Councils of Churches serve as agencies in which the churches not only work together, but also seek together to find and make more fully manifest the unity of the church.

Councils of churches have their special role in the economy of the Church. By establishing local, state, national, and world councils of churches, we have taken important steps toward unity, but unity has not thereby been accomplished. We must clearly realize that what we have done so far represents only the first feeble steps in the direction of unity. It has been suggested that we will take a leap forward if we consider that a council of churches is as much a church as one or another of the denominations.[29] While there has been some support in our Commission for this general view, our conclusion is that councils of churches are not and should not claim to be churches. It is our conviction that for councils of churches to claim that they are the still imperfect yet actual nuclei of the One Church would not be to further the cause of Christian unity but to add a new denomination or denominations to the spectrum. At the Oberlin Conference it was said, "...in North America we know by experience that efforts toward unity have been very productive of new and acute divisions."[30] The road to our present denominational divisions was a long and hard one, and the road to genuine Christian unity through the enlargement of areas of theological agreement and the reunion of churches cannot be by-passed. Councils of churches are not churches; they are improvisations made necessary because of the divided status of the churches. They are expedients, divinely guided, many of us believe, but provisional. They stand in the prophetic tradition, called into being for a particular function at a particular time for a particular need. The councils of churches are catalysts for the reunion of churches; though they may not invade the freedom of communions and make their unitive decisions for them, they can and should invade the consciences of the denominations in the name of the One Lord and press them to add to cooperative service, serious concern for union.

The council of churches movement will fulfill its important ecclesiological task better if it recognized that it has often exhibited a profound lack of concern for essential aspects of the Church. Just as in the case of individual denominations, so also councils of churches have at times reflected the thrust to organization for organization's sake. The movement has at times become an escape from the hard questions of genuine unity in faith. As a report of the World Council's Commission on Institutionalism and Unity has put it:

> Institutionalized co-operation may become fixated and thus be a hindrance to more advanced steps of church unity. Such institutional drift does not assure the unity we seek or need or the unity that Christ wills.[31]

The council of churches movement itself in need of self-criticism and purification, which must take the form of increasingly direct confrontation of the question of the reunion of the Church (as distinguished from the cooperation of churches). As they press the ecclesiological question, the councils of churches cannot expect to remain unchanged themselves.

The pathway to unity that is suggested in this report is one that demands much patience. As Archbishop Arthur Michael Ramsey has said:

> Yet just as the way of holiness cannot be hurried, and the way of truth cannot be hurried, so too there is concerning unity a divine patience. Guarding ourselves against confusing divine patience and our human sloth, we know that there is a divine patience, to be imitated in our patience with others, in our patience with ourselves, and in our patience with God's agelong patience. Patience includes the will to see that an apparent set-back in some scheme may be our call to go into things more deeply than before. Patience includes, above all, the will to expect that God's blessing upon our own cherished plans may not in His wisdom be separated from His disciplining us in holiness and in truth.[32]

The pathway to unity also calls for a willingness to lose life to save it. As the section on unity at the New Delhi Assembly declared, "The achievement of unity will involve nothing less than a death and a rebirth of many forms of church life as we have known them."[33] But the prospect of the self-transcendence of denominations and councils of churches by structures which far more fully manifest the unity of the Church is not a cause for regret but for rejoicing. Following the way of the Lord brings both peace and joy to his people.

The pathway to unity is one that also demands courage and boldness. A paragraph from the Report on the Section on Unity at New Delhi makes a fitting conclusion:

> In this situation are we not constrained by the love of God to exert pressure on the limits of our own inherited traditions, recognizing the theological necessity of what we may call 'responsible risk'? We emphasize the word 'responsible': for such actions must be taken with sincere respect for our confessional position and with the full attempt to explore

with the Christian communion to which we belong the meaning of what we are doing. Clearly, also, the responsible risk will be different according to our different convictions. Nevertheless, unless there is this preparedness to seek for responsible ways of breaking through to fresh understandings, we cannot hope to be shown the way to that growing unity which we know to be God's will for us. Responsible use of local situations to explore such possibilities is a challenge in every place.[34]

## Notes

1. Paul S. Minear, ed., *The Nature of the Unity We Seek: Official Report of the North American Conference on Faith and Order, September 3-10, 1957, Oberlin, Ohio* (St. Louis: Bethany Press, 1958), p. 153.

2. On the early councils, see C.J. Cadoux, *The Early Church and the World* (Edinburgh: T. & T. Clark, 1925, 1955); J.N.D. Kelly, *Early Christian Doctrines* (London: A. & C. Black, 1958). A detailed bibliography on ecclesiology in the patristic period is given by B. Altaner, *Patrology*, trans, by Hilda C. Graef (New York: Herder & Herder, 1960), pp. 32f.

3. The term "conciliar," although sometimes used of present-day developments, is reserved in this document to refer, according to the technical usage of church historians, to the movement and period indicated here.

4. For treatments of the Conciliar Movement, cf. Jacob, E.F. *Essays in the Conciliar Epoch* (Mancester University Press, 1953); Tierney, B., *Foundations of the Conciliar Theory* (Cambridge: Cambridge University Press, 1955); collection of source readings in Petry, R.C., *A History of Christianity; Readings in the History of the Early and Medieval Church* (Englewood Cliffs, N.J.: Prentice Hall, 1962); on some important figures in the Conciliar Movement, cf. Connolly, J.L., *John Gerson Reformer and Mystic* (Louvain: Librairie Universitaire, 1928); Morrall, J.B., *Gerson and the Great Schism* (New York: Barnes and Noble, 1961); Brett, H., *Nicholas of Cusa* (London: Metheun, 1932); R.C. Petry, "Unitive Reform Principles of the Late Medieval Conciliarists," in *Church History* XXXI (June 1962), pp. 164-181.

5. Cf. John T. McNeill, *Unitive Protestantism: A Study in Our Religious Resources* (New York: Abingdon Press, 1930); cf. also his compact treatment "The Ecumenical Idea and Efforts to Realize It, 1517-1618," in Ruth Rouse & Stephen Neill, eds., *A History of the Ecumenical Movement, 1517-1948* (Philadelphia: Westminster Press, 1954), pp. 27-67.

6. Cf. Jaroslav Pelikan, "Luther's Attitude Toward Church Councils," in Kristen E. Skydsgaard, ed., *The Papal Council and the Gospel* (Minneapolis: Augsburg Publishing House, 1961), pp. 37-60.

7. Cf. Sidney E. Mead, "Denominationalism: The Shape of Protestantism in America," *Church History*, XXIII (1954), 291-320.

8. Winthrop S. Hudson, "Denominationalism as a Basis for Ecumenicity: A Seventeenth Century Conception," *Church History*, XXIV (1955), 32. Cf. also Hudson's *American Protestantism* (Chicago: University of Chicago Press, 1961), pp. 33-48.

9. "'The True American Union' of Church and States: The Reconstruction of the Theocratic Tradition," *Church History*, XXXVIII (1959), 56f.

10. Some powerful minority voices were opposed to voluntary concepts of the church and to the nondenominational voluntary societies, but the latter won out in most of the burgeoning American denominations. Resistances developed to cooperative work that have sometimes been unreflectively carried over to the quite differently oriented cooperative work of the twentieth century.

11. W.A. Visser 't Hooft, *The First Assembly of the World Council of Churches* (London: S.C.M. Press, 1949), pp. 53-4. (In italics in the original.)

12. A summary of ecumenical discussion of these themes will be found in the interim report of the Commission on Christ and the Church of the Faith and Order Commission of the World Council of Churches: *One Lord, One Baptism*, (Minneapolis: Augsburg Publishing House, 1961).

13. Cf. Ross W. Sanderson, *Church Cooperation in the United States: The Nation-Wide Backgrounds and Ecumenical Significance of State and Local Councils of Churches in Their Historical Perspective* (New York: Association of Council Secretaries, 1960). See also J. Quinter Miller, *Christian Unity: Its Relevance to the Community* (Shenandoah Publishing House, 1957); Robert Lee, *The Social Sources of Church Unity: An Interpretation of Unitive Movements in American Protestantism* (New York: Abingdon Press, 1960), Chap. 5; Raymond A. Gray, "The Ecumenical Necessity; Distinctive Contributions of Local Councils of Churches and the Faith and Order Movement to the Achievement of Christian Unity" (S.T.M. thesis, Union Theological Seminary, New York, 1958).

14. This is similar to the original Basis of the World Council of Churches, which was defined by the Evanston Assembly as performing three functions: (1) "It indicates the *nature* of the fellowship which the churches in the Council seek to establish among themselves. For that fellowship, as a fellowship of churches, has its own unique character." (2) "It provides the *orientation point* for the work which the World Council itself undertakes. The ecumenical conversations which take place in the World Council must have a point of reference. Similarly the activities of the Council must be submitted to an ultimate norm and standard." (3) "It indicates the *range* of the fellowship" which the churches in the Council seek to establish. While the Basis is "less than a confession, it is much more than a mere formula of agreement. It is truly a basis in that the life and activity of the World Council are based upon it."

15. *Growing Together: A Manual for Councils of Churches* (New York: National Council of the Churches of Christ in the U.S.A., 1955), p. 21.

16. At the time of the survey, there were an estimated 316 local councils in the U.S.A. with paid staff, and 610 with volunteer staff. Constitutions available in the Office for Councils of the Churches for study numbered 332, of which 105, chosen at random sampling, were analyzed.

17. In addition to attention to the National Council of Churches of Christ in the U.S.A., the constitutions of some 62 other national councils of churches were scanned. The patterns do not seem to be greatly dissimilar from those in the U.S., though while 20 accepted the evangelical basis, as many more have some more extended confessional basis.

18. E.g., a study of the St. Louis Metropolitan Church Federation which was undertaken in preparation for the Oberlin Conference reported that "...the Federation has not, in almost a half century of history, provided, nor been urged to provide opportunities for discussions of faith and order." Elmer J.F. Arndt, "Summary of Findings," North American Conference on Faith and Order; Study Grist and Gist; #15, p. 2.

19. The translation of the Latin is, in sequence, "outside the walls," "in a certain sense," "a church outside the church."

20. "Towards an Ecumenical Theology," *Ecumenical Review*, XIII (1960-61), 219.

21. *Against Heresies*, Book III, chap xxiv.

22. See the Report of the Section on Service of the New Delhi Assembly of the World Council of Churches: Visser 't Hooft, W.A., ed., *The New Delhi Report* (New York: Association Press, 1962), pp. 93ff.

23. Although concern for the unity of the faith is a concern for all churches, there are certain churches which understand that missionary or evangelistic tasks cannot be carried out except on the basis of prior unity of faith.

24. "The Ecclesiological Significance of Inter-church Diakonia," *Ecumenical Review*, XIII (1960-61), pp. 193, 195.

25. Minear, ed., *The Nature of the Unity We Seek*, p. 169.

26. Minear, ed., *The Nature of the Unity We Seek*, p. 169.

27. John H. Van Lierop, ed., *Church and Unity in the Pacific Northwest* (Portland, Oregon: Greater Portland Council of Churches, 1962), p. 93.

28. Visser 't Hooft, ed., *The New Delhi Report* (New York: Association Press, 1962), pp. 116f.

29. Cf., e.g., Henry P. Van Dusen, "The Significance of Conciliar Ecumenicity," *Ecumenical Review*, XIII (1959-60), pp. 310-318.

30. Minear, ed., *The Nature of the Unity We Seek*, p. 175.

31. *The Old and the New in the Church* (Minneapolis: Augsburg Publishing House, 1962), p. 87.

32. "Unity, Holiness and Truth," *Ecumenical Review*, XIV (1961-62), p. 190.

33. Visser 't Hooft, ed., *The New Delhi Report*, p. 117.

34. Visser 't Hooft, ed., *The New Delhi Report*, p. 117.

# Faith and Order Commission Report on the Application for Membership in the NCCC of the Universal Fellowship of Metropolitan Community Churches*

In the fall of 1981 the National Council of Churches approved a new Preamble and Purpose for its constitution, calling the Council from the stance of a "cooperative agency" to that of a "community of communions." For some, this was too much to ask of a Council with such a weak emphasis on theology and the church uniting heart of ecumenism. For others this was a hope for a new direction to the council's life, growing beyond an activist, coalitional style towards a more conscious ecclesiological approach to its role in reconciling the member communions. The style of decision making and membership rules have yet to be revised to reflect this constitutional shift.

During the same month an application for membership in the Council came from a community, new on the ecclesiological spectrum, as Christian history goes. The Universal Fellowship of Metropolitan Community Churches is a communion founded some 15 years ago with a special ministry to those who have been alienated from their churches because of their sexual orientation. While the community has a wide range of ministries, and does not discriminate according to sexual orientation or perspective on human sexuality, its unique origin and context has focused discussion around a number of issues relating to its openness to an understanding of Christian anthropology by no means universally accepted in the Christian tradition.

For a communion to be admitted to the National Council, the questions of numbers of members and congregations, legal status and theology are reviewed by a Constituent Membership Committee. On the basis of a recommendation by that committee a vote is taken on the eligibility of the communion for membership by the Governing Board of the Council. This Board consists of about 270 delegates from the thirty-two member communions of

*Mid-Stream 22 (1983) 453-67.

the Council. Should the communion prove eligible, six months later the member communions (32) vote on membership. If the results of these two votes are positive, then the full board votes on membership. Many communions have been voted eligible but have not put themselves forward for membership. Some communions have been discouraged from applying for membership and at least one other communion, the Swedenborgian Church, has been engaged in dialogue with the Commission on Faith and Order before its application was considered.

When the Membership Committee gave its recommendation on the UFMCC to the Council in May, 1982, there were those on the Board who were unfamiliar with this community and who had never engaged them in ecumenical dialogue. There were others who were quite familiar with them, but had never engaged other churches in the Council in ecumenical dialogue over the issues involved. There were still others who, without benefit of orientation, had no history of the ecumenical movement and had not had the opportunity to internalize the new Preamble and Purpose or learn the ecclesiological and ecumenical stances of other member communions in the Council. There were those in each of these groups, nonetheless, who were quite prepared to make a decision on the spot without benefit of more extensive dialogue than the Governing Board debate period.

In order to provide for wider dialogue between the member churches of the Council, between representatives of these churches and the UFMCC and the Governing Board members, and between church leaders, Governing Board members and the constituency of the churches, a resolution was put forward to allow for more time and also provide a mechanism for initiating this dialogue. While all parties were urged to exercise pastoral concern for all involved, the specific task of providing a forum for dialogue on the issues of ecclesiology and ecumenical fellowship was assigned to the Commission on Faith and Order. This Commission of the Council is charged with the task of promoting the visible unity of the Church through theological dialogue on the church uniting/church dividing issues that must be resolved before full unity in faith can be realized. As the following report indicates, the task of this commission was not to review the work of the Constituent Membership Committee, nor to persuade communions as to the appropriate vote. Indeed, it is this mandate that has been most difficult for the secular press to clarify. The time line allotted was one year, an extremely short time to engage thirty-two different communions in a serious ecumenical dialogue on an extremely wide array of issues.

While the "ecclesiological and ecumenical fellowship" issues seemed to some as narrow, for the more biblically and theologically oriented traditions, these issues cover a full range of justice, anthropological and pastoral concerns which cannot be isolated from either sexuality or Council membership. On the floor of the Governing Board there was strong opposition voiced to seeing this issue as a Faith and Order issue. However, as the dialogue report shows, every church represented in the dialogue considered it to be a "church uniting/church dividing" issue. There were others who objected to ecclesiology being introduced since they considered ecclesiological language to be "contentless language." One can judge from this report and the background papers whether this is indeed the case for any of the communions involved.

The Faith and Order Commission consists of theologians appointed by the member communions of the Council, and representatives of other churches like the Roman Catholic, Southern Baptist, the three non-member Lutheran bodies, Christian Reformed, and Church of God (Anderson, IN). It unanimously approved a process directed by a steering committee of four of its members: William G. Rusch (Chair), Lutheran Church in America; Lauree Hersch Meyer, Church of the Brethren; John Brandon, African Methodist Episcopal; and Alexander Doumouras, Greek Orthodox Archdiocese of North and South America. The process called for the appointment of theologians by member communions of the Commission and the production of papers on the issues—papers that were to be informed by a mass of material provided from member Communions on ecclesiology, ecumenical fellowship and sexuality and from local ecumenical agencies as well as by the new Preamble and Purpose. These papers were distributed among the theologians for review and discussion at the first dialogue in November, 1982. The papers and the subsequent report of that dialogue (Part II of attached documentation) were shared with the representatives of the UFMCC who met with representatives from the first dialogue in December 1982. This group drew up a report (Part III of attached documentation). The complete documentation including all the papers submitted and the two reports were sent to the members of the Commission in preparation for a March 1983 meeting at which it was discussed and a final report (Part I of attached documentation) was formulated.

The report intends to clarify the issues so that constructive dialogue can take place and the churches might be able to understand one another and the Council more clearly as they prepare for voting. Other processes have been designed for furthering dialogue, and the vote on eligibility has again been postponed until November, 1983. This report was given to the Governing Board for its May 1983 meeting, though there has been no formal discussion of it in the Governing Board context.

Brother Jeffrey Gros, F.S.C.
*Director, Commission on Faith and Order*
*National Council of Churches of Christ*

## REPORT TO THE GOVERNING BOARD

*This report was presented to the Governing Board of the National Council of Churches of Christ from the Commission on Faith and Order on the application for membership of the Universal Fellowship of Metropolitan Community Churches.*

## I. Commission on Faith and Order Report* Mercy Center, Burlingame, California March 11-14, 1983

*Response to the Request of the Governing Board to Faith and Order*

1) The Commission on Faith and Order has called together two dialogues, one among representatives of member communions, the other between representatives of this group and representatives of the Universal Fellowship of Metropolitan Community Churches (UFMCC), the results of which are contained in this report (Part III). The 19 papers of member communions and of the UFMCC are available to the Governing Board upon request. The Commission has done studies before on the occasion of the application of the Swedenborgian Church. This time we have been asked to study questions of ecclesiological and ecumenical fellowship that have been raised by this community's application for membership.

2) Like the apostles at the Council of Jerusalem in Acts 15, we have found ourselves dealing with a wide range of issues affecting the unity of the churches and impinging on the pastoral, theological and political realities of church life.

3) We are drawn more deeply into a common search for unity with each other. More recently we have moved into dialogue and experience with the UFMCC. We have seen our task not as making recommendations on eligibility—the Constituent Membership Committee's task, or on membership—the member communion's prerogative, but on clarifying the issues of ecclesiology and ecumenical fellowship as they have emerged in the life of the Council.

*Reflections and Recommendations from the Commission Meeting*

## A. Ecclesiological Reflections

4) In the statements prepared by the member communions, in the two dialogue reports, and in our conversations, a critical issue has been identified

---

*As a Commission we submit the following report with reservation in that we believe the process did not give us sufficient time to engage the theological task adequately.

in relation to understanding the nature of the NCCC itself and, more specifically, the meaning of membership within the Council.

5) While no single ecclesiology has been presupposed as a test for
membership by different communions within the Council, the "revised
Preamble and Statement of Purpose" (1981) appears to be moving toward a
more formal position regarding the vision of conciliar unity and its ecclesial
implications:

> The NCCC in the USA is a community of Christian communions which,
> in response to the Gospel as revealed in the Scriptures, confess Jesus
> Christ, the incarnate Word of God, as Savior and Lord. These commu-
> nions covenant with one another to manifest ever more fully the unity of
> the Church.

6) Compare this statement, for example, with the earlier affirmation by
the WCC in 1950 (Toronto) which sets forth an intentionally neutral position
regarding the relationship of ecclesiology and membership within a council:

> The member churches of the World Council consider the relationship of
> other churches to the holy catholic church which the creeds profess as a
> subject for mutual consideration. Nevertheless membership does not
> imply that each church must regard the other member churches as
> churches in the true and full sense of the word.

> The member churches of the World Council recognize in other churches
> elements of the true church. They consider that this mutual recognition
> obliges them to enter a serious conversation with each other in the hope
> that these elements of truth will lead to a recognition of the full truth and
> to unity based on the full truth.

7) Within the present member communions of the National Council
there exists a diversity of opinion and perspectives based upon one's own
theology or tradition regarding the ecclesiological requirements for membership. Somehow these differences of perspective have continued to exist side-
by-side within the NCCC over several decades.

8) It seems clear that for some member communions, there would be
no theological problem in accepting the UFMCC for membership based upon
their own understandings of its ecclesiology, and also their understanding of
the nature of membership within the NCCC.

9) For others, there are theological problems because of their understandings of the UFMCC's ecclesiology, and also their understanding of the
nature of membership. Several member churches have expressed serious
reservations about the UFMCC as a church. It is clear that within the NCCC,

however, those same churches might also express similar judgments about present member churches with whom they are now in covenant and have a long history of valuable and responsible relationships. The diversity of positions is not only in relation to the UFMCC, but also to the issue of the meaning of membership itself.

10) The Commission therefore concludes that it cannot with one voice make a recommendation regarding the application of the UFMCC for membership in the NCCC based upon ecclesiology. And, whatever action the Governing Board takes on this application, the Faith and Order Commission believes an urgent and continuing issue for discussion is that of the nature of the ecclesial fellowship within the Council as set forth in its revised preamble and statement of purpose. As presently stated, the Preamble and Purpose of the NCCC could be interpreted to allow for either a positive or a negative vote on this matter.

## B. Continuing Theological Issues

11) The discussion of ecclesiological issues and the nature of the ecumenical fellowship of the NCCC led to an identification of an ever-increasing number of theological areas needing further investigation and discussion. Some of these areas were already spelled out in the report on the Dialogue between Representatives of the NCCC and UFMCC. Of particular note were three areas highlighted in the San Francisco discussion: anthropology; limits of legitimate diversity; responsibility for pastoral ministry.

12) *Anthropology:* A basic issue underlined in the dialogues is that of theological anthropology. Church tradition has held that man and woman were created in God's image, expressing that image through complementarity of male and female sexuality. Some recent theological interpretations stress relationship and community as the expression of God's image, seen through partnership and community among human beings of different sexes and of the same sex. The UFMCC represents this newer understanding of theological anthropology that needs further discussion.

13) *Limits of Legitimate Diversity in the NCCC:* The question of limits of diversity underlines not just the issue of valid signs of the Church, but also the different views of how limits are set. Some draw the limits according to certain ecclesiological criteria of their tradition such as creeds, sacraments, orders. Others understand the limits in terms of the central affirmation of the church applying for membership that it is a community of faith in the Lord Jesus Christ. The limit is thus set by the church applying for membership in the light of its own ecclesiology, rather than by the member churches.

Beyond what is required for membership by the NCCC constitution, there is the continuing issue of how limits are set.

14) *Responsibility for Pastoral Ministry:* The application of the UFMCC raises many issues concerning pastoral ministry among constituent congregations, as well as with, to and by the gay and lesbian community. Some churches already engaged in this ministry would welcome the UFMCC as a partner in ministry. Others find that the presence of the UFMCC would further polarize their own membership and make pastoral ministry less possible. Both the opportunities and the tensions of pastoral ministry to these different groups were clear as we sought to respond to the UFMCC request.

## C. Sharing Fellowship

15) Members of the Commission confess our complicity in these issues that divide us. Fear of homosexuality has brought many to evade, judge and reject gay men and lesbian women. When our churches have failed to extend compassion and nurture, guilt and failure are often expressed as hostility. Under rejection many homosexuals have turned from existing churches and have come together in a new Christian community.

16) We confess therefore also that what divides many churches in the NCCC from the UFMCC is not only our diverse views of church. Many in the churches are struggling with appropriate ways of ministry to and with gay men and lesbian women.

17) As in earlier dialogues, being together with members of the UFMCC helped us know them better. During our San Francisco meeting, many of our members visited and worshiped with congregations of the UFMCC and participated in Christian community with them. Many witnessed their faith, and experienced the UFMCC as a warm, healing community whose fellowship and mission embraced us and reached out to others. Many of us shared in liturgy, singing, prayer, the Word, the eucharist. Many talked and ate together and were moved and blessed by their ministry to us.

*Specific Recommendations*
18) We recommend:
To the members of the Governing Board:
A) In light of our experience of the importance of personal interaction, that you engage in dialogue with and experience the worship of UFMCC congregations in order better to consider the ecclesial character and quality of ministry of this community.

To the Governing Board:
B) In order that the UFMCC and the NCCC member communions recognize that the member churches are seriously addressing pastoral needs in this area, exploration be made of a pastoral letter to the NCCC member churches and the UFMCC reflecting the pastoral and political concerns emanating from this dialogue.

C) Because this application highlights the discrepancy between the intentions of the new Preamble and Purpose and the membership process, that dialogue with member communions be entered into to illuminate this discrepancy. One possible result could be a further understanding of one another and one another's theology, ecclesiology and pastoral approaches.

To Faith and Order:
D) Recognizing that continuing dialogue on theological issues requires regular interaction, that some means to be found so that the UFMCC can continue to discuss issues with us (e.g. liaison status, etc.).

## II. Theologian's Study Report: Seamen's Institute, New York, NY November 12-13, 1982

1) This report represents responses to some of the specific questions engendered in our member churches by the application of the UFMCC for membership in the NCCC in the U.S.A. It is in no way considered to be a theological statement of the Commission on Faith and Order, the NCC or especially of the member churches gathered to reflect on the questions raised. Rather it is a distillation of some of the issues offered to the UFMCC for its reflection in preparation for a December 1982 dialogue with representatives of our member churches and to the member communions of the NCC as a report of our brief discussion together. It is the clear consensus of this group that this is truly a Faith and Order issue, that is a Church uniting/ Church dividing issue which touches on questions of ecclesiology and the nature of the ecumenical fellowship, and which can only be resolved by our member churches by careful attention to the Preamble and Purpose of the NCCC and its emphasis on the church uniting mission of our presence together in Council.

2) We do not presume any authority in this paper for or to our churches, and we recognize that the member churches and the National Council are not charged with the responsibility for certifying before God or before our own membership the legitimacy of any church that applies for membership. We are clear that the vote of the Governing Board and the member communions nei-

ther legitimates nor calls into question the legitimacy of a community of Christians whether the vote is negative or positive. Such a vote, whatever the outcome, does indicate the seriousness with which the applying community has been taken by the National Council and its member communions.

3) Likewise, we clearly recognize the differing theological and constitutional bases by which members of the council are empowered to remain in membership with one another, and respect these differences in confession of our dividedness and acknowledge that it is God alone who finally judges our reality as churches and our decisions regarding one another and new members in our community. Our own styles of interpretation are brought to the Preamble and Purpose and to the documents of other communities of Christians within and without our community of churches, so that we are led to expect different perceptions of Council relationships, before our own understanding of the Christian faith.

4) In response to the question "Is the UFMCC a 'church qualifying for membership' as understood within the meaning of the Preamble and Purpose of the Constitution of the NCC?" we seem to arrive at very different responses. Some would say:

> a) that according to the purpose of the NCC and in the understanding of the UFMCC as presented in their documentation they would find it impossible to conclude that the UFMCC is a "church qualifying for membership." It needs to be kept in mind that this conclusion is based on the different theological perspectives in such communions as Lutheran, Eastern and Oriental Orthodox, American Baptist, African Methodist Episcopal, Christian Methodist Episcopal, Moravian, some Presbyterians and the United Church of Christ. This conclusion comes from different ecclesiological understandings of member communions in the light of the Preamble and Purpose of the NCC. (The United Church of Christ is compelled to respond in the negative already because of the framing of the question in terms of belief, that is, as a "test of faith." Frederick Herzog.)
>
> b) that the UFMCC do fulfill the requirements because at the core of their life they have an evangelical commitment to the Gospel of Jesus Christ. Moreover they bring a unique commitment to ministry to homosexuals. This conclusion, likewise, comes from different perspectives in such communions as the United Methodist, the Friends, the Christian Church (Disciples of Christ) and some other Presbyterians.
>
> c) that the issue is not clear and would only become so—so that a judgment could be made—when the experience together with this community would lead them to know or not to know this community as a "church." For those churches the judgment cannot be made in an experiential vacuum on the basis of statements of belief. This is the position of the Church of the Brethren.

5) The second question relates to the impact of the admission of the UFMCC to the ecumenical fellowship as our member churches relate to one another, to the National Council and to the UFMCC. "Would the present and future church uniting ability of the Council be strengthened or weakened by the admission of this community?"

6) It is evident that within the member churches there are differences over issues related to sexuality, and that the admission or non-admission of this community to the Council would have serious implications for their own internal life and its unity. In some cases, admission would have a negative impact on their own ability to hold fellowship; in others it would affect their union negotiations with other churches; in still others it would have an influence on current internal discussions of sexuality. For some, non-admission would indicate that sexuality takes precedence over affirmation of the Gospel as the operative organizing principle in the life and work of the churches.

> a) For some churches the admission of the UFMCC would weaken, if not damage irreparably the NCC as a vehicle for Christian unity. For some this might even include withdrawal from membership.
> b) Others would recognize the diminution that could occur in the ecumenical life of the Council because of this new member but feel the need to affirm ecumenical inclusiveness in spite of the difficulties.
> c) Some would recognize a commitment to a full range of ecumenical relationships. While tension on existing relationships would need to be taken into consideration, the importance of ecumenical inclusiveness would require incorporating this community. For these churches the question is not a justice issue, but a question of expanding the unity of the church wherever the Gospel is being preached and pastoral care is being given, even at the risk entailed for a unity already achieved.
> d) Others feel a church coming into being around the organizing principle of homosexuality cannot be recognized as enhancing the unity of the church because of the narrowness of the organizing principle.
> e) Others would hold to the "church" reality of this community, in light of the Preamble and Purpose, but are concerned for maintaining the community of churches which already exist within the NCC.
> f) Some feel that inclusion of this communion would enhance a fuller expression of the unity of the church.

Some churches find themselves ascribing to more than one of the above positions.

7) The third question was "What is an appropriate pastoral ministry to gay and lesbian persons by the churches of the NCC?"

> a) Some felt that admission of this community, the UFMCC, to the NCC was an appropriate means of expressing pastoral care for gay and les-

bian persons to whom member churches have not found means of ministering within their own communities.

b) Most people in the discussion responded positively to the following pastoral comment made by Thomas Hopko:

Pastoral ministry to homosexual persons in our particular culture is very difficult, and the complexities do not allow for a simple formulation. The very nature of pastoral ministry is personal and contextual, and decisions are made with pastoral *ekonomia* on the basis that it is the heterosexual monogamous marriage that is normative.

It is too simple to say that the only possible pastoral judgment is to tell homosexual persons to repent or get out of the church. Often this is neither necessary nor possible.

Nor on the other hand, can ministry be simply defined as affirming, celebrating, and even sacramentally consecrating homosexuality as a blessing from God, for all Christians to recognize.

The homosexual Christian, struggling with his or her homosexuality, who to death continues to be involved in acts with some sense of pathos before God, may be closer to God than the self-righteous straight person who says, "To hell with all of them."

The drama of the human soul, the life before God, the complexities of the matter, do not allow us to conclude either that the authentic pastoral ministry is simply to exclude all active homosexuals from the community of the church, or that a church can understand its ministry as simply affirming and celebrating homosexuality.

c) It was felt important to make clear that there is a distinction between homosexual orientation and the expression of such orientation in behavior. Men and women are to be affirmed as persons no matter what their sexual orientation. The church must also reach out in ministry to those persons who act out a homosexual orientation in behavior. This ministry takes on different forms depending on the theology, discipline and ethos of our different churches, while the pastoral care given to homosexual Christians in their life within our churches varies according to the style of pastoral ministry in our different communions. Likewise the importance of a ministry that can confirm and support the homosexual person was affirmed in all our churches, though the means and content of that support differed from one communion to another. (The American Baptist representative, George Peck, registered some hesitancy on this last sentence.)

8) Finally, a series of concerns was lifted up for the reflection of our member churches, the UFMCC and the members of the Governing Board:

a) All of our communions, though sadly not all of our members, deplore violations of the civil rights of homosexual persons, and any violence, contempt or vilification directed towards these, our sisters and brothers, as persons, individually or collectively. There is a consensus that homosexual persons are to be fully acknowledged as persons, as are heterosexual persons, though we differ on the moral evaluation of sexual expression. It appears that none of our churches clearly affirms homosexual expression in behavior, though that affirmation is among the range of options in some of our communions. (The Jewish and Christian traditions as interpreted by church officials have some responsibility for the sinful contempt in which certain heterosexual Christians have held homosexual persons. Phillip Mullen for the Philadelphia Friends)

b) The second concern to be raised was to ask the member communions what constructive forms of relationship in dialogue and cooperation in ministry would be possible with the UFMCC were their application for membership in the NCC not voted positively. All the churches present indicated that there was a wide range of relationships with groups—Christian and non-Christian—other than membership in the NCC.

c) Recognizing the positive obligations of the NCC to reach out in dialogue to all persons, including non-member groups and churches, the third concern was to ask the NCC what appropriate relationships might be developed were this application not to receive a positive vote.

A number of examples emerged in the discussion, among which were: observer status on the Commission of Faith and Order and other units of the Council, collaboration to decrease the emotional overtones with which member churches and congregations approach questions related to sexuality, an invitation to the UFMCC to demonstrate its interest in other ministries within the Council than those relating directly to sexuality.

9) Finally, our small study group wishes to confess on behalf of ourselves and our member churches that we have not done all we could to reach out to the UFMCC and to the homosexual persons in our own faith families. We believe that as churches and individuals we must search in God's grace to find effective ways to approach these, our neighbors, in ministry and dialogue.

## III. Report of the Dialogue between Member Churches of the NCCC and the UFMCC: Alma Mathews House, New York, NY, December 10-11, 1982

*Preface*

1) On December 10-11, 1982, representatives of several member communions of the National Council of Churches and representatives of the Universal Fellowship of Metropolitan Community Churches met to discuss Faith and Order issues related to the UFMCC application for membership in

the NCCC. This report summarized the agreement, recommendation, and points of disagreement among those representatives. The report is to be read along with the accompanying documents, which include the report of the November 12-13 meeting of theologians from NCCC member communions. That report formed the basis for the December dialogue.

2) The dialogue was congenial and was dominated by a spirit of prayer and mutual concern. The agreements reached are brief. We confess that many issues are still outstanding and that the two-day dialogue did not allow us to treat these concerns at the depth warranted.

3) This report is for the use of the NCCC's Commission on Faith and Order, the leaders of the member communions, the Department of Ecumenical Relations and Board of Elders of the UFMCC, and after the March meeting, the members of the NCCC Governing Board. It is not to receive wider circulation at this time.

Co-Chairs:
R. Adam DeBaugh   UFMCC
William Rusch       NCCC

*A. Areas of Agreement*

4) The participants in this dialogue understand that the UFMCC's reason for being is to proclaim the Gospel of Jesus Christ.[1]

The UFMCC affirms that love is good, that it is from God and that it is blessed since God is love and loves everyone. The UFMCC also affirms that one of God's created possibilities for loving includes physical, sexual loving between people of the same gender. The UFMCC grounds this affirmation in what it takes to be the undeniable facts of human experience and observations drawn from the social sciences, and considers their affirmation as compatible with the biblical message. The churches of the NCCC must take this testimony of the UFMCC most seriously, since in the past some communions have come to accept positions which their founders had originally denied.

5) The participants of this dialogue recognize their common faith commitment to Jesus Christ as Savior and Lord. In this context, we are all engaged in the process of exploring the theological dimensions of our nature as Christian persons, male and female, created in the image of God, and striving to live in responsible relationship with one another and the rest of creation. Therefore, it is vital for the churches of the NCCC to remain in intentional dialogue with the UFMCC on these issues in order to enhance fuller participation of the Christian community in articulating our visions through sharing our understandings of sacred scripture, tradition, theology, and experience.[2]

6) The UFMCC and the churches of the NCCC are struggling with common issues. It would be of mutual benefit to work collaboratively on

these issues that face all Christian churches and society today. In particular, this collaboration would help us address the ways such theological issues as image of God, orders of creation and theological anthropology affect the following:

a) A theology of sexuality;

b) Our understanding of human nature as it helps us to address current social questions of maleness/femaleness, gender roles, changing family structure;[3]

c) Ways in which historical dualism of male/female and spirit/body in the Christian tradition have shaped Christian faith and practice.

7) *Recommendation:* The participants from the member churches of the NCCC urge the Executive Committee of Faith and Order to invite representatives of the UFMCC to the March meeting of Faith and Order to discuss the issues related to the UFMCC application.

## B. Areas of Disagreement

8) On a number of issues under consideration, the participants in the dialogue did not reach agreement. These are significant issues and we recommend that the Commission on Faith and Order and the member communions of the NCCC give them serious consideration. We feel further discussion could assist mutual understanding.

a) What is the central question presented by this application? Many people in our churches believe that the question here is about homosexuality; others would say homosexuality is not the pivotal issue although it must be dealt with.

b) What are the limits of legitimate diversity that can be tolerated within the NCCC? Are the theological and practical differences between the UFMCC and the member churches acceptable differences or do they cross the bounds of legitimate diversity?

c) What are the theological and practical implications of recognizing the UFMCC as a "church eligible for membership"? Some question the possibility of the establishment and continuation of a church around the UFMCC understanding of human nature.

d) What would be the effects of a yes or no vote on the unity and inclusiveness of the NCCC? On the churches' understanding of ecumenism? On the member churches themselves?

e) What would be the effect of a positive or negative vote on the UFMCC and its community? Of particular concern is whether a negative vote might be the reason for increased violence against homosexual people and/or increased antireligious feeling in parts of the gay/lesbian community.

f) What methods do we appropriate to interpret the Bible? How do we use scripture in responding to these and other issues?

g) What are the sources of authority in our traditions for theology and for authentic Christian living? What is the place of scripture, tradition, experience, reason?

h) How do we define what is normative in our traditions? How can we clarify for one another our understanding and application of our norm: i.e., legal, ideal, sociological or other?

i) What do our various traditions teach about the role of genital sexuality outside of monogamous marriage? How do these teachings compare with contemporary Christian practice? What implications do these teachings have for the UFMCC rite of holy union?

j) In what ways can the churches receive ministry from Christians, such as homosexuals who are on the margin of the larger Christian community?

(This is a somewhat abbreviated summary of the issues discussed during the dialogue.)


## Notes

1. William G. Rusch wrote on December 17, 1982: "In my opinion these lines express the UFMCC's statement of its reason for being. I understand the meaning of those lines to be that all the dialogue participants heard this articulation of the UFMCC's reason for being by UFMCC participants."

2. William G. Rusch, December 17, 1982: "I wish to point out that others besides the UFMCC are working on these issues, including persons within NCCC member churches. The dialogue should include many others besides the UFMCC. I do not hear the text speaking against this, but I do not want to leave the impression that the UFMCC is the only possible dialogue partner for the issues raised in paragraphs B and C."

3. This comment from one of the drafters may serve to clarify the parameters of the discussion of the first two points:

"Contemporary life poses 'new questions' to traditional Christian teachings on the family, social relationships and gender roles. Specifically, modern Christian experience encompasses new forms of both institutional and informal relationships (for example, significant numbers of single parents: children in joint custody; extended families which do not have as a center a 'nuclear' family; long-term heterosexual and homosexual partnering without legal marriage). Also, a vast array of choices have developed which enlarge our historical understandings of the kinds of attitudes, work and behavior appropriate to women and men.

"As a result, many people in our churches seek a 'theology of sexuality' which integrates our traditional insights from scripture with our understanding of present experience. Further, this theology must speak clearly, compassionately and responsibly in our society on specific issues which have never before confronted churches in the forms we are now witnessing."

# A Report of the Bilateral Study Group of the Faith and Order Commission of the National Council of Churches*

During the past decade, the ecumenical movement has witnessed notable achievements in theological consensus-building. National and international bilateral dialogues have started to bear fruit after long years of patient and systematic attention to issues that have divided churches for generations. Simultaneously, multilateral dialogues have issued consensus-building statements such as the agreement on *Baptism, Eucharist and Ministry* produced by the Faith and Order Commission of the World Council of Churches.[1] Cumulatively considered, these agreements indicate that the ecumenical movement has reached the stage for moving beyond finding commonalities and formulating consensus; the ecumenical movement has now reached the stage of proposing to the churches a new agenda for proceeding to the reception of these results and for proposing common action based upon this new level of ecumenical agreement.

For example, church union negotiations, seemingly a dead issue during the 1970's, have recently come to fruition is such instances as the formation of the Presbyterian Church (USA) and the Evangelical Lutheran Church in America.[2] In addition, the Consultation on Church Union, after 25 years work, has reached a significant level of maturity with its formulation of a basic theological consensus and a proposal on covenanting which recommends that its member communions undertake the establishment of a covenant-communion.[3]

In this present climate of theological convergence and ecclesiological rapprochement, a recurring theme is that of seeking to understand more clearly the path to unity—of describing not only the goal we seek, but also the character and components of this goal as Christian communions and traditions attempt to journey from separation to reconciliation. For example, during the 1970's considerable debate was occasioned by some who claimed

*John Ford, ed., "A Report of the Bilateral Study Group of the Faith and Order Commission of the National Council of Churches," *Mid-Stream* 28 (1989) 115-35.

that the bilateral and conciliar approaches to unity set rival priorities for the ecumenical movement; while the strategies proposed are admittedly different, the various types of dialogue—bilateral, conciliar, church union etc.—seem to complement, rather than compete, with one another.

To date, various findings about the nature of unity have emerged in contemporary ecumenical conversations. Some of these findings take the form of theological ideas; other findings are more in the shape of Christian commitment. Some of these findings stem from reflection upon historical data; other findings are derived from the experience of ecumenical dialogue. Some of these findings suggest ways for resolving the divisive issues of the past, while others attempt to chart paths for the future.

These findings are not merely speculative ideas formulated by individual ecumenists; these findings are experiential insights born of the dialogical interaction among ecumenically minded Christians. These findings seem to represent parameters—consistently recurring concepts and convictions—underlying a plethora of agreed statements and consensus texts. Such findings need to be explicitly recognized and tested as churches begin to take official action in receiving, claiming, and implementing the results of the ecumenical dialogues in which they have been formally involved; such findings need to be explicitly validated as churches move toward greater oneness in the life, faith, and mission of the church.

Like every ecumenical consensus, the present set of ecumenical findings has a special history, both organizational and experiential. Simply stated, these findings are the product of the "Bilateral Study Group" of the Faith and Order Commission of the National Council of Churches. After spending a three-year period (1982-84) studying particular topics in documents issued by bilateral and multilateral dialogues,[4] the group turned its attention to an exploration of "underlying factors" or "basic assumptions" that seemed to be implicitly operative within many of these documents, yet had not generally received the direct attention they seemed to merit.

The present list of findings thus represents the result of a collective reflection that has attempted to go beyond particular issues to a formulation of less obvious but equally important assumptions that seem to be implicitly operative in ecumenical dialogue. The following 34 findings are clustered under four headings: 1) conversion, 2) the nature of the unity that we seek, 3) the faith and order of the church, and 4) the future of ecumenical dialogue.

While it is comparatively easy to present a list of findings, it is much more difficult to convey the sense of ecumenical fellowship that the group experienced in the course of discussing differences and seeking consensus. Suffice it to say then that these findings emerged not simply from the group's study of the texts issued by various dialogues at both the national and international levels, but more importantly from the group's semi-annual conversations over a three-year period (1984-87).

During this triennium, the Bilaterals Study Group was again chaired by Daniel Martensen (Lutheran Church in America), while Christopher Schreck (Roman Catholic Church) served as secretary. The discussion papers, from which the findings were eventually derived, were originally written by Joseph Burgess (American Lutheran Church), John Ford (Roman Catholic Church), Julia Gatta (Episcopal Church), Meg Madson (American Lutheran Church), J. Robert Nelson (United Methodist Church), and Robert Welsh (Disciples of Christ); in addition, material was used from Michael Kinnamon's book, *Truth and Community,* and suggestions received from Thaddeus Horgan were included. Besides those already mentioned, regular participants in the discussions during the triennium included: David Cubie (Church of the Nazarene), Richard Harmon (Southern Baptist Convention), Gerald Moede (United Methodist Church), Dayalan Niles (United Methodist Church), William Rusch (Lutheran Church in America), Jerry Sandidge (Assemblies of God) and Robert Stephanopoulos (Greek Orthodox Church); also contributing to the discussions were Mark Ellingsen (Strasbourg Ecumenical Institute), Efstathios Mylonas (Greek Orthodox Church), and, Jeffrey Gros, Alexandra Brown, Thomas Dandelet, Barbara Henninges, and Stephanie Yazge,[5] staff members of the Faith and Order Commission. John Ford edited the findings for publication.

## Aspects of Conversion in Ecumenical Dialogue[6]

Finding 1: *A Christian's commitment to ecumenism seems to begin with a "holy discontent" over the division and divisiveness among Christians.*

Christians from many different traditions and in many different places have come to the awareness that their disunity seriously damages the proclamation of the gospel and provides a stumbling block to Christ's mission in the world. Ecumenically-minded Christians have come to recognize that their disunity contradicts Christ's will for his church. The realization that the separation among Christians is a radical deviation from the gospel parallels the realization that one's personal life needs a radical "change of heart." The realization of the sinfulness of disunity among Christian is the beginning in ecumenism of a conversion, similar to a conversion in the very life of Christian faith.

Finding 2: *Because "ecumenical conversion," like every real conversion, is always the work of the Holy Spirit, its precise course cannot be determined in advance.*

Conversion is as crucial to ecumenism as it is to the Christian life itself. Ecumenism requires us to live in a paradoxical tension: we need to be ever loyal to the faith which "has been received," yet at the same time ever willing, under the impulse of grace, to "change our hearts." Indeed, while desiring a radically altered ecclesial situation from the one we now know, we need to be grateful to the church which has nourished and guided us to date. Like every conversion, ecumenism requires that we allow for the possibility that God may speak to us not only directly, but also through others; we must be prepared to admit that the Word of God may come to us through our partners in dialogue. Ecumenical dialogue should be approached in the same way as we approach prayer: ready to have our hidden sins and blindness exposed, ready to be shown that God's truth and goodness are always greater than we had imagined.

Finding 3: *Ecumenical "conversion" is, at least in part, the process whereby God changes us through our dialogue partners.*

Without receptivity to our dialogue-partners, there can be only simultaneous monologues—speaking without really listening—or unsatisfying debates—speaking without reciprocal understanding. Thus reciprocity is crucial to our ecumenical conversations, because there can be no genuine ecumenical dialogue if we do not come to the discussion willing to listen, willing to understand and willing to be changed in the process. Ecumenical dialogue implies receptivity to change, to conversion.

Finding 4: *Ecumenical dialogue opens the possibility for an expanded vision of faith.*

Although the gift of Christ has been given once for all, none of our separate traditions—nor even all of them together—can ever exhaust the meaning of the unfathomable revelation of Christ. Even when a church claims all the gifts of grace bestowed by Christ, its members should recognize the divine mandate for unity among all Christians. Precisely because our different denominational traditions have focused upon and developed different aspects of that revelation, we can in the course of dialogue come to an appreciation and acceptance of some parts of the one great Tradition that may be undeveloped or latent in each of our particular traditions.[7] Thus, through our dialogue with Christians whose traditions have developed in relative isolation from our own, we can be brought to see aspects of the gospel with a new and sharper clarity.

Finding 5: *Authentic ecumenism, like authentic conversion, is a deepening of both our basic commitment to Christ and our appreciation of the traditions of our respective churches.*

Ecumenism, like conversion, does not require us to jettison our critical faculties, nor to betray our deepest convictions, nor to mitigate our loyalty to what is true and good within our respective traditions. Relying on God as the source of all truth, the new insights that we receive in the graced movement of ecumenical conversion presumably will not negate, but rather enrich, the truth already revealed to us and communicated through the churches of which we are members. Our mutual sharing of the faith that each of us has received through our respective churches leads us to a deeper appreciation of the gifts of our own tradition as well as a greater awareness of the gifts that are to be found in other churches.

Finding 6: *Ecumenical dialogue requires us to speak the truth in love.*

The whole process of ecumenical dialogue, like that of conversion in the primal sense, involves a turning to God in humility and neediness, an eagerness to hear and to respond to God's Word when it is addressed to us through the give-and-take of ecumenical engagement. Thus, when dialogue is sufficiently probing, we allow ourselves to come under judgment for those aspects of our traditions that are deficient, misconstrued, or misapplied. Thus ecumenical asceticism requires that, speaking the truth in love, we not shrink from serving as an instrument of divine judgment and grace for our dialogue partners.

Finding 7: *Ecumenical dialogue, like conversion, should be accompanied by repentance.*

To approach ecumenical dialogue in a spirit of repentance will not, of course, make all the theological, ecclesiastical, and practical obstacles to unity instantly evaporate. But ecumenical dialogue, with its vision of the church ecumenical, does bring to light our secret ecclesiastical self-sufficiency, our reluctance to relinquish denominational isolationism. Thus ecumenism is an "ascetical activity," which begins with what ascetical theology calls the "purgative way," by a change of heart, advances by the "illuminative way," as we discover fresh aspects of the fullness of Christ, and it reaches its culmination in the "unitive way" when we realize that the unity God is forging with us comes through divine self-emptying, through *kenosis*.[8]

## The Nature of the Unity that We Seek

Finding 8: *The unity we seek is a gift of God.*

The search for Christian unity begins with the understanding that our oneness in Christ is basically a gift offered by God, not something that can be achieved by our designs or by human effort alone. The search for unity means that ecumenists must come to grips with diversity through an acceptance of others that must not serve as a cover for a rugged individualism in which each person is covertly looking out for his or her own denominational tradition at the expense of others; rather, the acceptance of diversity requires an active welcoming, a sincere reaching out to embrace the diversity of graces within other churches as genuine gifts to be received within the whole Christian community for the upbuilding of the church and its mission to the world. In seeking unity, Christians need to ask not only what gifts their tradition might contribute, but also what charisms their tradition needs to receive.

Finding 9: *Christian unity is vital to the church's mission of proclaiming the gospel so that all might believe.*

It is not merely a matter of historical coincidence that the major impetus for the ecumenical movement in the 20th century originated with people involved in missionary activity. The preaching of the gospel has frequently been frustrated by the divisions among Christians. Not only were prospective converts confused by apparently competing versions of Christianity, they were also scandalized that those who preached a message of divine love and ecclesial fellowship were in fact so alienated from each other. How can non-Christians be expected to accept the gospel as long as its preachers seem not to practice what they preach?

Finding 10: *Christian unity must be both visible and eucharistic.*

While recognizing that our unity will never be fully complete this side of the eschaton, Christian churches must still strive to achieve a visible and organic expression of oneness in Christ as a witness to the power of God's love to reconcile a broken, divided, and alienated world. Christians then should not be satisfied with an invisible unity based merely upon mutual good will, or a facile agreement to disagree without being disagreeable, or even on the belief that the sole ecclesial reality is an invisible church. Rather, the unity which we seek needs to be as real and visible as the gathering of family members at a common meal. Such unity needs to take the form of "one fully committed fellowship, holding the one apostolic faith, preaching the one Gospel, breaking the one bread, joining in common prayer, and having a corporate life reaching out in witness and service to all."[9] Such creedal, eucharistic, and kerygmatic unity further requires a mutual recognition of one another's baptisms and ministries as well as a commitment to a common process of collegial decision-making for the sake of the proclamation of the gospel.

Finding 11: *Like the gospel on which it is based, Christian unity is directed toward the entire human community.*

In their quest for unity, Christians have discovered that their denominational boundaries have frequently served as barriers excluding people, rather than as frontiers of a new land welcoming all those seeking freedom and salvation in Christ Jesus. Accordingly, the unity sought by churches must be inclusive of the entire human community with its racial, cultural, social and economic diversity. Far from imposing a rigid uniformity, the search for genuine unity calls upon the church to become truly universal, by reaching out to all people in every place, Thus, along with such typical questions as "How can we build the consensus needed for the unity?" we need to address the question, "How can we build sufficient trust to live together with great diversity?"

Finding 12: *Christian unity must be a clear witness to God's liberation and reconciliation.*

Christian unity is not merely a matter of achieving theological consensus, much less of brokering some type of ecclesiastical amalgamation. Authentic unity must effectively proclaim the gospel message of freedom and forgiveness. Obviously, this proclamation can be made in many different ways according to the challenges of particular situations; however, in the minds of many ecumenists, the litmus test for Christian unity is its ability to speak out against every kind of injustice and oppression in our society and our world.

Finding 13: *The unity that we seek rests on agreement in essentials, but permits diversity regarding subordinate matters.*

In searching for unity, Christians have come to understand how important it is to distinguish those issues that are primary and essential (and thus requiring clear agreement) from those that are secondary and subordinate (about which diversity is not only allowed but welcomed). Nonetheless, such a distinction is far easier to make than to apply. Ecumenists still debate where, so to speak, to draw the line between the primary or obligatory and the secondary or subordinate. It is clear, however, that in the past churches have often made the secondary obligatory, while sometimes allowing the primary to become obscured. In their continuing search for unity, church leaders must humbly yet honestly ask themselves: "Which of our doctrines are so essential that they must be maintained, even at the cost of continued disunity?"

Finding 14: *Christian unity requires a commitment to seeking the truth.*

Ecumenism is not simply an attitude of polite but vacillating tolerance nor a casual acceptance of ambiguous or divergent positions for the sake of ecclesiastical harmony. Those working for Christian unity must be fully committed to searching for truth, not simply to formulating the lowest common denominator of consensus. Essential to the pursuit of Christian truth is the recognition that our grasp of the saving truth of Jesus Christ is ever limited, never final: we are ever seekers after, never owners of, the absolute truth of Christ. Our task is to conform to God's truth, not to insist that everyone else conform to ours.

Finding 15: *Our search for unity rests on a common foundation: our faith in Jesus Christ.*

Our baptism into Christ already unites us as members of one family of faith. Ecumenically-minded Christians are therefore convinced that their partners in dialogue already live in the grace of God. Thus, Christians seeking unity through ecumenical dialogue are not seeking to bring their dialogue-partners to faith, rather they are searching for ways to understand, express, and live their common faith more truly. Thus, at the heart of genuine ecumenical dialogue is the conviction that all of our denominational differences are ultimately secondary to the unity we share as a result of our common experience of grace through faith in Jesus Christ.

Finding 16: *The search for Christian unity, like Christianity itself, is a commitment to a pilgrimage.*

In a sense, the ecumenical movement is not only the search for a set of essential Christian truths but also a methodology for understanding the implications of God's call for unity among all Christians. Accordingly, ecumenism is an invitation, a summons to, a way of living that dares to live trustfully with differences in the Christian community, not as a result of polite tolerance but on the basis of a shared commitment to the continuously creating, redeeming and sustaining God. Ecumenical commitment demands an expansion of horizons wherein Christians attempt to see the world from the viewpoints of their ecumenical partners and so to a broader vision of the church and society that they presently have.[10]

## The "Faith and Order" of the Church[11]

Finding 17: *Many denominational presentations of the Christian faith now seem obsolete or one-sided.*

The word "faith" sometimes refers to a personal belief or conviction, an attitude of trust and commitment; "faith" can also refer to the content or object of belief, as expressed in doctrines and creeds. The two senses are necessarily intertwined insofar as personal belief is given public expression and corporate professions of faith rest on the faith of individual believers.

The many different communions that have entered the ecumenical forum have brought with them a large quantity as well as an extensive variety of corporate expressions of their faith; confessions, creeds, catechisms, canonical dogmas, theological doctrines, liturgies, prayers, hymns, ecclesiastical traditions, exegetical styles and hermeneutical principles, plus an undefinable element called "ethos." All of these expressions are intended to serve, albeit in different ways, as bearers and communicators of the "faith once delivered to the saints."

As the result of many years of analyzing and comparing this tremendous quantity and diversity of expression, ecumenists have concluded that many of the theological viewpoints and polemical positions that were once characteristic of denominational presentations of the Christian faith were prompted by specific historical situations and by particular cultural viewpoints; insofar as these situations have changed and these viewpoints are no longer tenable, their original expressions are either obsolete or one-sided and should no longer be retained in their original form.

Finding 18: *Underneath apparently divergent expressions of faith, there is often a basic commonality.*

As theological convergence has become more pronounced, participants in ecumenical dialogue have come to recognize that underneath expressions that are apparently irreconcilable, there is often a basic commonality. In effect, denominational separations have frequently produced a divergence in theological viewpoint, liturgical practice, and church order that is reflected in ecclesiastical documents; this divergence in expression has often given the impression that differences are greater than they actually are. Insofar as all confessional documents are intended to witness to the one apostolic faith, there is frequently a basic commonality that needs to be rediscovered and appropriated. Consequently, ecumenists today are concerned about not only what divides us as Christians, but also what unites us as Christians.

Finding 19: *Operating within each ecclesial tradition is a gradation or hierarchy of truths.*

In practice, if not in theory, churches have sometimes given the impression that all their teachings have equal merit. Ecumenical discussion has made theologians much more aware not only of different degrees in the binding force of particular disciplinary provisions, but also gradations of importance within the area of doctrine itself. Ecumenists have come to recognize within their own ecclesial tradition a hierarchy of truths wherein some teachings seem more essential, others less so. While such an insight seems to promise tremendous ecumenical possibilities, to date its implications have only been sketched.[12]

Finding 20: *The beliefs which are actually held by many of the sincere faith-*
*ful are often different from the official doctrines of their own*
*church bodies.*

One should avoid stereotyping "faith" as being only the formal, doctrinal confessions, articles and creeds of particular communions; in fact, one
should note the wide diversities of personal faith as professed by individual
members of the same church. Quite often, agreements on matters of personal
faith transect denominational boundaries. This is the case even within some
churches that have the strictest definitions of orthodoxy and magisterial
teaching. This phenomenon suggests that there is a basis for Christian unity
in fact as well as in theory.

Finding 21: *Ecumenists in officially sponsored dialogues should seek unity*
*on the basis of what is formally taught by their sponsoring*
*churches.*

Ecumenists engaged in official ecumenical discussions are searching
for a common understanding of the Christian faith as it is formally professed
by their respective churches, in contrast to what is accepted by individuals or
groups or movements within their churches. The purpose of genuine ecumenism is neither to draw people away from the formal teachings of their
communions nor to fabricate a brand new ecumenical faith to supercede such
teachings. The purpose, rather, is to search for some basic areas of agreement
and criteria for evaluating the differing understandings of faith. That common search brings us repeatedly back to the meaning of apostolicty: "What is
the apostolic faith and what does it mean today?"

Finding 22: *The "order" of the church has a variety of meanings: the very*
*being as well as the communal, structural and functional ele-*
*ments of the church.*

Some convergence in understanding the "order" of the church has
already been achieved. On the one hand, those who once spoke of the body
of Christ in purely spiritual terms have come to understand that the body is
not an invertebrate, but needs a skeletal structure which belongs as much to
the nature of the church as its spirit does. On the other hand, many of those
who had been accustomed to thinking of "order" as the institutional reality of
the church have come to appreciate its personal and collective character, as a
fellowship in Christ and a community of the Holy Spirit.

The "order" of the church is neither a negotiable sociological option,
nor a necessary organizational bureaucracy; there is an essential, if enigmat-
ic, counterpoint of freedom and form. Whatever the shape (or *Gestalt*) into
which the church may evolve from the diverse patterns that are presently
proximate manifestations of unity, some of its present structures and expres-

sions of freedom will probably be modified but not wholly eliminated, for their elimination would be a loss to the wholeness, or catholicity, of the church.

Finding 23: *A fundamental issue in ecumenical dialogue is the relationship between Christ and the church.*

While Christians agree that they are saved by Christ alone, they disagree about the role of the church in regard to the process whereby an individual comes to salvation. In general, the Catholic tradition sees the church as a necessary instrument in the process of salvation: the church is *the* sacrament of salvation and thus the divinely established mediator of the sacraments and the interpreter of scripture. In contrast, the Protestant tradition tends to see salvation as taking place in the church but not through the church: the church is *a* humanly constituted place where the grace of Christ empowers each individual to understand the implications of scripture for his or her daily life.

Ecumenical discussion about the nature of the church has produced considerable agreement about the need for authority and structure; for example, many would agree that "a ministry of *episkopé* is necessary to express and safeguard the unity of the body" of Christ;[13] nonetheless, if there really is a fundamental difference in understanding the nature of the church, the adoption of similar ecclesial structures and compatible forms of decision-making may only be concealing, not resolving, an underlying problem of a basic ecclesiological difference.

## Considerations for Future Ecumenical Dialogue

Finding 24: *Ecumenical dialogue needs to give more specific attention to understanding the nature of doctrinal development.*

Rather surprisingly, a theory of doctrinal development is absent from explicit consideration in most ecumenical dialogues. This omission may be due to the fact that theological interest in doctrinal development only emerged in the 19th century—long after the Reformation, and even longer after the separation between the eastern and western churches. Insofar as most bilateral conversations have focused on the issues that created the original divisions, theological advances that have occurred since these separations have sometimes been overlooked.

This omission may also be related to the fact that doctrinal development is still a *quaestio disputanda*—a question for discussion in theological circles. While theologians generally consider doctrinal development an indisputable fact, they have to date been hard pressed to present a consistent theory. Consequently, doctrinal development has yet to achieve an established place within denominational dogmatics in the same way as specific doctrines such as faith and justification, Eucharist and ministry, etc. Even in those ecumenical dialogues which have treated such development-related issues as revelation and doctrine, the problem of doctrinal development seems to have received only peripheral attention, however much one suspects that presuppositions about the nature of doctrinal development lurk behind all church-dividing questions.

Finding 25: *In the search for appropriate contemporary expressions of the Christian faith, doctrinal development seems to be an essential, though implicit, ecclesiological premise.*

In seeking to preach the gospel to the contemporary world, most churches, whether of Catholic or Protestant traditions, seem to assume that doctrine develops, albeit in different though seemingly complementary ways. On the one hand, catholicity is frequently understood as the church's divinely given ability to encompass all peoples of all times and all places; just as Christianity itself has known a series of developments: Hebraic, Hellenic, Latin, European, Asian, African, etc., so too genuine catholicity implies an inherent capability of future ecumenical growth. On the other hand, for Protestants, the principle *semper reformanda*—the need for continual reform—implies that the task of reforming the church is inevitably a continual responsibility; not only has the church needed reform in the past, the church will need to reform its denominational divisiveness in preparation for an ecumenical future.

Finding 26: *The quest for Christian unity may be the next crucial phase in the development of doctrine.*

Given the fact that doctrinal developments in the past have included a generous measure of intramural dissension, ecumenists should really not be surprised if and when their quest for unity creates controversy. Indeed, if the history of doctrinal development furnishes any precedent, one should expect that the quest for ecumenical agreement will at times be both problematic and painful. Accordingly, it seems imperative for ecumenists to address the question of doctrinal development much more explicitly than has been the case to date.

Finding 27: *The achievements made through ecumenical dialogue during the past two decades are considerably indebted to the use of the historical-critical method.*

Following the example of biblical scholars and theologians, ecumenists have successfully employed the historical-critical method within the context of a believing community affirming the primacy of biblical authority. Theological breakthroughs in ecumenical dialogue seem to depend on the results of applying historical-critical method not only in biblical research, but also in historical studies; for example, without the scholarly reassessment, and in many instances revision, of polemical interpretations of the Reformation, many of the long-standing issues would still seem unresolvable.

By the same measure, the absence of an adequate historical consciousness in some theological discussions, along with the lack of appropriate ecclesiastical organs for evaluating such discussions, have had negative results not only for ecumenical dialogue but also for theological development within particular churches. Indeed, one reason for the opposition to ecumenical consensus statements seems to stem from perspectives that insist on particular denominational readings of church history. By clinging to time-conditioned positions in the face of apparently more faithful interpretations, church members may easily diminish the power of God's revelation to speak through these texts to the contemporary world.

**Finding 28:** *Ecumenists need to assess carefully the potential liabilities of the historical-critical method for ecumenical dialogue.*

While the use of the historical-critical method has led to the resolution of many long-standing church-dividing (or at least to their recasting in a new form), this method is not always appreciated by many church members. In effect, ecumenists seem to be basing their ecumenical consensus on historical-critical premises which some members of their churches simply do not share.

Accordingly, ecumenists need to examine more explicitly the limitations of the historical-critical assumptions operative in achieving ecumenical consensus, not only to avoid the pragmatic danger that ecumenists are outdistancing their coreligionists but also to avert the possibility that the theoretical assumptions used to resolve past disagreements may simultaneously be sewing the seeds of future division.

**Finding 29:** *Ecumenical consensus is easier to describe than to define.*

In fact, different understandings of consensus are currently operative in ecumenical dialogue, thereby giving rise to possible misunderstandings about what agreement has or has not been reached.

For example, consensus can be envisioned as a broad spectrum where each communion can find its place, sometimes through sharing common parts of that spectrum with other communions, sometimes by contributing a distinctive increment to that spectrum. Within such a spectrum, consensus implies that each communion finds what it considers essential to faith and is able to recognize a measure of commonality with, while simultaneously benefiting from, the contributions of other traditions.

Or to use a different image, consensus can be described as an ecumenical household of faith, where each communion would participate in the life of the whole family, while maintaining appropriate personal space. In terms of such a household image, each denomination would experience the support derived from sharing a common family life, while simultaneously contributing the gifts unique to its denominational heritage.

While these and similar images seem helpful for descriptive purposes, they are less satisfactory for specifying either the requisite extent of commonality or the permissible latitude of diversity. For example, if it is comparatively simple to say that for the sake of unity all communions must agree on some basic parameters within an otherwise broad spectrum, it is quite difficult to specify what those parameters are and where the endpoints of such a spectrum must be. Similarly, if each communion has the right and the responsibility to develop its particular gifts as a unique contribution to the whole household of faith, how does one harmonize the diversity of these gifts within a genuinely unified community?

Finding 30: *Ecumenical consensus statements inevitably admit of a diversity of acceptable interpretations.*

In recent years, bilateral and multilateral agreements have been intentionally drafted in such a way that ecumenists from a diversity of backgrounds have been able to acknowledge that such statements are acceptable in terms of their own denominational dogmatics. However, when such acceptance is critically examined, one finds that the same statement is being interpreted in notably different ways. Thus, while a consensus statement may have achieved a commonality of expression, immediately beyond that apparent consensus is a diversity of interpretation.

While practically all denominations allow diversity, to a greater or lesser degree, in the interpretation of their dogmatic statements, the question remains how wide a latitude is permissible before diversity in interpretation effectively destroys real commonality in consensus? At what point does apparent convergence become real divergence? This phenomenon—commonality in expression but diversity in interpretation—underlines the need for greater care in determining the nature and limits of consensus. Otherwise the most carefully crafted ecumenical consensus is likely to come unravelled in the subsequent wake of divergent interpretations.

Finding 31: *Consensus in theory can allow diversity in practice.*

Ordinarily when one thinks of consensus in theory, but diversity in practice, one has in mind variations on a theme, for example, the Eucharist may be celebrated in different languages according to different rites. But can diversity run deeper?

For example, while basic consensus about the meaning of baptism has enabled practically all denominations to recognize the validity of baptisms conferred in other churches, apparently unresolvable disagreement remains regarding the age at which baptism should be conferred. Consequently, even if "the differences between infant and believers' baptism become less sharp when it is recognized that both forms of baptism embody God's own initiative in Christ and express a response of faith made within the believing community," the simultaneous acceptance of two different baptismal practices, based on two different theological interpretations, raises the question whether consensus in theory can allow compromise in practice.[14]

Finding 32: *Ecumenists need to determine whether "compromise for the sake of unity" is problematic or paradigmatic.*

To some ecumenists, consensus in theory accompanied by compromise in practice seems at best problematic. For example, insofar as the apparent agreement about the meaning of baptism obviously unravels when it comes to the actual age for conferring baptism, the purported consensus is at best suspect. To others, such compromise seems paradigmatic, insofar as it affords a prototypical instance of a consensus in principle which admits of varying forms of implementation. In other words, if two different practices concerning the age for admission to baptism—representing two divergent theological understandings of baptism—are recognized as being in accord with the gospel and Christian tradition, what is the meaning of the ecumenical consensus that has been achieved? And—granting that one cannot really speak of consensus without acknowledging the existence and legitimacy of diversity—to what extent is diversity in either theory or practice permissible, without implicitly destroying the basic consensus?

Finding 33: *The development of a basic ecumenical consensus seems as critical for the contemporary church as Christological and trinitarian development was for the early church.*

In future records of the history of Christianity, the 20th century may become known as "the century of ecumenism," just as the fourth century is now known for its Christological developments. What remains to be seen is whether the 20th or 21st century can develop a basic ecumenical consensus—the fundamental doctrinal agreement that is necessary if the unity of the churches is to be achieved with both sincerity and fidelity. In some respects, the 20th century is better equipped with theological resources than was the fourth; in other respects, the 20th century is at a disadvantage, not only in terms of historical distance from the early church, but because of the highly pluralistic climate in which we live. Yet the ecumenical task seems no less urgent to the present age than the resolution of Christological questions was to the early church.

Finding 34: *The quest for Christian unity relies on a process where answers can be discovered only through the painstaking, and at times painful, process of dialogue.*

While many Christians might instinctively hope that the answers to ecumenical questions could be delineated *a priori* by a careful definition of terms, in fact, the answers may only be discoverable through ecumenical dialogue. In similar fashion, many church members and church administrators would like not only to know the destination but to see the shape and seaworthiness of the ecumenical ship before boarding it. But are such expectations realistic? Ecumenists have come to realize that ecumenical questions are shaped by a variety of social, cultural, geographical, and demographic factors; consequently, ecumenical questions are raised today in ways quite different from their classical dogmatic formulations. Thus, ecumenists have come to ask: Is the search for Christian unity, like Christianity itself, basically a pilgrimage?

## A Concluding Word

On the basis of their experience in dialogue, the members of the Bilaterals Study Group feel that these findings about the nature of unity must find their way into the commitments of the churches if there is to be further ecumenical progress. It is then the hope of the Bilaterals Study Group that churches (if they have not done so already) will come to accept the findings presented above; it is also hoped that other ecumenical groups will be able to add their own findings to this admittedly partial and preliminary list.

Indeed the growing volume of theological agreements and common texts, as well as bilateral and multilateral consensus statements, indicates that Christians stand at a creative moment in the life of the ecumenical movement. Christians seem to be finding that diversity is no longer a reason for division insofar as unity is no longer seen to require uniformity.

## Appendix 1:
## Faith and Order

*Background:* In ecumenical circles, it is customary to compare and contrast three dimensions of the World Council of Churches: 1) The Mission movement, which is primarily concerned with giving witness to the gospel, represents what the church *preaches.* 2) The Life and Work movement, which is involved in projects of service, education, and justice, is concerned with what the church *does.* 3) The Faith and Order movement, which studies the nature of the church and its teachings, expresses what the church *is.*

The ecumenical movement has attempted to channel these three different streams into a united current of witnessing, doing and being so that the catholicity (or wholeness) of the church will be fully realized and manifested. The numerous bilateral and multilateral dialogues which have taken place since 1965 as an aftermath of the Second Vatican Council have been principally concerned with the questions of Faith and Order; however important, such theological questions are but a part of the church's life as a whole.

*Terminology:* Although the antecedents of the expression, "faith and order," go back to the 17th century, the present ecumenical significance dates from 1910, when Bishop Charles H. Brent of the Episcopal Church chose this phrase to identify the new movement for unity. Since that time, people have discussed and disputed the meaning of the two words and their interrelationship. The need to translate the expression into other languages pointed up the problem. There was no problem in translating "faith" as *foi* (French), *Glaube* (German), or *fe* (Spanish); but "order" was not as easy to translate. At first the French used *organisation,* but this was later replaced with *constitution:* the mere structural organization of the church said too little about its nature or essence. In German, "order" was first expressed as *Ordnung,* but this lacked the right connotation and eventually gave way to *Kirchenverfassung,* which indicated both the concept and polity of the church. In Spanish, one still hears both *constitución* and *orden.* Similar ambiguities continue in English, where the meaning of "order" is seldom clear.

The difficulty of finding precisely the right word is not only a matter of language but also a problem in ecclesiology, namely, differing conceptions of what the church is. Accordingly, recent ecumenical studies have tried to clarify the meaning of both "faith" and "order." For a time, the word "order" was distinguished from "organization" in a philosophical way, the former referring to the essential being of the church in contrast to its external form. Another approach was based on the meaning of "event" and "institution" in the New Testament. The first, a more Pauline emphasis, was associated with the Holy Spirit's "eventful" work in gathering believers solely on the basis of their faith into being God's people; the second, a Petrine view, emphasized the organic, sociological reality of the body of Christ, wherein faith is expressed in community. Since extensive biblical evidence supports both types of ecclesiology, the ecumenical problem is to decide whether these concepts of order are necessarily at odds with each other, or whether the church in its wholeness comprehends both.

**Appendix 2:**
**Three Types and Criteria of Church Order**

What is the relationship between one's belief about the nature of the church and the actual "order" of the church? Are ecclesial faith and ecclesiastical order entirely separable, or essentially one, or reciprocally interactive? In other words, how is the church's "polity" influenced by particular teachings of faith and vice versa?

Three types of response have been given to these questions depending on varying emphases and appeals to three different criteria: 1) the New Testament, 2) tradition, and 3) innovative traditions.

1) The first typology is found in those churches which claim to derive their order or polity solely from the New Testament. Such a claim presents a hermeneutical problem, because the New Testament is neither simple nor consistent in it presentation of the apostolic church.

For example, those who discern in the New Testament a church which is primarily, or even exclusively, a structurally loose but personally adhesive fellowship of faith and love find congregational polity both compelling and satisfying. The main strength of this polity is that it can lead to a mutual sharing of life in the *koinonia* (community) in respect to love, worship and service; the sacraments (or ordinances) of baptism and the Lord's Supper are cherished and celebrated in the simple manner described in the New Testament; the members of the church respond to each other's needs as well as to those of the community in which they live. A major weakness of congregational polity is its independence; a self-defining local church may lack the support of, as well as correction by, other churches; on occasion a church relying on congregational polity has turned into an anarchic assembly of believers with a highly individualistic faith and notorious internal disputes.

2) The second typology is found in those churches which claim to derive their order from both the New Testament and the tradition of the church. Such a claim presents a further hermeneutical problem, insofar as the history of the church has known a variety of "orders" or "polities" which claim to represent the authentic tradition coming down from the apostles.

For example, while the church's order is seen to depend on the Bible as read and interpreted by the church through its doctors and councils, the crucial question is: which doctors and councils are authoritative? Nonetheless, this typology finds considerable strength in its unquestioning belief that the Holy Spirit guides the church through the course of history; in particular, the knowledge of revealed truth is guarded by the succession of apostolic representatives, the bishops; moreover, the church is conceived as the body of Christ, who is sacramentally present within the community through celebration of the Eucharist and the other sacraments. A recurrent weakness of an episcopal polity is that it can easily lead to an unwarranted authoritarianism; simultaneously, a major temptation for a sacramentally oriented church is a perfunctory ritualism.

3) The third typology is found in those churches which claim to derive their order of polity not only from the New Testament and the tradition of the church, but also from what might be called "innovative tradition": the new events, new movements, and new personalities that leave enduring marks on the churches that welcome them. Such a claim compounds the hermeneutical problem insofar as the history of the church has known a variety of innovations.

For example, while some innovations have come to be generally accepted by many churches, others have been rejected by some churches, and still other innovations that were once common in most churches have been allowed to fade away. What then are the criteria for discerning which innovations should be adopted, which rejected, and which discarded? The major strength that accrues to churches which welcome innovations is their ability to respond eagerly and usually effectively to the changes in the world about them; such churches can be sensitive to the impetus of the Holy Spirit acting within their midst. Nonetheless, such resiliency can have a high price; that of adopting the ephemeral as normative and adapting the gospel to the latest fashion.

All three of these church-types (*tupoi*) stand upon loyalty to the gospel of Jesus Christ, however variously they interpret it: by claiming to base their order directly on the apostolic pattern alone, or in light of both the New Testament and tradition, or in tandem with the exigencies of the age. If nearly all church orders to some extent display aspects of all three types, long lasting church divisions have frequently been due to differing and opposing beliefs about the ecclesial configuration of the New Testament, the authority of tradition, and the legitimacy of particular innovations.

Ecumenical studies and common experiences of unity during the past decades have brought theologians of widely different backgrounds somewhat closer toward agreement on the meaning of biblical teaching, the necessity of tradition and innovative development as determinants of the shape of both faith and order. There has been enough progress in these areas to permit hope for further convergence, but the omega point of full unity still seems remote.

John Ford, editor

## Notes

1. Faith and Order Paper 111 (Geneva: World Council of Churches, 1982); this document is also available in a number of publications, including *Growth in Agreement; Reports and Agreed*

*Statements of Ecumenical Conversations on a World Level,* edited by Harding Meyer and Lukas Vischer, *Ecumenical Documents* 2 (New York/Ramsey; Paulist Press; Geneva: World Council of Churches, 1984), pp. 465-503.

2. The Presbyterian Church (U.S.A.) resulted from the union of the (southern) Presbyterian Church, U.S. and the (northern) United Presbyterian Church in the U.S.A. The newly formed Evangelical Lutheran Church in America resulted from the union of the American Lutheran Church, the Lutheran Church in America and the Association of Evangelical Lutheran Churches.

3. *Digest of the Proceedings of the Sixteenth Meeting of the Consultation on Church Union* (Baltimore, November 26-30, 1984) Volume XVI, edited by Gerald F. Moede (Princeton: Consultation on Church Union, 1986) pp. 243-269.

4. The papers from the first phase of the work of the "Bilaterals Study Group" were published by the *Journal of Ecumenical Studies* 23/3 (Summer, 1986) 361-544.

5. It seems appropriate to note that the participants from the American Lutheran Church and the Lutheran Church in America are now members of the newly formed Evangelical Lutheran Church in America.

6. Portions of this section are based on Julia Gatta's "The Threefold Rule of Prayer: A Paradigm for Ecumenical Spirituality," *Vision: Oikoumeme* 4 (March 1987), pp. 6-11; reprinted in *Ecumenical Bulletin* 83 (May/June, 1987) 15-23.

7. The distinction between Tradition and traditions was given classic expression by *The Fourth World Conference on Faith and Order: Montreal 1963,* edited by P.C. Rodger and Lukas Vischer (New York: Association Press, 1964), p. 50: "By *the Tradition* is meant the Gospel itself, transmitted from generation to generation in and by the Church, Christ himself present in the life of the Church. By *tradition* is meant the traditionary process. The term *traditions* is used in two senses, to indicate both the diversity of forms of expressions and also what we call confessional traditions, for instance the Lutheran tradition or the Reformed tradition."

8. In the history of spirituality, the three ways are 1) the "purgative" way of beginners trying to rid themselves of sinful habits, 2) the "illuminative" way of those attempting to grow in virtue, and 3) the "unitive" way of those seeking perfect union with God; cf. E.E. Larkin, "The Three Spiritual Ways," *The New Catholic Encyclopedia* 14:835-836.

9. *The New Delhi Report: The Third Assembly of the World Council of Churches,* 1961, edited by W.A. Visser 't Hooft (New York: Association Press, 1962), p. 116.

10. For further discussion of this finding, see John Ford, "Bilateral Conversations and Denominational Horizons," *Journal of Ecumenical Studies* 23 (Summer, 1986) 518-528, and Meg Madson, "Hermeneutics and Theological Method," *ibid.* 529-544.

11. For background information on "Faith and Order," see appendix 1.

12. For further discussion, see William Henn, "The Hierarchy of Truths Twenty Years Later," *Theological Studies* 48 (1987) 439-471.

13. *Baptism, Eucharist and Ministry,* "Ministry" 23, p. 25; also see the discussion of "Three Types and Criteria of Church Order" in Appendix 2.

14. *Baptism, Eucharist and Ministry,* "Baptism" #12C, p. 5; it should be noted that the traditional terminology, "infant and believers' baptism," is inconsistent insofar as it contrasts a chronological concept with a theological concept; for a chronological comparison, it would be more appropriate to speak of "infant baptism" and "adult baptism"; since a theological comparison presupposes that every genuine baptism involves believers, it would seem better to speak of infant baptism as a baptism of "corporate faith" and to speak of adult baptism as a baptism of "personal confession."

# Report of the Harlem (1988) Consultation on Unity and Renewal with Black Churches in the USA*

On August 27-31, 1988, over 40 Christians from the African-American Christian community and from churches around the world came together in Harlem, New York, to discuss the African-American Christian contribution to the Unity of the Church and the Renewal of Human Community study of the World Council of Churches (WCC) Commission on Faith and Order. The consultation was prepared for, and graciously hosted by, African-American representatives of the historic black churches in the United States and African-Americans in predominantly white Protestant and Catholic churches.[1]

The basis for the discussion was a paper, "An African-American Perspective on the Unity of the Church and the Renewal of Human Community," with one specialized paper reflecting the black Roman Catholic perspective as an appendix. The paper was prepared by a United States-based committee and focused primarily on the WCC Faith and Order Unity and Renewal text, "The Church as Mystery and Prophetic Sign," while taking account also of the reports from WCC Faith and Order Unity and Renewal consultations on "The Ecclesiological Significance of the Churches Involvement in the Issues of Justice" held in Singapore and Porto Alegre, Brazil.

The purposes of the consultation were to encourage a dialogue between WCC Faith and Order and the black churches in the United States, and to make a contribution, reflecting the unique experience and insights of these black churches, to the WCC Faith and Order "Unity and Renewal" study. Additional recommendations are made for the churches and for the wider ecumenical movement.

In addition to discussion and reflection on the documents produced for the consultation, we shared the concrete experiences of specific ministries of the churches in Harlem and Brooklyn. We worshiped together in the black

*Mid-Stream 28 (1989) 412-20.

churches of Harlem. We experienced the manner in which the Christian faith energized leaders in a program to liberate persons from the bondage of addiction to drugs. We were called to a Christian understanding of the roots of this problem, and how the resources of our faith could bring hope and liberation. We surveyed the rich resources for black history, literature and culture, including the contribution of the black churches, in the Schomberg library. We saw the service of the black churches in holistic healing through a visit to a Harlem hospital. We witnessed the role of the black churches in housing, senior citizens, education, social outreach, preaching, evangelism and social justice ministries in a variety of churches and institutions in Harlem and Brooklyn. Daily we shared the deep spirituality of the black church experience through devotions, fellowship and testimony.

During the last day of our consultation we were shocked and saddened to receive news of the bombing of the offices of the South African Council of Churches and shared our prayers and solidarity with Bishop Manas Buthelezi, a participant in our consultation, and our fellow Christians in South Africa in the face of this outrageous and tragic act.

The report and recommendations from our meeting are rooted as much in the praxis of church ministry as in the theoretical researches of black scholarship. We celebrate the vitality of the Spirit even as we record our recommendations. The reports from the three groups represent a variety of thinking from a diverse group of African-American churches. They also reflect the thoughts and experiences of persons from the various churches throughout the world who attended the consultation.

The report is in the spirit of the black Catholic bishops who wrote:

> Black spirituality, in contrast with much of western tradition, is holistic. Like the biblical tradition, there is no dualism. Divisions between intellect and emotion, spirit and body, action and contemplation, individual and community, sacred and secular are foreign to us. In keeping with our African heritage, we are not ashamed of our emotions. For us the religious experience is an experience of the whole human being, both the feelings and the intellect, the heart as well as the head. Moreover, we find foreign any notion that the body is evil. We find our own holistic spiritual approach to be in accord with the scriptures and the logic of the incarnation.[2]

## Report from Group One: Mystery

The term "mystery" used in the WCC Faith and Order study program "The Unity of the Church and the Renewal of Human Community" has been nuanced in many ways by a variety of traditions. In this connection "mystery" is perceived among African-Americans in their daily experiences, joined by trans-historical realities of the presence of God.

Mystery is blackness being rejected, yet living with hope and struggle. Mystery is suffering in a communal unity which transcends religious affiliation. Some in this solidarity of communal suffering seek and find empowerment through the redemptive suffering symbolized by the cross of Jesus, which was freely chosen by the sufferer. Mystery is experiencing God's providence, lifting up cultural diversities and conveying the gospel for the good of the nations, in spite of and because of those diversities. Mystery is renewal of the Church through God's action for justice on behalf of the world. The word "mystery" reveals God's action in the world, and consequently reveals the sinfulness of any practices of racial exclusivity within the Church. "Mystery" is experiencing the manner in which a remnant people can help to reform the whole family of God. In a most important manner, mystery is expressed apocalyptically as a reversal of fortune in which those who are "nobodies" in the estimation of society will become "somebodies" through God's action.

For future reflection and action, the term "mystery" must be enriched through at least two motifs:

## 1) Spirituality

First, the spirituality of black people, especially the language of worship, needs to be amplified. The black experience is rooted in the language of worship. That is one reason why poetic expressions and metaphors are powerful expressions of the theological tradition of black people. Like the expression of the mystery of "transubstantiation," in worship blacks have expressed the mystery of "transformation." In worship African-Americans experience how the "last can be first," how oppressed can be victorious, how broken bodies can be transformed into a victorious people. "A maid, a slave...becomes what they are: somebody special" among God's children in worship.

For the black church, therefore, the Church as mystery is not only a trans-historical reality, but a "place." Because for it there is no radical separation between sacred and secular, the black church is understood less as mystery than as a *place* where a group of people gather at a particular time to reflect on life's experiences and celebrate anticipated victories, as well as to thank God for victories already achieved. When blacks gather for worship, the prayer is real: "Thank you, Lord, for allowing us to assemble one more time." This is a truly meaningful part of any prayer, for the mystery is that those living at the edge of constant death can be and were kept by God's providence. Death is always near, imminent and immediate; yet in worship the mystery of the alliance between God and human beings is sealed in prayer, song, sermon and testimony.

## 2) Blackness

Second, mystery must be enriched through stressing the theme of "blackness." Blackness and the disunity of the Church go hand-in-hand. Not because blacks created the disunity—the black church has never practiced racism—but because for the white church, blackness is symbolic. It is symbolic of a white church throwing out, segregating and rejecting a people *because* of their blackness. In documents emanating from the World Council some would like to see the term black, which is repugnant to many, used as a prophetic sign, transforming the concept so that "black" is seen as beautiful. We must *affirm* what is, for many in the Church, a bad sign and transform that sign into a good one.

This does not mean rejecting or segregating others, or compromising one's personhood in an attempt to make one acceptable to others. For teaching purposes, the need in our documents is to affirm that "separatist" movements in the body of Christ arose because of the issue of blackness being repugnant to some and being affirmed by others.

## Consequences of "mystery" through black eyes

Persons who live out the mystery will be empowered to affirm their personhood in the midst of suffering, while affirming in love the personhood of the human family. The mystery of reconciling love goes through the process of liberation. This is especially true of persons who have been oppressed by those who do not consider those whom they are oppressing as their equals. Love does not mean passivity in the face of racial intolerance; rather it means actively resisting all demeaning action's against one's personhood.

There is unmerited suffering, in the face of which one cannot sit passively by without taking action. There is also redemptive suffering for which one assumes the posture of the cross, taking on the role of "no power" as did Martin Luther King, Jr. Suffering which comes in an effort to bring justice for others is mysterious; yet it can be redemptive. This is the fundamental lesson of Jesus' life, death and resurrection, and it is basic to the faith and life of black churches, who strive to be Christ-like in word and deed.

## Christ-likeness

While the churches in the African-American tradition consistently confess their sin and call for repentance on the part of their own members, it would be less than realistic to suggest that those who have been oppressed and victimized by others have no obligation to raise a prophetic word about the racial exclusivism which has greatly contributed to the disunity of the Church.

Of course the prophet is not exempt from human sinfulness. But this does not distract from the authentic, prophetic call to repentance, the offer of God's grace; or, if this is refused, from the doom proclaimed for unrepentant and rebellious people. The prophetic word is real and trustworthy not because of the prophet's faithfulness but because of God's righteousness.

Christ-like persons are called to follow Christ "outside the gates" (Heb. 13:12). Metaphorically speaking, "outside the gates" is a place where people are marginalized from society and even from the universal Church; yet the African-American churches have been able to survive and live through crises which, by nature, were destructive of life. "Outside the gates" in black churches one experiences the irony of humor, even when humor is least expected. There is found there a mystery of "freedom" in the midst of enslavement. Like Christ, the African-American church has experienced transcendence over the immediacy of potentially devastating historical experiences.

The reign of God on earth as in heaven is a part of the prayer of Jesus. This prayer has been inculcated in the hopes and aspirations of the black church. In the tradition of Jesus Christ, the black church expresses the mystery of the reign of God through showing love instead of hatred towards those who placed unmerited suffering upon them. This does not mean that rage is not part of the African-American experience, but there appears to be in the African-American tradition a strong tendency which says, "Let's not aim our hatred at the system which is itself unjust." This strand of tradition in the black church reveals the reign of God which aims for liberation of the oppressed, and for a spirituality which keeps resentment from becoming self-destructive hatred.

## Report from Group Two: Sign

For our discussion it is important to remember the ambiguity of the concept of the Church as "sign." It can best be explained by contrasting the description of the Church as it is often experienced as a historical institution—broken and fragmented (descriptive)—with what the Church is called to be (prescriptive).

The African-American church is a sign that the wider Church often refuses to see; yet it points to the mystery of God, the power of God to transform and empower a people who have been despised and rejected. It is a sign to call the Church to unity and to point out ways to human renewal.

While the African-American church is a positive sign for justice and liberation, the issues raised by women who are ordained but have difficulty in finding equally-paid positions, or who have to struggle for inclusion in decision-making processes and in positions of power, encourage the African-American church to be self-critical.

In spite of, and because of, sin in the Church as institution, God is operative in human history, in the world. To be a true sign, faithful to its calling, the Church must be concretely the Word made flesh. Racism as well as sexism and classism must be on the agenda of the churches' search for greater visible unity. All of these examples of brokenness are church-dividing issues, and represent corporate sin in the Church as human institution.

### Personal and communal aspects of the sign

The Word made flesh is personal and communal. If a sign is to be effective it must begin with the individual; but the individual is never whole without the community. The African statement: "I am because you are" picks up both the personal and communal aspect of the motivation which sparks the corporate sign of relationship and inclusivity which characterizes the African-American church.

The black church recognizes that an adequate sign, one with integrity for the wider community and Church, begins with personal conversion and being empowered by the Holy Spirit. But while sign for the world must begin with the personal, if it stops there then it is ineffective, still-born. The personal must assume social consequences. Through the years the African-American church has become a beacon of hope by stressing both aspects, asking, on the one hand, "Have you got good religion?" and affirming to the world, on the other hand, "Satan, your kingdom must come down!"

### Nature of the sign

The nature of the sign which the African-American church brings to the unity of the Church and the renewal of humankind is functional. In its function as "sign" the African-American church points to injustice and unrighteousness existing within both the Church as "people of God" and the world. As a sign, it has stressed the importance of struggle and redemptive suffering in the process of reconciliation, not only specifically for the black church but more generally for Euro-American churches.

## Sign and hope

The African-American church testifies through its experience that "the Lord will make a way somehow": this people has experienced victories in Christ. Based on its memory of God's action on its behalf, similar to the Exodus experience of the Jewish heritage, the black church continues the struggle, assured of God's victory for righteousness—the overcoming of racism in the Church and in the world.

## Report from Group Three: Suggestions for the WCC Faith and Order Commission, the Ecumenical Movement and the Black Churches

The following suggestions for future reflection and action were offered by the members of this group.

*1. For the steering group of the WCC Faith and Order Study Program on "The Unity of the Church and the Renewal of Human Community":*
1) In the discussion of the document "Church as Mystery and Prophetic Sign," black church involvement should be encouraged at every stage. Resources for this include this report as well as the preparatory paper and its appendices prepared for this meeting.

2) The first two sections of this report should be given equal weight with the contribution of all other churches to this process.

3) The results of this consultation should be shared with white churches in the United States of America and white United States leadership in the WCC Commission on Faith and Order.

4) The input of Pentecostal and other African-American Christians absent from this meeting should be sought in this process.

5) Leadership from the consultation with black churches should be invited to make a presentation to the Faith and Order Standing Commission in Boston, September 2-9, 1988.

*2. Additional implications and suggestions*
In discussing the implications of this consultation for the churches and the institutional ecumenical movement we found that many important issues

surfaced which went beyond the specific study programme on "The Unity of the Church and the Renewal of Human Community." This section will outline the implications of our reflections in the meeting for: (i) the general work of the Commission on Faith and Order of the WCC; (ii) the role of the black churches within the WCC; (iii) the responsibilities of African-American Christians, and their churches, within the ecumenical movement; (iv) concerns specific to the United States churches and the ecumenical movement, relative to the black churches.

*In order to improve black church participation in WCC Faith and Order, it was suggested that:*

    1) Diminished United States church participation, including black churches, in Faith and Order due to expanding Third World participation should be compensated for by the present type of specialized consultation.

    2) Work should continue to include women and persons of color in the WCC Faith and Order Commission.

    3) Ways should be found to include the church-dividing issues raised by the African-American churches in the WCC Faith and Order agenda-setting process.

    4) A pool of names of African-American Christians with a diversity of competencies for Faith and Order writing and consultations should be developed.

    5) A full variety of theological methods should be used in the various WCC Faith and Order studies.

*In order to enhance black church participation in the World Council as a whole, it was suggested that:*

    1) The black churches, the United States churches and World Council leadership should support the black church liaison committee of the United States Conference of the World Council of Churches.

    2) World Council leadership should explore ways of financing full participation on the part of the black churches.

    3) World Council leadership should explore ways of bringing minorities, ethnic and caste groups together in participation.

    4) Ecumenical leadership should take account of the contributions of black church women, especially in connection with Ecumenical Decade of the Churches in Solidarity with Women.

*In order to enhance the black churches' commitment to their ecumenical vocation, it was suggested that:*

    1) The black churches should find ways to communicate to their mem-

bers the reality of the ecumenical movement and in particular "The Unity of the Church and the Renewal of Human Community" Study.

2) The specific work and programs of the NCCCUSA and the WCC should become part of the life of the black churches.

3) The black churches should make available to Faith and Order and the ecumenical movement scholars and leaders to provide an authentic witness to this tradition.

4) African-American Christians should come together to discuss their differences and to deepen their unity.

5) Ways should be found for incorporating the gifts of local congregations within the ecumenical movement.

*In order to strengthen the presence of black churches in the ecumenical movement in the United States, it was suggested that:*

1) The Partners In Ecumenism program of the NCCC should be supported.

2) Black church participation in the United States' Faith and Order and other programs of the NCCC should be supported.

3) The National Council, the Catholic Bishops' Conference and the black churches should be encouraged to deepen black Protestant and Catholic dialogue.

4) Efforts by the NCCC to deepen black church engagement at every level of its life should be supported.

5) The dialogue between black and Orthodox churches in the United States, facilitated by local, regional and the National Councils of Churches, should be encouraged.

**Recommendation as voted and approved in plenary**

The following recommendation from Group Three was approved by the final plenary session of the consultation:

> We the members of the World Council of Churches' Faith and Order Commission and representatives of the black churches meeting at the Abysinnian Baptist Church in Harlem, New York, recommend that:
> 1. The process of reflection by black churches and black Christians on the unity of the Church and the Renewal of Human Community Study Program should be continued.
> 2. Representatives of the World Council of Churches' Faith and Order Commission and the black church liaison group of the United States Conference of the World Council of Churches should develop a plan for

implementing the above recommendation, including provisions for staffing and funding.

## Notes

1. The terms "Afro-American" church and "black" church, which point to the same reality, are used alternatively throughout this document. This represents the different usages among consulation participants to describe the church.

2. "What We Have Seen and Heard," *Origins* 14 (October 1984): 277.

# The Holy Spirit Consultation: A Summary Statement

On October 24-25, 1985 a consultation was held at Holy Cross Greek Orthodox School of Theology, Brookline, Massachusetts, to consider the similarities and differences among the Christian churches concerning our faith in the Holy Spirit. The consultation used the Klingenthal Memorandum "The *Filioque* Clause in Ecumenical Perspective," Klingenthal, 1979 (*Spirit of God, Spirit of Christ*, Faith and Order Paper No. 103, Lukas Vischer, ed. [Gcncva, 1981]) as a reference point for its work. To many in the ecumenical movement, this memorandum appears to open new pathways toward resolution of the *filioque* question.

The papers prepared for the consultation addressed the place of the Holy Spirit in the trinitarian theology and life of various Christian traditions. Those of us who participated in the consultation represented an ever-wider diversity of Christian traditions. We were some fifty-five pcople, from the following Christian communions: Baptist, African Methodist Episcopal Zion, Brethren, Eastern and Oriental Orthodox, Episcopal, Holiness, Lutheran, Mennonite, Moravian, Pentecostal, Presbyterian/Reformed, Quaker, Roman Catholic, Swedenborgian, United Church of Christ and United Methodist. We met in the hope that, while dealing with our historic divisions and contemporary differences, we might recognize common areas of experience and thought concerning the Holy Spirit and also might serve the contemporary needs of thc whole Christian Church which seeks ever anew to give authentic witness to the Holy Spirit.

Three main areas of concern emerged in the discussions of the consultation: a) the *filioque* question, b) the naming of God, and c) the dynamic polarity between apostolic doctrine (creed) and apostolic life (experience). What follows, including the recommendations, is a summary of these discussions representing central issues raised by the papers, key points of discussion, and individual opinions. It is offered neither as an agreed statement nor

*Theodore Stylianopoulos and Mark Heim, eds., *Spirit of Truth: Ecumenical Perspectives on the Holy Spirit* (Brookline, MA: Holy Cross Orthodox Press, 1986) 187-97.

as an expression of a consensus on any major issue, but rather as a contribution to the ongoing ecumenical conversation on the apostolic faith and life.

## A. Filioque

1. The theological use of the *filioque* in the West was directed against any form of Arian ontological subordination of the Son to the Father and in this perspective is fully valid according to the theological criteria of the Eastern tradition.

2. In the West the *filioque* has been used to stress a) the consubstantial unity of the Trinity, b) the divine status of the Son, and c) the intimate relationship between the Son and the Spirit.

3. These points are also integral elements of Eastern trinitarian theology anchored in the Cappadocian teaching of *perichoresis* ("mutual indwelling") of the Persons of the Trinity. This teaching is reflected in the Nicene-Constantinopolitan Creed which professes an equal worship and glorification of the Persons of the Holy Trinity.

4. A fundamental and wide agreement exists between Eastern and Western trinitarian doctrine affirming the complete reciprocity and mutuality of the Son and the Spirit in their eternal relations (immanent Trinity) as well as their manifested action in creation, Church and society (economic Trinity).

5. Christ is both the bearer and the sender of the Spirit. The Spirit of God is in every way also the Spirit of the Son.

6. The Eastern tradition has long affirmed the teaching on the "monarchy" of the Father, that is, "the Father is the sole principle ('αρχή) source (πηγή) and cause ('αιτία) of divinity." (Klingenthal Memorandum)

7. The Western tradition has historically wished to show itself as much attached to this principle as the East. In affirming the *filioque* the Western tradition never thought that the "monarchy" of the Father was called in question.

8. However, the Eastern tradition has viewed the *filioque* as unintentionally compromising the "monarchy" of the Father, a doctrine which is enshrined in the Cappadocian teaching and reflected in the Nicene Creed which declares that the Spirit "proceeds from" or "goes forth out of" ('εκπορευόμενον) the Father.

9. The Eastern tradition has seen its own trinitarian approach as more consistently biblical and personal, with careful avoidance of any modalistic tendencies which compromise the uniqueness of each of the divine Persons.

10. Many contemporary Eastern theologians have felt that the *filioque* subordinates the Spirit to the Son, and thereby depersonalizes the Spirit.

11. Contemporary Eastern theologians have often pointed out what they consider to be consequences of the *filioque*: authoritarianism, institutionalism, clericalism, etc. One is hard pressed to demonstrate that such conditions actually are the result of the *filioque*. The very same patterns can be found in most churches, with or without the *filioque*. Nonetheless, a feminist theologian from the West thought that the critique of the *filioque* in this perspective by the East was essentially correct.

12. In the Western tradition the *filioque* was intended to indicate that the Son was involved in the procession of the Spirit, though only in a secondary manner, leaving the "monarchy" of the Father intact. Anything the Son contributes to the procession of the Spirit he receives from the Father. Western theologians have maintained that the Nicene Creed's concern in declaring that the Spirit proceeds from the Father was not to determine the relationship of origin but the divinity of the Spirit.

13. Eastern trinitarian thought as expressed by Gregory of Nyssa, Gregory the Cypriot and Gregory Palamas, conceives of the Son as *mediating*, but not *causing*, the Spirit's procession from the Father. On this nuanced difference hangs the whole weight of centuries of controversy between the Eastern and Western churches. This is also the reason why the Orthodox cannot accept the conjunction "and" in the *filioque* clause ("from the Father *and* the Son") which signifies a joint cause in the procession of the Spirit.

14. The opinion from among the Orthodox was expressed that the specifically Augustinian approach implicit in the *filioque*, namely that the Son is in some sense cause, would have to be recognized as doctrinally erroneous because it compromises the doctrine of the "monarchy" of the Father.

15. According to one Western opinion a considerable segment of Eastern theologians have recognized the integral relationship of the *filioque* to Western theological systems. According to this same opinion within that system the preservation of the *filioque* is an acceptable position. The truth and the intent asserted in the *filioque* has been held by the West since the fourth century. To transfer the *filioque* out of the theological culture of the West and insert it into the Eastern framework is a violation of the integrity of the Eastern theological culture.

16. Photios, Patriarch of Constantinople, who is recognized as a saint in the Orthodox Churches, proposed the formula "the Spirit proceeds from the Father alone." Yet this difference in teaching over against the *filioque* did not cause the breaking of communion between the Eastern and Western churches.

17. The question was asked whether the churches of the East and West would not be able to live together in a united church while the West retains the *filioque* as an authentic part of its theological identity. But others raised

the question whether or not this approach would imply an avoidance, not resolution, of the *filioque* question.

18. The Klingenthal Memorandum gave a number of suggested formulations which might bridge the differences between East and West, among them "the Spirit proceeds from the Father of the Son," and "the Spirit proceeds from the Father through the Son." These formulae would safeguard the "monarchy" of the Father while at the same time affirming the active participation of the Son in the eternal procession of the Spirit from the Father.

19. It was noted that there is no possibility for some of the churches to promote the use of an alternate text of the Creed as long as there is a demand that the *filioque* be recognized as theologically erroneous.

20. Fruitful for further study are the specific implications of the Augustinian and Cappadocian approaches to the Trinity and theology in general, that is, the practical implications for the role of the Spirit in creation, the Church and society today.

21. On the agenda of both East and West is the integration of the "full and constant reciprocity of the Incarnate Word and the Holy Spirit" (Klingenthal Memorandum) into theology, catechesis and preaching.

22. The warning not to carry too far the distinctions between the economic and immanent Trinity, or between the temporal mission and eternal procession, is well taken.

23. The differences between the East and West in the matters of the *filioque* do not constitute a "great divide." Together East and West confess the Holy Trinity, and share broad agreement regarding the work of the Spirit. These commonalities are embedded in the liturgies and theological traditions of both communities.

24. Moving beyond the question of the *filioque,* the churches should give attention to enlarging the Church's theology of the Holy Spirit. The churches should manifest an openness to the experience of the Spirit, which could lead to actualization of the power of Christ's resurrection among the whole people of God.

## B. The Naming of God

1. A series of questions were posed: How do we name God? Are there limits in the language of faith? How do we recognize and then overcome such limits? How does one understand the overwhelming masculine nature of the image conveyed in naming God "Father, Son and Holy Spirit"?

2. The Puritan tradition has spoken of God in anti-analogical fashion. Therefore, if God be King, then let there be no earthly kings or dominions. Under such a God creaturely life is life among a commonality of equals.

3. An analogical fashion of speaking would assume that if God be King, then earthly kings and dominions are archetypes of the heavenly superior. Under such a God, creaturely life would take on structures of subordination and superordination.

4. The *imago Dei* language presumes an analogy between creator and creature. More explicitly, the *imago Dei* is the *imago Trinitatis*. The divine community forms, informs and transforms the human community and personality. The *imago Trinitatis* shapes, sanctions, and challenges a specific community. Subordination within the divine community might be analogically used to justify subordination within the human community. Similarly, equality, solidarity and mutuality within the divine community might be used to challenge human communities to be as equal, as mutual, and as supportive.

5. Gender categories constitute only one kind of language in which *imago Dei* is expressed. Personal language for God need not be sexual; when it is, however, it should be balanced: male and female, masculine and feminine.

6. Many Western theologians felt that feminine ways of naming God should be accessible to all. The use of feminine names for God could be liberating both for men and women within various communities.

7. The triune God both embraces and extends beyond our categories of male and female.

8. The question was raised whether language about God could be anything but analogical? What about the form of address: "the God beyond knowing...whom we call Father"?

9. The names given God describe "person," that is, who God is, but also "relation," that is, how God is, both within the Godhead and in acting toward creatures.

10. Communions give varying weight to the names of God and their valence in identifying person or relation. Gregory of Nyssa and Gregory the Theologian maintain that all names of God describe activities of God, while the titles "Father" and "Son" have a different status signifying the eternal Persons of the Father and the Son.

11. Some churches name God in terms of what the creature can expect from God.

12. Feminist theologians of various confessional allegiances emphasize the relational significance of the title. Insofar as the begetting function of God is the chief content of the name "Father," God may be named "Mother."

13. A suggestion was made that the real issue of language is not creed but Gospel.

14. Also of concern is how God names us in relation to the triune God, within the community of the faithful, and before the whole of creation. The

relationship between who God is and who we are is dialogical. In communication with God we discover both who we are and who God is. This discovery forms our bearing toward God, ourselves, our communities, and our world.

15. All theological language is provisional and a mere human attempt to grasp the mystery. While formed and informed by tradition, theological language is also shaped by context. There must be a dynamic interaction between scripture, tradition, and context. The problem is to adjudicate among the possibly competing claims of each. The issue finally is one of discernment: Which names are inspired by the Spirit? Which are not?

### C. Creed and Experience

1. We recognize that the difficulties inherent in the *filioque* cannot be reduced simply to the conceptual. What is at issue is also the experience of the Spirit. Here experience is understood both as personal and ecclesial. This experience takes place within the context of a specific theological culture which differs from other authentic theological cultures. While recognizing the plurality of such cultures, we also want to affirm the large area of shared faith in the Spirit.

2. If one proceeds from experience, then the *filioque*, and the larger trinitarian question, becomes increasingly problematic for large segments of the population, female but also male. Increased recognition of women's experience, and the unacceptability of a God presented in purely male categories, or in two-thirds male, one-third female, will help defuse a highly charged atmosphere in many churches.

3. Taking experience as a point of departure and looking at creedal statements such as the *filioque,* some classical Pentecostals would regard creeds as expressions of "sectarianism" and "formalism," whether orthodox or not. Nevertheless, most classical Pentecostal churches have statements of faith, many of them borrowed from the historic creeds.

4. Some Pentecostal churches see their experience of the Spirit, including "the baptism in the Holy Spirit," as a significant ecumenical event, an invitation for the walls of sectarian denominationalism to fall.

5. Though classical Pentecostalism is no longer identified simply with the lower socio-economic groups (it now touches all classes), the presence of so many classical Pentecostal churches among the oppressed classes and ethnic minorities poses the question: Has the experience of the Spirit of these groups been given the kind of theological and ecumenical attention it deserves.

6. The experience of the churches from the Holiness tradition contains

elements which are typical of classical Pentecostal churches, such as an orientation to social justice issues, and a more gradual or growth approach to spiritual maturity. Like the classical Pentecostals, they are concerned that the agreement on the *filioque*, and on the broader issue of the Nicene Creed, will not adequately state the implications of life in the Spirit as viewed from their experience.

7. The presence of the charismatic renewal in so many of the historic churches has raised questions. There is recognition that charismatic groups within the historic churches have added to the quality of that church's spiritual experience. They have also posed a question to the churches about the nature of spiritual formation which the groups need to take seriously, even while it is recognized that such groups have at times been divisive.

8. Some charismatic Christians and some classical Pentecostal churches are impatient with the discussion of the *filioque* because they fail to see that there is anything experiential at stake. Therefore they are inclined to see this particular discussion as too narrowly focused, an ecclesiological dispute from the past without the hope of it contributing to a richer understanding of God's presence among us now. Yet they would welcome reconciliation between the historic churches on this divisive issue.

9. It is known that many of the debated formulae in the doctrine of the Trinity and affirmations about the Holy Spirit were worked out in the midst of ecclesiastical and socio-political controversies. Trinitarian theology is the foundation for Christian anthropology and ecclesiology. Ecclesiology includes a normative theory of how God wants humans to live together in community. Thus it has implications for how Christian life is to be ordered in social, political, familial, and cultural communities.

## D. Reflections and Recommendations

1. Participants were in general agreement that reception of the Klingenthal Memorandum and its recommendations by the churches represented the most hopeful path toward resolution of the *filioque* question.

2. What we share in regard to the trinitarian faith is greater than what divides us. East and West share a trinitarian faith which is expressed in the Nicene Creed, used by many of the churches.

3. Both East and West recognize that the Trinity is a mystery which exceeds all of our conceptual tools. Given the common faith of East and West, excessive precision is to be avoided. There has been, since the fourth century, a general understanding that the specific quality which distinguishes the generation of the Son from the procession of the Spirit eludes us. We live with the lack of precision here. We are even warned against prying (Gregory

the Theologian, *Fifth Theological Oration*, 8: "What, then, is procession? Do you tell me what is the unbegottenness of the Father, and I will explain to you the physiology of the generation of the Son and the procession of the Spirit, and we shall both of us be frenzy-stricken for prying into the mystery of God. And who are we to do these things, we who cannot even see what lies at our feet, or number the sand of the sea, or the drops of rain, or the days of eternity, much less enter into the depths of God, and supply an account of that nature which is so unspeakable and transcending all words.") Could not the same kind of imprecision be accepted with regard to the way the Son is involved in the procession of the Spirit from the Father? This is posed as a question to the churches rather than a demand.

4. The *filioque* question should not be isolated from its proper context, which is trinitarian doctrine. It should be seen that the doctrine of the Trinity is not a matter of heavenly metaphysics, but of the presence of the Father through the Son in the Holy Spirit touching history and the Church. Beyond the scriptures the roots of trinitarian doctrine are Christian experience, piety, and liturgy. If trinitarian doctrine returns to these primary sources of Christian experience, and re-experiences the development of trinitarian doctrine in history, much will be done to bring the *filioque* question out of its isolation. The study project of the National Council's Faith and Order Commission is promising in this regard.

5. A renewal of trinitarian piety and theology will demonstrate that issues raised by the *filioque*, far from being academic questions, touch the deepest roots of theological formulation, liturgical practice, and pastoral life.

6. The churches need to look again at the way Christ and Spirit (christology and pneumatology) stand in a relation of mutuality and reciprocity.

7. In approaching the *filioque* no attempt should be made to transfer what is proper in one theological culture to a different theological culture to which it is quite foreign.

8. It is the view of some that a more stringent and narrower agreement should not now be demanded than the chief participants at the time of the break up of the communion between the East and West were prepared to live with.

9. The West needs to recognize that the unilateral introduction of the *filioque* into the Creed, even given the differing ecclesiologies of East and West, was not only offensive at the time of its introduction, but continues to be so today. The West has failed to understand that this is not just to impose a Western theological view on the whole Church, but turns the Creed, which has a unitive function, into a source of division. Nor do Westerners usually grasp the significance of the Creed for the East, where it plays a larger role than it has historically in the West. Further, Westerners do not seem fully to

grasp the offense when a liturgical text is changed without the consent of others to whom the text also belongs.

10. We recommend that the churches of the West allow their congregations, as an alternate, the liturgical use of the ancient text of the Creed before the addition of the *filioque*. This is looked upon as an interim, rather than a final, solution.

11. Both East and West recognize that there is a proper nonontological subordination of the Spirit to the Son, as there is of the Son to the Father. What is not sufficiently realized in the West is that there is in Western theologies and piety a systematic subordination of the Spirit to the Son which does not give due respect to the mutuality and reciprocity which should exist between Christ and the Spirit. A thorough study of a wide variety of New Testament texts on the Spirit will be helpful in correcting this imbalance.

12. Both East and West need to recognize that one should not idealize one's own tradition, while caricaturing the other.

13. The Spirit is neither just an ornament of piety nor liturgical tinsel. Attention should be given not only to the relation of the Spirit to the Father and the Son, but to the role of the Spirit in creation, the political and economic orders. The Spirit should not be banished to the realm of piety, or imprisoned in liturgical formulations.

14. The issue of naming God is grave, and it touches the dignity of both women and men. No one should be under any illusion as to the deep seriousness of the issue. A solution calls for the involvement of women and men from the whole spectrum of academic and theological disciplines.

15. Though the state of the question of naming God was quite different in the fourth century, attention should be given to the norms established in the trinitarian, christological, and pneumatological controversies. For instance, Gregory the Theologian rejected the logic which says that God is male just because the vocabulary of "Father" is used. (Speaking somewhat in derision, Gregory asks, "Perhaps you would consider our God to be a male, according to the same arguments, because he is called God and Father..." *Fifth Theological Oration,*7.)

16. Primary religious symbols which arise out of human experience are not unlimited and are not expendable. Therefore there is the necessity of preserving those that are central to the living tradition while at the same time purging them of oppressive elements.

17. The use of the *imago Trinitatis* as a model for naming God is to be commended. The exploration of such an avenue would be more fruitful if it were accompanied by a trinitarian ecclesiology, where equality of persons does not rule out diversity of functions and a measure of non-sexual subordination.

18. The traditional christological paradigm for ecclesiology should be

set in its proper trinitarian context. Taking the trinitarian community as model enables one to see the pneumatological moment as co-constitutive of the Church. The pneumatological dimension does not belong to a second moment, as an energizer of an already existing structure. This more trinitarian model is also to be fostered because it provides ways of dealing with the question of authority and obedience.

19. Those from the historic churches who are somewhat new to the experiential pneumatology need to set aside preconceptions, and the supposition that the experiential can be communicated conceptually. While remaining true to their own ethos, an openness to both pre-literary and post-literary ways of approaching religious reality is to be encouraged.

20. Those from the classical Pentecostal and Holiness churches should explore ways of expanding their definition of experience. Many would find it helpful if they would communicate to other Christian brethren the wisdom they have found in the biblical hedges against an undisciplined experiential approach to God's presence in history. Their own wisdom and pastoral experience in this area is much more nuanced and sophisticated than is generally known.

21. The bearers of a more experiential pneumatology, such as the classical Pentecostals and the Holiness churches, belong integrally to the history of the Spirit. Without their presence, both formally and informally, in the theological dialogue, the ecumenical endeavor must necessarily remain truncated and impoverished.

22. The trinitarian discussions include the question of how normative ideas are related to the social fabric. Further discussion of the Holy Spirit and the apostolic faith needs to include reflection on the various methodologies in dealing with this relationship, examination of the historical and social context of the formulations, and the presuppositions brought to the discussion by participating communions and their theologians. Ecclesiology, social theory and the basis for the political witness of the whole People of God need to be seen in their nuanced relationship to the trinitarian faith.

# Faith to Creed Consultation Summary Statement*

## Introduction

We have sought to explore issues that would lead to a common understanding of the social and historical context for the development of the Nicene-Constantinopolitan Creed. We came together as representatives of diverse Christian communions with many personal and scholarly perspectives on this period in our common history. We also attempted to hear the various voices within the period itself and to move closer to shared understanding of the fourth-century expression of the apostolic faith as confessed in the creed.

## I. The Creed in Its Fourth-Century Context

Considering the creed in its fourth-century context broadened our understanding of its meaning.

–Monastic spirituality with its triad of prayer and worship, faith and theology, and ethical practice in daily life was an integral part of that context. This context must be seen as part of the meaning of the creed.
–The complex theological ferment from 325 to 381 included a struggle to develop sound teaching in trinitarian terminology. The creed was elaborated in the context of these developing trinitarian terms in a dynamic process of conciliar debate, consensus in the church, and subsequent retrospective appropriation.
–Before and after Nicaea, various similar local creeds were used in the churches. They were used in the process of Christian formation in the catechumenate and baptism, which entailed basic ethical as well as doctrinal instruction. Creeds were meant for personal profession of faith as well as for corporate reaffirmation of faith in the act of worship.

*Mark Heim, ed., *Faith to Creed. Ecumenical Perspectives on the Affirmation of the Apostolic Faith in the Fourth Century* (Grand Rapids: Eerdmans, 1991) 198-204.

−A conciliar tradition already existed before Nicaea. Bishops of particular churches met regularly to resolve issues.

−In the need to interpret Scripture to explicate faith, the creed served as a bridge, expressing the truth of Scripture in contemporary fourth-century terms.

## II. Perspectives That Shape Our Approach to the Fourth Century

In our discussions we became keenly aware that we tend to import into the fourth century questions that are at the center of our own traditions' life and history.

−Many issues regarding creeds and confessions, their status and function, seem to reflect the experience of the Reformation and Counter-Reformation period more than that of the early church.

−Christian groups that have experienced persecution and domination at the hands of other Christians in control of political power sometimes read the fourth century in terms drawn from those experiences.

−Churches that regard themselves as in direct continuity with the conciliar process that formed the creed tend to see the fourth century through the model of development toward the fully realized structures and theology that came afterward.

Our understanding of the creed's content and character is strongly colored by our own current ecclesial contexts.

−Those for whom the creed today plays a regular and integral role in liturgy, personal prayer, baptism, eucharistic celebration, and instruction tend to perceive its nature in the fourth century quite differently than those for whom the creed is known primarily as a historical document or a source for theological and doctrinal study.

−Experience of an ecumenical context, whether of worship with other Christians or of study and discussion such as we have enjoyed in this meeting, changes our perspective on the fourth century and the creed in the fourth century.

Most of us have implicitly or explicitly learned a perspective toward the fourth century context of the creed as part of our own ecclesial identity. Becoming mutually aware of these perspectives and of the realities in the fourth century that each of them both illuminates and obscures is one necessary step toward a common explication of the creed.

## III. Creed, Church, and Empire

Different perspectives on the development of church life in the fourth century, and especially of the Nicene-Constantinopolitan Creed, seemed to be influenced by different assessments of how faithful believers thought God wanted them to relate *ecclesium* and *imperium*. A major issue was to what extent and in what ways these developments were the product of the church and to what extent and in what ways they were the product of the temporal powers, specifically of the Roman *imperium*. The relative influence of each of these forces also seemed to be evaluated differently. For some the greater the influence of the *imperium,* the more negative their evaluation of the creed. For others, the amount of imperial influence had relatively little effect on their estimate of the creed's value. Still others viewed the political authority as a providential part of God's nurturing of the church.

Similar questions and evaluations concerned the extent to which the creed and related developments were issues only for an elite group in society and/or the church or for the common people as well. Related questions were raised concerning the extent to which these developments furthered the aims of the imperial power (e.g., did the evolving Nicene-Constantinopolitan Creed help Constantine and his successors unify the Empire?) and the extent to which they may have strengthened the church to resist imperial power. Once again, however, the relation of the church to imperial power was evaluated differently. The church's recognition of, alliance with, or use of imperial power was valued positively by some and negatively by others.

Finally, there were different perceptions as to whether with the conversion and rule of Constantine a shift took place in the life of the church, and if so how great a shift took place. Some saw it as involving a far-reaching reversal of the relationship of the church to society. Others saw it as a more continuous outgrowth of developments of the preceding centuries whereby the gospel further permeated the world. In general those who saw the Constantinian period as a radical shift tended to evaluate it negatively, while those who saw it as a more natural outgrowth tended to evaluate it positively.

## IV. Ethical Dimensions of the Creed

Questions were raised concerning the ethical implications and presuppositions of the creed.

For some participants, its lack of explicit ethical content is what would stand in the way of their being able to affirm the Nicene-Constantinopolitan

Creed as a common expression of the faith. For some of these there was the issue of whether the gospel, in which the ethical commitment is central, was not marginalized or distorted in the process of the formation of this creed or in the place it held subsequently.

Still other participants represented an emerging openness within several traditions including that of the radical Reformation to the trinitarian orthodoxy of the Nicene-Constantinopolitan Creed as an essential theological framework and grounding for a political and social ethic.

Others in our group viewed the creed as part of and connected to an emerging theological-ethical tradition as the church faces a complex culture.


## V. Language, Gender, and Creed

A major discussion took place on language and gender. We recognized that many things that trouble us today were normal and taken for granted in the fourth century, such as the use of male imagery in the creed. The significance of language and gender, of great importance today, is a concern within and among the churches. The following considerations and views figured in our conversation:

–The language and thought categories of the creed (and the fourth century) were formative for the church. Many believed that they have kept women in powerless places and today impede women from hearing the gospel as a saving word.
–Jesus, Paul, and the monastic thinkers lived by paradigms different in part from the prevailing uniform religious norms about them, especially regarding women's place and value. That encourages us in seeking an alternative rather than a uniform vision of the "way things should be."
–We know relatively little about the implicit and explicit effects of early Christian theology and christology on how women were viewed and valued. We need to examine early Christian texts on their own terms in order to see how our problem is and is not related to their views and presuppositions.
–The creed is a distinctive way of expressing who this God we worship is. It is problematic to change the historical words of the creed's text or references to the Trinity. It is also problematic that women lack the direct gender-affiliation to God afforded men.
–Speaking of God as father is normative; not speaking of God as mother is not normative, though we disagreed on the desirability of this usage in public worship and prayer.
–It is a matter of concern to both women and men whether males are ontolog-

ically and iconically related to God in ways women are not. Churches and Christians find and validate their different normative views in the traditions of this and earlier eras or in a revisionist, contextual reading of this era.

## VI. Additional Issues

We agreed that there were several issues that did not receive extensive attention but were significant and required more work.

–Although we explored many of the divisive issues that have arisen in relation to the creed, we did not give as much attention to the specific nature of the unique and authoritative status that the creed received and the process that led to this status. The nature of this special status and function deserves more historical and theological discussion.

–We recognize the need for more discussion of the way the creed does and might function in our churches today.

–We acknowledged that there are many groups whose perspectives on the creed would enrich our discussion but that were not represented in our consultation, including Pentecostals and traditional black churches.

–Another topic that requires further work is the normative character of the creed and the extent to which this character attaches primarily to the paradigmatic, cognitive, propositional content on the one hand and the extent to which it attaches to a covenantal and ecclesial participation on the other.

–We recognize the need for further study of the specific conciliar context that produced the creed, particularly with reference to its social, political, economic, and ethical dimensions.

–Some representatives of traditions identifying with the radical wing of the Reformation wondered whether the more ontological categories in the creed themselves have distorted the messianic particularity of Jesus and whether there might be alternative modes of theologizing that preserve the discipleship ethic as integral to christology.

## Conclusion

We all acknowledged the power of this creed to bring us into conversation with each other concerning issues of central importance to our faith: how to talk to God, trinitarian ethics, the relation of the church to temporal powers. Even in our disagreements we experienced the capacity of the creed to unify us by directing our attention to the faith we share.

# Index

# OTHER VOLUMES IN THE
# ECUMENICAL DOCUMENTS SERIES

Volume I: **Doing the Truth in Charity** (1982), edited by Thomas F. Stransky and John B. Sheerin—includes Vatican documents and papal statements on ecumenical concerns, 1964-1980.

Volume II: **Growth in Agreement** (1984), edited by Harding Meyer and Lukas Vischer—provides reports and agreed statements of bilateral and multilateral ecumenical dialogues on the world level.

Volume III: **Towards the Healing of Schism** (1987), edited and translated by E.J. Stormon—includes public statements and correspondence between the Holy See and the Ecumenical Patriarchate, 1958-1984.

Volume IV: **Building Unity** (1989), edited by Joseph A. Burgess and Jeffrey Gros—includes joint statements, with Roman Catholic participation, of bilateral and multilateral dialogues on the regional and national levels, especially in the U.S.A.